Communications in Computer and Information Science 1269

Commenced Publication in 2007
Founding and Former Series Editors:
Simone Diniz Junqueira Barbosa, Phoebe Chen, Alfredo Cuzzocrea,
Xiaoyong Du, Orhun Kara, Ting Liu, Krishna M. Sivalingam,
Dominik Ślęzak, Takashi Washio, Xiaokang Yang, and Junsong Yuan

More information about this series at http://www.springer.com/series/7899

Henry Muccini · Paris Avgeriou ·
Barbora Buhnova · Javier Camara ·
Mauro Caporuscio · Mirco Franzago ·
Anne Koziolek · Patrizia Scandurra ·
Catia Trubiani · Danny Weyns ·
Uwe Zdun (Eds.)

Software Architecture

14th European Conference, ECSA 2020
Tracks and Workshops, L'Aquila, Italy, September 14–18, 2020
Proceedings

Springer

Editors
Henry Muccini (iD)
University of L'Aquila
L'Aquila, Italy

Barbora Buhnova (iD)
Faculty of Informatics
Masaryk University
Brno, Czech Republic

Mauro Caporuscio (iD)
Department of Computer Science
Linnaeus University
Växjö, Sweden

Anne Koziolek (iD)
Karlsruhe Institute of Technology
Karlsruhe, Germany

Catia Trubiani (iD)
Gran Sasso Science Institute
L'Aquila, Italy

Uwe Zdun (iD)
Faculty of Computer Science
University of Vienna
Vienna, Austria

Paris Avgeriou (iD)
University of Groningen
Groningen, The Netherlands

Javier Camara (iD)
Department of Computer Science
University of York
York, UK

Mirco Franzago (iD)
University of L'Aquila
L'Aquila, Italy

Patrizia Scandurra (iD)
University of Bergamo
Dalmine, Italy

Danny Weyns (iD)
Department of Computer Science
KU Leuven
Leuven, Belgium

ISSN 1865-0929   ISSN 1865-0937   (electronic)
Communications in Computer and Information Science
ISBN 978-3-030-59154-0   ISBN 978-3-030-59155-7   (eBook)
https://doi.org/10.1007/978-3-030-59155-7

This Springer imprint is published by the registered company Springer Nature Switzerland AG
The registered company address is: Gewerbestrasse 11, 6330 Cham, Switzerland

Preface

The European Conference on Software Architecture (ECSA) is the premier European conference that provides researchers and practitioners with a platform to present and discuss the most recent, innovative, and significant findings and experiences in the field of software architecture research and practice.

This year's technical program included a doctoral symposium track with its own keynote, a gender diversity in software architecture & software engineering track with its own keynote, and a tool demos track. ECSA 2020 also offered nine workshops on diverse topics related to the software architecture discipline. ECSA 2020 also included a research track, three keynote talks, and an industry track, included in a volume by Springer LNCS. In addition, ECSA 2020 featured a journal first track partnering with the *Journal of Software and Systems*, Elsevier, and the *IEEE Software Magazine*.

ECSA 2020 received 103 contributions to all tracks. We received 11 workshop proposals, 4 doctoral symposium submissions, 3 gender diversity papers, 7 tools demos, 1 tutorial, and 4 journal first contributions.

The workshops took place on the two days before the ECSA 2020 main conference and the program included the following nine workshops:

- Third International Workshop on Context-aware, Autonomous and Smart Architecture (CASA 2020)
- 5th Workshop on Continuous Software Engineering (CSE 2020) and 6th International Workshop on Quality-Aware DevOps (QUDOS 2020)
- Third International Workshop on moDeling, vErification and Testing of dEpendable CriTical systems (DETECT 2020)
- 4th Workshop on Formal Approaches for Advanced Computing Systems (FAACS 2020) and First International Workshop on Model-Driven Engineering for Software Architecture (MDE4SA 2020)
- 4th International Workshop on Engineering IoT Systems: Architectures, Services, Applications, and Platforms (IoT-ASAP 2020)
- Second Workshop on Systems, Architectures, and Solutions for Industry 4.0 (SASI4 2020)
- 6th International Workshop on Automotive System/Software Architectures (WASA 2020)

All workshops together received a total of 58 papers. Each workshop had an independent Program Committee, which was in charge of selecting the papers. Out of the 58 submissions, 28 papers were selected to be presented at the workshops.

The doctoral symposium track had its own keynote provided by Radu Calinescu, from the Department of Computer Science at the University of York, UK, who talked about "Going the extra mile to publish your research in a top venue."

The gender diversity in software architecture track had also its own keynote provided by Paola Inverardi, from the Information Engineering, Computer Science, and

Mathematics Department, University of L'Aquila, Italy. Professor Inverardi, who was rector of the University of L'Aquila from 2013 to 2019, is in a unique position to report about the state of the implementation of gender equality policies at Italian universities, a topic of great interest to ECSA's audience.

We are grateful to the members of the tracks and workshop Program Committees for helping us to seek submissions and provide valuable and timely reviews. Their efforts enabled us to put together a high-quality program for ECSA 2020. We would like to thank the members of the Organizing Committee of ECSA 2020 for playing an enormously important role in successfully organizing the event with several tracks and collocated events, as well as the workshop organizers, who made significant contributions to this year's successful event.

July 2020

Paris Avgeriou
Barbora Buhnova
Javier Camara
Mauro Caporuscio
Mirco Franzago
Anne Koziolek
Henry Muccini
Patrizia Scandurra
Catia Trubiani
Danny Weyns
Uwe Zdun

Organization

General Chair

Henry Muccini — University of L'Aquila, Italy

Steering Committee

Muhammad Ali Babar	The University of Adelaide, Australia
Paris Avgeriou	University of Groningen, The Netherlands
Tomas Bures	Charles University, Czech Republic
Rogério de Lemos	University of Kent, UK
Laurence Duchien	CRIStAL, University of Lille, France
Carlos E. Cuesta	Rey Juan Carlos University, Spain
David Garlan	Carnegie Mellon University, USA
Paola Inverardi	University of L'Aquila, Italy
Patricia Lago	Vrije Universiteit Amsterdam, The Netherlands
Antónia Lopes	University of Lisbon, Portugal
Ivano Malavolta	Vrije Universiteit Amsterdam, The Netherlands
Raffaela Mirandola	Politecnico di Milano, Italy
Henry Muccini	University of L'Aquila, Italy
Flavio Oquendo (Chair)	IRISA, University of South Brittany, France
Ipek Ozkaya	Carnegie Mellon Software, USA
Jennifer Pérez	Universidad Politecnica de Madrid, Spain
Bedir Tekinerdogan	Wageningen University, The Netherlands
Danny Weyns	KU Leuven, Belgium
Uwe Zdun	University of Vienna, Austria

Program Committee Chairs

Research Track

Ivano Malavolta	Vrije Universiteit Amsterdam, The Netherlands
Ipek Ozkaya	Carnegie Mellon Software, USA

Industry Track

Anton Jansen	Philips, The Netherlands
Olaf Zimmermann	Hochschule für Technik Rapperswil, Switzerland

Conference Track Chairs

Doctoral Symposium

Patrizia Scandurra	DIIMM, University of Bergamo, Italy
Danny Weyns	KU Leuven, Belgium

Tool Demos

Paris Avgeriou	University of Groningen, The Netherlands
Barbora Buhnova	Masaryk University, Czech Republic

Gender Diversity in Software Architecture and Software Engineering

Javier Camara	University of York, UK
Catia Trubiani	Gran Sasso Science Institute, Italy

Workshop Organization Chairs

CASA

Claudia Raibulet	Universitá degli Studi di Milano-Bicocca, Italy
Khalil Drira	LAAS-CNRS, CNRS, Université de Toulouse, France
Mariagrazia Fugini	Politecnico di Milano, DEIB, Italy
Patrizio Pelliccione	University of L'Aquila, Italy, and Chalmers — University of Gothenburg, Sweden
Genaína N. Rodrigues	University of Brasilia, Brazil

Joint CSE/QUDOS

Robert Chatley	Imperial College London, UK
Katja Kevic	Microsoft, UK

DETECT

Yassine Ouhammou	LIAS, ISAE-ENSMA, France
Abderrahim Wakrime	Mohammed V University, Morocco

Joint FAACS-MDE4SA

Matteo Camilli	Free University of Bozen-Bolzano, Italy
Stéphanie Challita	Inria, France
Alessio Bucaioni	Mälardalen University, Sweden
Amleto Di Salle	University of L'Aquila, Italy
Ludovico Iovino	Gran Sasso Science Institute, Italy
Peng Liang	Wuhan University, China

IoT-ASAP

Romina Spalazzese	Malmö University, Sweden
Marie Platenius-Mohr	ABB Corporate Research, Germany

Ilias Gerostathopoulos   Vrije Universiteit Amsterdam, The Netherlands
Steffen Becker   University of Stuttgart, Germany

SASI4

Rafael Capilla   Rey Juan Carlos University, Spain
Klaus Schmid   University of Hildesheim, Germany
Patrizio Pelliccione   University of L'Aquila, Italy,
                              and Chalmers — University of Gothenburg, Sweden
Andreas Burger   ABB Corporate Research, Germany
Pablo O. Antonino   Fraunhofer IESE, Germany

WASA

Darko Durisic   Volvo Car Corporation, Sweden
Stefan Kugele   Technische Hochschule Ingolstadt, Germany
Yanja Dajsuren   Eindhoven University of Technology, The Netherlands
Miroslaw Staron   Chalmers – University of Gothenburg, Sweden

Organizing Committee

Workshop Chairs

Mauro Caporuscio   Linnaeus University, Sweden
Anne Koziolek   Karlsruhe Institute of Technology, Germany

Proceedings Chair

Mirco Franzago   University of L'Aquila, Italy

Web Chair

Karthik Vaidhyanathan   Gran Sasso Science Institute, Italy

Journal First Chair

Uwe Zdun   University of Vienna, Austria

Publicity Chairs

Stéphanie Challita   Inria, France
Juergen Musil   TU Wien, Austria

Student Volunteer Chairs

Roberta Capuano   University of L'Aquila, Italy
Jamal El Hecham   IRISA, France

Virtualization Chairs

Claudio Di Sipio   University of L'Aquila, Italy
Luca Traini   University of L'Aquila, Italy

Contents

DETECT - 3rd International Workshop on Modeling, Verification and Testing of Dependable Critical Systems

FAACS-MDE4SA - Joint Workshop on Formal Approaches for Advanced Computing Systems and Model-Driven Engineering for Software Architecture

ECSA 2020 Doctoral Symposium Track

ECSA 2020 Doctoral Symposium Track

Continuing a long tradition of the European Conference on Software Architecture (ECSA), the doctoral symposium at ECSA 2020 offered PhD students an opportunity to provide feedback on their research projects in the broad field of software architecture. The symposium accepted submission from both students at early and advanced stages of their research. Students were encouraged to present their research settings, goals, methods, (preliminary) results, and a critical reflection on their work, by interacting closely with established researchers in their specific areas. Despite the logistic challenges faced due to the COVID–19 pandemic that significantly affected the organization of the conference this year and transformed it into a virtual event, the symposium facilitated students disseminating their research and obtaining constructive feedback on their current research and future research directions.

Every submitted paper was reviewed by at least three members of the Program Committee. The evaluation was based on technical quality of the submission, including clarity, adequacy of the problem tackled, position to related work, self-contained solution description, expected results and evaluation plan, the overall quality, originality of the submission, the novelty of the research approach, and relevance to ECSA 2020. For this edition, we received high-quality submissions, and after a thorough review process, four contributions were accepted for presentation during the conference. Dr. Radu Calinescu gave an inspiring keynote talk on "How to get your research published in a top software engineering venue" that was appreciated by the students as well senior participants.

We thank the ECSA Organizing Committee for their continuous support. Our particular gratitude goes to the Doctoral Symposium Committee members for all their support in evaluating the submissions and guiding the next generation of researchers in the field of software architecture in their initial steps as research professionals and academics. Thanks also to the PhD students who contributed and actively participated and discussed their research projects. We also express our appreciation to the keynote speaker for accepting our invitation. All who contributed enabled us to have a particularly interesting symposium providing constructive input to the students and continuing to develop a spirit of collaborative research in the software architecture community.

Organization

Doctoral Symposium Chairs

Danny Weyns   KU Leuven, Belgium, and Linnaeus University,
Sweden

Patrizia Scandurra   DIGIP, University of Bergamo, Italy

Doctoral Symposium Program Committee

Jesper Andersson	Linnaeus University, Sweden
Francesca Arcelli	Università degli Studi di Milano-Bicocca, Italy
Steffen Becker	University of Stuttgart, Germany
Laurence Duchien	University of Lille, France
Carlo Ghezzi	Politecnico di Milano, Italy
Nicole Levy	Cedric, CNAM, France
Leonardo Mariani	Università degli Studi di Milano-Bicocca, Italy
Raffaela Mirandola	Politecnico di Milano, Italy
Elena Navarro	University of Castilla-La Mancha, Spain
Flavio Oquendo	IRISA, UMR, CNRS, Université de Bretagne-Sud, France
Jennifer Pérez Benedí	Universidad Politécnica de Madrid, Spain
Ralf H. Reussner	Karlsruhe Institute of Technology, Germany
Florence Sedes	Paul Sabatier University, France
Elvinia Riccobene	University of Milan, Italy
Marjan Sirjani	Malardalen University, Sweden
Chouki Tibermacine	University of Montpellier, France
Uwe Zdun	University of Vienna, Austria

Additional Reviewers

Henry Muccini
Antonela Tommasel

A Semiautomatic Approach to Identify Architectural Technical Debt from Heterogeneous Artifacts

Boris Pérez[1,2]([⊠]) [ID]

[1] Universidad de los Andes, Bogotá, Colombia
br.perez41@uniandes.edu.co
[2] Univ. Francisco de Paula Santander, Cúcuta, Colombia
borisperezg@ufps.edu.co

Abstract. Architectural Technical Debt (ATD) is a metaphor used to describe decisions taken by software architects to accomplish short-term goals but possibly negatively affecting the long-term health of the system. However, ATD doesn't receive enough attention for the architect teams because it is hard to identify, to measure, to prioritize, and its value is related to long-term maintenance and evolution of a system. In this research, we propose a model-driven approach that focuses on building a binary classification model for ATD identification based on the information gathered from artifacts produced during architecture design. This model will allow software architects to support the managing of conscious and unconscious ATD in their software projects. This proposal focuses on TD at the architecture-level only without considering source code. The effectiveness of this proposal will be evaluated using case studies and expert interviews.

Keywords: Architectural technical debt · Software architecture · Architectural technical debt management · Model-driven architecture

1 Introduction

Companies related to software development have an increasing pressure to improve their effectiveness in each new deployment, by reducing time or resources, and at the same time, delivering a high-quality solution capable of keeping functional in the long term [3,18]. This leads to software teams to take decisions to accomplish short-term goals but possibly affecting negatively the maintainability of the system [3]. Furthermore, these decisions could be made consciously (i.e. to promote certain quality attributes over others) or could be made unconsciously (i.e. lack of knowledge) [8].

This kind of design decisions when system-wide quality attributes (QAs) of a system, particularly maintainability and evolvability, are consciously or unconsciously compromise, is called Architectural Technical Debt (ATD) [27]. According to Ernst et al. [7], architecture debt is the most common source of

H. Muccini et al. (Eds.): ECSA 2020, CCIS 1269, pp. 5–16, 2020.
https://doi.org/10.1007/978-3-030-59155-7_1

TD. Typical ATD includes violations of best practices, consistency, and integrity constraints of the software architectures [18,27]. If ATD is left unchecked, it can cause expensive repercussions such as making it difficult and slow to add new business value [3]. Xiao et al. [26] stated that most time in the overall maintenance effort is consumed by paying interest on ATD.

Despite its importance, ATD doesn't receive enough attention for the architect teams because it is hard to identify, to measure (it is not easily visible), and its value is related to long-term maintenance and evolution of a system [3,11]. Also, there is a lack of time, a lack of effective tools, a lack of knowledge, and a lack of strategies to get to know what kind of information needs to be collected [17]. Discovering ATD items early in the software life cycle could save a significant amount of maintenance costs [18].

Some approaches for dealing with ATD are focused on individual activities within an overarching process of ATD management [18,26,27], or covering all ATD management activities [13]. However, these approaches are focused on the source code, which may lead to significant rework in order to repay the ATD [12], or relies heavily on interviews with the architecture team.

The goal of this research project is to define and develop a novel semiautomatic ATD identification technique able to support the management of candidate ATD items, and in doing so, supporting architects in making impact-conscious decisions. This approach is relying on architectural models (C&C, Deployment) and heterogeneous artifacts produced during the software architecture design stage together with machine learning techniques. The validation of this approach will be carried on through real industry cases. This work aims to answer the following research questions:

- RQ1: Can information extracted from architectural models and heterogeneous artifacts improve the identification of ATD items in comparison with traditional methods?
- RQ2: Which artifacts are more useful to provide indicators of ATD?
- RQ3: Is it possible to establish a relationship between the evolution of architectural elements and the ATD items injected into the architecture?
- RQ4: How supervised machine learning techniques can support the identification of ATD items?

The research study will include the implementation of the approach and its validation.

2   Related Work

During the past years, several approaches have been proposed to support the identification of ATD [25]. Martini et al. [18] developed a holistic framework for the semi-automated identification and estimation of Architectural Technical Debt in the form of non-modularized components. They run in parallel a refactored version of the component and a not refactored version of the component.

The evaluation was done by comparing the source code, by analyzing the history and the parallel development and maintenance efforts for both systems.

Díaz-Pace et al. [6] used link prediction (LP) techniques to inferring likely configurations of architectural smells. This approach considers a module structure as a network, along with information from previous versions, and applies link prediction techniques. It seeks to predict the appearance of new dependencies in the next system version. Li et al. [15] proposed to use software modularity metrics based on a single version of source code, to calculate ATD. Modularity metrics Index of Package Changing Impact (IPCI) and Index of Package Goal Focus (IPGF) were identified with a high correlation with ANMCC (the average number of modified components per commit). A higher ANMCC indicates more ATD in a software system.

Current approaches for architecture technical debt identification are mostly based at code level analyzing and monitoring [5]. Such approaches rely on the analysis of ATD symptoms to detect specific types of ATD such as architectural antipatterns and smells among architectural components [18], modularity analysis [19], dependency analysis [5] among others. These approaches are focused on code analysis. These approaches can only provide some insights about ATD presence, but it is not possible to confirm whether it is actual ATD nor provide ATD measures [18]. Architectural decisions are an important source of ATD, and some of them are not reflected in the code, for example, immature or obsolete technologies used, their rationale, or architecture nonconformance [2, 27].

Li et al. [27] proposed a decision-based ATDM (DATDM) approach. This process is based on architecture decisions and an ATD conceptual model. This approach is based on human knowledge and therefore, requires a strong presence of software architects. This ensures that ATD identification and measurement is carried out in the most formal and complete way. However, as said in [2], ATD identification and assessment need to be performed with a minimum of human intervention. Besker et al. [3] acknowledged that practical ATD Management (ATDM), with an architectural focus, lacks empirical studies.

Therefore, the research community stated three important requirements on ATD management: (i) To perform identification and assessments with as little human intervention as possible [2], (ii) to develop approaches dealing with artifacts different to source code [12], and (iii) to discover and pay ATD early in the software lifecycle [26].

3   Work Plan

The goal of this research project is to define and develop a novel semiautomatic ATD identification technique able to support the management of candidate ATD items (consciously or unconsciously), and in doing so, supporting architects in making impact-conscious decisions. This work followed three research activities: (i) A systematic review of the literature, (ii) a survey of the state-of-the-practice of causes, effects, monitoring, payment and preventive practices of TD in software projects, and (iii) an approach to support software architects in dealing with ATD.

3.1 Systematic Literature Review

The overall goal of this literature review is to identify, classify, and understand the current state of the art in the field of ATD management. This activity followed the guidelines of Kitchenham et al. [10] and was conducted in the light of the following research questions:

- RQ1: Which approaches to ATDM have been used by both industry and research community?
    - RQ1.1: What are the characteristics of these approaches?
    - RQ1.2: Which artifacts and data sources have been proposed in these approaches?
    - RQ1.3: Which evaluations have been performed in these approaches?
- RQ2: Which ATDM activities are supported in these approaches?

"Software architecture" and any synonyms, and "debt" were defined as search terms. We targeted the search query only to the title to reduce the number of studies from domains different than software development. The search was conducted in January 2019, and include papers from 2010 to 2018. Results obtained with this SLR demonstrate an important interest in looking for ways to deal with ATD. We started with 520 studies, to end up with 20 primary studies via a classification methodology dedicated to ATD management. From our analysis, we could establish that ATD identification and measurement are the most studied activities in the literature. Source code is the most used source of information in order to perform these activities, and interviews and meetings are used to support the insights of the proposals. We can also confirm that a proposal to manage ATD with an architectural focus is missing.

Similar systematic reviews can be found in the literature. Li et al. [12] performed a systematic mapping study of the research work published from 1992 to 2013 on TD and TD management. This study classified TD into 10 types, 8 TDM activities were identified, and 29 tools for TDM were collected. Code debt and architectural debt were the most selected TD types. Alves et al. [1] also performed a systematic mapping study to investigate the current state of the art of TD as well as TD management in practice. In this study, 100 works, dated from 2010 to 2014, were evaluated. They found 15 TD types, been design debt and architecture debt as the most selected one.

Systematic reviews focused on ATD can be found in [3,25]. Verdecchia et al. [25] performed a systematic mapping study for identifying, classifying, and evaluating the state of the art on ATD identification. Starting from 509 potentially relevant studies, they ended up analyzing 47 primary studies. ATD identification techniques were classified according to the level of abstraction (source code packages being the most selected), type of ATD, analysis type (architectural antipatterns and smells being the most selected), analysis input (source code being the most selected), among others. The secondary study of Besker et al. [3] is the closest to ours by focusing exclusively on ATD. This study inspected 42 studies to conceive a novel descriptive model aimed to provide a comprehensive interpretation of the architectural TD phenomenon. Their model identified the main characteristics of ATD in four groups: The importance of ATD, ATD Checklist, ATD Impediments, and ATD Management.

Our study differs from theirs by focusing on ATD management (approaches and activities supported), by having different research questions and focus, and by using a more recent period: from 2010 to 2018. None of the studies aims directly at the characterization of existing approaches for ATD management: characteristics, artifacts and data sources, evaluations, and supported activities. Therefore, conducting this research was a required activity to support our research.

3.2   Survey of the State-of-the-Practice on TD

As part of this study, it was required to understand not only what literature is saying about TD but also the state of practice and industry trends in the TD area. This activity was performed as a part of InsighTD project, which is a globally distributed family of industrial surveys initiated in 2017. Its goal is to gather relevant data about the state of practice of TD and to improve the understanding of TD management. To date, researchers from 11 countries (Brazil, Chile, Colombia, Costa Rica, Finland, India, Italy, Norway, Saudi Arabia, Serbia, and the United States) have joined the project. In this survey, data gathering was done using an online anonymous questionnaire (28 questions). Invitations were sent to software practitioners through LinkedIn, industry-affiliated member groups, mailing lists, and industry partners, as invitation channels.

Several studies have been performed since 2017, including the InsighTD project creation [24], analysis on the causes and effects of TD in agile software projects [23], understanding how practitioners react to the presence of debt in the Chilean software industry [21], among others [9,22]. For example, in [20], Pérez et al. identified refactoring, improve testing and improve design as the most cited practices for TD payment. Also, it was possible to establish a relationship between the age of the software systems and the amount of cited cases of *refactoring*. Software systems with *less than 1 year* (70.6%) of development tend to use more refactoring than software systems with *more than 10 years* (29.4%) of development. Finally, it was identified that refactoring is the main payment practice used by development teams to pay off the debt no matter what caused it to be injected.

3.3   Supporting Software Architects

This section presents a semiautomatic model-driven approach that focuses on building a binary classification model for ATD identification based on the artifacts produced during architecture design. This model will allow software architects to support the managing of conscious and unconscious ATD in their software projects. At the same time, newly identified or justified ATD cases may be used as inputs to the classification model. It is worth to mention that this model will identify candidates of ATD items, and the software architects will be responsible for confirming or rejecting these candidates. We seek to provide the architect with information that he did not have before, and that he/she can now use to make more impact-conscious decisions.

This proposal focuses on TD at the architecture-level only without considering source code. It is expected to work with software teams having several versions of the architecture and several heterogeneous artifacts. According to a study made as a part of InsighTD, we found that almost 59% of the respondents employ a mixing methodology based on traditional and agile approaches.

The core element of this proposal is the Block of Interest (BoI). A BoI represents the evolution of architectural elements during the software design. A BoI is composed of facts, where each fact represents a change in an architectural element (i.e., component), together with its characteristics. This proposal consists of three (3) stages, and eight (8) steps (Fig. 1). These stages are iterative and could be performed multiple times during the life cycle of the project. An iteration will depend on the software architects' team.

Currently, steps 1, 2, and 3 are developed. Step 4 is in progress. Steps 5 and 6 require the manual participation of software architects, and the application is already supporting these two steps. This proposal can work without step 4, focusing only on changes over architectural elements. However, step 4 is used to enrich the decisions taken by software architects and therefore, it is relevant to find justification of architectural decisions. Steps 7 and 8 are still to be developed. Strategies for organizing information for use by the ML model are being evaluated.

Stage 1. Extraction. This stage focused on reviewing artifacts produced during the architecture design stage, extracting information (step 1), and representing them in abstract models (step 2). Each artifact requires a specific procedure to extract its information, and a specific meta-model to represent them. Meta-models are stored in XMI, and designed on Ecore[1]. The meta-model for a component and connector model is presented in Fig. 2. Architectural models (Component & Connector, and Deployment) are required to be designed in Draw.io or LucidChart. Architectural decisions are required to be described using a specific ADR template (title, motivators, decision, alternative, among others). Commits logs also require a specific template defining elements such as type, scope, subject, and body. We plan to analyze which artifacts, by itself or together with another artifact, could provide better hints of ATD presence (RQ2).

Steps 1 and 2 are presented in separate ways because the information extracted from architectural models is used to create the BoI, and information extracted from heterogeneous artifacts is used to enrich the BoI. These artifacts are loaded through a web user interface,m and then steps 1 and 2 are done in an automatic fashion.

Stage 2. Synthesis. This is the core stage in our proposal and its goal is to build an ATD map over the architecture, based on changes in the architectural

---

[1] (Meta)model of Eclipse Modeling Framework (EMF).

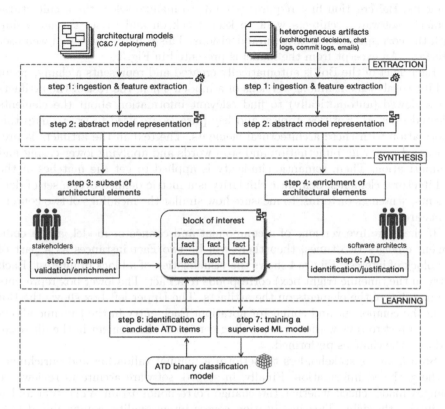

Fig. 1. Overview of the proposal

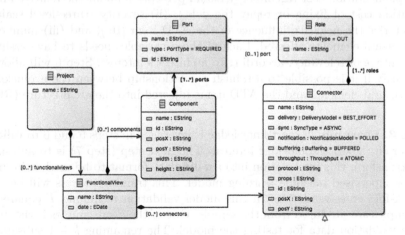

Fig. 2. Component and connector abstract model

elements. BoI creation first requires (step 3) to manual select the architectural elements software architects want to keep track on and to set a relationship with the corresponding architectural decisions. This is made through a web user interface. An excerpt from the model is presented in Fig. 3.

Each Fact of the BoI is automatically created and represents a change in an architectural element among versions of a model. Then, the rest of the artifacts are reviewed (automatically) to find relevant information about the elements selected (step 4). Entities, topics, and key phrases are used to try to map this information with these architectural elements. The text in the artifacts is pre-processed removing punctuation and stop words and applying lower-casing and lemmatization. Then, semantic similarity is applied to get the matches of the architectural elements. Semantic similarity is a metric defined over a set of documents, sentences or terms, to measure how similar the meanings of two content items are.

If there are five versions of a component and connector model, and a component changes two times, then there will be two Fact instances as a part of the block of interest. Figure 4 shows the visualization of a block of interest. Each entry in the timeline (right box) corresponds to a Fact. The lower box represents the matches of the elements on the artifacts. The Upper left box shows the BoI using the component and connector notation. Each entry in the timeline allows the architect to review the corresponding version of the element in the diagram, and also the changes performed.

Step 5 allows stakeholders to perform a manual validation and enrichment of the gathered information. Finally, in step 6, software architects review the changes made, check whether the change corresponds to an ATD item and if so, justify the debt. This justification covers intentionality, compromised QA, rationale, payment practice, among others proposed by Li et al. [14]. Software architects can measure the impact of the ATD item based on three variables: (i) Implementation cost (architect personal perception about the relative implementation cost of fixing or repay the debt), (ii) severity (three-level scale to characterize the negative influence of the ATD item [16]); and (iii) number of architectural elements affected. Each of these variables needs to have assigned a percentage of relevance, according to architect's interest. Step 6 will allow us to identify if it is possible to establish a relationship between the evolution of architectural elements and the ATD items injected into the architecture (RQ3).

Stage 3. Learning. Expert knowledge is leveraged in steps 5 and 6 to validate and enrich (label) the block of interest. The next step (step 7) is to automatically transform this information into a valid data format to be used as input to train a supervised machine learning model. This training process will be done using k-fold cross-validation. In this model validation technique, k equal-sized subsamples are produced from the sample. One of the k subsamples is then used as the validation data for testing the model. The remaining $k - 1$ subsamples are used as training data. This process is repeated k times.

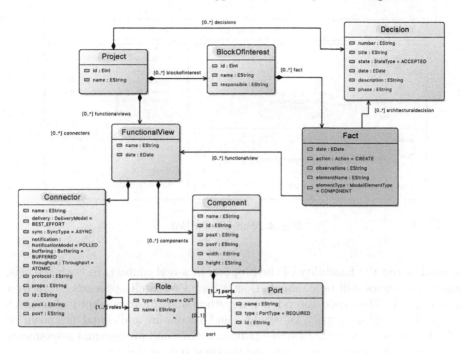

Fig. 3. Model core

The output of this step is a binary classification model, where the target variable (0,1) is an indicator if the element contributes to increase TD. Facts, with all the information related, are used as predictors for this model. The most facts used as predictors, the better the accuracy of the model. During this step, different supervised machine learning algorithms will be tested to identify which one offers the best accuracy (RQ4).

After the model reaches an acceptable level of accuracy, it can be used (step 8) by software architects to support the identification and rationale of candidate ATD items injected into the software architecture. This step will present a detailed list of all candidate ATD items found in the models and artifacts used to design the software architecture.

The main idea is to iterate over the list of Facts previously identified as ATD items and to compare them with a newly created Fact via a classification model. If all information surrounding the Fact is similar, then, the newly created Fact will be marked as a candidate ATD item. Software architects will be responsible to accept or reject the candidate. This way, we will be able to answer if information extracted from architectural models and heterogeneous artifacts can improve the identification of ATD items in comparison with traditional methods (RQ1).

To assess the applicability of this approach, we plan to conduct a set of validations, both in academic and industrial settings. The academic setting will be used to support the training step of the model. The industrial setting will

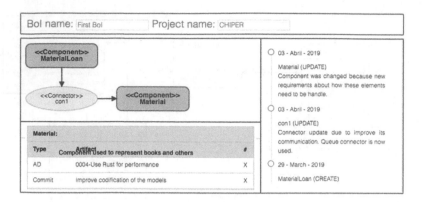

Fig. 4. Web UI of a BoI

be used to test the feasibility of the proposal in a real context. In both settings, expert interviews will be conducted, as a useful research approach to uncover knowledge [4]. The expert interview is a method of qualitative empirical research designed to explore expert knowledge, and to obtain additional unknown or reliable information, authoritative opinions serious and professional assessments of the research topic, in this case, architectural technical debt.

4   Expected Results

As researchers on software architecture, we hope that this proposal can be widespread in the software architects community, to support them during the decision-making process by making visible the ATD present in the architecture of software systems. We hope that this proposal could be used by the local software architects, and then by the global community. This proposal will be freely available through an online repository for two reasons: (i) to support its widespread, and (ii) to allow its improvement through collaboration with the scientific community.

We expect that new architectures and new artifacts can be included as inputs for the training step of the machine learning model, to improve the accuracy of the ATD identification process. We plan to keep researching machine learning techniques to identify which one can provide better accuracy in ATD identification.

We hope that the doctoral symposium helps us to improve and enrich this proposal, through the feedback on the used research methods, and references and guidance related to the work we are developing.

Acknowledgments. The author is working under the supervision of Prof. Darío Correal.

References

1. Alves, N.S., Mendes, T.S., de Mendonça, M.G., Spínola, R.O., Shull, F., Seaman, C.: Identification and management of technical debt: a systematic mapping study. Inf. Softw. Technol. **70**, 100–121 (2016)
2. Avgeriou, P., Kruchten, P., Ozkaya, I., Seaman, C.: Managing technical debt in software engineering (dagstuhl seminar 16162). In: Dagstuhl Reports. No. 4, Schloss Dagstuhl-Leibniz-Zentrum fuer Informatik (2016)
3. Besker, T., Martini, A., Bosch, J.: Managing architectural technical debt: a unified model and systematic literature review. J. Syst. Softw. **135**, 1–16 (2018)
4. Bogner, A., Menz, W.: The theory-generating expert interview: epistemological interest, forms of knowledge, interaction. Interviewing Experts, pp. 43–80. Palgrave Macmillan, UK, London (2009). https://doi.org/10.1057/9780230244276_3
5. Brondum, J., Zhu, L.: Visualising architectural dependencies. In: 2012 Third International Workshop on Managing Technical Debt (MTD), pp. 7–14 (June 2012)
6. Díaz-Pace, J.A., Tommasel, A., Godoy, D.: Towards anticipation of architectural smells using link prediction techniques. In: 2018 IEEE 18th International Working Conference on Source Code Analysis and Manipulation (SCAM), pp. 62–71. IEEE (2018)
7. Ernst, N.A., Bellomo, S., Ozkaya, I., Nord, R.L., Gorton, I.: Measure it? manage it? ignore it? software practitioners and technical debt. In: Proceedings of the 2015 10th Joint Meeting on Foundations of Software Engineering, pp. 50–60. ESEC/FSE 2015, ACM, New York, USA (2015)
8. Falessi, D., Cantone, G., Kazman, R., Kruchten, P.: Decision-making techniques for software architecture design: a comparative survey. ACM Comput. Surv. (CSUR) **43**(4), 33 (2011)
9. Freire, S., et al.: Surveying software practitioners on technical debt payment practices and reasons for not paying off debt items. In: Proceedings of the Evaluation and Assessment in Software Engineering, pp. 210–219. EASE 2020, Association for Computing Machinery, New York, USA (2020)
10. Kitchenham, B., Brereton, O.P., Budgen, D., Turner, M., Bailey, J., Linkman, S.: Systematic literature reviews in software engineering - a systematic literature review. Inf. Softw. Technol. **51**(1), 7–15 (2009)
11. Kruchten, P.: Strategic management of technical debt: tutorial synopsis. In: 2012 12th International Conference on Quality Software, pp. 282–284 (August 2012)
12. Li, Z., Avgeriou, P., Liang, P.: A systematic mapping study on technical debt and its management. J. Syst. Softw. **101**, 193–220 (2015)
13. Li, Z., Liang, P., Avgeriou, P.: Chapter 9- architectural debt management in value-oriented architecting. In: Economics-Driven Software Architecture, pp. 183–204. Morgan Kaufmann, Boston (2014)
14. Li, Z., Liang, P., Avgeriou, P.: Chapter 5- architecture viewpoints for documenting architectural technical debt. In: Software Quality Assurance, pp. 85–132. Morgan Kaufmann, Boston (2016)
15. Li, Z., Liang, P., Avgeriou, P., Guelfi, N., Ampatzoglou, A.: An empirical investigation of modularity metrics for indicating architectural technical debt. In: Proceedings of the 10th International ACM Sigsoft Conference on Quality of Software Architectures, pp. 119–128. QoSA 2014, ACM, New York, USA (2014)
16. Marinescu, R.: Assessing technical debt by identifying design flaws in software systems. IBM J. Res. Dev. **56**(5), 1–9 (2012)

17. Martini, A., Besker, T., Bosch, J.: The introduction of technical debt tracking in large companies. In: 2016 23rd Asia-Pacific Software Engineering Conference (APSEC), pp. 161–168 (December 2016)
18. Martini, A., Sikander, E., Madlani, N.: A semi-automated framework for the identification and estimation of architectural technical debt: a comparative case-study on the modularization of a software component. Inf. Softw. Technol. **93**, 264–279 (2018)
19. Nord, R.L., Ozkaya, I., Sangwan, R.S., Koontz, R.J.: Architectural dependency analysis to understand rework costs for safety-critical systems. In: Companion Proceedings of the 36th International Conference on Software Engineering, pp. 185–194. ICSE Companion 2014, ACM, New York, USA (2014)
20. Pérez, B., et al.: What are the practices used by software practitioners on technical debt payment? results from an international family of surveys. In: To appear in the Proceedings of the 3rd International Conference on Technical Debt. TechDebt, ACM (2020)
21. Pérez, B., et al.: Familiarity, causes and reactions of software practitioners to the presence of technical debt: a replicated study in the chilean software industry. In: 2019 38th International Conference of the Chilean Computer Science Society (SCCC), pp. 1–7 (2019)
22. Rios, N., et al.: Hearing the voice of software practitioners on causes, effects, and practices to deal with documentation debt. In: Madhavji, N., Pasquale, L., Ferrari, A., Gnesi, S. (eds.) REFSQ 2020. LNCS, vol. 12045, pp. 55–70. Springer, Cham (2020). https://doi.org/10.1007/978-3-030-44429-7_4
23. Rios, N., Mendonça, M.G., Seaman, C., Spinola, R.O.: Causes and effects of the presence of technical debt in agile software projects (2019)
24. Rios, N., Spínola, R.O., Mendonça, M., Seaman, C.: The most common causes and effects of technical debt: first results from a global family of industrial surveys. In: Proceedings of the 12th ACM/IEEE International Symposium on Empirical Software Engineering and Measurement, p. 39. ACM (2018)
25. Verdecchia, R., Malavolta, I., Lago, P.: Architectural technical debt identification: the research landscape. In: International Conference on Technical Debt (TechDebt) (2018)
26. Xiao, L., Cai, Y., Kazman, R., Mo, R., Feng, Q.: Identifying and quantifying architectural debt. In: Proceedings of the 38th International Conference on Software Engineering, pp. 488–498. ICSE 2016, ACM, New York, USA (2016)
27. Zengyang Li, P.L., Avgeriou, P.: Architectural technical debt identification based on architecture decisions and change scenarios. In: 2015 12th Working IEEE/IFIP Conference on Software Architecture, pp. 65–74 (May 2015)

Big Data and Machine Intelligence in Software Platforms for Smart Cities

Mubashir Ali(✉) iD

DIGIP, University of Bergamo, Bergamo, Italy
mubashir.ali@unibg.it

Abstract. Information and communication technologies (ICT) are playing an important role in the development of software platforms for Smart
Cities to improve city services, sustainability, and citizen quality of life.
Smart City software platforms have a significant role to transform a city
into a *smart city* by providing support for the development and integration of intelligent services. Big data analytics is an emerging technology
that has a huge potential to enhance smart city services by transforming city information into city intelligence. Despite this,it has attracted
attention in a rather restricted range of application domains, and its
joint application with self-adaptation mechanisms is rarely investigated.

In this Ph.D. research, in collaboration with the Smart Cities and
Communities Lab. of the Italian national agency ENEA, we focus on
the design and development of a software platform for smart city based
on *self-adaptation,* as realized in the IBM MAPE-K (Monitor, Analyze,
Plan, and Execute over a shared Knowledge) control loop architecture
model, and on *machine intelligence,* as provided by a big data analytics
framework. This last is introduced in between the analysis and planning
modules of the MAPE-K control loop model. We will evaluate the effectiveness of the proposed approach with a real showcase in the public
lighting domain.

Keywords: Smart city platform · Big data analytics · Self-adaptation

1 Introduction

More than half of the world population is living in the cities [13]. So facilitating
the city residents with better services and managing the services offered in the
city is an important task for the city managers. In this regard, many countries
are working in the development of Smart City projects. The rapid integration
in the field of Information and Communication Technology (ICT) and Internet of Things (IoT) is playing a significant role in making a city "smart". The
Smart City concept has been widely and variously defined by the industry and

This Ph.D. research is conducted in collaboration with the Smart Cities and Communities Lab. of the Italian national agency ENEA.

academia. According to [4,19], Smart City is the integration of social, physical and IT infrastructures to improve the quality of city services. The primary objective of the Smart City projects is to improve the city infrastructure by making use of ICT and IoT solutions and providing smart services to the citizens. The most common smart services offered usually are effective traffic and parking management, safety and security, environmental monitoring, to name a few. The storage and analysis of this heterogeneous multimodel urban data is crucial for a variety of goals, but traditional database management systems cannot help to achieve these goals. The recent development in the big data technologies and analytic techniques have made possible to get insight from raw data and derive useful hidden patterns on how people use cities that can be used for the development of novel intelligent smart services.

Development of intelligent smart services is equally important for citizens as well as for the business organizations. Lopez et al. [14] have identified and reviewed existing intelligent business and management models in the big data era. They stated that "Intelligence" is understood as a process of gathering, analyzing, interpreting, and disseminating high-value data and information at the right time for use in the decision-making process. No doubt, big data tools are very essentials for the storage and aggregation of large scale heterogeneous multimodel data, but computationally intensive machine intelligence and data analytics solutions are required to extract the hidden useful information that pro facilitate the city planners [9,12].

Public lighting energy management is one of the most crucial problems for smart cities [18]. Public lighting is one of the biggest energy consumers, especially public buildings such as government, health, and educational institutes have a high usage frequency [24]. However, the applications of big data analytics in this domain are limited.

Most of the studies reported in the literature rely on a very limited amount of historical data and are unable to process large amounts of urban data intelligently based on machine learning as well as big data platforms. Existing systems also lack of support for the identification of KPIs (Key Performance Indicators) – such as lighting KPIs (e.g., power per square meter, power per inhabitant, power per lighting spot, dimming KPIs, etc.) and KPIs for anomalies detection (outlier detection) – and forecasting models (such as time series prediction and anomaly prediction). With the aim of supporting city decision making processes and overcome these shortcomings, more intelligent systems based on big data analytics are required.

The goal of this PhD research project is to design and develop a novel big data analytic framework to support the decision making process in self-adaptive smart city software platforms, and therefore provide more intelligent city services. The proposed generic analytical framework will initially be validated in the public lighting domain to address the above highlighted limitations of the existing systems.

In order to achieve such a goal, the following main research questions are formulated:

- **RQ1:** How big data analytics and self-adaptation mechanisms can be integrated in smart city software platforms?
- **RQ2:** Which machine learning and deep learning algorithms are more suitable to support decision making in self-adaptive smart city software platforms?
- **RQ3:** Which big data technology stack and performance metrics are useful for the public lighting data analysis?
- **RQ4:** Which artifacts and emerging standards are more useful to provide KPI for smart cities and how these can be quantitatively measured?

2   Related Work

The state-of-the-art includes two main streams of research: (i) big data analytics for smart city platforms, and (ii) works about smart city services reported in the public lighting domain.

Big Data Analytics in Smart City Platforms. The role of big data in the development of smart cities is undeniable [10]. Big data analytics is an emerging technology that has a huge potential to enhance smart city services by transforming city information into city intelligence. Despite this, it has attracted attention in a rather restricted range of application domains, and its joint application with self-adaptation mechanisms is rarely investigated. The big data analytics has been actively used in the development of smart city software architecture, in this section, existing state-of-the art on smart city software architectures adopting big data analytics and self-adaptation are discussed.

Azzam et al. [2] proposed the architecture of the *CitySPIN* project for the development of smart services. The platform of the *CitySPIN* is assisted with methods and techniques, which are based on Semantic WEB and Linked Data technologies for the acquisition and integration of heterogeneous data of different formats (structured, unstructured, and semi-structured), including open data and social data. The *CitySPIN* project is based on a three-layered architecture: 1) back-end layer, which is responsible for data collection, pre-processing and data integration, 2) service layer, which provides the services of analysis by applying queries and prediction model. The prediction model is based on machine learning algorithms to facilitate the prediction by using historical data that can assist in decision making, and 3) front end layer or presentation layer, which facilitate the users to interact with the system and perform different kinds of analysis of their need.

In another study [17], a *CityPulse* framework is presented for the development of smart city services by enabling the integration of heterogeneous data streams, interoperability, (near-) real-time data analytics, and applications development in a scalable framework. The CityPulse framework is composed of a powerful data analytics module, which is empowered to perform intelligent data aggregation, quality assessment, event detection, contextual filtering, and decision support. All the components of the *CityPulse* have been developed as reusable entities and application development is facilitated by open APIs.

Pedro et al. [16] proposed a project called *CityAction* in the context of smart city, which facilitate the city managers to take actions/decisions on the bases of real-time city data. The main objective of the project is to support the design and development of an integrated platform that has the ability to combine city data coming from different sources with heterogeneous devices and perform intelligent data analysis. The architecture of the *CityAction* is based on four independent layers: 1) Device layer, in which IoT sensors, actuators and communication gateways correspond to different vertical systems, 2) M2M Connectivity layer, which is responsible for the devices interconnection to the internet, 3) Middleware layer, this layer has the responsibility to integrate several blocks like data broker, monetization, data management and analytics, vertical management M2M management, and API management, 4) Application layer that also has an ability to incorporate the open data to enrich the application portfolio. Mohamed et al. [5] came up with another approach to transform big data into a smart data. In this study, they introduced a system called *CityPro*. The architecture of the *CityPro* is discussed for surveillance system. In the architecture of the *CityPro*, a federated star-schema is used in the storage repository and repository only store the summarized data instead of huge amount of data.

In another study [6], an approach is discussed for the development of next-generation big data applications. they have proposed a *CAPIM* (Context-Aware Platform using Integrated Mobile services) platform, which is design to automate the process of collecting and aggregating the context information on a large scale. An intelligent transportation system is developed by using *CAPIM* platform, which helps the user and city managers to understand the traffic problems of their city. In another interesting study, Paula et al. [21] proposed a simple and scalable *hut* architecture to extract the valuable historical insights and actionable knowledge from IoT data streams. The developed *hut* architecture support both historical as well as real-time data analysis. It is applied on two real-world applications scenarios in smart city environment such as transportation and energy management. The implementation of the *hut* architecture is based on the open source components and can be replaced or customized according to the need. In another study [20], authors proposed a system called CrowdNav to enable self-adaptation in a complex large scale software-intensive distributed system by using big data analytics. The novel contribution of the developed system is to use the operational data, which is generated at run-time for adaption and the seamless integration of self-adaptation with latest Big Data technologies.

Smart Public Lighting. Our proposed smart city software architecture will initially be validated in the public lighting domain, so hereafter we have presented some notable studies reported in the public lighting domain. Marijana et al. [24] proposed an approach to address the issues of energy efficiency of the public buildings. The contribution of this approach is two-fold: 1) apply machine learning models to predict the energy consumption of the public building, a real dataset of Croatia that composed of 17,000 public buildings is used for experimental evaluation. Three well known ML methods i.e. deep neural network, RPart decision tree, and random forest were used, and it is observed that random forest produce the highest accuracy, and 2) an architecture of an intelligent machine learning based energy management system called: MERIDA that is composed of six layers i.e. i) big data collection, ii) data pre-processing, iii) ML models for prediction, iv) data interpretation and visualisation, v) decision making, and vi) benefits. This proposed study has extended and modified the approaches presented in [11,15,22].

In another study [15], authors proposed an advanced IoT based intelligent energy management system for public buildings. The architecture of the proposed system consists of three modules: 1) data collection module 2) data integration module, and 3) prediction models/rules and action plans. In the first module of the proposed system, authors introduced five pillars such as building's data, energy production, energy prices, weather data, and end-users' behavior. In data integration module, a semantic framework for data integration is proposed, which is based on Ztreamy system, a Python-based semantic service and Optimus ontology is also created. The third module integrates prediction models, rules, and a MariaDB database that is used to store the results. In [11], authors discussed an IoT based system comprised of three-layered architecture. The identified IoT layers are: (1) the perception layer that is composed of internet-enabled devices (sensors. cameras, GPS, RFID, etc), (2) the network layer, which is responsible to forward data from perception layer to the application layer, and (3) the application layer, which process the data coming from previous two layers and suggest better power's distribution and management strategies. Authors stress that Supervisory Control and Data Acquisition (SCADA) systems are the core of decision making in smart grid, and these systems are used for real-time monitoring and control over the power grid.

Galicia et al. [8], proposed a machine learning based ensemble method for predicting time series big data. The ensemble model is composed of a decision tree, gradient boosted trees, and a random forest. The system is implemented by using MLib library of the Apache Spark framework to ensure the scalability and suitability for big data. The experimental evaluation is performed on two different datasets i.e. Spanish electricity consumption data of 10 years, and Australian solar data. The experimental results showed that dynamic ensemble model provides best prediction results in comparison with static ensemble and individual ensemble members.

In another similar study [23], a deep learning based approach is proposed for big data time series forecasting. The deep feed forward neural network is used with Apache Spark platform for distributing computing. The system is evaluated on a real-world dataset composed of electricity consumption in Spain and authors observed that deep learning is one of the best technique to process big data time series along with the decision tree, in term of scalability and accuracy. In [22], an intelligent building management system is proposed to manage the public sector buildings of Croatia.The system is based on a three layered architecture, which collects building data, their energy, water consumption, monitor consumption indicators, detects anomalies or irregularities, sets energy efficiency targets and reports energy and water consumption savings.

An IoT and big data analytics based smart home energy management system is presented in [1], in which IoT devices are installed with home appliances to collect the energy consumption data, then collected data is forward to a centralized server for further processing and analysis. The proposed system has utilized off-the-shelf business intelligence (BI) and big data analytics software components to manage energy consumption. In [7], authors presented an adaptive lighting system for smart city environment. The developed system has an ability to autonomously control the lighting level of a street lamp by exploiting the vehicles data (car, bus, bike motorcycle) and pedestrian traffic in the targeted area. The system is making use of locally installed controllers, motion sensors, video cameras and electronic devices for video processing. Authors reported that by using this proposed system up to 65% energy can be saved in comparison of tradition street lamp system.

From a preliminary state-of-the-art review, it seems there does not exist a general smart city software platform designed by the joint application of big data analytics and self-adaptation mechanisms. It has also been observed that most of the software architectures for smart city services, which support adaptability, do not explicitly adopt a MAPE-K control loop architecture for self-adaptation.

3 Proposed Approach

This section presents a preliminary outline of a *big data-driven self-adaptive software architecture* to Support smart city decision making (see Fig. 1). The main modules of the proposed architecture are the Knowledge repository, Monitor, Analysis, Planning, Execute, and the Analytical framework. This last is the major focus of our research effort, together with the concrete realization and evaluation with respect to the public lighting domain. The function of each module is described in the following paragraphs.

Knowledge Repository. It is composed of a urban big data lake and by the useful knowledge and analytical models' results produced by the MAPE modules and by the analytical framework.

Monitor Module. It consists of static and dynamic data collection frameworks and of a real-time data stream processing and integration middleware. For example, the *Monitor* component may collect data from the lighting managed system PELL (Public Energy Living Lab), a project started by ENEA in 2014[1]. The primary objective of the PELL system is to collect, handle, organize and evaluate the dynamic and static strategic data of urban energy-intensive infrastructures (public lighting and public buildings). PELL brokers and gateway act as a sensors to update the monitor module.

---

[1] https://www.pell.enea.it/enea/.

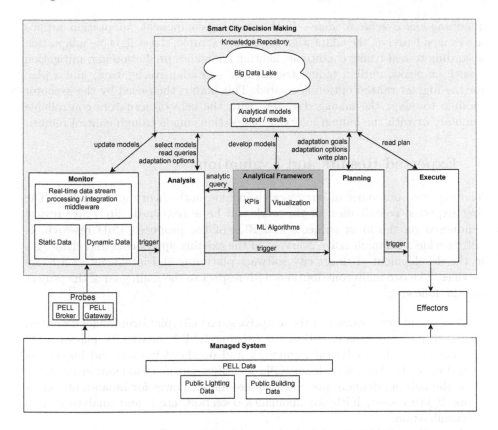

Fig. 1. Proposed adaptive smart city software architecture

Analysis Module and Analytical Framework. The analysis module analyzes the up to date knowledge to determine whether adaptation is required or not. In order to support dynamic adaptation, we have introduced an analytical framework in between the analysis and planning phases of the MAPE-K loop. The analytical framework consists of KPIs management tools, machine learning (ML) algorithms and city visualization dashboards. Different machine learning techniques such as supervised learning, unsupervised learning and reinforcement learning will be investigated for providing descriptive, predictive and prescriptive analysis. Since the performance of the machine learning models is highly dependent on the quality of data, different data pre-processing techniques will be applied to transform unstructured data into structured form. The analysis module could formulate analytical queries to the analytical framework in order to get the desired analysis, then their output/results are provided to the analysis component by making them available into the knowledge repository. Once the analysis components have performed the required analysis, it may trigger the planning module.

Planning and Execute Modules. In the planning component, adaptation options are ranked based on the adaptation goals (for example, street lighting adaptation according to real traffic conditions, lighting anomalies prediction and mitigation – such as peaks, outlier, faults, trends, etc. – in adaptive lighting) and a plan for the highest ranked option is created. This plan is then used by the executor module to adapt the managed system with the help of actuators controllable remotely or with the human interventions/actions made trough control rooms.

4   Expected Results and Evaluation

The expected outcomes of our research include both theory and practice. The first expected contribution of the work will be a systematic literature review conducted on the main subjects and RQs of the proposed PhD research. It will provide a comprehensive overview of the existing approaches and challenges in the development of smart city software platforms and intelligent smart city services. The two main contributions with respect to the main goal of the project are the following:

– Design and development of the adaptive smart city platform model described in the previous section within the existing ENEA smart city platform [3], focusing on the analytical framework and on the definition and implementation of the ML algorithms, KPIs identification and calculation (such as, in the lighting domain, power for square meter, power for inhabitant, power for lighting spot, KPIs for anomalies detection, etc.), and analytical data visualization.
– Evaluation of the proposed platform with a real-world smart city use case in the domain of public lighting. Intelligent analysis of the PELL public lighting data (such as descriptive, predictive, and prescriptive analysis) will be conducted.

5   Conclusion

In this paper, we have presented a research summary of a PhD project. We presented the design of our proposed smart city software architecture and highlighted the challenges in the existing smart city software platforms. The proposed architecture model is based on big data-driven software self-adaptation. We have also discussed the modules of proposed architecture with respect to big data analytics and the self-adaptation mechanism that we intend to use, namely the MAPE-K loop. We will evaluate the effectiveness of proposed approach into a PELL project use case.

Acknowledgement. This research program is supported in part by the Italian agency ENEA and the Italy's Lombardy Region.

References

1. Al-Ali, A.R., Zualkernan, I.A., Rashid, M., Gupta, R., AliKarar, M.: A smart home energy management system using iot and big data analytics approach. IEEE Trans. Consum. Electron. **63**(4), 426–434 (2017)
2. Azzam, A., et al.: The citySPIN platform: a CPSS environment for city-wide infrastructures (2019)
3. Brutti, A., et al.: Smart city platform specification: a modular approach to achieve interoperability in smart cities. In: Cicirelli, F., Guerrieri, A., Mastroianni, C., Spezzano, G., Vinci, A. (eds.) The Internet of Things for Smart Urban Ecosystems. IT, pp. 25–50. Springer, Cham (2019). https://doi.org/10.1007/978-3-319-96550-5_2
4. Caragliu, A., Del Bo, C., Nijkamp, P.: Smart cities in Europe. J. Urban Technol. **18**(2), 65–82 (2011)
5. Dbouk, M., Hakim, M., Sbeity, I.: CityPro: from big-data to intelligent-data; a smart approach. In: BDCSIntell, pp. 100–106 (2018)
6. Dobre, C., Xhafa, F.: Intelligent services for big data science. Future Gen. Comput. Syst. **37**, 267–281 (2014)
7. Gagliardi, G., et al.: A smart city adaptive lighting system. In: 2018 Third International Conference on Fog and Mobile Edge Computing (FMEC), pp. 258–263. IEEE (2018)
8. Galicia, A., Talavera-Llames, R., Troncoso, A., Koprinska, I., Martínez-Álvarez, F.: Multi-step forecasting for big data time series based on ensemble learning. Knowl. Based Syst. **163**, 830–841 (2019)
9. Habibzadeh, H., Kaptan, C., Soyata, T., Kantarci, B., Boukerche, A.: Smart city system design: a comprehensive study of the application and data planes. ACM Comput. Surv. **52**(2), 1–38 (May 2019). https://doi.org/10.1145/3309545
10. Hashem, I.A.T., et al.: The role of big data in smart city. Int. J. Inf. Manag. **36**(5), 748–758 (2016)
11. Jangili, S., Bikshalu, K.: Smart grid administration using big data and wireless sensor networks. Int. J. Adv. Res. Sci. Eng **6**, 629–636 (2017)
12. Juan, Y.K., Wang, L., Wang, J., Leckie, J.O., Li, K.M.: A decision-support system for smarter city planning and management. IBM J. Res. Dev. **55**(1.2), 1–3 (2011)
13. Lea, R.J.: Smart cities: an overview of the technology trends driving smart cities (2017)
14. López-Robles, J.R., Otegi-Olaso, J.R., Gómez, I.P., Cobo, M.J.: 30 years of intelligence models in management and business: a bibliometric review. Int. J. Inf. Manag. **48**, 22–38 (2019)
15. Marinakis, V., Doukas, H.: An advanced IoT-based system for intelligent energy management in buildings. Sensors **18**(2), 610 (2018)
16. Martins, P., Albuquerque, D., Wanzeller, C., Caldeira, F., Tomé, P., Sá, F.: Cityaction a smart-city platform architecture. In: Arai, K., Bhatia, R. (eds.) FICC 2019. LNNS, vol. 69, pp. 217–236. Springer, Cham (2020). https://doi.org/10.1007/978-3-030-12388-8_16
17. Puiu, D., et al.: Citypulse: large scale data analytics framework for smart cities. IEEE Access **4**, 1086–1108 (2016)
18. Radulovic, D., Skok, S., Kirincic, V.: Energy efficiency public lighting management in the cities. Energy **36**(4), 1908–1915 (2011)
19. Robert, G., et al.: Will the real smart city please stand up? City **12**(3), 303–320 (2008)

20. Schmid, S., Gerostathopoulos, I., Prehofer, C., Bures, T.: Self-adaptation based on big data analytics: a model problem and tool. In: 2017 IEEE/ACM 12th International Symposium on Software Engineering for Adaptive and Self-Managing Systems (SEAMS), pp. 102–108. IEEE (2017)
21. Ta-Shma, P., Akbar, A., Gerson-Golan, G., Hadash, G., Carrez, F., Moessner, K.: An ingestion and analytics architecture for iot applied to smart city use cases. IEEE Internet of Things J. 5(2), 765–774 (2017)
22. Tomšić, Ž., Gašić, I., Čačić, G.: Energy management in the public building sector-isge/isemic model. Energija 64(1–4) (2015)
23. Torres, J.F., Galicia, A., Troncoso, A., Martínez-Álvarez, F.: A scalable approach based on deep learning for big data time series forecasting. Integr. Comput. Aided. Eng. 25(4), 335–348 (2018)
24. Zekić-Sušac, M., Mitrović, S., Has, A.: Machine learning based system for managing energy efficiency of public sector as an approach towards smart cities. Int. J. Inf. Manag. 102074 (2020)

Decentralized Self-adaptation in Large-Scaled Systems of Systems

Daniel Matusek[✉] [ID]

Institute of Systems Architecture, Chair of Computer Networks, Technische
Universität Dresden, 01069 Dresden, Germany
daniel.matusek@tu-dresden.de

Abstract. Today's distributed applications require steady maintenance. To tackle this problem, so-called self-adaptive systems (SAS) can
be used to change the behaviour automatically to adapt to a changing
environment and context. Open challenges remain when those SAS get
combined with Systems of Systems (SoS). SoS can get partitioned in multiple sub-parts as a result of errors or connection faults which rises the
need for a decentralized self-adaptation approach in SoS. In this doctoral
paper, those open challenges are discussed and explained using a scenario
of self-driving vehicles. Ideas for solving the problems are presented and
the evaluation method of using the Webots simulation environment is
explained. Solving the problems of self-adaptive SoS will enable robust
adaptations in large-scale systems.

Keywords: Self-adaptive systems · Decentralized systems · Robust ·
Distributed systems · Systems of systems

1 Motivation

Today's distributed applications require steady maintenance. To tackle this problem, so-called self-adaptive systems (SAS) could be used to change the behaviour
automatically [1]. Solving the problem of adapting systems to changing context
and its environment would allow for nearly perpetual running systems [2]. SAS
can monitor themselves and their environment and analyse the state to adopt
the internal structure and behaviour to the changed context. Many proposed
systems use a central instance to control adaptation across multiple devices.

Systems of systems (SoS) are large interconnected collaborative systems [3],
which consist of multiple autonomous systems. They work together to achieve a
common goal, but the individual subsystems can have their own goals, too. Due
to numerous participants from different manufacturers heterogeneity is introduced into those systems. During the lifetime of an SoS, communication errors
or internal errors can occur, which impacts the coordination of self-adaptation
and disturbs a trouble-free procedure. Due to connection faults, new subsystems
can emerge and a system gets partitioned in even more parts. Due to multiple
autonomous parts and heterogeneity of the system, a centralized approach for

© Springer Nature Switzerland AG 2020
H. Muccini et al. (Eds.): ECSA 2020, CCIS 1269, pp. 27–37, 2020.
https://doi.org/10.1007/978-3-030-59155-7_3

self-adaptation in SoS is not suitable due to possible bottlenecks, communication overhead and a single-point-of-failure.

A decentralized solution for coordinating adaptations increases robustness and allows for improving the scalability of those systems [4]. Recently researchers proposed first approaches for the decentralized coordination of adaptations [5]. By developing a communication protocol to invoke adaptations decentrally, the need for a central instance was superseded. This approach has not been yet adopted for SoS, where the overall system structure is more complex than in a plain distributed system. Current approaches [5] rely on disturbance-free communication and correct working nodes, which might not be suitable in an SoS when many participants are involved. Enabling decentralization for self-adaptation in SoS would help to make those systems more robust and solving the remaining research challenges.

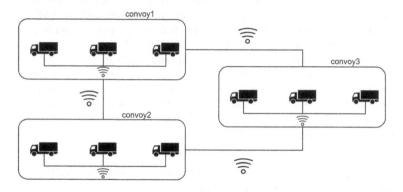

Fig. 1. Introduction of the scenario

Problem Scenario. To describe the problems which arise when combining self-adaptation and SoS, a scenario of a self-organizing [6] SoS is presented (see Fig. 1). The SoS consists of trucks, which span convoys or partitions of convoys on a network of highways. Convoys are organized towards a common goal and work together to optimize their results and fulfilment of the task. Each convoy can communicate with all the other convoys and the trucks can communicate with the other trucks in their convoy. In Fig. 1 the communication between trucks and convoys is indicated. Those connections could be disturbed and prevent the message exchange between participants, or even lead to the isolation of single trucks because they cannot connect to other peers. The subsystems get divided into multiple subparts and partitions are emerging. Those subparts should be able to work for their own to keep the whole system running. Split trucks from their convoy should now organize themselves together and continue to realize their system goal and possibly connect to their originating convoy later. Figure 3 shows a connection error for *convoy1*, where the right truck cannot communicate with others at this moment. This results in missing messages about ongoing adaptations by other trucks even in the same convoy. A truck or convoy might not adapt to a new or changed goal.

Scenario System Model. For the scenario and throughout the thesis, assumptions must be made about the underlying system model to understand the identified challenges and preliminary research questions. First, a decision about the form of coordination and knowledge sharing, i.e. if every participant must know about each other and if every participant must learn about all adaptations and changes in the system. Since the member of the SoS can change dynamically, the participants do not necessarily need to know about every single truck in the system.

To perform adaptations, member of the SoS must agree on or decline the adaptation, which leads to a decision whether we need a strong consensus to adapt as one or if subparts are allowed to adapt without the agreement of other subsystems or nodes. Since the scenario is considered a large-scale system, it would be a drawback if all nodes of the SoS must have agreed on an adaptation. Therefore adaptations without the agreement of all other participants are possible.

Next to the aforementioned constraints for the regarded types of SoS, additional properties must be met by the designed scenario. We use the characteristics described by Wätzold et al. [7]. The SoS is open, which allows for new participants during run-time and also allows for leaving members. The system is heterogeneous, which means that different types of members can be part of the system, e.g. different manufacturers. Self-adaptivity is a mandatory property. Next, it is a dynamic system because its internal structure can be varying during runtime. The subsystems in the SoS work collaborative to achieve a common goal but can work independently if they are on their own. Decentralization is a key aspect in this example to ensure higher availability when convoys move independently [8]. A central coordination instance is a single point of failure and if this central instance is not reachable due to shortages or connection issues, adaptations could not be invoked. Besides that, we eliminate a single point of trust and allow multiple instances to make decisions instead of trusting only one central node. Additionally, decentralized control allows for better scalability [4], which is crucial in a scenario of self-driving trucks, where the number of participants is unknown upfront.

2   Foundations

During the thesis, the notion of roles will be used to develop a solution for the problem of robust, decentralized SAS. With the help of roles, we can express the context-dependent and collaborative behaviour of objects, which is crucial for self-adaptive SoS. This approach has been proposed by Charles W. Bachmann [9] in 1973. To describe roles, their objects and properties, Steimann introduced 15 features which apply for role-based infrastructure [10]. Kuehn et al. [11] surveyed several approaches for role-based programming languages and defined an extended understanding of roles, in addition to those from Steimann

[10]. An object enriched with a role can act according to its played role and extends its original behaviour by the properties of the role. A big advantage of this concept is the ability to dynamically change the role of an object during runtime. This enables run-time adaptation which supersedes the need for long maintenance breaks and downtimes. An object (a so-called natural type), which could be e.g. a real-world entity, can play one or more roles and so change the behaviour, functions and abilities. Functionality could be loaded during run-time and would allow for a nearly perpetual runtime if we took aside arising errors or bugs. Those are some of the properties that can be exploited in the research of self-adaptive software systems. To develop role-based applications, a role-based domain-specific language called SCROLL was developed, which is based on scala and allows for dynamic dispatch [12].

Weißbach et al. [5] introduced an algorithm for coordinated decentralized adaptations. Every node has its adaptation manager (AM) which is responsible for invoking adaptations on the node runtime and is communicating with the AM on other nodes. The structure is indicated in Fig. 2. The adaptation coordination is managed by the AM on a higher layer. The adaptation process is performed transactionally and atomically, which means that only if every participant agrees and successfully prepares the adaptation, it will be executed. Otherwise, the changes will be rolled back. Every AM is allowed to invoke an adaptation if necessary. The implementation and concept from Weißbach et al. [5] are using a local role application runtime called LyRT[1] [13,14] on their nodes, which naturally allows for the run-time adaptations of the objects.

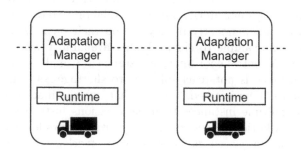

Fig. 2. Adaptation Manager in decentralized protocol

The protocol from Weißbach et al. [5] performing adaptations in an atomic and transactional way. This fits the concept of ACID (atomicity, consistency, isolation and durability) properties for database systems. This ensures that an adaptation is only successful if the whole change is applied for every participant. A contrary concept are BASE (Basic Availability, Soft-State, Eventual consistency) database transactions, which ensures that some level of availability is guaranteed and the data might not be the most current. Eventual consistency

---

[1] https://github.com/nguonly/lyrt-with-transaction.

ensures, that the system will reach some guaranteed state eventually, but not necessarily at every moment.

Conflict-Free Replicated Data Types (CRDTs) is a distributed data structure which allows for the automated synchronisation of distributed replicated data sets. CRDTs can be used offline and are not dependent on their latency. E.g., two parties share a common file and have an offline copy each. They are allowed to work offline on them and to make changes. When they both are online again, the replicas will get synchronised in the background automatically. CRDT enable the concept of eventual consistency of BASE, because the replicated datasets are not consistent if the participants are not connected, but synchronise afterwards.

3 Research Gap and Research Questions

In the following section, identified problems of the existing work and related research questions will be presented which will be tackled in the next years. Limitations are presented and discussed.

Subsystems in SoS can be the result of errors and connection faults, which partition the system. Those emerged subsystems could now perform adaptations to provide useful services within each partition. Each partition then takes its own independent adaptation decisions and thus, the subparts drift away from a globally consistent configuration. As a consequence, after reintegrating the subparts synchronization might be necessary to unite all system parts back to a single system. This challenge was already indicated by Weyns et al. [15]. This results from the independence of SoS because subsystems want to achieve their goals. Projecting this onto the scenario, *Convoy1* and *convoy2* from Fig. 1 could both trigger adaptations which affect the whole SoS including *convoy3*. Those changes can be contradictory to each other, which affects the system negatively. Considering the protocol from Weißbach et al. [5], concurrent adaptations could be even invoked by every single truck. This leads to the first research question: **RQ1.** How are concurrent adaptations in multiple subsystems handled?

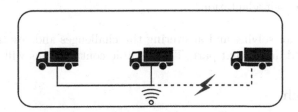

Fig. 3. Connection error in a convoy

Resulting inconsistency and a possibly false state of the system as a cause of connection errors is another challenge to tackle. Due to missing information because of a connection error, a truck or convoy might have wrong routing information and keep moving towards a wrong goal. Using the Weißbach protocol to perform a decentralized adaptation, the adaptation would be aborted since the disconnected truck could not respond to the request. For our scenario, aborting a change might not be the optimal solution regarding self-optimization. Inconsistency is tolerable to a certain point, but it must be dealt with.

RQ2. How can we recover a consistent state in an SoS after a self-adaptation was performed when a node or connection failed?

Another aspect to investigate is the distribution of leaders in the SoS [16] and the hierarchy of decentralized SoS. In the decentralized coordination protocol from Weißbach et al. [5] each AM can act as a coordinator in the system. The problem is illustrated in Fig. 1. With the protocol in its current form, every truck can invoke changes for the whole system regardless of its convoy. It is questionable if this is suitable for SoS, where a system is divided into multiple subsystems because it raises the communication overhead and increases the chance of concurrent adaptations.

RQ3. Which degree of decentralization is suitable for the adaptation coordination in SoS?

Investigated approaches for decentralized adaptations use the concept of atomic adaptation transactions for performing the distributed adaptations [5]. It is questionable if this is the right procedure if we consider large systems with a high amount of nodes. A truck in *convoy1* could trigger an adaptation to change the behavior of the other trucks in *convoy2* or *convoy3*. An example is route optimization for the other convoys. With atomic adaptation transactions following the ACID principle, if one of the convoys or trucks did not accept the change or revoked it, the whole adaptation will be rolled back. Even if the other convoy would profit from it, the change would not be executed.

RQ4. How do non-atomic adaptation transactions supporting a notion similar to eventual consistency behave in comparison to atomic adaptation transactions for decentralized self-adaptation?

Approaches for solving and answering the challenges and research questions will be presented in the next part. The possible contributions will be discussed.

4   Approach

The presented approach from Weißbach et al. [5] will be used as a foundation to develop decentralized self-adaptation in SoS and to introduce more robustness. In the following section goals for the elaborated problems will be presented.

Regarding **RQ1**, the problem of concurrent adaptations must be solved by a synchronization mechanism which compares the originating and resulting states of adapted nodes. The approach for **RQ2** is related to the first, since the result of both problems is missing synchronisation of the knowledge about the global state and an inconsistent or erroneous global state.

A procedure for failed nodes and connections between trucks and convoys must be developed which reestablishes consistency when subparts they get connected again or when concurrent adaptations were performed. Two possibilities can be investigated for this. The first can be used to address both **RQ1** and **RQ2**. In chapter two, CRDTs were introduced, which are mainly used for systems like e.g. Google Documents, which allow for collaborative work and working with offline copies [17]. It would be interesting to apply the concept of CRDTs to self-adaptive SoS. The current state of nodes and application could be treated like a shared dataset, which is replicated on multiple then. In case of a disconnection and possible resulting concurrent adaptations, those changes will be translated into a form similar to changes for CRDTs and after reconnection or finished adaptations, the changes can be synchronized again. Since this is an early stage of research, a deeper investigation on how to use CRDTs for self-adaptive SoS is necessary. In the case of a disconnected node which does not notice an upcoming adaptation (**RQ2**), the protocol from Weißbach et al. [5] could also be extended to replay adaptations when nodes are available again and if the adaptations were not concurrent. If a truck in a convoy failed, the other participants of the convoy are responsible to resend all missed messages. For whole convoys, the nearest convoy should trigger the recovery. This solution approach requires the disconnected subsystem or single node to remain in its original state before it came to an error, to ensure that no adaptations or changes will be overwritten.

Another identified problem regarding decentralized self-adaptation in SoS in the scenario is the leader election. The decentralized protocol from [5] allows every participant of the system to invoke adaptations and all nodes are treated equally. We will investigate if every AM of a subsystem should be able to communicate with others SoS, or if each subsystem has a leader which is responsible for inter-subsystem communication. We will compare the impact of different amount of leaders in an SoS and different hierarchies, or if equal members in an SoS regardless of the different subsystems are the right approach. For a hierarchical approach, a correct leader election mechanism must be chosen. This could be either a random decision or a sophisticated leader election mechanism. An exemplary algorithm for decentralized distributed systems was presented by Mo et al. [18]. The proposed way is stable even on position changes of the devices which is important for the scenario of self-driving trucks or if the topology adapts, which is very important for SoS. Their approach also makes assumptions about the correct moment in time when the leader must be switched. Additionally, we will analyse the needed hierarchical structure for efficient adaptations in SoS. A possible leader distribution and hierarchy is shown in Fig. 4. Each convoy has a leader now, which is responsible for the communication with the other convoys. For the internal structure of a convoy, each node is equal, but with this approach, the communication overhead for the whole system is reduced. The leader is indicated in orange. Leader change as proposed in [18] is important, since a leader can get disconnected in a subsystem, which is shown in *convoy1* in Fig. 4. Another truck must lead the convoy from now on. In combination with leader election, it is necessary to detect if partitioning occurred and which nodes belong to which partition. The next step would then be a leader election in that partition.

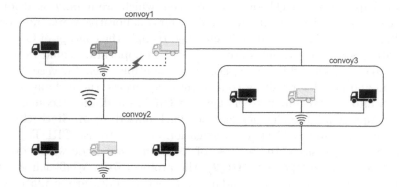

Fig. 4. Leader election in SoS

The existing decentralized adaptation protocol [5] uses atomic adaptation transactions for performing adaptations and follows the ACID principle. Since this approach introduces some limitations for self-adaptive SoS as explained in the chapter before, we will investigate the impact of the BASE concept for those transactions, which is motivated by modern database systems[2]. The current adaptation mechanism would allow a certain level of inconsistency and errors of nodes which participate in a transaction. It will be necessary to define a limit of tolerance for the eventual consistency and which states are still valid system states. A strong consensus is not necessary then. This would allow for error tolerance during the adaptation phase since the work focusses on large-scale systems where errors are more likely to happen than in a small system, and only the affected parts must be recovered.

5   Methodology

As explained in the previous sections, the identified challenges will be deeper investigated using the scenario of self-driving trucks. We will simulate those trucks using the Webots[3] Simulation environment. First, the overall scenario without error-solving mechanisms must be implemented to evaluate the behaviour of the system in its initial state. Afterwards, the error cases which were explained in Sect. 3 will be integrated into the system to check the impact

---

[2] https://neo4j.com/blog/acid-vs-base-consistency-models-explained/.
[3] https://cyberbotics.com/.

of the errors and to have a basis for evaluating the contributions of the thesis. The next step will be the investigation of a leader election and decentralization hierarchy to elaborate on the impact of many potential concurrent leaders which may invoke adaptations contrary to each other. After that, a concept will be created to use BASE transactions instead of ACID to allow for fault-tolerance in the system. For that, the protocol from Weißbach et al. [5] must be extended and modified. The designed concept will be evaluated using the scenario and proper benchmarks regarding errors and performance. We will evaluate the reliability of the decentralized adaptations in the subsystems and evaluate the impact on performance and communication overhead with different amounts of leaders in the SoS. An assessment of successful synchronization of diverged states must be done.

The scenario will be using a role runtime on the trucks in the convoys. This allows us to easily change the behaviour of the objects during run-time as a result of an adaptation. Generally, we will consider run-time adaptation for this project to decrease downtimes and keep the system running.

Those steps and improvements will result in robust self-adaptation in SoS using decentralization.

6 Future Work and Research Plan

Since the thesis is in an early stage, the next time will be used for deeper systematic literature research. The focus will be on decentralized coordination techniques, especially non-atomic techniques. Besides that, literature regarding concurrency in distributed systems will be evaluated. In parallel, a prototype of the mentioned idea will be implemented to evaluate intermediate results and to reschedule the plan if necessary. To test preliminary results, the simulation environment with Webots will be set up. Publications are planned for comparing the impact of ACID vs. BASE for decentralized adaptations and the efficiency of fewer leaders in subsystems of the SoS.

Following milestones are planned for the rest of the PhD time:

– **Q4/2020**: Finished deeper literature work and final research questions
– **Q3/2021**: Implemented improved algorithms for decentralized adaptations
– **Q4/2021**: Evaluation of the results using Webots
– **Q1/2022**: Begin of write-down
– **Q3/2022**: Handing in the finished thesis

7 Conclusion

In this doctoral project paper, the motivation and challenges in the field of SoS with decentralized self-adaptation were presented. Current problems and challenges were discussed and the state-of-the-art approaches were analysed. It was shown that there are still open fields of interest and issues regarding self-adaptation in partitioned SoS. The approaches for tackling the challenges were outlined and milestones for the PhD project have been introduced.

Acknowledgement. This work is funded by the German Research Foundation (DFG) within the Research Training Group Role-based Software Infrastructures for continuous-context-sensitive Systems (GRK 1907).

References

1. de Lemos, R., et al.: Software engineering for self-adaptive systems: a second research roadmap. In: de Lemos, R., Giese, H., Müller, H.A., Shaw, M. (eds.) Software Engineering for Self-Adaptive Systems II. LNCS, vol. 7475, pp. 1–32. Springer, Heidelberg (2013). https://doi.org/10.1007/978-3-642-35813-5_1
2. Weyns, D., et al.: Perpetual assurances for self-adaptive systems. In: de Lemos, R., Garlan, D., Ghezzi, C., Giese, H. (eds.) Software Engineering for Self-Adaptive Systems III. Assurances. LNCS, vol. 9640, pp. 31–63. Springer, Cham (2017). https://doi.org/10.1007/978-3-319-74183-3_2
3. Maier, M.W.: Architecting principles for systems-of-systems. Syst. Eng. 1(4), 267–284 (1998). https://doi.org/10.1002/(SICI)1520-6858(1998)1:4⟨267::AID-SYS3⟩3.0.CO;2-D
4. Weyns, D., Malek, S., Andersson, J.: On decentralized self-adaptation: lessons from the trenches and challenges for the future. In: Proceedings - International Conference on Software Engineering, pp. 84–93 (2010). https://doi.org/10.1145/1808984.1808994
5. Weisbach, M., et al.: Decentralized coordination of dynamic software updates in the Internet of Things. In: 2016 IEEE 3rd World Forum on Internet of Things, WF-IoT 2016, pp. 171–176 (2017). https://doi.org/10.1109/WF-IoT.2016.7845450
6. Ferscha, A.: Collective adaptive systems. In: UbiComp and ISWC 2015 - Proceedings of the 2015 ACM International Joint Conference on Pervasive and Ubiquitous Computing and the Proceedings of the 2015 ACM International Symposium on Wearable Computers, pp. 893–896. Association for Computing Machinery Inc, New York, USA (2015). https://doi.org/10.1145/2800835.2809508
7. Wätzoldt, S., Giese, H.: Modeling collaborations in adaptive systems of systems. In: ACM International Conference Proceeding Series, vol. 07–11-September. Association for Computing Machinery (2015). https://doi.org/10.1145/2797433.2797436
8. Casadei, R., Viroli, M.: Collective abstractions and platforms for large-scale self-adaptive IoT. In: Proceedings - 2018 IEEE 3rd International Workshops on Foundations and Applications of Self* Systems, FAS*W 2018, pp. 106–111. Institute of Electrical and Electronics Engineers Inc. (2018). https://doi.org/10.1109/FAS-W.2018.00033
9. Bachman, C.W., Daya, M.: The role concept in data models. In: Proceedings of the Third International Conference on Very Large Data Bases - Volume 3, VLDB 1977, pp. 464–476. VLDB Endowment (1977)
10. Steimann, F.: On the representation of roles in object-oriented and conceptual modelling. Data Knowl. Eng. 35(1), 83–106 (2000). https://doi.org/10.1016/S0169-023X(00)00023-9
11. Kühn, T., et al.: A metamodel family for role-based modeling and programming languages. In: Combemale, B., Pearce, D.J., Barais, O., Vinju, J.J. (eds.) SLE 2014. LNCS, vol. 8706, pp. 141–160. Springer, Cham (2014). https://doi.org/10.1007/978-3-319-11245-9_8
12. Leuthäuser, M.: Scroll - a scala-based library for roles at runtime. In: Proceedings of the 3rd Workshop on Domain-Specific Language Design and Implementation (DSLDI 2015) (2015)

13. Taing, N., et al.: Run-time variability of role-based software systems. In: MOD-ULARITY Companion 2016 - Companion Proceedings of the 15th International Conference on Modularity, pp. 137–142. Association for Computing Machinery, Inc (2016). https://doi.org/10.1145/2892664.2892687
14. Taing, N., et al.: Consistent unanticipated adaptation for context-dependent applications. In: Proceedings of the 8th International Workshop on Context-Oriented Programming, COP 2016, pp. 33–38. Association for Computing Machinery Inc, New York, USA (2016). https://doi.org/10.1145/2951965.2951966
15. Weyns, D., Andersson, J.: On the challenges of self-Adaptation in systems of systems. In: 1st ACM SIGSOFT/SIGPLAN International Workshop on Software Engineering for Systems-of-Systems, SESoS 2013 Proceedings, pp. 47–51. ACM Press, New York, USA (2013). https://doi.org/10.1145/2489850.2489860
16. Lesch, V., Krupitzer, C., Tomforde, S.: Emerging self-integration through coordination of autonomous adaptive systems. In: 2019 IEEE 4th International Workshops on Foundations and Applications of Self* Systems (FAS*W), pp. 6–9. IEEE (2019). https://doi.org/10.1109/FAS-W.2019.00016
17. Preguiça, N., Baquero, C., Shapiro, M.: Conflict-free Replicated Data Types (CRDTs) (2018). https://doi.org/10.1007/978-3-319-63962-8_185-1
18. Mo, Y., Beal, J., Dasgupta, S.: An aggregate computing approach to self-stabilizing leader election. In: 2018 IEEE 3rd International Workshops on Foundations and Applications of Self* Systems (FAS*W) (2018). https://doi.org/10.1109/FAS-W.2018.00034

Systematic Approach to Engineer Decentralized Self-adaptive Systems

Federico Quin$^{(\boxtimes)}$

Katholieke Universiteit Leuven, Leuven, Belgium
federico.quin@kuleuven.be

Abstract. Self-adaptation is a widely accepted approach to deal with uncertainties that are difficult to anticipate before deployment. We focus on architecture-based adaptation that relies on a feedback loop that reasons over architectural models of the system at runtime to make adaptation decisions. In particular, we study decentralized self-adaptive systems where self-adaptation is realized through multiple coordinating feedback loops. Such decentralization is crucial for systems where adaptation decisions cannot be made in a centralized way, such as in large scale Internet of Things (IoT). State of the art in this area is limited to either conceptual ideas or solutions dedicated to particular settings. This paper outlines a research project targeting the research question: "how to model and realize decentralized feedback loops that are capable to guarantee compliance of system goals in an efficient way despite uncertainties the system faces?" We plan to answer this question in two stage. First, we study commonalities and variability of decentralized self-adaptive systems leveraging on patterns and coordination mechanisms, and reify our insights in a framework. Second, we study language support for the design and implementation of decentralized self-adaptation, capitalizing on the outcome of the first stage. To ensure guarantees for the qualities we will found our work on formal techniques. To ensure efficiency, we will combine statistical techniques with machine learning. We plan to validate the research results in two domains: IoT and multi-cloud systems.

Keywords: Self-adaptation · Architecture-based adaptation · Decentralization · Formal techniques · Machine learning

1 Introduction

Self-adaptation equips a software system with the capabilities of dealing with changing conditions during operation. These changing conditions are versatile and are commonly referred to as uncertainties. We focus on architecture-based adaptation that relies on a feedback loop that reasons over architectural models of the system at runtime to make adaptation decisions. A well known way to realize self-adaptation is MAPE-K introduced by IBM (Monitor-Analyze-Plan-Execute sharing knowledge) [22]. Pioneering contributions in this area are the

© Springer Nature Switzerland AG 2020
H. Muccini et al. (Eds.): ECSA 2020, CCIS 1269, pp. 38–50, 2020.
https://doi.org/10.1007/978-3-030-59155-7_4

Rainbow framework [16], Models@Runtime [34] and the three layer architecture model that is inspired by robot architectures [25].

The upcoming generation of software systems increasingly consists of a large number of loosely composed distributed entities. An example of such a system is an Internet-of-Things application that comprises a large number of IoT sensors. To deal with adaptation, a centralized feedback loop can be constructed that manages the overall adaptation of the individual smaller networks, ensuring that the goals of the system are met. Yet such centralized solution may require substantial communication draining resources such as bandwidth and energy. Alternatively, the IoT network can be split up into smaller networks. Each smaller network can then be equipped with a feedback loop that coordinates and handles adaptation decisions locally. We focus our research around the latter approach where self-adaptation occurs in a decentralized fashion.

Engineering decentralized self-adaptive systems brings a whole heap of challenges with itself. Tasks such as coordination between feedback loops, knowledge sharing or making sure that system goals remain satisfied make the design of these systems difficult. Currently mostly conceptual ideas and tailored solutions have been proposed to engineer decentralized self-adaptive systems. This PhD research project aims for a systematic and reusable engineering approach.

This brings us to the research problem that we base our research on:

How to model and realize decentralized feedback loops that are capable to guarantee compliance of system goals in an efficient way despite uncertainties the system faces?

The remainder of this paper discusses related work, it gives an overview of the scientific approach we plan to follow in this PhD research project, we sketch the intended solution and how we plan to evaluate it, we list the expected contributions and conclude with a critical reflection on the planned research.

2   Related Work

We start with a discussion of related work. We focus on selected work that applies architecture-based adaptation to decentralized systems to gain an understanding of the current state of the art solutions. We also take a look at work that uses formal approaches to realize architecture-based adaptation to further build our own research upon. Lastly, we cover some work in the related areas of multi-agent systems and executable models as these will also play a key role in our research.

2.1   Decentralized Approaches to Architecture-Based Adaptation

A pioneering work on decentralized adaptation is [17] that uses the Alloy language to express structural constraints among software components. Component managers automatically configure the components according to the overall architectural specification. The approach uses reliable broadcast to maintain local copies of the configuration and coordinate component managers, restricting scalability. Later the authors introduced a gossip protocol to overcome the limitations of the centralized approach [38]. K-Components [10] reifies the system's architecture as a configuration graph whose nodes represent components and edges represent connectors. A configuration manager monitors events, plans the adaptations, validates them, rewrites the graph and adapts the underlying system. Malek et al. [27] use an auction-based coordination mechanism to find the appropriate deployment architecture under changing operating conditions. Hebig et al. [19] present a UML profile to support the design and interplay of control loops of adaptive systems at the architectural level. Weyns et al. [45] describe key attributes of decentralized adaptive systems derived from a number of case studies, and argues for an inter-disciplinary approach where the body of work of the multi-agent system community offers a promising starting point to tackle the challenges of decentralized adaptations. Vromant et al. [41] extend MAPE loops with support for inter-loop and intra-loop coordination, and Weyns et al. [46] further elaborate on how multiple MAPE loops can be coordinated. A simple notation is presented for MAPE loop interactions that is used to describe several patterns of interacting MAPE loops. GoPrime [9] offers a decentralized middleware for self-assembly of distributed services. GoPrime exploits a gossip protocol to achieve decentralized information dissemination to maintain an assembly of services that fulfills global quality-of-service and structural requirements. Gru [14] provides microservice architectures with a variety of decentralized autonomic operations without changing the implementation of the services themselves. Stack et al. [37] introduce self-healing concepts to autonomic cloud management systems. They propose and evaluate a layered master-slave architecture to assure proper quality control in hierarchical cloud architectures.

The solutions in these works are mostly limited to conceptual ideas (for example a position paper [41] on inter- and intra-feedback loop communication) or provide only limited applicability (for example [37] which specifically proposes a master-slave architecture). We further discuss how we will build upon these works in Sect. 4.

2.2   Formal Approaches to Architecture-Based Adaptation

Zhang et al. [47] present a process to create formal models for adaptive systems, verify the models and automatically translate the models into executable programs. Model-based testing is used to guarantee conformance between models and programs. In follow up work [48], a dynamically adaptive program is modeled as a collection of steady-state programs and a set of adaptations that realize transitions among the programs in response to environmental changes. To handle state explosion, the authors propose a modular model checking approach, but apply it only at design time. Epifani et al. [11] uses a discrete time Markov chain to represent the possible execution flows of a system at runtime. The probabilities that represent uncertainties are dynamically updated based on observations, using a Bayesian estimator. Calinescu et al. [6] argue for the use of quantitative verification at runtime for adaptive systems and in [7] the authors apply the approach to achieve quality goals for service-based systems. Formally specified requirements are automatically analyzed using runtime model checking techniques to identify and enforce optimal service configurations and resource allocation. Ghezzi et al. [18] introduce adaptive model-driven execution to mitigate uncertainties. A Markov decision model of the system, that is generated from UML interaction diagrams, specifies the probability distribution of the different execution paths of the system. The model is executed by an interpreter that drives the execution of the system to guarantee the highest utility for a set of quality properties. Calinescu et al. [5] present DECIDE, an approach to decentralize feedback loops that uses quantitative verification at runtime to assure quality-of-service requirements in the presence of change.

2.3   Executable Models and Multi-agent Systems

Multi-agent Systems. The body of work developed by self-organization and multi-agent system research offers an immense source of knowledge to tackle some of the difficult problems in decentralized adaptive systems. We highlight a few examples. Sharing complete knowledge in a decentralized setting constrains scalability, as for example discussed in [17]. Kota et al. [24] show that agents that are capable of reasoning about when and how to adapt using only their history of interactions provides a very robust approach to deal with change in decentralized settings. Weyns et al. [42] elaborate on the exploitation of coordination patterns from multi-agent systems as a basis to support adaptation in decentralized settings. Providing system-wide assurances in decentralized settings is challenging. Law-Governed Interactions [29] is one approach that contributes to the problem of assurances in decentralized systems. Nallur et al. [30] propose a mechanism for decentralized adaptation in multi-agent systems called clonal plasticity. This approach is particularly suitable for slow changing systems. Arcaino et al. [4] propose a framework, inspired by Abstract State Machines in the multi-agent systems domain, to specify distributed and decentralized adaptation control in self-adaptive systems.

Executable Models. Executable models are primarily used in model-driven engineering with the aim to test and measure particular properties of a system based on the execution of an abstract representation of the system; a well-known example is Executable UML [28]. Ctrl-F [3] introduces a domain-specific language to describe and verify adaptation behaviors of component-based architectures. Similarly to Executable UML, the specifications are not directly executed but compiled to an implementation in a general purpose programming language. Our interest is on executable models to the runtime. There are only a few examples of executable modeling languages proposed for adaptive systems. EUREMA [40] supports the specification of feedback loops and their coordinated execution. EUREMA is based on the notion of mega-model, but currently lacks a formal underpinning. ActivFORMS [20] supports direct execution of feedback loop models (specified as networks of timed automata). The models can be verified before deployment and executed at runtime realizing adaptation of a managed system via probes and effectors.

2.4 Related PhD Studies

Shmelkin [36] aims to provide answers on how inter- and intra-loop communication should happen in distributed and decentralized self-adaptive systems. Kluge [23] envisions a model-driven architecture for self-adaptive systems where structured context is explicitly modeled. Entities in this architecture are modeled as message-passing processes that fulfill a specified role. This role results in dynamic relationships and behavior with other entities in the system, with the aim of having an intuitive formulation of adaptations in the system.

3   Scientific Approach

The research will be conducted over a period of 3 to 4 years. We follow an incremental process in three stages based on Design Science (inspired by [15]) as shown in Fig. 1. In the first stage, it is crucial that we obtain a complete overview of the state of the art of research on decentralized self-adaptive systems. To that end we first conduct a systematic literature review [21] on this subject. Based on the insights collected from the literature study, in the second stage, we will identify commonalities and variability of solutions and use that as input for the design of a framework for decentralized self-adaptive systems. We plan to demonstrate the applicability of the framework to applications in the domains of IoT and Cloud. In the third stage, we will leverage the knowledge obtained from the first two stages to define language primitives for an executable modeling language of decentralized self-adaptive systems. Similarly to the framework, we will demonstrate the applicability of the language by applying it to the two domains.

In addition to the use cases on IoT and Cloud, we also plan to empirically validate our research results by conducting experiments with MsC students. More details on this can be found in Sect. 4.1. We will disseminate our findings via the publication of high-quality papers and provide software engineers with knowledge and open source tools to design decentralized self-adaptive systems.

4   Solution: Framework and Executable Language

We will consolidate the knowledge we obtained from the literature review into a framework. We plan to identify recurring patterns that are presented and used in these solutions and identify commonalities and variability in existing work. This allows us to design and realize a framework that supports the design of decentralized self-adaptive systems. Based on the insights derived from this effort and its evaluation, we will then consolidate the knowledge into language constructs for an executable modeling language to further help the design and implementation of decentralized self-adaptive systems.

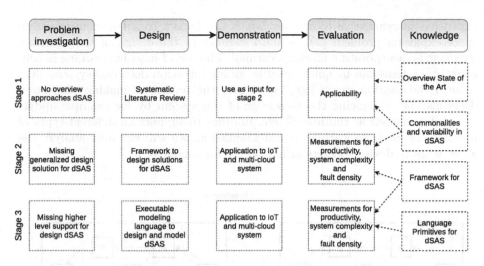

Fig. 1. Design of the research (dSAS short for decentralized self-adaptive system).

Framework. The framework is centered on two main aspects. The first aspect focuses on the realization of decentralized adaptation decisions by providing the appropriate interfaces to facilitate this. An important observation here is that decentralized adaptation can be constructed in multiple ways. Figure 2 shows an example scenario where two feedback loops need to make planning decisions by coordinating each of their planners. The proposed framework makes sure that the planners have the required interface to effectively decide on adaptation plans. Another example is presented in Fig. 3, where the feedback loops both have a local knowledge component and share a distributed knowledge component. Similarly, the framework should provide interfaces to support this scenario. The second aspect the framework focuses on is the way coordination is conducted. Here we are mainly concerned with the protocols used for communication, as well as the data that has to be communicated to properly coordinate the feedback loops. We will leverage on FORMS [44] as a starting point of the specific information that will need to be transmitted to ensure that proper coordination is possible.

Language Primitives. The executable modeling language will provide high-level modeling primitives to specify interactions between multiple feedback loops and high-level modeling primitives. Our focus will be on the identification of language primitives that we plan to embed in an existing core language, in particular timed automata for which extensive expertise is available in our research group. As a first element of the language, we place an emphasis on the models being executable, and thus no further coding of the feedback loops being necessary, avoiding error prone coding. As a second element, we focus on the use of statistical verification techniques rather than exhaustive techniques. The main reason for this decision is that statistical techniques are not as computationally expensive as exhaustive techniques, which are known to suffer from the state space explosion problem [20]. A third element in the design of the modeling language is incorporating machine learning. The use of machine learning in self-adaptive systems can be quite versatile: aiding intrusion-detection systems [31], reducing adaptation spaces [39], taking over the process of making adaptation decisions [33], enhancing the knowledge of the system by for example updating quality models at runtime [8], etc. In order to support all different types of use-cases of machine learning in self-adaptation, we will carefully analyze the approaches to devise concrete primitives in the language.

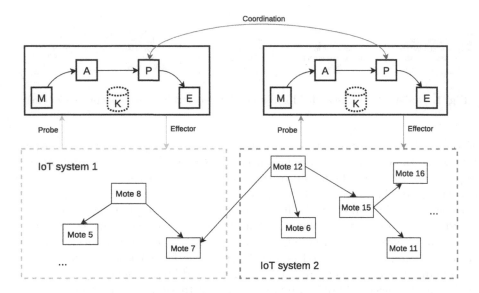

Fig. 2. Decentralized planning with multiple feedback loops

4.1   Evaluation

We plan to evaluate both the framework and the executable modeling language by realizing decentralized self-adaptive systems in the Internet of Things and Multi-Cloud domains respectively. The evaluation methodologies we intend to use are self-developed evaluation cases and case studies. In the evaluation cases, we will define metrics to compare the results with related approaches. In order to compare the effectiveness of our solution we will conduct case studies in MsC courses and thesis projects on the engineering of decentralized self-adaptive systems. In those case studies we aim to qualitatively evaluate the framework or executable modeling language. Measures that present themselves here are the time required to engineer those systems, as well as the complexity of the resulting systems (using established software metrics such as cyclometric complexity).

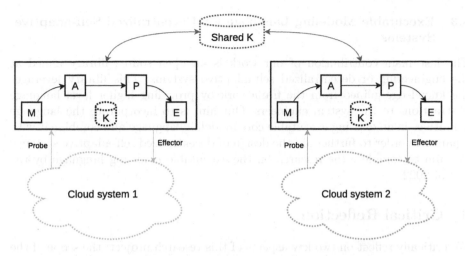

Fig. 3. Local and remote knowledge components with multiple feedback loops

5   Expected Contributions

We split up the expected contributions of this research into 3 parts, corresponding to the different stages and progression of the research.

5.1   State of the Art Overview of Decentralized Self-adaptive Systems

The first contribution of our work is a state of the art overview of the design and application of decentralized self-adaptive systems. This state of the art overview will be conducted by performing a systematic literature review [21]. We aim to publish a conference research paper presenting the findings from the literature review as a contribution to the self-adaptation community by the end of 2020.

5.2   Framework for Decentralized Self-adaptive Systems

A second contribution of our work will be an open source framework which supports the engineering and design of decentralized self-adaptive systems. An important note here however is the scope of applicability of the framework to a specified family of systems with inherent self-adaptation capabilities and particular uncertainty types and dynamics. The framework provides a higher level abstraction than application specific solutions, by supporting different decentralized system topologies and coordination tasks (see examples in Sect. 4). We plan to finalize and present the framework by the end of 2021.

5.3   Executable Modeling Language for Decentralized Self-adaptive Systems

The last main contribution of our work is an open source library aimed at the engineering of decentralized self-adaptive systems. This library leverages the knowledge gained from the framework by providing higher level language abstractions to the system engineers. Our aim is to incorporate the language primitives in an existing executable core modeling language and combine it with a parser in order to further aid the design of decentralized self-adaptive systems. We aim to complete the research on the executable modeling language by the end of 2022.

6   Critical Reflection

We critically reflect on two key aspects of this research project: the scope of the research and complexity management of the research.

Scope. In line with current research in self-adaptive systems, see e.g. [7,13,35], we assume that the managed system is available and equipped with basic facilities for consistent adaptation (probes to support monitoring, effectors for adding/removing elements, etc.), for which we can rely on existing solutions. We target systems for which dynamics in the environment are significantly slower than execution of adaptations and communication. We focus on runtime uncertainties that are related to parameters of the system or the environment [12,26,32] as well as structural uncertainty [43]. So called "unknown unknowns" that typically require evolution of the managing system are out of scope of this research. We also assume that the system provides effectors with discrete settings to adapt the system (or these parameters can be discretized). As we rely on statistical techniques for decision making of adaptations, we assume that the behavior of the managed system is stochastic and that the distributions of the variables that represent uncertainties in the runtime models of the system and the environment are known or can be determined. These assumptions determine the class of systems and the scope of problems that we target in this research. Example applications of this class are interactive service-based applications, applications deployed on mobile vehicles, and IoT applications. Out of scope are real-time systems and systems with entities that pursue their own goals. These systems require dedicated solutions (e.g., real-time operating systems) or pose specific trust challenges (e.g., establishing trustworthiness among elements).

Complexity. It is well known that decentralization of software systems is a challenging problem [46]. The need to handle uncertainty relying on statistical techniques and machine learning adds to this complexity. To tackle this complexity we organized this research project in phases, enabling us to work in an iterative manner where the complexity of the problem is gradually exposed and tackled. We will collaborate with members of the imec-DistriNet research group where ample expertise is available on key aspects of this research project, such as software architecture, coordination mechanisms, and language design. On the formal side, we will collaborate with the team of Radu Calinescu of York University, UK [1] with whom our research group has a long running collaboration. Finally, for the evaluation in the domain of the Internet of Things, we will work together with our partners of the Networked Embedded Software group at imec-DistriNet as well as with VersaSense, a provider of IoT solutions [2].

7 Conclusion

The engineering of decentralized self-adaptive systems is a complicated and multi-faceted endeavor. A vast amount of considerations have to be taken into account to (1) design and (2) ensure proper operation at runtime of these systems. In this paper we outline our PhD research project which aims to hide design complexities from system engineers by abstracting them away in the form of a newly proposed framework and executable modeling language. Both the framework and the language will be validated in the IoT and Cloud domains.

Acknowledgements. This research project is supported by the KU Leuven C1 grant "Trustworthy Decentralized Self-Adaptive Systems".

References

1. https://www.cs.york.ac.uk/people/raduc
2. https://www.versasense.com/
3. Alvares, F., Rutten, E., Seinturier, L.: High-level language support for reconfiguration control in component-based architectures. In: Weyns, D., Mirandola, R., Crnkovic, I. (eds.) ECSA 2015. LNCS, vol. 9278, pp. 3–19. Springer, Cham (2015). https://doi.org/10.1007/978-3-319-23727-5_1
4. Arcaini, P., Riccobene, E., Scandurra, P.: Formal design and verification of self-adaptive systems with decentralized control. ACM Trans. Auton. Adapt. Syst. **11**(4), 1–35 (2017)
5. Calinescu, R., Gerasimou, S., Banks, A.: Self-adaptive software with decentralised control loops. In: Egyed, A., Schaefer, I. (eds.) FASE 2015. LNCS, vol. 9033, pp. 235–251. Springer, Heidelberg (2015). https://doi.org/10.1007/978-3-662-46675-9_16
6. Calinescu, R., Ghezzi, C., Kwiatkowska, M., Mirandola, R.: Self-adaptive software needs quantitative verification at runtime. Commun. ACM **55**(9), 69–77 (2012)
7. Calinescu, R., Grunske, L., Kwiatkowska, M., Mirandola, R., Tamburrelli, G.: Dynamic QoS management and optimization in service-based systems. IEEE Trans. Softw. Eng. **37**(3), 387–409 (2011)
8. Calinescu, R., Rafiq, Y., Johnson, K., Bakundefinedr, M.E.: Adaptive model learning for continual verification of non-functional properties. In: 5th ACM/SPEC International Conference on Performance Engineering (2014)
9. Caporuscio, M., Grassi, V., Marzolla, M., Mirandola, R.: GoPrime: a fully decentralized middleware for utility-aware service assembly. IEEE Trans. Softw. Eng. **42**(2), 136–152 (2016)

10. Dowling, J., Cahill, V.: The k-component architecture meta-model for self-adaptive software. In: Yonezawa, A., Matsuoka, S. (eds.) Reflection 2001. LNCS, vol. 2192, pp. 81–88. Springer, Heidelberg (2001). https://doi.org/10.1007/3-540-45429-2_6

11. Epifani, I., Ghezzi, C., Mirandola, R., Tamburrelli, G.: Model evolution by run-time parameter adaptation. In: 31st International Conference on Software Engineering. IEEE, USA (2009)

12. Esfahani, N., Kouroshfar, E., Malek, S.: Taming uncertainty in self-adaptive software. In: 19th ACM SIGSOFT Symposium and the 13th European Conference on Foundations of Software Engineering. ACM (2011)

13. Filieri, A., Tamburrelli, G., Ghezzi, C.: Supporting self-adaptation via quantitative verification and sensitivity analysis at run time. IEEE Trans. Softw. Eng. 42(1), 75–99 (2016)

14. Florio, L., Nitto, E.D.: Gru: an approach to introduce decentralized autonomic behavior in microservices architectures. In: 2016 IEEE International Conference on Autonomic Computing (ICAC) (2016)

15. Fotrousi, F.: Combining user feedback and monitoring data to support evidence-based software evolution. Ph.D. thesis, Blekinge Institute of Technology, Karlskrona, Sweden, April 2020

16. Garlan, D., Cheng, S.W., Huang, A.C., Schmerl, B., Steenkiste, P.: Rainbow: architecture-based self-adaptation with reusable infrastructure. Computer 37(10), 46–54 (2004)

17. Georgiadis, I., Magee, J., Kramer, J.: Self-organising software architectures for distributed systems. In: 1st Workshop on Self-Healing Systems. ACM (2002)

18. Ghezzi, C., Pinto, L.S., Spoletini, P., Tamburrelli, G.: Managing non-functional uncertainty via model-driven adaptivity. In: 2013 35th International Conference on Software Engineering (ICSE) (2013)

19. Hebig, R., Giese, H., Becker, B.: Making control loops explicit when architecting self-adaptive systems. In: 2nd International Workshop on Self-Organizing Architectures. ACM (2010)

20. Iftikhar, M.U., Weyns, D.: Activforms: active formal models for self-adaptation. In: 9th International Symposium on Software Engineering for Adaptive and Self-Managing Systems. ACM (2014)

21. Keele, S., et al.: Guidelines for performing systematic literature reviews in software engineering. Technical report, Ver. 2.3 EBSE Technical Report. EBSE (2007)

22. Kephart, J.O., Chess, D.M.: The vision of autonomic computing. Computer 36(1), 41–50 (2003)

23. Kluge, T.: A role-based architecture for self-adaptive cyber-physical systems. In: 15th International Conference on Software Engineering for Adaptive and Self-Managing Systems (2020)

24. Kota, R., Gibbins, N., Jennings, N.R.: Decentralized approaches for self-adaptation in agent organizations. ACM Trans. Auton. Adapt. Syst. 7(1), 1–28 (2012)

25. Kramer, J., Magee, J.: Self-managed systems: an architectural challenge. In: Future of Software Engineering (FOSE 2007), pp. 259–268 (2007)

26. Mahdavi Hezavehi, S., Durelli, V., Weyns, D., Avgeriou, P.: A systematic literature review onmethods that handle multiple quality attributes in architecture-based self-adaptive systems. Inf. Softw. Technol. 90, 1–26 (2017)

27. Malek, S., Mikic-Rakic, M., Medvidovic, N.: A decentralized redeployment algorithm for improving the availability of distributed systems. In: Dearle, A., Eisenbach, S. (eds.) CD 2005. LNCS, vol. 3798, pp. 99–114. Springer, Heidelberg (2005). https://doi.org/10.1007/11590712_8

28. Mellor, S.J., Balcer, M., Jacoboson, I.: Executable UML: A Foundation for Model-Driven Architectures. Addison-Wesley Longman Publishing Co. Inc., USA (2002)
29. Minsky, N.H., Ungureanu, V.: Law-governed interaction: a coordination and control mechanism for heterogeneous distributed systems. ACM Trans. Softw. Eng. Methodol. 9(3), 273–305 (2000)
30. Nallur, V., Cardozo, N., Clarke, S.: Clonal plasticity: a method for decentralized adaptation in multi-agent systems. In: 11th International Symposium on Software Engineering for Adaptive and Self-Managing Systems. ACM (2016)
31. Papamartzivanos, D., Gómez Mármol, F., Kambourakis, G.: Introducing deep learning self-adaptive misuse network intrusion detection systems. IEEE Access 7, 13546–13560 (2019)
32. Perez-Palacin, D., Mirandola, R.: Uncertainties in the modeling of self-adaptive systems: a taxonomy and an example of availability evaluation. In: ACM/SPEC International Conference on Performance Engineering (2014)
33. Porter, B., Filho, R.R.: Losing control: the case for emergent software systems using autonomous assembly, perception, and learning. In: 2016 IEEE 10th International Conference on Self-Adaptive and Self-Organizing Systems (SASO) (2016)
34. Blair, G., Bencomo, N., France, R.: Models@ run.time. Computer 42, 22–27 (2009)
35. Salehie, M., Tahvildari, L.: Self-adaptive software: landscape and research challenges. ACM Trans. Auton. Adap. Syst. 4(2), 1–42 (2009)
36. Shmelkin, I.: Monitoring for control in role-oriented self-adaptive systems. In: 15th International Conference on Software Engineering for Adaptive and Self-Managing Systems (2020)
37. Stack, P., Xiong, H., Mersel, D., Makhloufi, M., Terpend, G., Dong, D.: Self-healing in a decentralised cloud management system. In: 1st International Workshop on Next Generation of Cloud Architectures. ACM (2017)
38. Sykes, D., Magee, J., Kramer, J.: FlashMob: distributed adaptive self-assembly. In: 6th International Symposium on Software Engineering for Adaptive and Self-Managing Systems, SEAMS 2011, pp. 100–109. ACM (2011)
39. Van Der Donckt, J., Weyns, D., Quin, F., Van Der Donckt, J., Michiels, S.: Applying deep learning to reduce large adaptation spaces of self-adaptive systems with multiple types of goals. In: 15th International Conference on Software Engineering for Adaptive and Self-Managing Systems (2020)
40. Vogel, T., Giese, H.: Model-driven engineering of self-adaptive software with EUREMA. ACM Trans. Auton. Adapt. Syst. 8(4), 1–33 (2014)
41. Vromant, P., Weyns, D., Malek, S., Andersson, J.: On interacting control loops in self-adaptive systems. In: 6th International Symposium on Software Engineering for Adaptive and Self-Managing Systems. ACM (2011)
42. Weyns, D., Georgeff, M.: Self-adaptation using multiagent systems. IEEE Softw. 27(1), 86–91 (2010)
43. Weyns, D.: Software engineering of self-adaptive systems. In: Cha, S., Taylor, R., Kang, K. (eds.) Handbook of Software Engineering, pp. 399–443. Springer, Cham (2019). https://doi.org/10.1007/978-3-030-00262-6_11
44. Weyns, D., Malek, S., Andersson, J.: Forms: a formal reference model for self-adaptation. In: 7th International Conference on Autonomic Computing. ACM (2010)
45. Weyns, D., Malek, S., Andersson, J.: On decentralized self-adaptation: lessons from the trenches and challenges for the future. In: Software Engineering for Adaptive and Self-Managing Systems, pp. 84–93. ACM (2010)

46. Weyns, D., et al.: On patterns for decentralized control in self-adaptive systems. In: de Lemos, R., Giese, H., Müller, H.A., Shaw, M. (eds.) Software Engineering for Self-Adaptive Systems II. LNCS, vol. 7475, pp. 76–107. Springer, Heidelberg (2013). https://doi.org/10.1007/978-3-642-35813-5_4
47. Zhang, J., Cheng, B.H.C.: Model-based development of dynamically adaptive software. In: 28th International Conference on Software Engineering. ACM (2006)
48. Zhang, J., Goldsby, H.J., Cheng, B.H.: Modular verification of dynamically adaptive systems. In: 8th ACM International Conference on Aspect-Oriented Software Development. ACM (2009)

ECSA 2020 Tool Demos Track

ECSA 2020 Tool Demos Track

It is our pleasure to welcome you to the tool demos track of the 14th European Conference on Software Architecture (ECSA 2020). The aim of the ECSA 2020 tool demos track is to provides an opportunity for both practitioners and researchers to present and discuss the most recent advances, ideas, experiences, and challenges in the field of software architecture by means of live tool demo presentations.

We solicited two categories of tool demo contributions addressing any aspect of tool support. These were tools used in practice, whether from vendors, industry, or open source projects, and research tools and demos from academic or industrial research environments. We welcomed tools raging from early prototypes to in-house or pre-commercialized products.

We received seven submissions, which underwent a peer-review process with three reviews each (single blind). Out of these seven submissions, five were accepted to be presented at the conference, where four of them had all positive (or borderline) scores (positive on average), and one had a combination of positive/borderline/negative scores (borderline on average) and was accepted conditionally to make sure that the concerns of the reviewers are properly addressed. We would like to thank all the authors for their time in preparing high-quality submissions.

Last, we would like to express our gratitude to the Tool Demos Program Committee for the dedication and great work during the tools selection process, and the whole organization team of ECSA 2020 for making ECSA 2020 a successful conference despite the COVID-19 challenges that resulted in moving the conference to the virtual format.

Organization

Tool Demos Chairs

Paris Avgeriou   University of Groningen, The Netherlands
Barbora Buhnovas   Masaryk University, Czech Republic

Tool Demos Program Committee

Rami Bahsoon   University of Birmingham, UK
Tomas Bures   Charles University Prague, Czech Republic
Daniel Feitosa   University of Groningen, The Netherlands
Ilias Gerostathopoulos   Technical University of Munich, Germany
Elisa Yumi Nakagawa   University of São Paulo, Brazil
Elena Navarro   University of Castilla-La Mancha, Spain
Jennifer Perez   Universidad Politécnica de Madrid, Spain
Claudia Raibulet   Università degli Studi di Milano-Bicocca, Italy
Rodrigo Santos   UNIRIO, Brazil
Michael Stal   Siemens, Germany
Danny Weyns   KU Leuven, Belgium

Additional Reviewers

Maria Istela Cagnin
Thiago Bianchi

Voyager: Software Architecture Trade-off Explorer

Jason Mashinchi and Javier Cámara[✉]

Department of Computer Science, University of York, York, UK
jason.mashinchi@alumni.york.ac.uk, javier.camaramoreno@york.ac.uk

Abstract. Software engineers must ensure that systems under development are endowed with software architectures that enable them to meet their requirements. Apart from functionality, systems also have to satisfy extra-functional requirements that may include behavioural constraints that the software must adhere to, as well as qualities to optimise such as performance, availability, and energy efficiency. These qualities are often inter-dependent and heavily influenced by the structure of the system. This results in poorly understood multi-dimensional design spaces, in which trade-offs among qualities are not evident when making architectural decisions. This paper presents *Voyager*, a tool which allows engineers to visualise architectural configurations and explore the trade-offs among their quality attributes in a multi-dimensional design space. The tool produces contextual visualisations to facilitate trade-off analysis, providing engineers with a streamlined way of understanding architectural design spaces, using an approach that combines architectural structure with multi-dimensional data visualisations. A user study was conducted to evaluate the effectiveness of the tool. Results show that participants achieved a significantly higher accuracy in a shorter time span and had a better user experience when using *Voyager*, with respect to an existing comparable tool.

Keywords: Software architecture · Visualisation · Trade-offs · Quality attributes

1   Introduction

Software is extensively used across the globe today, forming a key part of many industries with applications that range from safety-critical aviation to social networking. All software must meet its requirements – i.e. must be able to achieve its intended purpose, by performing functions required of it and meeting whatever behavioural constraints that exist [12]. For example, a piece of software may be required to calculate the speed a car is travelling, with a constraint that it must deliver a result within 10 ms of receiving an input. There are many correct ways to develop software, and many possible architectural structures that allow the software to achieve its goal, each with its own benefits and trade-offs.

© Springer Nature Switzerland AG 2020
H. Muccini et al. (Eds.): ECSA 2020, CCIS 1269, pp. 55–67, 2020.
https://doi.org/10.1007/978-3-030-59155-7_5

A key challenge for software engineers is to understand the properties of the architectural design space, to allow them to make better design decisions with well-grounded knowledge about the trade-offs amongst concerns (e.g. cost, reliability) and the architectural constraints [4]. More often than not, the architectural design space is poorly understood, as it is not easy to represent the trade-offs that exist between desirable quality attributes and the structure of possible architectural configurations in an accessible way. Understanding this design space is useful for developing optimal software, as different configurations entail different trade-offs that software architects have to make.

Visualisation is a useful tool for developing an understanding of data. However, visualising architectural design spaces is challenging because of the multi-dimensional nature of the problem (quality metrics used for comparison often go beyond three dimensions), and the difficulty in relating explicitly structure and quality trade-offs.

This paper presents *Voyager*[1] – a tool that primarily focuses on the needs of software engineers, by combining trade-off analysis with software architectural structure visualisation. As quality metrics of architectural configurations depend on their structures, it is helpful for architects to understand and easily analyse both side-by-side. Existing tools focus on either architecture visualisation (e.g. AcmeStudio [15]), or architectural trade-off analysis (e.g. ClaferMoo [11]), unlike *Voyager* which offers a novel combination of the two, enabling engineers to narrow design spaces and find better configurations more effectively.

While *Voyager* is designed primarily for software architecture analysis, the multi-dimensional trade-off analysis features are more general purpose, so it can also be applied to other related areas with multi-dimensional data to analyse results from variable configuration spaces (e.g. software product lines [6], quantitative verification [8]). In addition, *Voyager* has extensibility features that enable integration with external tools which can act as a data source and provide additional visualisations to appear in the user interface.

2   Background and Related Work

Architecture refers to the high-level aspects of the software, such as its overall organisation, the individual components and their functionality, and the relationships and interaction between them [4]. There are many alternative software architectures that can be used to realize a software system, each with its own set of quality characteristics [10]. Selecting one of a possible set of alternative approaches to the software architecture entails carrying out a set of design decisions which have to be informed by a clear understanding the design space, including trade-offs amongst relevant quality attributes.

To inform this selection, some tools such as Prism-MW [7], ArchJava [1] and Aura [16] facilitate modelling a set of correct architectural configurations to analyse, without much support for optimisation. Work in multi-dimensional

---

[1] The source code, user study data and a video demonstration of the *Voyager* tool is located online at: https://github.com/jasonmash/voyager.

architecture optimisation approaches is plentiful and varied in classes of techniques employed [2], with some recent approaches enabling automated synthesis of sets of correct configurations with associated quality metrics [5]. However, these tools are not designed to facilitate systematic and interactive exploration of their output, which is often difficult to understand and cumbersome to explore. The output of these tools can be used as input for *Voyager*, which offers trade-off and architectural structure visualisations that help software engineers understand and analyse these sets of multidimensional architectural data.

As each architectural configuration consists of a structured set of components, individual architectures can be visualised and analysed using tools such as AcmeStudio [15] and SoftArchVis [13]. These tools allow visualising the software architectures to give a better understanding of how each configuration is composed and their attributes. However, these tools are limited to visualising one architectural configuration at a time, reducing their effectiveness for understanding and analysing the design space and quality trade-offs. *Voyager* incorporates basic structural diagramming tools alongside its trade-off analysis functionality, and also provides an extensions interface that allows external tools to add new static or dynamic architectural visualisations.

Other existing tools such as ClaferMoo [11] and TradeMaker [3] are good for comparing amongst many configurations, providing charts such as 2D bubble plots and matrices representing the distribution of configurations in relation to their quality attributes. However, these do not include architectural structure information, making it difficult to understand how the quality attributes relate to the architecture itself. *Voyager* incorporates the design space visualisations and trade-off analysis tools, alongside architectural structure visualisations, showing each when contextually appropriate, without requiring any user configuration.

Finding an architecture design that meets all quality requirements while balancing the trade-offs from dependent quality attributes requires multi-objective optimisation, a process that generates sets of Pareto optimal solutions (i.e. solutions for which no alternative solution that is better in one property and equally as good with respect to all others, exists [14]). Although some of the existing architecture optimisation approaches can generate Pareto-optimal solutions, none of the surveyed tools incorporates algorithms to calculate the Pareto frontier for user-selected quality attributes from a raw data set. Our tool is able to do that, making clear which configurations are Pareto-optimal for the selected attributes.

In summary, existing tools are effective for analysing either a single architecture at a time, or multiple correct architectures but without any explicit link to architectural structure. In contrast, our tool combines the benefits of trade-off analysis with that of software architectural structure visualisation to enable better understanding of architectural design spaces.

3 Voyager

Voyager is designed to support architects during evaluation of architecture design quality and satisfaction of stopping criteria when optimising architectures, helping them in understanding the design space and potentially providing feedback for the generation of new design alternatives (Fig. 1, right).

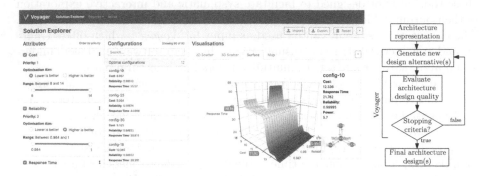

Fig. 1. (left) screenshot of Solution Explorer in *Voyager* and (right) architecture optimisation workflow (adapted from [2])

3.1 Implementation

The tool is implemented using open source web technologies, delivering a cross-platform application that runs in a browser. The tool is implemented using TypeScript (typescriptlang.org), a superset of JavaScript, which utilises extra compilation steps to add features such as type checking that improve developer productivity. Additionally, open source libraries such as Vue.js (vuejs.org), Bootstrap (getbootstrap.com) and ECharts [9] are used to construct the user interface, alongside several other libraries listed in the code. While the tool is designed to run entirely within a browser, all computation and data processing takes place locally, and data is persisted across browser sessions to ensure *Voyager* behaves like any other locally installed application.

To ensure the quality of the *Voyager* tool, a suite of end-to-end and unit tests has been developed, using the Cypress (cypress.io) and Mocha (mochajs.org) libraries respectively.

3.2 Solution Explorer

The core functionality of *Voyager* is found in the "Solution Explorer", enabling users to study a set of architectural configurations and their trade-offs using context-appropriate visualisations, alongside relevant sorting and filtering tools. The Solution Explorer page is split into three columns, each showing attributes, configurations and visualisations respectively for the current data set. An example is shown in Fig. 1 (left), for a set of configurations that have cost, reliability, and response time quality attributes.

3.3 Quality Attributes

The left-hand most "Attributes" pane includes the set of quality attributes inferred from the imported architecture configurations, and it has been designed to allow software architects to straightforwardly reduce the architectural design space. This is accomplished by allowing users to: select, filter and sort configurations based on the values of their quality attributes; to set an optimisation aim (i.e. whether higher or lower values are better for the attribute); and to narrow down the range of acceptable values for a given attribute. Changing these properties updates the list of configurations and any currently visible visualisations in real-time, ensuring users get instant feedback on how changes to the design space affect the possible architectural solutions for the given data set.

3.4 Architectural Configurations

The centre of the screen contains a list of configurations that meet the requirements specified in the attributes pane. The configurations are grouped together based on Pareto optimality, where optimal architectures on the Pareto frontier are placed at the top, followed by non-dominant solutions below. Configurations are sorted according to their attribute values, the order of which is determined by the attribute optimisation aim (e.g. when higher values are better, those configurations are placed first). This effectively shows architects which of the possible structures are best suited for further consideration.

A single configuration can be selected, showing the "Selected Configuration" panel to the right. This presents each quality attribute value for the selected configuration, and a radar chart of these values relative to those of other configurations, alongside any visualisations of its software architecture.

By default, *Voyager* shows an architectural structure graph, representing each component within the architecture and the connections between them. This chart allows the user to hover over individual elements for further details and can be panned and zoomed. Additional architectural visualisations from external tools can be shown in the selected configuration panel, by providing these in an image or html-based format using the *Voyager* extensions interface. These architectural visualisations help users understand the design space, by enabling users to quickly compare possible configurations and identify which style of architectures are better or worse, which components have which trade-offs, etc.

3.5 Design Space Visualisation

Using visualisations is an effective way of understanding data sets, as it allows humans to intuitively identify patterns and trends, and spot outliers. *Voyager* shows visualisations of the design space in the rightmost panel, including data points for each visible configuration after the attribute filters have been applied. This allows users to gain an understanding of the relationships between quality attributes and therefore whether trade-offs exist.

Software architecture quality attributes, like any other data, are easy to visualise when there are one, two or three attributes to analyse, making use of graphs such as scatter plots, bar charts and 3D surface plots. However, as it is common with software architectures, there are often more than three dimensions of data to process, presenting a challenge as we cannot simply add additional dimensions to graphical visualisations, being fundamentally limited to 3D space. Therefore, *Voyager* makes use complex visualisations that encode additional data into the space we are able to perceive, applying projections onto the data where necessary, and utilising additional properties such as colour, size and position where appropriate.

The visibility of each visualisation in the UI is context-dependent, as their effectiveness depends on the number of configurations and the number of dimensions of attributes, determined by the selected attributes and filters. Each visualisation updates in real-time as filters are adjusted, which means users do not have to manually press refresh (or similar) like existing tools. This reduces cognitive load, by allowing users to focus their thought processes on their data, rather than on how to get the software to do what they want it to.

The visualisations shown in the visualisations panel have been selected according to their usability, clarity and function. These include bar/line charts, 2D/3D scatter plots, surface plots, configuration maps and radar charts.

Each visualisation has a dropdown menu in the top right corner, providing options such as exporting to image files, and switching between projections of 3D charts (e.g. orthographic and perspective). All visualisations include additional information in tooltips for each data point – e.g. 3D scatter plots include information about where the mouse is along each axis, and which configuration is highlighted. In addition, selecting a point provides architectural structure diagrams, acting as an effective tool for comparing architectural structure and quality attributes side-by-side (c.f. Fig. 1, left).

3.6   Reports

Voyager contains reporting functionality to allow users to save any visualisation included in the application into a report for future reference. Report visualisations contain a snapshot of their source data to ensure their content is not modified by any data manipulation performed elsewhere in the application. Users can create one or more reports, each with a unique title, to group together multiple visualisations that can be labelled - this provides a straightforward mechanism for comparing between multiple architectures.

3.7   Data Sources and Extensibility

Voyager makes use of common file formats such as .csv and .json to allow users to import and export data from the application easily, enabling the use of various other tools for data collection and preparation. The state of the application can be exported directly from the user interface, and re-imported at a later date to restore the application exactly to its previous state, resulting in an output file that can be shared amongst interested parties when collaborating.

Voyager offers an extension interface, allowing third party tools to integrate with the tool by providing lists of configurations and associated customised visualisations in static (image) or dynamic (html/js) formats. Communication between *Voyager* and external tools is accomplished using HTTP requests, with the requirement for external tools to implement a REST API that returns JSON data for specified endpoints. This technology choice was made because HTTP is a widely supported protocol, with easy implementation across many programming languages.

4 Evaluation

During development, *Voyager* has been validated with existing data sets, including the Tele Assistance System (TAS) exemplar (a service-based system) [17], showing indication of its potential to analyze trade-offs in preliminary user experiments. To further validate that *Voyager* meets the goal of providing engineers with a user-friendly tool for visualising software architectures and exploring their trade-offs, we have conducted a user study to quantify its effectiveness.

4.1 User Study Design

We constructed a user study consisting of a set of questions related to a software architectural trade-off analysis scenario. Participants are asked to make use of tools including *Voyager* and other existing comparable software to analyse the provided data for a given scenario. This allows for the collection of quantitative data that is used to compare and measure the effectiveness of our tool.

Each scenario used in the user study include sets of architectural configuration data, containing both quality attribute values and a representation of the architectural structures for each configuration. Participants are asked questions requiring them to find optimal architectural configurations for the data set, by performing tasks such as filtering, sorting, clustering and correlation to identify any trade-offs between quality attributes. Participants also must make use of individual architectural structure visualisations to compare between two or more potential configurations. The data sets used contained many configurations with cost, battery life, range and reliability quality attributes, each with representative trade-offs between each.

To establish a baseline prior ability of each participant, and to ensure they have a chance to familiarise themselves with the type of problem they are being asked to solve, the first section of the user study consists of a background task which all participants complete. This background task contains a scenario and set of questions, alongside a basic spreadsheet tool that presents the data and only offers basic data analysis tools including sorting and filtering.

Following the completion of the background task, the participants are randomly allocated one of two possible tools for use on further, more difficult questions. One of these tools is *Voyager*, and the other is ClaferMoo Visualizer [11]

- a directly comparable tool with similar aims. This tool was selected for use in this study because: it provides a user interface that can be used to solve the same class of problems as *Voyager*, it is easily available and widely used, and it can be populated with fundamentally the same data set as *Voyager*.

The same scenario, data set and questions are used regardless of the allocated tool, with slight terminology adjustments to account for the differences between the tools (i.e. a *Voyager* "configuration" is called a "variant" in ClaferMoo). This second analysis task is intentionally more difficult than the background task, and contains additional quality attributes and configurations to analyse.

Each scenario consisted of four questions, each formulated to cover a comprehensive range of tasks users typically accomplish when conducting analytic activities, and also to provide quantitative data to be used to compare and measure the effectiveness of our tool. For each question, timing data was captured to understand how long it takes users to complete allocated tasks for each tool.

Question	Rationale
1. Identify the configuration with the lowest cost	A straightforward question to get participants familiar with the tool user interface. Requires them to use the UI to find a single configuration with the lowest value for one quality attribute
2. Identify one (or more) configurations with the highest possible battery life and highest possible range within the same configuration	This question is designed to get participants thinking about trade-offs, as the data set contained no obvious answers, as in this case, increased range meant reduced battery life. Participants could make use of the tabular or graphical representations of all configurations, as well as sorting tools to find those configurations that were on the Pareto-front for this problem
3. Identify one (or more) configurations that have the highest possible battery life, then the highest possible range where the reliability is greater than [threshold]	This question requires participants to make use of more advanced functionality within each tool, including filtering, to identify configurations on the Pareto-front for this problem. Participants were told that sorting/filtering/visualisation tools could be used
4. Identify any common features present in configurations that have a battery life greater than [threshold] and a cost less than [threshold]	This question was designed to get participants to make use of architectural structure visualisation tools, to identify any components and connections that were common within a similar class of configurations

The responses collected from each participant are validated using a numerical score for each question, representing the number of correct answers achieved out of the total set of correct answers. For the questions where optimal configurations need to be identified, the set of correct answers is the set of Pareto-optimal configurations matching the specified goal.

Following the completion of each scenario within the user study, we asked participants a series of usability questions to gather their opinion and therefore a measure of their perception and confidence of how well they performed on the task for each tool. Participants were asked (i) how they found the task, (ii) how well they thought they did, and (iii) how easy the tool was to use. The answer options for these questions took the form of a 5-point Likert scale, with the results being stored as 0 being a strongly negative answer, 3 being neutral, and 4 being a strongly positive answer.

To determine whether a response we received from a participant was valid (and not filtered out), we made use of the following criteria: (i) the participant completed all questions, (ii) all answers to the question were in the expected data formats, (iii) timing data was present for every question, and (iv) the participant reported no problems completing the study.

4.2   Experiment Design

We recruited 47 participants to complete the user study of various backgrounds and abilities. Of the 47 participants who started the user study, 32 participants fully completed the study and provided results that were valid for further analysis and contained no invalid answers according to the verification criteria above.

To ensure we understood our participants background experience, they were asked to provide their current occupation, educational study level, and their level of study in STEM-related subjects. Numbers of participants at each STEM education level were as follows: Secondary: 1; Post-Secondary: 9; Bachelor's Degree: 5; Master's Degree (or higher): 17.

A web-based tool was developed to conduct the user study. This was necessary to embed a spreadsheet tool, *Voyager* and ClaferMoo Visualizer in a seamless user interface, which ensured the only technical requirement participants had to comply with was access to a modern desktop-sized web browser.

The total cohort of participants was split into two equally-sized groups, each of which was allocated either the *Voyager* or ClaferMoo Visualizer tool. In total, 16 participants (50% of the total) completed the task using *Voyager*, and 16 participants completed the task using ClaferMoo Visualizer. All 32 participants completed the background task using the embedded spreadsheet.

To balance the effects of education levels amongst participants, their allocation to groups was entirely random. This led to the unintended effect of one group having a slightly higher average education level than the other, which may have resulted in an overestimate of the difference in outcomes between the groups in the results. To account for this, a statistical T-Test was performed making use of the background task data, which did not show a statistically significant difference in the scores achieved between the two groups ($p = 0.691$, with mean values of: 5.1 for Voyager, and 4.9 for ClaferMoo participants; where the maximum score was 8). A review of each participant's occupation showed these were well balanced between groups, as similar numbers of participants with relevant occupations were present in each group (e.g. engineers, computer specialists).

The independent variable of this experiment was the tool used to complete the same scenario. The dependent variables we measured were: correctness, confidence, user perception, and time to complete each task. Correctness was measured using the scores achieved per question, while confidence and perception were measured using the usability questions.

The hypotheses for this experiment were as follows:

1. Given the same data set and questions, participants would identify more correct answers in a shorter time period using *Voyager* compared to those using an existing tool.
2. Participants would find *Voyager* subjectively easier to use and would be more confident in their results compared to using a spreadsheet or a comparable existing tool.

4.3   Analysis and Results

The results of the user study support both hypotheses of the experiment. This data is publicly accessible alongside the source code. A two-sample, one-sided statistical t-test was used to calculate a measure of whether there was a significant difference between two sets of data, making use of the output p-value, which shows a significant result if it is less than 0.05. A p-value represents the probability of observing a result at least as extreme as the observed results, assuming that the null hypothesis is true (equal means). A smaller p-value means there is a smaller probability that the null hypothesis is true, providing stronger evidence in favour of the alternative hypothesis.

Participants using *Voyager* achieved a higher average score, in less time than those who used ClaferMoo Visualizer, given the same questions and data set. The mean average scores and durations for the tool questions are shown below, in addition to the p-values obtained using a t-test as described above.

	Total score (% correct)	Duration (mins)
Voyager	57	8.4
ClaferMoo visualizer	38	10.9
T-Test (p-value)	0.0133	0.0391

Performing a statistical t-test shows there is a significant difference between both tools for the total score with mean averages of 57% for Voyager, and 38% for ClaferMoo, with $p = 0.0133$. Likewise for timing data (total time to complete tool questions), with mean averages of 8.4 min for Voyager and 10.9 min for ClaferMoo, with $p = 0.0391$. These p-values allow us to reject the null hypothesis, and conclude there is not evidence in support of equal means. This shows a statistically significant difference for both dependent variables, indicating that the hypothesis that the *Voyager* tool allows users to achieve higher accuracy answers in a shorter time period is correct. Broken down by question, in every case, participants using *Voyager* achieved a higher mean average than those who used ClaferMoo Visualizer.

The results from the usability questions that measured user perception and confidence also support the hypothesis that *Voyager* was subjectively easier to use compared to a spreadsheet and existing tools. A statistical t-test for each of the questions asked was conducted, comparing the results from *Voyager* to those from both the spreadsheet and ClaferMoo tasks. The results are as follows:

Question	Mean average			T-test (p-value)	
	Spreadsheet	ClaferMoo	Voyager	Spreadsheet	ClaferMoo
How easy was the tool to use?	2.19	1.13	2.69	0.03627	0.00002
How did you find the task?	1.94	1.44	2.38	0.00904	0.00134
How well do you think you did?	2.38	2.25	2.81	0.01339	0.05330

For the user perception measures (how easy was the tool to use?, how did you find the task?) - it is clear that *Voyager* has a higher mean average than both a spreadsheet and ClaferMoo Visualizer, and this is statistically significant for in both cases ($p < 0.05$). This means users found *Voyager* easier to use, and found completing the same task easier using *Voyager*.

For the question quantifying how confident users felt about their answers (how well do you think you did?), *Voyager* had statistically significant difference compared to the spreadsheet ($p = 0.01339$) with a higher mean average, but there was not a significant difference compared to ClaferMoo Visualizer ($p = 0.05330$, which is greater than 0.05) despite its higher average. This is a clear contrast to the actual scores achieved on both tools, where there was a statistically significant difference in the results.

5   Discussion and Future Work

Voyager is a trade-off exploration tool designed for supporting effective analysis and understanding of multi-dimensional design spaces. The tool delivers a user-friendly, flexible and robust interface, offering a novel solution that combines multi-dimensional quality attribute analysis with architectural structure visualisation – neither of which appear to have been combined into a single tool before. It makes use of modern web technology to deliver clear 2D and 3D data visualisations, offering a maintainable and reliable codebase fit for future use and expansion. *Voyager*'s extensibility features enable flexible integration with other tools, opening up the potential to serve a much larger set of use-cases (e.g., software product lines).

Our user study shows *Voyager* is effective for use with multi-dimensional architecture trade-off problems, having obtained results that show it had a significantly better user experience compared with existing comparable tools, allowing participants to achieve higher accuracy of answers in a shorter time span.

There is scope for future work - including implementing new visualisation ideas (e.g. hierarchical structure exploration, parallel coordinate charts, conditional formatting etc), encouraging open source contributions, and offering enhanced support for external tool integration.

Acknowledgements. The authors would like to thank everyone who kindly volunteered to participate in the user study.

References

1. Aldrich, J., Chambers, C., Notkin, D.: ArchJava: connecting software architecture to implementation. In: Proceedings of the 24th International Conference on Software Engineering, ICSE 2002, pp. 187–197, May 2002
2. Aleti, A., Buhnova, B., Grunske, L., Koziolek, A., Meedeniya, I.: Software architecture optimization methods: a systematic literature review. IEEE Trans. Softw. Eng. **39**(5), 658–683 (2013)
3. Bagheri, H., Tang, C., Sullivan, K.: Trademaker: automated dynamic analysis of synthesized tradespaces. In: Proceedings of the 36th International Conference on Software Engineering, ICSE 2014, pp. 106–116. ACM, New York (2014)
4. Bass, L., Clements, P., Kazman, R.: Software Architecture in Practice, 3rd edn. Addison-Wesley Professional, Upper Saddle River, NJ (2012)
5. Cámara, J., Garlan, D., Schmerl, B.R.: Synthesizing tradeoff spaces with quantitative guarantees for families of software systems. J. Syst. Softw. **152**, 33–49 (2019)
6. Clements, P., Northrop, L.: Software Product Lines: Practices and Patterns. Addison-Wesley Professional, Reading, MA (2001)
7. Hinton, A., Kwiatkowska, M., Norman, G., Parker, D.: PRISM: a tool for automatic verification of probabilistic systems. In: Hermanns, H., Palsberg, J. (eds.) TACAS 2006. LNCS, vol. 3920, pp. 441–444. Springer, Heidelberg (2006). https://doi.org/10.1007/11691372_29
8. Kwiatkowska, M.: Quantitative verification: models, techniques and tools. In: 6th Joint Meeting on European Software Engineering Conference and the ACM SIGSOFT Symposium on the Foundations of Software Engineering: Companion Papers, pp. 449–458. ACM (2007)
9. Li, D., et al.: ECharts: a declarative framework for rapid construction of web-based visualization. Vis. Inform. **2**(2), 136–146 (2018)
10. Mahdavi-Hezavehi, S., Galster, M., Avgeriou, P.: Variability in quality attributes of service-based software systems: a systematic literature review. Inf. Softw. Technol. **55**(2), 320–343 (2013)
11. Murashkin, A., Antkiewicz, M., Rayside, D., Czarnecki, K.: Visualization and exploration of optimal variants in product line engineering. In: Proceedings of the 17th International Software Product Line Conference, pp. 111–115. ACM (2013)
12. Mylopoulos, J., Chung, L., Nixon, B.: Representing and using nonfunctional requirements: a process-oriented approach. IEEE Trans. Softw. Eng. **18**(6), 483–497 (1992)

13. Sawant, A.P., Bali, N.: Softarchviz: a software architecture visualization tool. In: 4th IEEE International Workshop on Visualizing Software for Understanding and Analysis, pp. 154–155, June 2007
14. Sayyad, A.S., Ammar, H.: Pareto-optimal search-based software engineering: a literature survey. In: 2013 2nd International Workshop on Realizing Artificial Intelligence Synergies in Software Engineering, pp. 21–27, May 2013
15. Schmerl, B., Garlan, D.: AcmeStudio: supporting style-centered architecture development. In: Proceedings of the 26th International Conference on Software Engineering, ICSE 2004, pp. 704–705 (2004)
16. Sousa, J.P., Garlan, D.: The aura software architecture: an infrastructure for ubiquitous computing (2003)
17. Weyns, D., Calinescu, R.: Tele assistance: a self-adaptive service-based system exemplar. In: 2015 IEEE/ACM 10th International Symposium on Software Engineering for Adaptive and Self-Managing Systems, pp. 88–92 (2015)

A Decision Support System for Pattern-Driven Software Architecture

Siamak Farshidi[1]([✉])(iD) and Slinger Jansen[1,2](iD)

[1] Department of Information and Computer Science, Utrecht University,
Utrecht, The Netherlands
{s.farshidi,slinger.jansen}@uu.nl
[2] School of Engineering Science, LUT University, Lappeenranta, Finland

Abstract. The selection process of architectural patterns is challenging for software architects, as knowledge about patterns is scattered among a wide range of literature. Knowledge about architectural patterns must be collected, organized, stored, and quickly retrieved when it needs to be employed. In this tool paper, we introduce a decision support system that uses a decision model for supporting software architects with the pattern selection problem according to their requirements, including functional and quality requirements. The decision model is built based on a technology selection framework for modeling multi-criteria decision-making problems in software production. Twenty-four software architects in the Netherlands have evaluated the tool. They confirm that the tool supports them with their daily decision-making process.

Keywords: Architectural patterns · Pattern-driven software architecture · Multi-criteria decision-making · Decision support system · Decision model

1 Introduction

Software architecture is fundamental for the development of a software product and plays an indispensable role in its success or failure as software architecture deals with the base structure, subsystems, and interactions among these subsystems [4]. Software architecture design can be viewed as a decision-making process: software engineers consider a set of alternative solutions that could solve a system design problem, and select the set that is evaluated as the optimal [14].

Software architecture is the composition of a set of architectural design decisions, concerns, variation points, features, and usage scenarios that address various system requirements, including functional and quality requirements [2]. Each architectural design decision is made with a design rationale [6], which represents the knowledge that provides the answers to questions about the design decision or the process followed to make that decision.

An architectural pattern describes high-level structures and behaviors of software systems and addresses a particular recurring problem within a given context

© Springer Nature Switzerland AG 2020
H. Muccini et al. (Eds.): ECSA 2020, CCIS 1269, pp. 68–81, 2020.
https://doi.org/10.1007/978-3-030-59155-7_6

in software architecture design [3]. Architectural patterns aim to satisfy several requirements and help to document the architectural design decisions [1]. So that selecting architectural patterns is a subset of architectural design decisions [22], and it is a challenging task for software architects, as knowledge about patterns, such as their application domains and their interactions with quality attributes, is scattered among a wide range of literature [18]. Thus, a decision support system (DSS) is needed to support software architects with architectural pattern selection intelligently.

In this article, we present a DSS for Pattern-Driven Architecture, which assists software architects in selecting the best fitting set of patterns. The DSS asks architects for their requirements in terms of functional requirements and quality concerns. Accordingly, several sets of architectural patterns are returned that match these requirements. Subsequently, architects can start tweaking the requirements to find the most suitable set of patterns for their design. The DSS is based on several well-known software engineering concepts, such as the ISO/IEC software quality models and the MoSCoW prioritization technique. Architects will indicate their preferences using primary selections such as 'The application *must have* high availability' and 'The application *could have* accessibility'. Using a literature study, we have assessed how patterns perform on these quality criteria. The DSS bundles this knowledge and provides architects with an interactive and collaborative decision tool.

We regard building a software architecture as a decision-making process [17]: (1) Stakeholders with their requirements are engaged. (2) Scenarios are captured. (3) Architectural patterns are identified to address requirements. (4) Potential combinations of patterns are explored. (5) Architects evaluate the combinations of patterns (alternative solutions). If the alternative solutions do not meed the requirements, they are reworked and requirements revisited. (6) An architecture is drafted using the identified patterns (alternative solutions), viewpoints, and perspectives. (7) Different architectural alternatives for refining the draft are explored, and architectural decisions are made to select among them. (8) The architecture is evaluated with stakeholders. Finally, if the architecture does not fulfill stakeholder requirements, the architecture design is reworked and requirements possibly revisited (see Fig. 1). While this process has been a reliable method for producing architectures, it strongly depends on the architect's limited knowledge and experience, who may have experience with only a small number of patterns. Thus, we envision a process where the architect is supported by tools to enhance her knowledge of the patterns available for particular design problems.

Recently, we designed a framework [8] for supporting software developers and architects (decision-makers) with their multi-criteria decision-making (MCDM) problems in software production. An MCDM problem deals with evaluating a set of alternatives and considers a set of decision criteria [15]. In this tool paper, we introduce a decision model, based on the framework, for the patterns selection problem. The DSS employed the decision model to support software architects with the pattern selection problem. Accordingly, we believe that the DSS can be used in steps (1–5) to facilitate the decision-making process for software architects (see Fig. 1).

The rest of this tool paper is organized as follows. Section 2 outlines a brief description of the DSS components and explains the constituent parts of the decision model. Section 3 presents the DSS and its application through a real-world example. Section 4 positions the DSS, among other tools and MCDM approaches, in the literature. Finally, Sect. 6 presents the evaluation of the DSS and summarizes this tool paper.

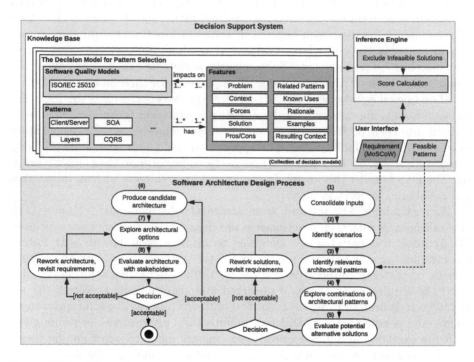

Fig. 1. This figure shows that the DSS can be deployed in the software architecture design process to support the software architects with the pattern selection problem [7,17].

2   Decision Support System

A DSS is an information system that comprises domain-specific knowledge and decision models to assist decision-makers by offering knowledge about a set of alternatives [20]. In this tool paper, the DSS integrates key aspects of knowledge-driven and model-driven DSSs [16] to store and organize the extracted knowledge regarding architectural patterns systematically facilitate the decision-making process. Note, for the sake of simplicity, we use *patterns* to refer "architectural patterns".

Additionally, we follow the framework [8] for modeling decision problems in software production as MCDM problems. The framework applies the six-step decision-making process [15] to build decision models for MCDM problems. The knowledge base of the DSS is a collection of decision models for different MCDM problems [7,9–11]. According to the framework, the decision model for the pattern selection problem contains three sets (including Patterns, Software Quality Models, and Features) besides the mapping among the elements of these sets (see Fig. 1).

- **Patterns:** Patterns are the building blocks that, when assembled, can provide complete solutions for an architect's problem (see Fig. 1). Patterns have relationships to each other. For example, patterns can be alternatives to each other, for example, *Interpreter*, *Rule-Based System*, and *Virtual Machine* [1]; Moreover, some patterns can also be complementary and combined. For instance, the *Client-Server* pattern can be combined with the *Broker* pattern [12].

- **Software Quality Models:** A set of quality attributes, such as Availability and Security, should be defined in the decision model. We employed the *ISO/IEC 25010* standard [13] as a domain-independent quality model. The key rationale behind using this software quality model is that it is a standardized way of assessing a software product's quality. Moreover, it describes how easily and reliably a software product can be used.

- **Features:** Each pattern has a set of features, for instance, "centralized governance" is a feature of the "Client-Server". We identified the following types of features through a Systematic Literature Review (SLR) [11]. We reviewed *21,373* articles, and finally, *232* high-quality primary studies have been selected for performing the knowledge extraction process. Note, such feature types can be found in most patterns, even with different titles. (1: Problem) Descriptions of the problems indicating the intent in applying patterns. (2: Context) The preconditions under which patterns are applicable. (3: Forces) Descriptions of the allied forces and constraints. (4: Solution) Static structures and dynamic behaviors of patterns. (5: Resulting Context) The post-conditions after a pattern has been applied. (6: Examples) Some sample applications of patterns. (7: Rationale) An explanation/justification of each pattern as a whole. (8: Related Patterns) The relationships among patterns. (9: Known Uses) Known applications of patterns within existing systems. (10: Pros/Cons) Pros and cons of employing patterns.

- **Mappings:** We identified the impacts of 29 patterns on 40 quality attributes based on a series of expert interviews with twelve senior software architects at different software producing organizations in the Netherlands [11]. Moreover, The mapping between the patterns and the features was investigated with the SLR and the experts.

Decision-Makers, such Software architects and developers, prioritize their requirements based on the MoSCoW prioritization technique [5], and then they send the requirements through the user interface of the DSS to the inference engine. Figure 3 shows the user interface of the DSS.

Inference Engine: The DSS has an inference engine that receives inputs from the user interface. Next, it excludes all infeasible solutions, those that do not support "Must-Have" features or those that support "Won't-Have" features, and then it ranks the feasible solutions based on the number of "Should-Have" and "Could-Have" features that they support. In other words, requirements with *Must-Have* or *Won't-Have* priorities act as hard-constraints and requirements with *Should-Have* and *Could-Have* priorities act as soft-constraints. The inference engine assigns a non-negative score to each alternative solution based on the well-known Sum of Weights Method [7], and finally, it returns a shortlist of feasible patterns (solutions) to the user interface.

3   A Practical Running Example

The DSS is accessible through the following link: (https://dss-mcdm.com). After login to the system, a software architect should select the "Software Architecture Pattern Selection" to create an instance of the decision model.

This section presents a real-world example of the pattern selection process. We asked a software architect at AFAS Software, a software producing organization in the Netherlands, to define their software architecture from a high-level of abstraction; then, we used the DSS and the decision model to capture the architect's concerns and requirements; next, the DSS generated a set of solutions accordingly.

Fig. 2. The architects describe their case in the context description screen. The tool uses text matching to automatically extract a subset of features from the description to get the architect started.

Case Description - The software architect described AFAS software as follows: *AFAS Software is a Dutch vendor of Enterprise Resource Planning (ERP) Software with more than 500 employees. AFAS has the goal of automating business* *processes found in a diverse range of companies. It supports business processes such as invoicing, project management, payrolling in a single integrated software system. The current AFAS product, called AFAS Profit, is a traditional client-server application with a relational database for storing and retrieving customers' management data, such as business models and ontologies. AFAS Profit is a complete, integrated ERP system used by more than 10000 small and medium-sized enterprises. For example, Ernst & Young, Kwik-Fit, LeasePlan, Oad Reizen, Sandd, and Wibra, are already employing AFAS Profit to automate their business processes. Figure 2 shows the description of the decision-making problem in terms of the case title and description; moreover, the logo of the company can be attached to the "case description".*

Fig. 3. Represents how a decision-maker can define the requirements based on the MoSCoW prioritization technique.

Case Definition - The software architect defined AFAS Profit as *a web-based solution that is consistent with the user experience of the windows client but feels web-native to customers. AFAS Profit is configurable by customers in their styling to match their logo and business style.* AFAS Profit has the following characteristics: (1) It is a combination of a client or frontend portion that interacts with the user and a server or back-end portion that interacts with the shared resource. The client process contains solution-specific logic and provides the interface between the user and the rest of the application system. The server process acts as a software engine that manages shared resources. (2) All data are centralized on a single server, simplifying security checks, including updates of data and software. (3) It supports a higher degree of flexibility and security, compared to the previous solution. (5) Its performance has increased significantly, compared to the previous solution, as tasks are shared between servers.

The architect stated that *"Functional Correctness", "Resource Utilization", "Configurability", "Accessibility", "Reliability", "Availability", and "Scalability" are the main quality concerns. Additionally, "technology agnostic", "modern web application", and "reusability of the business logic" are the key requirements of AFAS profit. Figure* 3 *shows the "case definition" of AFAS Profit. The software architect assigned the MoSCoW priorities (Must-Have, Should-Have, Could-Have, and Won't-Have) to the requirements. Note, the data type the features can be either Boolean or Non-Boolean. For instance, "handling user input" is a Boolean feature, which means that a pattern either supports it or not. However, the level of support of "Availability" or "Scalability", as two Non-Boolean features, of a pattern can be "High", "Medium", or "Low".*

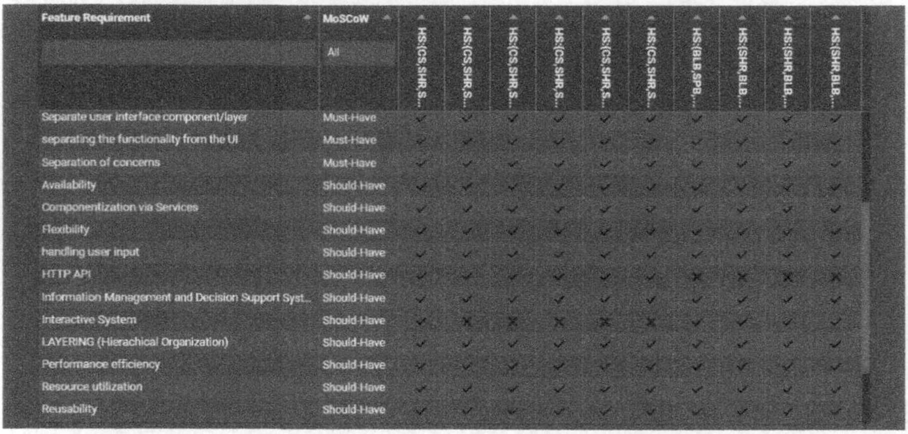

Feature Requirement	MoSCoW	HS:(CS,SHR,S...	HS:(CS,SHR,S...	HS:(CS,SHR,S...	HS:(CS,SHR,S...	HS:(CS,SHR,S...	HS:(CS,SHR,S...	HS:(BLB,SPB,...	HS:(SHR,BLB,...	HS:(SHR,BLB,...	HS:(SHR,BLB,...
	All										
Separate user interface component/layer	Must-Have	✓	✓	✓	✓	✓	✓	✓	✓	✓	✓
separating the functionality from the UI	Must-Have	✓	✓	✓	✓	✓	✓	✓	✓	✓	✓
Separation of concerns	Must-Have	✓	✓	✓	✓	✓	✓	✓	✓	✓	✓
Availability	Should-Have	✓	✓	✓	✓	✓	✓	✓	✓	✓	✓
Componentization via Services	Should-Have	✓	✓	✓	✓	✓	✓	✓	✓	✓	✓
Flexibility	Should-Have	✓	✓	✓	✓	✓	✓	✓	✓	✓	✓
handling user input	Should-Have	✓	✓	✓	✓	✓	✓	✓	✓	✓	✓
HTTP API	Should-Have	✓	✓	✓	✓	✓	✓	✗	✗	✗	✗
Information Management and Decision Support Syst...	Should-Have	✓	✓	✓	✓	✓	✓	✓	✓	✓	✓
Interactive System	Should-Have	✓	✗	✗	✗	✗	✗	✓	✓	✓	✓
LAYERING (Hierachical Organization)	Should-Have	✓	✓	✓	✓	✓	✓	✓	✓	✓	✓
Performance efficiency	Should-Have	✓	✓	✓	✓	✓	✓	✓	✓	✓	✓
Resource utilization	Should-Have	✓	✓	✓	✓	✓	✓	✓	✓	✓	✓
Reusability	Should-Have	✓	✓	✓	✓	✓	✓	✓	✓	✓	✓

Fig. 4. Illustrates part of the case evaluation by the DSS. Ticks (✓) in a row signify that the feature is supported by the corresponding patterns, and crosses (✗) symbolize that the patterns do not support the feature.

Case Evaluation - The software architect stated that *AFAS Profit architecture is based on a combination of the "Client-Server", "Publish-Subscribe", and "Layers" patterns. The main rationales behind these design decisions are (1) the frontend can be easily replaced or upgraded, and every module of the business logic, in the back-end, can be reused. (2) The web client communicates over HTTP with the server, so it is possible to choose different technologies for the web client. (3) They can implement a Content Management System (CMS) to make the web client configurable in style and layout. (4) While the data is requested through communication with the server, preventing stale data, the CMS parts are published with some delay, making it possible to cache the style and layout for fast retrieval.*

The inference engine gets the requirements and evaluates the alternative patterns in its knowledge base accordingly. As each pattern supports only a limited set of features, the inference engine has to generate feasible solutions (combinations of patterns). Note, finding a subset of patterns that support all hard-constraints can be formulated as the set cover problem. The DSS uses an algorithm based on the set cover problem to generate several feasible solutions when all patterns in its knowledge base do not support the entire list of hard-constraints of a decision-maker. For instance, Fig. 4 shows that the DSS could not find any patterns that address all the AFAS Profit requirements so that it generated a set of solutions consist of multiple patterns.

Feasible Solution	Explanation
HS:{CS,SHR,SPB,LAY,C2}	1 - CLIENT-SERVER (CS) 2 - SHARED REPOSITORY (SHR) 3 - SPACE-BASED (SPB) / CLOUD-BASED 4 - LAYERS (LAY) 5 - COMMAND AND CONTROL (C2)
HS:{CS,SHR,SPB,LAY,MIK}	1 - CLIENT-SERVER (CS) 2 - SHARED REPOSITORY (SHR) 3 - SPACE-BASED (SPB) / CLOUD-BASED 4 - LAYERS (LAY) 5 - MICROKERNEL (MIK)
HS:{CS,SHR,SPB,LAY,SOA}	1 - CLIENT-SERVER (CS) 2 - SHARED REPOSITORY (SHR) 3 - SPACE-BASED (SPB) / CLOUD-BASED 4 - LAYERS (LAY) 5 - SERVICE-ORIENTED ARCHITECTUE (SOA)

Fig. 5. Shows top-3 solutions for AFAS Profit.

Patterns tend to be combined to provide greater support for the reusability during the software design process [19]. A pattern can be blended with, connected to, or included in another pattern. For instance, the *Broker* pattern can be connected to the *Client-Server* pattern to form the combined *Client-Server-Broker* pattern [12]. Figure 5 shows top-3 solutions for AFAS profit. The solutions support all requirements with Must-Have priorities and do not support Won't have requirements (hard-constraints). Note, the DSS generated almost similar solutions that the experienced software architects at AFAS came up with. Note that the DSS sorts its suggestions based on their scores so that top-3 solutions can be considered the most valuable suggestions.

The DSS Reports - In the knowledge extraction phase for building the decision model, we observed multiple inconsistencies regarding the impacts of patterns on quality attributes. Some studies reported adverse impacts of a particular pattern on a quality attribute. For instance, *efficiency* can be considered as both strength and liability of the *Pipes and Filters* pattern. We applied fuzzy logic to aggregate the extracted knowledge regarding the potential impacts of patterns on quality attributes. In the implementation of the score calculation (trade-off) phase of the DSS, the impact values range from -2 to $2+$. Accordingly, the patterns with more liabilities score lower than those that have more strengths. Note, quantifying the impact of a particular pattern on the quality attributes is complicated because quality attributes are system-wide capabilities. Generally,

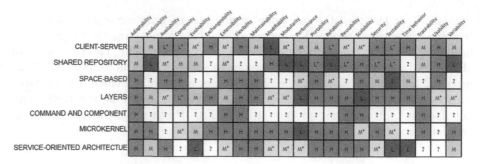

Fig. 6. Show a subset of the mapping between features and patterns used by the DSS to generate solutions for AFAS profit. The primary source of knowledge to build this mapping is the SLR. We employed Fuzzy logic to gain some agreement among the selected studies to calculate the values [11]. Note: High (H), Medium (M), Low (L), Unknown (?).

they cannot be evaluated entirely until the whole system can be evaluated. The DSS evaluates alternative solutions according to decision-makers' quality concerns. Figure 6 shows the impacts of the single solutions for AFAS profit on a subset of quality attributes.

Figure 7 illustrates a decision structure based on AFAS profit requirements. The DSS automatically generates such decision structures according to the requirements of decision-makers. The first level of the decision structure (Domain) indicates the goal of the decision-making process. The second level denotes the relevant quality attributes that impact the prioritized requirements, which are signified in the third level (requirements). The last level (Feasible Solutions) shows a list of feasible patterns for the decision domain.

4   Related Work

In the SLR [11], we reviewed selected *232* high-quality primary studies for performing the knowledge extraction process. The knowledge base of the SLR, including the primary studies and extracted knowledge, is available as a technical report on the following web page: http://swapslr.com. We realized that researchers introduced a variety of tools and MCDM techniques to address the pattern selection problem. Notably, there are few tools available for software architects. Architecting is a knowledge-intensive practice, so it can be hard to find the best way to support architects with the right knowledge at the right time. A subset of tools for supporting software architects with their design decisions are presented as follows: *Archium* (www.archium.io) is a visualization tool that produces a view on the functional dependencies between architectural design decisions. It is not an automatic pattern detection or selection, but visualizing the dependencies can help software architects identify such patterns. *ArchReco* (www.cs.ucy.ac.cy/sielis) provides a design environment that software architects can draw diagrams with pre-defined shapes that exist in a palette. The description of the shapes is part of a contextual element set that ArchReco's processes suggest the most suitable context-based recommended design patterns. Such Design Patterns are retrieved from several data sources and filtered according to the contextual information that is processed when software architects request recommendations. *Sirius* (www.obeodesigner.com/en/product/sirius) is a tool that enables software architects to graphically design complex systems while keeping the corresponding data consistent (architecture, component properties, etc.). *AKB* (www.se.jku.at/akb-knowledge-sharing) is an implementation and extension of the Architecture Haiku concept, a one-page design description. AKB supports software architects with capturing and sharing of architectural knowledge based on architecture profiles.

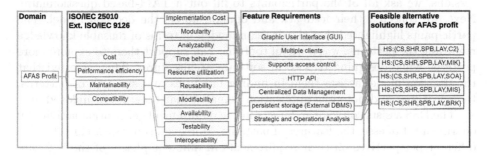

Fig. 7. Shows part of the decision structure for the AFAS profit that was generated by the DSS. The domain of the decision-making process is "Finding the best fitting set of patterns for AFAS profit". The qualities are based on the ISO/IEC 25010 [13] quality model. The software architect (decision-maker) defined the feature requirements. The DSS suggested feasible alternative solutions for AFAS profit (last level). Note, the mapping between the qualities and the features was based on domain experts' knowledge; moreover, the relationships among features and patterns were determined based on the SLR [11].

The DSS enables software architects to document their drawings and design rationales. We implemented a design studio based on the Unified Modeling Language concepts to store design decisions while the decision-making process. The main difference between the DSS and such tools is that it supports software architects with their decision-making process. In other words, the DSS provides a discussion and negotiation platform to enable software architects to make group decisions. Furthermore, the DSS can be used over the full life-cycle and can co-evolve its advice based on evolving requirements. Software architects can prioritize their functional requirements and quality concerns using the MoSCoW prioritization technique through the user interface of the DSS. Then, the DSS generates a set of feasible solutions that address the requirements.

5   Evaluation

We carried out a study with 24 software architects and developers in the Netherlands to assess the user acceptance of the decision support system and the decision model based on the Technology Acceptance Model. Firstly, we formed 12 groups of two individuals according to their expertise and the companies that they were working with. Next, we introduced the decision model within the DSS portal and presented some of its applications. Then, we assigned the problem definitions of two real-world software architectures to the groups and asked them to design two solutions for the problems. The groups used the decision model within the DSS platform to help them with (1) defining the requirements based on the MoSCoW prioritization technique, and (2) finding the best fitting set of patterns. The group sessions lasted between 45 to 60 min. At the end of the sessions, we ask all of the participants to fill out a TAM-based questionnaire; Next, we collected their feedback and opinion about the decision model. The participants highlighted that the decision model, in terms of reusable knowledge regarding the patterns, was a useful tool that can support them to explore more patterns while designing real-world software architectures. They asserted that the decision model assists them in finding liabilities and strength of patterns, their features, and potential application domains that they have employed in.

The DSS assists software architects in the requirements elicitation activity by offering a list of essential features of patterns. Moreover, software architects have different perspectives on their requirements in different phases of the Software Development Life-Cycle. They might want to consider generic domain features in the early phases of the life-cycle, whereas they are interested in more technical features as their development process matures. Therefore, the DSS might come up with various solutions for a software architect in different phases of its software development life-cycle. As the choices of a decision-maker are stored in the DSS knowledge base, it does not cost a significant amount of time to rerun the decision-making process. In a typical scenario, an architect will tweak her decisions and values to assess her choices have on the desired set of patterns. Software architects sometimes have to select a particular set of patterns because of legacy technology choices. Sometimes vendor lock-in makes a customer dependent on a vendor for products and services, unable to use another vendor without substantial switching costs. An example of a pattern that has been trending in recent years is the *Microservices* pattern (see [11]). *Microservices* advantages can tempt architects to consider it as a hammer and convert every design decision into a nail.

Patterns and quality attributes are not independent and have significant interaction with each other. Such interactions can be observed as trade-offs between quality attributes. Software architects need to select and employ an optimal set of patterns to satisfy quality concerns. For instance, some studies assert that *Reusability* is a strength and *Scalability* is a liability of the *Layers* pattern (see [11]). If an architect is looking for both qualities, she has two options: choose another (set of) pattern(s) or use *tactics* to improve *Scalability*. System quality is best exposed in production, independent of whether system quality has been made explicit. We recall that well-known authors, such as Wiegers and Beatty [21], classify quality attributes as external (exposed at the run time/in production, e.g., performance) and internal (exposed at design time, e.g., modifiability). If architects do not think about performance, the system will still expose its performance in the field. The knowledge around the quality of a system under design is hard to gather without *in the field* experiences; however, experience with similar patterns in other systems provides invaluable insight into the inherent qualities of a new system. The DSS recommends patterns that exhibit similar quality behaviors when purely implemented (without tactics) in different systems and that this knowledge can be used by architects to make informed design decisions. We consider it future work to further explore these relationships between patterns and the way in which these communicating properties are best communicated to architects, having to choose from a set of complex solutions.

The tool has been designed using the .Net framework. While it has been optimized somewhat, the tool will sometimes still perform slowly, with end-user wait times of around 5 s, which is workable, but not ideal. One of the challenges is the solution space: for recommending solutions (combinations of patterns), the problem's search space is huge, consisting of 29 patterns and 188 features. For instance, for a solution with three patterns, the problem's search space is found to contain $\sim 29 \times 28 \times 27 \times 188$ possible problem states.

6   Conclusion

In this tool paper, we present a DSS besides a decision model for architectural pattern selection. The DSS suggests feasible patterns for particular cases based on the quality concerns and functional requirements of decision-makers. The DSS[1] is accessible through the following link: (https://dss-mcdm.com). We consider it future work to ensure that the knowledge base remains up to date, for instance, through a wiki-mechanism. Thus, software architects can consider the DSS as a source of knowledge and reliable assistance while making decisions regarding the best-fitting set of patterns for their software architectures. Additionally, we should enhance the DSS with a learning module that improves its learnability aspect in the future.

It is presently impossible to assess which patterns are compatible and frequently used in combination, even though practically all systems implement more than one pattern. The knowledge base of the DSS contains individual patterns that solve particular parts of a design problem. The inference engine uses an algorithm based on the set cover problem to generate several feasible solutions when all patterns in its knowledge base do not support the entire list of hard-constraints of a decision-maker.

In our studies, we have dealt with different kinds of architectures, with a slight bias towards enterprise resource planning systems. We consider it as future

---

[1] Please watch a demo video of the DSS through this link: https://youtu.be/AhfGYpwpJSQ.

work to apply the tool to problems in other domains, such as Internet of Things, gaming, or media systems.

References

1. Avgeriou, P., Zdun, U.: Architectural patterns revisited-a pattern language. In: European Conference on Pattern Languages of Programs (2005)
2. Bosch, J.: Software architecture: the next step. In: Oquendo, F., Warboys, B.C., Morrison, R. (eds.) EWSA 2004. LNCS, vol. 3047, pp. 194–199. Springer, Heidelberg (2004). https://doi.org/10.1007/978-3-540-24769-2_14
3. Bushchmann, F., Meunier, R., Rohnert, H., Sommerlad, P., Stal, M.: Pattern-oriented software architecture-a system of patterns. Adv. Softw. Eng. Knowl. Eng. **1**, 1–487 (1996)
4. Clements, P., Kazman, R., Klein, M., et al.: Evaluating Software Architectures. Tsinghua University Press, Beijing (2003)
5. DSDM Consortium: The DSDM Agile Project Framework Handbook. Ashford, Kent (2014)
6. Dutoit, A.H., McCall, R., Mistrík, I., Paech, B.: Rationale Management in Software Engineering, 1st edn., p. 434. Springer, Heidelberg (2007). https://doi.org/10.1007/978-3-540-30998-7
7. Farshidi, S., Jansen, S., De Jong, R., Brinkkemper, S.: A decision support system for cloud service provider selection problems in software producing organizations. In 2018 IEEE 20th Conference on Business Informatics (CBI), vol. 1, pp. 139–148. IEEE (2018)
8. Farshidi, S., Jansen, S., de Jong, R., Brinkkemper, S.: A decision support system for software technology selection. J. Decis. Syst. **27**, 98–110 (2018)
9. Farshidi, S., Jansen, S., De Jong, R., Brinkkemper, S.: Multiple criteria decision support in requirements negotiation. In: The 23rd International Conference on Requirements Engineering: Foundation for Software Quality (REFSQ 2018), vol. 2075, pp. 100–107 (2018)
10. Farshidi, S., Jansen, S., España, S., Verkleij, J.: Decision support for blockchain platform selection: three industry case studies. IEEE Trans. Eng. Manage. **PP**, 1–20 (2020)
11. Farshidi, S., Jansen, S., van der Werf, J.M.: Capturing software architecture knowledge for pattern-driven design. J. Syst. Softw. **169**, 110714 (2020)
12. Harrison, N.B., Avgeriou, P.: How do architecture patterns and tactics interact? A model and annotation. J. Syst. Softw. **83**(10), 1735–1758 (2010)
13. ISO. IEC25010: systems and software quality requirements and evaluation (SQuaRE). International Organization for Standardization, vol. 34, p. 2910 (2011)
14. Lago, P., Avgeriou, P.: First workshop on sharing and reusing architectural knowledge. ACM SIGSOFT Softw. Eng. Notes **31**(5), 32–36 (2006)
15. Majumder, M.: Multi criteria decision making. Impact of Urbanization on Water Shortage in Face of Climatic Aberrations. SWST, pp. 35–47. Springer, Singapore (2015). https://doi.org/10.1007/978-981-4560-73-3_2
16. Power, D.J.: Decision support systems: a historical overview. In: Handbook on Decision Support Systems, vol. 1, pp. 121–140. Springer, Heidelberg (2008). https://doi.org/10.1007/978-3-540-48713-5_7
17. Rozanski, N., Woods, E.: Software Systems Architecture: Working with Stakeholders Using Viewpoints and Perspectives. Addison-Wesley, Boston (2012)

18. Tang, A., Liang, P., Van Vliet, H.: Software architecture documentation: the road ahead. In: The 9th Working IEEE Conference on Software Architecture, pp. 252–255. IEEE (2011)
19. Ton That, M.T., Sadou, S., Oquendo, F., Borne, I.: Composition-centered architectural pattern description language. In: Drira, K. (ed.) ECSA 2013. LNCS, vol. 7957, pp. 1–16. Springer, Heidelberg (2013). https://doi.org/10.1007/978-3-642-39031-9_1
20. Wang, H.: Intelligent agent-assisted decision support systems: integration of knowledge discovery and knowledge analysis. Expert Syst. Appl. **12**(3), 323–335 (1997)
21. Wiegers, K., Beatty, J.: Software Requirements. Pearson Education, London (2013)
22. Zimmermann, O.: Architectural decisions as reusable design assets. IEEE Softw. **28**(1), 64–69 (2010)

Gropius — A Tool for Managing Cross-component Issues

Sandro Speth[1]([✉])(iD), Uwe Breitenbücher[2](iD), and Steffen Becker[1](iD)

[1] Institute of Software Engineering, University of Stuttgart,
Stuttgart, Germany
{sandro.speth,steffen.becker}@iste.uni-stuttgart.de
[2] Institute of Architecture of Application Systems, University of Stuttgart,
Stuttgart, Germany
uwe.breitenbuecher@iaas.uni-stuttgart.de
https://www.iste.uni-stuttgart.de/rss/
https://www.iaas.uni-stuttgart.de/

Abstract. Modern software systems often are structured as distributed component-based architectures, such as microservice architectures. However, such systems come with significant challenges in cross-component issue management. Each component usually manages its issues in an independent issue management system, and conventional issue management systems only have a project-specific scope. Therefore, issues that affect multiple components or propagate across various components cannot be displayed. Furthermore, issues cannot be linked semantically to issues in other components. Instead, emergency solutions, such as a URL to the other issue, must be used. This makes it challenging to recognize cross-component dependency information. This paper presents Gropius, a tool for integrated management of cross-component issues. Gropius graphically models such cross-component issues together with the system architecture in a notation similar to a UML component diagram. Additionally, other research and industry efforts to manage such issues are discussed and compared to Gropius.

Keywords: Issue management · Integration · Service-oriented architecture · Component-based architecture · Bug tracking · Microservices

1 Introduction

Today's systems usually consist of several externalized components, such as microservices, which together form an application. Although such a distributed application has many advantages, the complexity of the application also leads to several challenges and problems during development as identified by Mahmood et al. [9]. For example, there is a lack of showing inter-dependencies of components. Additionally, since each component is developed by an independent team, often several teams which might not know each other meet at the

© Springer Nature Switzerland AG 2020
H. Muccini et al. (Eds.): ECSA 2020, CCIS 1269, pp. 82–94, 2020.
https://doi.org/10.1007/978-3-030-59155-7_7

interfaces between the components. In particular, issue management comes with the high potential for risk, since dependencies between the various components can lead to the propagation of bugs or other issues along the call chain through the components. To fix such an issue, the original component must be identified, and the bug must be fixed there. It is, therefore, necessary to be able to communicate such cross-component issues efficiently and effectively across individual component boundaries. For this, the architectural dependencies must be documented together with the issues. However, conventional issue management systems only work on a project-specific scope and thus fail to provide a cross-component view. In these conventional issue management systems, the dependencies between several issues of different components cannot be represented semantically. The only solution to create a link is to provide a URL to the linked issues. This makes it impossible to visualize dependencies of an issue on different components, as well as the architectural dependencies of the affected components on each other. Also, issue propagation is difficult to identify along with the issue by following the links instead of graphically. For the management of such cross-component issues, therefore, an appropriate syntax is required that models issues together with the dependency view of the architecture. For this purpose, we have developed Gropius, a system for integrated management of issues which affect different independently developed components. In Gropius, components, their dependencies to each other, as well as cross-component issues can be visualized and modelled in a graphical notation similar to a UML component diagram. Linking and propagation of issues, therefore, can be identified more easily. By applying the adapter pattern, Gropius acts as a wrapper over traditional issue management systems and can consequently create and manage issues in the issue management systems of all affected components. In this work, we describe the architecture and functionality of Gropius. Additionally, other approaches to manage cross-component issues are discussed and compared to our approach. Besides, there is a short introduction video for Gropius[1].

The remainder of the paper is as follows: Sect. 2 briefly explains the problem of issue management in component-based systems, provides a problem use case and discusses how this use case can be solved with the cross-component issue management system Gropius. Afterwards, the architecture of Gropius with particular regard to and the graphical CrossComponentIssueModeller are outlined in Sect. 3. Section 4 discusses related research and industry efforts to manage issues which are affecting several components or projects. Additionally, we compare these approaches with Gropius. Finally, we conclude in Sect. 5.

2 Problem Statement and Use Case

Modern systems usually consist of many independently developed components, such as in the widely used microservice architecture style. The components are specified by contracts and form the composable building blocks for a more extensive software [11,13]. Components offer interfaces to the outside world, which can

---

[1] https://youtu.be/dRhDINDbMkc.

be consumed by other components to use the exported functions. Thus, components can be provided and used without understanding the internals. However, the consumption of such interfaces also creates dependencies between the independent components of the system.

Mahmood et al. have described in [9] some problems and challenges that occur in such component-based systems. One of the main challenges they identify is the lack of adequate tracking of bugs and faults in such systems. They point out that issues in such systems must be tracked back to the original component and at the same time adequately managed in all dependent components. Additionally, Mahmood et al. show a lack of inter-dependency between components.

Since the components are each developed and maintained by independent teams, the ownership and resulting rights do not belong to the developers of the interface consuming components. Besides, bug reports and other types of issues for each component are managed in an independent issue management system (bug tracker). However, due to the dependencies across components, issues can be propagated across components along the call chain using the consumed interfaces. For example, if a component's functionality fails due to a bug, the dependent components will also be affected by the bug at runtime because the consumed interfaces do not fulfil their contracts.

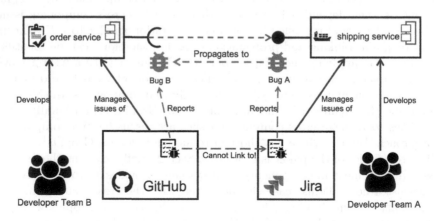

Fig. 1. A use case for a problematic issue management for two components of a webshop implemented as a microservice architecture

Imagine a use case of a part of a webshop implemented with a microservice architecture as shown in the component diagram of the Fig. 1. The order and shipping services are components of the system, with the shipping service providing an interface that is consumed by the order service. Both components are developed by independent teams and manage the issues of their components in different issue management systems (e.g. GitHub and Jira). Assuming a bug occurs in the shipping service's interface, the dependent functionality of the order service will also be affected at runtime. The bug, therefore, propagates via the consumed interface from the shipping service to the order service and creates another bug there. Bug reports can be created for the corresponding bugs in both issue management systems. However, as described in [9], the resulting bug must be traced back to its original component. To make this possible, the bug report of the resulting bug should link to the bug report of the original bug, since the fixing of the bug in the order service depends on the fixing of the bug in the shipping service. Since conventional issue management systems have a project-specific scope and, therefore, can only track issues within a component, issues cannot link to issues in other issue management systems. The bugs of both components must consequently be communicated and synchronized by the development teams via e-mail, meetings or other tools, which leads to a significant communication effort. Therefore, a system is needed that enables issue management for independently developed components while using the actual issue management systems of the components.

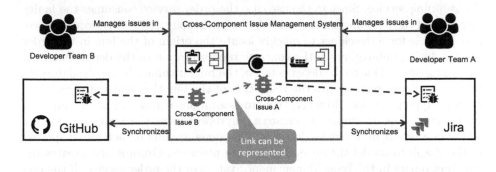

Fig. 2. Overview of the cross-component issue management system *Gropius*

For this purpose, we have designed Gropius, the integrated cross-component issue management system. Figure 2 shows how Gropius can be used to manage and synchronize issues across different components. Instead of using the conventional issue management systems, all issues of the components of a project can be modelled and managed using a graphical notation in Gropius, which is introduced by Speth in [12]. This allows development teams to create issues that affect multiple components and link semantically to other issues across components, rather than just specifying a URL or the ID of an issue. Gropius propagates changes to issues to the actual issue management systems of the components and synchronizes with them. Gropius thereby operates as a wrapper over the different issue management systems and links them to a single joint UI. The figure shows how components and their dependencies are modelled in the `CrossComponentIssueModeller` together with the issues in a system architecture graph. The components are represented in a syntax that is very similar to a UML component diagram to highlight dependencies across components more clearly. Additionally, Gropius can distinguish whether an issue directly affects a component or its interface and display this in the graph at a suitable position.

Dependencies between issues are modelled not only textually in the description of the issue, but also graphically, making them easy to identify.

The use case described above can now be solved very easily with Gropius. A project manager can create a project for the webshop in Gropius and create the components of the project (order service and shipping service). To synchronize Gropius with the actual issue management systems, each component links to the respective issue management system and the information about what type of issue management system (e.g. Jira) is involved. To ensure that the components are not only created individually but also to show the dependencies across components, the interface of the shipping service can be created in the graph and consumed by the order service. This allows Gropius to display the architecture of the webshop project, similar to a UML component diagram. After the components have been created, Gropius shows a project member, e.g. a developer, all open issues of the component in the graph. This allows a developer of the order service to quickly identify if a bug report exists for the interface of the shipping service. Since in the use case the order service consumes the faulty interface of the shipping service, and the bug is propagated to the order service, it is possible for a developer to quickly locate the origin of the bug in the order service during debugging via the concrete representation of the dependencies of the components. Due to the dependency of the bug, it cannot be resolved directly by the developer but requires the resolution of the bug that affects the interface of the shipping service. However, this cross-component bug can be documented via Gropius. The developer can create a bug report using the graph and point it to the bug report on which he depends. This semantic link is then also displayed in the graph to model the dependency more precisely. Gropius also creates the new bug report in the Issue Management System of the order service. If the bug report of the shipping service interface is closed, the graph will show the bug in green and signal the order service development team that the dependent bug can now be fixed.

3   Architecture

This section describes the general architecture of the Cross-Component Issue Management System *Gropius* [6]. As depicted in Fig. 3, the system is divided into front-end, back-end and databases, whereby the back-end is connected to the actual issue management systems of the components via adapters. The system, therefore, forms a kind of shared wrapper over other issue management systems. We present the front-end with particular regard to the graphical notation of cross-component issues in Sect. 3.1. The back-end is explained in more detail in Sect. 3.2. We look at the use of the adapter pattern to synchronize issues to the corresponding issue management systems. Finally, we discuss in Sect. 3.3 the persistence and synchronization of cross-component issues managed by Gropius.

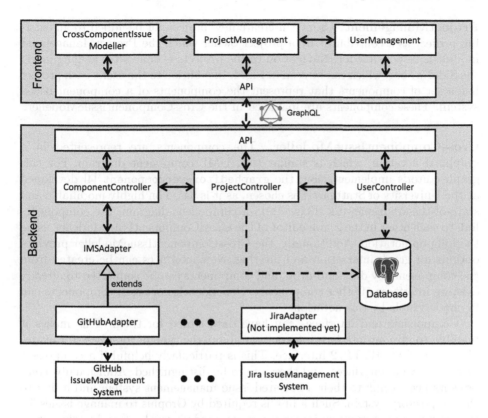

Fig. 3. Architecture of the cross-component issue management system

3.1   Front-End and the Graphical CrossComponentIssueModeller

The front-end is written as a web application in Angular, taking into account modern tools and technologies. It consists of three main modules responsible for user management (UserManagement), project and component management (ProjectManagement), and the modelling and management of cross-component issues (CrossComponentIssueModeller). The main view with expanded project menu and CrossComponentIssueModeller is depicted in Fig. 4.

UserManagement. The UserManagement module takes care of the registration, authentication and authorization of users. A user has to authenticate himself for the supported issue management systems. This can be done using credentials or access tokens. Since Gropius is a wrapper over other issue management systems, this step is particularly crucial for propagating user actions to the actual systems. Authentication between front-end and back-end is done using JSON Web Tokens, a modern standard for bearer tokens for client authentication [7].

ProjectManagement. Users can create new projects or be added to an existing project as a contributor by a project owner which the ProjectManagement module is responsible for. Navigation to the projects is done after logging in via the SideNav bar, which can be seen in Fig. 4. In addition to the users, each project has a set of components that represent the components of a component-based system. These components are managed in the CrossComponentIssueModeller.

CrossComponentIssueModeller. The components are represented in a graphical notation, which is similar to a UML component diagram. For this graph editor's implementation, the `grapheditor-webcomponent` [4] developed at the University of Stuttgart was chosen, as it is based on highly modifiable and state-of-the-art framework d3.js. As in a component diagram, the components link to each other in the graph editor of the CrossComponentIssueModeller using the lollipop notation. Additionally, the CrossComponentIssueModeller provides options for graph interaction and filtering. New interfaces can be created from the components by drag-and-drop, and components can be connected to already existing interfaces of other components. Dependencies between components can be made visible by this notation.

Components and interfaces can have data stored for them. This makes it possible to give an interface information about the type of interface, for example, a REST via HTTP/2 interface. This is particularly helpful if a component provides several interfaces, and these are to be distinguished. Additionally, components need a link to their associated issue management system and a link to their repository system. Such a link is required by Gropius to manage issues for the components. Actions on issues are propagated via the back-end to the actual issue management system. The required repository is stored so that a developer

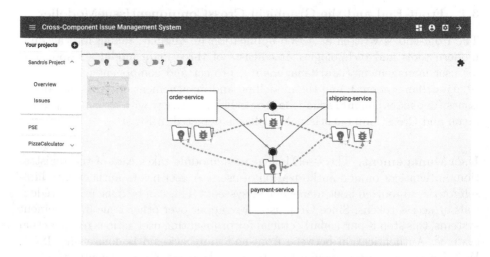

Fig. 4. Front-end view which shows an open project and the `CrossComponent IssueModeller`

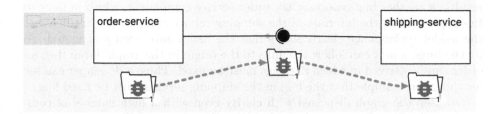

Fig. 5. Problem use case managed in the cross-component issue management system *Gropius*

can link issues to the source code or other artefacts in the repository of the component from Gropius. This is particularly important if a cross-component issue is to link to artefacts of another component, for example, the source code of an interface that is being consumed.

Issues are attached to the node for the respective components that are affected by the issues. If an issue affects a component's interface, the issue is displayed directly at the interface instead of at the component. The user can drag-and-drop for each component or interface individually to determine whether the issues should be displayed below, above, to the left or right of it. For a better overview, issues are collected in folders that can be opened by clicking. There are three main categories, feature requests, bug reports and unclassified issues. Feature requests are displayed with a blue bulb, bug reports with a red bug and unclassified issues with a question mark. Since the CrossComponentIssueModeller displays issues next to the components in the graph, links between different issues, especially issues of different components, can be displayed graphically. This allows a user to identify if issues are propagated across multiple components quickly. If several components have the same issue, this is displayed in the graph for all affected components. In contrast, in the data storage, it is only one object that references all affected components as locations. To prevent all issues from being displayed at the same time, a user can hide the different types of issues in the graph using toggle switches. Additionally, a user can use the notification toggle slider to display only those issues for which the user receives notifications from the underlying issue management system. Notifications include, for example, the user's selection in comments on an issue or when the user is assigned to an issue.

Consider the problem use case from Sect. 2. Figure 5 shows the graph of the CrossComponentIssueModeller for the use case. It displays the two components for an order service and a shipping service. The shipping service component provides an interface that is consumed by the order service component. Additionally, the figure depicts three bug reports. The first bug report concerns the shipping service component. Due to this bug, a second bug arises at the interface of the component. In the graph, the bug report at the interface points to the bug report at the component. Since the order service component consumes the interface of the shipping service component, the bug also propagates to this component. This results in another bug report for the order service component, which in links to the bug report in the interface of the shipping service component. In this view, the modelling language clearly shows that the issues have been propagated. To fix the bugs, a user can follow the links to the origin in the graph. From this, an order can be derived in which the bugs must be fixed. Thus, a developer can see for the given example that the bug in the shipping service must be fixed first.

To keep the graph displayed with clarity even with a high number of components, the CrossComponentIssueModeller offers the possibility to zoom in the graph or to move in the view of the graph by drag-and-drop. Additionally, all components and interfaces can be moved via drag-and-drop and thus arranged differently. The resulting layout is user-specific. Thus, each user can define the layout in the dependency graph of the components individually concerning his own needs. To ensure that the overview of the entire application can always be kept, a minimap in the upper left corner of the CrossComponentIssueModeller shows the entire graph in small size. It covers the parts displayed in the current view of the graph with a slightly transparent coloured rectangle.

If a user prefers a traditional list of issues instead of the dependency graph of the system's components and the display of dependencies across issues, he can switch to the list tab. There, all components and their issues are displayed in lists. It is easier to see issue details, such as the title, but information such as dependencies on issues in other components is wholly lost.

3.2 Backend and Adapter

The back-end and front-end communicate via GraphQL, a modern query language for APIs, which facilitates further development of the API over time [5]. Corresponding to the front-end, there are three modules for user management, project management and components. The UserController persists user data in the database and queries it. The ProjectController stores components and contributors to a project and how the components of the project are connected. A component can occur in several projects. The ComponentController ensures that for each component of a project, the issues can be queried, updated and new issues created via a uniform interface, the IMSAdapter. The cross-component issues are mapped to common issues in the actual issue management systems.

The use of the adapter pattern allows writing adapters specifically for any issue management system. As a consequence, Gropius can also support emerging issue management systems. The abstract IMSAdapter defines a uniform interface. The correct specific adapter can be selected and bound at runtime. In order to support a new issue management system, a developer can write a specialized adapter for the newly supported issue management system. This specialized adapter inherits from the abstract IMSAdapter. In this way, the adapters provide the interface that is consumed by the component controller. The user's credentials, such as an access token, must be stored in the database for authentication with the underlying issue management systems. In the case of GitHub, for example, Gropius acts as a GitHub app via the adapter and can, therefore, perform operations on behalf of the users on the actual issue management systems. This enables Gropius to act as a wrapper over the various component issue management systems. For other issue management systems, the adapter must follow the respective API terms of use. If the issue management system allows Gropius to perform operations directly with the user's credentials, Gropius can perform the operations without intermediate steps as if the user would perform them in the actual issue management system.

3.3   Persistence and Synchronization

The Gropius cross-component issue management system allows users to create and manage issues for the affected components. Each action, e.g. update of an issue, is propagated by Gropius on behalf of the user to the corresponding issue management systems of the components. This means that issues created in Gropius are stored persistently in the issue management systems of all affected components. The credentials of the user, such as an access token, are used for the respective issue management system that the user provides to Gropius. Depending on the issue management system, Gropius then acts as a registered app, as in the case of GitHub. The issue created by Gropius thereby appears as if it had been created by the user directly in the actual issue management system. An issue created by Gropius on the use-case's order service's GitHub repository is shown in Fig. 6. The issue body contains the actual description and additional metadata, which are interpreted by Gropius. The issue shown is a bug report, which refers to another component's issue with a *Depends* relation. If an issue is changed in the component's issue management system, Gropius can take this change into account when it next requests the issues. Even if this issue affects several components, Gropius propagates the changes made to the issue management systems of all components. If an issue is changed directly in the actual issue

Fig. 6. Bug report created by *Gropius* in the name of user *spethso* for the order service component of the use case

management system, this change will be recognized by Gropius the next time a Gropius user queries the issue. Then, Gropius propagates the change to the other issue management systems accordingly. Therefore, cross-component and regular issues are synchronized in both directions.

4   Related Research and Industry Efforts

There are various efforts for cross-component issue management. In a Redmine forum [10] it is discussed how an issue can be related to several projects. The proposed solution is to create a common (Redmine) task for all projects and subtasks for the respective affected projects. This solution is only feasible if all projects are in the same Redmine project. In component-based systems, however, each component usually manages its issues in an independent issue management system, for example, a separate Redmine project for each component. Therefore, this approach is not a practical solution for our use case.

Also, various Atlassian forums [2,3] discuss approaches to manage issues that affect multiple projects. In the proposed *Structure* plugin, Jira data from multiple Jira projects can be managed and filtered together in a spreadsheet-like UI. A significant disadvantage of this plugin is that ownership permissions are required for each project. Since components are usually developed and maintained externally, the plugin cannot usually be used for component-based systems. Another proposed solution is to create a simple Jira project with several Scrum Boards for individual projects (components). As described above, such an approach is not applicable for component-based systems.

The Jira Plugin *Backbone Issue Sync* [8] allows the synchronization of an issue across multiple Jira projects. As in Gropius, a user can decide which issue should be synchronized. However, the plugin is limited to Jira. Other issue management systems like GitHub or Redmine are not supported. With the use of adapters, Gropius can support different issue management systems and is, therefore, better suited for multiple components from different systems.

Multi Project Picker [1] is another Jira plugin that allows you to manage issues across multiple components. The Multi Project Picker plugin removes the limitation that an issue can only belong to one Jira project. Instead, an issue can be assigned to multiple projects using comma-separated projects in a form field. Also, as in Gropius and the Backbone Issue Sync, a user can specify for each issue which projects are affected. However, similar to the Backbone Issue Sync plugin, the plugin is limited to Jira projects and, therefore, not universally applicable as with Gropius.

5   Conclusion

Distributed component-based systems come with some challenges. One major challenge is tracking bugs and faults across components to the original component and adequately managing the issue in all affected components. Since each component usually has an independent issue management system, cross-component issues cannot be managed appropriately with conventional issue management systems. As a result, developers must communicate such issues using other means, such as e-mails or meetings. Another challenge is the identification of interdependencies of such independently developed components. We have developed Gropius to address these challenges. Gropius is a tool for integrated management of cross-component issues. In Gropius, the components of a component-based architecture and their dependencies are displayed in a graphical notation similar to UML component diagrams. Issues and their cross-component dependencies can be visualized in the graphical notation together with the affected components. This allows a developer to manage cross-component issues and track issues across multiple components. Changes to issues, as well as newly created issues, are propagated and synchronized via Gropius to the actual conventional issue management systems of the components so that existing components with their own issue management system can be imported without any problems. In contrast to other research and industry efforts, Gropius supports any issue management system via adapters instead of a single one. Consequently, Gropius enables integrated cross-component issue management via a uniform interface.

References

1. Multi project picker—atlassian marketplace. https://marketplace.atlassian.com/apps/1211709/multi-project-picker?hosting=server&tab=overview
2. Atlassian: how do others work with issues affecting multiple projects (2020). https://community.atlassian.com/t5/Jira-questions/How-do-others-work-with-issues-affecting-multiple-projects/qaq-p/399950
3. Atlassian: solved: Share one issue "ticket" across multiple projects ... (2020). https://community.atlassian.com/t5/Jira-Software-questions/Share-one-issue-quot-ticket-quot-across-multiple-projects-and/qaq-p/407534
4. Bühler, F.: Grapheditor—mico grapheditor documentation 0.5.4 documentation. https://mico-grapheditor.readthedocs.io/en/stable/#
5. Foundation, G.: Graphql—a query language for your API. https://graphql.org/
6. Gropius: a cross-component issue management system for component-based architectures. https://github.com/ccims
7. Jones, M., Bradley, J., Sakimura, N.: RFC 7519: Json web token (jwt). IETF, May 2015
8. K15t: Backbone issue sync for jira (2020). https://www.k15t.de/software/backbone-issue-sync-for-jira
9. Mahmood, S., Niazi, M., Hussain, A.: Identifying the challenges for managing component-based development in global software development: preliminary results. In: 2015 Science and Information Conference (SAI), pp. 933–938. IEEE (2015)

10. Redmine: relating an issue to multiple projects - redmine (2020). https://www.redmine.org/boards/1/topics/21939
11. Reussner, R.H.: Modeling and Simulating Software Architectures: The Palladio Approach. MIT Press, Cambridge (2016)
12. Speth, S.: Issue management for multi-project, multi-team microservice architectures. Master's thesis, University of Stuttgart (2019)
13. Szyperski, C., Gruntz, D., Murer, S.: Component Software: Beyond Object-Oriented Programming. Pearson Education, London (2002)

SecoArc: A Framework for Architecting Healthy Software Ecosystems

Bahar Schwichtenberg[✉] and Gregor Engels

Paderborn University, Paderborn, Germany
{bahar.schwichtenberg,gregor.engels}@upb.de
https://www.cs.uni-paderborn.de/dbis

Abstract. In recent years, prominent software companies have succeeded to grow by creating ecosystems of third-party providers and users around their software platforms. The overall well-functioning of such ecosystems is referred to as *ecosystem health* that is the result of a complex and variable range of architectural design decisions at business and technical levels. Despite a body of work considering the architecture of software ecosystems, there is still a lack of solid methods with a precise foundation to facilitate architectural decision-making by providing automated techniques and tools. To fill this gap, we present *SecoArc*, which is a pattern-centric ecosystem modeling framework for architecting healthy software ecosystems. SecoArc makes the architectural knowledge of well-established ecosystems available. In this paper, we focus on the SecoArc modeling language, analysis technique, and a ready-to-use tool. SecoArc enables platform providers to design architectural variabilities, assess the architecture concerning the quality attributes of ecosystem health, and deeply compare several competing architectures. We show the application of the SecoArc framework in a case study.

Keywords: Software ecosystems · Architectural analysis · Software architecture

1 Introduction

Nowadays leading software companies such as Apple grow by transforming their software products, e.g., iOS, to platforms with the open application programming interfaces (APIs) that are exposed to third-party providers so that they can develop software on top of the platforms. To this end, the companies create large ecosystems of third-party providers that are in service to a community of users. Literature refers to such ecosystems as *software ecosystems* [1]. Often online marketplaces such as Apple App Store[1] are used to make the third-party developments available to the users.

This work was partially supported by the German Research Foundation (DFG) within the Collaborative Research Center "On-The-Fly Computing" (CRC 901). In addition, we would like to thank Sayanti Kundu for the valuable work during the implementation of SecoArc.

[1] https://www.apple.com/ios/app-store, Last Access: June 20, 2020.

© Springer Nature Switzerland AG 2020
H. Muccini et al. (Eds.): ECSA 2020, CCIS 1269, pp. 95–106, 2020.
https://doi.org/10.1007/978-3-030-59155-7_8

Despite some companies being successful, there is still a lack of systematic knowledge to create software ecosystems. Platform provider is the keystone to ensure the health of the entire ecosystem by suitable architectural decision-making. Ecosystem health refers to its overall performance and sustainable well-functioning. It is the result of a complex design space of architectural variabilities comprising business and technical decisions and their interdependencies [2]. For example, platform providers observe user feedbacks very differently (if at all), e.g., in terms of binary rating, star rating, reviewing given by verified or anonymous users. In the lack of systematic knowledge, platform providers face irreversible consequences of suboptimal architectural decision-making mainly because they fail to deal with the architectural variabilities and deciding on a final set of architectural decisions that lead to the creation of a healthy ecosystem [3]. Examples of such consequences are going out of budget or continually falling into technical debt [4]. Technical debt happens when software development processes are sped-up by making fast but unconsolidated decisions, in the hope of a solid reconstruction in future [5]. A solution to overcome the lack of knowledge would be to make architectural knowledge of well-established ecosystems available for future use.

In this paper, we present a pattern-centric approach specific to the domain of software ecosystems called SecoArc [6] for designing and analyzing ecosystem architecture. The goal of the SecoArc framework is to assist platform providers in enhanced architectural decision-making while creating software ecosystems. The architectural knowledge provided by SecoArc is derived from several exhaustive studies of the well-established ecosystems and the related literature in our previous work [7,8]. Platform providers can use the *SecoArc modeling language* to specify the ecosystem architecture and the *SecoArc architectural analysis technique* to analyze the architecture with respect to the quality attributes of ecosystem health. This paper is an extension of our previous work [9], where the enactment of SecoArc in a case study is presented. The focus of this paper is mainly on modeling and analyzing activities and the tool-support. Specifically, we introduce the multifaceted result of architectural analysis that is categorized into four perspectives, i.e., *pattern suggestion*, *pattern conformance*, *quality attribute fulfillment*, and *decision conformance*. These results aim at enhancing architectural decision-making by (a) raising awareness about the strategic directions that the design decisions in an architecture are facilitating and (b) enabling platform providers to appraise their decision-making on the basis of existing ecosystems so that they can accordingly orient themselves through the process of decision-making.

The paper is structured as follows: First, Sect. 2 introduces the challenges that a solution to the problem needs to overcome. Section 3 presents the SecoArc framework. Section 4 elaborates on the modeling and analyzing activities performed in the case study. In Sect. 5, it is discussed how the SecoArc framework overcomes the challenges. Section 6 discusses related work, which is followed by Sect. 7 that concludes the paper and addresses future research directions.

2   Challenges

Investigation of the research problem related to *the lack of systematic architectural knowledge to create healthy software ecosystems* can be linked to three main challenges that are addressed within the scope of this paper.

C1: Dealing with Architectural Variability
When transforming a software product to an open platform, platform providers face an overwhelming range of architectural variabilities. Despite considerable amount of work on variability mechanisms in software engineering [10], these mechanisms are not applied for the domain of software ecosystems because architectural variabilities of software ecosystems are distributed among different disciplines such as computer science, business and information systems [3]. The solution for the problem needs to provide insight into different types of variable design decisions so platform providers can create custom designs based on them.

C2: Specifying Ecosystem Architecture
Existing modeling approaches such as general-purpose languages like Unified Modeling Language (UML) [11] and enterprise architecture modeling (EAM) like ArchiMate [12] do not directly capture design decisions of software ecosystems. In practice, the high abstraction and the amplitude of notations result in laborious and time-consuming work while specifying an ecosystem architectural specification. A modeling approach to specify ecosystem architecture needs to efficiently capture the key architectural characteristics of software ecosystems.

C3: Assessing Ecosystem Health
Platform providers are currently limited to textual templates, which use natural languages, to assess ecosystem health. Using such templates is tedious and leads to ambiguity. While textual templates can be used as complementary documentation, they lack a formal foundation to serve the basis for an automated analysis technique or tool. The solution needs to enable the assessment of ecosystem health in platform providers' contexts. Specifically, specific measurements that facilitate quantitative implications about the quality of the architecture should be introduced. More importantly, this should enable platform providers to compare the suitability of several architectures based of variabilities.

3   The SecoArc Framework

In this section, we present an *architectural ecosystem modeling framework* called *SecoArc* to overcome the challenges (C1-C3). The goal of the framework is to support platform providers in architectural decision-making while creating software ecosystems. The architectural knowledge provided by SecoArc is derived from the examination of more than 100 well-established ecosystems in practice as our previous study [7,8]. In the following, first, we give an overview of the

SecoArc architecture. Afterward, two main building blocks, i.e., the modeling language and architectural analysis technique, are presented.

3.1   Overview of Architecture

Figure 1 demonstrates an overview of the components of the SecoArc modeling language and the SecoArc architectural analysis technique. These components are implemented using the Eclipse Modeling Framework (EMF) and the Sirius framework. `Platform provider` is the human actor, who interacts with the `modeling workbench` to design the ecosystem architecture or analyze the architecture. The `modeling workbench` uses a domain-specific language. The language includes a `metamodel` that represents the SecoArc abstract syntax. It holds the description of software ecosystems. The concrete syntax is a set of `visual notations` for modeling the ecosystem architecture. Furthermore, the semantics is expressed by a set of `constraints`.

The `Platform provider` can use the `modeling workbench` to analyze the architecture by means of the `architectural analysis technique`. The analysis technique comprises three main components: `Context matching` provides design recommendations based on the platform provider's organizational context. `Decision matching` analyzes the suitability of a single architecture whereas `architecture comparator` compares more than one competing architectures with each other. Finally, a `report of analysis` is generated and provided to the `platform provider`. The rest of this section elaborates on each component.

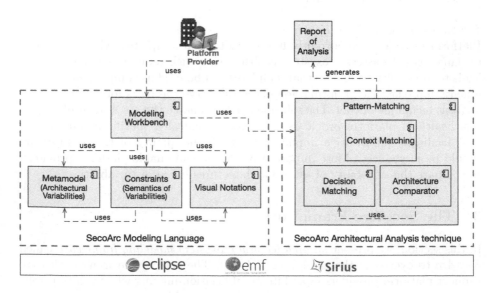

Fig. 1. SecoArc architecture

3.2   Modeling Language

SecoArc provides a modeling language to specify ecosystem architecture. The main objectives of the language are to (a) capture the domain knowledge of software ecosystems, including the architectural variabilities, and (b) provide a basis for the architectural analysis. In the following, we elaborate on the main constituents of the modeling language. The complete lists of visual notations and elements of the metamodel can be found in the SecoArc specification in [6].

Metamodel. The abstract syntax of the language is presented by a metamodel that comprises the domain knowledge of software ecosystems. It includes the description of human actors and their relations. Besides, the architectural variabilities are captured in terms of three types of elements, i.e., the elements of business, application, and infrastructure architectures [7]. The metamodel contains some semantics that is related to the well-formedness rules. An example is *the ecosystem architecture should have at least one platform provider.*

Visual Notations. SecoArc introduces visual notations that form the concrete syntax of the modeling language. The notations can be used to design ecosystem architecture in the modeling workbench. While both visual and textual notations have their own advantages and disadvantages, the reason to choose visual notations for the SecoArc concrete syntax refers to the users of SecoArc that are platform providers, who are often in management positions. They would like to capture main ideas efficiently without being confronting with overwhelming details. With this respect, visual notations surpass textual representations in hiding unwanted complexity [13].

Constraints. The semantics of the SecoArc language is defined by using rules that are statically checked on models. In SecoArc, these rules are implemented as Object Constraint Language (OCL) constraints. The constraints pertain to the structure of the ecosystem and should be obeyed by the architecture. These constraints capture the semantics of the architectural variabilities. For instance, *if the choice of service execution is defined as "remote execution on the cloud", then there must be infrastructure elements in the architecture that support this task.* The OCL constraints can be found in the source code of SecoArc. For the sake of brevity, we refer interested readers to the repository that is linked on the SecoArc website [6].

3.3   Architectural Analysis Technique

The SecoArc architectural analysis technique follows a rule-based pattern-matching approach that checks the architecture designed in the modeling workbench with respect to the knowledge of three architectural patterns.

In our previous work [8], we identify three architectural patterns for software ecosystems namely *open source software (OSS)-based ecosystem, partner-based ecosystem*, and *resale software ecosystem*. The patterns are based on an examination of ecosystems from a diverse range of application domains. In a nutshell, each pattern characterizes a prominent strategic ecosystem development approach that is dominantly used in practice to gear the ecosystem functionality to certain business objectives. In the OSS-based ecosystem, the platform provider aims at attracting developers of open-source software. The ecosystem is open to innovation. Software failure is not threatening human lives. In the partner-based ecosystem, the software is highly commercialized as well as extensively tested, as failures can cause severe financial or safety damages. Thereby, the platform provider develops a network of carefully selected partners. Only the partners can extend the platform functionality. In the resale software ecosystem, the number of third-party providers is noticeably high. In this situation, the platform provider empowers third-party providers with tools and techniques to develop software independently. Furthermore, the ecosystem is equipped with software features like rating and ranking that enable users to efficiently access high quality software as the number of third-party developments grows. Detailed processes of pattern identification are given in [8].

The tabular representation on the right side of Fig. 2 shows that each pattern is characterized using a high-level business objective. Furthermore, the patterns help platform providers with certain contextual factors address the quality attributes of ecosystem health. The concrete sets of design decisions in the middle determine the linkage between the ecosystem architecture and the quality attributes. During the architectural analysis, platform provider's organizational context and design decisions in the architecture are respectively matched against the contextual factors and the design decisions of the patterns. In the following, we refer to the components of the analysis technique shown in Fig. 1 and explain how they handle the pattern-matching tasks.

Context Matching. Each pattern is associated with a specific type of platform provider with certain organizational characteristics using four contextual factors, i.e., company size, market size, domain criticality, and commerciality. The `context matching` compares the contextual parameters provided by the platform provider with the contextual factors of the patterns. This results in a *pattern suggestion* that shows which pattern would suit the platform provider's organizational characteristics the most.

Decision Matching. Each pattern is described using a concrete set of architectural design decisions. The `decision matching` matches the decisions of the ecosystem architecture against the decisions of the patterns. The results of this matching are categorized into three perspectives, i.e., *pattern conformance, quality attribute fulfillment*, and *decision conformance*. Here, according to the number of matched decisions, percentages of decision conformance and thereby the pattern conformance are calculated. Furthermore, the quality attribute fulfillment is the extent that each quality attribute is fulfilled by considering the matched decisions associated with that quality attribute.

Architecture Comparator. The `architecture comparator` uses the results of `decision matching` to generate a comparative view for analysis of more than one architecture. In the comparative view, results of the pattern conformance, quality attribute fulfillment, and decision conformance for more than one architecture are calculated.

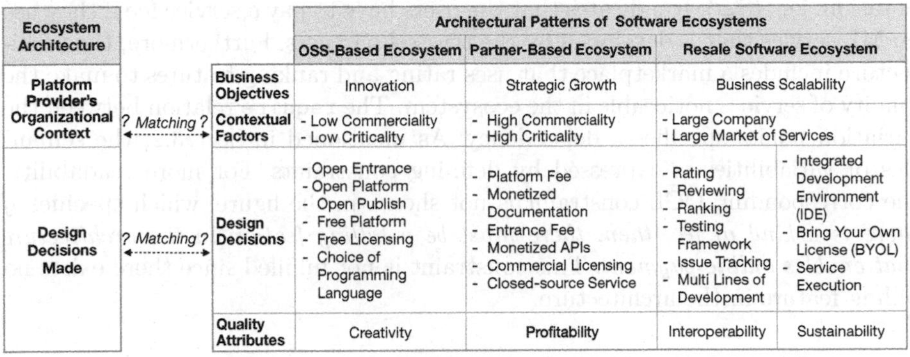

Ecosystem Architecture			Architectural Patterns of Software Ecosystems		
			OSS-Based Ecosystem	Partner-Based Ecosystem	Resale Software Ecosystem
Platform Provider's Organizational Context	? Matching ?	Business Objectives	Innovation	Strategic Growth	Business Scalability
		Contextual Factors	- Low Commerciality - Low Criticality	- High Commerciality - High Criticality	- Large Company - Large Market of Services
Design Decisions Made	? Matching ?	Design Decisions	- Open Entrance - Open Platform - Open Publish - Free Platform - Free Licensing - Choice of Programming Language	- Platform Fee - Monetized Documentation - Entrance Fee - Monetized APIs - Commercial Licensing - Closed-source Service	- Rating - Reviewing - Ranking - Testing Framework - Issue Tracking - Multi Lines of Development	- Integrated Development Environment (IDE) - Bring Your Own License (BYOL) - Service Execution
		Quality Attributes	Creativity	Profitability	Interoperability	Sustainability

Fig. 2. The pattern-matching performed by the architectural analysis technique

4   Case Study: On-The-Fly Computing

We apply the SecoArc framework within the scope of *CRC 901 On-The-Fly Computing*[2]. On-the-fly computing is a paradigm to provision custom-made software services on the basis of market platforms that individually compose third-party services for every user request using machine learning (ML) techniques. In the case study, the provider of an on-the-fly computing market designs and assesses the suitability of two alternative architectures using SecoArc. The detailed procedure of the case study is presented in our previous work [9]. In this section, we introduce the alternative architectures. Afterward, we elaborate on the modeling activities and results of the architectural analysis.

Architecture #1 describes an open ecosystem, where anyone can use the platform as a user, or to extend the platform's functionality as a third-party provider. The platform provider uses the public Git repository for the source codes.

Architecture #2 concerns a semi-open ecosystem, where the platform provider distinguishes commercial trusted partners from the mass number of third-party developers. The partners can commercialize their developments. In return, they need to deliver high quality software. To ensure the quality of software delivered by the partners, the platform provider uses an online marketplace that includes rating and ranking features.

---

[2] https://sfb901.uni-paderborn.de/, Last Access: June 20, 2020.

4.1   Architectural Modeling

Figure 3 shows how a variability, i.e., `Fee`, is realized in the metamodel. According to the knowledge of variabilities, `fee` is a typical variation point in software ecosystems [7]. The metamodel indicates this variability using inheritance relationships between `Fee` and its three variants. At the bottom, *Architecture #2* is partially shown. `Fee` is realized as `Service Fee` and modeled using the SecoArc notation, i.e., (S€). It indicates that the users have to pay a service fee if they use an ML service that is developed by the trusted partners. Furthermore, the architecture includes a marketplace that uses rating and ranking features to make the quality of services noticeable in the ecosystem. The `require` relation between the variation points specifies a dependency. As mentioned in Sect. 3.2, the semantics of variabilities is expressed by defining constraints. For more readability, the corresponding OCL constraint is not shown in the figure, which specifies *if there is a kind of fee, then, there must be a billing feature in the architecture that enables online payment*. This constraint is not fulfilled since there exists no billing feature in the architecture.

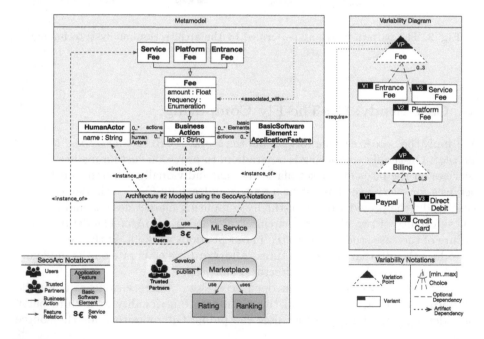

Fig. 3. The relations between the viabilities, metamodel, and architecture (for readability purposes, only relevant parts of the models and their relations are shown.)

4.2   Analysis Results

As mentioned in Sect. 3.3, the results of the architectural analysis is provided using four perspectives, i.e., pattern suggestion, pattern conformance, quality attribute fulfillment, and decision conformance. In the following, we elaborate on these results in the context of the case study.

a) Pattern Suggestion Perspective. Pattern suggestion is the result of the component `context-matching`. The provider of the on-the-fly computing platform specifies the software functionality as non-critical and free-to-use. Thereby, the analysis suggests the OSS-based ecosystem pattern. This implies the pattern is mostly applied by providers, who allow free and open access to their non-critical platforms. In the modeling workbench, typical ecosystem development strategies and the architectural design decisions of the OSS-based ecosystem are given.

b) Pattern Conformance Perspective. In contrary to the pattern suggestion, the result of pattern conformance depends on the design decisions. Figure 4 shows the result of pattern conformance. *Architecture #1* and *Architecture #2* respectively conform to the OSS-based ecosystem and resale software ecosystem patterns the most. The percentages show the extent to which the ecosystem architecture matches to the decisions of the patterns. By referring to the exemplary ecosystems, the platform provider can orient themselves through the process of decision-making.

	OSS-based Ecosystem	Resale Software Ecosystem	Partner-based Ecosystem
Architecture #1	100 %	33.3%	0 %
Architecture #2	50 %	88.8%	66.6%
Exemplary Ecosystems	Mozilla, Eclipse, Apache Cordova	Apple, Adobe, Salesforce	SAP, Symantec, Citrix

Fig. 4. Result of the pattern conformance

c) Quality Attribute Fulfillment Perspective. This perspective is the result of decision-matching. Figure 5 demonstrates the result for *Architecture #1* and *Architecture #2*. *Architecture #1* clearly supports creativity mainly due the high openness and free usage of the platform. *Architecture #2* enhances sustainability and interoperability, due to the decisions that strengthen the feedback loop between the users and providers, e.g.., by including rating and ranking features.

d) Decision Conformance Perspective Decision conformance facilitates a detailed view to the whole pattern-matching (cf. Fig. 2). Figure 6(a) presents a comparative view of this part of the results. In addition, in the modeling workbench, a detailed *report of analysis* is provided that lists the design decisions that are (not) realized in the architecture. Figure 6(b) presents a part of the analysis report for *Architecture #2* that provides details on two design decisions, i.e., rating and BYOL. Using this knowledge, the platform provider can actively

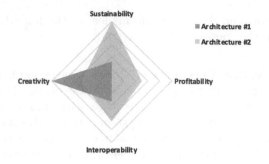

Fig. 5. Result of the quality attribute fulfillment

decide on the decisions that are not considered in the architecture and their absence degrades certain quality attributes. For example, interoperability can be improved in *Architecture #2* by including BYOL.

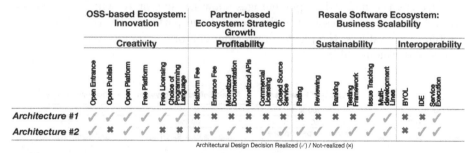

	OSS-based Ecosystem: Innovation						Partner-based Ecosystem: Strategic Growth						Resale Software Ecosystem: Business Scalability								
	Creativity						Profitability						Sustainability						Interoperability		
	Open Entrance	Open Publish	Open Platform	Free Platform	Free Licensing	Choice of Programming Language	Platform Fee	Entrance Fee	Monetized Documentation	Monetized APIs	Commercial Licensing	Closed Source Service	Rating	Reviewing	Ranking	Testing Framework	Issue Tracking	Multi-development Lines	BYOL	IDE	Service Execution
Architecture #1	✓	✓	✓	✓	✓	✓	✗	✗	✗	✗	✗	✗	✗	✗	✗	✗	✓	✓	✗	✗	✓
Architecture #2	✓	✗	✓	✓	✗	✗	✗	✓	✓	✗	✓	✓	✓	✓	✓	✓	✓	✓	✗	✓	✓

Architectural Design Decision Realized (✓) / Not-realized (✗)

(a) Realized and Not-realized Decisions of *Architecture #1* and *Architecture #2*

Rating	Decision Realized	Rating improves discoverability of high quality extensions when the market grows. This supports business scalability.
Bring Your Own License (BYOL)	Decision Not-realized	Services providers from other ecosystems might already licensed their services. BYOL facilitates the legal process that allows service providers to integrate external licenses in your ecosystem.

(b) Part of Report of Analysis for *Architecture #2*

Fig. 6. Result of the decision conformance

5   Discussion

We revisit the challenges introduced in Sect. 2 to discuss how they are addressed by the SecoArc framework. C1: The SecoArc metamodel, visual notation, and constraints embed the knowledge of architectural variabilities in business, application, and infrastructure levels. Therefore, by using the language, platform providers are relieved from being aware of all the variabilities and their interdependencies. C2: Using the SecoArc modeling language, platform providers can specify ecosystem architecture whereas the rich domain knowledge of software ecosystems is made available in a structured way. C3: The SecoArc analysis technique enables the assessment of ecosystem health by making the knowledge of well-established ecosystems reusable. The analysis technique automates the process of pattern-matching so that platform providers can check the health of their ecosystems and compare them with the existing ecosystems.

6 Related Work

In this section, we discuss related work that aims at facilitating modeling and/or analyzing software ecosystems. Woods and Bashroush [13] propose an architectural description language for large and complex information systems. It provides visual notations for experiments inside an industrial project, which are conventions agreed upon among the project members. Furthermore, Christensen et al. [14] conceptualizes the design and analysis of ecosystem architecture in telemedicine. Business and software aspects are respectively described using natural languages and UML deployment diagrams. However, the relations between the business and software aspects are not specified. Bosch and Bosch-Sijtsema [15] introduce ESAO for analysis of ecosystems. It is a conceptual framework to describe design decisions using natural languages. ESAO captures strategic, architectural, and organizational aspects at the enterprise and ecosystem levels. There, the linkage to business objectives is not clarified. The major shortcoming of the mentioned works is the lack of formality as the ecosystem architecture is mainly described using natural languages.

Sadi et al. present a design and analysis approach [16] using an i* modeling technique. The resulting models capture actors, tasks, and business goals. Despite having similar motivations to our work, this work only concerns collaborations. Thereby, the models are quite high-level. Our work includes software and infrastructure elements, and their relations to the actors. A lack of tool-support hampers the applicability of this work. Furthermore, the analysis technique concerns openness requirements, which is a different focus than our work.

7 Conclusion and Future Work

The novel architectural approach of creating software ecosystems by opening the platforms to third-party providers has been applied in practice in recent years. However, there is still a lack of systematic architectural knowledge to create healthy software ecosystems. In the lack of knowledge, platform providers have to bear consequences of suboptimal architectural decision-making. In this paper, we present SecoArc that aims at facilitating model-based design and analysis of software ecosystems. Using SecoArc, platform providers can design, analyze, and compare competitive architectures while assessing the quality attributes of ecosystem health. In the future, quality attributes concerning the governance and evolution of running ecosystems should be considered. This includes capturing dynamic semantics and quality rules related to the behavior of the actors and architectural elements. Generating meaningful code from the high-level description of the architecture is another challenge to be addressed as future research directions.

References

1. Bosch, J.: From software product lines to software ecosystems. In: International Conference on Software Product Line, pp. 111–119. CMU (2009)
2. Mhamdia, A.B.H.S.: Performance measurement practices in software ecosystem. Int. J. Prod. Perform. Manage. **62**(5), 514–533 (2013)
3. Manikas, K.: Revisiting software ecosystems research: a longitudinal literature study. J. Syst. Softw. **117**, 84–103 (2016)
4. Build an in-house enterprise app store without breaking the budget (2016). http://searchcloudapplications.techtarget.com/answer/Build-an-in-house-enterprise-app-store-without-breaking-the-budget
5. Digkas, G., Lungu, M., Chatzigeorgiou, A., Avgeriou, P.: The evolution of technical debt in the apache ecosystem. In: Lopes, A., de Lemos, R. (eds.) ECSA 2017. LNCS, vol. 10475, pp. 51–66. Springer, Cham (2017). https://doi.org/10.1007/978-3-319-65831-5_4
6. SecoArc, July 2012. https://sfb901.uni-paderborn.de/secoarc
7. Jazayeri, B., Zimmermann, O., Engels, G., Kundisch, D.: A variability model for store-oriented software ecosystems: an enterprise perspective. In: Maximilien, M., Vallecillo, A., Wang, J., Oriol, M. (eds.) ICSOC 2017. LNCS, vol. 10601, pp. 573–588. Springer, Cham (2017). https://doi.org/10.1007/978-3-319-69035-3_42
8. Jazayeri, B., Zimmermann, O., Küster, J., Engels, G., Szopinski, D., Kundisch, D.: Patterns of store-oriented software ecosystems: detection, classification, and analysis of design options. In: Lathin American Conference on Pattern Languages of Programs. ACM (2018)
9. Jazayeri, B., Schwichtenberg, S., Küster, J., Zimmermann, O., Engels, G.: Modeling and analyzing architectural diversity of open platforms. In: Dustdar, S., Yu, E., Salinesi, C., Rieu, D., Pant, V. (eds.) CAiSE 2020. LNCS, vol. 12127, pp. 36–53. Springer, Cham (2020). https://doi.org/10.1007/978-3-030-49435-3_3
10. Galster, M., Weyns, D., Tofan, D., Michalik, B., Avgeriou, P.: Variability in software systems—a systematic literature review. IEEE Trans. Soft. Eng. **40**(3), 282–306 (2014)
11. OMG. Unified Modeling Language™ (UML®) Version 2.5. (2017). https://www.omg.org/spec/UML
12. The Open Group. ArchiMate® 3.0.1 Specification (2017). http://pubs.opengroup.org/architecture/archimate3-doc/
13. Woods, E., Bashroush, R.: Modelling large-scale information systems using ADLs—an industrial experience report. J. Sys. Softw. **99**, 97–108 (2015)
14. Christensen, H., Hansen, K.M., Kyng, M., Manikas, K.: Analysis and design of software ecosystem architectures-towards the 4S telemedicine ecosystem. Inf. Soft. Tech. **56**(11), 1476–1492 (2014)
15. Bosch, J., Bosch-Sijtsema, P.: ESAO: a holistic ecosystem-driven analysis model. In: Lassenius, C., Smolander, K. (eds.) ICSOB 2014. LNBIP, vol. 182, pp. 179–193. Springer, Cham (2014). https://doi.org/10.1007/978-3-319-08738-2_13
16. Sadi, M.H., Yu, E.: Accommodating openness requirements in software platforms: a goal-oriented approach. In: Dubois, E., Pohl, K. (eds.) CAiSE 2017. LNCS, vol. 10253, pp. 44–59. Springer, Cham (2017). https://doi.org/10.1007/978-3-319-59536-8_4

SQuAT-Vis: Visualization and Interaction in Software Architecture Optimization

Sebastian Frank(✉)📵 and André van Hoorn📵

Institute of Software Technology, University of Stuttgart,
70569 Stuttgart, Germany
sebastian.frank@iste.uni-stuttgart.de

Abstract. Optimization of software architectures is a complex task that can not be fully automated. For this reason, software architecture optimization approaches often require human architects to participate in the optimization process, e.g., by selecting architectural candidates. Nevertheless, most of these approaches fail to support architects in solving their tasks as they provide no or insufficient visualization and interaction techniques. Thus, architects usually have to invest time and effort to find a (not ideal) solution themselves.

In this paper, we present SQuAT-Vis — a tool that can be plugged into software architecture optimization approaches and allows architects to investigate (intermediate) results visually. SQuAT-Vis has been developed based on four common use cases in the domain and to be compatible with the technologies used by SQuAT, a state-of-the-art software architecture optimization approach. Nevertheless, SQuAT-Vis is conceptually intended to be modular and compatible with other approaches as well. Such a tool is, therefore, an important contribution to the domain of (interactive) software architecture optimization.

1 Introduction

Software architecture optimization approaches, like SQuAT [19] and Per-Opteryx [15], exist to support architects in exploring design alternatives to reach a higher software quality, e.g., for performance and modifiability. For example, maintenance often contributes 40% to 80% of the costs to a software system [11], which makes modifiability a critical property of a software system.

However, software architecture optimization in practice is rarely fully automated. Instead, it relies on heuristics or the participation of human architects to solve the domain's challenges. One challenge is the exponential growth of the design space with an increasing number of requirements and architectural elements, making an investigation of the whole design space often infeasible [2]. Therefore, interactive approaches, like ArchE [7] or DesignBots [6], require the architect to select tactics to be applied and, thus, to guide the search. Another challenge is the conflict between quality attributes [4], which requires making trade-offs. Thus, architects have to express their preferences, e.g., in Per-Opteryx [15] by selecting the final candidate from a set of Pareto-optimal alternatives.

© Springer Nature Switzerland AG 2020
H. Muccini et al. (Eds.): ECSA 2020, CCIS 1269, pp. 107–119, 2020.
https://doi.org/10.1007/978-3-030-59155-7_9

Human architects have to perform essential tasks in the (interactive) optimization process, which are elaborated in this work, namely, selecting candidates, deciding on the termination of the optimization, identifying changes, and explaining results. However, visualization and interaction techniques are not provided by common software architecture optimization approaches. Therefore, the SQuAT-Vis tool presented in this paper intends to close this gap and avoids that architects have to invest time and effort in repeatedly developing (non-optimal) solutions on their own. To achieve this, SQuAT-Vis displays information about goal satisfaction and architectures in three connected views.

This paper gives an overview of the tool's design and implementation. It also provides a high-level summary of a previously conducted evaluation [10]. Artifacts, including the source code, are provided as supplementary material [9]. Additionally, a video [8] is provided. The remainder of this paper is structured as follows: Sect. 2 describes related works. The mentioned use cases, which SQuAT-Vis is designed for, are outlined in Sect. 3. Key concepts and decisions are explained in Sect. 4, while Sect. 5 describes SQuAT-Vis's views for the investigation of design alternatives. Then, Sect. 6 focuses on the tool's architecture and technologies, and Sect. 7 briefly summarizes the conducted evaluation. Finally, this work is concluded in Sect. 8.

2 Related Work

To the best of our knowledge, a visualization approach specifically designed to support architects in software architecture optimization does not exist. We examined a selection of sophisticated software architecture optimization approaches, namely DesignBots [6], ArchE [7], PerOpteryx [15], ArcheOpterix [1], SQuAT [19], and AQOSA [17]. All of these approaches provide none or limited visualizations to support architects. SQuAT [19] and PerOpteryx [15] provide results in textual form. ArchE [7] uses traffic light glyphs to display goal satisfaction. However, this simplified representation provides limited information. The works of AQOSA [17] and ArcheOpterix [1] use scatter plots to visualize the Pareto front. However, only a limited number of goals can be shown in a scatter plot, and not all optimization approaches are based on Pareto optimality.

While there seems to be no specific solution for software architects, there are many visualization tools that can be seen as partial solutions. Visualization approaches for specific optimization methods exist, e.g., GAVEL [12] allows visual comprehension of optimization processes based on genetic algorithms, which are, for example, used in PerOpteryx [15]. For multivariate data, generic tools like the Trade Space Visualizer [23] help to discover the relationship between variables. However, they require the architect to have a basic understanding of visualization, to perform manual efforts, and are unable to visualize software architectures. For software architectures, graphical modeling editors are usually available, e.g., the Palladio Bench for the Palladio Component Model [3]. However, these editors are designed for modeling single architectures, not for comparison and examination of multiple architectures.

In the more general, related interactive optimization domain, visualization and interaction techniques have been investigated before. Jones [14] examines how to use bar charts, pie charts, graph-based, and matrix-based visualizations for displaying optimization models, algorithms, and solutions. The advantages and disadvantages of bar charts, star plots, petal diagrams, and metroglyphs, among others, are discussed by Miettinen [18] for the visualization of decision-making problems. While the development of SQuAT-Vis benefited from these works' insights, the visualization of software architectures is not covered by them at all.

3   Use Cases

We developed SQuAT-Vis to assist architects in typical use cases of software architecture optimization. The foundation for identifying these use cases is the general optimization process in software architecture optimization, as described by Aleti et al. [2] and illustrated in Fig. 1. The optimization process starts with an initial architecture representation; then, new design alternatives are generated, and the alternatives' quality is evaluated. These activities are repeated until a defined stopping criterion is satisfied. Then, one or more candidate(s) are presented.

We extended the process by the activity of selecting a single, final design and the activity of implementing the necessary changes. We then identified activities that implicitly or explicitly require interaction with the architect in at least one software architecture optimization approach. The resulting use cases are explained in the following and enumerated in Fig. 1 in the order of appearance.

3.1   Candidate Selection

This use case describes that the architect has to reduce a set of architectural candidates to a subset. Interactive approaches allow the architect to express her preferences by selecting candidates during the optimization for a more directed search, e.g., ArchE [7] requires the architect to decide on the quality trade-offs in the next step. Approaches that present alternatives, e.g., Pareto-optimal solutions like in PerOpteryx [15], expect the architect to make the final choice by expressing her preferences in the end. This use case requires the architect to perform comparisons of several candidates with respect to the satisfaction of the optimization goals.

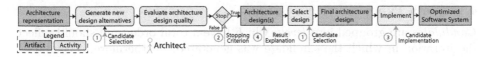

Fig. 1. Software architecture optimization process (based on Aleti et al. [2]) with the investigated use cases for interaction colored in red (Color figure online)

3.2   Stopping Criterion

In this use case, the architect has to decide whether she accepts the proposed candidate(s) or wants the optimization process to continue. Approaches like SQuAT [19] explicitly ask the architect for this decision, while others, e.g., PerOpteryx [15], expect a stopping criterion to be defined beforehand. However, the architect still has to implicitly make this decision as she can rerun the process with the outputs of a previous execution as the inputs. Again, the decision requires comparisons of several candidates with respect to optimization goal satisfaction, but also architectural and evolutionary information, e.g., parents of candidates, to judge whether another iteration is likely to improve the solution.

3.3   Candidate Implementation

In practice, the outcome of the optimization process should be the optimized software system. Therefore, the architect needs to understand which (architectural) changes she has to apply, e.g., which component needs to be allocated to which server. Although software architecture optimization approaches do not always explicitly show this information to the architect, the difference between the initial and final candidates can usually be investigated with graphical modeling editors. Therefore, this use case is not the main focus of SQuAT-Vis but is still considered due to its high practical relevance.

3.4   Result Explanation

Software architects often do not want to implement the proposed solution blindly. Trust is of high importance, especially in highly automated software systems [16]. Therefore, being able to understand which architectural changes lead to the satisfaction of goals or how goals influence each other is essential to accept a solution and get more insights about the system. This use case requires combining different kinds of information, i.e., goal satisfaction values and architectural properties.

4   SQuAT-Vis Concepts

This section gives insights into key concepts of SQuAT-Vis. Section 4.1 describes the elements from the domain of software architecture optimization, which are then mapped to visualizations, as described in Sect. 4.2. Finally, Sect. 4.3 introduces grouping and tagging of candidates. Further, minor concepts, also regarding interaction, are mentioned in Sect. 5 and shown in a provided video [8].

4.1   Data Types

Candidates are grouped into *levels*, which have a total order and should reflect the iteration in which the candidate was generated. Furthermore, a candidate can have a *parent*, which is another candidate that served as a basis for its creation. Apart from that, a candidate has two essential purposes. It represents an *architecture* and can be evaluated with respect to the optimization *goals*.

Architectures. Software architectures can be diverse, making it hard to select suitable elements and properties to model them. Thus, our selection is based on the Palladio Component Model (PCM) [3] as it is designed to model software architectures and predict their quality. *Components* were chosen as a means to describe partitions of software and *links* to indicate (static) dependencies between components. Furthermore, *allocations* describe to which *resource containers*, which represent servers, components are deployed to. The resource containers can consist of *resources*, which are characterized by a real-value, e.g., the clock rate of a central processing unit.

Goals. Software architectures are optimized with at least one *goal* in mind, usually referring to the architecture's quality attributes. As goals and their metrics can be various, e.g., in terms of units and optimization direction, we followed the approach of SQuAT to use *utility values*. Thus, the goal satisfaction has to be mapped into a utility value space, with values ranging from 0 (unsatisfied) to 1 (satisfied). All candidates have to know the utility value for each goal.

4.2   Visualizations

As described before, SQuAT-Vis has to visualize information about goals and architectures. While the first consists of multivariate data, the latter consists of rather relational data.

For *visualization of multivariate data*, we considered several visualizations, e.g., the ones mentioned by Miettinen [18]. Some of them are illustrated in Fig. 2, namely (a) scatter plot matrices, (b) bar charts, (c) parallel coordinates plots, (d) radar charts, and (e) petal diagrams. For goal satisfaction, we selected (a) scatter plot matrices and (d) radar charts as they complement each other well. Scatter plot matrices consist of one scatter plot for every combination of goals, showing one goal on each axis, while the candidates are represented as circles. Thus, they scale well with the number of candidates, but badly with the number of goals. The opposite holds for radar charts, which arrange multiple goals represented by axes in a circle. The candidates are represented as polylines, which have intersections with the axes according to their goal satisfaction. Therefore, they are compact and strengths and weaknesses can be interpreted based on the shape. A limited set of candidates can even be placed in the same visualization.

We also interpret resource specifications as multivariate data. Therefore, we chose to visualize them as (c) parallel coordinates plot. This visualization offers a trade-off between the required space and scalability with the number of architectures.

According to Salameh et al. [22], *visualizations of architectural data* are most often graph-based or matrix-based. For this reason and as it fits relational data, graph-based node-linked diagrams are used to visualize components, links, and allocations. As comparisons of candidates are important to support the use cases

Fig. 2. Visualization types for multivariate data

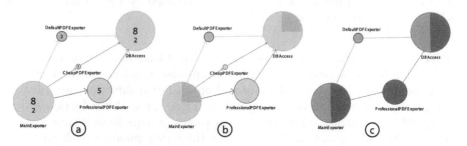

Fig. 3. Variations of node-link diagrams for visualizing multiple architectures

described in Sect. 3, we allow for merging several architectures into one visualization by scaling the size of the elements with the number of their appearance. Furthermore, coloring can be used to highlight candidates. Figure 3 illustrates three variations of the modified graphs. Variant ⓐ is text-based, while variant ⓑ uses a pie-chart for highlighting, e.g., there are two candidates using the *DefaultPDFExporter* and both are highlighted, while all eight candidates use the *MainExporter*, including the two highlighted candidates. Variant ⓒ is intended for the comparison of a small number of candidates, with one color assigned to each. In the example, both candidates use the *MainExporter*, but one uses the *DefaultPDFExporter*, while the other uses the *ProfessionalPDFExporter*.

4.3 Groups and Tags

All candidates in SQuAT-Vis can be grouped or tagged. Figure 4 shows the default colors and icons for the groups and tags. The architect can assign candidates to four groups that have different purposes. The *current* group highlights candidates temporarily. Candidates can also be *marked* for further investigation or *selected* as the desired result. Each candidate in the *comparison* group can get an individual color for more detailed comparisons of candidates in the comparison mode.

The architect can not assign tags as they describe the inherent properties of the candidates. The *initial* candidate given as an input to the optimization is tagged. As candidates that do not dominate each other, so-called *Pareto*-optimal candidates, can be of high interest, they are tagged as well. For approaches that can suggest candidates based on other techniques, e.g., negotiation in SQuAT [19], the *suggested*-tag is available.

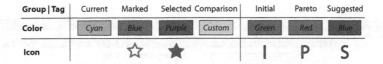

Group|Tag	Current	Marked	Selected	Comparison	Initial	Pareto	Suggested
Color	Cyan	Blue	Purple	Custom	Green	Red	Blue
Icon		☆	★		I	P	S

Fig. 4. Overview of the groups, tags, and their associated colors and icons

5   SQuAT-Vis Views

The previously described visualizations and variations of them are composed to form coordinated views [21] to allow the architect to investigate different aspects of a set of candidates. SQuAT-Vis also provides administrative views to select projects and to summarize their status, but only the three views focusing on visualizations are presented in the following. The *Population View* (Sect. 5.1) gives an overview of goal satisfaction of the whole population, while the *Candidates View* (Sect. 5.2) focuses on individual candidates. The *Architecture View* (Sect. 5.3) visualizes properties of the candidates' architectures.

5.1   Population View

The Population View (Fig. 5a) should give an overview of the whole population of candidates and allow for an efficient preselection.

Like the other views, the Population View is equipped with a (a) navigation toolbar at the top. It allows to switch between the views and provides the option to send *selected* candidates back to the software architecture optimization tool for further optimization. Furthermore, the (b) side toolbar is a means to inspect and control the available candidates, their group membership, and tags.

The remainder of the view mainly consists of two parts. The (c) magnified scatter plot gives an overview of all candidates with respect to the satisfaction of two goals. In the example, most candidates (almost) satisfy goal *m1*, but there is a much wider range for goal *p2*. The scatter plots for all combinations of goals are shown in the (d) scatter plot matrix, and each plot can be selected to be displayed as (c) magnified scatter plot.

This view is a comparatively compact representation of all candidates, enabling the architect to identify patterns in the scatter plots. Furthermore, the color of circles and rings indicates group membership and tagging, as described in Sect. 4.3. Evolutionary information is also displayed, as candidates of the most recent level are colored black, and candidates of previous levels are colored gray. Arrows show how candidates evolved from their parents.

One major drawback of the scatter plot representation is that candidates have to be represented as circles in every scatter plot. This makes it hard to investigate specific candidates with respect to all their goal satisfaction values. While highlighting by colors already mitigates this disadvantage, the (e) radar charts provide a more compact representation for *current* candidates.

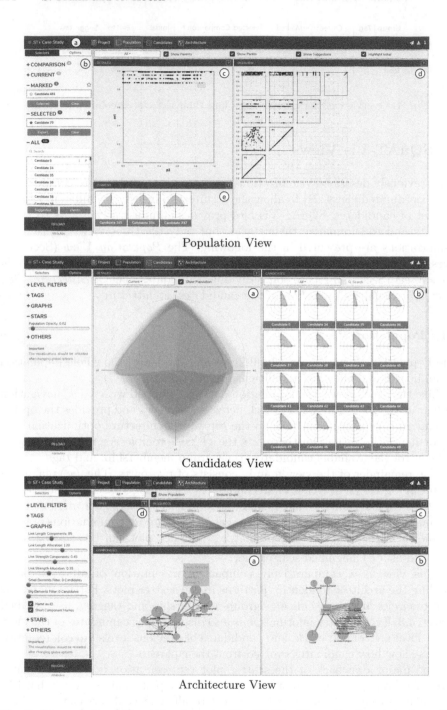

Population View

Candidates View

Architecture View

Fig. 5. Screenshots of the main views in SQuAT-Vis. They visualize data from the *ST+ Case Study* [19], which is available as part of the supplementary material [9].

5.2   Candidates View

The Candidates View (Fig. 5b) is intended for the comparison of a few candidates with respect to their goal satisfaction. Therefore, it complements the Population View, which focuses on giving an overview of the whole population.

The (a) big radar chart is intended to make comparisons between few candidates. One of the four groups can be chosen to display all candidates of the group in the same visualization. For the comparison group, they are shown in their color. In addition, all candidates can be shown with low opacity in the background to give the architect an impression about the goal satisfaction in the whole population, e.g., in the example, the dark area in the top indicates that goal $m1$ is much more often (almost) satisfied than the other three goals.

All candidates are shown in (b) the list of candidates visualized as radar charts. This list can be filtered based on names, tags, and groups. It also shows the tags and groups for each candidate and provides some interaction points, e.g., a right-click menu to modify the group composition.

5.3   Architecture View

The purpose of the Architecture View (Fig. 5c) is to examine the architectural properties of the whole population or groups. Therefore, it should help architects in finding explanations for the results of software architecture optimization.

The view consists of four parts. One part is the (a) node-link diagram for components and dependencies, as described in Sect. 4.2. A (b) variation, with rectangles as resource containers to visualize the allocation of components, is also displayed. Both node-link diagrams are equipped with additional features and interaction techniques. We applied a force-directed layout, with configurable parameters, to improve the arrangements of nodes and links. Elements can be filtered, dragged, moved to the front, hovered to show additional information, and their corresponding candidates are added to the current group if they are clicked.

A (c) parallel coordinate plot shows the active candidates as black, partially transparent lines, while the *current* candidates are highlighted. This feature allows to compare the *current* candidates to the population and make patterns visible, e.g., most candidates using a particular component could have a fast CPU.

To also make the influence on the goal satisfaction visible, a (d) radar chart is displayed. Similar to the big radar chart in the Candidates View, it shows several candidates simultaneously but is limited to the current group. In the shown example, it is evident that the highlighted candidates do overall satisfy three goals well, but not the fourth.

6   Architecture and Technologies

SQuAT-Vis has been initially designed to be compatible with SQuAT's technologies but aims to be modular and loosely coupled. Figure 6 illustrates its design.

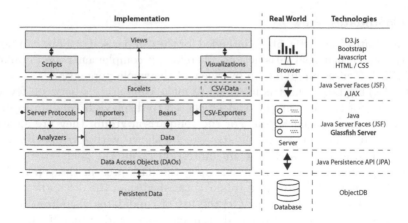

Fig. 6. Overview of the SQuAT-Vis system architecture and technologies

For the front-end, the JavaScript visualization library D3.js [5] is used to generate the visualizations due to its flexibility, big community, and the number of available templates to build on. The use of JavaScript for the implementation of the interaction techniques comes consequently with this decision. The utilization of web technology comes with the option of running a (central) SQuAT-Vis server remotely; then, architects need nothing but a browser to use the application.

The back-end is implemented based on Java Enterprise Edition (JEE), which has been chosen as it is a mature, scalable, and still maintained technology for developing web applications. To assure the loose coupling, SQuAT-Vis listens to an open port to communicate with software architecture optimization approaches, which can use a provided Java-library to follow predefined communication protocols. As the prototype focuses on SQuAT [19], only an importer for PCM [3] instances is available. Analyzers allow to enrich the received data, e.g., to tag Pareto-optimal candidates. The results are stored in a database and provided via Beans and Facelets as it is common in JEE applications.

The interface of SQuAT-Vis only expects information about goals and architectures and does not assume a specific optimization process. Therefore, it is conceptually compatible with various architecture optimization approaches. However, two significant limitations arise from the current implementation as it (i) uses the Java Socket API and (ii) lacks Non-PCM importers.

7   Evaluation

This section summarizes a previously conducted evaluation of SQuAT-Vis [10], which is fully described in the supplementary material [9]. We investigated (i) whether SQuAT-Vis can support architects in the use cases introduced in Sect. 3 and (ii) the tool's scalability with the number of candidates. Section 7.1 outlines the setup of the experiment and Sect. 7.2 summarizes results.

7.1 Description

Following the suggestion of Isenberg et al. [13], we conducted a qualitative evaluation based on a case study. We asked two experts and one non-expert of the field to watch a video tutorial and solve four tasks based on the four use cases described in Sect. 3 for each of two case study data sets. The $ST+$ [19] data set consisted of 554 candidates, 5 basic components, and 4 goals. The bigger data set is based on the Common Component Modeling Example (CoCoME) [20] and consisted of 1193 candidates, 51 components, and 8 goals. The participants answered a questionnaire consisting of 99 questions regarding their expertise, their performance in solving the tasks, and their overall impression of SQuAT-Vis. Besides, we conducted measurements of loading times for both data sets with increasing numbers of active levels for all the three views (see Sect. 5).

7.2 Results and Discussion

Except for the implementation of a candidate, all use cases were encountered by the participants before. The non-expert did only partially solve the tasks or not report any results, which leads to the conclusion that SQuAT-Vis should be used by experts. The experts (partially) solved all tasks regarding candidate selection and stopping criteria and were satisfied by their results and the support by SQuAT-Vis. For *CoCoME*, no expert solved a task regarding candidate implementation and result explanation. However, for $ST+$, some explanations were identified. The experts fully agreed that SQuAT-Vis is an important contribution to the field. They especially liked the Candidates View, the grouping concept, and the comparison mode. Their critique focused on the Architecture View, which has been rated as "not intuitive". The experts also suggested additional features, e.g., showing response values instead of utility values. The results of the scalability evaluation suggest displaying at most between 609 and 942 candidates to achieve view loading times of 10 s or less.

8   Conclusion

We presented SQuAT-Vis, a tool that provides connected views to visualize and interact with the results of software architecture optimization. It focuses on four previously defined, general use cases of human architects in the domain, namely the selection of candidates, whether to stop the optimization, implementing changes, and explaining results. Therefore, it visualizes goal satisfaction and architectures. The results of an expert user study [10], summarized in this paper, indicate that SQuAT-Vis is useful for candidate selection and deciding on the stopping criteria, while also offering limited support in explaining results. Furthermore, the prototype can handle up to several hundred candidates efficiently. Therefore, SQuAT-Vis can be seen as an important building block to support architects in (interactive) software architecture optimization. However, future work is required to improve the compatibility of SQuAT-Vis with more software architecture optimization approaches, conduct a more general evaluation of its applicability, and identify further improvements.

Acknowledgement. This work has been partially supported by the German Research Foundation (HO 5721/1-1) and the Baden-Württemberg Stiftung.

References

1. Aleti, A., Bjornander, S., Grunske, L., Meedeniya, I.: ArcheOpterix: an extendable tool for architecture optimization of AADL models. In: ICSE MOMPES, pp. 61–71. IEEE (2009)
2. Aleti, A., Buhnova, B., Grunske, L., Koziolek, A., Meedeniya, I.: Software architecture optimization methods: a systematic literature review. TSE **39**(5), 658–683 (2013)
3. Becker, S., Koziolek, H., Reussner, R.: The Palladio component model for model-driven performance prediction. JSS **82**(1), 3–22 (2009)
4. Boehm, B., In, H.: Identifying quality-requirement conflicts. IEEE Softw. **13**(2), 25–35 (1996)
5. Bostock, M.: D3.js. https://d3js.org
6. Diaz-Pace, J.A., Campo, M.: Exploring alternative software architecture designs: a planning perspective. IEEE Intell. Syst. **23**(5), 66–77 (2008)
7. Diaz-Pace, A., Kim, H., Bass, L., Bianco, P., Bachmann, F.: Integrating quality-attribute reasoning frameworks in the ArchE design assistant. In: Becker, S., Plasil, F., Reussner, R. (eds.) QoSA 2008. LNCS, vol. 5281, pp. 171–188. Springer, Heidelberg (2008). https://doi.org/10.1007/978-3-540-87879-7_11
8. Frank, S.: SQuAT-Vis showcase video. https://youtu.be/YUGujyR0jA8
9. Frank, S.: Supplementary material. https://doi.org/10.5281/zenodo.3454747
10. Frank, S.: Techniques for visualization and interaction in software architecture optimization. Master's thesis, University of Stuttgart (2019)
11. Glass, R.L.: Frequently forgotten fundamental facts about software engineering. IEEE Softw. **18**(3), 112 (2001)
12. Hart, E., Ross, P.: GAVEL-a new tool for genetic algorithm visualization. TEVC **5**(4), 335–348 (2001)
13. Isenberg, T., Isenberg, P., Chen, J., Sedlmair, M., Möller, T.: A systematic review on the practice of evaluating visualization. TVCG **19**(12), 2818–2827 (2013)
14. Jones, C.V.: Visualization and optimization. JOC **6**(3), 221–257 (1994)
15. Koziolek, A., Reussner, R.: Towards a generic quality optimisation framework for component-based system models. In: CBSE, pp. 103–108. ACM (2011)
16. Lee, J.D., See, K.A.: Trust in automation: designing for appropriate reliance. Hum. Factors **46**(1), 50–80 (2004)
17. Li, R., Etemaadi, R., Emmerich, M., Chaudron, M.: An evolutionary multiobjective optimization approach to component-based software architecture design. In: CEC, pp. 432–439. IEEE (2011)
18. Miettinen, K.: Survey of methods to visualize alternatives in multiple criteria decision making problems. OR Spectr. **36**(1), 3–37 (2012). https://doi.org/10.1007/s00291-012-0297-0
19. Rago, A., Vidal, S., Diaz-Pace, J.A., Frank, S., van Hoorn, A.: Distributed quality-attribute optimization of software architectures. In: SBCARS, p. 7. ACM (2017)

20. Rausch, A., Reussner, R.H., Mirandola, R., Plasil, F.: The Common Component Modeling Example, vol. 5153. Springer, Heidelberg (2008). https://doi.org/10.1007/978-3-540-85289-6
21. Roberts, J.C.: State of the art: coordinated & multiple views in exploratory visualization. In: CMV, pp. 61–71. IEEE (2007)
22. Salameh, H.B., Ahmad, A., Aljammal, A.: Software evolution visualization techniques and methods-a systematic review. In: CSIT, pp. 1–6. IEEE (2016)
23. Stump, G., Yukish, M., Martin, J., Simpson, T.: The ARL trade space visualizer: an engineering decision-making tool. In: MA&O, p. 4568. AIAA (2004)

ECSA 2020 Gender Diversity
in Software Architecture and Software
Engineering Track

ECSA 2020 Gender Diversity in Software Architecture and Software Engineering Track

It has been widely demonstrated that diversity in gender, culture, religion, and country, is a key factor to success, competitiveness, and innovation in software development. In the case of gender diversity, the role of traditionally underrepresented genders in the computing area has increasingly gained importance in the emerging information age. However, setting up gender-balanced teams in ICT companies as well as in STEM universities and research centers is still hard to realize in practice, even if everyone acknowledges the importance of achieving gender diversity for the success of projects.

Following the success of past editions, the 4th Special Track on Gender Diversity in Software Architecture & Software Engineering is part of the 14th premier European Conference on Software Architecture (ECSA 2020). The gender diversity track provides a forum for discussions about how to better achieve diversity in SE/STEM. People from all genders and backgrounds are invited to participate in this track. Students, industry professionals, academics, and other leaders in computing are welcome to promote networking and technical discussion to motivate the participation and visibility of underrepresented genders in STEM degrees and industry.

This year, the track received three submissions. Each one of them was thoroughly reviewed by at least three Program Committee members. After discussion, two out of the three submissions were accepted. In this edition, the track incorporated a mix of presentations and a panel to discuss current and future issues in the field by leading experts from academia. One of the highlights of the track was Professor Paola Inverardi's keynote talk. Professor Inverardi, who was rector of the University of L'Aquila, Italy, from 2013 to 2019, is in a unique position to report about the state of the implementation of gender equality policies at Italian universities, a topic of great interest to ECSA's audience.

Organization

Gender Diversity in Software Architecture and Software Engineering Chairs

Javier Camara
University of York, UK

Catia Trubiani
Gran Sasso Science Institute, Italy

Gender Diversity in Software Architecture and Software Engineering Program Committee

Aldeida Aleti
Monash University, Australia

Paolo Arcaini
National Institute of Informatics, Japan

Francesca Arcelli
Università degli Studi di Milano-Bicocca, Italy

Kyungmin Bae
Pohang University of Science and Technology, South Korea

Amel Bennaceur
The Open University, UK

Lidia Fuentes
Universidad de Málaga, Spain

Ilias Gerostathopoulos
Vrije Universiteit Amsterdam, The Netherlands

Antonia Lopes
University of Lisbon, Portugal

Paulo Mendes Maia
University of Ceara, Brazil

Claudio Menghi
University of Luxembourg, Luxembourg

Liliana Pasquale
University College Dublin and Lero, Ireland

Chouki Tiebermacine
University of Montpellier, France

Danny Weyns
KU Leuven, Belgium

Girl-Friendly Computer Science Classroom: Czechitas Experience Report

Barbora Buhnova[1,2](✉) and Lucia Happe[3]

[1] Czechitas, Prague, Czech Republic
baru@czechitas.cz
[2] Masaryk University, Brno, Czech Republic
buhnova@fi.muni.cz
[3] Karlsruhe Institute of Technology, Karlsruhe, Germany
lucia.happe@kit.edu

Abstract. The under-representation of girls within software engineering has far-reaching consequences, from social to economical. For the moment, curriculum design is being widely discussed as the essential factor that teachers can adapt to influence their education's inclusiveness. However, in building an inclusive learning environment, effective pedagogy is even more crucial, fostering controlled work with students' strengths, weaknesses, interest in the topic, sense of belonging, and experience of success. In this paper, we collect effective strategies for building a girl-friendly classroom environment that is inclusive towards novice computer science learners, and we pair them with the practical experience from a successful education NGO called Czechitas, specialized in female-tailored computing courses.

Keywords: Computer science education · Girls · Secondary grade · Learning environment · Czechitas

1 Introduction

The growth of interest in computer science (CS) and information technology (ICT) is a unique opportunity to widen the reach of CS education, resulting in a more diverse population of students. Realizing this potential is however challenging as we still know very little about how to teach CS to a broader audience more effectively, and how CS teaching shall adapt to the ways in which different people learn.

When looking at the gender diversity specifically, secondary education is being understood as the life-altering time period, where the self-selection of girls away from CS and other STEM subjects happens [27]. For many girls, this period is characterized by their first contact with CS and ICT subjects, in an environment where boys are ahead in their knowledge and tend to monopolize the instructor's time and set the standard pace within the classroom [29,34].

It is being shown [24] that novice learners learning complex topics benefit from support, explicitly guided tasks and activities, as well as specific and timely

© Springer Nature Switzerland AG 2020
H. Muccini et al. (Eds.): ECSA 2020, CCIS 1269, pp. 125–137, 2020.
https://doi.org/10.1007/978-3-030-59155-7_10

feedback [20,28]. In the presence of more experienced learners, the need is not always easily noticed. The frustration from the missing experience of success within the mixed secondary-school environment might make the novice learners (many of which tend to be female) drop the course concluding that it is too late for them to start with CS. That is why it is vital to invest deliberate effort in building an environment that is supportive of novice learners, having a direct effect on recruitment and retention of girls in CS.

Although many intervention programs have been implemented, gender diversity in practice has not improved significantly [3]. The low effectiveness of the interventions seem to suggest that the recommendations proposed in research are not reaching practice [15]. Indeed, publications that report on practical and actionable implementation of recommendations for girl-friendly classroom design are very rare [18].

In this paper, we explore existing research recommendations for building girl-friendly CS classroom environment benefiting novice secondary-grade learners, and put them in perspective with practical recommendations collected from lecturers of Czechitas, a nonprofit organization providing female-tailored CS courses. In the paper, we specifically explore the strategies that make the classroom environment less hostile and more welcoming to female novice learners.

The structure of the paper is as follows. In Sect. 2, we discuss the theoretical background of the work, followed with a short description of Czechitas in Sect. 3. The methodology of the study is outlined in Sect. 4, and the actual collection of effective recommendations is given in Sect. 5. Section 6 concludes the paper.

2   Research Background on Gender Tendencies

Although many different factors are being reported as necessary in increasing girls' interest and commitment in computer science [19], in the case of novice learners on the secondary level of education, the friendliness and inclusiveness of the environment appears to play the crucial role [26]. While such a safe environment benefits any novices, certain aspects make it benefit specifically the spectrum of students that are being left behind by the current style of CS education, which are more often girls than boys. Hence although talking explicitly about girls, the recommendations studied in this paper are meant to all secondary-grade CS novices who exhibit the skill set and tendencies statistically more typical for girls, irrespective of gender.

The distribution of differences in gender tendencies is in psychology described by the Bell curve of gender tendencies [4] illustrated in Fig. 1. The y-axis might characterize e.g., the generalist vs. specialist skill set, factual vs. intuitive thinking, focus on target vs. perspective, tendency towards short-term high-intensity commitment vs. long-term sustained commitment, or simply the intensity of self-identification with keywords such as agreeableness, assertiveness, enthusiasm, compassion, or contextualized tendency towards prioritization, integration, competition, inclusion, and others [32]. Although the average values of the male vs. female distribution might not be very different, and sizeable overlaps exist, the numbers of male and female individuals with different tendencies are substantial, which is why gender diversity boosts creativity and success in software engineering industry.

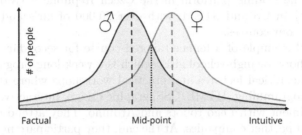

Fig. 1. Bell curve of gender tendencies [4].

Many of the differences in gender tendencies, such as the different approach to problem solving, are supported by neurological research. For instance, when girls try to understand the problem space, they tend to holistically characterize the domain to a greater detail as a web of an extensive array of potential factors [6,8,35]. Doing so, they might appear to be stuck and feel anxiety when being pushed by the teacher to move on quickly [14]. On the other hand, boys have a higher tendency to approach the problem by eliminating issues and approaching them in isolation [16]. Both the strategies have their advantages, and they work best in combination [4]. However, in the contexts of male-dominated computer science classrooms, the teachers without explicit attention and effort to notice it could unintentionally fall into the thinking that successful solutions are the ones linked with the problem-solving strategy that is more common for boys.

The fact that girls prefer safer environment without pressure, competition, with more time for their assignments and to rehearse and recall what they are learning at their own time, place, and pace, might be misinterpreted by the teacher as the fact that girls are weaker in computing, which is not the case. When girls are given the conditions they need to master computing, they achieve exceptional results, and later excel in the industry, where diverse individuals are needed to build various teams, involved in product design, implementation, testing, or management [17].

3   Practice Background on Czechitas

Czechitas [9,10,13] is a Czech non-profit organization founded in 2014 with the vision to bring tech closer to girls, and girls closer to tech. Since then, this idea has attracted a strong community of volunteers, tech professionals, and tech companies. It has turned into a rich portfolio of female-tailored courses in software engineering, including software architecture, web development, mobile app development, data science, testing, digital marketing, and many more. While initially established to provide female students with an opportunity to put their hands on coding, it now aims at achieving a major social change.

Thanks to the success of Czechitas education activities, consisting of hundreds of courses each year all around the Czech Republic, Czechitas has become recognized as the leading platform in the Czech Republic actively addressing gender diversity in CS and STEM, with over 20,000 of girls and women who graduated from our courses.

A successful example of a female-tailored course for secondary grade is the IT Summer School for high-school girls, which is a week-long program that consists of both theoretical lectures and practical workshops where the girls learn the basics of programming, HTML/CSS, graphic design, interactive game development, experiment with Lego robots and Arduino. They attend excursions at universities and partner companies. At the end, they participate in a hackathon, in which they are able to develop their own team IT project.

4   Methodology

As our study has both the research and practice elements, the methodology in this section details both, focusing on building a girl-friendly environment. To keep the focus, we are deliberately not including topics such as the effects of role models, curriculum design, or practical relevance of the education, which are all essential in gender-sensitive education. Instead, our focus in this paper is solely on the education environment.

Collecting Recommendations from Research: We have performed a literature search to understand the practices to create girl-friendly CS classroom recommended by research, including recommendations for inclusive pedagogy as well as the inclusive environment. We have covered the following research databases in the search: ACM Digital Library, IEEE, Google Scholar, Springer, Wiley Online Library, and Eric. The initial search generated hundreds of articles on diverse topics targeted to understand the causes, consequences, and solutions to gender distribution in STEM. We filtered the results and included the ones that provide insights or guidance on possible girls-friendly classroom design strategies in secondary education specifically, as the experiences in this time period have a crucial impact on the career perception in computing defined as software engineering or informatics.

Collecting Experience from Practice: To collect the best practices used by teachers in the Czechitas courses, we have organized two workshops in two Czech major cities, with 20 participants (teachers) each, including a moderated discussion with four most experienced lecturers in each workshop. The lecturers who were interviewed at the workshop all had at least two years of experience with lecturing Czechitas female-tailored courses. The workshops were organized as an open discussion forum among more and less experienced teachers to exchange knowledge on effective girl-friendly classroom design and organization strategies.

Table 1. Strategies making classroom environment inclusive of novice female learners

Recommendation (Rec.)	Goal of the strategy
1. By creating safe environment	
1.1. Support non-competitive culture [5,7]	Minimising building of classroom hierarchy hostile to girls
1.2. Hold lessons creating a sense of belonging [12]	Increasing awareness about what is happening in the classroom
1.3. Create opportunities for exchange [2,5,12,22]	Building the sense of belonging
1.4. Avoid technical obscurity in discussions [30]	Improving understanding
2. By segregation	
2.1. Provide all-female educational programs [5,12,19,33]	Allowing girls to get more instruction time
2.2. Split classes by experience not gender [22,29,31]	Working against the monopolization of instructor time by the most experienced students
3. By personalised learning	
3.1. Introduce easy methods for students to report on struggle [21]	Intervening to limit frustration
3.2. Plan time constraints to regularly check on class [1,21]	Intervening as needed to give personalized feedback
3.3. Use self-efficacy interventions [21,23,25]	Avoiding disengagement

5   Recommendations on Girl-Friendly Classroom Design

For more than 20 years, the research community, governmental, and educational institutions undertake diverse interventions aimed at increasing gender diversity in CS education, yet with little progress [18]. We believe that better transfer among research and practice provides an opportunity to address this challenge, not only by identifying causes and consequences and identifying possible interventions, but also by translating them into practical and actionable teaching practices, and learning back from them. Our argumentation is based on a review of research literature as well as on our own practical experience with teaching CS. We have examined the literature recommendations on how to teach CS to a broader audience more effectively and how CS teaching can adapt to gender tendencies observed in girls. In response to this research question, we aggregated a set of effective measures and strategies into three main categories, summarized together with their identified recommendations from literature in Table 1, and discussed in relation to our practical observations in the remainder of this section.

5.1   By Creating Safe Environment

Recommendations from Research: The sense of belonging seems to be the essential factor in achieving a safe environment allowing female novice learners to express themselves freely. What are the experiences necessary to feel that we belong? The research suggests that girls need: (1) to be able to succeed and be represented on all levels of classroom hierarchy; (2) to understand, share and exchange their classroom experiences; (3) to know that their experience is typical and expected; and (4) the language, art of expression used and goals followed in the classroom to be understandable and relevant to them.

The Rec. 1.1. [5,7] suggests using strategies to minimize competitive culture, which often feels threatening to girls. This can be achieved by instilling growth mindset and explaining strategies for success explicitly to girls and boys the same (to fight the hostile art of competition based on previous computing competence), as well as including assignments requiring skills usually hold by girls as well. The Rec. 1.2. [11] suggests reflecting on what's happening in the classroom, creating a transformative culture of shared experience. This could include collaborative lesson planning or debriefing discussions to explain the expectations. The teachers and tutors can especially share their own experiences with success and failure in computing tasks, how they feel using technology, what they expect of it, and what impact it has on their life or society. Shared experience combined with emphatic speech and authentic interest in what students are experiencing can rapidly increase the sense of belonging. The Rec. 1.3. [2,5,12,22] suggests that the classroom organization should include opportunities for exchange, communication of expectations, welcoming chat, and additional field trips and extracurricular activities targeted on girls but not necessarily segregated. Research [2] here shows that girls still believe that it is necessary to have masculine characteristics to succeed in CS. Providing them with non-stereotypical experiences in the classroom fights this dangerous belief. The Rec. 1.4. focuses on increasing the sense of belonging by avoiding technical obscurity in the language used in the classroom. Here, literature suggests that girls loose orientation quickly when many abstraction levels are mixed, and tend to fall in frustration when they feel the art of expression is strange and not relevant to them. Speech sensible to this, holding one abstraction level and informing the class by its change limits the frustration and fights the disengagement of girls in the classroom.

Experience from Czechitas: Creating a safe environment with a strong spirit of belonging is the essential characteristic of all Czechitas female-tailored courses and events. To this end, we implement several practices that have, over time, proved to have a significant impact on attracting girls to engage in learning programming and software engineering. As we find this crucial, we have a person in each course who checks for the right atmosphere, so that it is not the task of the lecturer who needs to focus on the teaching. In addition to that, besides the main lecturer, there is a team of 4–6 mentor assistants present in each course, ready for individual assistance to anybody struggling with their assignments.

Czechitas courses are characterized with a very informal atmosphere where the girls are navigated to get to know each other, and where we deliberately flatten the feeling of hierarchy between them and the lecturers, to remove the initial fear of asking questions and make it natural to be honest and open about individual learning difficulties. E.g., at each course, we spend some informal time together, which is strengthened by coffee breaks to which everybody contributes with the food they bring and share with others. After each course, the participants are invited to join our Facebook community, with specialized groups for different learning themes, where they can continue exchanging knowledge, following learning tips shared by others, and finding help if they struggle with their coding ideas and projects. Long-term courses have their own Facebook group, often paired with a Slack channel for a tighter connection.

Best Practices Emphasized by the Lecturers:

- Within a three-month course, dedicate one lesson in a month to a different kind of learning, e.g., outdoors in a park, sharing learning difficulties and successful attempts in overcoming them, tips, and tricks of discovered online learning platforms.
- Ease the atmosphere in the course by employing fun in the learning process. A good way is to use funny GIFs and memes in presentations as ice breakers. Another effective way is tandem teaching, where a pair of lecturers teach together while interacting in a friendly way to ease the atmosphere.
- Foster interaction via ways that are easy to join and add dynamics to the lesson. A good way is to stand up and move instead of just sit and raise hands. Interactive polls and dynamic word clouds also work well. If hand-raising is used, add funny elements to it, for instance, by using the hand like a clock hand to indicate on a scale 1–11 (as in hours on the clock) how well one understands a concept.
- Deliberately create opportunities for the participants to engage with assistant mentors on-site during the day to assist those who need help.
- To avoid technical obscurity and ease the understanding of difficult concepts, use analogy with the real world, and share tips for useful analogies with other lecturers. For instance, a data type can be explained as a post item type – one can fit different content into a package, an envelope, or a postcard. There is some data one can fit in a postcard as well as a package, but one is more appropriate than the other.

5.2   By Segregation

Recommendations from Research: The main goal of segregation of students based on gender in Rec. 2.1. [5,12,19,33] or on previous experience in Rec. 2.2. [22,29,31] is to provide all students with a fair share of instruction time and more suitable instruction form. More experienced students, in this case usually boys, tend to monopolize the teacher's time, computer labs, and the curriculum material. The teachers who do not make an explicit effort to provide a girl-friendly environment will unintentionally end-up promoting a male-oriented classroom. Dealing with such an environment, girls tend to give up and take a more passive and only observing position in a computer lab. This way, girls voluntarily give up their instruction time. Being in this circle of feeling misplaced and frustrated in the CS classroom, there is only a little that can spark girls' motivation and interest in CS. The hypothesis is that girls need a safe environment and community of other girls or a community of other girls or boys that are science-affine, similarly experienced, and welcoming. The study in [33] shows that the boys often limited girls' involvement in the classroom assignments and did not accept their ideas; over time, this has the potential to diminish girls' desire to participate. Both teachers and curriculum developers should consider how to guide students to productive and fair group work in the CS classroom.

Experience from Czechitas: While for primary-grade children, we do not observe any significant benefits of girls-only classes, for secondary-grade (especially the upper-secondary) and older girls and women, the positive effect of girls-only learning options is enormous. That is visible in the interest in the courses (multiple times higher than their capacity), open interaction happening within the class, as well as the commitment to continue with CS. Based on our experience, the girl-only environment benefits namely the novice learners who start with CS later than their peers. In our perception, the girl-only environment acts best as an incubator to build confidence and commitment to computing, while there shall be deliberate effort to integrate the learners in a mixed environment when ready. To this end, we encourage and support girls to form teams together with the lecturers or mentors, and register to mixed-gender IT hackathons, to experience success in the mixed environment too.

Best Practices Emphasized by the Lecturers:
- In the presence of more experienced learners within the classroom, keep the focus on the less experienced ones, while the more experienced can form a group around one of the assistant mentors, who shall have special assignments ready for them.
- If such a grouping is expected, adapt the seating of students accordingly (by experience) since the beginning. To do this, add a game at the beginning of the lesson, via which the students form the groups by experience organically themselves.
- Engage the more experienced learners in assisting their less experienced peers. Invite them explicitly in doing so during moments in which it is evident that some students are ready with their assignments while others might need help.

5.3 By Personalised Learning

Recommendations from Research: The goals of personalized learning are to: (1) provide self-efficacy interventions if needed; (2) calibrate self-evaluation of girls by encouragement and feedback; (3) and limit frustration. The Rec. 3.1. [21] suggests that teachers should introduce easy methods for students to report when

they are struggling, and they fell in traps in their work, where they need help
to continue. Many students, especially girls, are not comfortable with asking for
help, demanding attention, and struggle quietly in the CS classroom. Organizing
the classroom in a way that it is easy to ask for help diminishes these barriers.
The Rec. 3.2. [1, 21] shows that teachers need to be aware of students who frequently lose focus and intervene as needed. The standard strategy is to make
sure to scan the room frequently and allow some struggles before assisting students to allow them to think and learn on their own, but introduce constraints
on frustration, especially early in the course. The work in [25] shows that girls
respond to performance feedback early in the course, revising their self-efficacy
beliefs. The implication of this result is crucial as it suggests that responses
to early failures could be causing female students to disengage from CS very
early. Understanding how the self-efficacy feedback loop operates in girls could
modify pedagogical approaches by introducing early and targeted self-efficacy
interventions to improve girls' retention in CS. Too early failures decrease motivation to continue and retention of girls in the computer science courses rapidly.
Thus the solution here is to provide students with an innovative environment
and culture, early mentoring, and specially planned success experiences [25, 30].
Teachers can create opportunities for success and mentor girls to succeed early.
The Rec. 3.3. [21, 23, 25] highlights the importance of incorporating opportunities
for self-efficacy interventions and for self-evaluation in CS classroom. Teachers
should engage students in self-assessment opportunities and monitor them for
any inconsistencies that should be regularly reflected on. This reflection will help
students evaluate their performance and capabilities more objectively and more
accurately. Especially for girls, it is imperative as girls tend to underestimate
their performance in comparison to boys more often, which could be a huge
liability in the CS classroom.

Experience from Czechitas: The need for personalized learning is in Czechitas further emphasized by the fact that we provide extra-curricular education,
mixing students with different backgrounds and from different schools in one
classroom. Hence, we needed to develop a method to monitor each student's
progress and adapt their learning path accordingly for the most effective outcome. The monitoring part of the method is based on the system of colorful
sticky notes used by the students (stick visibly to their laptops) to share their
status, namely: (1) I am done with the primary assignment and work already on
the bonus assignment, (2) I am still working on the primary assignment and do
not want to be disturbed, (3) I am still working on the primary assignment and
would appreciate help, (4) I am also done with the bonus assignment and would
appreciate some guidance on what else I can be working on before the group is
ready to move on. The adaptation part of the method is based on pre-designed
sets of primary and bonus assignments, together with the ability of the lecturer
to find the right moment to move on to the next topic, while those who might be
left behind are helped individually by assistant mentors so that they catch up
with the leading group. In each classroom, there is typically one main lecturer
and 4–6 assistant mentors, who, besides individualized help, also encourage the

students who are struggling. Besides the on-site personalized learning management, we make sure that the students who might be slower are supported with study material upfront (so that they can familiarize themselves with the topic) and in many courses also a video recording afterward (so that they can recall the coding assignments and repeat them individually home for the stronger effect of the learning).

Best Practices Emphasized by the Lecturers:

- Do not rely on the sticky notes only, learn to read the eye contact and understand if somebody needs help.
- Ask progress questions that do not discourage the slower learners.
- Design bonus assignments so that they deepen the primary assignment knowledge, not introduce new knowledge.
- Prepare tips for complementary online resources for those who are ready with bonus assignments too early.
- Be ready to skip some course content if the group appears to need more time for the assignments than the lecturer expected. Decide in time what parts can be skipped so that the course does not appear unfinished.
- Be ready to add more content to the course on the fly if the group is faster than the lecturer expected.
- Within a three-month course, offer voluntary lessons once a month aimed solely at repeating the parts of the content that might not be fully understood by slower students.
- Avoid context switching, i.e. follow one core scenario or project the whole day or course, which the lecturer keeps coming back to.
- Work with the assumption that the students might be watching their screen at any point in time, which means that they can easily miss what is displayed on the lecturer's screen. Make sure to comment verbally on everything you do on the screen.
- Define sections of the course with an inclusive start, i.e., where even those who got lost in the previous section can resume and continue with others.
- Make pauses for the students to take notes so that they do not need to take notes parallel to the lecturer speaking. Explain how to take notes and what to note given the material that is provided as part of the course.
- When writing the code, do not delete the pieces of code written previously. Comment them out so that the students can come back to them later and reconstruct the lesson's story.

6   Conclusion

How the future of software engineering plays out will depend on our ability to support more cultural and gender diversity in computer science classrooms. As the richness of computing as intellectual endeavor starts to be explicitly visible in the curriculum and the offer of fields to study, the diversity of the students will increase, and the culture will evolve. To ease the process, the teachers need to be provided with the toolset for building an inclusive CS classroom environment. In the paper, we have contributed to building such a toolset via a survey of effective pedagogical interventions to create a more inclusive learning environment for girls in the field of computer science, which we have accompanied by experience from practice, namely from a successful educational NGO, called Czechitas.

Acknowledgements. The writing of this article was supported in part by Vector Stiftung, Project "Mädchen für Informatik begeistern" at Karlsruhe Institute of Technology (KIT).

References

1. Al-Khalifa, H.S., Faisal, H.R., Al-Gumaei, G.N.: Teaching mobile application development in 20 hours for high school girls: a web-based approach. In: 2019 IEEE Global Engineering Education Conference (EDUCON), pp. 16–21. IEEE (2019)
2. Anderson, L., Edberg, D., Reed, A., Simkin, M.G., Stiver, D.: How can universities best encourage women to major in information systems? Commun. Assoc. Inf. Syst. **41**(1), 29 (2017)
3. Annabi, H., Lebovitz, S.: Improving the retention of women in the IT workforce: an investigation of gender diversity interventions in the USA. Inf. Syst. J. **28**(6), 1049–1081 (2018)
4. Annis, B., Nesbitt, R.: Results at the Top: Using Gender Intelligence to Create Breakthrough Growth. Wiley, Hoboken (2017)
5. Arroyo, A.E.N.: Gender and Scratch: Exploring Support for Online Gendered Settings. Ph.D. thesis, The Pennsylvania State University (2018)
6. Blum, D.: Sex on the Brain: The Biological Differences Between Men and Women. Penguin Books, London (1998)
7. Boston, J.S., Cimpian, A.: How do we encourage gifted girls to pursue and succeed in science and engineering? Gift. Child Today **41**(4), 196–207 (2018)
8. Brizendine, L.: The Female Brain. Morgan Road Books, New York (2006)
9. Buhnova, B., Jurystova, L., Prikrylova, D.: Assisting women in career change towards software engineering: experience from Czechitas NGO. In: Proceedings of the 13th European Conference on Software Architecture-Volume 2, pp. 88–93 (2019)
10. Buhnova, B., Prikrylova, D.: Women want to learn tech: lessons from the Czechitas education project. In: 2019 IEEE/ACM 2nd International Workshop on Gender Equality in Software Engineering (GE), pp. 25–28. IEEE (2019)
11. Burns, H.D., Lesseig, K.: Empathy in middle school engineering design process. In: 2017 IEEE Frontiers in Education Conference (FIE), pp. 1–4. IEEE (2017)
12. Burns, H.D., Lesseig, K., Staus, N.: Girls' interest in stem. In: 2016 IEEE Frontiers in Education Conference (FIE), pp. 1–5. IEEE (2016)
13. Czechitas: Website. https://www.czechitas.cz
14. Decety, J., Jackson, P.L.: The functional architecture of human empathy. Behav. Cogn. Neurosci. Rev. **3**(2), 71–100 (2004)
15. DuBow, W.M., Ashcraft, C.: Male allies: motivations and barriers for participating in diversity initiatives in the technology workplace. Int. J. Gend. Sci. Technol. **8**(2), 160–180 (2016)
16. Fisher, H.: The First Sex: The Natural Talents of Women and How They Are Changing the World. Ballantine Books, New York (1999)

17. García-Peñalvo, F., Reimann, D., Tuul, M., Rees, A., Jormanainen, I.: TACCLE 3, O5: an overview of the most relevant literature on coding and computational thinking with emphasis on the relevant issues for teachers, Belgium, vol. 165123 (2016). https://doi.org/10.5281/zenodo
18. Gorbacheva, E., Beekhuyzen, J., vom Brocke, J., Becker, J.: Directions for research on gender imbalance in the it profession. Eur. J. Inf. Syst. **28**(1), 43–67 (2019)
19. Gürer, D., Camp, T.: An ACM-W literature review on women in computing. SIGCSE Bull. **34**(2), 121–127 (2002). https://doi.org/10.1145/543812.543844
20. Hattie, J.: The applicability of visible learning to higher education. Scholarsh. Teach. Learn. Psychol. **1**(1), 79 (2015)
21. Henry, J., Dumas, B.: Perceptions of computer science among children after a hands-on activity: a pilot study. In: 2018 IEEE Global Engineering Education Conference (EDUCON), pp. 1811–1817. IEEE (2018)
22. Hyrynsalmi, S., Sutinen, E.: The role of women software communities in attracting more women to the software industry. In: 2019 IEEE International Conference on Engineering, Technology and Innovation (ICE/ITMC), pp. 1–7. IEEE (2019)
23. Kallia, M., Sentance, S.: Are boys more confident than girls? the role of calibration and students' self-efficacy in programming tasks and computer science. In: Proceedings of the 13th Workshop in Primary and Secondary Computing Education, pp. 1–4 (2018)
24. Kirschner, P.A., Sweller, J., Clark, R.E.: Why minimal guidance during instruction does not work: an analysis of the failure of constructivist, discovery, problem-based, experiential, and inquiry-based teaching. Educ. Psychol. **41**(2), 75–86 (2006)
25. Lishinski, A., Yadav, A., Good, J., Enbody, R.: Learning to program: gender differences and interactive effects of students' motivation, goals, and self-efficacy on performance. In: Proceedings of the 2016 ACM Conference on International Computing Education Research, pp. 211–220 (2016)
26. Main, J.B., Schimpf, C.: The underrepresentation of women in computing fields: a synthesis of literature using a life course perspective. IEEE Trans. Educ. **60**(4), 296–304 (2017)
27. Murphy, A., Kelly, B., Bergmann, K., Khaletskyy, K., O'Connor, R.V., Clarke, P.M.: Examining unequal gender distribution in software engineering. In: Walker, A., O'Connor, R.V., Messnarz, R. (eds.) EuroSPI 2019. CCIS, vol. 1060, pp. 659–671. Springer, Cham (2019). https://doi.org/10.1007/978-3-030-28005-5_51
28. Narciss, S.: Designing and evaluating tutoring feedback strategies for digital learning. Digit. Educ. Rev. **23**, 7–26 (2013)
29. Siiman, L.A., Pedaste, M., Tõnisson, E., Sell, R., Jaakkola, T., Alimisis, D.: A review of interventions to recruit and retain ICT students. Int. J. Mod. Educ. Comput. Sci. **6**(3), 45 (2014)
30. Statter, D., Armoni, M.: Learning abstraction in computer science: a gender perspective. In: Proceedings of the 12th Workshop on Primary and Secondary Computing Education, pp. 5–14 (2017)
31. Vela, K.N., Bicer, A., Capraro, R.M., Barroso, L.R., Caldwell, C.: What matters to my future: stem int-her-est and expectations. In: 2018 IEEE Frontiers in Education Conference (FIE), pp. 1–7. IEEE (2018)
32. Weisberg, Y.J., DeYoung, C.G., Hirsh, J.B.: Gender differences in personality across the ten aspects of the big five. Front. Psychol. **2**, 178 (2011)
33. Wieselmann, J.R., Dare, E.A., Ring-Whalen, E.A., Roehrig, G.H.: "I just do what the boys tell me": exploring small group student interactions in an integrated STEM unit. J. Res. Sci. Teach. **57**(1), 112–144 (2020)

34. Willoughby, T.: A short-term longitudinal study of internet and computer game use by adolescent boys and girls: prevalence, frequency of use, and psychosocial predictors. Dev. Psychol. **44**(1), 195 (2008)
35. Zaidi, Z.F.: Gender differences in human brain: a review. Open Anat. J. **2**(1), 37–55 (2010)

Mining Gender Bias: A Preliminary Study on Implicit Biases and Gender Identity in the Department of Computer Science at the Technical University of Munich

Ana Petrovska[1]([✉]), Patricia Goldberg[1], Anne Brüggemann-Klein[1], and Anne Nyokabi[2]

[1] Department of Informatics, Technical University of Munich, Munich, Germany
{petrovsk,figueira,brueggem}@in.tum.de
[2] Siemens AG, Erlangen, Germany
anne.nyokabi@siemens.com

Abstract. The concept of implicit biases is widely seen in many different areas and is regarded as one of the main reasons for the gender disparity between students pursuing degrees in Computer Sciences. Since less than 20% of Computer Science students are female, the information about gender bias in this field is of extreme importance. This research aimed to investigate if and by how much the female students in our department are affected by likely gender bias in their academic life. The data collected in this research was used to evaluate the automatic association that students have towards a specific gender and the computer science field.

Keywords: Gender bias · Computer science · University and academia

1 Introduction and Motivation

Unconscious bias, also known as hidden or implicit bias [1], affects all of us. Very often, each of us, unconsciously and almost instantaneously assess the people around us based on their appearance, gender, and personality traits among others. However, excellence in education, science and research can only be achieved if we select from the broadest range of talents, and that is not possible if unconscious bias is narrowing down the field due to non-scientific reasons. Unconscious bias is a term from the field of psychology which describes the bias an individual has against another person or a situation [12].

Although unconscious bias can be harmless in some present-day situations, it often has damaging, long-lasting adverse effects. Concretely, it is related to labeling and burdening a specific group of people based on their gender, skin

A. Petrovska and P. Goldberg—these authors contributed equally.

color, age, religion, or country of origin. The process of labeling a person is automatic, and people develop these behaviors based on their background, past experiences, and general exposure to cultural attitudes and social stigmas against certain groups. The problem with unconscious bias is that when it affects our reasoning, leading us to make fewer fair decisions, especially in the matters that need rational thinking, deluding us from the true facts of the situations, and consequently preventing us from considering the bigger pictures. We cannot move towards narrowing the gender gap issue in the technical fields if we first do not comprehend the reasons that hold us back: the hidden, unconscious, non-rational biases that each individual (regardless the gender) has—on a personal level, which later propagates on an organizational level. Unconscious bias has been identified as the main reason for poor gender-balanced representation in the IT working environments, as well as the disproportion in the numbers of male versus female students pursuing degrees in Computer and Information Sciences worldwide, with around 20% of computer science degrees awarded to women [11]. Concretely, at the university where we conducted our study, the Technical University of Munich (TUM), the overall number of female students makes up to 34% in 2014 [8] and 36% in 2018 [7]. The numbers are somehow expected since we are a technical university with a strong focus on engineering and technical sciences, where the number of women is inherently lower. However, the disproportion of male and female students is more significant at the TUM Department of Computer Science, where only 19% of the students, 15% of the Ph.D. candidates and 11% of the professors are female [7].

Understanding the reasons for the immense gender gap and the disproportion in the numbers of our department has been the core motivation for this work. Mining the gender gap and the biases should potentially lead towards identifying the reasons behind the numbers, which should later enable us to take proactive measures for improving the current situation. In order to understand our biases, first, we need to be aware of them. Concretely, the idea behind this work initially originated from the previous efforts made towards increasing the awareness about the unconscious bias in the TUM Department of Computer Science—the *Unconscious Bias Awareness Training*, further explained in Sect. 2.1. The work presented in this paper, including the Unconscious Bias Awareness Training, has been conducted in the frame of Informatik-Forum Frauen (IFF)[1], also known as Women in CS @ TUM. IFF is an informal group at the TUM Department of Computer Science, working towards equal participation and support of women and other underrepresented groups at the department.

In previous research, Nosek et al. [9] studied the math-gender stereotype using a mixture of implicit and explicit tests to gather information about the math–gender relationship. Concretely, the authors investigated how the associations between 1) the feeling of belonging to a group for both genders (group membership) and 2) how well they identify themselves as part of that group (group identity), shapes one's individual preferences and performance. Depending on how strong these associations are, the attitudes towards math vary, cor-

---

[1] https://www.in.tum.de/en/current-students/equal-opportunity/.

responding in a more negative implicit and explicit math attitude for women but a more positive one for men. Stronger implicit math-male stereotypes were, bigger the negative impact on the women's attitude was. The authors concluded that associating the self with females and math with males made it difficult for women, even women who had selected math-intensive majors, to associate math with themselves. However, to the best of our knowledge, a similar study combining implicit and explicit tests, focusing on computer science-gender stereotypes, has not yet been conducted.

Inspired by the above mentioned Unconscious Bias Awareness Training and by the lack of available datasets containing information on the computer science-gender bias, the solution that this work proposes is an online questionnaire that can gather data from both implicit and explicit questions. Therefore, the problem that this work is solving is twofold. The first problem is from the field of psychology—the creation of the questionnaires that could collect information on the person's hidden biases, which could be later analyzed. We measured both the conscious and unconscious prejudice through explicit and implicit questionnaires, respectively. For the conscious measure, we have created explicit (self-reporting) questions on gender identity and questions relevant to the TUM Department of Computer Science. The self-report questions are particularly useful for cases in which we want to evaluate, not only what a person thinks, but also how one would explicitly present their ideas. The self-reporting questions are further explained in Sect. 3.1. As the unconscious measure, we used the Implicit Association Test (IAT) [4], further explained in Sect. 2.2. The second is a technical problem, for which we need to create an online surveying form that does not only collect the answers but also 1) collects the time that the respondent took for answering a specific question, and 2) the number of errors that the respondent makes while answering a question, which is of crucial importance for the analysis of the collected data and calculating the IAT results.

2   Previous Work

2.1   Unconscious Bias Awareness Training

To lessen the hidden bias consequences, the Informatik Forum Frauen (IFF) conducted Unconscious Bias Awareness Training within TUM Department of Computer Science. The goal of this training is to promote and increase awareness of our hidden biases through real-life experiments and examples. The training has been previously held in different setups inside the university reaching a broad range of people, for example, students, tutors, Ph.D. candidates or other lecturers, who participated in different workshops or pro-seminars [6].

2.2   Implicit Association Test

Previous work [1] has shown that in principle, the results from explicit or self-reporting questionnaires tend to be misleading, since the respondents are often (subconsciously) dishonest while answering the questions. In psychology, the proposed solution to this problem is a concept named "Implicit Social Cognition" [3], which served as a basis for developing the Implicit Association Test (IAT). IAT, initially developed and introduced in 1998 by Greenwald et al. [4] within the frame of social psychology, is a tool designed to measure and estimate one's unconscious or implicit bias towards a specific stereotypical group. Since then, it has been researched and used to investigate biases in several groups, most prominently focusing on gender and race. To address the issue of subconscious dishonesty that is present in the explicit questionnaire, IAT relies on the concept of time. Namely, faster response times are expected while pairing concepts that indicate stronger associations, for example male and computer science, compared with linking women and computer science, for which people usually take longer because of a weak mental association. While answering the IAT questionnaire, people need to connect terms that are rapidly shown to them, which makes it difficult to fake answers.

3   Method

3.1   Questionnaire Creation

Our questionnaire has two type of questions: explicit (self-reporting) questions further explained in Sect. 3.2, and implicit, IAT based questions, further explained in Sect. 3.3.

3.2   Explicit (Self-reporting) Questions

The first type of questions we developed was the Explicit Test. We created three sub-types of self-reporting question: *Gender Identity*, *Quality Ranking* and *Department Related* questions, classified into three categories: Matrix, Drag and Drop and Single Choice questions.

Gender Identity Questions. In order to have a better insight into who is completing the online questionnaire, we first asked two single choice questions on respondent's gender and their age. The respondents could identify with male or female gender, or could not disclose to which gender they identify with ("Rather not say" option).

The purpose of the gender identity questions was to classify the respondents and to extract their gender identity information. Table 1 shows the full list of questions. Using this type of information, we could better understand the person replying to the questionnaire, what are their personal views about their own gender, and how well are they identifying themselves with their gender. The gender identity questions are structured according to the Matrix category, in which the respondent were asked to answer if they *Strongly Agree, Agree, Disagree*, and *Strongly Disagree* with a given statement. We created eight gender identity statements in the matrix, with two different tones: "Positive" and "Negative".

Table 1. List of Gender Identity questions.

Nr.	Tone	Gender	Statement
1	Positive	1-Female	I feel I fit in with other Females in my department
		1-Male	I feel I fit in with other Males in my department
2	Negative	2-Female	I feel annoyed that I am supposed to do some things just because I am a Female
		2-Male	I feel annoyed that I am supposed to do some things just because I am a Male
3	Positive	3-Female	I feel comfortable being a Female in my department
		3-Male	I feel comfortable being a Male in my department
4	Negative	4-Female	I feel people interpret my behavior based on my gender
		4-Male	I feel people interpret my behavior based on my gender
5	Positive	5-Female	I feel that my personality is similar to most Females personalities' in my department
		5-Male	I feel that my personality is similar to most Males personalities' in my department
6	Positive	6-Female	I feel that the things I like to do in my spare time are similar to what most Females in my department like to do in their spare time
		6-Male	I feel that the things I like to do in my spare time are similar to what most Males in my department like to do in their spare time
7	Negative	7-Female	I sometimes think it might be more fun to be of opposite gender
		7-Male	I sometimes think it might be more fun to be of opposite gender
8	Positive	8-Female	I think I am a good example of being a Female
		8-Male	I think I am a good example of being a Male

Qualities Ranking. In the Qualities Ranking question the respondents were asked to rank ten given terms: *Smart, Emotionless, Geek, Confident, Disciplined, Independent, Principled, Opinionated, Attractive* and *Strong,* in the order they consider them as relevant qualities needed for success in their career or studies (most important at the top). This is a Drag and Drop question, with the most important quality ranked at the top.

Department Related Questions. The last type of self-reporting questions contained explicit questions about the Department of Computer Science at TUM in a Matrix form. This section was mainly designed to comprehend the student's perception of the department gender equality issues. The matrix contained eight statements, regardless of the gender of the respondent. The categories of responses are: *Strongly Agree, Agree, Strongly Disagree, Disagree* and *Not Applicable.* The last category was added since some students may have neither an advisor nor a supervisor, thus some statements were not applicable to those students. The list of statements is shown in Table 2.

3.3   Implicit Questions

The implicit questions are based on IAT [4,10]. In our work, we focus on two categories: Arts and Computer Science; and two targets: Female and Male. For each category/target, five words were chosen as representatives (see Table 3), and the respondents were asked to associate each word to the corresponding category or target. We collect the time and the number of errors a person did while associating a word to a target/category. The IAT developed was divided into seven association tasks, split into five steps, as shown in Fig. 1. Steps 1, 2 and 4 are practice sessions. The final hidden bias calculation was based only on the results from steps 3 and 5, disregarding the practice tasks.

Table 2. List of Department Related questions.

Nr.	Statement
1	Students in my department are treated equally by the staff regardless of their gender
2	I am confident that the staff of my department would address sexism
3	I have witnessed gender discrimination from the staff of my department
5	I feel that my professor treats men and women equally during the lectures
6	I feel that my supervisor/advisor aligns her/his research with mine
7	I feel that my supervisor/advisor helps me identify my training/development needs
8	I feel that my supervisor/advisor shows interest in my progress/success

Table 3. Words which represent the categories and the targets of the IAT.

Arts	Sculpture	Music	Theater	Painting	Melody
Computer Science	Programming	Technology	Code	Mathematics	Electronics
Female	Sister	Mother	Aunt	Grandmother	Daughter
Male	Brother	Father	Uncle	Grandfather	Son

The procedure of the association tasks is the following: the screen is divided into two parts, left and right. In the first step, the respondent needs to associate a term shown in the middle of the screen with Male on the left and Female to the right. In the second step, the term shown in the middle needs to be associated to a category—Computer Science and Arts to the left and right, respectively. The third step includes two consecutive critical association tasks, in which the participants need to associate words related to Male or Computer Science, and words related to Female or Arts. The fourth step was again a practice task, whose aim is to flip the targets, thus Female is located on the left side, while Male on the right. The last step, similarly to step three, had two critical association tasks but in this step Female is associated to Computer Science and Male to Arts.

4   Data Collection

With the permission of the TUM Data Protection Officer and the support from a few professors at the department, our questionnaire was filled in eight introductory and advanced lectures and practical courses, on bachelor and master level. We collected the data within a period of a month, and the students answered the questionnaire in-class supervised by at least one of the authors of this work and the lecturer of the course. In total, 457 students completed the questionnaire from which 184 (41%) were females, 267 (58%) were males, and 6 students (1%) did not identify their gender.

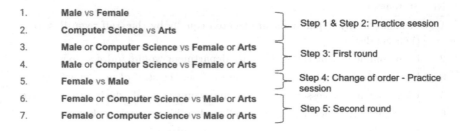

Fig. 1. Association tasks

5   Implementation of the Questionnaire

During our research we identified a lack of available—and ideally open-source— online survey tools that not only collect the respondents' answers but also the time each respondent takes to complete a section of the questionnaire. In our work, keeping track of the time was an essential factor, since calculating the IAT scores depends on the time that the respondents took to answer the question and the amount of errors that they made while doing so. The solution was to develop our own, in-house online questionnaire tool, which fulfills all the previously identified and elicited requirements that we had for our tool. The implementation of our questionnaire is open-source: https://gitlab.com/patygold3254/hiddenbias.

6   Results

In this paper, we explore the following two hypotheses:
Hypothesis 1: In the explicit questions, female and male students in our department give similar answers to the same question.
Hypothesis 2: In the implicit questions, each gender associates computer science easier with their own gender.

6.1 Data Exploration of the Explicit (Self-reporting) Questions

Gender Identity Questions. Figure 2 represents the percentage of replies for each statement from Table 1. The graph is sub-divided into Positive and Negative tone statements, and it is colored by the categories—from Strongly Disagree to Strongly Agree. The negative tone statements had the most accumulative percentage of Strongly Disagree and Disagree answers. Similarly, statements 1, 3 and 5 in the positive tone statements had the most accumulative percentage of Strongly Agree and Agree answers. Statements 2, 3 and 5 did not show a significant change in the answers among females and males respondents (less than 5% difference in each agreement level). In this question, the data collected did not represent a significant difference in responses among females and males.

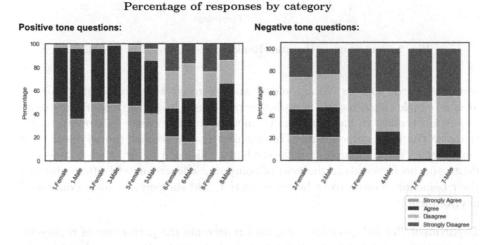

Fig. 2. Percentage of replies for each statement in the Gender Identity questions.

Qualities Ranking. Figure 3 shows the percentage of the words ranked in the *first place* by all of the respondents, divided by gender. Since the total number of respondents who did not identify with any gender was low (1%), the focus of this section will be only on the answers given by female and male respondents. The word with the highest percentage, among both female and male participants, was "Smart", which was ranked on a first place by 20% of the female and 30% of male respondents. On the contrary, the least amount of people ranked the word "Attractive" on the first place in their rankings. It is worth noting that the words "Emotionless", "Geek", "Opinionated" and "Strong" had twice the number of female respondents ranking it first place than male respondents.

Although the data collected from the *Gender Identity* questions do not show a significant difference between male and female respondents' answers, the data collected in *Qualities Ranking* does. This question shows a significant difference in adjectives which normally are used to describe the opposite gender. For

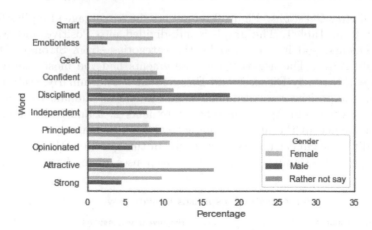

Fig. 3. Percentage of Qualities Ranking words ranked in first place.

example, words such as "Emotionless" and "Strong" that are normally associated as a male characteristic, were better positioned by female respondents as an important quality to have in order to succeed in their career or studies, rather than by the male respondents. This result shows a weaker gender identity of female students compared to male students, raising a theory that female students and professionals in the field of computer science, may be often adapting their behavior in order to be better accepted, and succeed in a male-dominated environment.

Department Related Questions. Figure 4 represents the percentage of replies for each statement related to the Department of Computer Science, colored by the category of the answer and sub-divided by the gender of the respondent. Statements 3, 6, 7 and 8 had almost 50% of the respondents answering as "Not Applicable". We could explain this by assuming that there are students that do not have a supervisor or advisor. However, statement 3 cannot be interpreted in the same way, as it was a question about gender discrimination. Furthermore, this sentence had the highest percentage of "Disagree" answers, leading, initially, to no conclusion from the answers. However, the conclusion that we could draw is that this question was either not well formulated or did not contain enough information to be answered, since more than a half of the respondents could not give a clear agree or disagree answer to it. Importantly, in the overall matrix, no great difference could be spotted while comparing the answers of different genders, therefore the perception of the department is similar to all the students.

6.2   Data Exploration of the Implicit Questions

The results of the implicit questions are calculated by counting the errors and response time of step 5 minus step 3 (see Fig. 1). If the result is negative, the winner is female, meaning that the respondent has an automatic association between Female and Computer Science. If the result is positive, the winner is male. The automatic association term refers to the hidden bias a person has of the target and the category. This association is subdivided into 4 classifications groups: "little to no", "slight", "moderate" and "strong". "Little to no" means that the respondent demonstrates hardly any automatic association to that gender and Computer Science, while "strong" means a strong association [1].

Percentage of department related responses by category

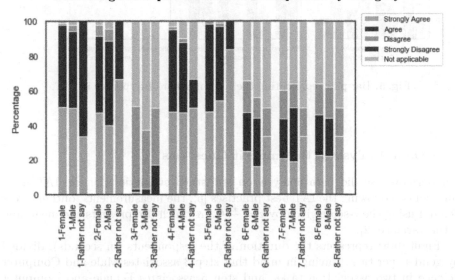

Fig. 4. Percentage of department related replies for each statement.

Figure 5 represents the distribution of the IAT results' variables collected from the respondents of our questionnaire. The x-axis represents the classification categories, while the y-axis—the number of responses in that category. Each bar plot represents the gender of the respondent, divided by "Female" (41% of the respondents), "Male" (58%) and "Rather not say" (1%). And the variable "Winner" represents the winner of the Implicit Association Test, explained above. It is worth noticing that 60% of female respondents showed an automatic association with Female and Computer Science, and this association is spread into the classification categories, varying from "little to no" until "strong". Meanwhile, 67% of male respondents showed a stronger automatic association with Male and Computer Science, having roughly the same intensity of classification categories. The data result, shown in Fig. 5, show that the majority of male respondents demonstrated a strong automatic association between Male and Computer Science. This result leads to the conclusion that men in the department of Computer Science at TUM have a stronger implicit association between

Male and Computer Science. Meanwhile, women have a less strong association between Male and Computer Science, tending to demonstrate actually a strong association between Female and Computer Science.

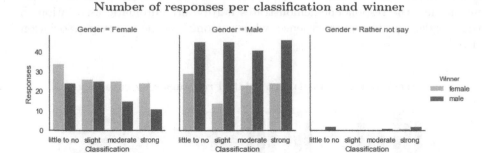

Fig. 5. Bar plot representing the total number of responses in IAT.

6.3 Data Analysis of the Implicit Questions

Furthermore, we did data analysis on statistical evaluations of the IAT measurements. Following the IAT best practises [5], the measurements' outliers were deleted using the z-score given by $z = \frac{x-\mu}{\sigma}$, in which μ represents the mean and σ the variance [2].

Figure 6(a) represents the duration of the respondents (in seconds), divided by gender, per task. Having in mind that step 3 associates Male and Computer Science in two association tasks, and step 5 associates Female and Computer Science in two tasks also, the boxplot shows a significant wider interquartile range (IQR) of the male respondents in step 5 comparing to female respondents. Therefore, the time range of male respondents when associating Female and Computer Science was bigger than the time range of female respondents. The

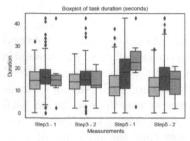
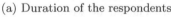

(a) Duration of the respondents

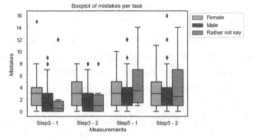

(b) Errors of the respondents

Fig. 6. Boxplot divided by gender, per task.

median of the male respondents in step 5 is significantly higher, comparing to their median in step 3. Figure 6(b) represents the errors per step, per respondent gender. While the boxplot for Females remains almost constant across tasks, the boxplot for the Males shows a higher IQR for step 5.

There are significant differences in the median and in the interquartile range of the duration and the number of errors when grouping the respondents per gender. This result leads to the conclusion that men take longer and make more errors than women while associating Female and Computer Science.

7 Conclusion

Since hidden biases are not trivial to measure, calculate and analyze, we propose explicit and implicit questions, based on which we collect data from our department to understand better if our students are affected by gender bias in their academic life. We have set up two hypotheses, which our results supported. Concretely, from the explicit self-reporting) questionnaire, our results showed that there is no significant difference in responses among female and male respondents on the *Gender Identity* and *Department Related* questions. Nevertheless, this differed in *Qualities Ranking*, where female students ranked characteristic usually linked to the opposite gender, as "Emotionless" and "Strong", as more important for success in their studies and careers.

Although society, media, and women's upbringing tend to picture men closer to computer science, or STEM in general, the results from our IAT questionnaire show that the majority of the of female students (60%) in our department associate computer science with female easier than with male, and 67% of the male respondents have a stronger automatic association with male and computer science. The results show that each gender associate computer science with their own gender more easily, but males do so more than females.

In summary, although we see a correlation of the respondent's gender with their hidden bias result, this study does not have sufficient data to conclude causality. As next steps we continue collecting and analyzing data from the department, that should enable us to do better statistics and draw better conclusions.

Acknowledgement. A special appreciation to everyone involved in the data collection.: Prof. Brügge, Prof. Seidl, Prof. Pretschner, Prof. Ott, Prof. Schulz, Prof. Jacobsen, T. Hutzelmann, N. Pezhman, M. Schüle, N. Hartmann, N.-M. Zarges, R. Palenta, D. Dzvonyar and L. Alperowitz.

References

1. Banaji, M.R.: Blindspot: Hidden Biases of Good People. Delacorte Press, New York (2013). https://search.library.wisc.edu/catalog/9910203165702121
2. Ghosh, D., Vogt, A.: Outliers: an evaluation of methodologies. In: Joint Statistical Meetings, pp. 3455–3460. American Statistical Association, San Diego (2012)

3. Greenwald, A.G., Banaji, M.R.: Implicit social cognition: attitudes, self-esteem, and stereotypes. Psychol. Rev. **102**(1), 4 (1995)
4. Greenwald, A.G., McGhee, D.E., Schwartz, J.L.: Measuring individual differences in implicit cognition: the implicit association test. J. Pers. Soc. Psychol. **74**(6), 1464 (1998)
5. Greenwald, A.G., Nosek, B.A.: Health of the implicit association test at age 3 (2001)
6. IFF: Unconscious Bias Training (2018). https://www.in.tum.de/en/current-students/equal-opportunity/projects/unconscious-bias-training/
7. TUM Department of Informatics: The Department of Informatics in Facts and Figures 2018 (2018)
8. Technical University of Munich: Diversity at tum, focus: Gender and family (2015)
9. Nosek, B.A., Banaji, M.R., Greenwald, A.G.: Math = male, me = female, therefore math ≠ me. J. Pers. Soc. Psychol. **83**(1), 44 (2002)
10. Nosek, B.A., Greenwald, A.G., Banaji, M.R.: Understanding and using the implicit association test: II. method variables and construct validity. Pers. Soc. Psychol. Bull. **31**(2), 166–180 (2005)
11. National Center for Science and Engineering Statistics: Women, minorities, and persons with disabilities in science and engineering: 2019. Technical report, National Science Foundation (2019)
12. Steele, C.M.: Whistling Vivaldi: And Other Clues to How Stereotypes Affect Us (Issues of Our Time). WW Norton & Company, New York (2011)

CASA - 3rd International Workshop on Context-aware, Autonomous and Smart Architecture

International Workshop on Context-aware, Autonomous and Smart Architecture (CASA)

The CASA@ECSA 2020 workshop aimed to bring together researchers and practitioners interested in modern systems implementing the required features for managing context-awareness, dynamicity, autonomy, and smart behavior. These features may be associated with small devices such as mobile phones and their related applications, as well as with big systems concerning transportation, airports, and cities. They are useful for a wide range of application domains including healthcare, e-government communication and social networks, smart grids, energy management systems, finance, conference management systems and learning, just to name a few examples.

The development of such solutions involves interdisciplinary and trendy concepts and skills concerning context-awareness, autonomy, adaptiveness, machine learning, Internet of Things, big data, integration and communication, networks, green and efficient energy consumption, and user-friendly access. In this context, software architectures play a fundamental role in the quality of development of such systems and the success of their deployment.

This workshop aims to discuss the fundamental principles of context-aware, autonomous, and smart solutions, the current architectural trends, and the future issues and challenges to be addressed at the architectural level. The workshop invites experts from industry and academic environments to share their solutions, ideas, visions, and questions about the design of software architectures for such solutions. We aim to enable discussions, partnerships, and collaborations among the software architects working on these topics.

CASA@ECSA 2020 received very interesting contributions from authors belonging to seven distinct countries, and the four best papers were accepted to be presented during this virtual event in September 2020 in the context of the 14th European Conference on Software Architecture (ECSA 2020).

The first paper entitled "State of the Practice Survey: Predicting the Influence of AI Adoption on System Software Architecture in Traditional Embedded Systems" is authored by Jasmin Jahic and Robin Roitsch. It investigates the perception of the artificial intelligence in industry and its impact, especially in embedded systems from an architectural point of view. The authors have interviewed various practitioners in different companies for the proposed survey.

The second paper entitled "Composition Algorithm Adaptation in Service Oriented Systems" is authored by Niranjana Deshpande and Naveen Sharma. It proposes the adaptation of composition techniques of services in service oriented architectures. The adaptation is performed for each user request. This solution leads to significant resource savings at runtime.

The third paper entitled "A Statistical Approach for Context-Awareness of Mobile Applications" is authored by Mai Abusair, Mohammad Sharaf, Antinisca Di Marco, and Paola Inverardi. It focuses on determining contextual situations that require adaptation in mobile contexts. The approach monitors the context, models the states of its variables, and determines whether a state requires or not an adaptation based on transition probabilities among states and the system quality.

The fourth paper entitled "A Reference Architecture for Personalized and Self-adaptive e-Health Apps" is authored by Eoin Martino Grua, Martina De Sanctis, and Patricia Lago. It proposes a reference architecture that enables artificial intelligence-based personalization and self-adaptation for mobile apps for e-Health. The architecture is based on multiple MAPE (Monitor, Analyze, Plan, Execute) loops operating at different levels of granularity and for different purposes.

The workshop program is enriched by the invited talk entitled "Handling Conflicting Requirements: a Primer" given by Prof. Paolo Ceravolo from Universitá degli Studi di Milano, Italy.

We would like to thank all the authors of the submitted contributions for their valuable proposals and the Program Committee members for their timely and accurate reviews. We would like to thank the ECSA 2020 workshops co-chairs, Anne Koziolek and Mauro Caporuscio, for their constant collaboration. Last but not least, we would like to thank the ECSA 2020 general chair, Henry Muccini, for his great work especially in this special 2020 edition.

Organization

Workshop Chairs

Claudia Raibulet   Universitá degli Studi di Milano-Bicocca, Italy
Khalil Drira   LAAS-CNRS, CNRS, Université de Toulouse, France
Mariagrazia Fugini   Politecnico di Milano, DEIB, Italy
Patrizio Pelliccione   Chalmers — University of Gothenburg, Sweden, and University of L'Aquila, Italy
Genaína N. Rodrigues   University of Brasilia, Brazil

Workshop Program Committee

Rodrigo Bonacin   Centro de Tecnologia da Informação Renato Archer, Brazil
Ovidiu Constantin   Oracle, Italy
Rafael Capilla   Rey Juan Carlos University, Spain
Liliana Dobrica   Politehnica University, Romania
Khalil Drira   LAAS-CNRS, CNRS, Université de Toulouse, France
Cédric Eichler   INSA Bourge, France
Paolo Falcarin   University of East London, UK
Mariagrazia Fugini   Politecnico di Milano, DEIB, Italy
Patrizio Pelliccione   Chalmers — University of Gothenburg, Sweden, and University of L'Aquila, Italy
Claudia Raibulet   Universitá degli Studi di Milano-Bicocca, Italy
Genaína N. Rodrigues   University of Brasilia, Brazil
Fatiha Saïs   Université Paris-Sud, France
Ramon Salvador Valles   Universitat Politècnica de Catalunya, Spain
Thierry Villemur   LAAS-CNRS, Université de Toulouse, France

State of the Practice Survey: Predicting the Influence of AI Adoption on System Software Architecture in Traditional Embedded Systems

Jasmin Jahić[1]([✉]) [iD] and Robin Roitsch[2] [iD]

[1] University of Cambridge, Cambridge, UK
jj542@cam.ac.uk
[2] NVIDIA GmbH, Würselen, Germany
rroitsch@nvidia.com

Abstract. Artificial intelligence (AI) is a very disruptive technology. When adopted by a software system, AI influences and significantly changes its architecture due to its complexity, as well as due to a need to adjust the existing system to use AI (e.g., adopt accelerators). This is particularly critical in traditional embedded systems as they focus on a tight coupling of software and hardware. In this paper, we present results of a survey on how well companies in embedded software domain understand AI, how they perceive its possible benefits, and how they discuss the adoption of AI and its influence on their software system architecture. The goal of this survey is to evaluate architectural techniques that companies currently use when trying to assess the influence of adopting AI and to discuss the adequacy of these techniques for this task.

Keywords: Artificial intelligence · Software architecture · System architecture · Embedded systems · Adequacy check

1 Introduction

Software systems today enjoy many benefits enabled by AI. Although these benefits are real and significant, in practice there is still a veil of mystery of what AI is capable of. Companies are still struggling to understand what kind of changes they need to introduce to their system architecture in order to adopt AI, and how these changes will affect system's non-functional properties. The reason for this is that AI is a very disruptive technology. It is not yet another framework to adopt in order to solve a particular problem. Instead, it introduces changes to software components, software design and development, data management (needed for training of AI models), and software system deployment. Furthermore, AI is still a new technology, with challenges related to testing, safety, and security. Therefore, adopting AI is a significant and risky architectural decision.

© Springer Nature Switzerland AG 2020
H. Muccini et al. (Eds.): ECSA 2020, CCIS 1269, pp. 155–169, 2020.
https://doi.org/10.1007/978-3-030-59155-7_12

In this paper, we present a survey performed among 51 embedded software system companies, which investigates what kind of analysis techniques industry uses for predicting the influence of adopting AI on their software system architecture. We also investigate what are the existing challenges in this regard, why the existing techniques are not well-suited for this purpose, and what would help architects in practice to overcome the existing challenges. The results of the survey indicate that AI is a complex technology, which imposes significant amount of changes on the existing components of system architecture and influences its most important quality aspects such is *safety*. The reasons why existing techniques for assessing the influence of architectural decisions fail are: i) lack of knowledge for applying AI in software systems, and ii) their inability to capture this lack of knowledge and indicate it to architects before making a decision.

This paper is organised in a following structure. Section 2 introduces related terms, definitions, and analysis approaches. Section 3 presents the questions driving this survey, and Sect. 4 presents results of the survey arranged according to these questions. Section 5 concludes this paper and presents potential for new analyses within the scope of this survey.

2   Related Work

2.1   AI, Neural Networks, and Machine Learning

One of definitions of artificial intelligence (AI) says that it is an intelligence of devices and machines that enables them to perceive their environment and take corresponding actions to fulfil their goals [10]. The computational backbone of AI are artificial neural networks [8]. Machine learning term refers to algorithms that build a mathematical model based on training data, enabling them to predict behaviour or make decisions without being explicitly programmed to do so [9].

There exist surveys that explore real benefits and myths around AI [1,2,5], as well as those that explore application benefits of AI in certain domains (e.g., in medicine [12]). To the best of our knowledge, none of the existing approaches investigates how suitable are the existing architecture techniques for investigating adequacy of AI and its influence on software system architecture.

2.2   Solution Adequacy Check and SWOT Analysis

Solution adequacy check (SAC) aims to build confidence in developed system architecture [7]. The SAC analyses how adequate is a system architecture design to meet its architecture drivers. SAC is based and derived from the Architecture Trade-off Analysis Method (ATAM) [6], which supports collecting and prioritizing architecture drivers and assists in evaluating an architecture against these. The Rapid Architecture Evaluation (RATE) method [7] is a SAC-based collection of evaluation methods supporting the development from early stages of requirements management up to code quality checks. The most important part of this architecture evaluation is the interpretation of the learned results about system design. By categorizing these to their corresponding natures, RATE enables evaluation of the outcome (i.e., influence and effect) of an architectural decision and rates the quality of system architecture that adopts such decision.

In contrast to RATE and especially to SAC, the Strength, Weakness, Opportunities, and Threats (SWOT) analysis [4,11] has its origin in strategic management and is a tool used for planning company strategies. It provides a comprehensive assessment of strengths and weaknesses as well as the opportunities and risks of a company. This technique aims to identify, on one hand, the internal company situation, on the other hand to evaluate possible chances and threats from external environment.

3 Survey Setup

3.1 Setup, Motivation, and Rationale

We have conducted this survey among 51 embedded software system companies from Austria, Germany, and Switzerland. The main motivation behind it is to understand how to predict the influence of a decision of adopting AI on properties of software systems. The influence can be reflected in terms of added value (e.g., improve quality properties, new functionality, new business cases, new applications), but it also can have negative effect. Often, there are sets of pre-requisite requirements that a system must fulfil. The new technology must not disturb these (e.g., non-functional requirements related to legacy, specific standards in industrial domain, and application type). Besides that, there could be commercial and organisational limitations and constraints stopping the adoption of a new technology (e.g., cost, a need to train the team, time for understanding necessary software and hardware changes). If these are misunderstood before making a decision, they can result in an architectural design with properties that do not satisfy system's requirements.

In order to understand if existing decision-making techniques for predicting influence of adopting a new technology are able to successfully guide architects through this process, we have surveyed how architects currently perform requirements engineering, how do they evaluate influence of adopting new technologies (e.g., decision making techniques such as adequacy check and SWOT analysis), and how they learn about new technologies.

Finally, we have offered to the survey participants several pre-defined choices of techniques that could enhance decision-making process to improve predicting the influence of AI adoption, and also asked them to specify their opinion. We were mainly focused on how to facilitate the process of predicting the influence of AI adoption (e.g., new types of analysis, training). Besides that, we wanted to know what architects need to understand about concrete properties, components, and processes of AI in order to predict how do they influence important design decisions of the system (e.g., data collection, deployment).

The survey questions are grouped into three categories. First (Sect. 3.2), we want to understand in which stage of adopting AI companies are, the internal level of knowledge that surveyed companies have about AI, what kind of benefits do architects expect from AI, and which of the good software architecture and engineering practices do architects use for decision-making and predicting the influence of the design decisions. The second category (Sect. 3.3) contains questions about particular requirements and limitations (e.g., safety) that are preventing companies from adopting AI, and what could help architects with the predicting the influence of a decision to adopt AI in their system. The third category contains questions related to profile of the companies that participated in the survey (see the summary in Sect. 3.4).

3.2 AI Knowledge, Expected Benefits, and Engineering Practices

Surveyed companies are at a different stage of adopting AI. In order to understand their AI-related expertise, we formulated the following questions:

1. Stage of AI adoption (possible answers: none, in evaluation, in development, existing and available, not clear)?
2. Internal knowledge about AI (possible answers: not existing, basic, intermediate, expert, *free text*)?
3. Presence of internal AI experts (possible answers: yes, no)?

Expected Benefits from Adopting AI:

1. Expected influence (e.g., added value) of adopting added-value from AI (possible answers: performance, new business cases, new customer base, improve competitiveness, new applications currently not possible with traditional programming approaches, *free text*)?
2. How could AI augment your product functionality (*free text*)?

Some development methodologies (e.g., V model [3]) could already help to reason about the effects that AI has on a system (e.g., through a proper requirements engineering process). In order to make architecturally significant decisions, there exist well-established analysis techniques that predict the influence of decisions on the system in terms of added value and negative side effects:

1. Requirements engineering approach (possible answers: internal brainstorming, internal workshops, discussion with domain experts, requirements exist, *free text*)?
2. How do you currently decide which is the most suitable hardware and software architecture for your product (*free text*)?
3. How do you evaluate new technologies with respect to their influence such is added value (possible answers: SWOT analysis, adequacy check, *free text*)?
4. How do you learn about emerging technologies (possible answers: suppliers, portals, blogs, fairs, conferences, magazines, *free text*).

3.3 Requirements, Limitations, and Decision-Making Process

Some of the most important architectural drivers in embedded software systems are cost, footprint, safety, and security. It is necessary not to disturb these requirements when adopting new technologies. In order to summarize what kind of requirements need to be met and what kind of limitations exist in companies, relevant to adopting AI, we have formulated the following questions:

1. Non-functional quality requirements (possible answers: safety, security, performance, standards, *free text*)?
2. Technical/commercial/organizational constraints (cost, team training, time for understanding software and hardware platforms, *free text*)?

In order to understand what could facilitate the decision-making process, we have created following questions:

1. What could facilitate the decision-making process for AI adoption (possible answers: information about AI in embedded systems, hands-on training, a tailored architecture adequacy check, dedicated consultation, *free text*)?
2. What would you need to understand about AI before adopting it to your system (possible answers: basic functionality of AI, how to design, development and usage of neural networks, data management for neural networks, deployment of neural networks, suitable target platforms, how to evaluate potential benefits of AI, *free text*)?

3.4 Company Profiles

The survey statistics show that we have covered a wide range of company sizes: 1 to 49 employees (15.69%), 50–999 (41.18%), 1000–4999 (23.53%), over 5000 (17.65%), while 1.96% of participants were not sure about their company size.

We are pleased to note that statistic shows that in our survey took part companies from 12 industrial domains (agriculture, automotive, avionics, autonomous machines, computer vision, defence, industrial applications, medical, smart home/city, public sector, energy, IT and Internet of Things (IoT)), covering 14 application fields (research and development, autonomous flying, automotive applications (driving, management), biometric application, image processing and vision, IoT platforms and connectivity, audio equipment, journalism, predictive maintenance, drilling services, energy management systems, lightning systems, industry 4.0 and robotics, medical devices).

4 Survey Results

4.1 Internal Knowledge of AI

The results of the survey show that AI is a technology that draws huge attention in industry (Fig. 1). Only less than 4% of the survey participants (2 companies) were not at all involved at any stage of AI adoption. The results also show that most of the companies are still in early stages of discussing AI and developing solutions based on it (more than 70% of companies are in these two stages, Fig. 1-a). AI is adopted in software systems by 13.73% of the surveyed companies. Very few companies (13.73% of them) consider that they have expert knowledge of AI in their teams (Fig. 1-b). This is an interesting result considering that more than 64% of the companies have dedicated AI experts (Fig. 1-c), and indicates a potential gap between skills that AI experts have and the skills that are needed for applying AI in software industry.

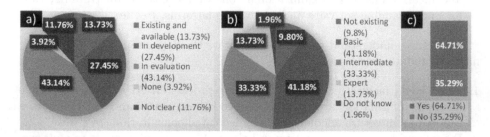

Fig. 1. a) Stage of AI adoption. b) Internal competences and knowledge about AI. c) Presence of dedicated AI experts.

4.2   Expected Benefits from Adopting AI

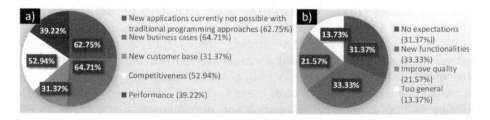

Fig. 2. a) Expected added-value from AI. b) Expected ways in which AI can augment product functionality.

When it comes to the discussion of influence that adopting AI potentially has, most architects are excited about possible benefits. On a higher abstraction level, when discussing general terms in which AI can bring added value (Fig. 2-a), architects mostly see the benefit of AI in enabling new business cases and enabling new applications which are currently not possible with the traditional programming approaches. It is also interesting to note that more than 50% of companies also selected *competitiveness* as the potential added value.

However, when asked about concrete ways in which AI can augment functionality of their system, architects struggled to describe concrete expected benefits. It is important to state that more than 30% of the answers communicated that architects do not see, at the moment, any possibility for AI augmenting functionality in their products, and that they simply do not need AI for that (Fig. 2-b). Furthermore, 13.73% of all answers were too generic (e.g., new functionalities). Other answers we have generalized into two categories. Around 33% of all companies have listed concrete functionalities which they expect AI to enable. These include predictive maintenance, pattern recognition and image processing, decision making, personalized systems, user assistance, and more human-alike functionality. Besides new functionalities, 21.57% of all answers were related to expected improvements in quality of functionality. Expected quality improvements include flexibility, adaptability, overall quality, performance, reduced software and product maintenance costs, efficiency, and improvements of algorithms in terms of increased accuracy while at the same time reducing implementation effort. From these answers we conclude that AI is still a very much misunderstood technology. It has been marketed well and from the marketing perspective practitioners have high expectations (e.g., competitiveness, new business cases). However, when it comes to listing concrete ways in which AI could potentially improve their system, we see that around 45% of the survey participants could not give a concrete answer (either none or too general). Although, theoretically, they see a huge potential of AI, they often do not see what kind of new functionalities this technology can enable, nor how can it increase quality of their products.

4.3   Existing Software Engineering and Architecture Practices

Requirements and architecture drivers are among the first produced artifacts needed for software architecture and describe its problem domain. The results of

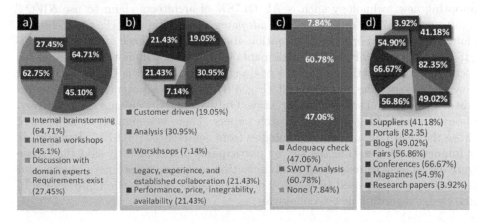

Fig. 3. a) Requirements engineering approach. b) Decisions-making techniques regarding suitable hardware and software technologies. c) Evaluation of influence on architecture when adopting new technologies (e.g, added-value). d) The most common mediums for learning about new technologies.

the survey show that companies have well established requirements engineering processes, and have established engineering practices for making decisions about software and hardware technologies that will help them to meet their requirements (Fig. 3). The results (Fig. 3-a) show that most of the companies use their internal capacities for listing the requirements (64.71% rely of internal brainstorming sessions, and 45.1% on internal workshop). A surprising result, in a positive sense, was that 62.75% of surveyed architects say that they also consult domain experts when formulating requirements for their products. Some of the surveyed companies also receive requirements from their customers (27.45%). When making decisions about appropriate hardware and software technologies (Fig. 3-b), around 30% of surveyed architects claim that they conduct some sort of analysis (e.g., SWOT, run benchmarks, state of the art review). Besides that, 21.43% answers claimed that the decision-making process is driven by software/hardware specifications and their attributes (performance, price, possibility to integrate, and availability). Also, 21.43% answers claimed that for making decisions they rely on established practices (legacy, experience, and established cooperation with suppliers).

Hence, we conclude that requirements engineering is a well-established discipline in the surveyed companies. Furthermore, architects often consult domain experts, which is particularly important for adopting new technologies such as AI. When making decisions about technologies, architects tend to perform certain analysis and make decisions according to general drivers present in this area (e.g., price, performance, legacy, and trustworthiness and reliability of suppliers).

The results of the survey regarding how the survey participants predict consequences of architectural decisions and their influence on software architecture in terms of added value and affected architectural properties (e.g. negative side effects) also indicate that there exist well-established techniques and processes in industry (Fig. 3). When reasoning about influence (e.g., compromising quality properties, potential incompatibility, effort) of an architectural decision of adopting new technology such is AI, 60.78% of architects claim to use *SWOT analysis*, and 47.06% claim to use *adequacy check* (Fig. 3-c). Some architects claim to use both. For more information about *adequacy check* and *SWOT analysis* see Sect. 2.2. Only 7.84% participants said that they do not use any analysis technique for evaluating influences of design decisions such is the adoption of a new technology. The second result (Fig. 3-d) indicates a potential gap between state of the art and state of the practice. Only 3.92% participants claim to learn about new technologies from research papers. There is a significant number of those that learn about new technologies from conferences (66.67%). However, it is important to note that the survey participants predominantly said that these were industrial congresses and rarely scientific conferences. Internet websites and technology portals, used by 82.35% of participants, remain the main source of knowledge regarding new technologies.

4.4 Quality, Technical, Commercial, and Organizational Requirements and Limitations

The survey's results show that the most important quality requirement of interest, when considering AI, is *performance* of the system (74.51% of participants stated so, Fig. 4-a). Besides *performance*, the results show that *safety* is the second most important quality requirement that companies must consider when adopting new technologies, such is AI (68.63% of all participants stated so). Survey participants also stated that, in context of *safety*, it is important to certify a system according to safety standards (e.g., ISO 26262). Besides these two, 56.86% of participants stated that *security* is an important quality requirement they need to consider. Some of the companies also need to consider limitations regarding sharing of personal data and functional safety. Besides these non-functional requirements, the survey participants expressed their concerns regarding time and effort needed for understanding AI-related software platforms (49.02%), understanding AI-related hardware platforms (47.06%), and time that is required to train their team in order to be able to use and integrate these platforms into their projects (45.1%). In that context, 39.22% of companies stated that they are concerned about potential costs that the adoption of AI technology will cause (Fig. 4-b). In summary, around two thirds of surveyed companies are worried how adoption of AI will affect their *performance*. Besides that, companies are worried if they will be able to certify their products due to the lack of AI-related standards, especially those related to *safety*. The results of the survey show that almost every second company is worried about the investment *costs* related to adopting AI.

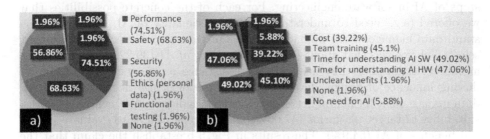

Fig. 4. When adopting AI, there are: a) Non-functional quality requirements that companies need to fulfill; b) Technical, commercial, and organisational constraints.

4.5 Enhancing Decision-Making Process for AI Adoption

In Sect. 4.3, we saw that 47.06% of the survey participants claim to use *adequacy check* when discussing influence of adopting new technologies (Fig. 3-c). However, when asked about what could enhance the decision-making process in order to facilitate the prediction of influence that the adoption of AI will have on a system (Fig. 5-a), majority of the participants (60.78% of them) selected *a tailored adequacy check*. Obviously, the existing adequacy check is not suitable for predicting the influence of adopting AI. Furthermore, the participants stated that they would need more information about how to apply and use AI in embedded systems (45.1%) and that hands-on training on AI technology would help them to assess the influence of AI adoption on their system (47.06%).

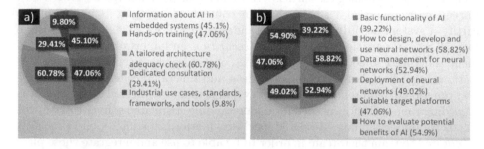

Fig. 5. a) Knowledge and techniques that could (further) facilitate adoption of AI. b) Concrete points that companies need to understand about AI to (further) adopt it.

In order to better understand what kind of concrete information companies would need in order to facilitate the decision making process and adopt AI (or adopt it further, as some surveyed companies have existing and available AI-based solutions), we have asked more concrete questions (Fig. 5-b). It seems that companies are indeed having a lack of knowledge about concrete application steps of AI in software engineering. For each of the concrete possibilities that we offered (e.g., need to understand basic functionality of AI, need to understand data management), we had a significant turn out of selections. The least selected choice was that about *basic functionality of AI* (39.22%). Besides that, architects claim that they need further assistance in understanding and predicting influence of design, development and use of neural networks (58.82%), data management for neural networks (52.94%), deployment of neural networks, suitability of target platforms (47.06%), and in general how to evaluate potential benefits of AI (54.9%). The results in Fig. 5-b establish the claim that the existing analysis techniques for guiding decision-making process and predicting the influence of decisions on software architecture (*SWOT, adequacy check*) are not suitable for exposing influence that AI will have on architecture of software system, because they simply do not capture these technology-specific, yet architecturally disruptive, aspects.

4.6 Survey Results According to the Existing Software Architecture Practices

In Sect. 4.3, we discussed existing software engineering and architecture practices that support engineers and architects when making decisions about adopting new technologies. The results (Fig. 3-c) show that 60.78% of the survey participants use *SWOT analysis*, and 47.06% of them claim to use *adequacy check* when making architectural decisions. While most of them use one or both of these, only 7.84% of the participants do not use any particular analysis.

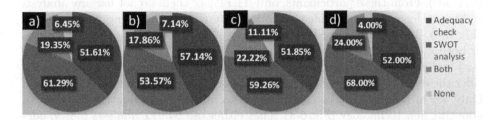

Fig. 6. Use of the existing analysis approaches among participants that consider that they also need: a) A tailored adequacy check for to facilitate adoption of AI. b) To additionally evaluate potential benefits of AI before adopting it. c) To additionally understand data management for neural networks. d) To additionally understand deployment of neural networks.

However, although they use these well-established architectural techniques, the survey participants stated that they need enhanced decision making processes i) to facilitate the adoption of AI, ii) to additionally evaluate potential benefits of AI, iii) to additionally understand data management needed for neural networks, and iv) to additionally understand deployment of neural networks.

When asked about knowledge and techniques that would facilitate the adoption of AI (see Sect. 4.5), 60.78% of the surveyed participants expressed a need for a tailored architecture adequacy check (Fig. 5-a), 45.1% stated that they would need more information about how to apply and use AI in embedded systems, and 47.06% of the survey participants said that hands-on training on AI technology would help them to assess the influence of AI adoption on their system. We focus on tailored architecture adequacy check (i.e., on those 60.78% surveyed participants), as it is the most desired technique and one that fits the best to the scope of architecture activities. Analysis of the survey results (Fig. 6-a) shows that only 6.45% of the participants, which consider that a tailored adequacy check would help them, do not use any analysis for discussing influence of adopting a new technology. Otherwise, all others that stated that they would need a tailored adequacy check is already using some sort of the analysis. From them, 61.29% are already using *SWOT analysis*, 51.61% are using *adequacy check*, and 19.35% are using both of these analyses. However, they still claim the need for a tailored adequacy check.

Existing analysis techniques should be able to guide architects through the process of making new decisions. However, 54.9% of survey participants claim that they need to additionally evaluate potential benefits of AI. From these participants, only 7.14% of them do not use any analysis technique for evaluating added value when it comes to making new decisions (Fig. 6-b). They either use *adequacy check* (57.14%), *SWOT analysis* (53.57%), or both analyses (17.86%). Therefore, we conclude that the existing analysis techniques are not suitable for evaluating additional benefits that AI introduces.

When it comes to data management, required for neural networks, 52.94% of the survey participants claim that they need to analyse this aspect further (Fig. 5-b). From these participants, only 11.11% of them do not use any analysis technique for evaluating added value when it comes to making new decisions (Fig. 6-c). They either use *SWOT analysis* (59.26%), *adequacy check* (51.85%), or both analyses (22.22%).

Finally, 49.02% of the survey participants claim that they need to further consider the effect of deployment of neural networks on their architecture (Fig. 5-b). Only 4% of them do not use any analysis technique for evaluating decisions of adopting new technology (Fig. 6-d). They either use *SWOT analysis* (68%), *adequacy check* (52%), or both analyses (24%). Those companies where AI experts are absent perceive their knowledge of AI as either non existing (27.78%) or basic (72.22%).

4.7   Survey Results According to Internal Knowledge that Companies Have Regarding AI

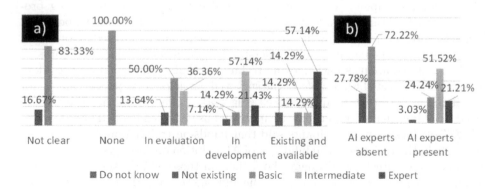

Fig. 7. Internal competences and knowledge about AI (*do not know, not existing, basic, intermediate, expert*) compared with: a) Stage of AI adoption, and b) presence of AI experts.

We have compared the perception that participants have about their internal level of competences and knowledge about AI against phase of adoption of AI (Fig. 7-a), and against presence of AI experts in their enterprises (Fig. 7-b). The results are as one would expect. Around 21% of participants that are in development stage of AI adoption perceive that they have expert knowledge of AI and 57.14% of them perceive that they have intermediate knowledge of AI. Around 57% of participants that work in organisations where AI is already available in systems perceive that they have expert knowledge of AI.

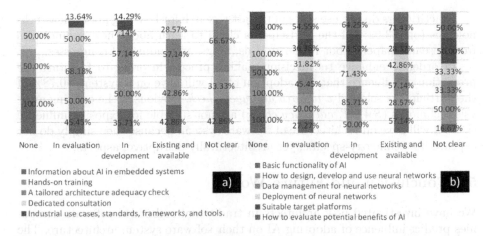

Fig. 8. Comparison between stage of AI adoption (*none, in evaluation, in development, existing and available, not clear*) against: a) Knowledge and techniques that could facilitate adoption of AI, and b) concrete points that companies need to understand about AI for (further) adopting it.

Finally, we have identified what kind of needs exist at different stages of AI adoption (Fig. 8). It is interesting to notice that 57.14% of surveyed participants, which claim to have AI available in their existing systems, stated that tailored adequacy check could help them to further facilitate adoption of AI (Fig. 8-a). Another interesting result is that as companies progress further with AI adoption, there is a greater need to evaluate potential benefits of this technology (Fig. 8-b): 54.55% of surveyed participants that are in evaluation phase of AI adoption said that they need to further understand AI benefits, against 64.29% of those that are in development phase, and 71.43% that are in phase where AI already exists in their systems. These companies might have adopted AI without considering its benefits, or they are struggling to justify benefits of AI adoption, or they are simply trying to find new use cases.

4.8   State of the Practice Summary

Companies that have AI experts perceive their knowledge about AI either mostly as basic (24.24%) and intermediate (51.52%), and expert by only 21.21% of these companies. This indicates a potential gap between skills that AI experts have with the skills that are needed for applying AI in software industry. The results of the survey show that companies have well-established requirements engineering processes, where they often consult domain experts (62.75% of them). Furthermore, they use well-established analysis techniques (*SWOT* and *adequacy check*) before adopting new technologies (only 7.84% participants do not use these). There were no other inputs from architects besides these two analyses.

Practitioners do not use state of the art research for learning about new technologies (only 3.92% of the participants claim to learn about new technologies from research papers), but rather portals, blogs, and industrial congresses.

In order to enhance the decision-making process in order to facilitate the prediction of influence that the adoption of AI will have on a system, 60.78% of the participants selected *a tailored adequacy check*. Obviously, the existing analysis techniques (*SWOT, adequacy check*) are not suitable for exposing influence that AI will have on architecture of software system, because they simply do not capture its technology-specific, yet architecturally disruptive, aspects.

5   Conclusion and Future Work

We have investigated how architects in traditional embedded software companies predict influence of adopting AI on their software system architecture. The results indicate two important challenges. Although companies these days have dedicated AI experts, there is obviously a gap in skills that these experts have with the needs for applying AI in software engineering. The second conclusion is that, although companies often use analysis techniques that should enable prediction of the influence of adopting AI in their systems, there is a need for more tailored analysis techniques that would expose concrete effects that AI adoption has on a system (e.g., drawbacks and benefits of AI adoption), and expose concrete categories in which a company has the lack of knowledge with respect to relevant AI properties, components, and processes. Such exposure would enable engineers and stakeholders in making more adequate decisions about AI adoption. The existing techniques are unable to capture this lack of knowledge and indicate it to architects in a form that would enable them to discard some AI-related decisions as inadequate.

In future, it would be very interesting to analyse dependencies between the stage in which company is when it comes to the adoption of AI with i) the expected added-value and ii) the decision-making process.

References

1. Bacon, L.: Benefits and challenges in the use of big data and AI. In: 2018 19th IEEE/ACIS International Conference on Software Engineering, Artificial Intelligence, Networking and Parallel/Distributed Computing (SNPD), p. 1 (2018)
2. Dasoriya, R., Rajpopat, J., Jamar, R., Maurya, M.: The uncertain future of artificial intelligence. In: 2018 8th International Conference on Cloud Computing, Data Science Engineering (Confluence), pp. 458–461 (2018)
3. Forsberg, K., Mooz, H.: The relationship of system engineering to the project cycle. In: INCOSE International Symposium, vol. 1, no. 1, pp. 57–65 (1991)
4. Ghaffari, K., Soltani Delgosha, M., Abdolvand, N.: Towards cloud computing: a SWOT analysis on its adoption in SMEs. Int. J. Inf. Technol. Converg. Serv. 4 (2014)
5. Kawakami, H., Hiraoka, T.: Contemplating AI technologies from the viewpoint of benefit of inconvenience. In: 2013 Conference on Technologies and Applications of Artificial Intelligence, pp. 335–336 (2013)

6. Kazman, R., Klein, M., Barbacci, M., Longstaff, T., Lipson, H., Carriere, J.: The architecture tradeoff analysis method. In: IEEE International Conference on Engineering of Complex Computer Systems (Cat. No. 98EX193), pp. 68–78 (1998)
7. Knodel, J., Naab, M.: Pragmatic Evaluation of Software Architectures. Springer, Switzerland (2016). https://doi.org/10.1007/978-3-319-34177-4
8. Kolata, G.: How can computers get common sense? Science **217**(4566), 1237–1238 (1982). https://science.sciencemag.org/content/217/4566/1237
9. Koza, J.R., Bennett, F.H., Andre, D., Keane, M.A.: Automated design of both the topology and sizing of analog electrical circuits using genetic programming. In: Gero, J.S., Sudweeks, F. (eds.) Artificial Intelligence in Design '96, pp. 151–170. Springer, Dordrecht (1996). https://doi.org/10.1007/978-94-009-0279-4_9
10. Poole, D., Mackworth, A., Goebel, R.: Computational Intelligence: A Logical Approach (1998)
11. Schawel, C., Billing, F.: Die Top 100 Management Tools, pp. 23–225. Gabler Verlag, Wiesbaden (2004)
12. Yeasmin, S.: Benefits of artificial intelligence in medicine. In: International Conference on Computer Applications Information Security (ICCAIS), pp. 1–6 (2019)

Composition Algorithm Adaptation in Service Oriented Systems

Niranjana Deshpande(iD) and Naveen Sharma(✉)(iD)

Rochester Institute of Technology, Rochester, NY, USA
{nd7896,nxsvse}@rit.edu

Abstract. Architecting and constructing software systems using Service Oriented Architecture (SOA) is a widely employed paradigm. Application functionality is commonly delivered by composing Internet communicable software components or services. Using SOA, applications are constructed by a well-defined composition process that implements composition logic to meet an application's functional and non-functional requirements. Various composition techniques have been proposed in the literature, with varying performance guarantees and resource usage. Service composition also has to adapt to unanticipated conditions posed by a highly dynamic environment due to changing services, evolving architectures, and user requirements. Current adaptive methodologies determine a composition technique at design time and adapt selection and binding of service at runtime. In this paper, we propose adaptation of composition techniques for each user request. Our data driven approach selects the best composition technique for a given application dependency graph. It learns adaptation rules from execution data and trades-off resource usage and solution quality of composition techniques.

Keywords: Service composition · Dynamic algorithm selection · Classifier-based selection

1 Introduction

Service Oriented Architecture (SOA) has become a widely used architectural paradigm in software engineering. Its popularity derives, in part, from its promise to deliver software applications as composable systems by designing and implementing modular software as communicating services. At the heart of actualizing these composable systems lies the service composition process.

Service composition is a complex task due to the following factors. First, service composition is Quality of Service (QoS) driven. This means a service composition technique must efficiently search and carefully select service candidates that not only meet the application's functional requirements but also non-functional QoS objectives satisfying user constraints. Second, the number of third-party services available that implement the same functionality has also dramatically increased [8]. Searching and selecting service candidates from a

© Springer Nature Switzerland AG 2020
H. Muccini et al. (Eds.): ECSA 2020, CCIS 1269, pp. 170–179, 2020.
https://doi.org/10.1007/978-3-030-59155-7_13

large number of services can quickly become time and memory-intensive. Furthermore, during an application's lifecycle, services evolve leading to changes in QoS that result in unexpected overall application behavior that is difficult to trace and correct manually [21]. Third, application functionality may also evolve at runtime, changing overall functional requirements. Thus, changing user needs and services make service composition a dynamic task. Software composition must adapt quickly and efficiently to meet user expectations.

Due to the dynamic nature of composition, it is not possible to anticipate how individual services may change and what effect their evolution has on overall global performance [18]. Thus, adaptation is necessary. Current adaptive methodologies [9,10,15] address QoS driven service composition by determining a composition technique to be used statically at design time and adapting local service selection and binding at runtime. Additionally, adaptation occurs at an individual service level using a set of predetermined rules and decision points. Current approaches do not consider adapting composition algorithms at runtime to save resources.

Given a wide variety of available service composition methods [16], we focus on this question: how can we determine the right method for a given service composition task? We postulate that the right method is the one that meets application QoS while managing compute resources needed for execution. Our goal is to improve composition using a data-driven classifier trained on past execution data that proactively selects the most appropriate composition algorithm for the current user request, learns adaptation rules from execution data to meet user QoS requirements and saves time and memory resource usage used for composition. We present preliminary results for our adaptive selection approach and report time and memory savings while meeting QoS requirements.

2 Related Work

Current adaptive service composition literature discusses different approaches to achieve QoS based SOA adaptation - some present new composition algorithms while others outline systems approaches for adaptation. Various adaptive composition algorithms are discussed in [13,16,22–24]. Each composition algorithm has different performance guarantees and uses different computational resources, so our approach outlines how to adaptively pick between several available composition algorithms for each user request.

Several QoS driven approaches have been proposed for self-adaptation of SOA systems [1,3–7,11,14,19,22]. While many self-adaptive QoS driven approaches for SOA systems [3,5–7,19] use service selection to adapt to changes in the environment, [4,22] propose techniques for architectural adaptation by dynamically adapting coordination patterns. Some current approaches for QoS driven composition such as [10,11,21] present platforms which use both service selection and dynamic coordination pattern selection as adaptation mechanisms.

MOSES [10] addresses adaptation at the individual and composite services by triggering adaptation reactively. The composition technique is a Linear Programming (LP) optimization algorithm chosen at design time. While LP algorithms provide optimal results, they can easily become resource intensive for larger compositions; different algorithms can be used for different user requests. Another approach, QoSMOS [9], maps composite services to abstract services and allocates resources to services for execution depending on desired solution quality. It does not consider resources consumed by the choice of composition algorithm - which is an important consideration. Our approach focuses on selection of the appropriate composition algorithm and proactively adapts the same to meet QoS and compute resource requirements.

The methods discussed above address adaptation at the service or workflow level but do not change the core composition mechanism. With such varied service composition approaches proposed, we focus on selecting the right technique at runtime for optimal composition. Composition technique selection depending on the complexity of composition and compute resources available has shown to provide solutions that meet user QoS requirements and have resource savings in [20]. In [20], the authors propose dynamic selection of composition algorithms to minimize processing time for submitted user requests. They do not propose adaptation, rather their focus is on recommending algorithms for a set of manually submitted batched user requests once invoked. Their approach minimizes processing time of batched user requests which is not indicative of real-time processing, making it less precise compared to adaptation on a per-request basis. Also, due to the highly dynamic service nature of composition environment, a scalable, runtime system is required to service user requests [8]. Our approach explicitly factors in memory and time requirements of individual algorithms along with user QoS constraints for individual requests.

Approaches for testing self-adaptive capabilities of SOA systems are presented in [14,17]. While [14] outlines an approach to testing how fault tolerant an adaptive SOA system is by injecting faults, in [17], details are provided about building in self-testing into applications allowing for validation at runtime. While recognizing the importance of runtime validation, in this paper, we do not focus on validation. We propose a new adaptation mechanism by choosing an appropriate composition algorithm for a user request keeping in mind environmental conditions. By proactively selecting the composition algorithm for each user request, we explicitly allow for trade offs between computational overhead and solution quality based on changing dependency graph characteristics, services and user constraints.

3   Solution Overview

Our main goal is to provide the best suited composition technique for each user request. The best suited composition technique is one that meets user QoS specifications within the time and memory resource alloted to it. Figure 1 shows a high level system overview. A user sends a request characterized by the minimum QoS requirements for the composed application to meet. A dependency graph depicting application functionality as a sequence of abstract tasks is assigned by the system based on the nature of each request. The system also allocates time and memory resources for the composition algorithm to use. These are gathered and sent to the composition algorithm selector which chooses from a portfolio of available algorithms. The selector proactively adapts which composition algorithm is to be used for each user request, by modeling performance of each algorithm and predicting the best possible algorithm given current context. Once a selection is made, the composition executor uses registered services to complete the user request.

3.1   Composition Algorithm Adaptation

As our main goal is to select the best suited composition algorithm, so we start by implementing a portfolio of algorithms. We run the algorithms on simulated user requests to collect data about their performance. This data is used by a data-driven selector to make decisions at runtime. We use a classifier trained on labeled data and evaluate its performance. These steps are described in detail next.

Portfolio of Algorithms. We implement 3 popular service composition algorithms - Multi Constrained Shortest Path (MCSP) [23], Ant Colony System(ACS) [24] and Genetic Algorithm (GA) [20]. Each belongs to a different class of algorithms used to solve service composition, using variable compute resources depending on desired solution quality. We use a grid search for ACS and GA hyper-parameters to determine the best performing configuration for each request. ACS, GA and MCSP use the L_p metric discussed in [24] as a utility function. The L_p metric measures utility of a calculated solution with respect to the optimal solution. It unifies all QoS metrics into a single quantity making it easier to understand. To simulate user requests, we generate sets of random QoS requirements and randomly assign dependency graphs. Each abstract task

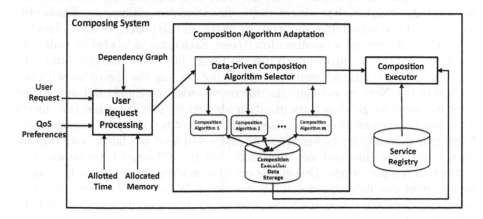

Fig. 1. High level system overview

in the dependency graph has its own concrete implementations of services. So, to simulate concrete service QoS metrics, we randomly sample the QWS [2] dataset. Each service is associated with 8 QoS metrics from the QWS dataset: response time, latency, reliability, availability, successability, compliance, best practices and throughput. Each attribute is weighted differently depending on user preferences. We generate weights for each of these attributes and compute resource allocations randomly. Thus, each composition algorithm receives a dependency graph, user QoS requirements, QoS weights and a set of concrete service QoS metrics to choose from. A composition algorithm selects a set of concrete service each corresponding to abstract service in the dependency graph such that it fills user requirements.

Training Classifiers. We choose classifiers as the data-driven composition algorithm selector component. As a machine learning based approach it learns trade-off rules from the data itself. By providing labels, we guide the classifier to arrive at the correct conclusion. Developers can guide the system to prioritize their requirements by changing labeling schemas. So, we empirically evaluate popular classifiers such as Support Vector Machines (SVMs), random forests, Logistic Regression and Discriminant Analyses. A grid search determines the best hyperparameters for each classifier. We select this subset of classifiers as they provide a good breadth of types of relationships that can be modeled between features. To evaluate classifiers, 5-fold cross-validation was performed along with a grid search for hyperparameters. A 70–30 train test split was used on a shuffled dataset to train the data and evaluate its accuracy. Time and memory resources were randomly assigned to each request. The test set is used to evaluate performance after a classifier is picked in Sect. 4.

Dataset Creation. Composition algorithm execution yields information about its performance. As seen from Algorithm 1 each dataset entry records composition algorithm used, original user and computed solution QoS requirements, assigned QoS weights, dependency graph characteristics, delivered solution utility, assigned and actual time and memory usage. In this paper, we use a classifier to decide which composition algorithm to use. Each entry is labeled according to the best composition algorithm to use. To assign labels, we first determine the algorithms that fulfill QoS requirements. If not, we use the algorithm with the highest utility. Next, we calculate the difference between assigned and actual time (and memory) usage of each composition algorithm. The algorithm that meets user requirements and best minimizes atleast one of two compute resources differences is chosen to be the algorithm of choice and used as a label. Note that we do not minimize time and memory usage, but the difference between assigned and actual resource usage. This allows our chosen algorithm to adapt flexibly as each request can be assigned variable resources. We use the labeled dataset to train classifiers and determine which one to use based on its accuracy and the F1 score.

Algorithm 1: Processing Historical Data Input to Classifier

Output: Trained classifier, $CLASSIFIER$
Function CLASSIFIERDATASET:

    for *each $UReq \in HistData$* **do**
        $W_{UReq} \leftarrow (num_{abs}, num_{cand})$
        $\overrightarrow{c\_res}_{UReq} \leftarrow (t_{assgn}, m_{assgn})$
        $w_{UReq} \leftarrow (w^1, w^2, ...w^n)$
        for $m \in compositionPortfolio$ **do**
            $utility \leftarrow funcLp(q_{sol}, q_{req})$
            $t \leftarrow t_m - t_{assgn}$
            $mem \leftarrow mem_m - mem_{assgn}$
            $datum \leftarrow (q_{req}, t, m, W_{UReq}, w_{UReq}, m)$
            $dataset \leftarrow dataset \cup datum$
        end
    end
    $labelled\_data \leftarrow getLabels(dataset)$
    $CLASSIFIER \leftarrow train(labelled\_data)$

---

4 Experimental Evaluation

To evaluate how well classifier-based selection performs, we simulate test sets of user requests randomly and randomly assign time and memory resources. We compare time and memory usage of the classifier-picked composition algorithm versus a naively picked algorithm that picks only based on solution utility. As our approach picks the algorithm meeting user constraints or the next best algorithm in case one is not available, we compare based on computational resources. We measure percentage of time and memory saved per request using both choices and report average values.

Collecting Composition Algorithm Execution Data. To collect execution data each composition algorithm is executed on randomly generated user requests. We implement three composition algorithms - MCSP [23], ACS [24] and GA [20]. Inputs to each composition algorithm are users constraints, weights corresponding to QoS preferences, an assigned dependency graph and randomly assigned time and memory resources. User constraints were randomly generated for each of the 8 QoS attributes as described previously. Dependency graphs of different sizes and structures were considered. Graphs having number of abstract services in [5, 10, 20, 30, 40] and number of candidate services in [5, 10, 15, 20, 25, 30, 35, 40] having three structures, sequential, structured and fully connected as described in [12], were generated. Each combination was tested and evaluated with different weights corresponding to each QoS attribute. The collected dataset is shuffled and split 70–30, 70% of it is used for training the classifier and 30% is used to test and evaluate classifier-based adaptation approach performance. Collected data is shuffled and split multiple times to give different train and test sets for variability. Multiple evaluations on test sets gives an accurate estimate of both individual classifier and classifier-based adaptation performance.

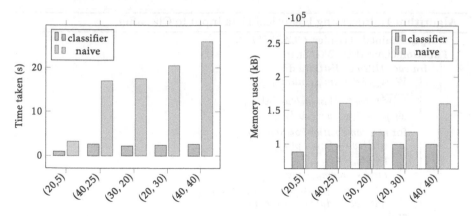

Fig. 2. Compute resources utilized by composition algorithm if chosen by our approach vs a naive approach

Classifier Selection. To select an appropriate classifier for our application, we empirically evaluate some popular options as seen from Table 1. Based on the results from Table 1, the top performing classifiers were Random Forest, Decision Tree and QDA. As seen from Table 1, Random Forest demonstrates good accuracy and F1-score. A high F1-score indicates that a classifier can correctly identify true positives, even in situations where there may be a class imbalance, making for a stable classifier. Thus, Random Forest is used for selecting composition algorithms. Random Forest uses 200 trees, a maximum depth of 6 and entropy as a splitting criterion.

Classifier-Based Adaptation Approach Performance. For our preliminary results, we implement three popular composition algorithms from existing literature and train a classifier to choose an appropriate composition technique per user request. To assess our technique's performance, we evaluate the percentage of time and memory resources saved by our classifier-based approach compared to a purely naive approach. The naive approach makes selections based purely on the expected solution utility, that is, it picks the composition algorithm that provides the highest possible utility. Our classifier considers expected solution utility, time and memory resources to select the composition algorithm. The classifier selects the composition algorithm that meets user requirements. In case none of the available algorithms can meet user requirements, it selects one

Table 1. Classifier accuracies

Classifier	Accuracy	F1 score	Classifier	Accuracy	F1 score
Random Forest	0.95	0.94	Logistic Regression	0.88	0.88
Decision Tree	0.94	0.93	SVM with rbf kernel	0.51	0.39
QDA	0.92	0.92	SVM with sigmoid kernel	0.52	0.35

that gives the best possible utility for a request. Hence, we evaluate performance based on gains in time and memory utilization. Figure 2 shows time and memory that would be utilized by a selected composition algorithm if chosen by a naive selector versus our approach. In the figure, we visualize compute resource usage for variably sized dependency graphs. Dependency graphs are characterized by a tuple (#abstract services, #candidate services per abstract service) Overall, considerable compute savings are observed. Using random forest as a classifier, we observed on average, 33% of time was saved compared to a naive approach across the requests we tested our approach on. We saw a similar savings in memory used, 24.8 %. These results indicate that our approach is able to select appropriate composition algorithms for unique user requests. Thus, our approach picks the a composition approach that delivers on user QoS requirements while using the resources allocated to it.

Composition Algorithm Selection Overhead. The selection algorithm itself takes negligible time to pick between different approaches. If we were to consider the total request processing time as a sum of the time taken to select a composition algorithm and execute it, the selection itself takes less than 1% of total processing time on average, which is negligible. Other overheads associated are time and memory resources used by the classifier, which are also negligible as compared to resources used for composition. Note that our classifier requires a labeled dataset.

5   Conclusion and Future Work.

In this work, we outline a data-driven approach for composition algorithm adaptation. Our classifier-based approach learns adaptation rules from past execution data and shows 95% accuracy on a random training dataset. Preliminary results demonstrate considerable compute resource savings for various solution utility requirements. We assume that changes in a dynamic environment are reflected in composition algorithm performance, so we will expand our experiments to more closely simulate more diverse user requests - in terms of dependency graphs and constraints. A limitation of using classifiers is the requirement of labels, which requires additional processing. In the future, we will expand our experiments to include other types of learning algorithms that do not require labels. In addition to this, we will deploy our approach as an online feedback loop to be used at runtime. More diverse composition algorithms will also be added, to analyze the bounds of scalability of our approach.

Acknowledgements. This material is based upon work supported by the National Science Foundation under Award No. 1943002.

References

1. Al-Helal, H., Gamble, R.: Introducing replaceability into web service composition. IEEE Trans. Serv. Comput. **7**(2), 198–209 (2014). https://doi.org/10.1109/TSC.2013.23
2. Al-Masri, E., Mahmoud, Q.H.: QoS-based discovery and ranking of web services. In: 2007 16th International Conference on Computer Communications and Networks, pp. 529–534, August 2007. https://doi.org/10.1109/ICCCN.2007.4317873
3. Ali, N., Solis, C.: Self-adaptation to mobile resources in service oriented architecture. In: 2015 IEEE International Conference on Mobile Services, pp. 407–414, June 2015. https://doi.org/10.1109/MobServ.2015.62
4. Alrifai, M., Risse, T.: Combining global optimization with local selection for efficient QoS-aware service composition. In: Proceedings of the 18th International Conference on World Wide Web, WWW 2009, p. 881–890. Association for Computing Machinery, New York (2009). https://doi.org/10.1145/1526709.1526828
5. Ardagna, D., Baresi, L., Comai, S., Comuzzi, M., Pernici, B.: A service-based framework for flexible business processes. IEEE Softw. **28**(2), 61–67 (2011)
6. Ardagna, D., Pernici, B.: Adaptive service composition in flexible processes. IEEE Trans. Softw. Eng. **33**(6), 369–384 (2007)
7. Ardagna, D., Mirandola, R.: Per-flow optimal service selection for web services based processes. J. Syst. Softw. **83**(8), 1512–1523 (2010). https://doi.org/10.1016/j.jss.2010.03.045. http://www.sciencedirect.com/science/article/pii/S0164121210000750. Performance Evaluation and Optimization of Ubiquitous Computing and Networked Systems
8. Bouguettaya, A., et al.: A service computing manifesto: the next 10 years. Commun. ACM **60**(4), 64–72 (2017). http://doi.acm.org/10.1145/2983528
9. Calinescu, R., Grunske, L., Kwiatkowska, M., Mirandola, R., Tamburrelli, G.: Dynamic QoS management and optimization in service-based systems. IEEE Trans. Softw. Eng. **37**(3), 387–409 (2011). https://doi.org/10.1109/TSE.2010.92
10. Cardellini, V., Casalicchio, E., Grassi, V., Iannucci, S., Lo Presti, F., Mirandola, R.: MOSES: a platform for experimenting with QoS-driven self-adaptation policies for service oriented systems. In: de Lemos, R., Garlan, D., Ghezzi, C., Giese, H. (eds.) Software Engineering for Self-Adaptive Systems III. Assurances. LNCS, vol. 9640, pp. 409–433. Springer, Cham (2017). https://doi.org/10.1007/978-3-319-74183-3_14
11. Cardellini, V., Casalicchio, E., Grassi, V., Lo Presti, F., Mirandola, R.: Towards self-adaptation for dependable service-oriented systems. In: de Lemos, R., Fabre, J.-C., Gacek, C., Gadducci, F., ter Beek, M. (eds.) WADS 2008. LNCS, vol. 5835, pp. 24–48. Springer, Heidelberg (2009). https://doi.org/10.1007/978-3-642-10248-6_2
12. Cardoso, J.: Approaches to compute workflow complexity. In: Leymann, F., Reisig, W., Thatte, S.R., van der Aalst, W. (eds.) The Role of Business Processes in Service Oriented Architectures. No. 06291 in Dagstuhl Seminar Proceedings, Internationales Begegnungs- und Forschungszentrum für Informatik (IBFI), Schloss Dagstuhl, Germany, Dagstuhl, Germany (2006). http://drops.dagstuhl.de/opus/volltexte/2006/821
13. Cho, J., Ko, H., Ko, I.: Adaptive service selection according to the service density in multiple qos aspects. IEEE Trans. Serv. Comput. **9**(6), 883–894 (2016). https://doi.org/10.1109/TSC.2015.2428251

14. Fugini, M.G., Pernici, B., Ramoni, F.: Quality analysis of composed services through fault injection. Inf. Syst. Front. **11**(3), 227–239 (2009)
15. Gomaa, H., Hashimoto, K., Kim, M., Malek, S., Menascé, D.A.: Software adaptation patterns for service-oriented architectures. In: Proceedings of the 2010 ACM Symposium on Applied Computing, SAC 2010, pp. 462–469. ACM, New York (2010). http://doi.acm.org/10.1145/1774088.1774185
16. Jatoth, C., Gangadharan, G., Buyya, R.: Computational intelligence based QoS-aware web service composition: a systematic literature review. IEEE Trans. Serv. Comput. **10**(03), 475–492 (2017). https://doi.org/10.1109/TSC.2015.2473840
17. King, T., Ramirez, A., Rodolfo, C., Clarke, P.: An integrated self-testing framework for autonomic computing systems. J. Comput. **2** (2007). https://doi.org/10.4304/jcp.2.9.37-49
18. Mutanu, L.: State of runtime adaptation in service-oriented systems: what, where, when, how and right. IET Softw. **13**, 14–24 (2019). https://digital-library.theiet.org/content/journals/10.1049/iet-sen.2018.5028
19. Schuller, D., Siebenhaar, M., Hans, R., Wenge, O., Steinmetz, R., Schulte, S.: Towards heuristic optimization of complex service-based workflows for stochastic QoS attributes. In: 2014 IEEE International Conference on Web Services, pp. 361–368 (2014)
20. Trummer, I., Faltings, B.: Dynamically selecting composition algorithms for economical composition as a service. In: Kappel, G., Maamar, Z., Motahari-Nezhad, H.R. (eds.) ICSOC 2011. LNCS, vol. 7084, pp. 513–522. Springer, Heidelberg (2011). https://doi.org/10.1007/978-3-642-25535-9_36
21. Wang, H., et al.: Integrating reinforcement learning with multi-agent techniques for adaptive service composition. ACM Trans. Auton. Adapt. Syst. **12**(2), 81–842 (2017). https://doi.org/10.1145/3058592. http://doi.acm.org/10.1145/3058592
22. Wang, L., Li, Q.: A multiagent-based framework for self-adaptive software with search-based optimization. In: 2016 IEEE International Conference on Software Maintenance and Evolution (ICSME), pp. 621–625, October 2016. https://doi.org/10.1109/ICSME.2016.16
23. Yu, T., Zhang, Y., Lin, K.J.: Efficient algorithms for web services selection with end-to-end QoS constraints. ACM Trans. Web **1**(1) (2007). http://doi.acm.org/10.1145/1232722.1232728
24. Zhang, W., Chang, C.K., Feng, T., Jiang, H.y.: QoS-based dynamic web service composition with ant colony optimization. In: 2010 IEEE 34th Annual Computer Software and Applications Conference (COMPSAC), pp. 493–502. IEEE (2010)

A Statistical Approach for Context-Awareness of Mobile Applications

Mai Abusair[1]([✉]), Mohammad Sharaf[1], Antinisca Di Marco[2],
and Paola Inverardi[2]

[1] An-Najah National University, Nablus, Palestine
{mabuseir,sharaf}@najah.edu
[2] University of L'Aquila, L'Aquila, Italy
{antinisca.dimarco,paola.inverardi}@univaq.it

Abstract. Context-aware systems are able to sense and adapt to the
environment. Mobile applications can benefit from context-awareness
since they incur to context changes during their execution. A detailed
understanding of the context is needed to know what a context-aware
system should sense and adapt to. This paper introduces a statistical
approach that helps in determining contextual situations that require
adaptation. The approach starts from monitoring mobile context variables values, modeling their states, and deducing from these models a
Markov chain model, where each state represents a contextual situation.
Depending on transition probabilities and system quality at each state
we can decide when it is necessary to apply context-awareness.

Keywords: Context-awareness · Contextual situation · Transition
probability

1 Introduction

Nowadays, most software systems adapt their behavior according to their context. Mobile applications have a huge context variability due to user mobility, diverse user preferences, and device capabilities. Context-awareness (that
leads to adaptation) have a great effect on the qualities of software systems, like
availability [2,13]. Therefore, in designing a system that is context-aware, only
relevant part of this environment (i.e. context) is considered. Determining the
relevant context is not easy. The complexity of the environment may involve
an enormous possibly relevant context. Accordingly, an approach is needed to
decide the context to be considered in designing context-aware systems [8,10].

In [3], we deal with understanding context variability. In particular, we introduce an empirical approach, based on an Android mobile application, that monitors the mobile phone context variables, and, by analyzing the monitored data, is
able to model the *context variables* and the *contextual situations* as UML State

© Springer Nature Switzerland AG 2020
H. Muccini et al. (Eds.): ECSA 2020, CCIS 1269, pp. 180–194, 2020.
https://doi.org/10.1007/978-3-030-59155-7_14

charts. In [2,13], we use *contextual situations* to analyze at each state the mobile application behaviors in terms of service availability and user satisfaction, and to determine consequently the appropriate adaptation strategy at each *contextual situation.*

This paper extends our work in [3]. It proposes a statistical approach, that after extracting the *contextual situations* from the mobile context variability, it builds a Markov chain model where each state represents a *contextual situation.* It computes the transition probability matrix for the different states. *The contextual situations* that receive more frequent transitions probabilities are candidates for applying adaptations at their state. The approach aims to save the effort of applying unnecessary adaptations, and, thus, mobile resources can be used more efficiently.

This paper is organized as follows: Sect. 2 presents a brief background, while Sect. 3 introduces the statistical approach. The approach is evaluated in a scenario described in Sect. 4. Finally, Sect. 5 concludes the paper.

2   Background

The recently developed software systems never stands on their own but they are connected to their environment. Context-aware applications require knowledge not only about user's current environment (e.g., location, time, or if the user is in quiet or noisy environment), but also about the specifications of the computing devices and resources being used (e.g, mobile device or notebook) [7,11]. Context-aware applications might also require knowledge about user's social situations (e.g., manager or co-worker). The application then adapts the Quality of Service or the presentation of information offered to the users according to the current context [2,4,13].

In the following sections, we briefly describe the context concepts and modeling, in Sects. 2.1 and 2.2, respectively.

2.1   Context Concepts

Context is defined in [1] as *"any information that can be used to characterize the situation of any person, place or object that is considered relevant to the interaction between a user and an application, including the user and application themselves"*. Context encompasses information like time, location, lighting, noise level, network capabilities and user status.

The context variability can be described using context concepts detailed in [3]. Recalling our work in [3], a *context variable* C can have several values *val,* these values can be discrete or can take a range of values. The *context variable* C general formula can be written as [9]:

$C \in \{val_1, val_2, ... val_z\}$ for discrete values

or

$C \in \{ [val_a, val_b], [val_c, val_d], .. \}$ for range of values

For instance, if B represents battery level, CN network connectivity, and LL light level. Then these *context variables* can be written as:

B $\in$ {SufficientBattery, NoSufficientBattery}
CN $\in$ {AvailableConnectivity, NoAvailableConnectivity}
LL $\in$ $\{[0, 150), [150, 300), [300, 1000), [1000, 10000]\}$

A *contextual situation* S can be defined by a group of *context variables* C and their values, under which a system will eventually run. If a *contextual situation* S is defined by x *context variables* C then S will be denoted as:

$$S = \{C_1(val_{C_1}), C_2(val_{C_2}), ..., C_x(val_{C_x})\}$$

Since each *context variable* C has different values val_C, different *contextual situations* may result from the same group of context variables. For instance, let us consider a *contextual situation* defined by battery state B and connectivity CN as described in the previous section, then possible *contextual situations* will be:

$S_1 = $ {B(SufficientBattery), CN(AvailableConnectivity)},
$S_2 = $ {B(SufficientBattery), CN(NoAvailableConnectivity)},
$S_3 = $ {B(NoSufficientBattery), CN(AvailableConnectivity)},
$S_4 = $ {B(NoSufficientBattery), CN(NoAvailableConnectivity)}

2.2   Context Modeling Approach

Modeling context variability is needed to understand the system environment. Our empirical approach, previously suggested in [3], is devised to model the context. The approach aims to derive the *contextual situations* from a context sensing application. The context sensing application can be any tool that is able to monitor a group of required *context variables* and collect their values while the device is running.

The approach [3] encompasses a group of steps: The first step of the approach requires to run the Android mobile application, namely *Context Sensing Application* (CSA), to sense *context variables*. In the second step, the collected data are shared and stored for analysis. The third step of the approach deals with the analysis of monitored data to build statechart models for each *context variables*, separately. Such models describe the *context variables'* states (represented by single values or range of values) and the probability to move from one state to another. The devised statecharts describe the evolution of the *context variables* over time. In the forth step, such *context variables'* models are lumped together and thus allows to realize the different *contextual situations* that might occur.

3   Statistical Approach for Context-Awareness

In this Section we will describe our statistical method that aims to realize the relevant context in designing context-aware mobile applications. The approach starts by reasoning on monitored *context variables* values to extract their possible states, detailed in Sect. 3.1. Then, from the *context variables* states, the *contextual situations* are deduced and formulated in a Markov chain model where each state represents a *contextual situation*, detailed in Sect. 3.2. After all, the transition probability matrix is computed, and by reasoning on its values, the candidates states to context-awareness are determined according to transitions probabilities received and their effect on the Quality of Service, detailed in Sect. 3.3. Figure 1 summarizes the approach.

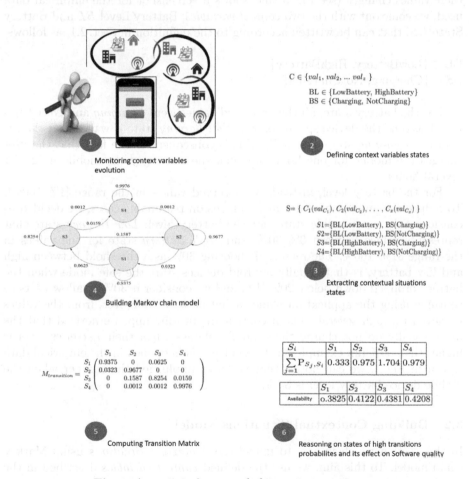

$C \in \{val_1, val_2, \ldots val_z\}$

$BL \in \{\text{LowBattery, HighBattery}\}$
$BS \in \{\text{Charging, NotCharging}\}$

1 Monitoring context variables evolution

2 Defining context variables states

$S = \{C_1(val_{C_1}), C_2(val_{C_2}), \ldots, C_z(val_{C_z})\}$

$S1 = \{BL(\text{LowBattery}), BS(\text{Charging})\}$
$S2 = \{BL(\text{LowBattery}), BS(\text{NotCharging})\}$
$S3 = \{BL(\text{HighBattery}), BS(\text{Charging})\}$
$S4 = \{BL(\text{HighBattery}), BS(\text{NotCharging})\}$

3 Extracting contextual situations states

4 Building Markov chain model

$$M_{transition} = \begin{array}{c} \\ S_1 \\ S_2 \\ S_3 \\ S_4 \end{array} \begin{array}{cccc} S_1 & S_2 & S_3 & S_4 \\ \left(\begin{array}{cccc} 0.9375 & 0 & 0.0625 & 0 \\ 0.0323 & 0.9677 & 0 & 0 \\ 0 & 0.1587 & 0.8254 & 0.0159 \\ 0 & 0.0012 & 0.0012 & 0.9976 \end{array}\right) \end{array}$$

S_i	S_1	S_2	S_3	S_4
$\sum_{j=1}^{n} P_{S_j,S_i}$	0.333	0.975	1.704	0.979

	S_1	S_2	S_3	S_4
Availability	0.3825	0.4122	0.4381	0.4208

5 Computing Transition Matrix

6 Reasoning on states of high transitions probabilites and its effect on Software quality

Fig. 1. A statistical approach for context-awareness

3.1   Defining Context Variables States

To define the *context variables* of a mobile application, we run a context sensing application to monitor and log the *context variables* values (we can use the app adopted in [3] or any other available app). Then, by applying analytical reasoning on the collected data, we can define the *context variables* states.

For simplicity, we show how *context variables* are defined using simple example. Recalling to what we have in [3], we show two *context variables* evolution, namely battery state and level. To define the *context variables*, the user was asked to run a context sensing application in the background of her mobile phone for one week. Then, the context log file is extracted. By analyzing the log file values, concentrating on the battery level and battery state values, and by reasoning on their values changes (see Fig. 3 that shows a screenshot for the empirical data used, we come out with the two *context variables*, Battery Level BL and Battery State BS, that can be written according to the definition in Sect. 2.1, as follows:

BL ∈ {LowBattery, HighBattery}
BS ∈ {Charging, NotCharging}

For the battery state, all the extracted values were *Charging* and *NotCharging*. The time the device spends on the *NotCharging* state is way longer than it is in the *Charging* state. Normally, this is consequent of the fact that the user charges the mobile for one hour and then she can enjoy the mobile usage for several hours.

For the battery level, instead, we observed values in the range [1%, 100%]. To reduce the number of states and to focus on reasonable cases, we decided to consider only two possible states for the battery level: *Low Battery* state that represents values between 0%–30%: and *High Battery* state for the values in the range 31%–100%. The reason of choosing 30% as a threshold between high and low battery, is that usually android devices start the safe mode when the battery dropped down below 20% [12], and we consider it 30% to allow users to continue using the application while saving battery. Moreover, from the values retrieved through several runs of context monitoring app, we noticed that the users usually do not charge their mobile phones when their batteries level is higher than 30% (an example on this evidence is happened in the empirical data shown in Fig. 3, we can notice that the user unplugged the charger when the mobile device battery level is 34%).

3.2   Building Contextual Situations Model

In this section we show how to model the *contextual situations* using Markov chain model. To this aim, we use the defined *context variables* described in the previous section to deduce the different *contextual situations*.

Accordingly, each state in the Markov chain model represents a super state that obtained from a combination of a certain number of *context variables* states (in this example the two states for battery level and battery state). The resulted

Markov chain model, called *contextual situation* model, models the run-time context evolution of a mobile context-aware software system.

We should note that sometimes not all the combinations are allowed, some *context variables* values cannot be met together (for example to have no internet connection and the ping process is success). Therefore, in order to build a consistent unique *contextual situation* model, only *contextual situation* that are feasible combinations of *context variables* states have to be considered. The feasibility of these combinations can be noticed by reasoning on the retrieved log file values.

Therefore, by considering the two *context variables*, Battery Level *BL* and Battery State *BS*, described in the previous section, we can deduce up to four different *contextual situations*. These are:

$S1 = \{$BL(LowBattery), BS(Charging)$\}$
$S2 = \{$BL(LowBattery), BS(NotCharging)$\}$
$S3 = \{$BL(HighBattery), BS(Charging)$\}$
$S4 = \{$BL(HighBattery), BS(NotCharging)$\}$

Thus, the Markov chain model will have four states (S1, S2, S3, S4). The transitions probability for these states are computed using the following formula [3]:

$$p_{s_i,s_j} = \frac{\#(v_i \to v_j)}{\#(v_i \to v_k) + \#(v_i \to v_j)} \tag{1}$$

where:

$\#(v_i \to v_j)$ represents the number of subsequent pair of records reporting in the first a value v_i falling into the state s_i and in the second a value v_j falling into the state s_j; $\#(v_i \to v_k)$, where k! = j, represents the number of subsequent pair of records reporting in the first a value v_i falling into the state s_i and in the second a value v_k falling in any state excluding s_j.

The probability to remain in the state s_i is set to $p_{s_i,s_i} = 1 - Sum(p_{s_i,s_j})$ where j is different from i. Figure 2 shows a simple example for computing transitions probabilities from context records, supposing the concern is to track simple network information every one hour.

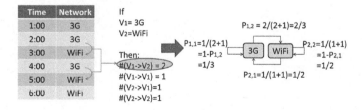

Fig. 2. An example on computing transition probabilities

Figure 3 has a screenshot for our extracted empirical data, that shows examples of some considered *contextual situations* state transitions (*contextual situations* states are represented using solid rounded rectangles). Figure 4 shows the *contextual situations* state transitions probabilities deduced from the values retrieved from the user running context sensing application.

3.3 Computing Transition Matrix

The Markov chain produced for the *contextual situations* is described using a transition matrix. By reasoning on the matrix values we are able to determine the *contextual situations* that receive high transitions probabilities.

Going back to the example illustrated in the previous section, and according to the *contextual situations* model produced Fig. 4, we build a transition matrix as follows:

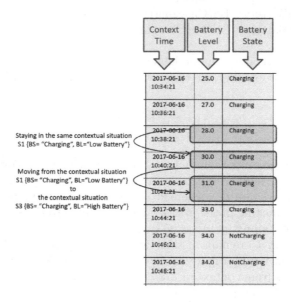

Fig. 3. Examples on contextual situations state transitions

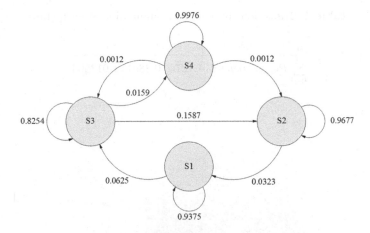

Fig. 4. Contextual situation Markov model for battery state and level

$$
M_{transition} = \begin{array}{c} \\ S_1 \\ S_2 \\ S_3 \\ S_4 \end{array}
\begin{array}{cccc}
S_1 & S_2 & S_3 & S_4 \\
\left(\begin{array}{cccc}
0.9375 & 0 & 0.0625 & 0 \\
0.0323 & 0.9677 & 0 & 0 \\
0 & 0.1587 & 0.8254 & 0.0159 \\
0 & 0.0012 & 0.0012 & 0.9976
\end{array} \right)
\end{array}
$$

For each *contextual situation* state S_i where $i \in [1, n]$, and n is the number of *contextual situations*, we will find the sum of the transitions probabilities that lead to it, including the transition probability from a state to itself. Table 1 shows the values computed at each state from the probabilities in the transition matrix example.

Accordingly, S_2 state, that represents the *contextual situation* that includes *low battery* and *not charging*, receives the highest transitions probabilities. Following it S_4 state, that represents the *contextual situation* that includes *high battery* and *not charging*. Then, S_1 and S_3, respectively.

The *contextual situations* that receive high transitions probabilities, comparable with other states, are good candidates for applying context-awareness at their states. This will help the analyst to shorten the probable *contextual situations* list for context-awareness. Moving to a given *contextual situation* more often, means that the analyst should take care about this *contextual situation* and its effect on the Quality of Service [6]. While, less frequent transitions to a given *contextual situations*, means that the system can rarely being exposed to this context, and, thus, the analyst can exclude this *contextual situations* from being relevant to context-awareness; making sure this will not have a critical effect on the Quality of Service of a system being studied. See Fig. 5 that summarises the realized relationships among *contextual situations* selection.

Table 1. Transitions probabilities summation at each state

S_i	S_1	S_2	S_3	S_4
$\sum\limits_{k=1}^{n} P_{S_k,S_i}$	0.9698	1.1276	0.8891	1.013504

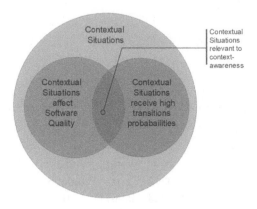

Fig. 5. Contextual situations that are relevant to context-awareness

Thus, referring to our work in [5,13], the Quality of Service must be measured in the different *contextual situations* to ensure it has a noticeable effect on the quality. For example, if the aim of applying context-awareness is to preserve service availability, then, the initially selected *contextual situations* (determined by transitions probabilities) must have noticeable effect on computing service availability in order to be considered in the adaptation strategy. In the following section, we clarify this and the whole approach by running it on a mobile application real example.

4   Running the Approach on OSApp Mobile Application

OSApp is an Android mobile application connected to the "OffSiteArt—Artbridge for L'Aquila" project[1]. The project aims to cover the scaffolding of the buildings in reconstruction after the 2009 earthquake with pieces of art of emergent artists selected under a call for art.

When the user runs the app while moving in the city center, she will have information about the pieces of arts around her as markers on google map. When she clicks on one of such markers, she will receive details of the piece of art and of the artist's biography, as high quality picture and video content [13]

---

[1] http://www.offsiteart.it.

As it is now, OSApp always sends to the user high quality pictures and videos without considering the different contexts under which the application is running due to the user mobility. However, the app may experience different connectivity conditions depending on the different network coverage available in the area; the device running it could have different battery status.

In order to clarify the approach described in Fig. 1, we will run an experiment on OSApp that shows how our statistical approach works.

While running OSApp, we run in the background of the mobile device a context sensing application that is able to monitor several environmental context [3]. After retrieving the log file, for simplicity, we choose to reason on two *context variables*; Network Connectivity (NC) and Battery Level (BL), and we define them with their values as follows:

$NC \in \{ GoodConnectivity, \ PoorConnectivity \}$
$BL \in \{ LowBattery, \ HighBattery \}$

Supposing that, when the download speed is less than 1 MB then NC is poor and when it is higher than 1 MB then NC is good. Also, when BL is less than or equal 30% then BL is low battery and when BL is more than 30% then BL is high battery.

If a *contextual situation* S will be described by the variables BL and NC, then 4 possible *contextual situations* will result:

$S_1 = \{NC(PoorConnectivity), \ BL(LowBattery)\}$
$S_2 = \{NC(PoorConnectivity), \ BL(HighBattery)\}$
$S_3 = \{NC(GoodConnectivity), \ BL(HighBattery)\}$
$S_4 = \{NC(GoodConnectivity), \ BL(LowBattery)\}$

The *contextual situations* model for the four states (S_1, S_2, S_3, S_4) is represented using Markov chain model, see Fig. 6. By reasoning on the log file context values, the transitions probabilities can be computed using the formula in Sect. 3.2.

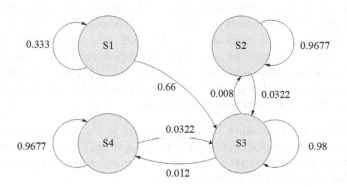

Fig. 6. Contextual situation model for battery level and network connectivity

The transition matrix is computed as follows:

$$M_{transition} = \begin{array}{c} \\ S_1 \\ S_2 \\ S_3 \\ S_4 \end{array} \begin{pmatrix} S_1 & S_2 & S_3 & S_4 \\ 0.333 & 0 & 0.666 & 0 \\ 0 & 0.9677 & 0.0322 & 0 \\ 0 & 0.008 & 0.98 & 0.012 \\ 0 & 0 & 0.0322 & 0.967 \end{pmatrix}$$

For each state we will find the sum of all transitions probabilities that lead to it, see Table 2.

Table 2. Transitions probabilities summation at each state in OSApp

S_i	S_1	S_2	S_3	S_4
$\sum_{k=1}^{n} P_{S_k, S_i}$	0.333	0.975	1.704	0.979

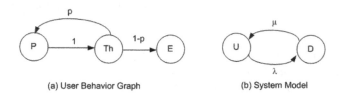

(a) User Behavior Graph   (b) System Model

Fig. 7. System model and UBG with loop

Back to the experiment, we want to modify OSApp in a way it will be context-aware application that preserves the User Perceived Service Availability ($UPSA$) [13]. In [14], the authors came with the concept of $UPSA$ that is defined as: *During a user interaction (session) with the system, the user issues multiple requests at different time points for different system resources. The unavailability of requested resource will cause the request to fail. The service availability is the probability that all requests are successfully satisfied during the user session.* In addition, the authors developed several models of $UPSA$ that consider different User Behavior Graphs (UBG) and system models. In this paper, for simplicity, we will reuse their $UPSA$ model coming from:

- UBG with loops that allow multiple requests in the user session; this UBG has three states: processing state P, thinking state Th and exit session state E, with a probability p that a user will make another request, and probability $1 - p$ that she will exit the session (see Fig. 7-(a)).
- A system model with two states, up state U and down state D, with constant failure rate λ and repair rate μ (see Fig. 7-(b)).

For the considered model, we recall the work in [13], the $UPSA$ formula is defined as follows:

$$\forall \, UP_k \in UP$$

$$UPSA_{T_b}^{S_a} = \frac{u_0 \cdot \frac{\lambda_p}{\lambda + \lambda_p} \cdot (1-p)}{1 - p \cdot [\frac{\lambda_p}{\lambda + \lambda_p} \cdot (\frac{\mu}{\lambda + \mu} + \frac{\lambda}{\lambda + \mu} \cdot \frac{\lambda_{Th}}{\lambda + \mu + \lambda_{Th}})]} \tag{2}$$

Where

- p user probability of interest in making requests
- $1\text{-}p$ probability that a user will end the session after thinking state
- λ_P is a rate that represents the number of requests per time unit the user makes to the system
- λ_{Th} is the rate associated to the thinking time state the user enters
- μ_0 instantaneous system availability [15]
- λ system failure rate
- μ system repair rate

Note that, in Formula 2 the system parameters and UBG probabilities are influenced by the *user profile* UP_k, *contextual situations* S_a and *tactics* T_b (i.e. app behavior). This means that we will have a $UPSA$ value for each UP_k, S_a and T_b. Indeed, if we have x user profiles UP, m tactics T, n contextual situations S, Where, $k \in [1, \text{x}]$, $a \in [1, \text{m}]$, $b \in [1, \text{n}]$. Then, $UPSA_{T_b}^{S_a}$ calculated for UP_k is the user perceived service availability for a user belonging to profile UP_k, deploying T_a tactic in S_b contextual situation.

In this experiment, we have one *user profile* (mid-age users whose ages are between 35–49 years) running OSApp in different *contextual situations* (S_1, S_2, S_3, S_4) and experimenting different *tactics* (app behaviors, $T1$ when OSApp sends high quality pictures and videos and $T2$ when OSApp sends low quality pictures and videos).

To compute $UPSA$, we asked mid-age users to run OSApp in its original behavior (sending high quality picture and videos $T1$) and to make different requests for information about pieces of arts under different *contextual situations*. Then, from the extracted *contextual situations* and requests log file, we are able to compute $UPSA$ for OSApp under different states, see Table 3.

Table 3. $UPSA$ for mid-age users running OSApp with high qualities

	S_1	S_2	S_3	S_4
$UPSA$	36.34%	0.3771	41.04%	39.22%

Table 4. $UPSA$ for mid-age users running OSApp with low qualities

	S_1	S_2	S_3	S_4
$UPSA$	38.25%	41.22%	43.81%	42.08%

Accordingly, by reasoning on the values in Table 2 and 3, we realize that:

- The *contextual situation* S_3 receives the highest transitions probabilities. In other words, the probability of the transitions from any of the specified states (S_1, S_2, S_3, S_4) to S_3 is high; comparable with other states. Moreover, the computed $UPSA$ value at S_3 is more than the values at other specified *contextual situations*. That means, if the $UPSA$ value at S_3 is accepted for us, then the default behavior for OSApp can be employed at S_3 state.
- The *contextual situation* S_1 receives the lowest transitions probabilities. Moreover, the $UPSA$ at S_1 has the lowest computed availability among other values. However, since the transitions probabilities from other states to S_1 is low, then, there could be no need to apply adaptations at this state to enhance the availability. Applying an adaptation at this state can waste efforts and usages of mobile resources.
- The *contextual situations* in S_4 and S_2 have very close, relatively high, transitions probabilities. Thus, we can consider applying adaptations at their state to enhance the $UPSA$.

If we want to enhance the $UPSA$, we can think of applying another behavior that deliver the same service but with different quality, like sending low quality pictures and videos. Table 4 shows the $UPSA$ computed at the different *contextual situations* if OSApp always sends low quality pictures and videos.

Accordingly, to preserve the $UPSA$ for a given user profile UP, OSApp can perform an adaptation strategy that at a given *contextual situation* S OSApp applies the *tactic* T that has the highest $UPSA$ [13], see Table 5. However, to save the effort of applying unnecessary adaptation, OSApp should consider the transitions probabilities, computed in Table 2, to decide when to apply adaptations. Thus, for OSApp to be context-aware system that adopts efficient adaptations and preserves $UPSA$, we can extract an efficient adaptation strategy

Table 5. Extracting efficient adaptation strategy for mid-age users running OSApp

	S1	S2	S3	S4
UPSA for T1	36.34%	37.71%	41.04%	39.22%
UPSA for T2	38.25%	41.22%	43.81%	42.08%
Adaptation strategy considering maximum UPSA (T1, T2)	T2	T2	T2	T2
Transitions probabilities $\sum$	0.333	0.975	1.704	0.979
Efficient adaptation strategy after considering transitions probabilities	Eliminated	T2	T1 (default behavior)	T2

(see Table 5) that applies at S_3 the default behavior (sending high quality pictures and videos $T1$), at S_2 and S_4 it applies the low quality behavior (sending low quality picture and video $T2$), and finally S_1 can be eliminated from the adaptation considerations, since it receives low transitions probabilities and it does not have a critical effect on $UPSA$.

5 Conclusion

This paper presents a statistical approach for context-aware mobile applications. We evaluated our approach by running it on OSApp. The approach is able to determine the *contextual situations* that are relevant to context-awareness by computing at their different states the transitions probabilities and software qualities.

The paper shows how efficient adaptation strategy can be extracted. The described adaptation strategy aims to perform changes in the mobile application behavior, at relevant *contextual situations*, to preserve the user perceived service availability taking into account an efficient use of mobile resources.

References

1. Abowd, G.D., Dey, A.K., Brown, P.J., Davies, N., Smith, M., Steggles, P.: Towards a better understanding of context and context-awareness. In: Gellersen, H.-W. (ed.) HUC 1999. LNCS, vol. 1707, pp. 304–307. Springer, Heidelberg (1999). https://doi.org/10.1007/3-540-48157-5_29
2. Abusair, M.: User- and analysis-driven context aware software development in mobile computing. In: ESEC/FSE 2017 Proceedings of the 2017 11th Joint Meeting on Foundations of Software Engineering, Paderborn, Germany, September 2017, pp. 1022–1025. ACM (2017)
3. Abusair, M., Di Marco, A., Inverardi, P.: An empirical approach for determining context of mobile systems. In: Proceedings of the 11th European Conference on Software Architecture: Companion Proceedings, pp. 71–77 (2017)
4. Abusair, M., Sharaf, M., Di Marco, A., Inverardi, P., Muccini, H.: An approach for developing context-aware mobile application. In: WomENcourage2019, Rome, Italy (2019)
5. Abusair, M., Sharaf, M., Muccini, H., Inverardi, P.: Adaptation for situational-aware cyber-physical systems driven by energy consumption and human safety. In: Proceedings of the 11th European Conference on Software Architecture: Companion Proceedings, pp. 78–84 (2017)
6. Autili, M., Di Benedetto, P., Inverardi, P.: Context-aware adaptive services: the PLASTIC approach. In: Chechik, M., Wirsing, M. (eds.) FASE 2009. LNCS, vol. 5503, pp. 124–139. Springer, Heidelberg (2009). https://doi.org/10.1007/978-3-642-00593-0_9
7. Dey, A.K.: Providing architectural support for building context-aware applications. Ph.D. thesis, Georgia Institute of Technology (2000)
8. van Engelenburg, S., Janssen, M., Klievink, B.: Designing context-aware systems: a method for understanding and analysing context in practice. J. Log. Algebr. Methods Program. **103**, 79–104 (2019). https://doi.org/10.1016/j.jlamp.2018.11.003. http://www.sciencedirect.com/science/article/pii/S2352220818300191

9. Eskins, D., Sanders, W.H.: The multiple-asymmetric-utility system model: a framework for modeling cyber-human systems. In: 2011 Eighth International Conference on Quantitative Evaluation of Systems (QEST), pp. 233–242. IEEE (2011)

10. Mikic-Rakic, M., Malek, S., Medvidovic, N.: Architecture-driven software mobility in support of QoS requirements. In: Proceedings of the 1st International Workshop on Software Architectures and Mobility, pp. 3–8. ACM (2008)

11. Muccini, H., Sharaf, M., Weyns, D.: Self-adaptation for cyber-physical systems: a systematic literature review. In: Proceedings of the 11th International Symposium on Software Engineering for Adaptive and Self-managing Systems, pp. 75–81 (2016)

12. Ravi, N., Scott, J., Han, L., Iftode, L.: Context-aware battery management for mobile phones. In: Sixth Annual IEEE International Conference on Pervasive Computing and Communications, PerCom 2008, pp. 224–233. IEEE (2008)

13. Abusair, M., Di Marco, A., Inverardi, P.: Context-aware adaptation of mobile applications driven by software quality and user satisfaction. In: Proceedings of the 2017 IEEE International Conference on Software Quality, Reliability and Security Companion, Information Assurance Workshop, Prague, Czech Republic, July 2017 (2017)

14. Wang, D., Trivedi, K.S.: Modeling user-perceived service availability. In: Malek, M., Nett, E., Suri, N. (eds.) ISAS 2005. LNCS, vol. 3694, pp. 107–122. Springer, Heidelberg (2005). https://doi.org/10.1007/11560333_10

15. Wang, D., Trivedi, K.S.: Modeling user-perceived reliability based on user behavior graphs. Int. J. Reliab. Qual. Saf. Eng. **16**(04), 303–329 (2009)

A Reference Architecture for Personalized and Self-adaptive e-Health Apps

Eoin Martino Grua[1]([⊠]) (iD), Martina De Sanctis[2] (iD), and Patricia Lago[1] (iD)

[1] Vrije Universiteit Amsterdam, Amsterdam, The Netherlands
{e.m.grua,p.lago}@vu.nl
[2] Gran Sasso Science Institute, L'Aquila, Italy
martina.desanctis@gssi.it

Abstract. A wealth of e-Health mobile apps are available for many purposes, such as life style improvement, mental coaching, etc. The interventions, prompts, and encouragements of e-Health apps sometimes take context into account (e.g., previous interactions or geographical location of the user), but they still tend to be rigid, e.g., by using fixed rule sets or being not sufficiently tailored towards individuals. Personalization to the different users' characteristics and run-time adaptation to their changing needs and context provide a great opportunity for getting users continuously engaged and active, eventually leading to better physical and mental conditions.

This paper presents a reference architecture for enabling AI-based personalization and self-adaptation of mobile apps for e-Health. The reference architecture makes use of multiple MAPE loops operating at different levels of granularity and for different purposes.

Keywords: Self-adaptive systems · Personalization · Reference architecture · Mobile apps · e-Health

1 Introduction

E-Health mobile apps are designed for assisting end users in tracking and improving their own health-related activities [28]. With a projected market growth to US$102.3 Billion by 2023, e-Health apps represent a significant market [12] providing a wide spectrum of services, i.e., life style improvement, mental coaching, sport tracking, recording of medical data [24]. The unique characteristics of e-Health apps w.r.t. other health-related software systems are that e-Health apps (i) can take advantage of smartphone sensors, (ii) can reach an extremely wide audience with low infrastructural investments, and (iii) can leverage the intrinsic characteristics of the mobile medium (i.e., being always-on, personal, and always-carried by the user) for providing timely and in-context services [9].

However, even if the interventions, prompts, and encouragements of current e-Health apps take context into account (e.g., previous interactions or geographical location of the user), they still tend to be *rigid* and not fully tailored to individual

H. Muccini et al. (Eds.): ECSA 2020, CCIS 1269, pp. 195–209, 2020.
https://doi.org/10.1007/978-3-030-59155-7_15

users, e.g., by using fixed rule sets or by not considering the unique traits and behavioral characteristics of the user. In this context, we see *personalization* [7] and *self-adaptation* [15, 27] as effective instruments for getting users continuously engaged and active, eventually leading to better physical and mental conditions.

In this work, we combine personalization and software self-adaptation to provide users of mobile e-Health apps with a better, more engaging and effective experience. To this aim, we propose a *reference architecture that combines data-driven personalization with self-adaptation*. The main design drivers that make the proposed reference architecture unique are: (i) the **combination of multiple *Monitor - Analyze - Plan - Execute* (MAPE) loops** [17] operating at different levels of granularity and for different purposes, e.g., to suggest users the most suitable and timely activities according to their (evolving) health-related characteristics (e.g., active vs. less active), but also to cope with technical aspects (e.g., connectivity hiccups, availability of IoT devices and third-party apps on the user's device) and the characteristics of the physical environment (e.g., indoor vs. outdoor, weather); (ii) the exploitation of our **online clustering algorithm** for efficiently managing the evolution of the behavior of users as multiple time series evolving over time. This online clustering algorithm has been already extensively tested in a previously published article [14], showing promising results by doing better than the current state-of-the-art.

The main characteristics of the proposed reference architecture are the following: (i) it caters the personalization of provided services to the specific user preferences (e.g., preferred sport activities); (ii) it guarantees the correct functioning of the provided features via the use of connected IoT devices (e.g., a smart-bracelet) and runtime adaptation strategies; (iii) it adapts the provided services depending on contextual factors such as environmental conditions and weather; (iv) it supports a smooth participation of domain experts (e.g., psychologists) in the personalization and self-adaptation processes; and (v) it can be applied in the context of a single e-Health app and by integrating the services of third-party e-Health apps (e.g., already installed sport trackers).

2   Background

The notion of *reference architecture* (RA) is borrowed from Volpato et al. [26], who define it as "a special type of software architectures that provide a characterization of software systems functionalities in specific application domains", e.g., SOA for service orientation and AUTOSAR for automotive. In the context of this study, a *self-adaptive software system* is defined as a system that can autonomously handle changes and uncertainties in its environment, the system itself and its goals [27].

For the definition of *personalization* we build on that by Fan and Poole [7] and define it as "a process that changes a system to increase its personal relevance to an individual or a category of individuals". Furthermore, to enhance personalization, we use CluStream-GT (standing for: CluStream for Growing Time-series) [14]. CluStream-GT was chosen for this RA as it is the state-of-the-art clustering algorithm for time-series data (especially within the Health domain). CluStream-GT works in two phases: offline and online. First, the *offline phase* initializes the algorithm with a small initial dataset; this is done either at design time or at the start of runtime. After, during the *online phase* the algorithm clusters the data that is being collected at runtime. Clustering allows the RA to group similar users together; where similarity is determined by the data gathered from the apps. This gives the RA a more sustainable and scalable method of personalization, without requiring to create individual personalization strategies but maintaining a suitable degree of personalization [14,19]. An example case where clustering can be used to aid personalization is with the use of cluster based Reinforcement Learning [13].

The *methodology* used for the design of our RA is the one presented by Angelov et al. [2].

3 Related Work

Several RAs for IoT can be found in the literature [1,3,4,10]. In particular, Bauer et al. [4] present several abstract *architectural views* and *perspectives*, which can be differently instantiated. The adaptation of the system's configuration is also envisioned, at an abstract level. IoT-A [3] aims to be easily customized to different needs, and it makes use of *axioms* and *relationships* to define connections among IoT entities. IIRA [1] is particularly tailored for industrial IoT systems. WSO2 [10] presents a layered structure and targets scalability and security aspects too. All of the above RAs are abstract and domain independent. As such, they do not address required features specific to the IoT-based e-Health domain. Moreover, they lack the needed integration with AI for personalization used to tailor interventions to the user's health-related characteristics.

Other works providing service oriented architectures (SOAs) focused on adaptation but neglected user-based personalization. E.g., Feljan et al. [8] defined a SOA for planning and execution (SOA-PE) in Cyber Physical Systems (CPS), and Mohalik et al. [22] proposed a MAPE-K autonomic computing framework to manage adaptivity in service-based CPS. Morais et al. [23] present RAH, a RA for IoT-based e-Health apps. RAH has a layered structure, and it provides components for the prevention, monitoring and detection of faults. Differently from RAH, our RA explicitly manages the self-adaptation of the e-Health mobile app, both at users- and architectural levels. Mizouni et al. [21] propose a framework for designing and developing context-aware adaptive mobile apps. Their framework lacks other types of adaptation, i.e., adaptation for user personalization and adaptation with other IoT devices – which is possible with our RA.

Lopez and Condori-Fernandez [20] propose an architectural design for an adaptive persuasive mobile app with the goal of improving medication adherence. Accordingly, the adaptation is here focused only on the messages given to the user and lacks the other levels of adaptation (environment adaptation, etc.) that our RA covers. Kim [18] proposes a general RA that can be used when developing adaptive apps and implements a e-Health app as an example. However, being it general, the RA lacks the level of detail present in our work, the integration of AI for personalization, and a way for involving domain experts in the app design and operation, which is essential in adaptive e-Health.

In summary, to the best of our knowledge, ours is the first RA for e-Health mobile apps that simultaneously supports (i) *personalization* for the different users, by exploiting the users' smart objects and preferences to dynamically get data about e.g., their mood and daily activities, and (ii) *runtime adaptation* to the user-needs and context in order to keep them engaged and active.

4   Reference Architecture

Figure 1 shows our RA[1] with the following stakeholders and components.

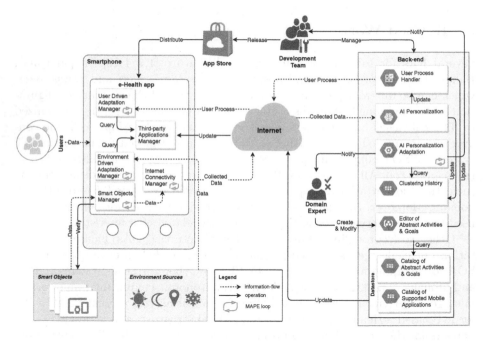

Fig. 1. Reference architecture for personalized and self-adaptive e-Health Apps

Users provide and generate the Data gathered by the e-Health app. At the first installation, the users are asked to input information to better understand their aptitudes. After an initial usage phase and data collection, the system has enough information to assign them to a cluster.

Smartphone is the host where the self-adaptive e-Health app is installed. In the mobile app, four components, namely *User Driven Adaptation Manager*,

---

[1] For the interested reader, we have defined the corresponding viewpoint here: http:// s2group.cs.vu.nl/casa-2020-technical-report/.

Environment Driven Adaptation Manager (*UD Adaptation Manager* and *ED Adaptation Manager* from here on, respectively), *Smart Objects Manager* and *Internet Connectivity Manager* implement a MAPE loop to dynamically perform adaptation. The *Third-party Applications Manager*, in turn, is responsible for the communication with third-party apps supported by the RA that can be exploited by the e-Health app both during its nominal execution and when adaptation is performed. It is also responsible for storing the user's preferences. Further details on these components are given in Sect. 5.

Smart Objects are devices, other than the smartphone, that the app can communicate with. They are used to gather additional data about the users as well as augmenting the data collected by the smartphone sensors. For instance, a smart-watch would be used by the app to track the user's heart-rate, therefore adding extra information on the real-time performance of the user.

Environment is the physical location of the user, and its measurable properties. It is used by the e-Health app to make runtime adaptations w.r.t. its current operational context and to the user's scheduled activities (see Sect. 5.5).

The back-end of our RA (right-hand side of Fig. 1) is `Managed` by a *Development team*. It additionally exposes an interface to the *Domain Expert* that is also involved in the e-Health app design and operation. The back-end contains the components needed to store the collected user data and to manage the user clusters. It also hosts components supporting the general functioning of the app.

User Process Handler is in charge of sending `User Processes` to the users, by taking care of sending the same User Process to all users of the same cluster. A *User Process* is composed of one or more *Abstract Activities*. These activities are inspired by the ones introduced in [5], although they differ both in the structure and in the way they are refined, as later explained. An *Abstract Activity* is defined by a vector of one or more *Activity categories* and an associated goal, with each vector entry representing a day of the week[2]. For the sake of space we leave the description of the formalization of the goal model to future work.

Each *Abstract Activity* is defined by the Domain Expert via the *Editor of Abstract Activities & Goals* and later stored in the *Catalog of Abstract Activities & Goals*. Each Activity category identifies the kind of activity the user should perform. As an example, the user can receive either a *Cardio* or *Strength* Activity category and so should perform an activity of that kind. More precisely, for each user, the Activity categories are converted to *Concrete Activities* at run-time via the use of the *UD Adaptation Manager* and based on the user's preferences. For instance, a cardio Activity category can be instantiated into different *Concrete Activities* such as running, swimming and walking. Moreover, if an *Abstract Activity* is composed of multiple Activity categories, all or some of type Cardio, they can be converted into different *Concrete Activities*. This implies that users who receive the same User Process will still be likely to have different *Concrete*

---

[2] Examples of Abstract Activities are shown here: http://s2group.cs.vu.nl/casa-2020-technical-report/.

Activities, therefore personalizing the experience to the individual user (this is further discussed in Sect. 5.2).

The *User Process Handler* receives `Updates` from (i) the *AI Personalization* and (ii) the *Editor of Abstract Activities & Goals* in order to send User Processes to their associated users. The AI Personalization `Updates` the *User Process Handler* every time a user moves from one cluster to another, while the *Editor of Abstract Activities & Goals* `Updates` it every time new clusters are analyzed by the Domain Expert (along with the new associated User Process). These updates guarantee that the *User Process Handler* remains up to date about the User Processes and their associated users.

AI Personalization sends an `Update` to the *Clustering History* component whenever a change occurs in the clusters. The *AI Personalization* component uses the CluStream-GT algorithm to cluster users into clusters in a real-time and online fashion [14]. It receives the input data from the e-Health app (see `Collected Data` in Fig. 1). More than one instance of CluStream-GT can be running at the same time. In fact, there is one instance per category of data. E.g., if the e-Health app is recording both ecological momentary assessment [25] and biometric data, one for the purpose of monitoring **mood** and the other for **fitness**, there will be two running instances of the algorithm.

AI Personalization Adaptation is in charge of monitoring the evolution of clusters and detecting if any change occurs. Examples include the merging of two clusters or the generation of a new one. To do so, it periodically `Queries` the *Clustering History* database. If one or more new clusters are detected, this component will `Notify` both the Development Team and the Domain Expert. The Domain Expert will examine the new information and add the appropriate User Process to the *Catalog of Abstract Activities & Goals* via the dedicated editor. In turn, the Development Team is notified just as a precaution so that it can verify if the new cluster is not an anomaly. The specifics of the corresponding MAPE loop are described in Sect. 5.1.

The role played by AI via the CluStream-GT algorithm is relevant in our RA as it strongly supports both personalization and self-adaptation, thus guaranteeing a continuous user engagement that is crucial in e-Health apps. Specifically, personalization is achieved by clustering the users based on their preferences and their physical and mental condition. This supports the RA in assigning appropriate *User Processes* to each user, and further adapt them to continuously cope with the current status of the user.

Clustering History is a database of all the clusters created by the *AI Personalization* component. For each cluster it keeps all of the composing microclusters with all of their contained information.

Editor of Abstract Activities & Goals allows the Domain Expert to create and modify *Abstract Activities* (and their associated goals) and to combine them as User Processes. This is achieved via a web-based interactive UI and the editor's ability to `Query` the *Catalog of Abstract Activities & Goals*. It is also the editor's responsibility to update the *User Process Handler* if any new User Process has been created and is currently in use.

Catalog of Abstract Activities & Goals is a database of all User Processes that the Domain Expert has created for each unique current and past cluster. When a new cluster is defined, the Domain Expert can assign to it an existing User Process from this catalog, or create a new one and store it.

Catalog of Supported Mobile Applications is a database containing the metadata needed for interacting with supported third-party mobile apps installed on users' devices. This database stores information such as the specific types of Android intents (and their related extra data) needed for launching each third-party app, the data it produces after a tracking session, etc. Indeed, our e-Health app does not provide any specific functionality for executing the activities suggested to the user (e.g., running, swimming); rather, it brings up third-party apps (e.g., Strava[3] for running and cycling, Swim.com[4] for swimming) and collects the data produced by the apps after the user performs the physical activities. The main reasons for this design decision are: (i) we do not want to disrupt the users' habits and preferences in terms of apps used for tracking their activities, (ii) we want to *build on* existing large user bases, (iii) we do not want to reinvent the wheel by re-implementing functionalities already supported by development teams with years-long experience.

Whenever the e-Health app evolves by supporting new applications (or no longer supporting certain applications), the *Catalog of Supported Mobile Applications* `Updates`, through the *Datastore*, the *Third-party Applications Manager*. The *Third-party Applications Manager* responsibility is to keep the list of supported mobile apps up to date and provide the corresponding metadata to the *UD Adaptation Manager* and the *ED Adaptation Manager*, when needed.

The e-Health app and back-end communicate via the Internet. Specifically, the communication from the e-Health app to the back-end is REST-based and it is performed by the *Internet Connectivity Manager*, which is responsible for sending the `Collected Data` to the *AI Personalization* component in the back-end. Communication from the back-end to the e-Health app is performed by the *User Process Handler* which is in charge of sending the `User Process` to the e-Health app via push notifications.

5 Components Supporting Self-adaptation

The RA has five components used for self-adaptation. To accomplish its responsibilities, each of these components implement a MAPE loop.

5.1 AI Personalization Adaptation

The main goal of the AI Personalization Adaptation is to keep track of the clusters evolution and to enable the creation of new User Processes. It does it through its MAPE loop depicted in Fig. 2. During its `Monitor` phase, the AI

---

[3] http://strava.com.
[4] http://swim.com.

Personalization Adaptation monitors the macro-clusters. In its **Analyze** phase it determines if there are changes in the monitored macro-clusters. To do so, the AI Personalisation Adaptation periodically queries the Clustering History database. It compares the current clusters with the previously saved ones. If any of the current ones are significantly different, then the AI Personalization Adaptation enters its **Plan** phase. The **Plan** phase gathers the IDs of the users and macro-clusters involved in these significant changes. Since this change involves the need of the creation of new User Processes for all of the users belonging to the new clusters the Domain Expert must be involved in this adaptation. To achieve this we have exploited the type of adaptation described in [11], which considers the involvement of humans in MAPE loops. In particular, in [11] the authors describe various cases in which a human can be part of a MAPE loop. AI Personalization Adaptation falls under what the authors refer to as: 'System Feedback (Proactive/foreground)'. This type of adaptation is initiated by the system which may send information to the human. The human (i.e. Domain Expert) uses this information to execute the adaptation (by creating the new User Processes necessary). To send the needed information to the Domain Expert, AI Personalization Adaptation takes the gathered knowledge from the **Plan** phase and gives it to **Execute**. **Execute notifies** (Fig. 1) both the Development Team and the Domain Expert about the detected cluster change(s) and relays the gathered information.

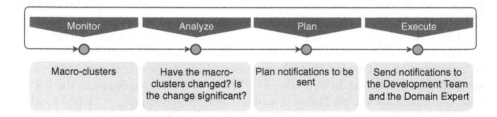

Fig. 2. AI Personalization Adaptation MAPE loop.

To determine if a cluster is significantly different from another we use a parameter *delta*. This parameter is set by the Development Team at design time and determines how different the stored information of one cluster has to be from another one to identify them as unique. The Development Team is notified as a precaution, to double check the change and verify that no errors occurred.

5.2 User Driven Adaptation Manager

The main responsibility of the UD Adaptation Manager is to receive the User Process from the back-end and convert the contained Abstract Activities into Concrete Activities. A Concrete Activity represents a specific activity that the user can perform, also with the support of smart objects and/or corresponding mobile apps. As an example, *running* is a concrete activity during which the user can exploit a smart-bracelet to monitor their cardio rate as well as a dedicated mobile app to measure the run distance and the estimated burned calories. A Concrete Activity is designed as a class containing multiple attributes that is stored on the smartphone. The attributes are:

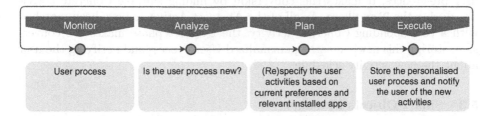

Fig. 3. UD Adaptation Manager MAPE loop.

- **Selectable**: is True if the UD Adaptation Manager or the ED Adaptation Manager can choose this Concrete Activity, when dynamically refining Abstract Activities; False otherwise. It is set by the user via the user preferences.
- **Location**: it specifies if the activity is performed indoors or outdoors. This attribute is used by the ED Adaptation Manager to choose the appropriate Concrete Activity according to weather conditions (see Sect. 5.5).
- **Activity category**: it defines what type of category does the Concrete Activity fall under. E.g., for a fitness activity, it specifies a cardio or strength training.
- **Recurrence**: it tracks how many times the user has performed the Concrete Activity in the past. It allows the UD Adaptation Manager to have a preference ranking system within all the selectable Concrete Activities.

For each user, the Concrete Activities are derived from their preferences stored in the Third-party Applications Manager. During its nominal execution, the UD Adaptation Manager is in charge of refining the Abstract Activities in the User Process into Concrete ones. To do this, it queries the Third-party Applications Manager and exploits its knowledge of the Concrete Activities and their attributes. After completing the task, the UD Adaptation Manager presents the personalized User Process to the user as a schedule, where each slot in the vector of Activity categories corresponds to a day. Therefore creating the personalized user schedule of Concrete Activities.

Refining a User Process is required every time that the user is assigned with a new process, to keep up with its improvements and/or cluster change. To this aim, a dynamic User Process adaptation is needed to adapt at run-time the personalized user schedule, in a transparent way and without a direct user involvement. Figure 3 depicts the MAPE loop of the UD Adaptation Manager.

Once it accomplishes its main task of refining the User Process, the UD Adaptation Manager enters the `Monitor` phase of its MAPE loop, by monitoring the User Process. The `Analyze` phase receives the monitored User Process from `Monitor`. `Analyze` is now responsible to determine if the user has been assigned a new User Process. If so, the UD Adaptation Manager converts the Abstract Activities in this new User Process into Concrete ones, taking into account the user preferences. It makes this conversion by finding suitable Concrete activities during the `Plan` phase. As all of the Abstract Activities have been matched with a corresponding Concrete activity, the `Execute` phase makes the conversion, storing this newly created personalized User Process and notifying the user about the new activity schedule.

5.3   Smart Objects Manager

This component aims to maintain the connection with the user's smart objects and, if not possible, find alternative sensors to make the e-Health app able to continuously collect user's data, thus to perform optimally. To this aim, it implements a MAPE loop, shown in Fig. 4, supporting the dynamic adaptation at the architectural level of the smart objects. The `Monitor` phase is devoted to the run-time monitoring of the connection status with the smart objects. Connection problems can be due to either the smart objects themselves, which can be out of battery, or to missing internet, bluetooth or bluetooth low energy connectivity. The `Analyze` phase is in charge of verifying the current connection status (received by `Monitor`) and see if the connection status with any of the smart objects has changed. During the `Plan` phase the MAPE will create a sequential plan of actions that the `Execute` will have to perform. All of the actions are aimed at re-establishing the lost connection or at finding a new source of data. For instance, if the smart-watch connected to the smartphone runs out of battery and the attempts to reconnect to it fail, the Smart Objects Manager will switch to sensors inbuilt in the smartphone (such as the accelerometer).

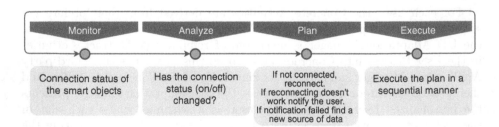

Fig. 4. Smart Objects Manager MAPE loop.

5.4   Internet Connectivity Manager

The main purposes of the Internet Connectivity Manager are to (1) send the `Collected Data` to the back-end and store them locally when the connection is missing, and (2) provide resilience to the e-Health app's internet connectivity. As shown in the MAPE loop in Fig. 5, during the `Monitor` phase the Internet Connectivity Manager runtime monitors the quality of the smartphone's internet connection. `Analyze` is then in charge of detecting whether a significant connection quality alteration is taking place. If so, the Internet Connectivity Manager enters the `Plan` phase and it plans for an alternative. The alternative can include switching the connection type or storing the currently collected data locally on the smartphone. As a new connection can be established, the component sends the data to the back-end to be used by the AI Personalization.

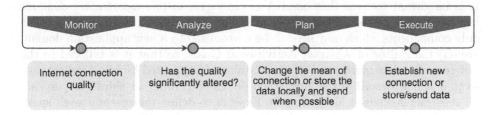

Fig. 5. Internet Connectivity Manager MAPE loop.

5.5   Environment Driven Adaptation Manager

One of the objectives of the e-Health app is keeping the users constantly engaged, to ensure that they execute their planned schedule of activities. To this aim, the ED Adaptation Manager plays an important role, which is essentially supported by its MAPE loop, depicted in Fig. 6. The purpose of this component is to constantly check whether the currently scheduled Concrete Activity best matches the runtime environment (i.e., weather conditions) the user is located in. To do so, the ED Adaptation Manager monitors in run-time the user's environment. The `Monitor` phase periodically updates the `Analyze` phase by sending the environment data. This phase establishes if the environment significantly changed. If so, it triggers the `Plan` phase that verifies whether the currently planned Concrete Activity is appropriate for the user's environment. If it is not, it finds an appropriate alternative and sends the information to `Execute`. `Execute` swaps the planned Concrete Activity with the newly found one and notifies the user of this change.

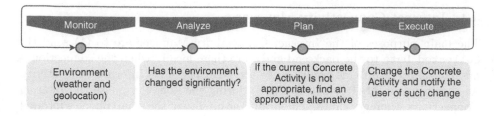

Fig. 6. ED Adaptation Manager MAPE loop.

6 Discussion

It is important to note that our RA is *extensible so to support other domains* beyond fitness and mood. On the client side no changes are required, whereas the only components which may need to be customized to a new application domain are: (i) the Editor of Abstract Activities & Goals, so that it is tailored to the different domain experts; and (ii) the Catalog of Supported Mobile Applications, so that it now describes the interaction points with different third-party apps.

Abstract Activities allow Domain Experts to define *incremental goals* spanning over the duration of the whole User Process. In addition, User Processes are defined at the cluster level (potentially including thousands of users) and can cover large time spans (e.g., weeks or months). Those features make the operation of the RA sustainable from the perspective of Domain Experts, who are not required to frequently intervene for defining new goals or User Processes.

Furthermore, through the conversion from Activity Categories to Concrete Activities, which takes place during the dynamic Abstract Activities refinement, we accommodate both *Type-to-Type* adaptation (e.g., from the *Cardio* Activity Category to the *Running* Concrete Activity) and the most common *Type-to-Instance* adaptation (e.g., by using the Strava mobile app as an instance of the *Running* Concrete Activity). Similarly, a *Type-to-Type* adaptation is reported by Calinescu et al. [6] presenting an approach where elements are replaced with other elements providing the *same* functionality but showing a superior quality to deal with changing conditions (e.g., dynamic replacement of service instances in service-based systems). In our approach, however, we go beyond, by replacing activities with others providing *different* functionality to deal with changing conditions. To the best of our knowledge, this adaptation type is uncommon in self-adaptive architectures, despite quite helpful.

The components of the RA running on the smartphone can be deployed in two different ways, each leading to a different business case. Firstly, those components can be integrated into an existing e-Health app (e.g., Endomondo[5] for sports tracking) so to provide personalization and self-adaptation capabilities to its services. In this case the development team of the app just needs to deploy

---

[5] http://endomondo.com.

the client-side components of the RA as a third-party library, suitably integrate the original app with the added library, and launch the server-side components. The second business case regards the creation of a new meta-app integrating the services of third-party apps, similarly to what apps like IFTTT[6] do. In this case, the meta-app makes an extensive usage of the Third-party Applications Manager component and orchestrates the execution of the other apps already installed on the user device.

Finally, we are aware that our RA is responsible for managing highly-sensitive user data, which may raise severe *privacy* concerns. In order to mitigate potential privacy threats, the communication between the mobile app and the back-end is TLS-encrypted and the payload of push notifications is encrypted as well, e.g., by using the Capillary Project [16] for Android apps, which supports state-of-the-art encryption algorithms, such as RSA and Web Push encryption. Eventually, we highlight that, according to the privacy level required by the Development Team, the components running in the back-end can be deployed either on premises or in the Cloud, e.g., by building on public Cloud services like Amazon AWS and execute them in a protected environment, e.g., behind additional authentication and authorization layers.

7   Conclusions and Future Work

In this paper we presented a RA for e-Health apps. Its goal is to combine AI-based personalization and self-adaptation. The RA achieves self-adaptation on three levels: (i) adaptation to the users and their environment, (ii) adaptation to smart objects and third-party applications, and (iii) adaptation according to the data of the AI-based personalization, ensuring that users receive personalized activities that evolve with the users' run-time changes in behavior.

As future work we are realizing a prototype implementing the RA and designing a controlled experiment to evaluate its effects on users' behavior and performance at run-time.

References

1. The industrial internet of things volume G1: reference architecture. Ind. Internet Consort. (2019). https://bit.ly/2talimM
2. Angelov, S., Grefen, P., Greefhorst, D.: A framework for analysis and design of software reference architectures. Inf. Softw. Technol. **54**(4), 417–431 (2012)
3. Bassi, A., et al.: Enabling Things to Talk: Designing IoT Solutions with the IoT Architectural Reference Model, 1st edn. Springer, Heidelberg (2016). https://doi.org/10.1007/978-3-642-40403-0
4. Bauer, M., et al.: IoT reference architecture. In: Enabling Things to Talk: Designing IoT solutions with the IoT Architectural Reference Model (2013)

---

[6] http://ifttt.com.

5. Bucchiarone, A., Lafuente, A.L., Marconi, A., Pistore, M.: A formalisation of adaptable pervasive flows. In: Laneve, C., Su, J. (eds.) WS-FM 2009. LNCS, vol. 6194, pp. 61–75. Springer, Heidelberg (2010). https://doi.org/10.1007/978-3-642-14458-5_4
6. Calinescu, R., Weyns, D., Gerasimou, S., Iftikhar, M.U., Habli, I., Kelly, T.: Engineering trustworthy self-adaptive software with dynamic assurance cases. IEEE Trans. Softw. Eng. **44**(11), 1039–1069 (2018)
7. Fan, H., Poole, M.S.: What is personalization? Perspectives on the design and implementation of personalization in information systems. J. Organ. Comput. Electron. Commer. **16**(3–4), 179–202 (2006)
8. Feljan, A.V., Mohalik, S.K., Jayaraman, M.B., Badrinath, R.: SOA-PE: a service-oriented architecture for planning and execution in cyber-physical systems. In: 2015 International Conference on Smart Sensors and Systems (IC-SSS), pp. 1–6 (2015)
9. Fling, B.: Mobile Design and Development: Practical Concepts and Techniques for Creating Mobile Sites and Web Apps. O'Reilly Media Inc., Sebastopol (2009)
10. Fremantle, P.: A Reference Architecture for the Internet of Things. WSO2 White paper (2015). https://bit.ly/2RMzCft
11. Gil, M., Pelechano, V., Fons, J., Albert, M.: Designing the human in the loop of self-adaptive systems. In: García, C.R., Caballero-Gil, P., Burmester, M., Quesada-Arencibia, A. (eds.) UCAmI 2016. LNCS, vol. 10069, pp. 437–449. Springer, Cham (2016). https://doi.org/10.1007/978-3-319-48746-5_45
12. Global Industry Analysts, Inc.: mHealth (mobile health) services - market analysis, trends, and forecasts (2019). https://tinyurl.com/rbvdtc3
13. Grua, E.M., Hoogendoorn, M.: Exploring clustering techniques for effective reinforcement learning based personalization for health and wellbeing. In: 2018 IEEE Symposium Series on Computational Intelligence (SSCI), pp. 813–820. IEEE (2018)
14. Grua, E.M., Hoogendoorn, M., Malavolta, I., Lago, P., Eiben, A.: Clustream-GT: online clustering for personalization in the health domain. In: IEEE/WIC/ACM International Conference on Web Intelligence, pp. 270–275. ACM (2019)
15. Grua, E.M., Malavolta, I., Lago, P.: Self-adaptation in mobile apps: a systematic literature study. In: IEEE/ACM 14th International Symposium on Software Engineering for Adaptive and Self-Managing Systems (SEAMS), pp. 51–62 (2019)
16. Hogben, G., Perera, M.: Project capillary: End-to-end encryption for push messaging, simplified. (2018). https://tinyurl.com/y8n8btoc
17. IBM: An architectural blueprint for autonomic computing. Technical report. IBM (2006)
18. Kim, H.K.: Architecture for adaptive mobile applications. Int. J. Bio-Sci. Bio-Technol. **5**(5), 197–210 (2013)
19. Kim, K., Ahn, H.: Using a clustering genetic algorithm to support customer segmentation for personalized recommender systems. In: Kim, T.G. (ed.) AIS 2004. LNCS (LNAI), vol. 3397, pp. 409–415. Springer, Heidelberg (2005). https://doi.org/10.1007/978-3-540-30583-5_44
20. Suni Lopez, F., Condori-Fernandez, N.: Design of an adaptive persuasive mobile application for stimulating the medication adherence. In: Poppe, R., Meyer, J.-J., Veltkamp, R., Dastani, M. (eds.) INTETAIN 2016 2016. LNICST, vol. 178, pp. 99–105. Springer, Cham (2017). https://doi.org/10.1007/978-3-319-49616-0_9
21. Mizouni, R., Matar, M.A., Al Mahmoud, Z., Alzahmi, S., Salah, A.: A framework for context-aware self-adaptive mobile applications SPL. Expert. Syst. Appl. **41**(16), 7549–7564 (2014)

22. Mohalik, S.K., Narendra, N.C., Badrinath, R., Le, D.: Adaptive service-oriented architectures for cyber physical systems. In: IEEE Symposium on Service-Oriented System Engineering, SOSE, pp. 57–62 (2017)
23. de Morais Barroca Filho, I., Aquino Junior, G.S., Vasconcelos, T.B.: Extending and instantiating a software reference architecture for IoT-based healthcare applications. In: Misra, S., et al. (eds.) ICCSA 2019. LNCS, vol. 11623, pp. 203–218. Springer, Cham (2019). https://doi.org/10.1007/978-3-030-24308-1_17
24. Paschou, M., Sakkopoulos, E., Sourla, E., Tsakalidis, A.: Health internet of things: metrics and methods for efficient data transfer. Simul. Model. Pract. Theory **34**, 186–199 (2013)
25. Shiffman, S., Stone, A.A., Hufford, M.R.: Ecological momentary assessment. Annu. Rev. Clin. Psychol. **4**, 1–32 (2008)
26. Volpato, T., Oliveira, B.R.N., Garcés, L., Capilla, R., Nakagawa, E.Y.: Two perspectives on reference architecture sustainability. In: Proceedings of the 11th European Conference on Software Architecture: Companion, pp. 188–194. ACM (2017)
27. Weyns, D.: Software engineering of self-adaptive systems: an organised tour and future challenges. In: Chapter in Handbook of Software Engineering (2017)
28. Williams, P.A.H., McCauley, V.: A rapidly moving target: conformance with e-health standards for mobile computing. In: 2nd Australian eHealth Informatics and Security Conference (2013)

CSE/QUDOS - Joint Workshop on Continuous Software Engineering and Quality-Aware DevOps

Joint Workshop on Continuous Software Engineering and Quality-Aware DevOps (CSE/QUDOS)

It is our great pleasure to welcome you to CSE/QUDOS 2020 – the joint 5th Workshop on Continuous Software Engineering (CSE 2020) and 6th International Workshop on Quality-Aware DevOps (QUDOS 2020), held virtually as part of the 14th European Conference on Software Architecture (ECSA 2020).

The QUDOS workshop provides a forum for experts from academia and industry to present and discuss novel quality-aware methods, practices, and tools for DevOps. On the other hand, the goal of the CSE workshop is to present and discuss innovative solutions, ideas, and experiences in the area of continuity along the entire software engineering lifecycle, hence, CSE. For the second time, the CSE and QUDOS workshops joined forces to foster cross-fertilization and bootstrap an even bigger, stronger community around the urgently emerging topics they are both addressing from different angles.

CSE/QUDOS 2020 is a one-day workshop. The workshop received eight submissions for full papers, three submissions for short papers, and two abstract submissions for industry talks. The quality of submissions was extremely high, leading us to accept four technical full papers, two short papers, and one industry abstract. These papers were selected by the program chairs based on the reviews provided by the CSE/QUDOS 2020 Program Committee members. In addition to the talks presenting the accepted papers, CSE/QUDOS 2020 featured an invited keynote and ample space was devoted to discussions on continuous software engineering and quality-aware DevOps.

We thank the Program Committee members, who helped with timely and constructive reviews, as well as each author and presenter for their contributions to the CSE/QUDOS 2020 workshop.

The joint CSE/QUDOS 2020 workshops were organized and technically sponsored by the Research Group (RG), the DevOps Performance Working Group of the Standard Performance Evaluation Corporation (SPEC RG), and the consortium of the EU project RADON. The workshop is also supported by the IFIP Working Group on Service Oriented Systems and the GI Working Group Microservices and DevOps.

Organization

Workshop Chairs

Robert Chatley   Imperial College London, UK
Katja Kevic   Microsoft, UK

CSE Steering Committee

Stephan Krusche   Technical University of Munich, Germany
Horst Lichter   RWTH Aachen University, Germany
Dirk Riehle   FAU Nürnberg, Germany
Andreas Steffens   RWTH Aachen University, Germany

QUDOS Steering Committee

Danilo Ardagna   Politecnico di Milano, Italy
Giuliano Casale   Imperial College London, UK
Andre van Hoorn   University of Stuttgart, Germany
Philipp Leitner   Chalmers — University of Gothenburg,
                                 Sweden

Workshop Program Committee

Bram Adams   Polytechnique Montréal, Canada
Maurício Aniche   TU Delft, Netherlands
Cor-Paul Bezemer   University of Alberta, Canada
Jan Bosch   Chalmers University of Technology, Sweden
Daniel Bryant   DataWire and InfoQ, UK
Jürgen Cito   TU Vienna, Austria
Thomas Kurpick   Trusted Shops GmbH, Germany
Shane McIntosh   McGill University, Canada
Brendan Murphy   Container Solutions, UK
Adrian Mouat   University of Oxford, UK
Cesare Pautasso   University of Lugano, Switzerland
Kayla Shapiro   Facebook, UK

Emma Söderberg   Lund University, Sweden
Damian Tamburri   TU Eindhoven, The Netherlands
Catia Trubiani   Gran Sasso Science Institute, Italy
Benji Weber   Snyk, UK
Uwe Zdun   University of Vienna, Austria

Collecting Service-Based Maintainability Metrics from RESTful API Descriptions: Static Analysis and Threshold Derivation

Justus Bogner[1]([✉]) [iD], Stefan Wagner[1] [iD], and Alfred Zimmermann[2] [iD]

[1] Institute of Software Engineering, University of Stuttgart, Stuttgart, Germany
{justus.bogner,stefan.wagner}@iste.uni-stuttgart.de
[2] Herman Hollerith Center, University of Applied Sciences Reutlingen,
Reutlingen, Germany
alfred.zimmermann@reutlingen-university.de

Abstract. While many maintainability metrics have been explicitly designed for service-based systems, tool-supported approaches to automatically collect these metrics are lacking. Especially in the context of microservices, decentralization and technological heterogeneity may pose challenges for static analysis. We therefore propose the modular and extensible RAMA approach (RESTful API Metric Analyzer) to calculate such metrics from machine-readable interface descriptions of RESTful services. We also provide prototypical tool support, the RAMA CLI, which currently parses the formats OpenAPI, RAML, and WADL and calculates 10 structural service-based metrics proposed in scientific literature. To make RAMA measurement results more actionable, we additionally designed a repeatable benchmark for quartile-based threshold ranges (green, yellow, orange, red). In an exemplary run, we derived thresholds for all RAMA CLI metrics from the interface descriptions of 1,737 publicly available RESTful APIs. Researchers and practitioners can use RAMA to evaluate the maintainability of RESTful services or to support the empirical evaluation of new service interface metrics.

Keywords: RESTful services · Microservices · Maintainability · Size · Complexity · Cohesion · Metrics · Static analysis · API documentation

1 Introduction

Maintainability, i.e. the degree of effectiveness and efficiency with which a software system can be modified to correct, improve, extend, or adapt it [17], is an essential quality attribute for long-living software systems. To manage and control maintainability, quantitative evaluation with metrics [9] has long established itself as a frequently employed practice. In systems based on service orientation [22], however, many source code metrics lose their importance due to the increased level of abstraction [4]. For microservices as a lightweight and fine-grained service-oriented variant [20], factors like the large number of small

© Springer Nature Switzerland AG 2020
H. Muccini et al. (Eds.): ECSA 2020, CCIS 1269, pp. 215–227, 2020.
https://doi.org/10.1007/978-3-030-59155-7_16

services, their decentralized nature, or high degree of technological heterogeneity may pose difficulties for metric collection and the applicability of existing metrics, which has also been reported in the area of performance testing [11]. Several researchers have therefore focused on adapting existing metrics and defining new metrics for service orientation (see e.g. our literature review [7] or the one from Daud and Kadir [10]).

However, approaches to automatically collect these metrics are lacking and for the few existing ones, tool support is rarely publicly available (see Sect. 2). This significantly hinders empirical metric evaluation as well as industry adoption of service-based metrics. To circumvent the described challenges, we therefore propose a metric collection approach focused on machine-readable RESTful API descriptions. RESTful web services are resource-oriented services that employ the full HTTP protocol with methods like `GET`, `POST`, `PUT`, or `DELETE` as well as HTTP status codes to expose their functionality on the web [23]. For microservices, RESTful HTTP is used as one of the primary communication protocols [20]. Since this protocol is popular in industry [5,26] and API documentation formats like WADL[1], OpenAPI[2], or RAML[3] are widely used, such an approach should be broadly applicable to real-world RESTful services. Relying on machine-readable RESTful documentation avoids having to implement tool support for several programming languages. Second, such documents are often created reasonably early in the development process if a design-first approach is used. And lastly, if such documents do not exist for the system, they can often be generated automatically, which is supported for popular RESTful frameworks like e.g. Spring Boot[4].

While formats like OpenAPI have been used in many analysis and reengineering approaches for service- and microservice-based systems [18,19,25], there is so far no broadly applicable and conveniently extensible approach to calculate structural service-based maintainability metrics from interface specifications of RESTful services. To fill this gap, we propose a new modular approach for the static analysis of RESTful API descriptions called RAMA (RESTful API Metric Analyzer), which we describe in Sect. 3. Our prototypical tool support to show the feasibility of this approach, the RAMA CLI, is able to parse the popular formats OpenAPI, RAML, and WADL and calculates a variety of service interface metrics related to maintainability. Lastly, we also conducted a benchmark-based threshold derivation study for all metrics implemented in the RAMA CLI to make measurements more actionable for practitioners (see Sect. 4).

2   Related Work

Because static analysis for service orientation is very challenging, most proposals so far focused on programming language independent techniques. In the context

---

[1] https://www.w3.org/submission/wadl.

[2] https://www.openapis.org.

[3] https://raml.org.

[4] https://springdoc.org.

of service-oriented architecture (SOA), Gebhart and Abeck [13] developed an approach that extracts metrics from the UML profile SoaML (Service-oriented architecture Modeling Language). The used metrics are related to the quality attributes unique categorization, loose coupling, discoverability, and autonomy.

For web services, several authors also used WSDL documents as the basis for maintainability evaluations. Basci and Misra [3] calculated complexity metrics from them, while Sneed [27] designed a tool-supported WSDL approach with metrics for quantity or complexity as well as maintainability design rules.

To identify linguistic antipatterns in RESTful interfaces, Palma et al. [21] developed an approach that relies on semantic text analysis and algorithmic rule cards. They do not use API descriptions like OpenAPI. Instead, their tool support invokes all methods of an API under study to document the necessary information for the rule cards.

Finally, Haupt et al. [14] published the most promising approach. They used an internal canonical data model to represent the REST API and converted both OpenAPI and RAML into this format via the epsilon transformation language (ETL). While this internal model is beneficial for extensibility, the chosen transformation relies on a complex model-driven approach. Moreover, the extensibility for metrics remains unclear and some of the implemented metrics simply count structural attributes like the number of resources or the number of POST requests. The model also does not take data types into account, which are part of many proposed service-based cohesion or complexity metrics. So, while the general approach from Haupt et al. is a sound foundation, we adjusted it in several areas and made our new implementation publicly available.

3   The RAMA Approach

In this section, we present the details of our static analysis approach called RAMA (RESTful API Metric Analyzer). To design RAMA, we first analyzed existing service-based metrics to understand which of them could be derived solely from service interface definitions and what data attributes would be necessary for this. This analysis relied mostly on the results of our previous literature review [7], but also took some newer or not covered publications into account. Additionally, we analyzed existing approaches for WSDL and OpenAPI (see Sect. 2). Based on this analysis, we then developed a data model, an architecture, and finally prototypical tool support.

Relying on a canonical data model to which each specification format has to be converted increases the independence and extensibility of our approach. RAMA's internal data model (see Fig. 1) was constructed based on entities required to calculate a wide variety of complexity, size, and cohesion metrics. While we tried to avoid unnecessary properties, we still needed to include all metric-relevant attributes and also to find common ground between the most popular RESTful description languages.

The hierarchical model starts with a `SpecificationFile` entity that contains necessary metadata like a title, a version, or the specification format (e.g.

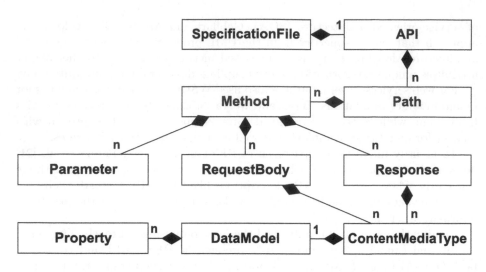

Fig. 1. Simplified canonical data model of RAMA.

OpenAPI or RAML). It also holds a single `API` wrapper entity consisting of a base path like e.g. `/api/v1` and a list of `Paths`. These `Paths` are the actual REST resources of the API and each one of them holds a list of `Methods`. A `Method` represents an HTTP verb like `GET` or `POST`, i.e. in combination, a `Path` and a `Method` form a service operation, e.g. `GET /customers/1/orders` to fetch all orders from customer with ID 1. Additionally, a `Method` may have inputs, namely `Parameters` (e.g. path or query parameters) and `RequestBodies`, and outputs, namely `Responses`. Since `RequestBodies` and `Responses` are usually complex objects of `ContentMediaTypes` like JSON or XML, they are both represented by a potentially nested `DataModel` with `Properties`. Both `Parameters` and `Properties` contain the used data types, as this is important for cohesion and complexity metrics. This model represents the core of the RAMA approach.

Based on the described data model, we designed the general architecture of RAMA as a simple command line interface (CLI) application that loosely follows the *pipes and filters* architectural style. One module type in this architecture is `Parser`. A `Parser` takes a specific REST description language like OpenAPI as input and produces our canonical data model from it. `Metrics` represent the second module type and are calculated from the produced data model. The entirety of calculated `Metrics` form a summarized results model, which is subsequently presented as the final output by different `Exporters`. This architecture is easily extensible and can also be embedded in other systems or a CI/CD pipeline.

The prototypical implementation of this approach is the RAMA CLI[5]. It is written in Java and uses Maven for dependency management. For metric modules, a plugin mechanism based on Java interfaces and the Java Reflection

---

[5] https://github.com/restful-ma/rama-cli.

API enables the dynamic inclusion of newly developed metrics. We present an overview of the implemented modules in Fig. 2.

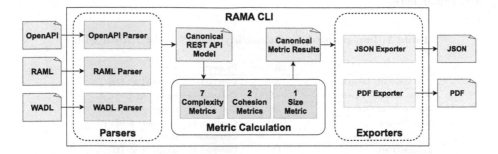

Fig. 2. Implemented architecture of the RAMA CLI (arrows indicate data flow).

For our internal data model, we used the *protocol buffers* format[6] developed by Google. Since it is language- and platform-neutral and is easily serializable, it can be used in diverse languages and technologies. There is also a tooling ecosystem around it that allows conversion between protocol buffers and various RESTful API description formats. From this created `protobuf` model, the necessary Java classes are automatically generated (`Canonical REST API Model` in Fig. 2).

With respect to input formats, we implemented `Parsers` for OpenAPI, RAML, and WADL, since these are among the most popular ones based on GitHub stars, Google search hits, and StackOverflow posts [15]. Moreover, most of them offer a convenient tool ecosystem that we can use in our `Parser` implementations. A promising fourth candidate was the Markdown-based API Blueprint[7], which seems to be rising in popularity. However, since there is so far no Java parser for this format, we did not include it in the first prototype.

The RAMA CLI currently implements 10 service-based maintainability `Metrics` proposed in five different scientific publications (see Table 1), namely seven complexity metrics, two cohesion metrics, and one size metric. We chose these metrics to cover a diverse set of structural REST API attributes, which should demonstrate the potential scope of the approach. We slightly adjusted some of the metrics for REST, e.g. the ones proposed for WSDL. For additional details on each metric, please refer to our documentation[8] or the respective source.

Finally, we implemented two `Exporters` for the CLI, namely one for a PDF and one for a JSON file. Additionally, the CLI automatically outputs the results to the terminal. While this prototype already offers a fair amount of features and should be broadly applicable, the goal was also to ensure that it can be

---

[6] https://developers.google.com/protocol-buffers.

[7] https://apiblueprint.org.

[8] https://github.com/restful-ma/rama-cli/tree/master/docs/metrics.

extended with little effort. In this sense, the module system and the usage of interfaces and the Reflection API make it easy to add new `Parsers`, `Metrics`, or `Exporters` so that the RAMA CLI can be of even more value to practitioners and researchers.

Table 1. Implemented maintainability metrics of the RAMA CLI.

Name	Abbrev.	Property	Source
Average Path Length	APL	Complexity	Haupt et al. [14]
Arguments per Operation	APO	Complexity	Basci and Misra [3]
Biggest Root Coverage	BRC	Complexity	Haupt et al. [14]
Data Weight	DW	Complexity	Basci and Misra [3]
Distinct Message Ratio	DMR	Complexity	Basci and Misra [3]
Longest Path	LP	Complexity	Haupt et al. [14]
Number of Roots	NOR	Complexity	Haupt et al. [14]
Lack of Message-Level Cohesion	LoC_{msg}	Cohesion	Athanasopoulos et al. [1]
Service Interface Data Cohesion	SIDC	Cohesion	Perepletchikov et al. [24]
Weighted Service Interface Count	WSIC	Size	Hirzalla et al. [16]

4 Threshold Benchmarking

Metric values on their own are often difficult to interpret. Some metrics may have a lower or an upper bound (e.g. a percentage between 0 and 1) and may also indicate that e.g. lower values are better or worse. However, that is often still not enough to derive implications from a specific measurement. To make metric values more actionable, *thresholds* can therefore play a valuable role [28]. We therefore designed a simple, repeatable, and adjustable threshold derivation approach to ease the application of the metrics implemented within RAMA.

4.1 Research Design

Since it is very difficult to rigorously evaluate a single threshold value, the majority of proposed threshold derivation methods analyze the measurement distribution over a large number of real-world systems. These methods are called benchmark-based approaches [2] or portfolio-based approaches [8]. Since a large number of RESTful API descriptions are publicly available, we decided to implement a simple benchmark-based approach.

Inspired by Bräuer et al. [8], we formed our labels based on the quartile distribution. Therefore, we defined a total of four ranked bands into which a metric value could fall (see also Table 2), i.e. with the derived thresholds, a measurement could be in the top 25%, between 25% and the median, between the median and 75%, or in the bottom 25%. Depending on whether lower is better or worse for the metric, each band was associated with one of the colors green, yellow, orange, and red (ordered from best to worst). If a metric result is

Table 2. Used metric threshold bands (colors are based on a metric where lower is better; for metrics where higher is better, the color ordering would be reversed).

Band	Color	Start	End
Q1	green	lower bound or minimum	1st quartile
Q2	yellow	1st quartile	2nd quartile / median
Q3	orange	2nd quartile / median	3rd quartile
Q4	red	3rd quartile	upper bound or maximum

in the worst 25% (red) or between the median and the worst 25% (orange) of analyzed systems, it may be advisable to improve the related design property.

To derive these thresholds per RAMA CLI metric, we designed an automated benchmark pipeline that operates on a large number of API description files. The benchmark consists of the four steps `Search`, `Measure`, `Combine`, and `Aggregate` (see Fig. 3). The first step was to search for publicly available descriptions of real-world APIs. For this, we used the keyword and file type search on GitHub. Additionally, we searched the API repository from APIs.guru[9], which provides a substantial number of OpenAPI files.

Once a sufficiently large collection of parsable files had been established, we collected the metrics from them via the RAMA CLI (`Measure` step). In the third step `Combine`, this collection of JSON files was then analyzed by a script that combined them into a single CSV file, where each analyzed API represented a row. Using this file with all measurements, another script executed the threshold analysis and aggregation (`Aggregate` step). Optionally, this script could filter out APIs, e.g. too small ones. As results, this yielded a JSON file with all descriptive statistics necessary for the metric thresholds as well as two diagram types to potentially analyze the metric distribution further, namely a histogram and a boxplot, both in PNG format.

To make the benchmark as transparent and repeatable as possible, we published all related artifacts such as scripts, the used API files, and documentation in a GitHub repository[10]. Every subsequent step after `Search` is fully automatable and we also provide a wrapper script to execute the complete benchmark with one command. Our goal is to provide a reusable and adaptable foundation for re-executing this benchmark with different APIs as input that may be more relevant threshold indicators for a specific REST API under analysis.

4.2   Results

We initially collected 2,651 real-world API description files (2,619 OpenAPI, 18 WADL, and 14 RAML files). This sample was dominated by large cloud providers like Microsoft Azure (1,548 files), Google (305 files), or Amazon Web

---

[9] https://apis.guru/browse-apis.
[10] https://github.com/restful-ma/thresholds.

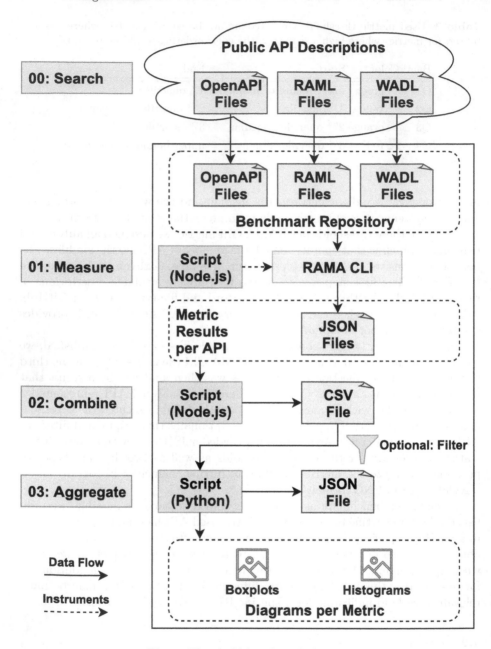

Fig. 3. Threshold benchmark design.

Services (205 files). Additionally, there were cases where we had several files of different versions for the same API.

A preliminary analysis of the collected APIs revealed that a large portion of them were very small, with only two or three operations. Since it seems reasonable to assume that several of the RAMA CLI metrics are correlated with size, we decided to exclude APIs with less than five operations (*Weighted Service Interface Count* < 5) to avoid skewing the thresholds in favor of very small APIs. Therefore, we did not include 914 APIs in the `Aggregate` step. Our exemplary execution of the described benchmark calculated the quartile-based thresholds based on a total of **1,737 public APIs** (1,708 OpenAPI, 16 WADL, and 13 RAML files). The median number of operations for these APIs was 15. Table 3 lists the thresholds for all 10 metrics of the RAMA CLI. Because of the sequential parsing of API files, the execution of the benchmark can take up to several hours on machines with low computing power. We therefore also provide all result artifacts of this exemplary run in our repository[11].

Table 3. Calculated metric thresholds from 1,737 API description files.

Metric	Top 25%	25% - 50%	50% - 75%	Worst 25%
APO	[0.20, 3.52]	]3.52, 4.60]	]4.60, 8.63]	]8.63, 21.63]
APL	[1.00, 2.50]	]2.50, 5.00]	]5.00, 8.00]	]8.00, 15.60]
BRC	[1.00, 1.00]	]1.00, 0.99]	]0.99, 0.60]	]0.60, 0.00]
DW	[4, 77]	]77, 167]	]167, 378]	]378, 41570]
DMR	[0.00, 0.26]	]0.26, 0.36]	]0.36, 0.48]	]0.48, 1.00]
LoC$_{msg}$	[0.00, 0.53]	]0.53, 0.62]	]0.62, 0.69]	]0.69, 1.00]
LP	[1, 3]	]3, 8]	]8, 10]	]10, 19]
NOR	[1, 1]	]1, 2]	]2, 3]	]3, 359]
SIDC	[1.00, 1.00]	]1.00, 0.64]	]0.64, 0.55]	]0.55, 0.00]
WSIC	[5, 8]	]8, 15]	]15, 31]	]31, 1126]

5   Limitations and Threats to Validity

While we pointed out several advantages of the RAMA approach, there are also some limitations. First, RAMA only supports RESTful HTTP and therefore excludes asynchronous message-based communication. Even though REST is arguably still more popular for microservice-based systems, event-driven microservices based on messaging receive more and more attention. Similar documentation standards for messaging are slowly emerging (see e.g. AsyncAPI[12]), but our current internal model and metric implementations are very REST-specific. While several metrics are undoubtedly valid in both communication

---

[11] https://github.com/restful-ma/thresholds/tree/master/results.
[12] https://www.asyncapi.com.

paradigms, substantial efforts would be necessary to fully support messaging in addition to REST. Apart from that, the approach requires machine-readable RESTful API descriptions to work. While such specifications are popular in the RESTful world, not every service under analysis will have one. And thirdly, relying on an API description file restricts the scope of the evaluation. Collected metrics are focused on the interface quality of a single service and cannot make any statement about the concrete service implementation. Therefore, RAMA cannot calculate system-wide metrics except for aggregates like mean, which also excludes metrics for the coupling between services.

Our prototypical implementation, the RAMA CLI, may also suffer from potential limitations. While we tried to make it applicable to a wide range of RESTful services by supporting the three formats OpenAPI, RAML, and WADL, there are still other used formats for which we currently do not have a parser, e.g. API Blueprint[13]. Similarly, there are many more proposed service-based metrics we could have implemented in the RAMA CLI. The modular architecture of RAMA consciously supports possible future extensions in this regard. Lastly, we unfortunately cannot guarantee that the prototype is completely free of bugs and works reliably with every single specification file. While we were very diligent during the implementation, have a test coverage of ~75%, and successfully used the RAMA CLI with over 2,500 API specification files, it remains a research prototype. For transparency, the code is publicly available as open source and we welcome contributions like issues or pull requests.

Finally, we need to mention threats to validity concerning our empirical threshold derivation study. One issue is that the derived thresholds rely entirely on the quality and relevance of the used API description files. If the majority of files in the benchmark are of low quality, the derived thresholds will not be strict enough. Measurement values of an API may then all fall into the Q1 band, when, in reality, the service interface under analysis is still not well designed. By including a large number of APIs from trustworthy sources, this risk may be reduced. However, there still may be services from specific contexts that are so different that they need a custom benchmark to produce relevant thresholds. Examples could be benchmarks based only on a particular domain (e.g. cloud management), on a single API specification format (e.g. RAML), or on APIs of a specific size (e.g. small APIs with 10 or less operations). As an example, large cloud providers like Azure, Google, or AWS heavily influenced our benchmark run. Each one of these uses fairly homogeneous API design, which influenced some metric distributions and thresholds. We also eliminated a large number of very small services with less than five operations to not skew metrics in this direction. So, while our provided thresholds may be useful for a quick initial quality comparison, it may be sensible to select the input APIs more strictly to create a more appropriate size- or domain-specific benchmark. To enable such replication, our benchmark focuses on repeatability and adaptability.

---

[13] https://apiblueprint.org.

6   Conclusion

To support static analysis based on proposed service-based maintainability metrics in the context of microservices, we designed a tool-supported approach called RAMA (RESTful API Metric Analyzer). Service interface metrics are collected based on machine-readable descriptions of RESTful APIs. Our implemented prototypical tool, the RAMA CLI, currently supports the specification formats OpenAPI, RAML, and WADL as well as 10 metrics (seven for complexity, two for cohesion, and one size metric). To aid with results interpretation, we also conducted an empirical benchmark that calculated quartile-based threshold ranges (green, yellow, orange, red) for all RAMA CLI metrics using 1,737 public RESTful APIs. Since the thresholds are very dependent on the quality and relevance of the used APIs, we designed the automated benchmark to be repeatable. Accordingly, we published the RAMA CLI[14] as well as all results and artifacts of the threshold derivation study[15] on GitHub.

RAMA can be used by researchers and practitioners to efficiently calculate suitable service interface metrics for size, cohesion, or complexity, both for early quality evaluation or within continuous quality assurance. Concerning possible future work, a straight-forward option would be the extension of the RAMA CLI with additional input formats and metrics to increase its applicability and utility. Additionally, our static approach could be combined with existing dynamic approaches [6,12] to mitigate some of its described limitations. However, the most critical expansion for this line of research is the empirical evaluation of proposed service-based maintainability metrics, as most authors did not provide such evidence. Due to the lack of automatic collection approaches, such evaluation studies were previously challenging to execute at scale. Our preliminary work can therefore serve as a valuable foundation for such endeavors.

Acknowledgments. We kindly thank Marvin Tiedtke, Kim Truong, and Matthias Winterstetter for their help with the threshold study execution and tool development. Similarly, we thank Kai Chen and Florian Grotepass for their implementation support. This research was partially funded by the Ministry of Science of Baden-Württemberg, Germany, for the doctoral program *Services Computing* (https://www.services-computing.de/?lang=en).

References

1. Athanasopoulos, D., Zarras, A.V., Miskos, G., Issarny, V., Vassiliadis, P.: Cohesion-driven decomposition of service interfaces without access to source code. IEEE Trans. Serv. Comput. **8**(4), 550–5532 (2015). https://doi.org/10.1109/TSC.2014.2310195
2. Baggen, R., Correia, J.P., Schill, K., Visser, J.: Standardized code quality benchmarking for improving software maintainability. Software Qual. J. **20**(2), 287–307 (2012). https://doi.org/10.1007/s11219-011-9144-9

---

[14] https://github.com/restful-ma/rama-cli.
[15] https://github.com/restful-ma/thresholds.

3. Basci, D., Misra, S.: Data complexity metrics for XML web services. Adv. Electr. Comput. Eng. **9**(2), 9–15 (2009). https://doi.org/10.4316/aece.2009.02002
4. Bogner, J., Fritzsch, J., Wagner, S., Zimmermann, A.: Assuring the evolvability of microservices: insights into industry practices and challenges. In: 2019 IEEE International Conference on Software Maintenance and Evolution (ICSME), pp. 546–556. IEEE, Cleveland, Ohio, USA, September 2019. https://doi.org/10.1109/ICSME.2019.00089
5. Bogner, J., Fritzsch, J., Wagner, S., Zimmermann, A.: Microservices in industry: insights into technologies, characteristics, and software quality. In: 2019 IEEE International Conference on Software Architecture Companion (ICSA-C), pp. 187–195. IEEE, Hamburg, Germany, March 2019. https://doi.org/10.1109/ICSA-C.2019.00041
6. Bogner, J., Schlinger, S., Wagner, S., Zimmermann, A.: A modular approach to calculate service-based maintainability metrics from runtime data of microservices. In: Franch, X., Männistö, T., Martínez-Fernández, S. (eds.) PROFES 2019. LNCS, vol. 11915, pp. 489–496. Springer, Cham (2019). https://doi.org/10.1007/978-3-030-35333-9_34
7. Bogner, J., Wagner, S., Zimmermann, A.: Automatically measuring the maintainability of service- and microservice-based systems: a literature review. In: Proceedings of the 27th International Workshop on Software Measurement and 12th International Conference on Software Process and Product Measurement on - IWSM Mensura 2017, pp. 107–115. ACM Press, New York (2017). https://doi.org/10.1145/3143434.3143443
8. Bräuer, J., Saft, M., Plösch, R., Körner, C.: Improving object-oriented design quality: a portfolio- and measurement-based approach. In: Proceedings of the 27th International Workshop on Software Measurement and 12th International Conference on Software Process and Product Measurement on - IWSM Mensura 2017, pp. 244–254. ACM Press, New York (2017). https://doi.org/10.1145/3143434.3143454
9. Coleman, D., Ash, D., Lowther, B., Oman, P.: Using metrics to evaluate software system maintainability. Computer **27**(8), 44–49 (1994). https://doi.org/10.1109/2.303623
10. Daud, N.M.N., Kadir, W.M.N.W.: Static and dynamic classifications for SOA structural attributes metrics. In: 2014 8th. Malaysian Software Engineering Conference (MySEC), pp. 130–135. IEEE, Langkawi, September 2014. https://doi.org/10.1109/MySec.2014.6986002
11. Eismann, S., Bezemer, C.P., Shang, W., Okanović, D., van Hoorn, A.: Microservices: a performance tester's dream or nightmare? In: Proceedings of the ACM/SPEC International Conference on Performance Engineering, pp. 138–149. ACM, New York, April 2020. https://doi.org/10.1145/3358960.3379124
12. Engel, T., Langermeier, M., Bauer, B., Hofmann, A.: Evaluation of microservice architectures: a metric and tool-based approach. In: Mendling, J., Mouratidis, H. (eds.) CAiSE 2018. LNBIP, vol. 317, pp. 74–89. Springer, Cham (2018). https://doi.org/10.1007/978-3-319-92901-9_8
13. Gebhart, M., Abeck, S.: Metrics for evaluating service designs based on SoaML. Int. J. Adv. Software **4**(1), 61–75 (2011)
14. Haupt, F., Leymann, F., Scherer, A., Vukojevic-Haupt, K.: A framework for the structural analysis of REST APIs. In: 2017 IEEE International Conference on Software Architecture (ICSA), pp. 55–58. IEEE, Gothenburg, April 2017. https://doi.org/10.1109/ICSA.2017.40

15. Haupt, F., Leymann, F., Vukojevic-Haupt, K.: API governance support through the structural analysis of REST APIs. Comput. Sci. Res. Dev. **33**(3), 291–303 (2017). https://doi.org/10.1007/s00450-017-0384-1
16. Hirzalla, M., Cleland-Huang, J., Arsanjani, A.: A metrics suite for evaluating flexibility and complexity in service oiriented architectures. In: Feuerlicht, G., Lamersdorf, W. (eds.) ICSOC 2008. LNCS, vol. 5472, pp. 41–52. Springer, Heidelberg (2009). https://doi.org/10.1007/978-3-642-01247-1_5
17. International Organization For Standardization: ISO/IEC 25010 - Systems and software engineering - Systems and software Quality Requirements and Evaluation (SQuaRE) - System and software quality models (2011)
18. Mayer, B., Weinreich, R.: An approach to extract the architecture of microservice-based software systems. In: 2018 IEEE Symposium on Service-Oriented System Engineering (SOSE), pp. 21–30. IEEE, Bamberg, March 2018. https://doi.org/10.1109/SOSE.2018.00012
19. Neumann, A., Laranjeiro, N., Bernardino, J.: An analysis of public REST web service APIs. IEEE Trans. Serv. Comput. **PP**(c), 1 (2018). https://doi.org/10.1109/TSC.2018.2847344
20. Newman, S.: Building Microservices: Designing Fine-Grained Systems, 1st edn. O'Reilly Media, Sebastopol, CA, USA (2015)
21. Palma, F., Gonzalez-Huerta, J., Moha, N., Guéhéneuc, Y.-G., Tremblay, G.: Are RESTful APIs well-designed? Detection of their linguistic (Anti)patterns. In: Barros, A., Grigori, D., Narendra, N.C., Dam, H.K. (eds.) ICSOC 2015. LNCS, vol. 9435, pp. 171–187. Springer, Heidelberg (2015). https://doi.org/10.1007/978-3-662-48616-0_11
22. Papazoglou, M.: Service-oriented computing: concepts, characteristics and directions. In: Proceedings of the 4th International Conference on Web Information Systems Engineering (WISE 2003), p. 10. IEEE Computer Society, Rome, Italy (2003). https://doi.org/10.1109/WISE.2003.1254461
23. Pautasso, C.: RESTful web services: principles, patterns, emerging technologies. In: Bouguettaya, A., Sheng, Q.Z., Daniel, F. (eds.) Web Services Foundations, pp. 31–51. Springer, New York (2014). https://doi.org/10.1007/978-1-4614-7518-7_2
24. Perepletchikov, M., Ryan, C., Frampton, K.: Cohesion metrics for predicting maintainability of service-oriented software. In: Seventh International Conference on Quality Software (QSIC 2007), pp. 328–335. IEEE, Portland (2007). https://doi.org/10.1109/QSIC.2007.4385516
25. Petrillo, F., Merle, P., Palma, F., Moha, N., Guéhéneuc, Y.-G.: A lexical and semantic analysis on REST cloud computing APIs. In: Ferguson, D., Muñoz, V.M., Cardoso, J., Helfert, M., Pahl, C. (eds.) CLOSER 2017. CCIS, vol. 864, pp. 308–332. Springer, Cham (2018). https://doi.org/10.1007/978-3-319-94959-8_16
26. Schermann, G., Cito, J., Leitner, P.: All the services large and micro: revisiting industrial practice in services computing. In: Norta, A., Gaaloul, W., Gangadharan, G.R., Dam, H.K. (eds.) ICSOC 2015. LNCS, vol. 9586, pp. 36–47. Springer, Heidelberg (2016). https://doi.org/10.1007/978-3-662-50539-7_4
27. Sneed, H.M.: Measuring web service interfaces. In: 2010 12th IEEE International Symposium on Web Systems Evolution (WSE), pp. 111–115. IEEE, Timisoara, September 2010. https://doi.org/10.1109/WSE.2010.5623580
28. Vale, G., Fernandes, E., Figueiredo, E.: On the proposal and evaluation of a benchmark-based threshold derivation method. Software Qual. J. **27**(1), 275–306 (2018). https://doi.org/10.1007/s11219-018-9405-y

Optimizing Parametric Dependencies for Incremental Performance Model Extraction

Sonya Voneva[1]([⊠]), Manar Mazkatli[1]([⊠]), Johannes Grohmann[2]([⊠]),
and Anne Koziolek[1]([⊠])

[1] Karlsruhe Institute of Technology, Karlsruhe, Germany
uzeci@student.kit.edu,
{manar.mazkatli,koziolek}@kit.edu
[2] University of Würzburg, Würzburg, Germany
johannes.grohmann@uni-wuerzburg.de

Abstract. Model-based performance prediction in agile software development promises to evaluate design alternatives and to reduce the cost of performance tests. To minimize the differences between a real software and its performance model, parametric dependencies are introduced. They express how the performance model parameters (such as loop iteration count, branch transition probabilities, resource demands, and external service call arguments) depend on impacting factors like the input data.

The approaches that perform model-based performance prediction in agile software development have two major shortcomings: they are either costly because they do not update the performance models automatically after each commit, or do not consider more complex parametric dependencies than linear.

This work extends an approach for continuous integration of performance model during agile development. Our extension aims to optimize the learning of parametric dependencies with a genetic programming algorithm to be able to detect non-linear dependencies.

The case study results show that using genetic programming enables detecting more complex dependencies and improves the accuracy of the updated performance model.

Keywords: Performance model (PM) · Parametric dependencies · Genetic programming (GP) · Agile development

1 Introduction

When software performance does not meet the predefined requirements, delays, higher costs, and failures on deployment may occur [26]. Thus, the approach of Software Performance Engineering (SPE) is crucial in today's software development process. Model-based Performance Prediction (MbPP), first introduced by

© Springer Nature Switzerland AG 2020
H. Muccini et al. (Eds.): ECSA 2020, CCIS 1269, pp. 228–240, 2020.
https://doi.org/10.1007/978-3-030-59155-7_17

Smith [22] under the name SPE, aims to avoid potential performance issues using a performance model of the considered system. This allows the reproduction of the time-critical behaviour of a system based on a simulation [19]. PMs allow the developers to judge the quality of their software components and the design alternatives without investing the effort of actually implementing and testing them.

To describe the specific implementation of the components better, *parametric dependencies* are introduced. They express the relation between input arguments of a service and the Performance Model Parameters (PMPs). The PMPs are represented by abstract source code characterizations like loop iterations count, branch transition probabilities, resource demands, and arguments of external service calls. The parameterization allows answering "what-if"- questions, like MbPP for unseen usage profiles or design alternatives. For example, if we detected that the resource demand of a specific service equals *its input argument * 5*, we can easily simulate the system under new conditions (new input).

One disadvantage of MbPP is that creating a PM and keeping it consistent with the source code during agile software development is a time-consuming task. Until recently, researchers have focused on automating the extraction of PMs, but two main flaws are found in existing works [3, 4, 13, 15, 23, 25].

- in order to extract the PM after some update in the code, the whole system must be instrumented and run, which causes high monitoring overhead and discards the manual changes that may be applied to the extracted PMs (e.g., refinements to PMs architecture or to PMPs).
- they don't examine how the PMPs depend on input data, i.e. the parametric dependencies, except [7, 13].

In the approach, proposed by Mazkatli et al. [17], Continuous Integration of Performance Model (CIPM), both issues are addressed by incremental extraction and calibration of PMs with parametric dependencies.

The incremental calibration of CIPM [18] covers, however, only linear dependencies. This work extends CIPM by (1) advanced estimation of the external calls' arguments, considering the parametric dependencies and (2) by optimizing all the detected dependencies using a genetic algorithm. For goal (1), we filter the dependency candidates by applying feature selection. We furthermore search for a dependency not only to the input arguments of a service, but, considering the data flow, to the return values of the previous external calls.

This paper is structured as follows: Sect. 2 gives an overview of the backgrounds of our work, Sect. 3 presents a code example to clarify the definition of parametric dependencies. In Sect. 4 we elaborate on the specific steps of our approach. Section 5 covers the evaluation part of the work. In Sect. 6 the related work in the scientific field is discussed. Finally, Sect. 7 concludes the paper and suggests some future work.

2   Foundations

This chapter contains the foundations of our approach. We discuss the different tools, libraries and algorithms, involved in the process.

2.1   Palladio

Palladio is an approach to model and simulate architecture-level PMs. Within Palladio, the Palladio Component Model (PCM) defines a language for describing PMs: the static structure of the software (e.g. components and interfaces), the behavior, the required resource environment, the allocation of software components, and the usage profile.

The PCM Service Effect Specification (SEFF) [20] describes the behavior of a component service on an abstract level using different control flow elements: internal actions (a combination of internal computations that do not include calls to required services), external call actions (calls to required services), loops, and branch actions. SEFF loops and branch actions include at least one external call, otherwise they are merged into the internal actions to increase the level of abstraction. To predict the performance measures (response times, central processing unit (CPU) utilization, and throughput) the architects have to enrich the SEFFs with PMPs. Examples of PMPs are resource demands (processing amount that internal action requests from a certain active resource, such as a CPU or hard disk), the probability of selecting a branch, the number of loop iterations, and the arguments of external calls.

Palladio uses the stochastic expression (StoEx) language to define PMPs as expressions that contain random variables or empirical distributions. StoEx allows to refer to variable properties (e.g. `NUMBER_OF_ELEMENTS`, `VALUE`, `BYTESIZE`, and `TYPE`). StoEx also supports calculations (e.g. `5*file.BYTESIZE`) and comparisons (e.g. `(x.VALUE > 8) ? 1 : 2`) [20].

2.2   Kieker

Kieker [9] is an extensible open-source application performance management tool, which allows capturing, analyzing and visualizing execution traces of source code. Monitoring probes are inserted into the source code without modifying it. They can be predefined and customized or dynamic and adaptive. We use Kieker with manually instrumented code to store monitoring records. For defining the structure of the records we use the Instrumentation Record Language (IRL) [10].

2.3   Algorithms

For detecting initial parametric dependencies we integrated two Machine Learning (ML) algorithms from the Java library Weka [8]. Linear regression is used for estimating dependencies which consists only of numeric values. Decision tree is adopted for all dependencies which contain numeric and nominal values.

For refining the initial dependencies we applied Genetic Programming (GP) [12]. It is a meta-heuristic machine learning technique which, inspired by the Darwinian principle of survival and evolution of the fittest, finds an optimal solution to a search problem. The definition of optimal is according to a predefined *fitness function*. Each potential solution is referred to as an *individual*. Furthermore, individuals consist of *genes*. GP is a special kind of genetic algorithm with genes, forming a tree structure.

In the following, the most important elements of GP will be described. A *gene repository* stores the genes, which itself is a base for creating a *chromosome repository*. The chromosome repository keeps all chromosomes. A chromosome is a potential solution of the problem, whereas the genes are the particles, of which that solution is composed. A set of chromosomes is called a *generation*.

A typical GP approach consists of multiple steps, which are repeated in many iterations. In the first iteration an initial generation is created from individuals in the chromosome repository. Next, the *crossover* and *mutation* take place. The process of crossover is analogous to biological crossover in human reproduction - parent chromosomes are recombined to form new children. Mutation is simply changing one or multiple genes of a chromosome to ensure genetic diversity.

The fitness function determines how "good"/"fit" an individual is. In order to define the fitness of an individual, domain expertise on properties of the expected optimal solution is required.

2.4   Continuous Integration of Performance Model

Continuous Integration of Performance Model (CIPM) is an approach to automatically keep the architectural PM consistent during the agile software development [17]. Its idea is to respond to the changes in source code by updating and calibrating the PM incrementally.

CIPM uses predefined consistency rules [14] that propagate the changes in source code to the PM using model-based transformations. Additionally, CIPM applies model-based instrumentation that instruments only the changed parts of source code to provide the required monitoring data for calibrating the new/updated parts of PMs.

After executing the source code, CIPM analyses the generated monitoring data to calibrate PMs incrementally [11,18]. The incremental calibration estimates the missing PMPs considering the (linear) parametric dependencies. For the detection of the parametric dependencies, CIPM uses ML algorithms like linear regression and decision tree, which may result in inaccurate parametrized PMPs if more complex dependencies exist.

CIPM updates also the deployment and usage parts of PMs to respond to the potential changes in deployment or usage profile. To validate the accuracy of the updated PM, CIPM starts the simulation and calculates the variation between the monitoring data and the simulation results to show the estimation error.

3   Parametric Dependencies Example

To illustrate the meaning of a parametric dependency, listing 1.1 will be examined. In this code piece, we have two components - A and B. The presented method from component A - serviceA() calls three services from its external component - B. This means that component A is the *requiring* component and component B is the *providing* component. As one can notice, the branch transition and the arguments of the external service calls depend on the arguments of serviceA().

The external calls in this scenario are the calls to serviceB1(), serviceB2() and serviceB3(). We try to estimate the dependency between each argument of an external call and the corresponding candidates for a dependency from the arguments of serviceA() or the data flow like the list result. The candidates for a dependency can be arguments from the same data type (as the external call argument) or arguments which have a characteristic from the same data type. For example, the candidates for the integer argument of the serviceB2 are the x.VALUE, y.VALUE and result.NUMBER_OF_ELEMENTS. These candidates are used to build a dataset which is the training set of our ML algorithms, which try to detect the dependencies. In PCM the dependencies can be represented as a *StoEx* (see Sect. 2.1). So, if the dependencies in this example are successfully detected the *StoEx*s would be: 4 * y.VALUE for the argument of the serviceB1(), x.VALUE ^ 2 + y.VALUE for the argument of the serviceB2() and result.NUMBER_OF_ELEMENTS for the argument of the serviceB3().

```
   public class A {
2
       private B componentB;
4
       public void serviceA(int x, int y, boolean b){
6          /* Some internal action */
           if(b){
8              /* Some internal action */
               List<Integer> result = componentB.serviceB1(4*y);
10             componentB.serviceB2(Math.pow(x,2) + y);
               componentB.serviceB3(result.size());
12         }
           . . .
14     }
   }
```

Listing 1.1. Example of a service (serviceA()) calling external services (serviceB1() and serviceB2() or serviceB3())

4   Approach

The proposed approach is part of the vision described by Mazkatli and Koziolek [17], see section Sect. 2.4. They describe a tool which automatically updates a PM, represented as PCM, from iterative source code changes. The incremental calibration [18] enriches the extracted PM with parametric dependencies of the form:

$$D_i(P) = (a * p_0 + b * p_1 + ... + z * p_n + C) \tag{1}$$

where $p_0, p_1..p_n$ are numeric service arguments or numeric attributes of the caller's arguments. $a..z$ are the weights of the input arguments and C is a constant. This work aims to additionally detect non-linear parametric dependencies for external call arguments and for all types of PMPs and to refine the linear dependencies.

In the following, we present an overview of our workflow (cf. Fig. 1).

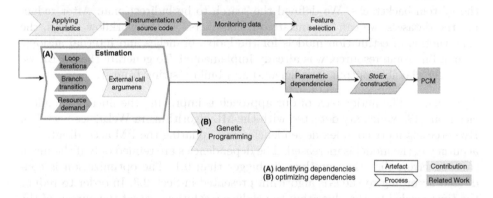

Fig. 1. Workflow of our approach

Preprocessing. We begin by applying some heuristics, similarly to [13], before monitoring the source code. The point is to reduce the monitoring overhead by recording only performance-relevant information. For example, if we have an input argument which has the type List<T>, we may not be interested in its specific elements. Therefore, we monitor only its size. In our approach, we defined which characteristics should be monitored for every data type which is handled.

Afterwards, the source code is instrumented using the framework Kieker, see Sect. 2.2, similarly to [18].

The collected monitoring data is one of the inputs needed for our dependency estimation approach. The other input is the PCM of the system. We can easily differentiate between the records of the PMPs, because Kieker stores them as separate types. We have monitoring record types for loop, branch, internal action demanding a resource, and an external call action. For example, a monitoring record for the latter contains information like external action id, service execution id, caller id, caller execution id, input parameters, return value, entry and exit timestamps. More information on this can be found in this Bachelor's thesis [24].

Feature Selection and ML Models. The monitoring records are then converted to datasets (for each PMP a separate one), which are valid as inputs for the algorithms of Weka [8]. We use this library for feature selection and then creating an estimation model for each PMP. We filter the dataset to remove all attributes which do not have an impact on the prediction quality. For judging this, the `ClassifierSubsetEval` class was chosen, which evaluates attribute subsets on training data. It uses a classifier to estimate the 'merit' of a set of attributes. In our case the classifiers are `LinearRegression` - for numeric values only, and `J48` - a decision tree, implementing the C4.5 algorithm ([21]), for both nominal and numeric values. The evaluator also needs a specified search technique. Our choice - `BestFirst` performs greedy hill climbing with backtracking; one can specify how many consecutive non-improving nodes must be encountered before the system backtracks. We defined the search to be bidirectional. After reducing the datasets, we can instantiate our classifiers. As the workflow shows, the construction of estimation models for the loops, branches and internal actions, demanding some resource, was already implemented. To generate the *StoEx*, we parse the classifier output (coefficients) and build a string from it.

Optimizing. The major part of our approach is improving the linear dependencies from [18], which are detected with the ML algorithms in Weka, see Sect. 2.3. By detecting more complex dependencies and updating the PM accordingly, the accuracy of the model is increased. The dependencies are refined only if the mean squared error, that they produce, is bigger than 0.1. The optimization is conducted according to the GP algorithm presented in Sect. 2.3. In order to reduce the time needed by the algorithm to produce a solution, we set the output of the above-mentioned ML algorithms as an initial parametric dependency (starting point of the genetic evolution).

Similarly to the approach of Krogmann et al. [13], we model genes as mathematical functions to express more complex dependencies. Figure 2 depicts an example of a gene. This is very beneficial for our approach since both, the *Abstract Syntax Tree (AST)* of the *StoEx* language and the genes of GP have tree structures and we are able to easily transform the initial *StoEx* into a starting individual for the GP.

Another worth-mentioning feature of the GP is the *fitness function*. In our implementation the fitness of an individual (mathematical expression) is judged according to its complexity (depth of AST) and prediction accuracy (mean squared error). Moreover, each algorithm run (evolution) is restricted by a maximum run time and a maximum number of generations - these limits are implemented as parameters of the algorithm.

In our work, we used the Jenetics library[1], written in Java, which provides a GP implementation. In contrast to other GP implementations, Jenetics uses

---

[1] https://jenetics.io/manual/manual-5.1.0.pdf.

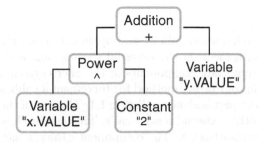

Fig. 2. Tree representation of the individual $x^2 + y$

the concept of an evolution stream for executing the evolution steps. Therefore, it is no longer necessary to perform the evolution steps in an imperative way.

The final step of the workflow is constructing the *StoEx* - this involves some string processing. Then, the *StoEx* is inserted in the PCM at the right place and as an output of our approach we deliver the PCM, enriched with the optimized parametric dependencies.

5   Case Study

Our evaluation is twofold. First, we judge the importance of feature selection and the accuracy of the initial estimated dependencies. Second, we evaluate the optimization technique GP. In the first part, we compare the accuracy and the complexity of the estimated dependencies when feature selection is used and when not. The results do not show a significant impact of using the feature selection for numerical variables in contrast to using it for nominal ones [24]. Therefore, due to lack of space in this paper we focus on the second part of the evaluation to show the most representative results.

5.1   Goal and Scenario

Our main research question is: *which PM is more accurate - with GP optimization or without?* To answer this question, we calibrate three different PMs: one with our approach, one considering only linear dependencies and the last one - without any parametric dependencies. For the calibration, we use a monitoring data generated by a usage profile P1. Then, we use the three models to predict the performance for unforeseen usage profile P2. To compare the prediction power of these PMs, we compare the predicted response times by the simulations with the actual response times that we can measure for P2. Both response times are distributions, therefore we use the following metrics to compare the similarity: Kolmogorov-Smirnov-Test (KS-Test) [6] that tests whether two empirical distributions come from the same underlying distribution, the Wasserstein metric [16] that quantifies the effort needed to transfer one distribution into the other, and conventional statistical measures. For both KS-Test and Wasserstein, the lower the value is, the higher is the accuracy of PM.

5.2   Setup

To answer the research question above we implemented an artificial example - a small application with focus on the external service calls with complex dependencies. The most important components of the micro-system are:

class A contains our target method for incremental calibration of the PCM - serviceA(). Its first part is shown in listing 1.1. The rest of the method consists of a loop and some other external service calls. This method has three arguments - int x, int y, and boolean b. The component class A has the PCM role of a *requiring* component - this means it requires some external services.

class B encapsulates six methods which are called by class A.So class B has the PCM role of a *providing* component. Each of these six methods has only one input argument and contains an internal action, which does some computations like calculating prime numbers or square root of 1000 numbers in an array. The arguments of the called methods in class B each have a different dependency to the service argument(s) of class A. To ensure variety we set different dependencies: linear, qudratic, cubic, negation, etc.

First, we apply a fine-grained monitoring using the following usage profile P1 to generate the required monitoring data for the calibration. For this, we ran serviceA() 500 times with ten simulated concurrent users. We chose the arguments x, y and b as follows: random integer from the set $[0..9]$, random integer from the set $[1,..10]$, and random boolean. With the described setup the monitoring itself took around 20 min. After this, we calibrated three different PMs - one only with distribution functions of the estimated PMPs (manually calibrated), one after learning the linear dependencies as described in [18] and one with more complex (optimized) dependencies as described in this paper.

Then, we start the simulation using the three PMs to predict the response time of serviceA() for the unforeseen usage profile (P2): i.e., changing the x parameter to a random integer from the set $[0..19]$, y parameter to random integer from the set $[1..20]$, and b to random boolean. We repeat the simulation 50 times for each PM to make the results more representative.

As a reference, we monitor serviceA() coarse-grained for the usage profile (P2), to create a validation set for the evaluation. Coarse-grained monitoring records the entry and exit times without the unnecessary monitoring overhead, like service id or arguments. Finally, we compare the simulation results with the actual monitoring data using the metrics defined in Sect. 5.1.

5.3   Results

First, we want to discuss the time aspect of calibrating a PMs with our approach and the benefits of doing this iteratively. We measured that identifying and optimizing all six dependencies between arguments of serviceA() and arguments of the external calls from class B takes around **35** s on average. A linear dependency is detected for around **4** s (with the ML algorithms) and a quadratic, for example, takes around **10** s, as it involves the optimization process. In a scenario, where only one input argument of an external service call is changed the iterative update of the PM, i.e. considering only the modified parts of the code, could save us a serious percentage of the optimization time.

Table 1 presents a comparison between the response times of serviceA() over 50 iterations according to the monitoring data and to the three PMs simulations. From each distribution, the quartiles, as well as the minimum, maximum, and average values are calculated. As the table shows, the performance prediction of the PM that is calibrated with our approach - optimizing parametric dependencies, is the closest prediction to the actual monitoring response time in comparison to the prediction of other PMs: PM that is calibrated with linear dependencies and PM that is distribution functions, where parametric dependencies for external service calls are not handled at all.

Table 1. Response times (in seconds) of the three PMs: first - parameterized only with distribution functions for the external call arguments, then - only with linear dependencies for all PMPs and finally - with more complex dependencies for all PMPs.

Distribution	Min	Q1	Q2	Q3	Max	Avg
Monitoring	0.009	0.217	0.59	1.318	2.589	0.825
Distribution functions	**0.021**	1.576	2.857	4.369	7.151	3.045
Linear functions	0.025	1.643	2.904	4.546	7.082	3.078
Optimized	0.111	**0.676**	**1.222**	**1.676**	**2.232**	**1.199**

In Table 2, again the simulations of the PMs are compared, but this time with different metrics - KS-Test [6] and Wasserstein [16]. As the numbers from Table 2 indicate, the **Optimized** PM improves the KS-Test value by **0.302** and the Wasserstein value by **1.255** on average. This improvement is roughly **two** times for the KS-Test value and **five** times for the Wasserstein value. These results confirm that the **Optimized** PM has the highest similarity to the actual system.

Table 2. Comparison of the metrics KS-Test and Wasserstein of the three models: first - parameterized only with distribution functions for the external call arguments, then - only with linear dependencies for all PMPs and finally - with more complex dependencies for all PMPs.

Metric	Distribution functions	Linear functions	Optimized
KS Q1	0.585	0.581	**0.278**
KS Avg.	0.595	0.592	**0.293**
KS Q3	0.608	0.601	**0.300**
WS Q1	1.527	1.535	**0.292**
WS Avg.	1.568	1.56	**0.313**
WS Q3	1.609	1.591	**0.339**

6   Related Work

Various approaches for extracting an architectural model based on static (e.g. [2,14]), dynamic (e.g. [3,4,23]), or hybrid analysis (e.g. [13]) exist. In comparison to our approach, the aforementioned approaches require monitoring overhead to extract consistent PMs during agile software development and do not keep the previous potential manual changes to PMs. Similarly to the approach of Krogmann et al. [13], we use GP to detect the parametric dependencies. In contrast to their work, we use the GP during an incremental calibration of PMs. This reduces the required overhead by GP to learn the dependencies, because our approach uses GP only to optimize the PMPs that have been changed in the recent development iteration and have a high cross-validation error by the used initial ML algorithms.

The following works also consider parametric dependencies. Grohmann et al. [7] introduce an approach to identify and to characterize [1] parametric dependencies for PMs using monitoring data from a running system. This monitoring data is then analyzed and correlations between different parameters are identified with the use of different feature selection approaches from the area of the ML. This approach does not represent the parametric dependencies as *StoEx* or support the iterative updates to PM. Courtois et al. [5] use multivariate adaptive regression splines to extract parametric dependencies. They perform dedicated performance tests to obtain the data on which they fit the regression splines. This approach also lacks the incremental fashion of PM construction.

7   Conclusion and Future Work

The contribution of this work is twofold. First, we presented an approach for the incremental estimation of external calls' arguments for CIPM, considering parametric dependencies. For this, we apply some feature selection algorithms to reduce the number of candidates for the proposed ML algorithms that identify (initial) dependencies.

The second part of our work is the optimization of the parametric dependencies for all types of PMPs using a GP algorithm, which refines the outputs of the ML algorithms (*PMPs as StoEx*) and eventually finds more complex dependencies than linear. To sum up, the implemented mechanism needs two inputs - a PCM and monitoring data from instrumented source code. The output of our algorithms are the *optimized PMPs as StoEx*, which are inserted in the PCM, so that at the end we enriched a PCM with parametric dependencies.

To evaluate the implemented technique, we ran the simulation for the artificial micro-system using three different PMs, parameterized in different ways, and compared between the response time of our target service according to the monitoring records and the simulated response times. The results show that the PM with optimized parametric dependencies has an accuracy of **two** times (Kolmogorov-Smirnov-Test value) and **five** times (Wasserstein metric) higher than a PM with linear or distribution functions only. This confirms that the optimization improves the accuracy of the PM.

Our approach promises to detect more complex dependencies during the incremental calibration to improve the accuracy of the iteratively updated PMs. Therefore, we plan to integrate our implementation with the implemented pipeline, proposed in [18], and to perform further evaluation using different case studies.

In future works we aim to develop an optimization mechanism which handles the dependencies of the nominal arguments as well, as our implementation lacks this feature. Additionally, we aim to extend our approach to detect the dependencies to the service arguments of composite data types. One idea in this direction is traversing all fields of the composite argument until reaching primitive ones.

References

1. Ackermann, V.: Blackbox learning of parametric dependencies for performance models from monitoring data (2018)
2. Becker, S., Hauck, M., Trifu, M., Krogmann, K., Kofron, J.: Reverse engineering component models for quality predictions. In: 2010 14th European Conference on Software Maintenance and Reengineering, pp. 194–197 (03 2010)
3. Brosig, F., Huber, N., Kounev, S.: Automated extraction of architecture-level performance models of distributed component-based systems. In: Proceedings of the 2011 26th IEEE/ACM International Conference on Automated Software Engineering, pp. 183–192. IEEE Computer Society (2011)
4. Brunnert, A., Vögele, C., Krcmar, H.: Automatic performance model generation for java enterprise edition (ee) applications. In: European workshop on performance engineering pp. 74–88 (09 2013). https://doi.org/10.1007/978-3-642-40725-3-7
5. Courtois, M., Woodside, M.: Using regression splines for software performance analysis. In: Proceedings of the 2nd International Workshop on Software and Performance, pp. 105–114 (2000)
6. Dodge, Y.: The Concise Encyclopedia of Statistics, Chapter Kolmogorov-Smirnov Test, pp. 283–287. Springer, New York (2008)
7. Grohmann, J., Eismann, S., Elflein, S., von Kistowski, J., Kounev, S., Mazkatli, M.: Detecting parametric dependencies for performance models using feature selection techniques. In: 2019 IEEE 27th International Symposium on Modeling, Analysis, and Simulation of Computer and Telecommunication Systems (MASCOTS), pp. 309–322 (2019)
8. Hall, M., Frank, E., Holmes, G., Pfahringer, B., Reutemann, P., Witten, I.H.: The WEKA data mining software: an update. SIGKDD Explor. Newsl. 11(1), 10–18 (2009)
9. van Hoorn, A., Waller, J., Hasselbring, W.: Kieker: a framework for application performance monitoring and dynamic software analysis. In: Proceedings of the 3rd ACM/SPEC International Conference on Performance Engineering. ICPE 2012 (2012)
10. Jung, R.: An instrumentation record language for kieker. Technical report., Kiel University (2013). https://doi.org/10.13140/RG.2.1.3655.5689
11. Jägers, J.P.: Iterative performance model parameter estimation considering parametric dependencies (2018)
12. Koza, J.R.: Genetic Programming: On the Programming of Computers by Means of Natural Selection. MIT Press, Cambridge, MA, USA (1992)

13. Krogmann, K., Kuperberg, M., Reussner, R.: Using genetic search for reverse engineering of parametric behavior models for performance prediction. IEEE Trans. Softw. Eng. **36**, 865–877 (2010). https://doi.org/10.1109/TSE.2010.69
14. Langhammer, M.: Automated Coevolution of Source Code and Software Architecture Models. Ph.D. thesis, Karlsruhe Institute of Technology, Karlsruhe, Germany (2017)
15. Langhammer, M., Shahbazian, A., Medvidovic, N., Reussner, R.H.: Automated extraction of rich software models from limited system information. In: 2016 13th Working IEEE/IFIP Conference on Software Architecture (WICSA). IEEE (2016)
16. Majewski, S., Ciach, M., Startek, M., Niemyska, W., Miasojedow, B., Gambin, A.: The wasserstein distance as a dissimilarity measure for mass spectra with application to spectral deconvolution. In: 18th International Workshop on Algorithms in Bioinformatics (WABI 2018) (2018)
17. Mazkatli, M., Koziolek, A.: Continuous integration of performance model, pp. 153–158 (04 2018). https://doi.org/10.1145/3185768.3186285
18. Mazkatli, M., Monschein, D., Grohmann, J., Koziolek, A.: Incremental calibration of architectural performance models with parametric dependencies. In: IEEE International Conference on Software Architecture (ICSA 2020) (2020)
19. Pooley, R.: Software Engineering and Performance: a road-map. In: ICSE-Future of SE Track, pp. 189–199 (2000)
20. Reussner, R.H., et al.: Modeling and Simulating Software Architectures- The Palladio Approach. MIT Press, Cambridge (2016)
21. Ruggieri, S.: Efficient c4.5. IEEE Trans. Knowl. Data Eng. 14(2), 438–444 (2002). https://doi.org/10.1109/69.991727
22. Smith, C.U.: Performance Engineering of Software Systems, 1st edn. Addison-Wesley Longman Publishing Co., Inc, Boston, MA, USA (1990)
23. Spinner, S., Walter, J., Kounev, S.: A reference architecture for onlineperformance model extraction in virtualized environments. In: Companion Publication for ACM/SPEC on International. Conference on Performance Engineering, pp. 57–62. Association for Computing Machinery, New York, USA (2016)
24. Voneva, S.: Optimizing parametric dependencies for performance model extraction. bachelor's thesis (2020). https://sdqweb.ipd.kit.edu/publications/pdfs/Voneva20a.pdf
25. Walter, J., Stier, C., Koziolek, H., Kounev, S.: An expandable extraction framework for architectural performance models. In: Proceedings of the 8th ACM/SPEC on International Conference on Performance Engineering Companion, pp. 165–170. ICPE 2017 Companion, ACM, New York, USA (2017)
26. Woodside, M., Franks, G., Petriu, D.: The future of software performance engineering, pp. 171–187 (06 2007). https://doi.org/10.1109/FOSE.2007.32

Data Pipeline Architecture for Serverless Platform

Chinmaya Dehury[1]([✉])(iD), Pelle Jakovits[1], Satish Narayana Srirama[1](iD),
Vasilis Tountopoulos[2], and Giorgos Giotis[2]

[1] University of Tartu, Tartu, Estonia
{chinmaya.dehury,jakovits,srirama}@ut.ee
[2] Athens Technology Center S.A., Athens, Greece
{v.tountopoulos,g.giotis}@atc.gr

Abstract. To provide cost effective cloud resources with high QoS, serverless platform is introduced that allows to pay for the exact amount of resource usage. On the other hand, a number of data management tools are developed to handle the data from a large number of IoT sensing devices. However, the modern data-intensive cloud applications require the power that comes from integrating data management tools with serverless platforms. This paper proposes a novel data pipeline architecture for serverless platform for providing an environment to develop applications that can be broken into independently deployable, schedulable, scalable, and re-usable modules and efficiently manage the flow of data between different environments.

Keywords: Serverless computing · Data pipelines · TOSCA · DevOps

1 Introduction

While moving towards a more matured utility computing to offer the computing resources on a on-demand basis with pay-as-you-go pricing model, Cloud Service Providers (CSPs) are designing and developing serverless platforms, such as AWS Lambda, Google Cloud Functions, etc. Here the cloud services are broken down to the level of individual functions triggered by different events.

This event-driven computing model uses container technology. For each function, a dedicated container is created that hosts the function and provides the necessary virtual resources. Such containers only need to run while the function is being executed and this enables developers and cloud consumers to pay for exact usage of the resources, even at the granularity of hundreds of milliseconds.

In the case of data-intensive cloud applications, it is necessary to efficiently handle the flow of huge data volume, using different data management tools /architectures, such as Apache Nifi [1], Apache Beam [4], Amazon data pipeline [3], data mesh, etc. For this matter, serverless platforms need to be mature enough to work with the data pipeline technologies. On the other hand, existing data pipeline architectures should be developed for integration purpose to

© Springer Nature Switzerland AG 2020
H. Muccini et al. (Eds.): ECSA 2020, CCIS 1269, pp. 241–246, 2020.
https://doi.org/10.1007/978-3-030-59155-7_18

invoke remote serverless functions. To fill this research gap, this paper presents a data pipeline architecture for the serverless platform using the Topology and Orchestration Specification for Cloud Applications (TOSCA) [5] standard. The goal is to allow developers to rapidly model, develop, and deploy data pipeline applications that are compatible with the serverless paradigm.

The rest of the paper is organized as follows. The proposed methodology for the data pipeline architecture is explained in Sect. 2 together with used technologies. Section 3 presents a possible use case of proposed architecture. Section 4 concludes the paper with the scope for further developments of the proposed architecture.

2   Methodology

This section discusses the overall concept of how to model data pipeline applications with the TOSCA language. It is important to note that TOSCA specification is not designed for modeling the flow of data. To fill up this gap, RADON consortium has proposed an architecture that includes the methodology of how data pipelines should be modeled and orchestrated [7].

TOSCA [5] is a recently developed standard focusing on the portability and interoperability of the cloud-based applications. The TOSCA-based application blueprint describes the structure and management aspects of the whole application. The structure of the applications is defined by a graph consisting of a set of nodes (to represent software components) and edges (to represent relationship among software components), collectively known as the *topology template*. Further, the standard allows the user to provide information that is enough to make automatic deployment and un-deployment of the applications, provisioning of the resources, and manage the life-cycle of the application etc. [8].

2.1   Pipeline Modelling

The modeling of the pipeline and general overview of the proposed architecture is presented in this section. It is essential to understand the general requirement of a data-pipeline based serverless application. Users should be able to seamlessly and efficiently integrate the serverless functions with different data sources and storage services to handle the data flow. The pipeline should provide a way to handle the data in an efficient manner. It should also consider the performance mismatch among the pipelines and facilitate a data buffering or queuing if needed.

The proposed architecture provides a set of TOSCA models to fulfill the requirements of serverless applications. Under the hood, open-source data management platform **Apache NiFi** [1] is used for automating the movement, routing, and transformation of data between different systems and services. NiFi introduces essential components such as processors, input ports, output ports and queues between processors. The processors are individual tasks for carrying out activities such as reading/writing the data from/to local and remote services, routing data to FaaS functions, modifying the content of data, etc. Currently only NiFi is supported but other data management platforms, such as **Amazon data pipeline** [3] can be introduces as an alternative. **Amazon data pipeline** [3] is a cloud service offered by Amazon to handle the movement and transformation of the data within the AWS cloud services, such as S3 buckets, different databases, AWS lambda functions, etc. This allows developers to schedule data analytics operations or configure data copying tasks to be invoked by different events. Furthermore, Ansible automation engine is used for implementing the life-cycle management commands (e.g. install, configure, start, stop) of the TOSCA models.

The hierarchy of developed TOSCA models (within RADON consortium) for data pipeline based applications for the serverless platform is presented in Fig. 1. It can be seen that the TOSCA models are mainly divided into three groups, under the umbrella of abstract node type *PipelineBlock*: *SourcePB*, *MidwayPB*, and *DestinationPB*. The detailed description of the above models is presented in the following sections.

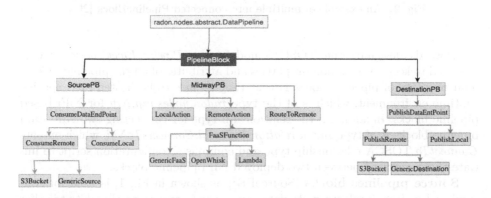

Fig. 1. TOSCA-based pipeline models hierarchy [2].

Modelling Basic Pipelines. Each pipeline acts like a black box, which receives some input, processes the input data, and then gives the desired output. A pipeline can also be used to redirect without any processing. Keeping that in mind, a basic pipeline unit, known as *PipelineBlock*, is created, as shown in the example Fig. 2. Each *PipelineBlock* consists of a queue to hold the incoming data, i.e., *DataIngestionQueue*, a dedicated queue to hold the output, i.e., *DataEmissionQueue*, and a sequence of one or more data analytics tasks between both the queues. Both the queues can be connected to data endpoints or another *PipelineBlock*. An example of how multiple *PipelineBlocks* can be used is presented in Fig. 2. The example consists of two *PipelineBlocks*: *PipelineBlock1*, and *PipelineBlock2*. The *PipelineBlock1* is responsible for invoking a serverless function after receiving the data from an external data end-point, and *PipelineBlock2* is responsible for pushing the processed data to an external storage component, i.e. S3Bucket. Here both the pipelines are independent and are very loosely coupled. For such feature, *PipelineBlock1* can be connected to any other Pipelines to bush the data or to further process the output from first pipeline. Similarly, *PipelineBlock1* can be replaced by other pipelines to invoke serverless function deployed in different cloud environment.

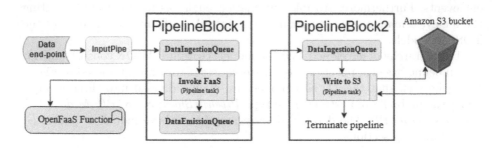

Fig. 2. An example of multiple interconnected PipelineBlock [2].

Towards designing the TOSCA models, the *PipelineBlock* node type is designed to keep the common properties and attributes of all the pipelines. Common property of pipeline blocks is that they *require* to be hosted on a specific runtime environment, which is of the type *radon.nodes.nifi.Nifi* for NiFi based pipeline blocks. In addition, the relationship type for connecting two NiFi data pipeline blocks is of type *radon.relationships.nifi.ConnectsToNifi*, which extents *ConnectTo* TOSCA relationship type and contains a configuration script to initiate the connection between two deployed NiFi pipeline blocks.

Source pipelines blocks (SourcePB), as shown in Fig. 1, is used for consuming data from local or remote data sources and *requires* passing data to other pipeline blocks. *SourcePB* is used to derive *ConsumeDataEndPoint* TOSCA node type, which in turn is used to derive: *ConsumeRemote* and *ConsumeLocal*. *ConsumeRemote* node type is used for consuming data from external sources and contains types such as *ConsS3Bucket* for reading data from AWS S3 buckets and *GenericSource* for reading data from a generic external storage. To read the data from the local file system, we have designed *ConsumeLocal* node type, which needs the value of the *directory*, indicating the path of the directory from where data need to be fetched.

Midway pipeline block (MidwayPB) is designed for intermediate data transformation or analytic tasks and it requires both incoming and outgoing connections from other node types. Three dedicated node types: *LocalAction*, *RemoteAction*, and *RouteToRemote* are derived from *MidwayPB*. *LocalAction* node type can be used to perform data processing tasks on local server. *RemoteAction* node type is used to invoke remote services to perform some processing operations on the data. Such as *FaaSFuntion* node type, which models functions from different serverless platforms. For example, under *FaaSFunction, Lambda* node type is created to invoke the AWS lambda function. Its basic properties are *function_name*, *cred_file_path* for credential file, *region* of the function etc. Similarly, node type to invoke Google Cloud Function can also be developed by deriving the *FaaSFunction* node type. *RouteToRemote* node type is designed to route data objects based on their characteristics. For instance, multiple serverless functions can be deployed to handle different image sizes, and images can be routed to different functions based on their size. One function can be designed to process only images smaller than 10 MB and another to handle images larger than 100 MB. In such scenarios, *RouteToRemote* node type can play a major role in routing images to the most appropriate FaaS functions.

Destination pipeline block (DestinationPB) is similar to *SourcePB* node type, with the main difference that *DestinationPB* is used to publish data to a data source or an external service. *PublishRemote* TOSCA node type can be used to publish the data to AWS S3Bucket (using *PubsS3Bucket*) or to a generic data end-point that can be accessed remotely (using *GenericDestination* node type). Similarly, to publish the data to the local file system, *PublishLocal* can be used, with the only minimum input being the *directory*, which indicates where to put the data in the local machine. This node type must have the *capability* to accept connection from either *SourcePB* or from *MidwayPB*.

3 Use Case: Tourism Promotion

A Mobile and web-based cloud application for tourism promotion, Viarota [6] can be seen as a potential application of the proposed architecture. Viarota provides optimal loyalty-based personalised tour plans developed within the RADON project [7]. To promote these tours, Viarota crawls the user's posts and views from different social media sources and tour related websites, such as Twitter, Facebook, Youtube, etc. The crawled data are then processed and stored in a database for providing aggregated reviews on the visits placed in the proposed tours. The data pipeline approach can be applied while crawling the data from different online sources, and process the crawled data by invoking different FaaS functions, etc. In this case, relevant pipelines, include data, such as the taxonomy concepts for the places of visit being included in the tours proposed for a touristic destination, their various combinations into tours, the automatically collected posts from various social media sources, which relate to what is said about the places and their index file, containing annotations, like the time of the posts, the inferred season, the sentiment expressed in them and eventually the reflected emotion. By applying the data pipeline approach, the whole application can be broken into multiple independent deployable, schedulable, scalable, and re-usable microservice-based modules. This would accelerate the development process of such a data-intensive application.

4 Conclusions and Future Works

In this paper, an architecture based on the data pipeline approach is proposed for the serverless platform. The architecture uses and extends the TOSCA specification for data pipeline based serverless applications. Apache NiFi is used as the underlined technology and Ansible as the automation engine for the implementation of the life-cycle of the serverless components. Different TOSCA nodes are proposed for consuming, publishing, and transforming data, including the utilization of remote serverless functions for analytical tasks.

Development of additional TOSCA nodes for a variety of functionalities, such as node type to handle the data movement through a secure channel, encrypting the data only in case of multi-cloud environment, etc. are the part of the future development plan of the proposed architecture. Further, a set of necessary TOSCA node types will be developed for the implementation of the Viarota solution based on data pipeline approach in order to support this application scenario in effectively managing the involved data pipelines and their movement across different cloud-based environments.

Acknowledgment. This work is partially funded by the European Union's Horizon 2020 research and innovation project RADON (825040).

References

1. Apache NiFi (2019). https://nifi.apache.org/. Accessed 21 October 2019
2. D5.5-Data-Pipeline-Orchestration-I, 16 July 2020 (2019). http://radon-h2020.eu/wp-content/uploads/2020/01/D5.5-Data-Pipeline-Orchestration-I.pdf
3. AWS data pipeline documentation (2020). https://docs.aws.amazon.com/data-pipeline/. Accessed 24 January 2020
4. Beam overview, 16 July 2020 (2020). https://beam.apache.org/
5. Topology and orchestration specification for cloud applications (TOSCA) standard v1.3 26 February 2020 (2020). https://docs.oasis-open.org/tosca/TOSCA-Simple-Profile-YAML/v1.3/TOSCA-Simple-Profile-YAML-v1.3.html
6. Viarota - enhance the travel experience of your visitors 25 June 2020 (2020). https://viarota.com/
7. Casale, et al.: Radon: rational decomposition and orchestration for serverless computing. SICS Softw. Intensive Cyber-Phys. Syst, August 2019
8. Kopp, O., Binz, T., Breitenbücher, U., Leymann, F.: Winery – a modeling tool for TOSCA-based cloud applications. In: Basu, S., Pautasso, C., Zhang, L., Fu, X. (eds.) ICSOC 2013. LNCS, vol. 8274, pp. 700–704. Springer, Heidelberg (2013). https://doi.org/10.1007/978-3-642-45005-1_64

Examination and Comparison of TOSCA Orchestration Tools

Anže Luzar[✉], Sašo Stanovnik, and Matija Cankar

XLAB Research, XLAB d.o.o., Pot za Brdom 100, 1000 Ljubljana, Slovenia
anze.luzar@xlab.si
https://www.xlab.si/research/

Abstract. The use of orchestration and automation has been growing in recent years. This can be especially evident in cloud infrastructures where OASIS TOSCA orchestration standard can be used to provide independence and prevent vendor lock-in. In this paper we examine different TOSCA compliant orchestration tools, test them with TOSCA templates and present a comparison between these tools. This comparison should be used to decide which tool is easier to use for both the companies and the developers according to their requirements.

Keywords: Comparison · Cloud computing · DevOps · Orchestration · Automation · Orchestrator · Orchestration tool · TOSCA

1 Introduction

Automation and orchestration tools usually do not draw the attention of developers who are independent or are working on smaller projects. However, for large companies and corporations they are of great significance, bringing business value through the possibilities to orchestrate and transfer applications throughout several cloud infrastructures. Although developers want complete independence from the target platforms, numerous cloud providers only provide compatibility and first–party support for their own services. This can create a significant impact on the effort and cost expenditure, associated with the migration of services to from one to another cloud platform. Companies therefore search for universal orchestration tools, which promise compatibility with many cloud providers. However, these often don't support specific functionalities within each of the supported cloud platforms. To pick the orchestrator and the accompanying tools means researching their advantages and also all their drawbacks. There currently seems to be no evident intersection between orchestration or automation support within the cloud services as orchestrators usually do not support deployment on all available cloud platforms and also do not support all possible automation tools. For this paper we delve into orchestration and set a goal to examine and compare different orchestration tools in order to make the decision process more straightforward. This paper presents the properties and use of several selected tools.

© Springer Nature Switzerland AG 2020
H. Muccini et al. (Eds.): ECSA 2020, CCIS 1269, pp. 247–259, 2020.
https://doi.org/10.1007/978-3-030-59155-7_19

1.1 DevOps and Orchestration

Development and Operations (DevOps for short) is an approach in information technology that emphasizes communication and integration between software developers and other IT experts and is used mostly for introducing automated software and infrastructure changes [7].

Orchestration is a sort of distributed automated configuration that includes monitoring and coordination of computer systems, application and services and thereby helps making the execution of complex tasks or task groups easier. The process of orchestration is used to solve the problem of connecting and arranging larger amounts of automated tasks in a desired workflow [14]. Within orchestration a workflow is defined (this is usually called a process of workflow orchestration) and consists of a sequence of automated tasks. Based on the orchestration targets there are many different types of orchestration and the ones that stand out the most are cloud orchestration, service orchestration and release orchestration [8].

It is important to distinguish orchestration from automation which are often confused. The execution of a task and the operations within, belongs to the automation, which aims to reduce the human factor in the processes that can be automated. On the other hand, the orchestration process aims to join the majority of already automated tasks and put them in a logical order which then results in the deployment of the complete application or services [3].

1.2 Orchestration Tools

Orchestrators or orchestration tools represent a wide set of complex IT software that is used to invoke the aforementioned process of workflow orchestration. These tools can be very specific – from deploying applications to setting up Docker containers. In order to pick the appropriate tool we should follow different criteria such as:

- the size of the company which is important when paying for tool licences,
- the operating systems used in the orchestrated system,
- whether the tool is open-source or commercial, where one should note that open-source tools are often supported by their community and that commercial tools offer professional support and can therefore be used in mission–critical IT systems [13].

The orchestration tools can often be scaled and can deliver highly complex applications and, as we repeat the tasks again and again, they become predictable and can be optimized. Apart from that, it is known that these tools reduce costs and errors (through repeatability of the orchestration process), increase productivity, save significant amount of time, make operations faster, minimize system down times etc. In the last few years there has been an enormous growth in cloud orchestration for several cloud providers (for instance Amazon Web Services, Microsoft Azure and Google Cloud Platform) where the orchestration process includes deploying applications, creating cloud resources (e.g. for storage), configuring networks, setting up virtual machines and so on. Organizations use orchestrators to migrate their applications to the cloud and in doing so they increase the accessibility, reduce times for healing the services in case of errors and make all their business processes faster [15].

1.3   OASIS TOSCA Standard

OASIS Topology and Orchestration Specification for Cloud Applications, or shortly TOSCA, is an open standard that defines the application topology within cloud infrastructures by dividing services into components and defining their connections, dependencies, capabilities and requirements. This makes the applications portable and independent of any cloud providers which corresponds to the DevOps theory of installing and delivering applications throughout their life cycle [11]. Apart from TOSCA there are other cloud orchestration standards such as Amazon AWS CloudFormation or OpenStack Heat, but they are specific and tailored to their platforms. CloudFormation seems to be more AWS oriented and Heat was designed for OpenStack and targets cloud workloads, whereas TOSCA is more general and meant for enterprise workloads and applications.

The TOSCA standard includes a special metamodel with a declarative domain-specific language that offers the definition of portable TOSCA documents called TOSCA templates and complete application packages (commonly called blueprints) which include templates with all the accompanying files needed for the deployment. All these files usually get packed into compressed artifacts called Cloud Service Archives or CSARs. TOSCA has a strictly defined system of types which for example includes node types, relationship types, their properties, attributes, interfaces, requirements and so on. The TOSCA standard can be used within different markup languages and the most common ones are YAML and XML. We centered ourselves around TOSCA Simple Profile for YAML that currently has four different versions (v1.0, v1.1, v1.2 and v1.3) [2].

There are currently many emerging and promising tools using TOSCA such as Alien4Cloud, Apache AriaTosca, CELAR, Cloudify, DICER, Eclipse Winery, MSO4SC HPC, Indigo, ONAP, OPEN-O, OpenBaton, OpenStack, OpenTOSCA, Opera, RADON, SODALITE, OPNFV, Puccini, SeaClouds, TosKer, Ubicity and so on. Some of them are completely compatibile with the standard and some others have extended it and defined their own DSL. However, TOSCA YAML templates have little practical value without their implementations. To provide these, different automation tools can be used, such as Ansible, Chef, Puppet, Salt, Juju, Jenkins, Vagrant, Bash, Docker and Terraform. TOSCA orchestrators are focused on connecting these tools with parsed TOSCA definitions so that tasks can be executed [12].

2   Testing the Orchestration Tools

For the analysis we have chosen xOpera, Ystia Yorc, IndigoDC and Cloudify orchestrators which all support TOSCA standard definitions. For the testing part we prepared a simple TOSCA template (see Fig. 1) for creating a directory with an example file. The template uses the latest TOSCA YAML profile version 1.3 (for the orchestrators which did not support this version we have changed it to lower ones). Here we defined one simple node type called `hello_type` with one input (which is set to `"Hello from TOSCA!"` at the beginning of the orchestration) and two paths to operations for creating (deploying) and deleting (undeploying).

```
1    tosca_definitions_version: tosca_simple_yaml_1_3
2
3    node_types:
4      hello_type:
5        derived_from: tosca.nodes.SoftwareComponent
6        interfaces:
7          Standard:
8            inputs:
9              content:
10                default: { get_input: content }
11                type: string
12            operations:
13              create: playbooks/create.yml
14              delete: playbooks/delete.yml
15
16   topology_template:
17     inputs:
18       content:
19         type: string
20         default: "Hello from TOSCA!"
21
22     node_templates:
23       my-workstation:
24         type: tosca.nodes.Compute
25         attributes:
26           private_address: localhost
27           public_address: localhost
28
29       hello:
30         type: hello_type
31         requirements:
32           - host: my-workstation
```

Fig. 1. TOSCA YAML template for testing.

For the operation actuators we used Ansible playbooks because Ansible is the easiest automation tool for setup and usage and also most of the TOSCA orchestrators prefer and support it. The example playbook we used for the `create` TOSCA interface operation is shown in Fig. 2. A similar playbook was used to implement `delete` TOSCA operation.

```
1        - hosts: all
2          gather_facts: false
3          tasks:
4            - name: Create the new folder structure
5              file:
6                path: /tmp/opera-test/hello
7                recurse: true
8                state: directory
9
10           - name: Create hello.txt and add content
11             copy:
12               dest: /tmp/opera-test/hello/hello.txt
13               content: "{{ content }}"
```

Fig. 2. Ansible playbook for the TOSCA create operation.

2.1 xOpera

xOpera is a project that includes opera tool which is a lightweight open-source TOSCA orchestrator compatible with TOSCA Simple Profile in YAML v1.3 [17]. As primary developers of opera we follow the UNIX convention of a minimal tool that does only one thing (e.g.. orchestration) and that one thing well instead of having a tool that can handle multiple tasks of different types. This orchestration tool uses Ansible to implement the TOSCA standard operations which means that operations like deploy and un-deploy run a set of actuators in the form of Ansible playbooks [4]. Opera is easily installed through a Python pip package that is available on PyPI (https://pypi.org/project/opera/). Opera only provides the client CLI interface so it can be used very quickly [17]. Our xOpera orchestration test where we used opera deploy and opera undeploy commands has been successful (see Fig. 3).

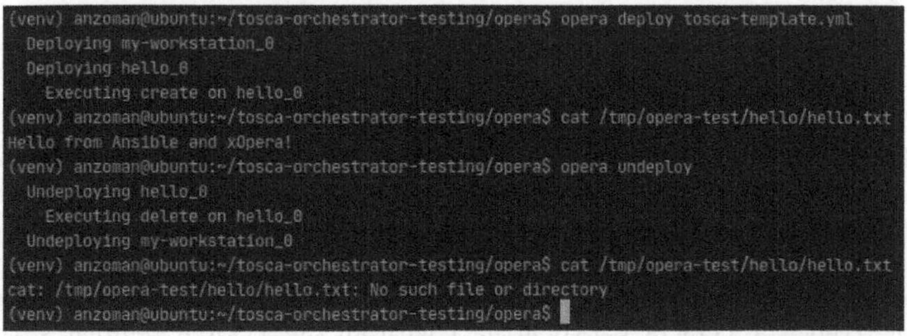

Fig. 3. The orchestration testing with xOpera.

2.2 Ystia Yorc and Alien4Cloud

Yorc is the High Performance Computing (HPC) TOSCA orchestrator which targets support for hybrid infrastructure applications such as Infrastructure as a Service (IaaS), HPC schedulers and Container as a service (CaaS). The important part of Yorc are the scaling of applications within TOSCA workflows [18]. Yorc has multiple set–up options. The usual way is to run its server on a remote virtual machine (such as an OpenStack VM) where we have to take care of the configuration of the server. This is also important if we want to properly interact with the open–source orchestration platform Alien4Cloud where Yorc is officially supported. An easier setup method that we used is to use the official Yorc Docker image and deploy the server in a Docker container. For interacting with the server we used a CLI client Yorc tool and downgraded the prepared TOSCA template to YAML version 1.2 which is the latest supported TOSCA version in Yorc. We also needed to pack our templates and playbooks in a zipped CSAR to be able to run the `yorc deployments deploy` command as shown in Fig. 4.

Fig. 4. Orchestration process result using Ystia Yorc.

Alien4Cloud (or a4c) stands for Application LIfecycle ENablement for Cloud or shorter Alien4Cloud which is an Atos open-source platform that facilitates managing complex applications and cloud services within companies and herewith also offers a tool for fast application deployment for users and developers. Alien4Cloud extends TOSCA Simple Profile in YAML along with all the TOSCA entities providing its DSL called Alien4Cloud DSL. The a4c orchestrator receives a TOSCA CSAR artifact with all the TOSCA templates, their implementations and the accompanying files as an input. The orchestration process depends on the a4c version we use. Apart from officially supported Ystia Yorc there is also a support for Cloudify 3, Cloudify 4, experimental support for Marathon tool (which is a meta framework for Mesos offering orchestration of clusters and Docker containers) and the support for Puccini orchestration tool in beta version. By supporting multiple orchestrators Alien4Cloud becomes more independent from the cloud provider and therefore tries to prevent so called vendor lock-in since multiple orchestrator includes the support for multiple cloud providers. The installation of a4c can be done on Linux or OS X with one curl command in terminal solely and then we can already access the tool's dashboard in the browser. There is a simple drag and drop topology modelling tool where we can use already prepared a4c roles from the TOSCA topology catalog. TOSCA definitions can be imported from Git and when modelling is done we can export a full TOSCA template or CSAR [1].

Because of numerous features that we found useful, we also decided to test the usage of a4c orchestration tool. After reshaping the TOSCA template to be compatible with Alien4Cloud domain specific language we have setup a4c platform in a Docker container and installed Yorc plugin to connect a4c with Yorc orchestrator. From there on the orchestration process was smooth as we packed our TOSCA templates into CSAR and initiated the deployment within the a4c platform.

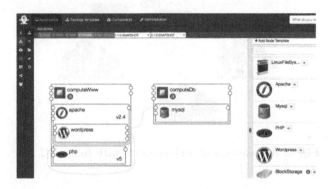

Fig. 5. Alien4Cloud topology modelling tool.

2.3   Indigo DC

IndigoDC is a TOSCA orchestration tool representing a Platform as a Service (PaaS) component which primarily offers setting up resources on cloud computing platforms like OpenStack or OpenNebula and also offers managing groups of computers using open–source Apache Mesos clusters [9]. The orchestrator was developed within a European Union Horizon 2020 project called INDIGO-DataCloud (INtegrating Distributed data Infrastructures for Global ExplOitation) which aimed to provide hybrid infrastructure and software in the form of IaaS and SaaS components. The speciality of this tool is that it uses a Service License Agreement (SLA) to choose the orchestration target and the order of the automated tasks with the help of a REST service called Cloud Provider Ranker that collects the data about available cloud providers and chooses one using different rules and algorithms [16]. For the testing part we have set up Indigo DC server locally in a Docker container and used the Orchent CLI client tool to interact with the orchestrator. Indigo uses Ansible playbook or roles for TOSCA operations but the supported version of TOSCA YAML is only 1.0 so we had to refactor our TOSCA template by providing minor changes to TOSCA interface operation definitions. From that point we had issues as the orchestrator was unable to initiate the deployment. The problem was also that for the orchestrator to work we would have to supply different cloud provider secret credentials (like for AWS, Azure and GCP) to the server which could raise some security issues. The configuration if Indigo Data Cloud orchestrator was not intuitive so from there we did not proceed with the testing.

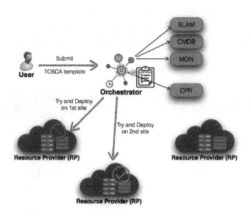

Fig. 6. Architecture of orchestration with IndigoDC [10]

2.4 Cloudify

Cloudify is an open-source framework for cloud orchestration with a built-in TOSCA orchestrator, modelling tool and monitoring software that offers modeling applications, optimizing their life cycle and deploying on numerous cloud providers [5]. Some of the components that can be a part of applications are included by default (for instance Nginx, Gunicorn, Flask, PostgreSQL, RabbitMQ and Pika), while others can be included through special plugins (for example Ansible and cloud plugins). Cloudify can be used by setting up a Cloudify Manager in a Docker container that acts as an orchestration server and then it can be interacted with using the Cloudify CLI. The other way is to use the Cloudify web component that represents a concept of Environment as a Service (EaaS) to provide reusable orchestration environments with the goal to reduce the bottleneck between orchestration, automation, CI/CD tools and cloud providers. The Cloudify orchestrator has moved beyond TOSCA, developing its own Cloudify DSL that is used to define its own application blueprints.

Therefore it offers Cloudify DSL versions 1.0, 1.1, 1.2 in 1.3 that are derived from corresponding TOSCA profiles. The DSL includes extended TOSCA definitions and plugins that can be used for TOSCA implementations (e.g. plugin definitions for Chef, Puppet, Ansible, Salt, ...). The other embedded TOSCA actuators can be in the form of Python, Bash, PowerShell, Ruby scripts and so on [6].

Fig. 7. Cludify dashboard.

For the testing part we used free testing license for Cloudify Labs (in Fig. 7), translated our TOSCA template to Cloudify DSL and used the prepared Ansible playbooks for creating and deleting the service. We packed all the files into a CSAR and uploaded it to the Cloudify labs web portal where we initiated the workflow and the deployment (see Fig. 8).

Fig. 8. Successful blueprint deployment via Cloudify Labs orchestrator.

3   The Comparison of TOSCA Orchestrators

During the testing of different orchestrators we created a comparison that would help us decide which tools are appropriate for the tested use case and to show the perspective that orchestrators have. The comparison is visible in Table 1 where we picked the most commonly occurring characteristics among these tools: release year, tool purpose, supported platforms, architecture, language, installation, license, supported automation tools, user interface, modeling tool, OASIS TOSCA compatibility, supported TOSCA profiles and supported cloud providers.

Table 1. Orchestration tools comparison table.

Aspect	Opera	Yorc	Indigo	Cloudify
Release year	2019	2017	2016	2012
Purpose	Minimalistic TOSCA orchestrator	HPC TOSCA orchestrator	TOSCA Paas orchestrator for cloud frameworks	Opensource TOSCA orchestration platform
Supported platforms	Linux, OS X, Windows	Linux	Linux	Linux, OS X
Architecture	Client	Server, client	Server, client	Server, client
Implemented in	Python	Go	Java	Python
Installation	Virtual environment and opera pip package	Server on an OpenStack VM or a Docker container	Server in a Docker container	Server on an OpenStack VM or a Docker container
Installation and usage difficulty	Easy	Medium	Hard	Medium
License	Apache License 2.0	Apache License 2.0	Apache License 2.0	Apache License 2.0
Supported automation tool	Ansible	Bash scripts, Ansible	Ansible	All (by default bash, Python, Ruby and other scripts and Ansible plugin
User interface	No	Yes	Yes	Yes
Modelling tool	No	Yes (Alien4Cloud)	No	Yes (embedded and Alien4Cloud)
TOSCA compatibility	Yes	Yes	Yes	No
Latest TOSCA profile version	TOSCA YAML 1.3	TOSCA YAML 1.2	TOSCA YAML 1.0, TOSCA NFV 1.0	Cloudify DSL 1.3 (derived from TOSCA 1.3)
Officially supported target cloud platforms	The support is performed by the user	AWS, OpenStack in GCP	AWS, Azure	AWS, Azure, GCP, OpenStack, vCloud(plugins)

Looking into the release year it is apparent that the newest orchestrator is xOpera and the oldest is Cloudify. Every tested orchestrator serves its own purpose such as: versatile and light-weight approach, supporting heterogeneous infrastructures (HPC, Cloud) for xOpera, HPC computing for Yorc, PaaS orchestrator for Indigo and open-source orchestration platform for Cloudify. All of the orchestrators support the Linux operating system and Cloudify has the additional support for OS X. Cloudify and xOpera are written in Python, Yistia Yorc in Go and IndigoDC is implemented in Java. All tools except xOpera require setting up an orchestration server which can reside in a Docker container. The installation process for xOpera consists of only installing it as a

Python package. Based on setup difficulty and usage we have categorized the xOpera orchestrator as easy to use, whereas Yorc and Cloudify were marked with medium difficulty. IndigoDC was the most problematic for usage because it consumed the biggest amount of time and at the end we were not able to use it for the orchestration. All analyzed orchestration tools have an open-source Apache 2.0 license. xOpera and Indigo are implementing the TOSCA standard by using Ansible as the automation tool, while Yorc offers Bash and Ansible. Cloudify is the most advanced in this aspect since it can be used with Python, Ruby or Bash scripts, with an embedded Ansible plugin or by using any other custom–defined plugin in order to use other automation tools like Chef, Puppet or Salt. Apart from xOpera, all of the tools provide a graphical user interface. Yorc and Cloudify also include a modelling tool for combining TOSCA entities and both are part of the Alien4Cloud platform. The orchestrators are fully compatible with TOSCA standard, except from Cloudify which uses its own DSL language, extending TOSCA standard definitions. Opera supports the latest TOSCA YAML profile version 1.3, Yorc supports YAML 1.2, Indigo used version 1.0 and also provides the support for TOSCA NFV network profile v1.0 and Cloudify also uses the latest TOSCA version since its DSL v1.3 is derived from TOSCA profile in YAML v1.3 but it also keeps the support for all the older TOSCA YAML versions. The xOpera orchestrator does not have any predefined cloud plugins and the user is required to provide the support himself based on TOSCA definitions and Ansible modules. Yorc explicitly supports OpenStack, AWS and GCP, whereas IndigoDC includes the support for AWS and Azure cloud providers. Cloudify can be connected to any cloud by using our custom plugins or the prepared plugins for AWS, Azure, GCP, OpenStack and VMware vCloud.

4   Results and Decisions

The aspects of the orchestration tool comparison they helped us to decide which tool is the best for our testing use case. For us the most important characteristics were the installation, which had to be easy and fast. This allows us to test the deployment right away and consequently requires the latest TOSCA compatibility to keep up with the latest TOSCA standard features. Our key purpose, the minimalistic TOSCA orchestrator, which can be used for simple client deployment without any scaling or HPC features can be achieved by opera as the most suitable tool for our experiment. That choice might not be the best for other use cases. The presented comparison aspects can guide developers through the choice of the best tool according to their own different requirements. For instance if HPC computing is needed, uses should consider Yorc, as it was developed especially for that purpose, or maybe xOpera orchestrator if they want to benefit from the latest TOSCA version. For example if we would want to deploy our application on several cloud providers along with the use of various automation tools and plugins, Cloudify would prevail as it offers the support for almost all these tools. Then there are special cases when developers want to create a model of their application in a graphical environment with all the visible connections between different components. Going this way opera is not the best choice, whereas Cloudify and Yorc along with Alien4Cloud modeling tool could stand out.

The next aspect that cannot be waved aside is the supported version of the TOSCA Simple Profile in YAML. Every version brings new syntax updates and features and it is important for the orchestrators to support the latest TOSCA versions in order to ensure the best possible cloud deployment process. There opera and Cloudify, which are based on latest TOSCA v1.3 are the most suitable. The security is also a big concern when picking these tools since engineers does not want to expose their cloud credentials (e.g. AWS secret keys, GCP service account keys etc.) to numerous possible treats and they want to be sure that the orchestrator or the service that is being used within will not copy or move credentials away from the local machine. Considering security, Cloudify seems as a good option as it provides so called secrets store which is a secure variable storage where the secrets are stored and called from as key-value pairs. On the other hand Yistia Yorc also turns out to be reliable in this perspective since it uses HashiCorp Vault to protect sensitive data. Apart from the fact that deployment with Indigo orchestrator did not work properly, this orchestrator has its own separated Identity and Access Management service which supports different cloud secrets and can be a good choice.

5   Conclusions and Future Work

Orchestration and with it, automation, are already important today, but will further gain importance, with the rise of 5G (and with it, edge). The latter will bring additional complexity basically on all infrastructure levels, as the number of connected devices and their capabilities will increase further. During our examination OASIS TOSCA turned out to be a promising standard with the ability to define and maintain application topology. Combined with orchestration tool and equipped with automation actuators TOSCA standard gets a practical use that can simplify multiple processes and can save a lot of precious time. All the orchestrators that we have tested were unique and had their own purpose whether this was HPC computing or PaaS interaction. Since we were not able to get IndigoDC to work, xOpera, Yorc and Cloudify were analyzed more in detail. Apart from Yorc being the official Alien4Cloud orchestrator, xOpera is also a tool with significant potential. From all the tools it was the easiest to install and to use. It does not have any embedded cloud plugins which is, in fact, not a negative thing since it then allows users to define this part as they wish. xOpera also supports the latest 1.3 version of TOSCA YAML which proves that the tool is being maintained and updated through time. Cloudify is a more enterprise solution and seems to be used by corporations which desire support and a user friendly environment, whereas xOpera is currently an open-source orchestrator in the making. This fact is also different from all the other tools, which seem to be in a mature state of development. It is evident that the orchestrator that will be most flexible and will follow the latest cloud trends with the support for the latest TOSCA version will have a good chance of dominating.

Acknowledgements. This paper has been partially supported by the European Union's Horizon 2020 research and innovation programme under Grant Agreement No. 825040 (RADON). The work described here has also been conducted within the European Union's Horizon 2020 Research & Innovation action SODALITE (project no. 825480).

References

1. Alien4cloud documentation. https://alien4cloud.github.io/ (2020). Accessed on 17 June 2020
2. Binz, T., Breiter, G., Leyman, F., Spatzier, T.: Portable cloud services using tosca. IEEE Internet Comput. **16**(3), 80–85 (2012)
3. Caballer, M., Zala, S., Lopez Garcia, A., Molto, G., Orviz Fernandez, P., Velten, M.: Orchestrating complex application architectures in heterogeneous clouds
4. Carbonell, M.: xopera: an agile orchestrator. https://www.sodalite.eu/content/xopera-agile-orchestrator (2019). Accessed on 24 June 2020
5. Cloudify. https://cloudify.co/ (2020). Accessed on 18 June 2020
6. Cloudify documentation center. https://docs.cloudify.co/ (2020). Accessed on 23 June 2020
7. Devops day. https://slovenia.iiba.org/sl/devops (2017). Accessed on 24 June 2020
8. Goldberg, J.: Workflow orchestration: an introduction. https://www.bmc.com/blogs/workflow-orchestration/ (2019). Accessed on 22 June 2020
9. Indigo - datacloud github. https://github.com/indigo-dc/ (2020). Accessed 21 June 2020
10. Indigo paas overview. https://www.slideshare.net/TheEOSChubproject/indigopaasoverview/ (2019). Accessed on 21 June 2020
11. Oasis tosca. https://www.oasis-open.org/ (2020). Accessed on 19 June 2020
12. Oasis tosca documentation. https://docs.oasis-open.org/tosca/ (2020). accessed on 19 June 2020
13. Orchestration & scheduling tools. https://www.plutora.com/ci-cd-tools/orchestration-scheduling-tools (2019). Accessed on 20 June 2020
14. Redhat. https://www.redhat.com (2020), accessed on 22 June 2020
15. Rouse, M.: What is cloud orchestration (cloud orchestrator)? https://searchitoperations.techtarget.com/definition/cloud-orchestrator (2017). Accessed on 26 June 2020
16. Salomoni, D., Campos, I., Gaido, L.: Indigo-datacloud: a platform to facilitate seamless access to e-infrastructures. Journal of Grid Computing **16**, 381–408 (2018). Accessed on 2020-6-21
17. xopera github repository. https://github.com/xlab-si/xopera-opera (2020). Accessed on 18 June 2020
18. Ystia project github. https://github.com/ystia (2020). Accessed on 20 June 2020

Auto-scaling Using TOSCA Infrastructure as Code

Matija Cankar[1](✉), Anže Luzar[1], and Damian A. Tamburri[2]

[1] XLAB d.o.o., Pod za Brdom 100, 1000 Ljubljana, Slovenia
matija.cankar@xlab.si
[2] Eindhoven University of Technology - JADS, s'Hertogenbosch, The Netherlands
https://www.xlab.si/research/

Abstract. Autoscaling cloud infrastructures still remains a challenging endeavour during orchestration, given the many possible risks, options, and connected costs. In this paper we discuss the options for defining and enacting autoscaling using TOSCA standard templates and its own policy definition specifications. The goal is to define infrastructure blueprints to be self-contained, executable by an orchestrator that can take over autonomously all scaling tasks while maintaining acceptable structural and non-functional quality levels.

Keywords: Cloud computing · Scaling infrastructures · Autoscaling · TOSCA · Orchestration · Function-as-a-Service · FaaS

1 Introduction

The cloud computing era fostered the emergence of ways to exploit the compute, storage, and network resources and provide new abilities to adapt dynamically the amount of the computing resources to the need of the application that relies on resource provisioning [8]. The aforementioned practice—defined as scaling of the resources [9]—has increasingly became more efficient and responsive to the current application load. On the one hand, two known approaches to scaling are nowadays used, with the first one making possible to *scale-in* or perform vertical scaling, which means that the capacities of the provisioned resources (CPU, RAM, etc.) are scaled up or down. The second is *scale-out* or performing horizontal scaling, which means that the number of units (e.g., virtual machine with specific amount of RAM, CPU, and storage) is enlarged or shrunk.

On the other hand, all cloud providers address the scaling of the leased virtual infrastructure in some way and mostly all do this by their own approach that differs mainly in configuration of this task. For example, the OpenStack [5] uses its own language called Heat, Amazon AWS uses CloudFormation [1] and some cloud management tools, like open-source representative called Slipstream [3] use their own techniques.

Besides the differences of the cloud providers, the approach to the scaling depends on the technology that powers the application. For example, applications based on Docker and Kubernetes allow for horizontal scaling. However,

© Springer Nature Switzerland AG 2020
H. Muccini et al. (Eds.): ECSA 2020, CCIS 1269, pp. 260–268, 2020.
https://doi.org/10.1007/978-3-030-59155-7_20

applications based on Function-as-a-Service (FaaS) [2] will mainly use a combination of vertical and horizontal scaling. Almost all public provides allow manually defined values for vertical scaling, while horizontal scaling is covered by the provider. Only in private open source cloud solutions, as Open-FaaS, both scaling approaches need to be performed by an external software.

To support the autoscalable orchestration of microservice applications intermixing FaaS, Container, and regular virtual-machine components that can be deployed on any provider we develop xOpera, an orchestrator capable of "speaking" with all cloud providers and technologies, addressing autoscaling in a policy-based fashion. On the one hand, interoperability is achieved thorough abstraction, which can be solved with the OASIS standard on "Topology and Orchestration Specification for Cloud Applications" (TOSCA) [4]. On the other hand, the policy-based facilities offered by xOpera only partially address the expected scaling capabilities and the approach shows several limitations.

We contribute to the state of the art and practice with experiences gained through the design and prototypization of xOpera—and its autoscaling features—which we expect to spark fruitful discussions and speedup the standardisation and practice of the auto-scaling definition of cloud applications.

The rest of this paper is structured as follows, first the problem of scaling and current support in TOSCA is presented. In Sect. 3 presents the concepts of scaling and the Sect. 4 proposes an approach and evaluation. The paper discusses ideas in Sect. 5 and is concluded with Sect. 5.

2   Problem Definition

The introduction section described different scaling approaches based on underlying technology. Performing (auto)scaling is complicated task that needs to take into account the state of the application before and after the scaling and perform all required steps to guarantee a safe transition between the states. The software performing this act needs to rely on a set of policies and thresholds that define scaling limits and duties. To perform the scaling on an appropriate moment, the scaling software needs to be subscribed on a messaging queue from monitoring and perform actions with the orchestrator. This tight integration between monitoring service, scaling service and orchestrator service makes the issue even harder and frequently is well solved only inside closed provider environments (Amazon AWS, Microsoft Azure, Google Cloud Platform, etc). This means that user is able to deploy application to one provider and use one approach of scaling, but moving this application to another provider will require manual re-configuration of deployment and scaling. Our aim is to depend on TOSCA standard and propose a way to define scaling at the deploy time, so the orchestrator will be able to create initial deploy on infrastructure and configuration of monitoring in a way that will be easily manageable in case of scaling.

2.1 Definition of Application Scaling

One most crucial agreement to be defined before forming the scaling approach is to determine *what scaling is* and *what is not*. The modification of the running application is scaling when *we can change the amount of resources without having a significant impact on the running application(s)*. In our case this means that scaling should not result in total un-deploy and redeploy of application but rather moving the functionality from one state to another without shutting down or re-deploying everything.

Based on aforementioned limits we focused on the three most general scaling approaches:

1. simple horizontal scaling, e.g., scaling of containers;
2. simple vertical scaling, e.g., FaaS scaling;
3. complex horizontal scaling, e.g., load balancer example.

In our proposal we consider all other scaling approaches that include more significant changes in the application as (re-)deploying of a new application and are therefore, out of scope.

Next two crucial agreements to be defined on scaling are determining a way to explain the scaling limitations and scaling actions. The TOSCA suggests the use of scaling policies to define scaling limitations and thresholds, as shown on Fig. 1. The current version of standard does not provide any details explaining how this data can be used in action therefore it is not obvious what is the job of a scaler, orchestrator or maybe some other tool. When the thresholds are reached something should happen, e.g., a scaler application should take care of it. To overcome this issue we propose a TOSCA which example tries to resolve this issue in Sect. 4.

```
1    tosca_definitions_version: tosca_simple_yaml_1_3
2    my_scaling_policy_1:
3      type: tosca.policy.scaling
4      description: Simple node autoscaling
5      properties:
6        min_instances: <integer>
7        max_instances: <integer>
8        default_instances: <integer>
9        increment: <integer>
```

Fig. 1. TOSCA YAML example from TOSCA v1.3.

3   Scaling Concepts

Most common approach to implement scaling is to use three components (see Fig. 2), namely orchestrator, monitoring and scaler. In this approach the scaler receives notifications from monitoring, defines next scaling state and instructs the orchestrator how to achieve this change. To describe this approach with a particular monitoring application and a TOSCA orchestrator would imply, that scaler encapsulates all knowledge about scaling and also about deploying. Scaler would need to a) receive monitoring notifications b) create a new TOSCA-application blueprint based on the defined policies and c) send the blueprint to the orchestrator. The downside of this idea is a division of the process lead between the orchestrator.

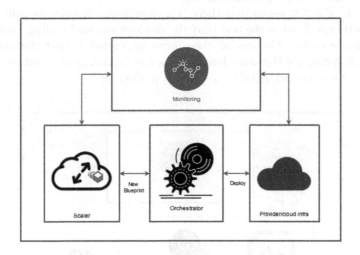

Fig. 2. Scaling using the scaler component.

For example – using the mentioned concept – when orchestrator receives the initial application blueprint in TOSCA CSAR, which we consider that it is an application package including all necessary information to spawn up and set application in runtime, it needs to a) deploy all application components, b) configure monitoring and c) define scaler. But after the initial orchestration of the application is done, the scaler overtakes the leadership and instructs the orchestrator how to proceed. This approach complicates the situations on two levels, first it is a requirement for a scaler, which is TOSCA compliant and can scale applications on various providers. The second issue raises when user sends a small update of the application configuration to the orchestrator which could be overridden by the scaler sending new TOSCA configuration to the orchestrate at the same time. Therefore, if something goes wrong and specifications are different in orchestrator and scaler it is not clear if the targeted application state is in the orchestrator or in the scaler.

4   Proposed Approach, Scaler Inside the Orchestrator

Our proposed approach eliminates the scaler and adds its functionality inside the orchestrator, as it is sketched in Fig. 3. This means that orchestrator would be the entity in charge of deploying and scaling application at any moment. In the initial deployment orchestrator deploys application, configures monitoring threshold and defines a TOSCA scaling policy with all scaling definitions. This means that monitoring would send notifications directly to the orchestrator when the thresholds would be reached. In this particular cases, orchestrator would run a `scale` command on the TOSCA blueprint (by executing the linked Ansible playbook) which would perform scaling.

From the Fig. 3 it seems that there is no significant change, we anticipate to solve two things. First is the one that the deployment and scaling process deal only with one entity. The second even more important is that the description of the scaling can use the same language as the deploying one and exploits the orchestrator engine and TOSCA actions to perform it.

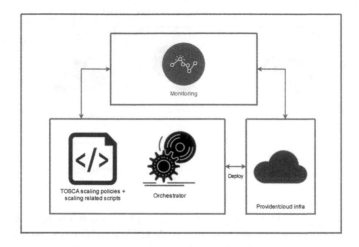

Fig. 3. Proposed architecture without scaler component, TOSCA defines everything and orchestrator is able to accept monitoring notifications.

An example of the proposed TOSCA scaling policy and scaling interface for our approach is shown in Fig. 4. Note that the example is simplified to emphasise only the crucial parts of an approach that can be used to fulfill scaling within the TOSCA orchestrator by configuring scaling in TOSCA YAML service template. In the first part of the listing in Fig. 4 – lines 1–22 – the OpenStack virtual machine presenting an initial application state is defined. Next block – lines 24–40 – presents the scaling policy, similarly that TOSCA standard suggests and was presented in Fig. 1. The property of CPU is defined to be monitored, and the initialisation is globally limited, not accepting values lower than 80. This threshold should be configured by the orchestrator in a particular monitoring tool as Prometheus. This monitoring configuration part is omitted from our example for brevity. The next part – lines 41–51 – defines the triggers that would initiate scaling procedures. A trigger affects our application, the openstack node, and calls the scaling operation. The important part of this TOSCA definition comes next – lines 53–61 – where we define scale operation called by trigger. This interface would call a specific Ansible script that orchestrator would process at the deployment phase. This `scale_out.yaml` script would perform scaling on an OpenStack VM e.g. deploy one additional instance to balance the load on the application. The rest of the TOSCA template on Fig. 4 – lines 63–79 – defines a topology template that initializes first VM and sets scaling policy properties.

In action the scale-up policy (`radon.policies.scaling.ScaleOut`) would be used when the CPU load would surpass the adjusted value (see `cpu_upper_bound`). When this would happen the policy could use targets key-word to filter out the node it applies to and use a TOSCA scaling trigger definition in order to call the defined TOSCA `scale` operation within the `radon.interfaces.scaling`. This interface operation would then pass on the amount by which to scale (see the `adjustment` parameter) to the Ansible play-book (`scale_out.yaml`) which would perform scaling on an OpenStack VM (for example it could deploy one additional instance so that the load would be bal-anced).

4.1 Proposed Experiment and Evaluation Plan

The implementation of the proposed concept is in progress and will be fin-ished and tested during RADON project [2]. For the orchestrator we will use xOpera [10] orchestrator with current support of TOSCA v1.3 and Prometheus [6] for monitoring. Currently in progress is finalising the possibility to scale FaaS applications, supporting vertical scaling of the requirements based on configuration update on the providers side, e.g. AWS, Azure or GCP. The next step is to support horizontal scaling with adding or removing container instances. The last step will be to support horizontal scaling of regular virtual machines.

The crucial step here is to define TOSCA types, namely nodes, policies and triggers in a way that will serve as a template to other applications. The outcomes will be tested by the RADON project partners providing template applications and industrial use-cases and the xOpera orchestrator community. The templates for scaling will be published in a publicly available TOSCA template library provided by RADON project and project GitHub repository [7].

Evaluation will be straight-forward with testing the designed TOSCA blue-print of a scalable application with the proposed orchestrator. If this combination will be able to scale application in a same way that scalers can, the verdict will be that the TOSCA standard yaml specification is strong enough to exploit the orchestrator in a way to act as a scaler. That approach simplifies the solution as we do not need special TOSCA scaler to scale TOSCA applications.

5 Discussion and Lessons Learned

Deploying application is a complex job with many tasks. Having the ability to use one IaC language, as TOSCA, is a commodity for a DevOps teams that deploy

```
1    tosca_definitions_version: tosca_simple_yaml_1_3
2
3    node_types:
4      radon.nodes.OpenStack.VM:
5        derived_from: tosca.nodes.Compute
6        properties:
7          name:
8            type: string
9          image:
10           type: string
11         flavor:
12           type: string
13         network:
14           type: string
15         key_name:
16           type: string
17       interfaces:
18         Standard:
19           type: tosca.interfaces.node.lifecycle.Standard
20           operations:
21             create:
22               implementation: playbooks/create.yaml
23
24   policy_types:
25     radon.policies.scaling.ScaleOut:
26       derived_from: tosca.policies.Scaling
27       properties:
28         cpu_upper_bound:
29           description: The upper bound for the CPU
30           type: float
31           required: false
32           constraints:
33             - greater_or_equal: 80.0
34         adjustment:
35           description: The amount by which to scale
36           type: integer
37           required: false
38           constraints:
39             - greater_or_equal: 1
40       targets: [ radon.nodes.openstack.VM ]
41       triggers:
42         radon.triggers.scaling:
43           description: A trigger for scaling
44           event: trigger
45           target_filter:
46             node: radon.nodes.openstack.VM
47           action:
48             - call_operation:
49                 operation: radon.interfaces.scaling.scale
50                 inputs:
51                   adjustment: { get_property: [ SELF, adjustment ] }
52
53   interface_types:
54     radon.interfaces.scaling:
55       derived_from: tosca.interfaces.Root
56       operations:
57         scale:
58           inputs:
59             adjustment: { default: { get_property: [ SELF, name ] } }
60           description: Operation for scaling.
61           implementation: playbooks/scale_out.yaml
62
63   topology_template:
64     node_templates:
65       vm1:
66         type: radon.nodes.OpenStack.VM
67         properties:
68           name: HostVM
69           image: centos7
70           flavor: m1.xsmall
71           network: provider_64_net
72           key_name: my_key
73
74     policies:
75       test:
76         type: radon.policies.scaling.ScaleOut
77         properties:
78           cpu_upper_bound: 90
79           adjustment: 1
```

Fig. 4. TOSCA YAML template example with scaling policy.

their applications to heterogeneous environment with multiple cloud providers. The deployment step is very well covered in TOSCA, while the ability to auto-scale application is not yet fully defined. During the process of creating the framework for developing, deploying and lifecycle management we realised that the latter, which includes scaling, is complex and fragile. Following the approach with *outside scaler* did not promise a stable solution. For example, in case of issues an interruptions during the application life-cycle management, it is not clear which state – scalers or orchestrators – is the desired one? It could be that scaler is in process to submit new application template to the orchestrator, or the orchestrator should update the scalers' configuration.

Exploring the solutions that would not be affected from aforementioned orchestrator-scaler leadership issue we focused on TOSCA definitions and propose the usage of TOSCA, which incorporates scaling definitions to be executed by orchestrator. The TOSCA standard will not require significant updates to use our approach, while some improvements of the TOSCA orchestrators will be necessary. Orchestrator cannot be stopped after the deploy (or particular re-deploy job), but needs to be alive and ready to accept the triggers from the monitoring system. This changes the way how the orchestrator should operate.

6   Conclusions and Future Work

To conclude, scaling and autoscaling are and will be desired functionalities within larger microservice applications e.g. AWS Lambda applications and applications using Docker containers. There are several ways of establishing scaling policies successfully but some of them can consume more time or require more tools than others. Instead of commonly used separate scalers this part can be moved to the orchestration process in order to facilitate this task and have universal approach to the application scaling. OASIS TOSCA standard provides promising scaling policies that can be supported in TOSCA orchestrators which can then use their own services to maintain the automatic scaling of application's resources and therefore relieve the end-users and the companies by keeping the applications constantly accessible.

Acknowledgements. This paper has been partially supported by the European Union's Horizon 2020 research and innovation programme under Grant Agreement No. 825040 (RADON).

References

1. Aws cloud formation (2020). https://aws.amazon.com/cloudformation/. Accessed 19 June 2020
2. Casale, G., et al.: RADON: rational decomposition and orchestration for serverless computing. SICS Softw. Intensive Cyber Phys. Syst. **35**, 77–87 (2019). https://doi.org/10.1007/s00450-019-00413-w

3. Janiesch, C.: Slipstream: live dashboarding for sap netweaver bpm ("galaxy"). Sap community network blog (2009). http://scn.sap.com/people/christian.janiesch/blog/2009/11/17/slipstream-live-dashboarding-for-sap-netweaver-bpm-galaxy

4. Lipton, P., Palma, D., Rutkowski, M., Tamburri, D.A.: Tosca solves big problems in the cloud and beyond!. IEEE Cloud Comput. 5(2), 37–47 (2018). http://dblp.uni-trier.de/db/journals/cloudcomp/cloudcomp5.html#LiptonPRT18

5. Openstack heat (2020). https://wiki.openstack.org/wiki/Heat. Accessed 19 June 2020

6. Prometheus (2020). https://prometheus.io/. Accessed 21 June 2020

7. Radon github repository (2020). https://github.com/radon-h2020. Accessed 29 June 2020

8. Sahare, S., Rojatkar Dr, D.V.: Cloud computing. Int. J. Trend Sci. Res. Dev. 1(6), 786–789 (2017). http://www.ijtsrd.com/engineering/electronics-and-communication-engineering/4685/cloud-computing/shubhangi-sahare

9. Wei, Y., Kudenko, D., Liu, S., Pan, L., Wu, L., Meng, X.: A reinforcement learning based auto-scaling approach for saas providers in dynamic cloud environment. Math. Probl. Eng. 2019, 11 (2019). https://doi.org/10.1155/2019/5080647

10. xOpera github repository (2020). https://github.com/xlab-si/xopera-opera. Accessed 20 June 2020

Towards Coordinated Autoscaling and Application Brownout at the Orchestrator Level

Ivan Kotegov and Antonio Filieri$^{(\boxtimes)}$ ⓘD

Imperial College London, London, UK
a.filieri@imperial.ac.uk

Abstract. Modern cloud applications are expected to continuously provide adequate performance, withstanding changing workloads, heterogeneous hardware, and unpredictable infrastructure failures. Autoscaling can automatically provision resources to match performance goals but may suffer from slower reaction times and risks of over-provisioning. Brownout mechanisms, on the other hand, empower applications with the ability to quickly dim out optional features, freeing computational resources to serve core functionalities with the desired performance level. However, modifying an application to include brownout capabilities may require invasive changes to the codebase and the need to expose ad-hoc interfaces to coordinate the interaction of the brownout dimmers and autoscaling actions, avoiding interferences that may destabilize the system. In this paper, we report on our preliminary results on the design of an application-agnostic control theoretical solution to integrate scaling and dimming capabilities at the orchestrator level. We implemented a prototype of our controller on top of Kubernetes and HAProxy to empower generic applications with coordinated autoscaling and brownout capabilities by dynamically controlling the number of active replicas and per-user access to optional API endpoints.

1 Introduction

Modern cloud applications are expected to adapt their behavior and resource allocations to continuously provide the desired quality of service in spite of unpredictable changes in their workloads and execution environments.

Most adaptation techniques rely on feedback loops to control and mitigate the effects of external phenomena on the performance of the controlled application. Feedback loops continuously measure the evolution of relevant quality figures of the running system, triggering adaptation actions when these measures deviate from acceptable ranges. Adaptation decisions, such as provisioning of additional resources or disabling optional software features, can be drawn based on a variety of methods, from casting the decision as an optimization problem to using machine learning to predict the most appropriate reactions [1].

Different methods require more or less accurate models of the relevant system behaviors (e.g., abstracted as queuing networks or difference equations), can

© Springer Nature Switzerland AG 2020
H. Muccini et al. (Eds.): ECSA 2020, CCIS 1269, pp. 269–274, 2020.
https://doi.org/10.1007/978-3-030-59155-7_21

adapt for a single or multiple goals and actuators, and provide different guarantees on the effectiveness, stability, and robustness of their decision processes [2].

Among the different adaptation paradigms considered in the field, in this paper we focus on autoscaling and brownout. Autoscaling aims at automatically allocating and deallocating computational resources as required by the application to match its performance goals. Microservices or FaaS are typical architectures that enable an application to increase its capacity by instantiating additional replicas. Brownout [3] is instead a form of graceful degradation where an application may adaptively disable optional features to reduce its computational fingerprint, releasing resources to serve core features at the required performance level. Brownout has also been used to improve the energy footprint of cloud applications [4], and resource utilization in cloud applications [5].

Differently from autoscaling, current brownout controllers require ad-hoc changes to the application codebase, increasing maintainability costs and development complexity. Furthermore, while provably effective and stable in isolation, deploying these two techniques simultaneously on the same application may induce coupling effects, where the actions taken independently by the two controllers may antagonize each other, possibly leading to oscillations.

In this paper, we present preliminary findings on our development of a control-theoretical adaptation mechanism to coordinate autoscaling and brownout decisions at the orchestrator level, with the goal of controlling the response time of an application. To coordinate the two controllers' actions to keep the response time at the desired values, we propose using a mid-range control architecture [6]. This enables the use of computationally efficient and provably stable PI controllers, coordinated to take advantage of the distinct speed, accuracy, and strengths of both autoscaling and brownout. We report on preliminary experimental results in support of our control design via a prototype implementation on top of Kubernetes and HAProxy.

2   Background

Feedback Control. Figure 1 represents a basic feedback loop. The controller C computes its control signal u as a function of the difference between the desired behavior – the *setpoint* (y_{sp}) – and the measured process behavior (y). This difference is called error (e). The process behavior is affected by both the control signal and external disturbances w. Even if the external disturbances are not explicitly modeled or only coarse information about them is available, their (relevant) effects on the process propagates through the measure y via the feedback loop, allowing the controller to reject the disturbances.

Controllers can be evaluated on several formal properties [7]. The three most relevant for this work are stability, settling time, and overshoots. A stable controller will eventually drive the process within a bounded distance from the setpoint, if feasible. Settling time is the time required to converge (up to a fixed accuracy) to the setpoint, while overshoots are related to transitory excessive reactions and should be limited.

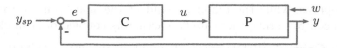

Fig. 1. Feedback control loop.

PID Controllers. Equation (1) formalizes the control law of a PID controller.

$$u(t) = \underbrace{K \cdot e(t)}_{\text{proportional}} + \underbrace{\frac{K}{T_i} \cdot \int e(\tau)d\tau}_{\text{integral}} + \underbrace{K \cdot T_d \cdot \frac{de(t)}{dt}}_{\text{derivative}} \tag{1}$$

where $e(t) = y_{sp}(t) - y(t)$ is the error, which the controller aims to minimize. A PID is tuned through the three parameters K, T_i, and T_d. K is the proportional gain. Higher values of K lead to "stronger" reactions, which may reduce the settling time of the closed loop, but could destabilize it. The integral term mitigates steady-state deviations form the setpoint that the proportional component cannot handle, it can, however, lead to overshoots. The integral action also helps to smooth the reaction to fast changes in the error. The derivative term can reduce the convergence time and increase stability, but it may induce the controlled system to follow error variations due to external disturbances. For our application, we will not use the derivative component ($T_d = 0$), preferring disturbance rejection over settling time. This setting is called the PI controller. PID controllers do not require an explicit analytical model of the process but can be tuned using human expertise or established heuristics [6]. While usually sub-optimally, PIDs can control several classes of nonlinear systems [5].

3   Coordinating Scaling and Dimming

Our goal is to consistently control the number of replicas allocated to an application (scaling) and the brownout of optional features (dimming). We will refer to the corresponding controllers as *scaler* and *dimmer*, respectively. Control should be placed at the orchestrator/load-balancer level, instead of modifying the application's logic, for a better separation of concerns. The control goal is to keep the average response time close to a prescribed setpoint.

Individually, both a scaler and a dimmer can be implemented using PI. The former actuated on the number of replicas, the latter regulating the rate at which access to optional features endpoints is allowed. However, if the two controllers act independently, they can interfere with one another, possibly leading to oscillations and destabilizing the system. For example, consider the measured response time exceeds the setpoint, the scaler can allocate an additional replica, while at the same time the dimmer may disable optional features, reducing computational demand. The reduced demand would trigger the scaler to deallocate excessive replicas, while the dimmer would at the same time restore optional features. In control terms, there are two actuators coupled on a single measure.

Mid-range Control. PI(D)s are single-input single-output (SISO) controllers, i.e., manipulating one actuator to control one measurement, and cannot be easily extended to control multiple inputs or multiple outputs. We can observe that the dimmer and the scaler have different dynamics. Dimmer decisions can be enforced quickly (access control) and have high resolution, deciding with high precision the rate at which optional features should be served. However, dimming can compensate only moderate load variations, since core application features are always served. Scaling, on the other hand, can compensate for larger variations by provisioning additional resources, but its actions have lower resolution and take longer to actuate.

This situation lends itself to the design of a *mid-range control* architecture [6]. This architecture is described in Fig. 2. The dimmer takes the measured response time and controls the rate at which optional features are served to reach the setpoint. The scaler, on the other hand, takes the control signal emitted by the dimmer and controls the number of provisioned replicas to keep the dimmer around the middle of its operational range (d_{sp}).

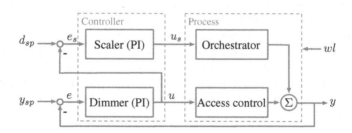

Fig. 2. Controller architecture.

When the error e exceeds the capabilities of the dimmer, its control signal u is likely to saturate to the top or the bottom of its range (i.e., either serving optional features to every user or to none). This deviation of u from its mid-range d_{sp} will then trigger the reaction of the scaler, which will allocate or deallocate replicas to bring the dimmer back to d_{sp} where it can limit serving optional features as needed for the new number of replicas. Both the dimmer and the scaler are PI controllers.

4   Preliminary Results

Implementation. We implemented the control architecture of Sect. 3 by extending HAProxy-Ingress, an open-source Kubernetes Ingress controller. Dimming is implemented by generating and dynamically updating the HAProxy's configuration defining access control lists (ACLs) for optional application features. The dimmer control signal represents the maximum number of requests a user (uniquely identified by session id) can make over a 30 s window before their requests to optional features get disabled. The range of the dimmer control signal is 1–1000. The scaler controls the number of pods in the cluster (1–6). Average response time is measured by HAProxy over the last 1024 requests.

Experiment. We adapted the JPetStore benchmark adding artificial optional features, similarly to [3]. The optional features simulate a random delay averaging 1 s. Kubernetes is deployed on a cluster of 6 i7-4790 workstations and uses Weave Net CNI. We used JMeter distributed testing with 6 instances to simulate users. Each simulated user generated a sequence of up to 1000 requests separated by a random delay between 1 and 100 milliseconds. Each user is randomly assigned a ratio between 0 and 50% denoting the proportion of optional features requested. The controllers have been tuned manually, with $K = 0.05$ and $T_i = 3$ for the dimmer and $K = 0.0025$ and $T_i = 1000$ for the scaler. The scaler uses a hysteresis of 2 min to allow for resource allocation and measurements update. The target mid-range for the dimmer is set to 600 ± 200.

Results. An example run is shown in Fig. 3. Time is reported in steps of 15 s. The top subfigures shows the number of active user sessions over time, and the measured response time and setpoint, respectively.

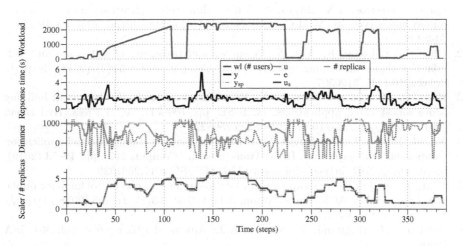

Fig. 3. Experiment results. From the top: workload wl in number of active user sessions; Response time (y) and its setpoint (y_{sp}); Dimmer control signal (u_d) and error (e_d); Scaler control signal (u_s) and corresponding number of replicas.

As observable in the figure, small variations in the workload are handled by the dimmer, without the intervention of the scaler (whose control signal is nonetheless tracking the deviation of u from its midrange). Larger variations and higher spikes (e.g., flash crowds) require the provisioning of more replicas, which is triggered when the dimmer signal u saturates towards 1; similarly, replicas are removed when u saturates towards 1000 (i.e., in our setup, serving optional features to all users). The two controllers coordinate their operations avoiding oscillations and bringing the average response time around or below the setpoint.

5   Conclusions

We presented preliminary results on the use of a mid-range control architecture to coordinate autoscaling and brownout at the orchestrator level. The use of PI controllers requires a few arithmetic operations to determine the control actions, avoiding the overhead of more complex multi-objective strategies [8]. However, in these experiments, the controllers have been tuned manually, which may require some expertise. Autotuning and adaptive PIs may provide better performance, in particular allowing to retuning the controllers to better fit the current workload trends, reducing settling time and overshooting phenomena [9].

References

1. Qu, C., Calheiros, R.N., Buyya, R.: Auto-scaling web applications in clouds: a taxonomy and survey. In: ACM Comput. Surv. **51**(4) (2018). https://doi.org/10.1145/3148149
2. Chen, T., Bahsoon, R., Yao, X.: A survey and taxonomy of self-aware and self-adaptive cloud autoscaling systems. ACM Comput. Surv. **51**(3) (2018). https://doi.org/10.1145/3190507
3. Klein, C., Maggio, M., Årzén, K.-E., Hernández-Rodriguez, F.: Brownout: building More robust cloud applications. In: ICSE, pp. 700–711. ACM Press, Hyderabad (2014).https://doi.org/10.1145/2568225.2568227
4. Xu, M., Dastjerdi, A.V., Buyya, R.: Energy efficient scheduling of cloud application components with brownout. IEEE Trans. Sustain. Comput. **1**(2), pp. 40–53 (2016). arXiv: 1608.02707. https://doi.org/10.1109/TSUSC.2017.2661339
5. Wang, C., et al.: Effective capacity modulation as an explicit control knob for public cloud profitability. ACM Trans. Auton. Adapt. Syst. **13**(1), 21–225 (2018). https://doi.org/10.1145/3139291
6. Åström, K.J., Hägglund, T., Astrom, K.J.: Advanced PID control, vol. 461. ISA (2006)
7. Filieri, A., et al.: Control strategies for self-adaptive software systems. ACM Trans. Auton. Adapt. Syst. **11**(4), 241–2431 (2017). https://doi.org/10.1145/3024188
8. Maggio, M., Papadopoulos, A.V., Filieri, A., Hoffmann, H.: Automated control of multiple software goals using multiple actuators. In: ESEC- FSE. ESEC/FSE 2017. ACM, August 2017. https://doi.org/10.1145/3106237.3106247
9. Maggio, M., Klein, C., Årzén, K.-E.: Control strategies for predictable brownouts in cloud computing. In: IFAC Proceedings Volumes. 19th IFACWorld Congress, vol. 47, no. 3, pp. 689–694, January 2014. https://doi.org/10.3182/20140824-6-ZA-1003.00669

DETECT - 3rd International Workshop on Modeling, Verification and Testing of Dependable Critical Systems

International Workshop on Modeling, Verification and Testing of Dependable Critical Systems (DETECT)

Critical systems are emerging research fields where the safety is dependent upon the precise operations of the system. With this in mind, software architecture is one of the most challenging topics for critically dependable systems since it requires integrating solutions from experts of various domains. Also, integration of components contributed by respective domain experts is one of the key challenges in engineering software architectures.

Critical systems are more and more used in different domains and under several forms (e.g., cyber-physical systems, embedded systems, real-time systems) and become more complex since they can be networked and composed of heterogeneous subsystems. Due to their heterogeneity and variability, critical systems require the expertise of a modeling, verification, and testing area to ensure their dependability and safety of their software architectures. The International Workshop on moDeling, vErification and Testing of dEpendable CriTical systems (DETECT) was organized in conjunction with the European Conference on Software Architecture (ECSA), hence it is mainly based on model-based system engineering paradigm and software architecture challenges.

DETECT 2020 would not have possible without the support and the cooperation of the Program Committee members and also the external reviewers, who carefully reviewed and select the best contributions. We would like to thank all the authors who submitted papers, the reviewers, and the Organization Committee members for their investment and involvement in the success of DETECT 2020. This volume contains the papers selected for presentation at the workshop. The acceptance rate was 40%. Indeed, DETECT 2020 received 15 papers from 8 countries (Algeria, Belgium, France, Germany, Morocco, The Netherlands, the UK, and the USA). The Program Committee selected six full papers. Each paper was reviewed by at least four to five reviewers and was discussed afterwards by the reviewers and the Program Committee chairs. EasyChair was used for the management of DETECT 2020 and it provided a very helpful framework for the submission and review processes.

Organization

Workshop Chairs

Yassine Ouhammou   LIAS, ISAE-ENSMA, France
Abderrahim Ait Wakrime   Mohammed V University, Morocco

Workshop Program Committee

Shaukat Ali   Simula, Norway
Youness Bazhar   ASML, The Netherlands
Alessandro Biondi   Scuola Superiore Sant'Anna, Italy
Mohamed Yassin Chkouri   Abdelmalek Essaâdi University, Morocco
Khalil Drira   LAAS-CNRS, Université de Toulouse, France
Rachida Dssouli   Concordia University, Canada
Mamoun Filali-Amine   IRIT, France
Abdelouahed Gherbi   ETS Montreal, Canada
Fahad Golra   Agileo Automation, France
Paul Gibson   Télécom SudParis, France
Emmanuel Grolleau   LIAS, ISAE-ENSMA, France
Geoff Hamilton   Dublin City University, Ireland
Jameleddine Hassine   KFUPM, KSA
Jérome Hugues   SEI CMU, USA
Gwanggil Jeon   Incheon National University, South Korea
Slim Kallel   University of Sfax, Tunisia
Tomasz Kloda   Technical University of Munich, Germany
Zakaria Maamar   Zayed University, UAE
Van-Hien Ngo   STE Hanoi University, Vietnam
Réda Nouacer   CEA, France
Mehrdad Saadatmand   RISE SICS Vasteraas, Sweden
Colin Snook   University of Southampton, UK
Laura Titolo   NASA, USA
Faiez Zalila   CETIC, Belgium

Measurement-Based Timing Analysis on Heterogeneous MPSoCs: A Practical Approach

Roy Jamil[1,2]([✉]), Emmanuel Grolleau[1]([✉]), Bernard Dautrevaux[2]([✉]),
and Antoine Bertout[1]([✉])

[1] LIAS, ENSMA, University of Poitiers,
1 av. C. Ader, BP40109, 86961 Futuroscope, France
{roy.jamil,grolleau}@ensma.fr, antoine.bertout@univ-poitiers.fr
[2] AC6, 21, Rue Pierre Curie, 92400 Courbevoie, France
{roy.jamil,bernard.dautrevaux}@ac6.fr
https://www.ac6.fr

Abstract. This paper explores and compares different execution time measurement methods on modern heterogeneous multiprocessor systems on chip (HMPSoCs). We consider different measurement factors, such as the resolution, accuracy, granularity and difficulty of implementation and use of each technique. Moreover, HMPSoCs add the dimension of inter core cluster communication which has so far received little attention. In this paper, we show how to evaluate inter-cluster communication and apply the method on several recent chips. Moreover, we characterize the cost of migration between different types of cores.

Keywords: Execution time measurement · Worst case execution time · Timing analysis · Real time · Heterogeneous multiprocessors

1 Introduction

Several types of programs have to meet timing constraints, especially in the real-time systems domain. For those, a timing analysis is required: it is measuring the duration of the execution of some code on a given platform. A safe way to compute a worst-case execution time (WCET) [18] of a program is called *static*: based on a fine grain model of the execution platform and the source or binary code, the worst-case behavior of each branching in the program combined with the worst-case behavior of the internal state of the platform is established [13,14]. Nevertheless, on modern platforms like heterogeneous MPSoCs, the static faces two major problems. The platform model for new platforms cannot be found in any timing analysis tool and adding them would require a very high amount of work. Moreover, if it were to be done, the possible interference at different

Supported by AC6.

H. Muccini et al. (Eds.): ECSA 2020, CCIS 1269, pp. 279–293, 2020.
https://doi.org/10.1007/978-3-030-59155-7_22

contention points (memory bus, memory banks, cache memory, heuristic components, etc.) would lead to a very high overestimation of the possible behavior of the program. Indeed, modern architectures tend to optimize average execution time at the cost of determinism. The other way to compute a worst-case or average execution time on a platform is called *dynamic*, and consists in measuring the actual execution time of the program under analysis on the target platform. This technique can be applied on a new platform, with the help of adapted development environments, like the one we present in this paper. This technique is not safe, since it is possible to observe, at some point in the lifetime of the system, some execution time that could be larger than the one measured during dynamic timing analysis. Nevertheless, for systems with less stringent timing constraints, called *soft* real-time systems, intensive dynamic measurement of the execution time could be sufficient, and often be the only applicable choice. Indeed, the execution time of an instruction may vary depending on the internal state of the processor. This state becomes more and more complex with the presence of heuristic components. As a result, it is becoming more difficult to predict the relevant parts of the processor's internal state that influence timing behavior. The execution of a piece of code is dependent not only on the value of its input data (for example, issuing different branching in tests) but also, given the exact same behavior (same branching conditions), this execution is dependent on the internal state of the CPU and memory, especially regarding local optimization of average execution time. These optimization techniques imply execution time variations, and may even worsen the worst-case execution time.

Typically, a processor handles each instruction in several steps (or stages): fetching, decoding, executing, writing, etc. For the same instruction, only one of these stages is used at the same time. In practice, available stages are used in parallel for other instructions. This leads to an overlap in the execution of instructions, known as *pipelining*. Since there may be dependencies between instructions (for example, a calculated value is required for a subsequent instruction), there may be interaction between instructions that are executed one after the other.

Most high frequency CPUs use a cache memory to accelerate average memory access time by storing values read from the memory. The locality of reference implies that an accessed instruction or data has a high chance to be accessed again, and the next access to a cached value will not necessitate to access the memory, reducing the execution time. Nevertheless, preemption will alter the cache content, and create cache related preemption delays, problem which has received a lot of attention in static analysis [1].

Moreover, in order to keep the pipeline filled in the program branches, processors commonly implement a branch prediction, its purpose is to predict what is executed after a conditional branch when the condition is not yet known. These processors then speculatively retrieve the instructions from the memory, which are ignored if the prediction turns out to be wrong. This often influences the behaviour of the cache in the most complex way.

On multicore architectures, sharing the same memory bus, or on multicore and manycore architectures sharing the same memory banks, execution on one core may interfere with execution on another core because of the contention of accesses to both the memory bus and memory banks.

Moreover, programs can require the use of external circuits, from external specialized computing units (e.g., Floating Point Unit - FPU, Graphical Processing Unit - GPU, Application Specific Integrated Circuits - ASICs, etc.), to external devices and peripherals, which work asynchronously from the computing cores and can also be shared among several cores (and thus among several executing pieces of code). For example, if the system has to access a peripheral by mapped addresses in memory, then the computation of the WCET should take both the time taken by the communication bus to access the peripheral and the response time of the device into account. This is also the case for memory. The response time of the device, memory or bus depends on their respective occupancy rates and on their arbitration policy, which is to often opaque.

On complex hardware architectures, it is not possible to know the actual, achievable, WCET of a system because it is too complex to determine. Indeed, there are many parameters to take into account and the overestimation compared to actual observable cases is too large to be useful. Moreover, if the evolution of technology for three decades has always prioritized the average computation time, being detrimental to the worst-case execution time. For example, if the WCET on a modern hardware platform overestimates tenfold the WCET compared to the actual observable WCET, what would be the point of using this platform compared to an older, slower, and simpler platform where the computed WCET would be closer to the actual observable WCET? We do not believe that using a platform at 5 or 10% of its capacity is acceptable. This is why we focus on dynamic measurement tools on modern platforms. One of the desired effects is to find the value as close as possible to the worst observable execution time.

1.1 Timing Analysis Methods

This paper focuses on measurement methods of execution times on modern computing platforms. Deployment of a program, along with its host operating system, configuration, and options, is time consuming. Moreover, several clocks, timers, and software Application Programming Interfaces (API), allow theoretically a programmer to measure the execution time of a piece of code. In this paper, we discuss these methods, in order for them to be used in a wider timing analysis method to obtain a worst-case execution time. This can be used in three of the four families of timing analysis methods that can be identified.

(1) Dynamic methods rely on intensive measurement on the platform.
(2) Static analysis is based on mathematical models that depends on both software and hardware with the same importance. It generally has two phases: the flow analysis determines all possible paths in the control flow graph of the program, and the time analysis evaluates the execution time of each of these paths. The hardware model allows to determine the execution time of the instructions individually. The software model represents the possible execution flows. The combination of these models with information on the

maximum number of times loops are iterated, the possible paths in the program, the frequency of execution of code parts, etc. gives a WCET estimate. As long as the models are correct, the WCET estimate is always reliable, even if it is greater than any observable execution time.

(3) Hybrid measurement-based analysis was first presented by Kirner et al. [9]. It is an industry standard technique, employed in commercial tools, that operates similarly to static analysis, except that it does not rely on a hardware model. Rather, it uses measurements to derive execution times of small program parts, before combining them using flow information in the WCET calculation. Although the WCET estimate is generally more accurate than that computed by static analysis, there is a possibility of underestimation if testing has not sufficiently stressed the execution times of the small program parts. Requiring intensive testing on the platform, the content of this paper can also be useful in this type of measurement.

(4) More recently, some research groups started to develop stochastic response time analysis methods, based on stochastic distributions on execution times [5], which could lead to consider the very rare occurrences of the simultaneity of worst-case program behavior with worst-case platform behavior as rare events, and reduce the under-utilization of modern platforms. Like dynamic methods, these methods require intensive testing and this paper also offers tooling for such type of measurement.

1.2   Measurement Techniques Characteristics

In order to measure execution time several methods exist that are each featuring a unique selection of attributes[17]. These include:

1. *Accuracy* represents how close the measured value is to the true value by using a measuring technique. In other terms, when retrieving an execution time there is always an error limit. The actual value is certainly between the measured value $+-$ the accuracy of the method.

2. *Difficulty* of using a technique is a subjective characteristic, it is the effort put in place to implement a method. For instance, if a given method requires the use of advanced materials (e.g., logic analyzer), it is typically less accessible to users than a purely software method.

3. *Granularity* represents the size of code which is possible to be measured, for example, some methods are able to measure the execution time per function, thread or process, other advanced techniques are able to measure the execution time of a single instruction [10]. Measurement, especially by software means, has an impact on the measure.

4. *Resolution* of a measurement with respect to time, is the hardware limitation associated with each method. For example, some physical timers have a resolution of one microsecond.

1.3   Contributions

We show how we help a user to obtain measurements on his programs using a new module that we are developing. For this tool, we tried to make the technique easy to use, requiring only the target hardware and the development computer, giving the highest possible resolution depending on the available clocks or operating system, then it retrieves the measurement data automatically through the debugger and exports it to a spreadsheet. The limitation, as with other dynamic methods, is the inability to know the accuracy. We plan to work on this limitation in future works. In the following section, the existing measurement methods are compared. Then, in the third section, a specific measurement method on heterogeneous MPSoCs is discussed.

2   Measurement Methods on a Core

2.1   Stopwatch

Using stopwatches is a basic method to measure the amount of time elapsed between the beginning and the end of a measurement. It requires a timing device, for example, a digital watch, started at the beginning, and stopped at the end of the measured piece of code. The stopwatch can be either external, where the watch does not affect the code being measured, or instrumented, where we have to add some code at the boundaries of the block of code being measured, altering the duration of the measured code.

The resolution and the accuracy of this method depends on the tool being used for the measurement. When running several times this code, the measurement data is to be stored somewhere in the memory or registers of the target hardware. There are two naive ways to handle it: (i) data stored locally during the measurement campaign, and sent to the host platform at the end, creates more memory stress and can interfere with the measurement itself, or be limited by local memory size, (2) data sent after each measure to the host computer, which can slow down the whole process. In both cases, the data is sent to the host computer using a connection between target and host (Ethernet, serial, etc.).

All these methods require therefore an additional code to recover the data which increases the complexity of the measurement system. But there is another way to retrieve data without adding any code. This method uses a debugging system based on a hardware debug probe and a software debugger. It allows the host machine to have a full view on the memory and the registers' values. It also makes possible to transfer the data recovery complexity from the measured system to the host machine where we can simply encapsulate it into a software part of an integrated development environment. We can then re-use it to do measurements on other systems, all the while taking advantage of the possibility of displaying the data on the host with statistics and graphs.

Regardless of the underlying stopwatch, many issues may occur due to the preemption and interrupts. During the measurement of a segment of code, an interrupt provokes false measurement value. We have two solutions to cope with this. The first consists in masking the interrupts at the beginning of a measurement and unmasking it at the end. But this solution is not applicable all the time, because masking is not always available and it could also affect the system behavior or modify its timing. The second solution is to simply discard values that do not make sense, for example when we have a duration much longer than other measurements most probably due to the interrupt. This solution must be applied carefully to avoid discarding a representative value.

In the next sub-sections, we derive the listing of the stopwatch code on several types of platforms.

2.2   Linux Time Tools

Linux provides many tools and functionalities to measure the elapsed time, with their own characteristics, advantages and disadvantages.

The linux commands `date` and `time` are two popular tools giving the execution time of the whole program. They cannot be used to measure the execution time of a specific function or a block of code. The main advantage of these tools is the ease of use. Nevertheless, they are not very accurate and have a relatively high granularity (a program). Gprof [7] is an open source profiling tool for Unix application, it is a part of the GNU project and can be used for profiling programs compiled with GCC. In order to gather measurement data, GProf needs code instrumentation, which can be done automatically using the GCC compiler by passing specific options.

For more accurate measurement with a finer granularity, POSIX clocks can be used. Two popular clocks are usually used:

1. CLOCK_REALTIME that represents the current wall clock which is affected by the modification of the system time-of-day clock.
2. CLOCK_MONOTONIC which represents the elapsed time since a fixed point in the past, this clock is not affected by changes in the system clock or a system reboot.

It defines two functions for the clock configuration, the first is used to get the resolution of the clock `clock_getres()`, which is implementation dependant, and has a precision up to a nanosecond. The second, `clock_settime()`, is used to set the time of a clock.

The function `clock_gettime()` returns the current value of the selected clock. This function should be used as a wrap to stopwatch in order to measure the segment of code, this is done by taking its value at the beginning and the end of the measured block, as shown below:

```
struct timespec start_time , stop_time ;
unsigned int measurement ;
clock_gettime (CLOCK _MONOTONIC, &start_time );

/* code to measure */

clock_gettime (CLOCK_MONOTONIC, &stop_time );
measure = (( stop_time . tv_nsec − start_time . tv_nsec ) +
( stop_time . tv_sec   − start_time . tv_sec )*1000000000u );
```

One of the drawbacks of this method is that we include the duration of clock_gettime() itself in the measurement. If the portion of measured code is short, this leads to a drastic overestimation.

2.3 C Standard Functions

Many functions defined in C language are available for measurement, these functions should be used like a stopwatch. The function clock() [8] determines the processor time used and the function time() [8] determines the current calendar time. The standard does not specify their resolution but indicates that they should be the implementation's best approximation.

2.4 Clock Cycles Counter

Most processors implement mechanisms and registers used for profiling and benchmarking purposes. These mechanisms are usually based on free running cycles counter, counting upward, where the value of the register will be incremented by one on each clock cycle, then it will be zeroed on overflow and generate an event. These mechanisms are on-chip physical components controlled by assembly instructions, and have a small overhead on the processing. On Intel architectures this counter is called Timer Stamp Counter (TSC), on the other hand, ARM based architectures use the clock cycles counter (CYCCNT), which is a 32-bits register. The counter is usually used like a stopwatch: its value is reset and it has to be started before the measurement.

2.5 Timer/Counter Chip

Processors' chips usually contain timers, that could be general purpose timers or any other timer type. These timers are based on counters either upward or downward. In both cases, they can be used to measure the execution time of a segment of code or a function by using it as a stopwatch. This technique requires an initialization phase before doing the measurement, during which the timer usually has to be configured by setting the source clock and other setup mentioned later on. These peripherals have many registers that provide different functionalities. In order to measure a portion of code, two types are required: the control registers and the counter value registers. The latter holds the maximum counting limitation which is usually based on registers size between 8 and 32 bits. The control functionalities vary among chips and types, and the ability to set it as an upward or a downward counter is usually available. Another common functionality is the possibility to specify the initial, start, stop and reset values, as well as setting a pre-scaler (clock divider) and the counting granularity. Giving a timer resolution, the higher the precision is, the lower the duration before an overflow. Let's suppose that the timer has 32 bits counter value registers, and has a source clock frequency 200 MHz meaning that its precision can get up to 5 ns. This implies that it will overflow after 21.47 s. With the pre-scaler, the clock can be divided by 2, 4, 6... so that measurement can be done for a longer duration, at the cost of precision. To avoid any kind of inaccuracy, it is always recommended to start with an estimated pre-scaler, and then reduce it to increase the precision, discarding values that show that an overflow occurred. In some cases, it is even recommended to measure a block of code with an estimated execution duration equal to 10% of the maximum value that can be held by the value registers. We can find these timers in two places. Either they are available as an external peripheral inside the chip or in all cores of the same type. On one hand, having the timer as an external peripheral has many advantages. Besides providing different functionalities not related to the measurement, we can benefit from the higher clock speed allowing more precision, in addition to size of the registers value. It is also more configurable without side effects on the system. This kind is used later on, to measure the inter processors message passing. But this type is much more specific to each board, making its usage less portable than other types. On the other hand, each processor usually provides a main timer that can be used for many purposes. The most common one is the tick generator of an operating system. In most cases, it is configured to have the same speed as the processor so the measurement can take place without any special kind of initialization. The measurement unit could be both in time or in cycles. The conversion is not immediate since some processors see their frequency dynamically modified depending on the load or core temperature. Such a timer should be used carefully because other components could be using it, and they might modify its configuration (for example FreeRTOS uses the Systick timer for its own purpose). This also implies that if an operating system is used, there is a high risk of inaccurate results. In such cases, it is recommended to use another method or another timer and certainly not changing its configuration in any way, because it will probably crash the operating system. One popular example of a timer used for measurement is the ARM Systick timer, that can be found in all ARM based microcontrollers from different manufacturers, allowing the code to be way more portable than the external timer. It is also easy to use [19].

2.6   Logic Analyzer

Logic analyzer is a solution to a particular class of problems. It is a versatile tool that can help with digital hardware debugging, design verification and embedded software debug. The data stored in the real-time acquisition memory can be used in a variety of display and analysis modes. Once the information is stored within the system, it can be viewed in many formats.

In order to use a logic analyzer two approaches are possible. The first one consists in connecting the probes to the CPU pins. The advantage of this approach is that it does not disturb the real-time code. At the same time, it is a very complicated method because the correlation between the logic analyzer measurement and the source code can only be done by reverse engineering.

The second one consists in sending strategic signals to an output port at the beginning and end of each code segment. These signals are then read as events by the logic analyzer. The code instructions that are enclosed within a macro make it easier to redefine the macro without affecting the application code. This method can be used for small systems as well as for large applications that use commercial real-time operating systems.

2.7   Experimental Comparison

We measured the execution time using different methods on three heterogeneous boards, the STM32MP157-DK2 from STMicroelectronics, it consists of a dual-core Cortex-A 650 MHz and a single core Cortex-M 209 MHz, and two boards from NXP, the i.MX7ULP (Cortex-A 500 MHz and a Cortex-M 200 MHz) and the i.MX8EVK (Cortex-A 1 GHz and a Cortex-M 240 MHz). We used the Adaptive Differential Pulse Code Modulation benchmark which is part of TACLe Benchmark suite [6], the test was repeated for at least one hundred times. In Fig. 1, we are showing as box plots the results obtained using three measurement methods: the ARM cycles counter (CYCCNT), ARM core timer (SYSTICK) and a peripheral timer that is specific to each board. The results are similar across all three methods. This shows a consistency that is reassuring since the only difference lies on the choice of the easiest method to implement.

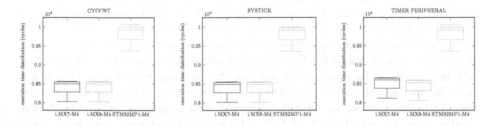

Fig. 1. Execution time distribution using different methods

Figure 2 shows the results of the same benchmark code but using the POSIX clock based measurement using `get_clocktime()` function on a Linux OS in normal load condition or in a stressed environment using the hackbench tool [20]. We can see that the results in a stressed environment are more spread than on normal load. The execution time when measured in nanoseconds varies a lot depending on the frequency of the processor, therefore, the i.MX7 500 MHz frequency is the slowest and the i.MX8 1 GHz is the fastest, though if we calculate the equivalent cycles count, it gives closer values.

We notice that the execution time on the i.MX8 board is faster on a stressed environment. This is due to the fact that Linux changes the frequency dynamically [15] depending on the processor's load. In this case, the frequency 1 GHz when normal load, while it is boosted 1.5 GHz in the stressed environment.

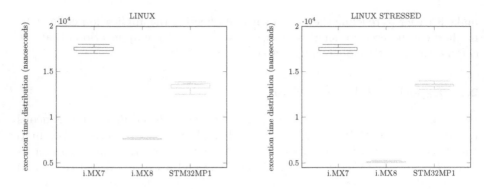

Fig. 2. Execution time distribution on Linux

3   Inter-core Timing Measurement

3.1   Heterogeneous Asymmetric Multicores

Until recently, most of the multicore platforms were homogeneous, including several identical cores able to access the main memory using the same bus, allowing a global scheduler to schedule the threads globally on every core. Following the market needs, several SoC manufacturers are nowadays proposing new heterogeneous multicore system where they combine at least two different types of cores, for example a microcontroller (MCU) and a set of microprocessors (MPU). This new technology is becoming very popular in the computing world, this is not only due to the fact that we can dedicate a processor to a specific function but also to the ability to use an entirely different OS on each core. SoC architects, are creating mixed types of processing cores for complex systems to perform sophisticated operations in an effective way, they combine MCU and MPU units on one multicore device. For example, we can find a SoC with quad-core ARM Cortex-A53, two ARM Cortex-R5 and a Field-Programmable Gate Array (FPGA) or another SoC with dual-core ARM cortex-A7 and an ARM Cortex-M4.

In a real-time context, those features stress the question of how to measure the execution time of an application that starts on a core then migrates through the inter processor communication mechanism then ends on another type of core.

3.2   Inter-core Communication Technologies

Heterogeneous asymmetric multi processor (AMP) cores have several components that permit inter-core communication, the most important one is the shared memory, we usually find exclusive memories for each group of the AMP cores and a shared memory [16], where they can access it simultaneously. This access needs other mechanisms to avoid a race condition and to allow synchronisation. This is where an inter cores signaling controller is implemented that triggers interrupts between the AMP cores, this controller is available in the STM32 family as Inter-Processor Communication Controller (IPCC) [16], which mainly consists of two parts – Interrupts management and the AHB interface. Each channel makes use of single status flags to indicate Send or Receive status of a processor. Communication between processors follows a simple and stream-lined approach using the IPCC. Before any message is passed, the channel flag is first checked to see whether it is free or occupied. Once the channel is free, a channel free interrupt is generated by the sender. The channel free interrupt is then masked after which the message can be written in the channel buffer. The channel status flag is also set to 'Occupied' that triggers an interrupt in the receiver side. The receiving side then checks which channel is occupied and masks the appropriate Channel Occupied Interrupt. This allows the data to be read by the receiver from the channel buffer. Once the operation is complete, the receiver sets the Channel status flag to Free and unmasks the Channel Occu-pied interrupt. For half-duplex communication, the processors follow a similar method to send and receive messages through the IPCC.

Another mechanism available in Asymmetric Multi Processor (AMP) archi-tectures is the hardware spinlocks [11], also known as hardware semaphores [16], which permits the exclusive access to the shared memory or a shared peripheral. These hardware means are often used by the software framework OpenAMP, that allows AMP systems to utilize the multi-processor configuration by allow-ing operating systems to interact and communicate with complex homogeneous or heterogeneous architectures.

With a large number of microcontroller cores being built on single integrated chips, it is becoming increasingly difficult for developers to fully utilize the avail-able underlying hardware. When it comes to homogeneous systems, the symmet-rical processing approach treats all the cores equally by evenly balancing the load among them. However, they cannot be scaled to handle heterogeneous architec-tures, that can host different operating systems and use different instruction sets. This is where the OpenAMP framework comes into the picture. It is an open-source project that mainly deals with changing the ways operating systems are designed to interact with existing hardware. The framework allows developers to install and deploy multiple operating systems, applications and software over homogeneous or heterogeneous architectures. They are scalable and allow the developers to utilize the available hardware.

OpenAMP is based on a master-slave concept that utilizes different proces-sors and load. The main components of an OpenAMP are mentioned below [2]:

1. Remoteproc: It is used to control the Life-Cycle Management of the different processors existing on the AMP architecture. It uses the software running on the master processor to control other remote processors in the architecture. It also can be used to allocate system resources and create virtual I/O (virtio) devices using the firmware resource table.
2. rpmsg: It is a virtio-based API that allows Inter-Process communication between software running on different processors in the AMP architecture. RPMsg devices are also called channels.

RPMsg-Lite is another method for communication between multiple cores in a heterogeneous. It is a lightweight implementation of the RPMsg that offers a code size reduction, API simplification, and improved modularity [12], we use this implementation on the NXP i.MX boards.

3.3   Measurement Methods

To measure the execution time of a program that runs on AMP multicores we should use techniques that are independent from any specific core. Furthermore, the cycle does not make sense, as long as the cores are not synchronized and each has its own frequency. This is the reason why we should use a time unit like the nanosecond or microseconds where we take the same time reference.

An on-chip external timer is a good choice in this case, as long as this peripheral could be controlled by all the AMP cores. It should be used like a stopwatch, where the start value is taken from the first core and then the end value from the last.

In the example shown in Fig. 3, we have two AMP cores. The start value is taken from the microcontroller (MCU) and the end value from the processor. Our measurement method includes the execution time on both the MCU and the processor parts, writing the message to the shared memory in addition to the latency due to the inter-processor communication mechanism.

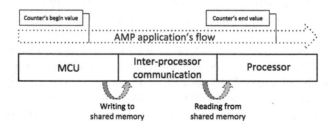

Fig. 3. AMP measurement using timer

Like any other measurement method based on the on-chip timer, one has to make sure to avoid the counter overflow as well as to decide on which core this timer should be initialized. The time unit is the timer's counter value, which can be converted to seconds based on the timer's frequency and prescaler.

In order to prepare for the test, we developed two applications each executed on a different core. The first sends a 512 bytes message to the second part which continues the execution. The external timer used for the measurement is initialized on the microcontroller's side, and it is possible to start, stop or read its counter's value on both sides.

The results shown in Fig. 4 demonstrate the execution time in nanoseconds of this application where benchmark parts were starting and ending on different

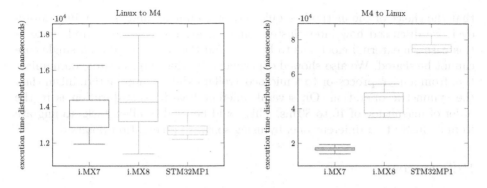

Fig. 4. Measuring the communication time for AMP application

cores. We can notice, on all boards, that sending a message from the microcontroller to the Linux operated microprocessor has higher latency but shows more determinism. The fact that there is more variation when Linux operates as the reader can be explained by the fact that the task waiting for the message, while having the highest priority, is in a waiting state. When the message arrives, it triggers an interrupt, which triggers the Linux kernel operations, that will put the task in a ready state, and call the scheduler. This is therefore suffering the variation of the kernel latency. When Linux acts as the sender, we observe very few variation, because when the counter is activated by the highest priority task, that then feeds the messaging's driver with the data to send, there is no scheduling decision to make.

3.4 Heterogeneous Migration

Currently, schedulers support migration only for symmetrical multiprocessing (SMP). In AMP system, these schedulers face many challenges, because they must deal with unrelated multiprocessor platforms, that usually have different instruction set architecture (ISA). Nevertheless, allowing migration could lead to a full resource utilization, because optimal global schedulers for heterogeneous platforms have been proposed in the literature [3,4]. Nevertheless, these global schedulers usually consider an instantaneous migration time. One simple solution consists of compiling the code for each architecture, then specifying the migration points in the code, allowing the migration from a cluster to another. This is where the necessary local data is transferred to the other side using OpenAMP to continue the execution.

4   Conclusion

In this paper we discussed several measurement methods both on a single type of core, for baremetal and Linux based pieces of code. We showed experimentally that most clock based measurement methods give similar results, this implicates that the choice of the methods should rely on simplicity and accessibility. Moreover, we discussed how inter-cluster communication can be measured, since in this case, an external clock has to be used and the timers used on a single core cannot be shared. We also showed experimentally that inter cluster communication from a microprocessor to a microcontroller exhibits more determinism than the symmetric operation. On several different boards, this duration is in the order of magnitude of 10 to 80 ms. This could be used to allow tasks to migrate from a cluster to a different one, by using software preemption points.

References

1. Altmeyer, S., Burguière, C.: Cache-related preemption delay via useful cache blocks: survey and redefinition. J. Syst. Architect. **57**(7), 707–719 (2011)
2. Baum, F., Raghuraman, A.: Making full use of emerging ARM-based heterogeneous multicore SoCs. In: 8th European Congress on Embedded Real Time Software and Systems (ERTS 2016) (2016). https://hal.archives-ouvertes.fr/hal-01292325
3. Bertout, A., Goossens, J., Grolleau, E., Poczekajlo, X.: Template schedule construction for global real-time scheduling on unrelated multiprocessor platforms. In: 2020 Design, Automation & Test in Europe Conference & Exhibition, pp. 216–221. IEEE (2020)
4. Bertout, A., Goossens, J., Grolleau, E., Poczekajlo, X.: Workload assignment for global real-time scheduling on unrelated multicore platforms. In: Proceedings of the 28th International Conference on Real-Time Networks and Systems, pp. 139–148 (2020)
5. Davis, R.I., Cucu-Grosjean, L.: A survey of probabilistic schedulability analysis techniques for real-time systems. LITES: Leibniz Trans. Embed. Syst., 1–53 (2019)
6. Falk, H., et al.: Taclebench: a benchmark collection to support worst-case execution time research. In: 16th International Workshop on Worst-Case Execution Time Analysis (2016)
7. Graham, S.L., Kessler, P.B., McKusick, M.K.: Gprof: a call graph execution profiler. SIGPLAN Not. **39**(4), 49–57 (2004). https://doi.org/10.1145/989393.989401
8. ISO: ISO/IEC 9899:2018 Information technology – Programming languages – C. pub-ISO, pub-ISO:adr, June 2018. https://www.iso.org/standard/68564.html
9. Kirner, R., Wenzel, I., Rieder, B., Puschner, P.: Using measurements as a complement to static worst-case execution time analysis. Intell. Syst. Serv. Mankind **2**, 8 (2005)
10. Lilja, D.J.: Measuring Computer Performance: A Practitioner's Guide. Cambridge University Press, Cambridge (2005)
11. Linux kernel: Hardware Spinlock Framework. https://www.kernel.org/doc/Documentation/hwspinlock.txt
12. NXP: RPMsg-Lite User's Guide. https://nxpmicro.github.io/rpmsg-lite/
13. Park, C., Shaw, A.C.: Experiments with a program timing tool based on source-level timing schema. In: Proceedings 11th Real-Time Systems Symposium, pp. 72–81. IEEE (1990)
14. Puschner, P., Koza, C.: Calculating the maximum execution time of real-time programs. Real-Time Syst. **1**(2), 159–176 (1989)
15. Spiliopoulos, V., Kaxiras, S., Keramidas, G.: Green governors: a framework for continuously adaptive DVFs. In: 2011 International Green Computing Conference and Workshops, pp. 1–8. IEEE (2011)

16. ST Microelectronics: STM32MP157 advanced Arm-based 32-bit MPUs (2019)
17. Stewart, D.B.: Measuring execution time and real-time performance. In: Embedded Systems Conference (ESC), vol. 141 (2001)
18. Wilhelm, R., et al.: The worst-case execution-time problem-overview of methods and survey of tools. ACM Trans. Embed. Comput. Syst. (TECS) 7(3), 36 (2008)
19. Yiu, J.: The Definitive Guide to ARM® Cortex®-M3 and Cortex®-M4 Processors. Newnes (2013)
20. Zhang, Y.: Hackbench (2008). https://people.redhat.com/mingo/cfs-scheduler/tools/hackbench.c

Awas: AADL Information Flow and Error Propagation Analysis Framework

Hariharan Thiagarajan$^{(\boxtimes)}$, John Hatcliff$^{(\boxtimes)}$, and Robby$^{(\boxtimes)}$

Kansas State University, Manhattan, KS, USA
{thari,hatcliff,robby}@ksu.edu

Abstract. The continued maturation of industry standard architecture description languages is providing a foundation for more sophisticated analyses earlier in the system engineering process. The Architecture Analysis and Design Language (AADL) and its supporting annotation sub-languages provide the ability to model system hardware/-software components as well as information flows within the system. Such flows include conventional notions of data/control flows, security-oriented information flows, and fault/error propagation paths that are supported by the AADL Error Modeling Annex (EMv2)—all of which are central to engineering safety/security-critical systems.

In this paper, we describe Awas – an open-source framework for performing information reachability analysis on AADL models annotated with flow annotations at varying degrees of details. The framework provides highly scalable interactive visualizations of flows with dynamic querying capabilities. To ease the process, we provide a simple domain-specific language to pose various queries for checking safety and security properties. We demonstrate the effectiveness of our approach by applying it on a collection of industrial models of safety/security-critical systems from the medical and avionics domains.

1 Introduction

Critical systems have become more complex and interconnected in recent years. The growing emphasis on the composition of components and systems into bigger systems provides unique challenges in developing real-world solutions. One way to cope with the scale of such systems is to adopt distributed development. However, when multiple vendors are involved, it is imperative to communicate the dependencies and responsibilities. Safety and security aspects of the system often span multiple organizations and many sub-systems. It is essential to have a common understanding of various dependencies in the system.

A common approach to developing systems of systems is to use a model-based system engineering (MBSE) methodology. Developing a system model enables

This work is supported in part by the US Army, by the DARPA CASE program, and by Software Engineering Institute.

the capturing of the overall architecture and assign responsibilities among stakeholders. In distributed development with multiple stakeholders, integration failure is a common concern. Identification and rectification of integration failures are expensive due to encountering integration failures late in the system integration process, which is after the development of individual components. Using a standardized architecture description language like the Architecture and Analysis Definition Language (AADL) provides an opportunity to analyze the system before considerable monetary investments, share a common vocabulary, model elements, and tools to design and implement a system. MBSE can also include code generation – ensuring the generated code captures the abstract model's safety and security critical properties.

In a multi-vendor development context, various notions of dependence analysis are key to gaining system understanding and supporting safety and security audits and assurance cases. In hazard analysis, the knowledge of fault propagation through the system due to dependencies facilitates developing better hazard mitigation strategies. Analyzing security aspects of the system requires comprehending the flow of information through data and control channels. Additionally, over the life cycle of the system, upgrading and re-integrating components requires an understanding of the impact of the changes. Addressing these challenges is best supported by a general-purpose dependence analysis infrastructure – where dependencies can be captured in and derived from models which align with the structure of the system to be deployed. Using a dependence analysis infrastructure, developers and analysts can better understand relationships and interactions between components in large scale systems.

The developers of AADL recognize these challenges and provided with language constructs to capture the flow of information within a component, between components, and between a platform and its functional sub-system. Additionally, AADL annex EMv2 enables the capturing of error flows in the system. However, AADL lacks tooling to visualize the end-to-end flow of information, especially in a large system. In a model with multiple sub-systems, abilities to navigate up and down the system hierarchy is advantageous. In hazard analysis of the medical system, although AADL provides tools to compute the flow of error, overlaying the calculated error flows on the system model can better communicate the hazardous scenario to an analyst. Finally, AADL needs support for dynamic interaction with the model and its dependence information, including the ability to specify and replay queries capturing relevant "what if?" scenarios.

In this paper, we present Awas, a general-purpose framework for scalable dependence analysis of AADL models that integrates AADL flows and EMv2 error propagations. Specific contributions of this paper are:

- General AADL model representation with different forms of information flow
- Scalable reachability analysis libraries
- Interactive visualization of AADL models with the ability to focus on particular concerns of developers and analysts
- General dependence framework for security and hazard analyses

– Evaluation of the suitability and scalability of the framework against examples
  from avionics and medical domains

The Awas tool and example AADL models, along with the tutorial materials,
are available as open-source content at [16]. Additionally, Awas is being applied
on the DARPA CASE project to analyze system-wide information flow properties
and on a US Army project to support risk management of interoperable medical
systems.

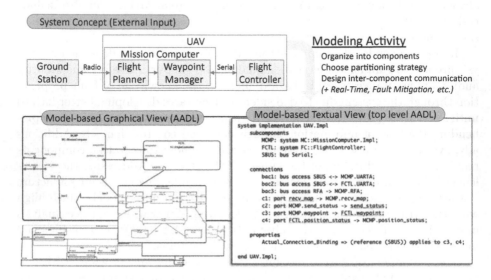

Fig. 1. A simple UAS example with AADL modeling artifacts

2   Background

In this section, we provide a brief overview of AADL, focusing on its various
forms of dependency and information flow relations. AADL concepts are illustrated using a simple Unmanned Aerial System (UAS).[1]

Figure 1 presents a high-level view of a fragment of the example system
(upper left) along with excerpts of AADL modeling artifacts. The system concept
consists of a UAV conducting surveillance. The UAV receives mission information (e.g., a map with collection targets) from the ground station and sends
status information to the ground station. The UAV includes a mission computer
and a flight controller. The mission computer computes waypoints from ground
station inputs. The flight controller acts upon these waypoints to advance the
surveillance task. The mission computer is inspired by US Air Force Research
Lab's Unmanned Systems Autonomy Services (OpenUxAS) [13].

---

[1] The simple UAS is adapted from an example used by the Collins Aerospace team
  on DARPA Cyber-Assured Systems Engineering (CASE) project – the authors are
  part of the Collins team on DARPA CASE.

```
1  system implementation UAS.Impl
2   subcomponents
3    GND: device GS::GroundStation;
4    UAV: system UAV::UAV.Impl;
5    RFB: bus RF;
6   connections
7    c1: port GND.send_map -> UAV.recv_map;
8    c2: port UAV.send_status -> GND.recv_status;
9    bac1: bus access RFB <-> GND.RFA;
10   bac2: bus access RFB <-> UAV.RFA;
11  properties
12   Actual_Connection_Binding => (reference
            (RFB)) applies to c1, c2;
13 end UAS.Impl;
```

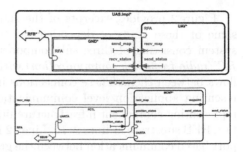

Fig. 2. Simple UAV system top level model – illustrating inter-component dependences

Fig. 3. Instance diagram of top level system and the UAV subsystem

AADL Overview: AADL is a SAE standardized architecture description language for modeling real-time embedded systems. AADL has both textual and graphical views as illustrated in Fig. 1. AADL modeling elements include software, middleware, and hardware and components along with various types of dependency relationships *between* them (inter-component dependencies) and *within* them (intra-component dependencies). Each modeling element can have a variety of AADL *properties* – modeling attributes that specify important characteristics of the element that may subsequently be leveraged for model analysis or code generation.

Inter-component Dependences: The most prominent inter-component relationships are *connections* which capture data and control flow between software components such as threads and processes (e.g., the flow of waypoint data between the mission computer and flight controller). Connections associate *ports* on sending and receiving components, and AADL includes different port categories to specify communication patterns between components (e.g., asynchronous message passing, synchronous shared memory). Relationships to/between middleware components can be captured using by specifying connections via *bus accesses* (intuitively, a feature on a software component indicating that it utilizes a communication substrate); for example, the mission computer and flight controller declare access to an AADL *bus* that models a serial bus communication medium. Finally, software elements such as threads/processes and connections can be allocated to middleware and hardware resources such as processors and buses using AADL *bindings*. These dependencies can have multiple layers. For example, a process can first be bound to a *virtual processor* used to model a partition in a hypervisor and then the hypervisor partitions can be bound to a *processor*. Similarly, a communication *connection* can be bound (transitively) through one or more *virtual buses* representing layers of abstraction and associated protocols in a protocol stack.

Figure 2 provides excerpts of the simple UAS AADL model that illustrate some of these kinds of dependencies. It captures the implementation of the system consisting of three sub-components of type *GroundStation*, *UAV*, and *RF (radio frequency communication)* with *connections* representing information flows between them. These connections include both: (a) port connections representing application level communication at lines 7–8, and (b) bus accesses representing component infrastructure utilization of the underlying communication RFB substrate at lines 9–10. Line 12 is an AADL *binding* specifying that the port based communication between the ground station and the UAV components is realized using the RFB bus at a lower level of abstraction.

The model information in Fig. 2 is part of what AADL terms a *declarative model* because it declares the architectural structure organized into a hierarchy using various AADL containment structures. In addition, the model may have multiple component implementation declarations for a given component type. Given a selection of particular component implementations, AADL tools will construct an *instance model* which instantiates the declarative model to a particular implementation configuration/instance while removing some of conceptual containment components to more directly associate connections between ports of components corresponding to actual hardware and software units. Figure 3 illustrates a portion of an instance model diagram for the system. Note that some of the dependence relations such as bindings, e.g., the realization of the connection *c1* and *c2* through the bus *RFB*, are not captured.

```
 1  system MissionComputer
 2    features
 3      recv_map: in event data port DataType.Impl;
 4      position_status: in event data port DataType.Impl;
 5      waypoint: out event data port DataType.Impl;
 6      send_status: out event data port DataType.Impl;
 7      UARTA: requires bus access UAV::Serial;
 8      RFA: requires bus access UAS::RF;
 9    flows
10      compute_waypoint: flow path recv_map -> waypoint;
11      compute_status: flow path position_status -> send_status;
12    annex EMV2 {**
13      use types UAS_Errors;
14      error propagations
15        recv_map : in propagation {wellformed_authenticated, wellformed_unauthenticated,
                  not_wellformed_authenticated, not_wellformed_unauthenticated};
16        waypoint : out propagation {wellformed_authenticated};
17      flows
18        wellformed_authenticated : error path recv_map{wellformed_authenticated} ->
                  waypoint{wellformed_authenticated};
19        unauthenticated_map : error sink recv_map{not_wellformed_unauthenticated,
                  wellformed_unauthenticated};
20        not_wellformed_map : error sink recv_map{not_wellformed_unauthenticated,
                  not_wellformed_authenticated};
21      end propagations; **};
22  end MissionComputer;
```

Fig. 4. AADL flow and error propagations annotations in mission computer

Intra-component Dependencies: AADL also provides multiple notions of intra-component dependences. The most basic of these are *flow specifications*, which model data and control flow relationships between a component's input and output ports. Figure 4 presents additional model details for the Mission Computer component. Line 10 uses a *flow* annotation to indicate that computing a waypoint will involve taking map information as input from the component's recv_map port and producing waypoints that will flow out of the waypoint port. Similarly, computing status information will take input from the position_status port and send information out of the send_status port. AADL does not define a precise semantics for flows, and it does not make an explicit distinction between data and control flow. Flow annotations may be given different interpretations by different analysis tools. For example, a latency analysis tool may consider a flow to model a single or collection of execution paths through the component source code, with an associated worse case execution time for the path. A security analysis tool may interpret the flow as a specification of information flow (e.g., a combination of data and control flow).

AADL includes other notions of flows that augment the basic flows above. For example, it provides an Error Modeling (EM) annex [15] to support multiple forms of model-based hazard analysis. In EM, *tokens* representing errors/faults and *error flow annotations* are added to model propagation of errors through a component. One can also use these annotations to model various types of security issues. For example, consider that the UAS system is designed to satisfy the following requirements.

1. Communications between Ground Station and UAV must be authenticated.
2. Commands from the Ground Station shall be checked for well-formedness before being used to compute coordinates for the Flight Controller.

These address two different integrity properties: a data authentication property and a data well-formedness property. While basic AADL flows capture flow channels from the Ground Station to the UAV flight controls, the requirements above reflect *properties of information* flowing along those channels. Specifically, somewhere along the channels the system needs trusted components to filter out malformed data and to authenticate data. To reason about both properties at once, one can use AADL error tokens to simulate/approximate a *cartesian abstract interpretation* that captures different combinations of well-formedness and authentication properties. We define the following four tokens EMv2 error tokens: *wellformed_authenticated, wellformed_unauthenticated, not_wellformed_authenticated,* and *not_wellformed_unauthenticated.*

In Fig. 4, lines 15–16 models that the mission computer component may receive any combination of error through its port *recv_map*. However, it may propagate only the *wellformed_authenticated* message to the flight controller – reflecting the fact that somewhere in the mission computer architecture security functions "filter out" malformed messages and unauthenticated messages. Line 18 shows the propagation of the token *wellformed_authenticated* received in the input port *recv_map* to the *waypoint* port (i.e., "good" information is allowed to flow through and form the basis of waypoints to the flight controller). On the other hand, the mission computer acts as a *sink* for (i.e., filters out) any token that indicates a "bad" message, (i.e., tokens *not_wellformed_unauthenticated*, *not_wellformed_authenticated* and *wellformed_unauthenticated*).

3   Awas Tool Architecture

Section 2 surveyed the diverse forms of inter- and intra-component dependence captured in AADL models, and Sect. 1 summarized the many uses of dependencies in developing and assuring safety and security critical systems. Awas provides (a) infrastructure that unifies AADL dependencies into a single graph-based framework, (b) algorithms for performing analysis and queries on dependence information, (c) APIs that allow other tools to access Awas algorithms and tailor them to specific concerns, and (d) interactive and scalable visualizations of dependence information and analysis results.

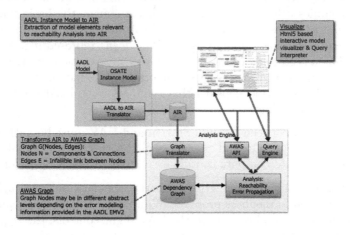

Fig. 5. AADL reachability analysis tool architecture

Figure 5 presents the Awas tool implementation architecture. Awas is a plug-in to the open-source Eclipse-based OSATE environment, the most popular AADL modeling tool. AADL instance models are translated through a JSON-based AADL Intermediate Representation (AIR), from which the Awas graph structures are extracted. Analysis and query algorithms work on the graph structures. The algorithms/queries can be directed and results obtained either through APIs or through the Awas visualization infrastructure.

For a given AADL instance model, Awas generates an HTML5-based interactive visualization. Awas algorithms, developed in Scala, are compiled to JavaScript and run directly in the browser – allowing queries and analyses to be executed independently of OSATE or other tool components requiring installation. Figure 6 shows an example visualization. Multiple panes can be opened to

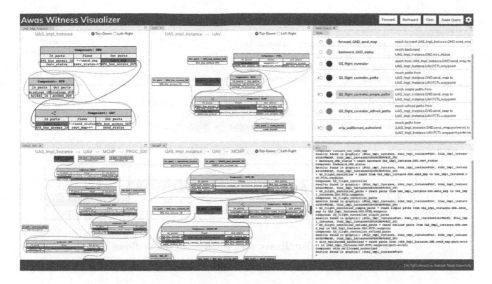

Fig. 6. Awas reachability visualizer and query interpreter

show dependencies and analysis results at different levels of the system architecture. The user can immediately launch and view various forms of forward and backward reachability analysis by selecting components, ports, and connections. Views can be configured by selected levels of detail (e.g., focusing on base connection dependencies, adding dependencies related to AADL bindings, adding AADL EM error flow information). In addition, AADL provides a query language (illustrated in the right pane of Fig. 6 that enables frequently used queries and queries corresponding to system requirements or auditing goals to be specified and easily replayed with a single click. The visualizer provides a dynamic read-eval-print-loop for the Awas query language (bottom right). Our industrial partners have found the HTML5-based Awas visualizers to be especially useful because they allow a system description to be easily distributed via the web or a zip file so that stakeholders can browse the architecture and its dependencies without having to install the complete OSATE infrastructure and associated AADL models.

4 Base Awas Dependence Graph and Visualization

The base Awas dependence visualization consists of components, each with a summary of its intra-component flows/dependencies, and AADL connections reflecting inter-component dependencies. Figure 7 illustrates how Awas captures intra-component information flows. The top of the figure illustrates the use of AADL's existing `flow` annotation in the AADL textual view to indicate that within the UAS mission computer software, information arriving at the `position_status` only flows to the `send_status` output port. The bottom of Fig. 7 shows this information in the Awas web-based visualizer.

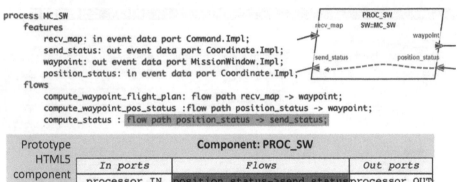

```
process MC_SW
   features
      recv_map: in event data port Command.Impl;
      send_status: out event data port Coordinate.Impl;
      waypoint: out event data port MissionWindow.Impl;
      position_status: in event data port Coordinate.Impl;
   flows
      compute_waypoint_flight_plan: flow path recv_map -> waypoint;
      compute_waypoint_pos_status :flow path position_status -> waypoint;
      compute_status : flow path position_status -> send_status;
```

Prototype	Component: PROC_SW		
HTML5	In ports	Flows	Out ports
component	processor_IN	position_status->send_status	processor_OUT
flow	position_status	recv_map->waypoint	send_status
visualizer	recv_map	position_status->waypoint	waypoint

Fig. 7. Awas visualization of intra-component flows

To capture inter-component dependencies and to support reachability analysis in various stages of modeling from an abstract model to a model with rich error behavior and nested components, Awas constructs a graph data structure similar to the Program Dependence Graph (PDG) [6], capable of capturing intra-/inter-component flows, and error flows. In the in-memory graph representation, both components and connections are represented as nodes. The edges connecting the nodes are considered infallible or passive similar to [19]. To interact with the visualization of underlying dependence graph, users simply click on a component or port and press a button to carry out basic queries such as "where in the system does information from this port/component flow?" (forward reachability in the dependence/constraint graph) or "what system elements are contributing information that flows into this port/component?" (backward reachability).

In the visualization of the UAS example in Fig. 8, the user clicks on the send_map port (in blue) of the Ground Station and presses the *Forward* button to invoke the dependence analysis and visualizer to display paths (in red) and associated ports and connections (in green) along which map information flows in the system. The visualization allows one to open multiple windows to show the results at different levels of the system hierarchy (in Fig. 8), the left window shows the top-level of the system, while the right two windows show the UAV and its mission computer subsystem). A simple scroll of a mouse wheel zooms into a particular system section or component of interest. Double-clicking on components drills down to their subcomponent models.

In AADL, a component can be refined by a sub-system where the information from a component's input port descend into the sub-system and accent back through the output port into the parent system. The intra-component flows defined in a component summarizes the information flow in the sub-system. In Awas, each system is expressed by a graph. In case of sub-system, the Awas graph includes the parent component's ports as nodes in the graph. Using these port-nodes a sub-system graph is connected to its parent component's graph.

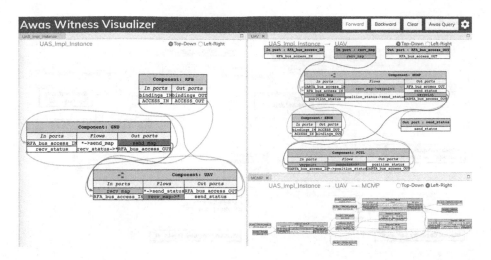

Fig. 8. Awas visualization of a forward slice (interactive forward dependence query) (Color figure online)

5 Property Propagation Graph and Visualization

Awas supports different forms of analyses that are layered on top of the base graphs and visualizations of Sect. 4. One such layering is the support for the AADL Error Modeling (EM) annex. In previous work, we illustrated how AADL EM and Awas could support safety analysis and risk management of medical devices [17]. In this section, we summarize how Awas can support visualizations of simple security analysis phrased in AADL EM.

Section 2 illustrated how AADL EM specifications could be used to capture authentication and message well-formedness properties related to the UAS example. Figure 9 shows an annotated screenshot of the Awas visualizer for the data security property analysis applied to this example. The figure illustrates flow properties of the system after adding flow controls that authenticate commands and filter out malformed Ground Station data. The top left quadrant shows the top level system architecture. The colored markups highlight the map port of the Ground Station and information flow channels into the UAV.

Figure 10 shows a simplified version of the system architecture for readability, overlaid with portions of Fig. 9 that capture key specifications and analysis results. The top left shows a magnification of the Ground Station visualization: the outgoing map port of Ground Station is annotated to indicate that a compromised Ground Station may send malformed map data or otherwise untrustworthy data or commands. Diving down into the UAS architecture in the top right of Fig. 9, the visualization shows map information flowing through UAV mission computer, with the bottom right showing the map information's path through mission computer components. The bottom left shows the details of the mission computer software architecture. To guard against the threats captured earlier in annotations for the Ground Station, the radio driver component was

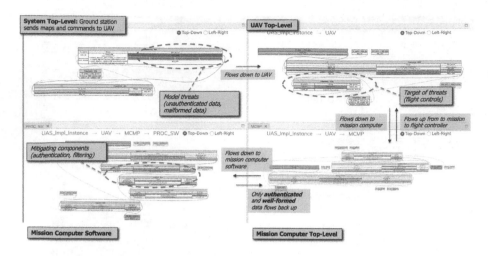

Fig. 9. Awas visualization of AADL EM-based security properties (Overview)

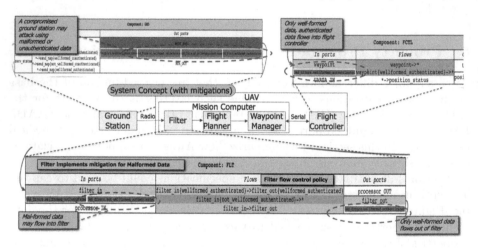

Fig. 10. Awas visualization of AADL EM-based security properties (Details) (Color figure online)

modified to authenticate the map and commands, and a filter component was added that drops map messages that are malformed.

Figure 10 zooms in on a summary of the filter flow policy, indicating that while "not well-formed data" flows into the filter, such data does not flow out of the filter (indicated by the ∗). In Fig. 9, the flow leaving the filter is visualized showing the path through the remainder of the software (where the map data is converted into waypoints) and mission computer (bottom right) all the way to the flight controls (top right). Figure 10 also shows a summary of the flows into the flight controller indicating that the desired properties are satisfied for the waypoint data – only waypoint data derived from authenticated and well-formed map data flows into the flight controls.

These examples illustrate a broader capability enabled by the synergistic interaction between AADL EM and Awas: a system can be analyzed for different safety and data security concerns that are relevant to a particular application (in the example, authentication and message formed-ness). These analyses do not need to consider details from scratch; instead they "piggyback" on the base flow channels and reason about whether or not desired properties exist at different points along those channels.

6   Awas Query Language

Previous sections focused on how users interacted with Awas by clicking and selecting various options within visualizations. This section provides a brief overview of the Awas query language, which can be used to codify commonly executed queries, architecture-oriented requirements, or audit objectives. Queries can be presented to Awas via loading a text file, entering text through the Awas visualizer REPL, or through the Awas APIs.

Forward Reachability: Awas forward reachability analysis answers the general question of "what are all the components (ports, connections) that depend on a component (port) of interest?". The query concept below from the Simple UAS is an example forward reachability.

Query Concept 1
If the ground station sends the map, where does information regarding the map flow? Also, where is it getting consumed?

This query concept can specified as an Awas query as follows:

```
forward_GND_send_map = reach forward UAS_Impl_Instance.GND.send_map
```

There are two parts on all Awas queries. The part of the query before the equals sign is the name of the query; that is, *forward_GND_send_map* is the query name. The part after the equal sign is the query expression. The query name stores the results of a query. Therefore, subsequent queries can be composed using the query name. The expression of a query is the part that gets evaluated against the model. The query expression starts with the keyword *reach* indicating that it is a reachability query. The following keyword *forward* dictates the direction of the reachability analysis. Finally, the canonical name of the port *send_map* serves as the criteria for the query.

Backward Reachability: Similar to the forward reachability described above, the user can compute the reachability against the flow of information using the backward analysis. Backward analysis can answer the question of "where does the information needed by a component of interest flow from?". Additionally, in case of a safety analysis, a backward analysis is useful in identifying the root causes of a hazard or failure. Backward reachability analysis is analogous to the backward program slicing [20].

Query Concept 2

From where does information needed to compute the recv_status flow from?

This query concept can be specified as an Awas query as follows:

```
backward_GND_status = reach backward UAS_Impl_Instance.GND.recv_status
```

Source and Target Reachability: Since forward and backward reachability computes a transitive closure, in a large system, the forward or backward analysis results may overwhelm the user. If the user concern is to check for the flow of information only up to a certain point in the system, then they can provide both source and the target in the query to obtain a more focused set of results. The counterpart of this operation in the implementation level is program chopping [7,14].

Query Concept 3

When the ground station is sending the map, how does it get to the flight controller?

This query concept is formalized as follows:

```
GS_flight_controller = reach from UAS_Impl_Instance.GND.send_map
                            to UAS_Impl_Instance.UAV.FCTL.waypoint
```

This query illustrates that the user can specify both the source and sink of the information flow using the keywords *from* and *to* . The result includes all the connections, components, and ports responsible for propagating information between *send_map* and *waypoint* ports.

Path Reachability: In the chopping analysis above, the result computed includes all the nodes that are contributing to the reachability of a target node from a source node. However, the result does not distinguish each sequence of nodes that traces a path from source to target. In some instances, it is useful to realize the results as paths. We compute the path similar to the *meet-over-all-path* solution in program analysis [8]. We split a path whenever there are more than one intra-component flows defined for a port and more than one edge leaving from a port. In case of absence of the intra-component flows we conservatively assume flows connecting every pair of input and output ports. This causes exponential number of paths and degrade the performance. However, the bigger question is, why would someone explore paths when the model is not mature enough to include intra-component flows? On the other hand, if the graph is strongly connected, there can be a large number of paths. In that case, we provide filtering mechanism based on the presence or absence of a node/port in the path using *all*, *some* and *none* keywords.

Query Concept 4

When the ground station is sending the map, is it always flowing through the filter?

This query concept is formalized as follows:

```
paths_FTL = reach refined paths from UAS_Impl_Instance.GND.send_map
                              to UAS_Impl_Instance.UAV.FCTL.waypoint
                  with none(UAS_Impl_Instance.UAV.MCMP.PROC_SW.FTL:port)
```

This query checks for the first requirement defined in Sect. 2. It identifies individual paths that can reach the port *waypoint* form port *send_map*, and among paths, it checks for the existence of a path without any of the ports form the filter (FTL) component. The keyword *refined* informs the query evaluator to ignore the paths using summary flows in the parent components. An empty result for the above query indicates that all the paths from *send_map* to *waypoint* passes through *FTL* component.

Error Reachability: Although the OSATE IDE provides several forms of hazard analysis to calculate the error propagation in an AADL model [2,10], it fails to *explain* and *visualize* the propagation of errors in the system. In our approach, we overlay the error propagation information on the Awas graph to provide evidence of an error affecting other components. To issue queries with error tokens, the Awas query language includes the ability to reference EM error tokens.

Awas computes the error propagation and transformation using a simplified version of Fault propagation and Transformation Calculus (FPTC) [19]. The reachability is first computed without the error information and then results are refined with error propagation.

Query Concept 5

Do only authorized and well-formed maps reach the flight controller?

This query concept poses the question whether issues such as *not_wellformed* or *unauthenticated* information originating from the ground station reach the flight controller. In essence, we are checking for the possibility of the situation where an adversary is capable of taking control over the UAV or the possibility of crashing the UAV due to corrupted data.

```
valid = reach paths from UAS_Impl_Instance.GND.send_map{
            UAS_Errors.wellformed_authenticated, UAS_Errors.not_wellformed_unauthenticated,
            UAS_Errors.not_wellformed_authenticated, UAS_Errors.wellformed_unauthenticated}
                to UAS_Impl_Instance.UAV.FCTL.waypoint{UAS_Errors.wellformed_authenticated}
```

The query specification captures that, even though the port *send_map* may propagate *wellformed_authenticated, wellformed_unauthenticated, not_wellformed_authenticated, not_wellformed_unauthenticated* only *wellformed_authenticated* reaches the port *way point*.

7 Evaluation

We evaluated Awas based on the reachability queries described in Sect. 6 applied to a collection of open source AADL models. Table 1 presents the performance data for various queries evaluated in both JVM and JavaScript platforms. On the JVM sections, we generated thirty queries using randomly picked criterion and evaluated each query thirty times to compute the average evaluation time for a model. For the JavaScript sections, we used the Google Chrome web browser as the execution platform and evaluated each query ten times to compute the average on a MacBook Pro with a 2.3 GHz Intel Core i7 process and 16 GB of memory.

Table 1. Experiment data

Models		Aircraft System	Display Manager	Flight Guidance System	Flight Guidance Two GPS	Isolette	Open PCA Pump	Communication	Router Speed Regulation	Simple UAV	AFRL UxAS	Wheel Break System
No. of Graphs		7	11	1	2	4	13	1	11	4	2	312
Max Depth of Nested Graph		4	3	1	2	3	5	1	2	4	2	8
No. of Components		32	40	5	11	14	49	6	35	18	38	455
No. of Connections		47	48	7	22	44	587	8	59	46	102	1666
No. of Ports		127	116	10	30	64	834	16	143	102	599	1834
No. of Nodes		104	140	14	37	79	1098	13	142	81	142	3473
No. of Edges		94	96	14	44	88	1176	16	152	110	206	3332
No. of Intra-component Flows		9	0	15	34	15	119	15	121	48	0	0
Average Time (ms)	Forward Node Reachability	JVM	<1	<1	<1	<1	1	102	<1	1	3	26	101
		JS	2	3	1	2	5	387	3	3	9	70	305
	Backward Node Reachability	JVM	<1	<1	<1	<1	2	173	<1	1	4	30	72
		JS	4	3	<1	2	6	410	1	3	11	78	199
	Source Node to Target Node	JVM	1	1	<1	1	4	326	1	2	8	68	164
		JS	5	5	2	4	10	1080	3	7	22	143	511
	Node Path Reachability	JVM	2	<1	<1	<1	2	-	<1	<1	7	33496	-
		JS	15	3	<1	<1	6	-	<1	10	35	-	-
	Forward Port	JVM	1	3	<1	2	14	653	<1	7	10	162	864
		JS	4	19	2	8	34	1974	2	14	21	311	2279
	Backward Port	JVM	<1	1	<1	<1	4	84	<1	<1	2	7	359
		JS	1	2	<1	2	9	165	<1	2	5	12	507
	Source Port to Target Port	JVM	3	5	1	3	21	876	<1	7	12	169	1343
		JS	4	18	4	10	42	2413	3	19	29	401	3006
	Port Path Reachability	JVM	4.8	7	1	5	18063	-	2	12	22	-	-
		JS	10	24	4	13	-	-	5	26	45	-	-

As can be observed from Table 1, Awas is capable of performing reachability analysis instantaneously even on large industry model such as the *Wheel break system* except for the path reachability. In the model *Speed regulation* path reachability computation is reasonably efficient due to the availability of intra-component flows. Elsewhere, in the *Isolette* model, due to the lack of intra-component flows, port path reachability is noticeably slower.

Our work demonstrates the feasibility of performing graph-based reachability analysis in a web browser, due to the recent improvement in the JavaScript execution engines [5].

It is difficult to empirically evaluate the useability and effectiveness of a tool like a Awas without a rigorous user study. For anecdotal evidence, we note that Awas handles a large subset of AADL and has been applied to industrial scale models including the Open PCA Pump models [3] – one of the largest and most complex publicly available AADL models (over 80 components, with 5–7 levels of architectural hierarchy. Once AADL flows annotations are added to a model, constructing an Awas visualization follows a very simple work flow: choose on option from an OSATE menu, specify a target folder, open the generated HTML index file in a browser. Our experience working with AADL on a number of projects is that even with small models it is easy to lose "situational awareness" (e.g., "what other things is this port connected to and what does it influence within the system?"). We have found Awas to be very useful to regain situational awareness and to support comprehension of model structure. The Awas web site [16] contains example models that can be immediately launched for browsing, and these example artifacts are supported by detailed walkthroughs and videos.

8 Conclusion and Future Work

AADL models capture many notions of dependence relevant for engineering safety and security systems, but up to this point the lack of tooling has been a barrier to effective leveraging of this information. With Awas, we have developed a framework that aggregates AADL's dependence information and provides analysis and visualization tools that enable engineers to better utilize that information for development and assurance of realistic systems.

AADL and Awas can contribute to more rigorous engineering practices that addresses challenges in developing certified software and systems [4]. For example, in recent work we have applied Awas to support hazard analysis and risk management activities required for certification of medical devices [3,17].

With our industrial partners, we are extending Awas to support other forms of analysis and projections of model and system information. This includes (a) supporting additional security analysis and threat modeling tasks that leverage model properties of components and connections added during security audits, (b) providing specifications and visualizations of flows between partitions in systems whose safety and security properties are established using a micro-kernel and separation kernel foundation [1,11], (c) visualization of coverage information (e.g., of ports, connections, and flow paths) from system tests and during live execution, (d) visualizations of counter-example paths resulting from model-checking activities and deductive verification techniques in AADL [9], and (e) integration of model-level information flows with source-code level information flows [12,18] and the ability to navigate freely between these.

References

1. Carpenter, T., Hatcliff, J., Vasserman, E.Y.: A reference separation architecture for mixed-criticality medical and IoT devices. In: Proceedings of the ACM Workshop on the Internet of Safe Things (SafeThings). ACM, November 2017
2. Delange, J., Feiler, P.: Architecture fault modeling with the AADL error-model annex. In: 2014 40th EUROMICRO Conference on Software Engineering and Advanced Applications, pp. 361–368. IEEE (2014)
3. Hatcliff, J., Larson, B., Carpenter, T., Jones, P., Zhang, Y., Jorgens, J.: The open PCA pump project: an exemplar open source medical device as a community resource. SIGBED Rev. **16**, 8–13 (2019)
4. Hatcliff, J., Wassyng, A., Kelly, T., Comar, C., Jones, P.L.: Certifiably safe software-dependent systems: challenges and directions. In: Proceedings of the on Future of Software Engineering (ICSE FOSE), pp. 182–200 (2014)
5. Herrera, D., Chen, H., Lavoie, E., Hendren, L.: Webassembly and javascript challenge: Numerical program performance using modern browser technologies and devices. Technical report, Technical report SABLE-TR-2018-2, Montréal, Québec, Canada (2018)

6. Horwitz, S., Reps, T., Binkley, D.: Interprocedural slicing using dependence graphs. ACM Trans. Program. Lang. Syst. (TOPLAS) **12**(1), 26–60 (1990)
7. Jackson, D., Rollins, E.J.: Chopping: a generalization of slicing. Carnegie-Mellon Univ Pittsburgh Pa Dept Of Computer Science, Technical report (1994)
8. Kildall, G.A.: A unified approach to global program optimization. In: Proceedings of the 1st Annual ACM SIGACT-SIGPLAN Symposium on Principles of Programming Languages, pp. 194–206. ACM (1973)
9. Larson, B.R., Chalin, P., Hatcliff, J.: BLESS: formal specification and verification of behaviors for embedded systems with software. In: Brat, G., Rungta, N., Venet, A. (eds.) NFM 2013. LNCS, vol. 7871, pp. 276–290. Springer, Heidelberg (2013). https://doi.org/10.1007/978-3-642-38088-4_19
10. Larson, B., Hatcliff, J., Fowler, K., Delange, J.: Illustrating the AADL error modeling annex (v. 2) using a simple safety-critical medical device. ACM SIGAda Ada Lett. **33**(3), 65–84 (2013)
11. Larson, B., Jones, P., Zhang, Y., Hatcliff, J.: Principles and benefits of explicitly designed medical device safety architecture. Biomed. Instrum. Technol. **51**(5), 380–389 (2017)
12. Ranganath, V.P., Hatcliff, J.: Slicing concurrent java programs using Indus and Kaveri. STTT **9**(5–6), 489–504 (2007). https://doi.org/10.1007/s10009-007-0043-0
13. Rasmussen, S., Kingston, D., Humphrey, L.R.: A brief introduction to unmanned systems autonomy services (UxAS). In: 2018 International Conference on Unmanned Aircraft Systems (ICUAS), pp. 257–268 (2018)
14. Reps, T., Horwitz, S., Sagiv, M.: Precise interprocedural dataflow analysis via graph reachability. In: Proceedings of the 22nd ACM SIGPLAN-SIGACT Symposium on Principles of Programming Languages, pp. 49–61. ACM (1995)
15. SAE AS-2C Architecture Description Language Subcommittee: SAE Architecture Analysis and Design Language (AADL) Annex Volume 3: Annex E: Error Model Language. Technical report, SAE Aerospace, June 2014
16. Thiagarajan, H., Hatcliff, J.: Awas user documentation. http://awas.sireum.org/. https://awas.sireum.org
17. Thiagarajan, H., Larson, B., Hatcliff, J., Zhang, Y.: Model-based risk analysis for an open-source PCA pump using AADL error modeling. In: Proceedings of the International Conference on Model-based Safety Analysis, September 2020
18. Thiagarajan, H., Hatcliff, J., Belt, J., Robby: Bakar Alir: supporting developers in construction of information flow contracts in SPARK. In: 2012 IEEE 12th International Working Conference on Source Code Analysis and Manipulation, pp. 132–137 (2012)
19. Wallace, M.: Modular architectural representation and analysis of fault propagation and transformation. Electron. Notes Theoret. Comput. Sci. **141**(3), 53–71 (2005)
20. Weiser, M.: Program slicing. In: Proceedings of the 5th International Conference on Software Engineering, pp. 439–449. IEEE Press (1981)

Formal Verification of Run-to-Completion Style Statecharts Using Event-B

Karla Morris[1]([✉]), Colin Snook[2], Thai Son Hoang[2], Geoffrey Hulette[1], Robert Armstrong[1], and Michael Butler[2]

[1] Sandia National Laboratories, Livermore, CA, USA
knmorri@sandia.gov
[2] ECS, University of Southampton, Southampton, UK

Abstract. Although popular in industry, state-chart notations with 'run to completion' semantics lack formal refinement and rigorous verification methods. State-chart models are typically used to design complex control systems that respond to environmental triggers with a sequential process. The model is usually constructed at a concrete level and verified and validated using animation techniques relying on human judgement. Event-B, on the other hand, is based on refinement from an initial abstraction and is designed to make formal verification by automatic theorem provers feasible. We introduce a notion of refinement into a 'run to completion' statechart modelling notation, and leverage Event-B's tool support for theorem proving. We describe the difficulties in translating 'run to completion' semantics into Event-B refinements and suggest a solution. We illustrate our approach and show how critical (e.g. safety) invariant properties can be verified by proof despite the reactive nature of the system. We also show how behavioural aspects of the system can be verified by testing the expected reactions using a temporal logic model checking approach.

Keywords: Run-to-completion · State-charts · Refinement

1 Introduction

Statecharts provide a graphical language, generalized from state machines, that is popular with engineers. Variants appear in Matlab Simulink/Stateflow [11] and the Ansys tools. Particularly attractive is providing accessibility to abstraction/refinement via Rodin/Event-B which has an intuitive metaphor in the Statechart semantics [12,13]. The hope is that engineers can better understand the origin of proof obligations in refinements and achieve formal guarantees earlier in their designs where it is most tractable. Our approach is focused on a mapping to Event-B where safety preservation is key. In our version of Statechart semantics, refinement means a subset of traces from an abstraction. This has the beneficial effect of preserving safety properties from abstraction to refinement and permits proofs to be discharged at the highest tractable level of abstraction where they are the easiest to discharge.

© Springer Nature Switzerland AG 2020
H. Muccini et al. (Eds.): ECSA 2020, CCIS 1269, pp. 311–325, 2020.
https://doi.org/10.1007/978-3-030-59155-7_24

Many incompatible definitions of refinement have been posed by others [4, 10] and that can lead to confusion. Though these separate refinements have different goals, all of which may be attractive to systems designers in different ways, they will not always preserve safety properties. From the Event-B vernacular it might be better to relabel these other approaches not as methods of model "refinement", but rather methods of model "elaboration". Preservation of safety across refinement requires only a few restrictions to the original [5] Statecharts (e.g. transitions cannot cross containment boundaries arbitrarily), but still allows for both parallel and hierarchical composition.

The work we will present here includes three refinement rules.

1. *Rule A:* Guard conditions on a transition can be strengthened; this can be done by adding textual guards to the transition, or changing the source of the transition to a nested state.
2. *Rule B:* Transitions can have additional actions, provided they do not modify variables appearing in the abstraction; this can be accomplished by adding textual action to the transition or by changing the target to nested state.
3. *Rule C:* A state-chart can be embedded within a state of another state-chart – sometimes called hierarchical composition or hierarchical refinement.

Via the translation explained in Sect. 5, these rules rely on the usual Event-B proof obligations to ensure that they do indeed yield refinements in the Event-B semantics. If an Event-B model B can be shown (via the construction rules of the Event-B language as well as the proof obligations) to refine another Event-B model A, then we know that every behavior of B is also a behavior of A. This definition yields a useful principle of preservation of safety – if we can show that a bad thing never happens in A, then we can add detail via refinements in B, knowing that the bad thing will continue to never happen in B. That is, Event-B refinements preserve safety properties in the sense of [9]. This makes refinement a useful technique in developing safety-critical systems: one can analyze a simpler abstract model for critical safety properties and then add detail to the model via refinements, secure in the knowledge that the safety properties will be preserved.

Although the autonomous drone example in this paper is based on the example described in [4], the definition of refinement used in that work is quite different from our own. This forces some differences in our refinement rules and consequently the way the example is developed. In [4] "refinement" is a transformation of the model which preserves reachability of a state with respect to sequences of inputs. However, this also allows the possibility of introducing new behaviors in the concrete model that the abstraction does not exhibit (more details are in Sect. 4). While this notion of refinement seems useful in certain contexts, unlike refinement in Event-B it does not guarantee preservation of safety properties. Therefore it should be considered less suited to development of safety-critical systems.

Section 2 provides background material. Section 3 discusses the Statechart concept of 'run to completion' and how it can be specified in Event-B. Section 4 introduces our example case study; a drone. Section 5 gives an outline of our translation from State-Chart XML (SCXML) to Event-B. Section 6 illustrates our approach to verifying safety invariant properties. Section 7 illustrates our approach to verifying control responses, and Sect. 8 concludes.

2 Background

2.1 SCXML

SCXML is a modelling language based on Harel state-charts with facilities for adding data elements that are modified by transition actions and used in conditions for their firing [16]. SCXML follows a 'run to completion' semantics, where trigger events[1] may be needed to enable transitions. Trigger events are queued when they are raised, and then one is de-queued and consumed by firing all the transitions that it enables, followed by any (un-triggered) transitions that then become enabled due to the change of state caused by the initial transition firing. This is repeated until no transitions are enabled, and then the next trigger is de-queued and consumed. There are two kinds of triggers: internal triggers are raised by transitions and external triggers are raised by the environment (non-deterministicly for the purpose of our analysis). An external trigger may only be consumed when the internal trigger queue has been emptied. We chose SCXML as our source language because it is relatively simple compared to some run to completion modelling languages yet has a well defined action language and simulation tool support.

2.2 Event-B

Event-B [1,6] is a formal method for system design. It uses *refinement* to introduce system details gradually into the formal model. An Event-B model contains two parts: *contexts* and *machines*. Contexts contain *carrier sets*, *constants*, and *axioms* constraining the carrier sets and constants. Machines contain *variables* v, *invariants* $I(v)$ constraining the variables, and *events*. An event consists of a guard denoting its enabled-condition and an action defining the value of variables after the event is executed. In general, an event e has the form: **any** t **where** $G(t, v)$ **then** $S(t, v)$ **end** where t are the event parameters, $G(t, v)$ is the guard of the event, and $S(t, v)$ is the action of the event.

Machines can be refined by adding more details. Refinement can be done by extending the machine to include additional variables (*superposition refinement*) representing new features of the system, or by replacing some (abstract) variables by new (concrete) variables (*data refinement*). Refinement in Event-B is reasoned on an event basis. A (concrete) event f refines an (abstract) event e if whenever f is enabled then e is also enabled (guard strengthening), and the action of f is the same or equivalent to e (where equivalence is given by some relationship defined in the invariants). New events are said to refine 'skip' (an implicit abstract event that did nothing), and therefore do not alter abstract variables. More information

---

[1] In SCXML the triggers are called 'events', however, we refer to them as 'triggers' to avoid confusion with Event-B.

about Event-B refinement can be found in [1]. Event-B is supported by the Rodin Platform (Rodin[2]) [2].

2.3   UML-B State-Machines

UML-B [14] provides a diagrammatic modelling notation for Event-B in the form of state-machines and class diagrams. The diagrammatic models relate to an Event-B machine and generate or contribute to parts of it. For example a state-machine will automatically generate the Event-B data elements (sets, constants, axioms, variables, and invariants) to implement the states. Transitions contribute further guards and actions representing their state change, to the events that they elaborate. State-machines are typically refined by adding nested state-machines to states. Each state is encoded as a boolean variable and the current state is indicated by one of the boolean variables being set to TRUE. An invariant ensures that only one state is set to TRUE at a time. Events change the values of state variables to move the TRUE value according to the transitions in the state-machine. While the UML-B translation deals with the basic data formalisation of state-machines it differs significantly from the semantics discussed in this manuscript. UML-B adopts Event-B's simple guarded action semantics and does not have a concept of triggers and run-to-completion. Here we make use of UML-B's state-machine translation but provide a completely different semantic by generating a behaviour into the underlying Event-B events that are linked to the generated UML-B transitions.

3   Run to Completion

The run to completion semantics is specified via an abstract basis that is extended by the model [12,13]. Figure 1 shows a state-chart representation of how the basis enforces the run to completion semantics on the model transitions.

The specification of this basis consists of an Event-B *context* and *machine* that are the same for all input models and are refined by the specific output of the translation. The basis context introduces a set of all possible triggers, SCXML_TRIGGER which is partitioned into internal and external triggers (e.g. FutureInternalTrigger and FutureExternalTrigger respectively), some of which will be introduced in future refinements. Each refinement partitions these trigger sets further to introduce concrete triggers, leaving a new abstract set to represent the remaining triggers yet to be introduced. For clarity, we use sets to abstractly represent the trigger queues. This does not affect safety verification but forces us to introduce fairness assumptions regarding trigger consumption in order to verify liveness properties. It would be relatively straight forward to properly model the trigger queues which are an implementation of this fairness property.

---

[2] An extensible toolkit which includes facilities for modelling, verifying the consistency of models using theorem proving and model checking techniques, and validating models with simulation-based approaches.

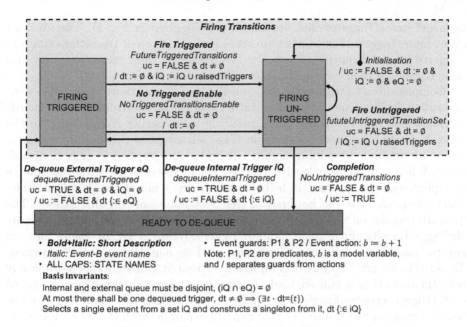

Fig. 1. Abstract representation of run to completion basis

Each of the transitions in the basis (see Fig. 1) represents an abstract event of the basis machine that describes the generic behaviour of models under a run to completion semantics. These events provide an abstraction that defines the altering of trigger queues and completion flag. Event-B refinement rules prohibit new events from modifying abstract variables (i.e. new events refine 'skip'). Hence, since SCXML transitions need to modify the trigger queues etc., used to capture the SCXML run to completion semantics, all events generated by translation of the specific SCXML model, must refine abstract events introduced for this purpose in the basis. The basis machine also declares variables that correspond to the currently dequeued trigger, dt, the queue of internal triggers raised by actions within the model, iQ, the queue of external triggers raised by the environment, eQ, and a flag, uc, that signals when a run to completion macro-step has been completed (no un-triggered transitions are enabled). Note that, for convenience, the currently dequeued trigger is modelled as a singleton set which may be empty (i.e. consumed) or contain the single trigger to be consumed.

The trigger queues and dequeued trigger are initialised to empty and uc is set to FALSE so that un-triggered transitions are dealt with via the futureUntriggeredTransitionSet event. This will subsequently enable completion and reset the uc flag to TRUE. The abstract event futureRaiseExternalTrigger represents the raising of an external trigger (not shown in the diagram). After completion, a queued trigger can be prepared for consumption by moving it to the dequeued trigger, dt. Internal triggers have a higher priority, since the external trigger queue is only dequeued if the iQ is empty (see dequeueExternalTriggered and dequeueInternalTriggered in Fig. 1). The abstract event futureTriggeredTransitions represents a combination of transitions that are triggered by the dequeued trigger, dt. The actions of these transitions may also raise triggers of their own in the internal trigger queue iQ.

Completion of triggered and untriggered transitions may be non-deterministically premature to allow future refinements to strengthen the guards of transitions (i.e. to disable them resulting in an earlier completion). In the process of refining a model, a designer takes advantage of this non-determinism in the abstraction by adding nested sub-states and explicit guards to transitions. When a refinement level is reached where the designer wants to enforce a requirement (i.e. prevent it being bypassed by a non-deterministic completion), the model needs to be *finalised* (see Sect. 5 for more on finalisation). The SCXML translation tool will then automatically strengthen the guards of events NoTriggerTransitionEnable and futureUntriggeredTransitionSet, to ensure that the run to completion sequence is not interrupted by non-deterministic behaviour. To do this we need to guard completion so that it cannot happen while any relevant transition is still enabled. To finalise a triggered transition, the guard of NoTriggerTransitionEnable is strengthened by adding the conjunction of the negated guards of all transitions that can fire in parallel with the transition being finalised. Similarly the guard of futureUntriggeredTransitionSet is strengthened by adding the conjunction of the negated guards of all untriggered transitions that can fire in parallel. It may seem that finalisation could cause an unmanageable explosion of guards. However, to fire in parallel, transitions must be contained in parallel regions and also be enabled by the same trigger (or be un-triggered). In practice, since most systems do not contain many parallel regions, the number of transitions that can fire in parallel is limited. Transition finalisation can be left until it is needed for the proof of a particular property and does not generate any new proof obligations since adding guards is a trivial refinement step. Finalisation is also needed in order to remove non-deterministic behaviours when the model is animated for validation purposes.

4   Description of the Sample Application

To illustrate the development and analysis process of a design using the previously described state-chart semantics, we will discuss a quadrotor helicopter or quadrotor application similar to the one presented by Syriani et al. [4]. The application will focus on the incremental design of some of the drone's required functionality. The constructed model must obey state-chart refinement rules listed in Sect. 1, these rules are proven within the Rodin tool. The structure of the state-chart for this model at each subsequent abstraction level restricts further the development of the model to refinements that obey the rules. This will allow us to prove properties of the model in a very strategic fashion, as properties proven of early abstraction levels are preserved in later refinements.

The first abstraction of the model shown in Fig. 2 captures the basic functionality of the drone. The model's initial state is OFF and as a result of the on and toTakeoff external triggers it transitions to the START and OPERATIONAL states respectively[3]. The drone reacts to the off external trigger by shutting down and subsequently transitioning to the OFF state. Within the OPERATIONAL state the drone will transition to FLY, DESCEND or LANDED state after the internal trigger toFly, toLand or landed is raised, respectively. In this abstraction, these internal triggers are raised non-deterministically in the system by functionality not currently defined. As additional details are incorporated into the model in later refinements some of that non-determinism is removed and replaced by transitions with actions that raised the previously defined internal triggers. It should be noted that this abstraction of the drone model includes a transition from TAKEOFF to DESCEND (dashed transition in Fig. 2). This allows for the drone to respond to a toLand trigger if it encounters some problems while in the TAKEOFF state. Syriani et al. [4] introduces this transition in later refinements under Rule 8 *path refinement rule*. This rule is inconsistent with our rules of refinement as it results in a concrete event with no corresponding behavior in the abstraction.

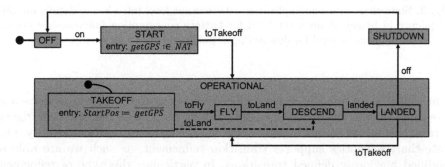

Fig. 2. State-chart of drone application. Abstract level including only generic behavior.

Figure 3 shows three subsequent refinements to the drone model. The first refinement of the model is shown in beige, as we refine the parent state TAKEOFF by applying *Rule B and C*. Under these rules we introduce child states and new model variables, similar to Rule 2 *basic-to-or state rule* defined by Syriani et al. [4] As part of this refinement we introduced an untriggered transition responsible for raising the toFly internal trigger, and therefore removed some of the non-determinisms in the abstraction.

The second refinement, the details of which are shown in green in Fig. 3, extends the capabilities within OPERATIONAL by using *Rule C* to make it a parallel state that controls flying and battery related functionality. This is the same as Rule 4 *and-state rule* defined by Syriani et al. [4]. The charge within the drone battery is control by the parallel BATTERYOP state. The functionality

---

[3] Transitions in Figs. 2–3 are labeled with trigger names (e.g. toTakeoff, toFly) not with event names as it is in UML-B.

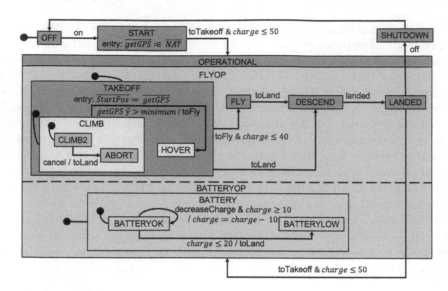

Fig. 3. State-chart of drone application. Refinement level introducing details for take off (shown in beige). Refinement level for battery consumption functionality (shown in green). Refinement level for descending capabilities, in case of emergency (shown in lilac).

is modeled by introducing a new model variable, charge, which is decreased as a response to the internal trigger decreaseCharge. The aforementioned trigger, is raised non-deterministically by some unspecified internal functionality. Our state-chart semantics supports transition refinement, as such we are able to modified previously defined transitions. In particular, this type of refinement allow us to add guards and/or actions to previously defined transitions. The strengthening of guards, *Rule A*, or additional actions, *Rule B*, are expressed in term of new model variables that contribute implementation details to the model. To ensure the drone operates with enough battery power we strengthen the guards of transitions to the FLY and TAKEOFF states. As part of this design stage we introduce a requirement to constrain drone operation to a battery charge of at least 20% capacity. This can be expressed as

$$(\text{BATTERYOK} = \text{TRUE}) \Rightarrow \text{charge} > 20\% \ .$$

Figure 3 shows the third refinement of the drone model, with features added in lilac. At this stage we use *Rule C* to introduce additional implementation details to ensure that under special circumstances (e.g. sensing of adverse environment or unexpected battery dropped) the drone is able to circumvent flying and proceed to an emergency landing. The previously described requirement can be expressed as

$$(\text{TAKEOFF} = \text{TRUE}) \Rightarrow (\text{BATTERYOK} = \text{TRUE} \lor \text{toLand}) \ .$$

To implement this new capability in the design the internal trigger cancel is introduced. The internal trigger cancel can be raised non-deterministically by some sensing capability, the details of which are not currently implemented. If the trigger is raised, the climbing process must be aborted and the drone descending sequence shall start. This refinement level is done differently from Syriani et al. [4], which follows Rule 7 *state extension rule*. The aforementioned rule requires a data remapping of the abstract states TAKEOFF, CLIMB and HOVER, which should be distinct from the states in this refinement, as the state ABORT is introduced. In contrast, we implement this refinement using a rule similar to Syriani et al.'s Rule 2 *basic-to-or state rule*, which introduces the concrete states CLIMB2 and ABORT to the abstract state CLIMB.

5   SCXML Translation to Event-B

The translation of a specific SCXML model to UML-B and Event-B, comprises the following stages:

- Firstly, a basis machine and context are created to embody the semantics of the SCXML language (Sect. 3). The basis provides variables and events to model the queue of triggers as well as abstract versions of events to model transitions firing. The basis is independent of the particular SCXML model which is added in subsequent refinements.
- Secondly, all possible combinations of each set of transitions that can fire together are calculated and corresponding events are generated, at appropriate refinement levels, that refine the abstract basis events. The transitions that can fire together are those that are triggered by the same trigger (or are both untriggered) and are in different parallel ('and') sub-states. If these transitions raise internal triggers, a guard, (e.g. $\{i1, i2, ...\} \subseteq$ raisedTrigger, where $i1, i2, ...$ have been added to the internal triggers set), is introduced to define the raised triggers parameter. The subset allows more triggers to be raised in later refinements. For triggered transitions, the trigger is specified by a guard that defines the value of the trigger parameter.
- Thirdly, the SCXML state-chart is translated into a corresponding UML-B state-machine whose transitions elaborate (i.e. add state change details to) the transition combination events that the transition may be involved in. A transition may fire in parallel with transitions of parallel nested state-machines that have the same (possibly null) trigger.
- Finally the UML-B state-machine is translated into Event-B by programmatically invoking the UML-B translator.

A tool to automatically translate SCXML source models into UML-B has been produced. The tool is based on the Eclipse Modelling Frameworkand uses an SCXML meta-model provided by Sirius [3] which has good support for extensibility. The UML-B state-machine is subsequently translated into Event-B using the standard UML-B translation which provides variables to model the current state and guards and actions to model the state changes that transitions perform. Further details of the translation are given in [12,13].

6 Verification of Safety Properties

In a state-chart model we naturally wish to verify properties P that are expected to hold true in a particular state S. Hence, all of the safety properties that we consider are of the form: S=TRUE ⇒ P , where the antecedent is implicit from the containment of P within S. There are two kinds of properties that we might want to verify in an SCXML state-chart; 1) properties concerning the values of auxiliary data maintained by the system and 2) constraints about the state of another parallel state-chart region. SCXML models represent components that react to received triggers and cannot be perfectly synchronised with changes to the monitored properties. Hence, P may be temporarily violated until the system reacts by leaving the state S in which the property is expected to hold. To cater for this we express P in a modified form P' that allows time for the reaction to take place. There are two forms of reaction that can be used to exit S; a) an untriggered transition, or b) a transition that is triggered by an internally raised trigger. For a), the modified property P' becomes P ∨ *untriggered transitions are not complete*, and for b) P' becomes P ∨ *trigger t is in the internal queue or dequeued* (where t is the internal trigger raised when the violation of P is detected). Hence P is checked only in stable states that are reachable according to the run-to-completion semantics.

In this section we illustrate a typical example of the type of properties that we imagine could be verified in a reactive SCXML system. All of the proof obligations are automatically discharged for our example. Since our models are strictly structured and proof obligations will always have this common form, we are optimistic that proofs will always discharge automatically. We model the safety property features at an early level of refinement where the models are relatively simple, so that the validity of verification conditions is clear. Detail is then added in later refinements which are proven (automatically) to preserve the previously verified safety properties. In our example, some auxiliary data is monitored by one state-chart region and while a parallel region refers to the state of the monitoring region. Hence the reaction consists of an un-triggered transition in the monitoring region which sends an internal trigger to the other region when it leaves the desired monitor state.

For our drone model, the safety property that we wish to verify is that the control system does not continue to take off or fly if the battery charge drops below a certain threshold (say 21%). By refinement level 1 we have developed the drone's state to the point where we distinguish the TAKEOFF and FLY states (Fig. 2). In refinement level 2 we therefore introduce the battery charge monitoring function along with the associated safety properties. A parallel state-chart region, with sub-states BATTERYOK and BATTERYLOW, is added to the state OPERATIONAL (Fig. 3). The BATTERYOK sub-state is used in the safety invariant of the TAKEOFF and FLY states. Thus we split the verification into two parts: a *type b* proof to show that the system reacts to the battery charge decreasing below 21% (an external event) by leaving the BATTERYOK sub-state, and a *type a* proof to show that when the system leaves the BATTERYOK state it subsequently (within the run to completion) leaves the FLY or TAKEOFF states. Both parts are described in more detail as follows.

System Reacts to the Low Battery Charge. An external trigger indicates that the battery charge has dropped by 10% and this is used by a self transition to decrement the controllers data value for charge. The BATTERYOK state is supposed to indicate that the battery charge is ok (>20%) and to ensure that it does, we add a state invariant to this effect (charge>20). When charge decreases to 20 (or less), an untriggered transition immediately reacts by switching to the BATTERYLOW state. To ensure that this reaction is not bypassed by the non-determinism that we incorporated to allow for future refinement, we flag it as finalised at refinement level 2. Finalisation means that we cannot strengthen its guards in future refinements as is normally permitted, since its reaction is needed to ensure the invariant is preserved. If the user forgoes the finalization, the property would not be verifiable at that refinement level and it will need to be verified in later refinements. After translation to Event-B via UML-B the invariant in state BATTERYOK is

$$(\text{BATTERYOK} = \text{TRUE}) \Rightarrow (\text{uc} = \text{FALSE} \vee \text{charge} > 20) \ .$$

The only events that can break this invariant are ones that make the antecedent become true or the consequent become false and we deal with these as follows: The transitions that enter state OPERATIONAL and initialise the BATTERY region by entering BATTERYOK (hence making the antecedent become true) contain the guard that charge>50 (since we do not allow the drone to take off unless the battery is well charged) and hence the invariant is satisfied. The self transition that decreases charge (and hence could potentially falsify the consequent) is guarded by uc = FALSE since it is a triggered transition, and hence the disjunction in the consequent ensures it remains true. The completion event NoUntriggeredTransitions of the basis machine resets uc = TRUE to indicate completion of the cycle and hence could potentially break the invariant. However, finalising the transition BATTERYOK_BATTERYLOW (that leaves BATTERYOK when charge>20 becomes false) means that the negation of its guard is added to the completion event by the translation. Since this transition fires when BATTERYOK = TRUE (i.e. its source state) and charge$\leq$20 the completion event is guarded by $\neg(\text{BATTERYOK} = \text{TRUE} \wedge \text{charge} \leq 20)$ which means that it does not fire when it could break the invariant (i.e. forcing the untriggered reaction to fire first).

System Subsequently Leaves the FLY or TAKEOFF States. The safety property of the TAKEOFF and FLY states can now be simply stated as BATTERYOK = TRUE. However, since this relies on a particular internal trigger (toLand) to make the appropriate reaction, we also need to specify that trigger as an attribute of the invariant in the SCXML model. After translation to Event-B via UML-B the invariant in state TAKEOFF becomes

$$(\text{TAKEOFF} = \text{TRUE}) \Rightarrow (\text{toLand} \in \text{iQ} \vee \text{toLand} \in \text{dt} \vee \text{BATTERYOK} = \text{TRUE}).$$

The invariant for the FLY state is similar with a corresponding antecedent. The transitions that enter TAKEOFF (which make the antecedent true) simultaneously enter BATTERYOK ensure the consequent is true. The only transition that enters FLY (which makes the antecedent of the FLY invariant true) comes from the TAKEOFF state and hence the consequent is already true. The transition that leaves BATTERYOK (making the last disjunct of the consequent false) raises the toLand trigger making the first disjunct true. Some transitions leave the superstates of BATTERYOK but these either simultaneously leave OPERATIONAL (the superstate of TAKEOFF and FLY), or re-enter BATTERYOK. The basis contains an event to dequeue the internal triggers which preserves the overall consequent because establishes the second conjunct as it falsifies the first (i.e. it removes toLand from the iQ but simultaneously adds it to dt). The only events that falsify the second conjunct are the transitions triggered by toLand which leave the TAKEOFF or FLY states making the antecedent false.

Hence, invariant properties that follow these suggested patterns are always automatically proven due to simple logic about the changes in state.

7   Verification of Control Responses

A model that has been proven to satisfy some invariant (e.g. safety) properties, may still not behave in a useful way. Therefore, as well as verifying invariant properties, we would like to verify the system's responsiveness. That is, we want to ensure that the controller responds to external triggers to make appropriate modifications to the system variables. These kind of live responses are difficult to prove via invariant preservation since they are temporal properties. While Event-B refinements have also been shown to preserve some liveness properties under certain conditions [7], there are not yet efficient supporting tools for the technique. Instead, we can express the property in Linear Temporal Logicand use the ProB[4] model checker to verify it.

In general, our liveness properties will have the following form:

$$G([\text{external\_trigger\_event}] \Rightarrow F\{\text{predicate}\}) ,$$

where the predicate concerns variables v that the system maintains, and may refer to old values old(v) that existed when the external trigger occurred. To specify a liveness property to be verified, a special Linear Temporal Logicelement is added to the SCXML model with attributes, property (a string of the above form) and refinement (an integer indicating the refinement level at which the property should be verified). The translator generates a separate 'branch' refinement for each Linear Temporal Logicproperty to be verified. In this special refinement, history variables are added to record the value at the state when the external trigger occurs, of any variables that are referenced as 'old' values. A text file is automatically generated containing the Linear Temporal Logicproperty to be checked. In this generated version, an assumption of strong fairness

---

[4] ProB is an animator, constraint solver and model checker for the B-Method. https://www3.hhu.de/stups/prob.

is added for all other events in the model. Without this assumption, the system may never achieve the expected response to a trigger. Therefore it corresponds to a requirement that the system can always make satisfactory progress and not become live locked. For simplicity we omit this assumption from the remaining examples.

$$\mathsf{SF}[\mathsf{e1}] \wedge \mathsf{SF}[\mathsf{e2}]\ldots \Rightarrow \mathsf{G}([\mathsf{external\_trigger\_event}] \Rightarrow \mathsf{F}[\mathsf{predicate}])$$

This property can be added into the ProB model checker LTL formula text field.

We illustrate the method with an example of a temporal property that we expect to hold in the drone SCXML system. The liveness property that we wish to verify is that, after an external trigger event decreaseCharge, the battery charge value should decrease in value.

$$\mathsf{G}\,([\mathsf{ExternalTriggerEvent\_decreaseCharge}] \Rightarrow \mathsf{F}\,\{\mathsf{charge} < \mathsf{old}(\mathsf{charge})\})\;.$$

However, we could not verify this property. The counter example traces that ProB provided gave us a better understanding of the reasons why. The property as stated is too strong (i.e. not true) for our model; there are additional conditions that need to be considered and added as part of the antecedent.

- Our model represented the trigger queues abstractly as sets which meant that the decreaseCharge trigger may never be dequeued. The standalone version of ProB allows strong fairness to be specified for particular parameter values but this does not work in the Rodin plug-in for ProB. In any case, a more accurate (concrete) representation of the queue fixes the problem and improves our model.
- The charge is not always decreased in response to the decreaseCharge trigger. The controller only monitors battery charge while in the BATTERYOK state and discards the trigger in other states. Also, the controller stops decreasing charge when it approaches 0. To cater for this we added a pre-condition BATTERYOK = TRUE $\wedge$ charge $\geq$10 to the LTL property.
- Even if this pre-condition is true when the trigger is raised, another trigger (e.g. off) may already be in the queue and take the controller out of BATTERYOK before the decreaseCharge trigger is dequeued. Again we strengthen the pre-condition off $\notin$ dt $\cup$ eQ of the Linear Temporal Logicexpression to avoid this situation.

After making these changes the final form of the Linear Temporal Logicproperty, which ProB was able to exhaustively check and confirm was as follows:

$$\mathsf{G}([\mathsf{ExternalTriggerEvent\_decreaseCharge}] \wedge \{\mathsf{BATTERYOK}{=}\mathsf{TRUE} \wedge \mathsf{charge}{\geq}10 \wedge$$
$$\mathsf{off}{\notin}\mathsf{SCXML\_dt}{\cup}\mathsf{SCXML\_eq}\} \Rightarrow \mathsf{F}\,\{\mathsf{charge} < \mathsf{old}(\mathsf{charge})\})\;.$$

8   Conclusion

Reactive Statecharts are useful and widely used by engineers for modelling the design of control systems. Event-B provides an effective language for formally verifying properties via incremental refinements. However, it is not straightforward to apply the latter to the former. We have demonstrated a technique for introducing refinement of reactive Statecharts that can be translated to Event-B for verification. Invariant properties about the expected coordination of states can be added and are interpreted with additional allowance for the reactions to take place. That is, they hold only after the reaction has taken place. Such invariants prove automatically with the existing Rodin theorem provers. We also demonstrate a complementary process for verifying expected reactions to environmental triggers that uses the Linear Temporal Logicmodel checker. Another kind of liveness property that would be useful to verify is that the 'run' converges to completion. I.e. transition loops and raised internal triggers do not introduce endless live-lock, but eventually terminate to allow the next external trigger to be consumed. This could also be verified using the Linear Temporal Logicmodel checker, however, in future work we will adopt the techniques suggested in [8] to verify liveness properties using the theorem provers.

These verifications do not validate that the model behaviour is useful. For this, the SCXML model should be animated so that its behaviour can be observed by a domain expert. Elsewhere [15] we have developed a 'Scenario Checker' tool and methods for animating pre-defined domain specific scenarios at various levels of abstract. In future work we will demonstrate the use of this tool for automatically executing the run to completion. In future work, we also intend to formalise the semantics of our extended SCXML notation in order to define its notion of refinement and correspondence to Event-B.

All data supporting this study are openly available from the University of Southampton repository at https://doi.org/10.5258/SOTON/D1475

Acknowledgements. Sandia National Laboratories is a multimission laboratory managed and operated by National Technology & Engineering Solutions of Sandia, LLC, a wholly owned subsidiary of Honeywell International Inc., for the U.S. Department of Energy's National Nuclear Security Administration under contract DE-NA0003525.

References

1. Abrial, J.R.: Modeling in Event-B: System and Software Engineering. Cambridge University Press, Cambridge (2010)
2. Abrial, J.R., Butler, M., Hallerstede, S., Hoang, T., Mehta, F., Voisin, L.: Rodin: an open toolset for modelling and reasoning in Event-B. Softw. Tools Technol. Transf. **12**(6), 447–466 (2010)
3. Eclipse Foundation: Sirius project website, March 2016. https://eclipse.org/sirius/overview.html
4. Syriani, E., Sousa, V., Lúcio, L.: Structure and behavior preserving statecharts refinements. Sci. Comput. Program. **170**(15), 45–79 (2019). https://doi.org/10.1016/j.scico.2018.10.005
5. Harel, D.: Statecharts: a visual formalism for complex systems. Sci. Comput. Program. **8**(3), 231–274 (1987). https://doi.org/10.1016/0167-6423(87)90035-9

6. Hoang, T.S.: An introduction to the Event-B modelling method. In: Industrial Deployment of System Engineering Methods, pp. 211–236. Springer (2013)
7. Hoang, T.S., Schneider, S., Treharne, H., Williams, D.M.: Foundations for using linear temporal logic in Event-B refinement. Form. Asp. Comput. **28**(6), 909–935 (2016). https://doi.org/10.1007/s00165-016-0376-0
8. Hudon, S., Hoang, T.S., Ostroff, J.S.: The Unit-B method — refinement guided by progress concerns. Softw. Syst. Model. **15**(4), 1091–1116 (2016). https://doi.org/10.1007/s10270-015-0456-2
9. Lamport, L.: Proving the correctness of multiprocess programs. IEEE Trans. Softw. Eng. **SE–3**(2), 125–143 (1977)
10. Maraninchi, F.: The Argos language: graphical representation of automata and description of reactive systems. In: In IEEE Workshop on Visual Languages (1991)
11. MATLAB: 9.7.0.1190202 (R2019b). The MathWorks Inc., Natick, Massachusetts
12. Morris, K., Snook, C., Hoang, T.S., Armstrong, R., Butler, M.: Refinement of statecharts with run-to-completion semantics. In: Artho, C., Ölveczky, P.C. (eds.) FTSCS 2018. CCIS, vol. 1008, pp. 121–138. Springer, Cham (2019). https://doi.org/10.1007/978-3-030-12988-0_8
13. Morris, K., Snook, C., Hoang, T.S., Hulette, G., Armstrong, R., Butler, M.: Refinement and verification of responsive control systems. In: Raschke, A., Méry, D., Houdek, F. (eds.) ABZ 2020. LNCS, vol. 12071, pp. 272–277. Springer, Cham (2020). https://doi.org/10.1007/978-3-030-48077-6_23
14. Snook, C., Butler, M.: UML-B: formal modeling and design aided by UML. ACM Trans. Softw. Eng. Methodol. **15**(1), 92–122 (2006). https://doi.org/10.1145/1125808.1125811
15. Snook, C., Hoang, T.S., Dghaym, D., Fathabadi, A.S., Butler, M.: Domain-specific scenarios for refinement-based methods. J. Syst. Arch. (2020). (to be published in)
16. W3C: State chart XML SCXML: State machine notation for control abstraction, September 2015. http://www.w3.org/TR/scxml/

A Simulator Coupling Architecture
for the Creation of Digital Twins

Thomas Kuhn[✉], Pablo Oliveira Antonino, and Adam Bachorek

Fraunhofer Institute IESE, Fraunhofer-Platz 1, 67663 Kaiserslautern, Germany
{thomas.kuhn,pablo.antonino,adam.bachorek}@iese.fraunhofer.de

Abstract. Digital Twins are digital representations of real-world entities. Their behavior resembles the behavior of the real entity at all times. They are candidates for the evaluation of complex adaptive embedded systems, for example in the domains of autonomous driving, or industry 4.0 production systems. However, as most simulators are specialized and only simulate selected aspects of a system with highest accuracy, the creation of a Digital Twin requires the coupling of simulators and their simulation models. Related work indicates that this is still a labor-intensive and manual task. In this paper, we present an architecture framework that transfers approaches from Component-Based Software Engineering to simulator coupling. Simulators are encapsulated as simulation components with defined interfaces. The creation of a Digital Twin is supported by orchestrating simulation components. We present the formal definition of simulation components and our simulation framework, as well as the rules for coupling simulation components into Digital Twins.

Keywords: Simulator coupling · Digital Twins · Components · CBSE

1 Introduction

Simulations are an integral part of the development and testing cycle of embedded systems. They are used in Hardware-in-the-Loop (HiL) testbeds to cover, for example, the simulation of system environments, as well as in virtual HiL setups that substitute physical parts of HiL testbeds with simulation models. With growing system complexity, simulations need to cover an increasing amount of effects. This is especially important, as architects need to keep nowadays much more system aspects into account, which include low-level aspects of target platforms, like communication busses [15]. With the upcoming use of Digital Twins for systems, Digital Twins provide simulation models that behave at all times like the real system under development [1], a single simulator cannot anymore ensure a simulation with sufficient accuracy. Instead, multiple, often specialized simulators, must be coupled to represent also complex system environments with sufficient accuracy.

Creation of a coupled simulation requires the semantic integration of simulation models from multiple simulators. Related work shows that this is still a manual task that

© Springer Nature Switzerland AG 2020
H. Muccini et al. (Eds.): ECSA 2020, CCIS 1269, pp. 326–339, 2020.
https://doi.org/10.1007/978-3-030-59155-7_25

requires the manual integration of proprietary interfaces to simulators. Simulator couplings are therefore often manually developed as tailored connectors between simulators. We did observe that while software interfaces to simulators often differ, the underlying Models of Computation and Communication (MOCC), which control the behavior of the simulation, are relatively harmonized. The behavior of most simulators conforms to a specific MOCC that specifies its simulation model. Environment simulators, for example, comply with a continuous time MOCC, while network simulators conform to discrete event MOCCs. We gave a brief overview on MOCCs and on the coupling of MOCCs into holistic simulations [2].

In this paper, we introduce our component-based approach specifically for the coupling of simulation components. It provides a defined encapsulation for simulators into Simulation Components (SCs) with defined interfaces. We describe Simulation Components (SCs), interfaces, views on simulation models, and coupling semantics. We furthermore describe the coupling of focused SCs into Digital Twins that address multiple system aspects, and discuss the re-use potential of SCs. Our goal is to raise attention to the need of unified interfaces for simulators, and to discuss our proposal for an open and accessible database for re-useable simulator interfaces. This will enable the creation of complex Digital Twins simply by instantiating and connecting SCs with compatible interfaces.

The remainder of this paper is structured as follows: Sect. 2 surveys related work. Section 3 describes our simulator coupling concept. Section 4 describes the realization of network simulation components with the ns-3 network simulator. Section 5 draws conclusions and lays out future work.

2 State-of-the-Art and State-of-the-Practice

Simulator couplings are used whenever a single simulator is no longer sufficient for a simulation task. Sommer, German, and Falko [3] illustrate a coupling between the discrete event network simulator OMNeT++, and the movement simulator SUMO. OMNeT++ is the simulation host and splits the coupled simulation into time steps. The coupling first simulates all network traffic, and then invokes SUMO to simulate node movements. SUMO provides node positions after each simulation step to OMNeT++ and therefore replaces the built-in node movement simulation of OMNeT++.

[5] documents the coupling of network simulation with components for power systems simulation. It simulates the impact of network delays to the overall system performance. The network simulation implements a frame level simulation that simulates the transmission of network frames between power system components. Recent works in simulator coupling illustrate the need of integrating simulators to simulate system effects that go beyond the abilities of the simulation model of a single simulator. The authors of [4] illustrate another bidirectional coupling of a vehicle simulator and (wireless) network simulation to support the development of autonomous driving vehicles. Another recent work with respect to simulator coupling is presented in [7]. The authors of [7] describe a coupling of mobility and network simulators to enable the evaluation of new communication protocols and concepts in a realistic context. [13, 16, 18] illustrate simulator couplings for the validation of automotive functions. [14] illustrates a virtual

environment for Ecosystem Admission, which addresses an even more advanced use-case. These works illustrate the need of future simulator couplings for highly automated and autonomous driving functions. [8] describes a co-simulation platform for smart grids that integrates the OPNET network simulator with the OpenDSS simulator for the simulation of power distribution networks. The simulation host is realized as MATLAB code that invokes both simulators according to the co-simulation model. OPNET provides the network simulation, while OpenDSS simulates the smart grid behavior. Similar to [5], the impact of a network to smart grid behavior is simulated by the coupling.

The authors of [9] describe an evaluation of energy efficiency of MIMO antenna arrays. It requires a physical layer simulation that covers radio propagation and short scale fading. The detailed simulation provides higher accuracy with respect to transmission errors due to interferences, but of course also requires significantly more calculations per simulation step.

In related work, there also have been previous attempts to define re-usable interfaces between simulators. Wegener et al. [4] documents a proposal for a common interface between mobility and network simulators, which is a common simulator coupling. The interface supports the execution of simulation steps, issuing of defined node movement commands, and communication of node positions to network simulators. The discussed simulator couplings illustrate open requirements for the integration of simulation models: The works presented in [3–5] only require (a less accurate) frame level communication to evaluate overall system and application performance. [9] requires a much more accurate network simulation with realistic radio propagation. [3] illustrates the substitution of a mobility simulation model with a more accurate simulation.

We have built on several approaches for the coupling of simulation models: The Functional Mock-up Interface (FMI) standard [10] is a standard for the packaging of simulation models. It defines Functional Mockup Units (FMU) that encapsulate simulation models with an interface. The FMI puts a focus on functional simulation. It realizes a discrete time coupling of simulation models that is extended with a mechanism to re-evaluate the simulation in case of detected discontinuities. Communication between FMUs is via the exchange of values after completed simulation steps. FMU however does not yet cover the connection of simulators with different MOCCs. It does also not encapsulate multiple simulation models in the same FMU. We use FMU as a foundation for our Simulation Component approach. The High-Level Architecture (HLA) [11] is another approach for the coupling of simulation models. It covers the execution of a distributed simulation, as well as the definition of object models.

3 Simulator Coupling Architecture

Related work indicates the need for the integration of different simulation models, and that simulator couplings are performed manually without a high degree of re-use. Component Based Software Engineering (CBSE) did increase re-use significantly. Combining simulators and their simulation models into a Digital Twin should be as easy as the re-use of software components.

3.1 Simulation Component-Based Digital Twins

CBSE encapsulates software functions into components that enforce the information hiding principle: component users use components through defined interfaces, the implementation of a component remains hidden. Users must not make assumptions regarding the implementation of a component that is not covered by an interface, and a component must not make any assumptions regarding its environment that is not covered by an interface. This enables re-use and, for example, the possibility to replace one component by another component with a compatible interface. We encapsulate simulators and their simulation models in re-useable Simulation Components. Figure 1 illustrates the elements of a Simulation Component (SC) for simulating a WiFi communication channel. An SC type is identified by a type name, e.g. *WiFi Channel*. Views provide access to the SC.

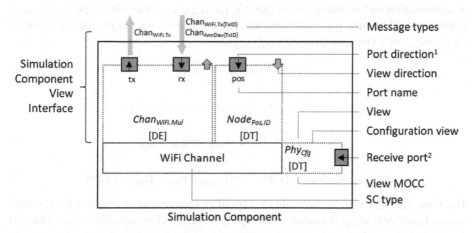

Fig. 1. Elements of a Simulation Component

Basic SCs encapsulate a simulator and its simulation models. Aggregated SCs encapsulate and combine other SCs. Similar to software components, an SC provides interfaces for inter-component communication. We define the set of interfaces to an SC as views on this component. A view provides a consistent access on simulation models of the encapsulated simulator. Complex simulators may provide multiple views to access their simulation models, simple simulators possible only provide a single view. Multiple views on the same simulation model enable access to this model on different levels of detail.

We distinguish provided, required, and configuration views. Provided views expose simulation data, and enable, for example, access to simulated node positions, or a simulated network. They are marked by an arrow that points away from the component. Required views receive data from other SCs. They are marked by an arrow that points towards the SC. We distinguish mandatory required views that must be connected for an SC to be operational, and optional provided views that support, for example, the optional substitution of a contained simulation model with another one. Configuration views enable the configuration of a simulation component. They are painted at the side of the SC.

Inter-SC communication is via messages. Views therefore consist of input and output ports that send and receive messages. A port is part of the view interface and defines a set of sent or received messages. Every view also defines the MOCC that its communication conforms to. Views of a basic SC always conform to one MOCC. Aggregated SCs, however, may contain multiple directors that control contained SCs according to different MOCCs. Views of aggregated SCs consequently may conform to different MOCCs. The illustrated example in Fig. 1 uses Discrete Time (DT) and Discrete Event (DE) MOCCs.

3.2 Simulation Components

We define a Simulation Component sc as tuple of a set of views SC_{Views}, and a name sc_{Name}. The set SC_{Views} contains all views of a Simulation Component. It consists of the defined interface for this view sc_{ViewIF}, the view type $sc_{ViewType}$, and an associated model of computation and communication (MOCC) $sc_{ViewMOCC}$. The view type $sc_{ViewType}$ is either a provided view (prv), an optional required view (req_o), a mandatory required view (req_m), or a configuration view (cfg).

$$sc = (SC_{Views}, sc_{Name}) \tag{1}$$

$$sc_{View} = (sc_{ViewIF}, sc_{ViewType}, sc_{ViewMOCC}) \tag{2}$$

$$sc_{ViewType} \in \{prv, req_o, req_m, cfg\} \tag{3}$$

$$sc_{ViewIF} = \{sc_{port.n}\}, \ sc_{port} = (p_{type}, p_{dir}), \ p_{dir} \in \{tx,rx\} \tag{4}$$

The view interface sc_{ViewIF} consists of a set of ports that realize communication endpoints. Every port sc_{port} is a tuple of the port type p_{type} and port direction p_{dir}. The port direction defines whether the port transmits (tx) or receives data (rx). A view may be added to an SC as a provided or a required view. The view interface sc_{ViewIF}, however, always defines ports and port directions from the viewpoint of a provided view.

Parameter ports (SC_{Ports}) provide configuration data and are always rx ports, thus, have no direction property. The port type p_{type} defines the message type for a port. Every port transmits or receives a set of message types t_{msg}.

$$p_{type} = \{t_{msg.m}\} \tag{5}$$

A message type t_{msg} is defined by a set of named message parameter T_{par}, and by a base message type t_{base}. A message parameter t_{par} is defined by a tuple of parameter name p_{name} and parameter type t_{type} along with a flag indicating if it is optional (p_{opt}). Message types inherit parameters from their base type. Refinement of inherited parameters is not permitted, with the exception of refining an optional message parameter to a mandatory parameter.

$$t_{msg} = (T_{par}, t_{base}, T_{meta}), \ t_{par} = (p_{name}, t_{type}, p_{opt}), \tag{6}$$

Message parameter types t_{type} are defined according to a type system. Our framework supports the primitive types *Float, Double, Integer, Boolean, String, Int8, Int16, Int32,*

Int64, as well as Maps, Structures, Sets, and Array types based on the supported basic types for inter-Simulation Component communication.

$$t_{meta} = (id_{meta}, t_{type}) \tag{7}$$

Messages may carry additional meta data in addition to the defined parameter, which is independent of message types. Component ports may require specific meta data properties to be present or guarantee meta data availability. This enables the extension of view types with additional information that is not directly related to a view, but, e.g., to a coupling. A common use for meta data is to add addressing information when creating 1:n, m:1, or n:m inter-component connections. SC interfaces define the set T_{meta} that contains the IDs and types (t_{type}) of required and always provided meta data properties.

A view furthermore defines a model of computation and communication (MOCC) in $sc_{ViewMOCC}$ which defines the communication semantics of that view.

3.3 Extending and Connecting Views

Views may be extended to add additional provided information. Extended views are permitted to add additional transmit ports, and to add additional transmitted messages to inherited transmit ports. Extending may also add additional meta data to messages at transmit ports. When a view is added as required view, extending adds additional dependencies that can only be satisfied by connecting an extended view. Provided views remain backwards compatible, i.e., they retain all information provided by base views.

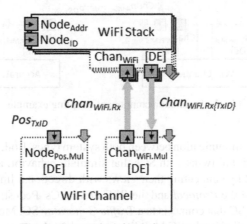

Fig. 2. Connecting simulation components

Simulation components are connected to Digital Twins by connecting provided to required views with directional links. An operational SC requires connection of all mandatory required views. A directional link always connects transmit ports to receive ports, as illustrated in Fig. 2.

Figure 3 above illustrates the coupling of Simulation Components into a Digital Twin that simulates an environment with cars and pedestrians. The coupling evaluates

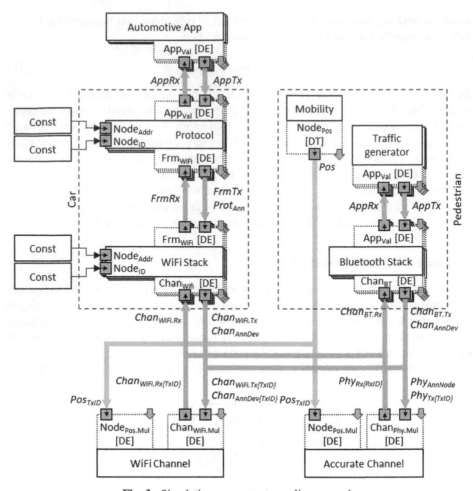

Fig. 3. Simulation component coupling example

interaction of WiFi communication between both system types. Both cars and pedestrians are represented by digital twins with SCs that simulate behavior, and WiFi interfaces. The SCs are coupled by connecting their views with directional links. Digital Twins of cars (Car_n) consist of the *Protocol* and the *WiFi Stack* SCs. Pedestrians are represented by a *Bluetooth Stack* SC that connects to a *Traffic Generator* SC. Movements of cars and pedestrians are controlled by the SC *Mobility*. Communication between SCs for protocol and WiFi simulation is via view Frm_{WiFi}. Wireless channel simulation is exposed as individual simulation component *WiFi Channel* and *Accurate Channel* to enable the use of simulation models with different accuracy. This enables a frame-based simulation in the large scale, as well as the evaluation of interferences between Bluetooth and WiFi communication that may share the same frequency bands.

In the illustrated example from Fig. 3, the connection between views $Node_{Pos}$ and $Node_{Pos.Mul}$ of *Mobility* and *Accurate Channel* connects views that conform to different

Models of Computation and Communication (MOCC). When coupling both views, the coupling must ensure correct coupling semantics to yield valid simulation results.

We have already described the foundations of MOCC coupling in [2]. Simulation component execution conforms to a MOCC that controls its execution. Directors implement MOCCs and control assigned Simulation Components. The nesting of directors enables the creation of nested simulations with coupled MOCCs (cf. [2]). An aggregated SC that defines multiple views internally contains directors that control the SCs realizing the views of the aggregated SC.

Coupling of two views with differing MOCCs is consequently performed based on the coupling semantics from [2]: Inter-SC communication is realized with messages. A view using a Discrete Time (DT) MOCC transmits a message from every transmit port at the end of every time step, and samples the most recently received value on all of its input ports. A view that uses a Discrete Event (DE) MOCC only transmits changed values on its output ports, and immediately reacts to changes on its input ports, conforming to the DE_{MOCC} (cf. [2]).

4   Application Example

The usability of our coupling approach depends on the applicability of SCs, in particular on their ability to harmonize the interfaces of simulation models from existing simulators. We therefore analyze the simulation models of the well-known ns-3 network simulator to provide evidence for this. We focus on the encapsulation of its WiFi simulation classes into SCs, and describe the views of the created SCs.

Figure 4 illustrates relevant classes of the ns-3 [17] simulator with respect to the WiFi simulation model. We grouped important ns-3 classes into Protocol simulation, Node simulation, simulation of Movements, WiFiMAC, WiFiPhy, and the WiFiChannel.

The ns-3 uses a discrete event simulation with a central scheduler that schedules events and controls message transport between the C++ classes that implements the ns-3 simulation models. The overall architecture of an ns-3 simulation resembles the communication stack architecture as defined by the ISO/OSI reference architecture [12]. All communicating ns-3 classes implement specific *send* and *receive* functions that pass *Packet* instances to higher and lower layers. Ns-3 *Packets* carry tags, headers and trailers in addition to frame payload to pass information between protocols across layers.

The ns-3 *Node* class implements a physical node and aggregates applications, protocols, and network devices. The *Channel* class and its subclasses implement the shared communication medium of a network. We chose the *YansWiFiChannel* as the simulation model for this evaluation. The *AdhocWifiMac* and *MacLow* classes implement WiFi medium access control protocol simulation. *WiFiPhy* is the base class of WiFi physical layer implementations while class *YansWifiPhy* implements the physical layer that matches the *YansWiFiChannel* implementation. The *MobilityModel* class simulates node movements and enables access to node positions.

Figure 5 illustrates the encapsulation of the groups of ns-3 classes from Fig. 4 into SCs for the simulation of WiFi MAC/Phy (*ns-3 WiFi*) and IP protocols (*ns-3 protocol*). The SC *ns-3 WiFi* encapsulates both WiFi MAC and Phy simulation, as we figured that the implementation of these simulation models often depends on each other. It therefore

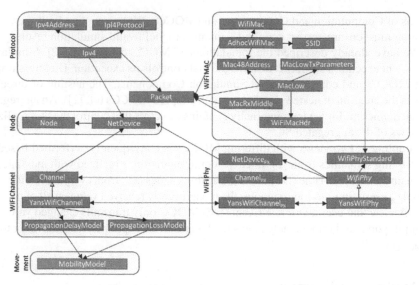

Fig. 4. Main ns-3 WiFi simulation classes

would not have been feasible to separate them into individual SCs. The WiFi MAC and Phy classes of ns-3 require a reference to an instance of the ns-3 node class. This and an instance of the *NetDevice* class (cf. Fig. 5) is therefore part of the ns-3 *WiFi* SC.

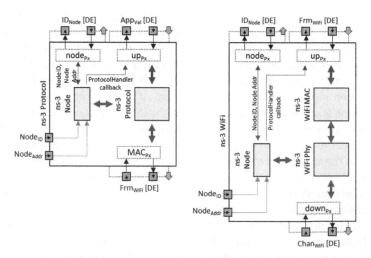

Fig. 5. Protocol and WiFi Simulation Components

We created generic, i.e., non-ns-3 specific message types for inter-SC communication, which are illustrated in greater detail in Table 1. Interfaces convert generic inter-component communication messages to ns-3 message types (e.g., *Packet*) that are expected by the ns-3 simulation model implementations. Most ns-3 simulation models require references to other parts of the protocol stack. For example, the *ns-3 WiFi* SC needs to register upstream protocols in the *ns-3 Node* instance to ensure its routing to upstream components. The ns-3 realizes this via a callback function *(ProtocolHandler-Callback)* that transports frames to protocol simulation models. The ns-3 WiFi SC must furthermore assign the 48 Bit MAC address of the WiFi interface to the ns-3 node, as well as a unique node ID.

Table 1. Message type definitions

Message type	Member	Type	Description
Pos	x	Double	Node x coordinate
	y	Double	Node y coordinate
	z	Double	Node z coordinate
AppTx	pkt	Packet	Packet data and metadata
AppRx	pkt	Packet	Packet data and metadata
WiFiTx	pkt	Packet	Transmitted WiFi frame
WiFiRx	pkt	Packet	Received WiFi frame
Chan$_{Wifi.Tx}$	pkt	Packet	Transmitted WiFi frame
Chan$_{Wifi.Rx}$	pkt	Packet	Received WiFi frame
Chan$_{AnnDev}$	protId	Int32	Protocol ID
ChanPhy.Tx	txWave	Double[]	Transmitted modulated frame
ChanPhy.Rx	rxWave	Double[]	Received modulated frame
.TxID	txID	Int64	Transmitter ID meta data

Our Simulation Component therefore defines a configuration view with parameter ports that enable configuration of the mandatory parameter *node ID* and *node Addr*. Protocol simulation models get a unique ID assigned, which is used internally to manage the *ProtocolHandlerCallback* function, and to address inter-SC component messages to the correct protocols, e.g., to realize the n:m link between *WiFi Stack* and *Protocol* in Fig. 3.

The SC *ns-3 Protocol* encapsulates the simulation models for the IP stack of the ns-3 simulator. It also uses an ns-3 node instance and must register upstream protocols similar to the *WiFi* SC. We decided to replicate the node instance in both SCs, as the ns-3 implementation did permit this. The existing ns-3 protocol classes make use of packet tags; adding tags to inter-component communication must therefore be possible for proper operation of ns-3 based Simulation Components. Figure 6 illustrates a technology-independent *Packet* type for inter-SC interaction that replaces the ns-3 specific *Packet* class. It is used for message types that are communicated through the views of SCs. The *Packet type* defines a unique ID (*uID*), a serialized payload (*data*), and additional meta data that is stored in a key/value map using structured types. The structured types

PktTag, ByteTag, Header, Trailer store ns-3 specific information that is not used by other simulators.

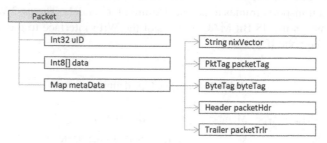

Fig. 6. Packet type for Simulation Component coupling

We decided to keep the native ns-3 types for the meta data, as it does not contain any negative impact data for our evaluation. Exporting parts of the meta data for message definitions of an extended view, however, could enable a tighter integration of other simulators. We leave this for future work.

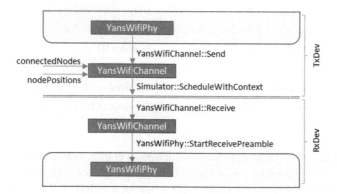

Fig. 7. ns-3 Phy and Channel interaction

Figure 7 details the interaction between ns-3 *YansWiFiPhy* and *YansWiFiChannel* components, which will become a border between two SCs. The *YansWiFiChannel* component requires a list of connected nodes, as well as connection to a mobility model that provides the subset of nodes that are in transmission range from the *YansWiFiPhy* component. The SC interface for the channel therefore must provide this information. We decided to introduce the *Chan$_{AnnDev}$* message for this (cf. Table 1).

Internally, the *YansWiFiChannel* uses the *Simulator::ScheduleWithContext* operation to pass ns-3 *Packet* instances between the sender and all receiver nodes. This function invokes the scheduler and is part of the discrete event implementation of the ns-3 simulator. The ns-3 scheduler therefore needs to be integrated with the discrete event MOCC of the Simulation Component to process incoming messages. We achieved that by implementing the simulation worker interface of FERAL that enables its integration into a hierarchically coupled simulation, as described in [2].

Figure 8 illustrates the Simulation Components that encapsulate ns-3 *WiFi Channel* and *Mobility* models in detail. It illustrates the component substructure with the ns-3 class groups from Fig. 7, interfaces, and main message flows.

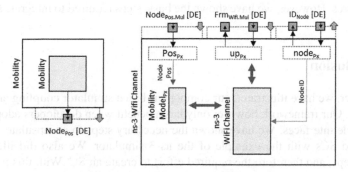

Fig. 8. Mobility and WiFi channel Simulation Components

Table 2 illustrates the detailed views definition for inter-SC communication that were illustrated in Fig. 3. Message types are detailed in Table 1. The inter-view communication messages include messages for communicating actual simulation events, e.g., the inter-component transmission of simulated wireless frames, as well as the transmission of meta data that includes node positions and registration of upstream protocols.

Table 2. View definitions for inter-SC communication

View	Message type	Description
$Node_{Pos}$	Pos	Node position (x,y,z coordinates)
$Node_{Pos.Mul}$	Pos_{TxID}	Node position with sender ID meta data
App_{Val}	AppTx	Transmitted (functional) application data
App_{Val}	AppRx	Received (functional) application data
Frm_{WiFi}	WiFiTx	Transmitted WiFi frame
Frm_{WiFi}	WiFiRx	Received WiFi frame
$Chan_{Wifi}$	$Chan_{Wifi.Tx}$	Transmitted WiFi frames
$Chan_{Wifi}$	$Chan_{Wifi.Rx}$	Received WiFi frames
$Chan_{Wifi}$	$Chan_{AnnDev}$	Announce WiFi device to channel
$Chan_{Wifi.Mul}$	$Chan_{Wifi.Tx.TxID}$	Transmitted WiFi frames with sender ID
$Chan_{Wifi.Mul}$	$Chan_{Wifi.Rx.RxID}$	Received WiFi frames with receiver ID
$Chan_{Wifi.Mul}$	$Chan_{AnnDev.TxID}$	Announce WiFi device to channel with sender ID
$Chan_{Phy.Mul}$	$Chan_{Phy.Tx.TxID}$	Transmitted modulated frames with sender ID
$Chan_{Phy.Mul}$	$Chan_{Phy.Rx.RxID}$	Received modulated frames with receiver ID
$Chan_{Phy.Mul}$	$Chan_{AnnDev.TxID}$	Announce device to channel with sender ID

In our evaluation, we illustrated the most important steps to encapsulate important simulation models of the ns-3 simulator as Simulation Components. We also illustrated that harmonized interfaces can transport data between simulation models with simulator-independent data structures. Simulator-specific information was encapsulated in meta data, and enabled the use of simulator-specific features in couplings. Harmonizing additional information that we encoded as simulator-specific meta data will enable additional features. However, we have shown the basic steps required to integrate simulation models.

5 Conclusion

In this paper, we have illustrated our component-based simulator coupling architecture framework. Our framework however only has a benefit when developers adopt the idea of re-useable interfaces. We have shown the necessary steps to encapsulate simulation models into SCs with the example of the ns-3 simulator. We also did illustrate the required steps, and therefore the required effort to create an SC. With this publication, we want to start a discussion regarding re-useable simulator interfaces to simplify future couplings. This is necessary, as the rapid creation of simulation environments will also become necessary in future, as future embedded systems will be operating in much more heterogeneous system contexts compared to already existing systems. They will require more sophisticated DTs as testing environments. As existing HiL settings cannot provide this flexibility, and traditional simulator couplings require too much effort for manual couplings, we believe that component-based approaches have the potential to simplify the creation of tailored simulator couplings significantly.

To support future simulator couplings, we are currently working on an implementation of this framework that will be made available for academic research. This framework will consist of core components that enable the coupling of programming languages, and implement the main aspects of the framework. It will furthermore provide integration components that simplify the integration of new simulators as simulation components.

References

1. Glaessgen, E.H., Stargel, D.S.: The digital twin paradigm for future NASA and U.S. Air Force Vehicles. In: 53rd Structural Dynamics and Materials Conference Special Session: Digital Twin, Honolulu, HI, US (2012)
2. Kuhn, T., Forster, T., Braun, T., Gotzhein, R.: FERAL — framework for simulator coupling on requirements and architecture level. In: Proceedings of the Eleventh ACM/IEEE International Conference on Formal Methods and Models for Codesign (MEMOCODE 2013), pp. 11–22. IEEE Computer Society, USA (2013)
3. Sommer, C., German, R., Dressler, F.: Bidirectionally coupled network and road traffic simulation for improved IVC analysis. IEEE Trans. Mob. Comput. **10**(1), 3–15 (2010). https://doi.org/10.1109/TMC.2010.133
4. Wegener, A., Piorkowski, M., Raya, M., Hellbrück, H., Fischer, S., Hubaux, J.-P.: TraCI: an interface for coupling road traffic and network simulators. In: Proceedings of the 11th Communications and Networking Simulation Symposium, CNS 2008 (2008). https://doi.org/10.1145/1400713.1400740

5. Nasiriani, N., et al.: An embedded communication network simulator for power systems simulations in PSCAD. In: 2013 IEEE Power & Energy Society General Meeting, Vancouver, BC, pp. 1–5 (2013). https://doi.org/10.1109/pesmg.2013.6672764
6. Llatser, I., Jornod, G., Festag, A., Mansolino, D., Navarro, I., Martinoli, A.: Simulation of cooperative automated driving by bidirectional coupling of vehicle and network simulators. In: 2017 IEEE Intelligent Vehicles Symposium (IV), Los Angeles, CA, pp. 1881–1886 (2017). https://doi.org/10.1109/ivs.2017.7995979
7. Schuhbäck, S., et al.: Towards a bidirectional coupling of pedestrian dynamics and mobile communication simulation. In: Proceedings of 6th International OM, vol. 66, pp. 60–67 (2019)
8. Sun, X., Chen, Y., Liu, J., Huang, S.: A co-simulation platform for smart grid considering interaction between information and power systems. In: ISGT 2014, Washington, DC, pp. 1–6 (2014). https://doi.org/10.1109/isgt.2014.6816423
9. Kim, T., et al.: Tens of Gbps support with mmWave beamforming systems for next generation communications. In: IEEE GLOBECOM 2013, December 2013, pp. 3790–3795 (2013)
10. Bertsch, C., et al.: FMI for physical models on automotive embedded targets. In: Proceedings of the 11th International Modelica Conference, Versailles, France, 21–23 September 2015, vol. 118. Linköping University Electronic Press (2015)
11. Dahmann, J.S., Fujimoto, R.M., Weatherly, R.M.: The department of defense high level architecture. In: Proceedings of the 29th Conference on Winter Simulation, pp. 142–149 (1997)
12. Zimmermann, H.: OSI reference model – the ISO model of architecture for open systems interconnection. IEEE Trans. Commun. **28**(4), 425–432 (1980)
13. Feth, P., Bauer, T., Kuhn, T.: Virtual validation of cyber physical systems. In: GI Conference on Software Engineering & Management, Dresden, Germany (2015)
14. Cioroaica, E., Chren, S., Buhnova, B., Kuhn, T., Dimitrov, D.: Towards creation of a reference architecture for trust-based digital ecosystems. In: ECSA 2019: Proceedings of the 13th European Conference on Software Architecture – vol. 2, September 2019
15. Antonino, P.O., Morgenstern, A., Kuhn, T.: Embedded-software architects: it's not only about the software. IEEE Softw. **33**(6), 56–62 (2016)
16. Marko, N., Ruebsam, J., Biehn, A., Schneider, H.: Scenario-based testing of ADAS - integration of the open simulation interface into co-simulation for function validation. In: Proceedings of the 9th International Conference on Simulation and Modeling Methodologies, Technologies and Applications (SIMULTECH 2019) (2019)
17. Riley, G.F., Henderson, T.R.: The ns-3 network simulator. In: Wehrle, K., Güneş, M., Gross, J. (eds.) Modeling and Tools for Network Simulation. Springer, Heidelberg (2010). https://doi.org/10.1007/978-3-642-12331-3_2
18. Baumann, P., Samlaus, R., Mikelsons, L., Kuhn, T., Jahic, J.: Towards virtual validation of distributed functions. In: Proceedings of the 2019 Summer Simulation Conference (SummerSim 2019), July 2019

Integrating Runtime Verification into an Automated UAS Traffic Management System

Matthew Cauwels$^{(\boxtimes)}$ (iD), Abigail Hammer$^{(\boxtimes)}$ (iD), Benjamin Hertz$^{(\boxtimes)}$ (iD),
Phillip H. Jones$^{(\boxtimes)}$ (iD), and Kristin Y. Rozier$^{(\boxtimes)}$ (iD)

Iowa State University, Ames, IA 50010, USA
{mcauwels,arhammer,benhertz,phjones,kyrozier}@iastate.edu

Abstract. Unmanned Aerial Systems (UAS) are quickly integrating into the National Air Space (NAS). With the number of registered small (under 55 pounds) UAS in the USA alone at over 1.5 million, and projected to expand rapidly, according to the Federal Aviation Administration (FAA), safety is a pressing consideration. Safe UAS integration into the NAS requires an intelligent, automated system for UAS Traffic Management (UTM). Even more than for manned aircraft, UTM must integrate runtime checks to ensure system safety, at the very least to make up for the lack of humans on board to employ the common-sense safety checks ingrained into the culture of human aviation.

We overview a candidate automated, intelligent UTM system and propose multiple integration points for runtime verification (RV) to ensure that each part of the UTM adheres to safety requirements during operation. We write, validate, and present patterns for formal requirements across multiple subsystems of this UTM framework. After encoding our requirements as flight-certifiable runtime observers in the R2U2 RV engine, we execute them in simulation across multiple real-life test flights supplemented with simulated data to cover additional cases that did not occur in flight. Lessons learned accompany an analysis of the efficacy and performance of RV integration into the UTM framework.

Keywords: UAS · UTM · Runtime Verification · R2U2

1 Introduction

The Federal Aviation Administration (FAA) forecasts Unmanned Aerial System (UAS) numbers to continue to "expand rapidly" over the next 20 years with over 90% of the growth from consumer-grade or professional-grade (non-model) UAS used for commercial or research purposes [5]. Given the considerable traffic this

K. Y. Rozier—Supported by NSF CAREER Award CNS-1552934 and NSF PFI:BIC grant CNS-1257011. Reproducibility artifacts: http://temporallogic.org/research/DETECT2020/.

© Springer Nature Switzerland AG 2020
H. Muccini et al. (Eds.): ECSA 2020, CCIS 1269, pp. 340–357, 2020.
https://doi.org/10.1007/978-3-030-59155-7_26

will generate and the pressing concern for safe integration into the National Air Space (NAS), additional traffic management is required on top of current safety regulations [6]. A recent candidate for an intelligent, automated UAS Traffic Management (UTM) system addresses these concerns [25].

One important consideration in such an automated system is how, and where, to integrate checks *during system operation* that continuously monitor for violations of system safety requirements, e.g., due to unexpected environmental conditions or other scenarios that could not be predicted and tested for during system design. This is especially critical given the automated nature of the systems involved: pilots and human ground controllers make numerous decisions in the control of commercial aircraft that serve as a foundation for their traffic management systems but are missing from UTM. For example, pilots regularly identify and dismiss off-nominal sensor readings and ground controllers operate under unstated assumptions, such as that the flight plans of two aircraft should never contain unsafe overlaps.

Runtime Verification (RV) provides checks that cyber-physical systems adhere to their safety requirements during operation. However, much of the research into RV has focused on increasing expressivity of monitored properties and operational reach of RV engines. The on-board resources, overhead, operational delays, and intrusive system instrumentation required to run these tools are incompatible with flight certification [12]. In response, the Responsive, Realizable, Unobtrusive Unit (R2U2), was designed to monitor sufficiently expressive properties, in real time, under hard resource constraints, with low-to-no overhead, and without system instrumentation that would violate flight certification [17]. Only three RV tools are flight-certifiable: R2U2, Lola [22], and Co-Pilot [16]; R2U2's flexible architecture was the easiest to adapt to our UTM system.

We examine the candidate UTM system [25], overviewing its design, implementation, and initial tests, e.g., with University of Iowa's (U of I's) Operational Performance Laboratory's (OPL's) Vapor 55 UAS flying over small, nearby airspace. We map out three subsystems where RV could be embedded within this UTM framework: on-board the Vapor 55, on-board each Ground Control System (GCS), and within the UTM cloud-based framework. However, the biggest bottleneck to the successful deployment of formal methods like RV is specification of the requirements under verification [19]. Building upon the runtime specification pattern categories of [19], we detail patterns for formal requirements specification across these subsystems and write, debug, and validate a covering set of temporal logic specifications. Using R2U2 to create runtime observers from this specification set, we deploy in simulation real-time RV over a set of real-life flight tests, expanding our data set to include realistic scenarios that were not able to be flown in real life. We examine the outputs from R2U2 and provide a roadmap for utilizing this data to robustify the UTM framework. Our case study details the process of RV integration for future adopters of systems like UTM.

Our contributions are as follows: (1) patterns useful for RV specifications across a real distributed UTM implementation; (2) a method for adding a single first-order operator to Mission-time Linear Temporal Logic (MLTL) specifications in an RV engine; (3) an open set of RV benchmarks from real-world UAS/GCS telemetry data; (4) an extensive experimental evaluation (124 specifications) of a distributed RV implementation in real-time; and (5) lessons learned from distributed RV specifications validation and refinement for a UTM system.

The remainder of this paper is organized as follows. Section 2 gives background information on MLTL and R2U2. Section 3 overviews the candidate UTM framework. Our formal specifications fill Sect. 4, including specifications specific to the on-board UAS, the GCS, and the UTM's cloud-based framework. To inform future practitioners, we detail their organization, discuss coverage metrics, and exemplify each specification pattern we found useful in our study. We also address the critical topic of specification validation and debugging. Section 5 describes our test scenario and graphs the outputs from R2U2 for specifications from six of our patterns. Section 6 concludes with lessons learned and next steps for RV integration into the future UTM system.

2   Preliminaries

Mission-Time Linear Temporal Logic. For all our specifications, our chosen language is Mission-time Linear Temporal Logic (MLTL) [11,17]. A variant of Metric Temporal Logic (MTL) [2], MLTL incorporates closed interval $I = [a, b]$ time bounds over a set of bounded natural numbers (i.e., $0 \leq a \leq b < +\infty$) on each temporal operator.

Definition 1 *(MLTL Syntax [11,17]). The syntax of an MLTL formula φ over a set of atomic propositions $\mathcal{AP}$ is recursively defined as:*

$$\varphi := \text{true} \mid \text{false} \mid p \mid \neg\varphi \mid \varphi_1 \wedge \varphi_2 \mid \varphi_1 \vee \varphi_2 \mid \Box_I\varphi \mid \Diamond_I\varphi \mid \varphi_1\mathcal{U}_I\varphi_2 \mid \varphi_1\mathcal{R}_I\varphi_2$$

where $p \in \mathcal{AP}$ is a Boolean atom (0/1), φ_1 and φ_2 are MLTL formulas, and I is a closed-bound interval $[lb, ub]$, where $lb \leq ub$.

For any two MLTL formulas φ_1 and φ_2, $\varphi_1 \equiv \varphi_2$ if and only if they are semantically equivalent. Since MLTL is derived from linear temporal logic (LTL), many of the semantics are the same: $\text{false} \equiv \neg\text{true}$, $\varphi_1 \vee \varphi_2 \equiv \neg(\neg\varphi_1 \wedge \neg\varphi_2)$, $\neg(\varphi_1\mathcal{U}_I\varphi_2) \equiv (\neg\varphi_1\mathcal{R}_I\neg\varphi_2)$ and $\neg\Diamond_I\varphi \equiv \Box_I\neg\varphi$. The only notable difference is that MLTL discards LTL's next ($\mathcal{X}$) operator, as it is semantically equivalent to $\Box_{[1,1]}\varphi$ [11]. A position $\pi[i]$, where ($i \geq 0$) is an assignment over $2^{\mathcal{AP}}$; $|\pi|$ represents the length of π.

Definition 2 *(MLTL Semantics [11,17]). The satisfaction of an MLTL formula φ, over a set of propositions $\mathcal{AP}$, by a computation/trace π starting from position i (denoted as $\pi, i \models \varphi$) is recursively defined as:*

- $\pi, i \models \text{true}$, $- \pi, i \models p$ *iff* $p \in \pi[i]$, $- \pi, i \models \neg\varphi$ *iff* $\pi, i \not\models \varphi$,
- $\pi, i \models \varphi_1 \wedge \varphi_2$ *iff* $\pi, i \models \varphi_1$ *and* $\pi, i \models \varphi_2$,
- $\pi, i \models \varphi_1\mathcal{U}_{[lb,ub]}\varphi_2$ *iff* $|\pi| \geq i + lb$ *and, there exists* $j \in [i + lb, i + ub]$ *such that* $\pi, j \models \varphi_2$ *and for every* $k < j$, $k \in [i + lb, i + ub]$, $\pi, k \models \varphi_1$.

Realizable Responsive Unobtrusive Unit (R2U2). Our R2U2 instrumentation uses two of that tool's main architectural layers: (1) signal processing and (2) temporal logic monitors. R2U2 has implementations in hardware (FPGAs), C++, and C; we choose the latter for embedding in the UTM. R2U2's architecture details appear in a tool overview [20], with additional details from past case studies in [7,10,13,17,23].

R2U2 reads relevant sensor readings off the main system bus, then passes them through lightweight, real-time atomic checkers that filter and discretize the sensor readings. Checks like "altitude < MIN" transform signals into Boolean atomics, e.g., true or false, that populate the atomic propositions in temporal logic formulas. Each MLTL formula encodes directly into an observer embedded on the target platform. The hierarchical tree of inputs, filters, atomic checkers, and temporal logic formulas comprise an *R2U2 specification observation tree.* Redundant branches of the tree can be combined through a pre-flight optimization step for efficiency and reducing encoding size. For example, suppose R2U2 is implemented on a fixed-wing UAS and has two separate specifications: (1) the UAS's landing gear will be stowed when it is above 1,000 ft, and (2) the UAS's speed will be within 300 mph to 400 mph when above 1,000 ft. Since both of these specifications require the altimeter reading to exceed 1,000 ft, a single Boolean operator can be passed to both temporal logic observers.

3   UTM System Definition

In parallel with NASA's third UTM Technical Capability Level [14], a hybrid university-industrial team proposed an intelligent, centralized UTM for low-altitude urban environments to coordinate UAS traffic in a safe and efficient way [25]. A high-level diagram of the proposed UTM system appears in Fig. 1.

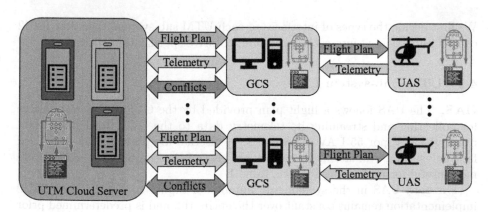

Fig. 1. An overview of the NSF funded cloud-based UTM[25]. (Color figure online)

Ground Control Stations (GCS) connect to the UTM Cloud Server and upload their proposed flight plan for approval. The UTM Cloud server performs pre-flight plan conflict detection using a dynamic geofencing algorithm [27]. The UTM then notifies the GCS if the flight plan is rejected or approved. If rejected, the GCS should submit a new flight plan until one is approved. When approved, the GCS streams the UAS's telemetry data to the server, which then performs an en route conflict prediction. If an en route conflict is predicted, the server will alert all GCS involved of the conflict, so that they may have enough time to submit a new flight plan and perform an avoidance maneuver.

There are many challenges to overcome before such a UTM would be incorporated into our NAS [3,18]. For example, an ongoing research question is how to handle uncooperative and hostile UAS in the UTM's airspace. One assumption of this UTM is that all UAS are non-hostile, i.e., no UAS is purposefully flying an unapproved flight plan. However, this UTM was designed to receive telemetry data from anyone who connects to it, regardless of flight plan status. While the details of how to maintain communication with both cooperative and uncooperative UAS is still ongoing research [24], RV can be used within this UTM to alert the operator to the presence of uncooperative UAS.

Another ongoing research question for UTMs is whether low-altitude airspace should be structured, e.g., with similar traffic patterns and rules as ground transportation [9]. Regardless of which approach is used, RV can be incorporated to alert users of dangerous or undesirable circumstances. For example, this UTM was developed for unstructured airspace, so it has more general operating range specifications, such as those that make sure that all UAS are within the UTM's airspace. Conversely, if a structured airspace was chosen, the structured ruleset can be formally verified using RV.

4   UTM Runtime Specifications

We first decide the types of interfaces to each UTM sub-system, then how R2U2 can be implemented into each subsystem, to drive specification elicitation.[1]

4.1   UTM Sub-system I/O

UAS. The UAS follows a flight plan provided by the GCS and is responsible for collecting and streaming its telemetry data to the GCS. Real flight data from OPL's Vapor 55 UAV helicopter's [1] internal log provides the data used for analysis and evaluation. The subset we chose is based on which signals were most useful for performing RV; see Table 1.

For each UAS in the system, the number of inputs to an on-board R2U2 implementation remains constant over the entire run and is predetermined prior

---

[1] Note that the list presented is not a comprehensive list of all our specifications; the full list can be found at http://temporallogic.org/research/DETECT2020/.

Table 1. Selected output signals from the UAS.

Signal	Description	Units
Pos{N, E, D}	Relative positional vector (North, East, Downward) from the home point.	{m, m, m}
Lat, Lon, Alt	GPS coordinate positions.	{DD, DD, MSL}
Roll, Pitch, Yaw	Euler angles of the UAS.	{deg, deg, deg}
P, Q, R	Euler angle-rates of the UAS.	{deg/s, deg/s, deg/s}
Vel{N, E, D}	Velocity vector of the UAS.	{m/s, m/s, m/s}
Acc{N, E, D}	Acceleration vector of the UAS.	{m/s^2, m/s^2, m/s^2}
Temp, TempE1/2	Temperature of the air and motors.	C
Pres	Atmospheric pressure.	hPa
Phase	Set of strings corresponding to preset phases of flight.	{<undefined>, Test actuators, Stationary, Hover, Cruise, Go to, Stop at, In flight, Landed}
Subphase	Set of strings corresponding to preset subphases of flight.	{Ready, Test, Takeoff, Manual, Waypoints, Home, Landing}
FlightMode	Set of strings corresponding to automatic and manual control.	{Automatic, Home}
RPM	RPM of the main motor.	–

to runtime. This makes implementations of R2U2 equivalent across all UAS, meaning that the time spent creating specifications for an individual UAS remains constant. This is assuming all UAS in a system are the same class, i.e., all single-rotor helicopter-style UAS with similar parameters.

GCS. The GCS has many responsibilities within the UTM system. It is responsible for: (1) submitting flight plans to the UTM; (2) directing and receiving telemetry data from an inflight UAS; (3) pre-processing and transmitting any telemetry data received from its UAS to the UTM; and (4) monitoring for any conflict alerts from the UTM. For our case study, we look only at implementing RV to monitor (1), (2), and (4). Due to limitations on the way the UTM's test data was produced, i.e., the Vapor 55 was only simulated during the UTM test, and because it would be identical to the UAS's R2U2 implementation, we omitted (3) from the GCS's R2U2 implementation.

A challenging aspect of the GCS is that the flight plan data must be continuously streamed to R2U2, since flight plans that are transmitted once across the GCS to the UTM are not saved anywhere in R2U2's memory (see Table 2). This made formatting R2U2's inputs from the GCS challenging; in particular, the number of waypoints within a GCS's flight plan can vary. This led to $NumTelem + NumFP + (NumWPsFP)(NumWP)$ total inputs from a GCS to R2U2, where $NumTelem$ is the number of telemetry inputs, $NumFP$ is the number of inputs from the flight plan, $NumWpsFP$ is the number of signals associated with each waypoint, and $NumWP$ is the number of waypoints within the flight

Table 2. Input and output signals from the GCS to the UTM

Signal	GCS I/O	Description	Units
Telemetry Signals			
ID	O	The flight plan ID of the telemetry transmission.	int
Time	O	The time stamp when the GCS transmits the telemetry to the UTM.	UNIX
wp{Lon,Lat,Alt}	O	The latitude, longitude, and altitude of the waypoint the UAS is currently flying toward.	DD/MSL
Lon,Lat,Alt	O	The UAS's measured longitude, latitude, and altitude.	DD/MSL
Vel	O	The UAS's velocity measurement.	m
Ang	O	The UAS's heading measurement.	deg.
Flight Plan Signals			
Signal	**GCS I/O**	**Description**	**Units**
fp_ID	I	The UTM's assigned flight plan ID for the approved flight plan.	int
Status	I	The UTM's response to the GCS's flight plan	{Approved, Rejected, Replaced}
Start	O	The start time of the flight plan.	UNIX
End	O	The estimated end time of the flight plan.	UNIX
Phase	O	The type of waypoint.	{START, STOP, CRUISE, HOME}
fp{Lon,Lat,Alt}	O	The specific waypoint's latitude, longitude, and altitude.	DD/MSL
Time_Filed	O	The time stamp when the GCS transmitted the flight plan to the UTM.	UNIX

plan. For our specific system, $NumTelem = 9$, $NumFP = 4$, $NumWpsFP = 5$, and $NumWP$ varies between 4 and 10 waypoints.

This variance in the number of inputs from one GCS to another led us to develop specifications that validate across *all* instances of $NumWP$. We accomplished this by adjusting R2U2's pre-processing layer to iterate across a loop of all instances of one variable (say, **Phase**) and determine if at least one violates a certain property. While this is not a full-fledged first-order logic [4,8], it leads to a mapping of multiple inputs to a single Boolean atomic input to R2U2 and acts like a single first-order operator to MLTL. At the sacrifice of precision, i.e., rather than knowing which exact waypoint was violating a property, R2U2 reports if at least one input is violating a property, which allows for easier automation and generality when incorporating R2U2 across iterative types of inputs (i.e., varying number of waypoints).

UTM Cloud Server. Since the UTM is implemented as a cloud-based, centralized server, it is in charge of consolidating all flight plan and telemetry information and determining whether any two UAS will conflict. Like the instances of R2U2 for the GCS, the number of inputs for the UTM varies: once with the number of waypoints in a flight plan and again with the number of UAS. Thus, the total number of inputs to an instance of R2U2 for the UTM can be calculated by $NumID(NumTelem + NumFP) + (NumWPsFP)(\sum_{i=0}^{NumID} NumWP[i])$, where $NumID$ represents the total number of flight plan IDs in the UTM and $NumWP[i]$ is the specific number of waypoints for flight plan i. This can lead to a large number of inputs for R2U2, i.e., 20 UAS with 4 waypoints each would be 580 inputs.

Similar to the GCS, to get traction on such a large number of inputs, we have designed our specifications similar to first order logic, i.e., *for all UAS* a certain property holds or *there exists a UAS* where a property is violated. Again, we trade expressiveness for performance: we retain real-time performance guarantees but only promise R2U2 will immediately alert the UTM operator of a violation, not identify the specific UAS responsible.

4.2 Coverage of Real-World Specification Types

To help organize our specifications, each one is categorized into one of six labels: (1) operating range, (2) sensor bounds, (3) rates of change, (4) control sequences, (5) physical model relationships, and (6) inter-sensor relationships. These categories resemble those of [19,26], though we add a level of granularity to several for ease of organization.

Operating Range. Every sensor to, and variable within, a given system has an expected *operating range* and should it fall below or exceed a given threshold, this may indicate a hazardous system state. For example, the proposed centralized UTM will cover a predefined airspace. Should a UAS stray beyond these operating limits of the UTM, an alert will be sent to the UTM operator to inform the corresponding UAS's GCS that they are reaching or exceeding a safety threshold of the system.

Sensor Bounds. Sensors and variables also have well defined *bounds* on the values they can return. For example, a UAS should never see latitude values that are meaningless (i.e., latitude measurements less than $-90°$ or greater than $90°$). These types of specifications may be used in conjunction with *Operating Range* specifications to help diagnose whether there is a user error (accidentally operating outside their airspace) or hardware failure (sensor returning bad data to the system).

Note that there is an implied $\Box$ operator outside all of the specifications due to the *stream-based* nature of R2U2 runtime observers. That is: R2U2 outputs a stream of verdicts indicating whether each specification holds starting at

Table 3. UAS, GCS, and UTM specifications investigated

Name	Description	MLTL Specification
UAS_RC_8	The difference between two consecutive pressure Pres readings cannot exceed a maximum rate of climb MaxPrevPres.	$\neg(\Box_{[0,3]}\neg(Pres\_leq\_MaxPrevPres \wedge Pres\_geq\_MinPrevPres))$
UAS_IS_1	Since the altimeter and the barometer both derive the air pressure, the error between these two measurements of pressure will be less than the MaxPresErr and greater than MinPresErr.	$(Pres\_lt\_MaxPresErr) \wedge (Pres\_gt\_MinPresErr)$
GCS_CS_7	The reference latitude LatWP and longitude LonWP will be contained within the set of waypoints given in the flight plan.	$wpLonLat\_eq\_fpLonLat$
GCS_PM_2	If a telemetry stream is reporting that the UAS's heading Ang is between 90° and 180°, then, if the UAS's velocity Vel is greater than 0 m/s, the UAS's latitude Lat should be decreasing while its longitude Lon should be increasing.	$\neg(Ang\_eq\_Quad4 \wedge Vel\_gt\_Zero) \vee (Lat\_geq\_PrevLat \wedge Lon\_geq\_PrevLon)$
UTM_OR_11	Every UAS's position will be bounded within the given airspace. All latitude Lat will be bounded between (41.6000°,41.6720°).	$\Box_{[0,3]}(Lat\_leq\_LatUB \wedge Lat\_geq\_LatLB)$
UTM_SB_3	Every UAS's position will exist on Earth GPS coordinates. All latitude Lat measurement's will be bounded by (−90°,90°) degrees.	$\Box_{[0,3]}(Lat\_leq\_MaxLatUB \wedge Lat\_geq\_MinLatLB)$

See http://temporallogic.org/research/DETECT2020/ for a compete set of specifications.

every discretized execution time stamp. Formally, $\forall i$, R2U2 gives a verdict as to whether $\pi, i \models \varphi$ in the form of a stream $\langle i, verdict \rangle$. So, even the purely propositional formulas are still asserting that a relationship holds, e.g., throughout a flight.

Rates of Change. Additionally, sensor's and variable's *rate of change* may also be bounded. For example, a UAS will have some maximum change in velocity between any two telemetry transmissions. Should it exceed this value, it may indicate that the UAS's transmission rate varied (e.g., a dropped transmission). Additionally, one could monitor to make sure there is change between two consecutive sensor measurements, or that the amount of variance between sensor measurements is not skewed in one direction or another, which could mean the UAS is under a cyber-attack, such as GPS spoofing.

Control Sequences. Because this system follows a rigorous series of stages, several specifications monitor that the system is adhering to its specified *con-*

trol sequence. For example, the intended sequence of states for the UTM is to: (1) receive a flight plan from a GCS, (2) approve or reject the flight plan, (3) if approved, issue the GCS a corresponding flight plan ID, and (4) the GCS transmits the telemetry data of the UAS with the corresponding flight plan ID. Many different hazardous situations can be made by removing or rearranging this intended sequence; thus, monitoring for any out-of-order sequences can help alert the system or the user to execute a mitigation action.

Physical Model Relationships. In many systems, there exist *physical relationships* between one or more combinations of sensors and actuators when commanding the system. For example, if a UAS is commanded to accelerate, the motors should respond accordingly to execute that command. These types of relationships can detect sensor calibration errors and ensure that sensors agree about the system's overall state.

Inter-sensor Relationships. To help diagnose failures, some systems may be able to invoke specifications that use multiple sensors, either of the same or different type, to measure common values. For example, the relationship between barometric pressure (obtained from an on-board barometer) and altitude (obtained from the GPS) allows for more than one way to measure altitude. RV can use these types of specifications to determine if both sensors agree. If they do not agree, then polling, or other system health management techniques, could be used to determine the faulty sensor and switch the primary source for the UAS altitude measurements.

4.3   Specification Validation

Because specification creation is a circular process [19], we chose to validate our list of RV specifications in a variety of ways. The first was a Matlab-based approach where we incorporated logged data for each subsystem into Matlab and validated the ways in which the Boolean atomics were created. The second was by uploading our MLTL runtime specifications for each individual subsystem into an open-source MLTL satisfiability checker [11] to perform specification debugging via checking each specification, its negation, and the conjunction of all specifications for satisfiability [21]. The third way these specifications were validated was by running the pre-recorded data into the R2U2 tool chain and checking to see if the specification held true over the system trace. If it did, we injected faults into the pre-recorded data and monitored R2U2's output to see if it correctly detected the faults. Of the list of 124 specifications we made for the UAS, GCS, and UTM, Table 3 presents six specifications that we feel encapsulate interesting properties about each subsystem.

5 Evaluation

The UTM test scenario consists of 20 UAS interacting with the UTM – OPL's Vapor 55 hardware-in-the-loop simulation and our 19 physics-based simulated flights – with the goal of testing the UTM's conflict detection logic. Of the 20 flight plans, 18 were conflict-free, one was designed to create a pre-departure conflict, and one deviated from the pre-approved flight plan, creating an en-route conflict. During the 42 min test, the UTM correctly detected and alerted both GCSs of the en-route conflict, with OPL's GCS submitting a new, conflict-free flight plan en-route.

Although we intended to have R2U2 embedded into the UTM system for this test, in practice this would have required enhancements to core functionalities and improving the networking capabilities of the UTM. However, all test data was recorded and put to use offline in refining our specifications and implementations of R2U2 into each subsystem. We argue that since R2U2 has previously been embedded and used in several successful aerospace applications [7,10,13,17,23], our offline, real-time simulations of this embedding perform representatively to an actual implementation. Note we plan to incorporate R2U2 into the UTM system for the next test.

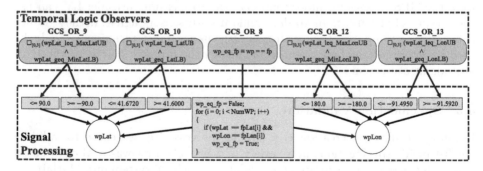

Fig. 2. A small observation tree from the GCS's R2U2 implementation. Two sensor values, `wpLat` and `wpLon`, are inputs to the signal processing layer, which pre-processes them into Boolean atomics for the temporal logic observers.

R2U2 was hosted on a Ubuntu 18.04 LTS operating system on an Intel Core i7-4810MQ CPU with a 2.80 GHz clock and 16 GB of RAM. Each subsystem of R2U2 was run independently, i.e., each subsystem was run with its own instance of R2U2 across its own input trace and no cross-platform communication was performed. Figure 2 shows an example of how specifications are encoded into R2U2's observations trees.

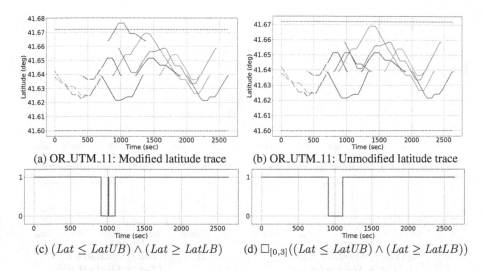

Fig. 3. Two instances of the UTM's R2U2 monitoring: a modified run (a) where one UAS (purple) temporarily exceeds the operating range bounds, and an unmodified run (b) where all UAS lie within the operating range (dashed lines). Both fault-injected runs show R2U2 identifies the corresponding violation of the specification; however, the output of the purely Boolean formula (c) bounces due to a missed telemetry transmission. To avoid a false positive, due to missing data, we add a temporal logic filter (d) that monitors for multiple subsequent nominal data sequences. (Color figure online)

Operating Range. As seen from Fig. 3, the UTM's R2U2 monitors and reports if the operating range bounds are satisfied for all of UAS's latitude measurements. As the original test data was fault-free, we injected a fault, which revealed a sudden spike in R2U2's output during the injected fault. This corresponds to a dropped transmission in the original data. Thus, we refine our specification to include an overarching $\Box_{[0,3]}$ operator, which acts as a sliding window temporal filter, to suppresses such output bouncing.

Sensor Bounds. Similar to Fig. 3, Fig. 4 shows the UTM's R2U2 monitoring and reporting if any of the UAS's latitude measurements exceed the sensor bound threshold of $(-90°, 90°)$. Similarly, the original data was fault free, so we injected a fault into one of the UAS's latitude measurements. Again, testing revealed transmission losses, so we added a $\Box_{[0,3]}$ filter to suppress any false positives triggered by missing data.

Rates of Change. The pressure recorded by a UAS's on-board barometer changes as it ascends and descends. Thus, we developed a specification to monitor change in pressure: the difference between two consecutive pressure readings are limited to ± 0.4 hPa (derived from the maximum rates of climb and descent

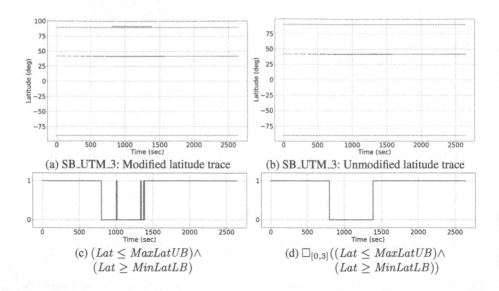

Fig. 4. Like Fig. 3, the top graphs show modified (a) and unmodified (b) input traces. Similarly, dropped telemetry transmissions cause output bouncing (c), so a $\Box_{[0,3]}$ filter is applied (d). (Color figure online)

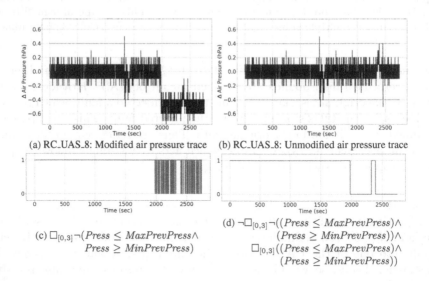

Fig. 5. Two instances of the UAS's R2U2 monitoring: (a) a modified trace where we injected a shift in the air pressure's rate of change, and (b) an unmodified trace where a few anomalies exceed the pressure rate of change bounds (dashed lines). Both outputs of the fault-injected run from R2U2 are shown; however, the output of the original formula (c) bounces due to noisy input jumping back within the margins. To remove this bouncing, we added another $\Box_{[0,3]}$ filter (d) to keep the current state until all outliers are filtered and the state has unquestionably changed. (Color figure online)

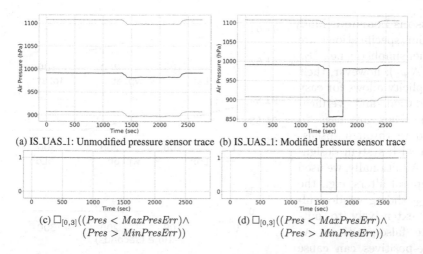

(a) IS_UAS_1: Unmodified pressure sensor trace (b) IS_UAS_1: Modified pressure sensor trace

(c) $\Box_{[0,3]}((Pres < MaxPresErr)\wedge$
$(Pres > MinPresErr))$

(d) $\Box_{[0,3]}((Pres < MaxPresErr)\wedge$
$(Pres > MinPresErr))$

Fig. 6. Two instances of the UAS's R2U2 monitoring: an unmodified run (a) where the pressure from the barometer remains within the error margins of the GPS's calculated atmospheric pressure (dashed lines), and a modified run (b) where the same data was injected with a fault by subtracting 100hPa from the barometer's atmospheric pressure reading. R2U2's output (c) acknowledges the error-free trace of (a), and (d) shows that R2U2 detects the violation from (b). (Color figure online)

[15]). Unlike our other specifications, Fig. 5 shows that we needed to include a conjunction of two $\Box_{[0,3]}$ filters to remove all output bouncing: one filters outlying violating verdicts and one filters outlying satisfying verdicts.

Control Sequence. The UTM's test scenario included one UAS deviating from its pre-approved flight plan. Figure 7 shows R2U2 correctly detecting this real-world deviation in real time.

Inter-sensor Relationship. The difference between the barometer's and GPS's pressure should be bounded within acceptable error. A comparison of the two sensors can help diagnose sensor failures (see [15] for more details). For example, Fig. 6 shows a side-by-side comparison of two pressure traces: an unmodified and a modified version with a fault injected from $t = 1500$ to $t = 1750$.

Physical Model Relationship. As shown in Fig. 8, when a UAS's heading is between 90° and 180° and its velocity is non-zero, then the UAS's latitude should be decreasing while its longitude is increasing.

Lessons Learned. Many of our specifications are rather simplistic, i.e., $\Box_{[0,3]}$ $(\varphi_1 \wedge \varphi_2)$; however, their simplicity allows for easy validation and verification. They are easy to validate through discussion with system designers. Additionally, we used temporal filters, e.g., the $\Box_{[0,3]}$ sliding window filter, extensively to mitigate false-positives. As false-positives can cause mistrust of the RV monitor, we built our specifications to err on the side of missing a fault. As seen in Sect. 5, if R2U2 sent a fault alert, the fault was clear for the human operators receiving the alert.

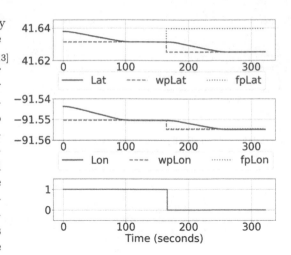

Fig. 7. The latitude (top) and longitude (middle) traces for an adversarial UAS, showing that the GCS is commanding it to a different waypoint (red, dashed line) instead of one from its approved flight plan (green, dotted line). Corresponding to the violation of CS_GCS_7 (Table 3), R2U2's output (bottom) shows it successfully detects this real-world fault. (Color figure online)

Many of our specifications encapsulate intuitive bounds and relationships for sensor values and variables that humans implicitly assume about a given system, i.e., latitude coordinates are bounded between $(-90°, 90°)$ and that events cannot end before they start. These "common-sense" specifications are often overlooked, yet they catch real faults, e.g., from variable overflow and underflow, sensor or wiring failures, and excessive noise. Our coverage categorization for specifications allowed us to enumerate many such sanity checks about the UTM system, which helped us achieve a reasonable covering set of specifications for the UTM's three sub-systems. In practice, this lead to R2U2 identifying a real-life fault where a data-translation error caused the UTM to register flight plans that ended before they started. Such an error would be obvious to human controllers but automated systems require RV to flag this impossibility. Future work is aimed toward creating automated tools for specification elicitation.

6   Conclusion

Before UAS can integrate into the NAS, we need to establish a provably safe, intelligent, and automated UTM system. To help facilitate this, we have integrated the state-of-the-art runtime verification tool R2U2 across the three different layers of an actual UTM implemen-

tation: on-board the individual UAS, in conjunction with each operator's GCS, and embedded into a centralized, cloud-based UTM server.
By validating and releas-
ing over 100 runtime
MLTL specifications, two
sets of recorded traces
from test flights of a
real-life UTM implemen-
tation, and the results
of checking those formu-
las, we contribute a large
benchmark suite. This
suite is useful for verification of the algorithms
and implementations of
future RV tools, provid-
ing both nominal and
faulty traces and realis-
tic sensor noise and out-
lier readings that chal-
lenge RV engines.

Additionally, we exem-
plify the real-world challenges of implementing
RV into a centralized,
high-traffic UTM. We

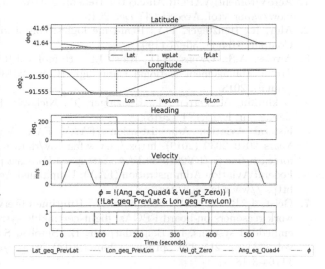

Fig. 8. Single instance of R2U2 on a simulated UAS
showing the latitude, longitude, heading, and velocity.
With assumptions of the UAS operating in North Amer-
ica and there is a relationship between heading and trajectory, then a relationship between velocity, heading,
and position can be verified. (Color figure online)

demonstrate real-time performance of extending MLTL formulas with a single first-order operator, where we validate whether a specification holds *for all*
UAS or if *there exists* a UAS that violates a specification. When refining our
specification set, we found sensor noise and outliers triggered false positives and
that a simple $\square_{[0,3]}$ around each critical sensor check eliminated these while only
slightly delaying the trigger of actual faults. Of our 124 specifications, two-thirds
contain this construct. This modification can be automatically inserted into specifications for real-life systems where false positives cannot be tolerated. Though
we verified a short (42 min) relatively small real-life system (26, 33-64, and 634
sensor inputs for the UAS, GCS, and UTM, respectively) we still found it hard
to manually write a sufficiently covering set of specifications. To ensure we did
not miss covering unstated assumptions, we used coverage metrics to brainstorm
our list of 124 specifications: variable coverage (every variable appears in at least
one specification) and pattern coverage (specifications follow each pattern from
[19]). Our experience informs an on-going project to enable more automated
specification elicitation.

References

1. AeroViroment: VAPOR All-electric Helicopter UAS. https://www.avinc.com/uas/view/vapor-vtol. Accessed 17 Dec 2019
2. Alur, R., Henzinger, T.A.: Real-time logics: complexity and expressiveness. Inf. Comput. **104**(1), 35–77 (1993)
3. Aweiss, A.S., Owens, B.D., Rios, J.L., Homola, J.R., Mohlenbrink, C.P.: UAS Traffic Management National Campaign II. In: 2018 AIAA SciTech, pp. 1–16, January 2018
4. Bakhirkin, A., Ferrère, T., Henzinger, T., Nickovic, D.: The first-order logic of signals. In: EMSOFT (2018)
5. Federal Aviation Administration (FAA): FAA Aerospace Forecast - Fiscal Years 2019–2039 (2019). https://www.faa.gov/data_research/aviation/aerospace_forecasts/media/FY2019-39_FAA_Aerospace_Forecast.pdf
6. Federal Aviation Administration (FAA): Unmanned Aerial Systems (UAS) (2020). https://www.faa.gov/uas/
7. Geist, J., Rozier, K.Y., Schumann, J.: Runtime observer pairs and bayesian network reasoners on-board FPGAs: flight-certifiable system health management for embedded systems. In: Bonakdarpour, B., Smolka, S.A. (eds.) RV 2014. LNCS, vol. 8734, pp. 215–230. Springer, Cham (2014). https://doi.org/10.1007/978-3-319-11164-3_18
8. Havelund, K., Peled, D., Ulus, D.: First order temporal logic monitoring with BDDs. In: FMCAD, pp. 116–123 (2017)
9. Hunter, G., Wei, P.: Service-oriented separation assurance for small UAS traffic management. In: INCS19, pp. 1–11 (2019)
10. Kempa, B., Zhang, P., Jones, P.H., Zambreno, J., Rozier, K.Y.: Embedding online runtime verification for fault disambiguation on Robonaut2. In: Bertrand, N., Jansen, N. (eds.) FORMATS. LNCS, pp. 196–214. Springer, Cham (2020). https://doi.org/10.1007/978-3-030-57628-8_12
11. Li, J., Vardi, M.Y., Rozier, K.Y.: Satisfiability checking for mission-time LTL. In: Dillig, I., Tasiran, S. (eds.) CAV 2019. LNCS, vol. 11562, pp. 3–22. Springer, Cham (2019). https://doi.org/10.1007/978-3-030-25543-5_1
12. The international conference on runtime verification. https://www.runtime-verification.org/ (2001-present)
13. Moosbrugger, P., Rozier, K.Y., Schumann, J.: R2U2: monitoring and diagnosis of security threats for unmanned aerial systems. In: FMSD, pp. 1–31, April 2017
14. NASA: Unmanned Aircraft System (UAS) Traffic Management (UTM). https://utm.arc.nasa.gov/index.shtml. Accessed 12 Mar 2020
15. NASA: Earth atmosphere model, May 2015. https://www.grc.nasa.gov/WWW/K-12/airplane/atmosmet.html
16. Pike, L., Wegmann, N., Niller, S., Goodloe, A.: Copilot: monitoring embedded systems. Innovations Syst. Softw. Eng. **9**(4), 235–255 (2013). https://doi.org/10.1007/s11334-013-0223-x
17. Reinbacher, T., Rozier, K.Y., Schumann, J.: Temporal-logic based runtime observer pairs for system health management of real-time systems. In: TACAS, pp. 357–372 (2014)
18. Rios, J., Mulfinger, D., Homola, J., Venkatesan, P.: NASA UAS traffic management national campaign: operations across Six UAS Test Sites. In: DASC, pp. 1–6 (2016)
19. Rozier, K.Y.: Specification: the biggest bottleneck in formal methods and autonomy. In: Blazy, S., Chechik, M. (eds.) VSTTE 2016. LNCS, vol. 9971, pp. 8–26. Springer, Cham (2016). https://doi.org/10.1007/978-3-319-48869-1_2

20. Rozier, K.Y., Schumann, J.: R2U2: tool overview. In: RV-CUBES, Seattle, WA, USA, vol. 3, pp. 138–156. Kalpa Publications, September 2017
21. Rozier, K.Y., Vardi, M.Y.: LTL satisfiability checking. Int. J. Softw. Tools Technol. Transfer (STTT) **12**(2), 123–137 (2010)
22. Schirmer, S.: Runtime monitoring with LOLA. Master's thesis, Saarland University, November 2016. https://elib.dlr.de/113126/
23. Schumann, J., Rozier, K.Y., Reinbacher, T., Mengshoel, O.J., Mbaya, T., Ippolito, C.: Towards real-time, on-board, hardware-supported sensor and software health management for unmanned aerial systems. IJPHM **6**(1), 1–27 (2015)
24. Wargo, C.A., et al.: Ubiquitous surveillance notional architecture for system-wide DAA capabilities in the NAS. In: 2018 IEEE Aerospace Conference, pp. 1–14 (2018)
25. Wei, P., Atkins, E.M., Hunter, G., Rozier, K.Y., Schnell, T.: Pre-Departure Dynamic Geofencing, En-Route Traffic Alerting, Emergency Landing and Contingency Management for Intelligent Low-Altitude Airspace UAS Traffic Management, July 2017. https://www.nsf.gov/awardsearch/showAward?AWD_ID=1718420
26. Zhao, Y., Rozier, K.Y.: Formal specification and verification of a coordination protocol for an automated air traffic control system. Sci. Comput. Program. **96**, 337–353 (2014)
27. Zhu, G., Wei, P.: Low-altitude UAS traffic coordination with dynamic geofencing. In: 16th AIAA Aviation Technology, Integration, and Operations Conference, June 2016

Dependability of Model-Driven Executable DSLs
Critical Review and Solutions

Akram Idani[(✉)][iD]

Univ. Grenoble Alpes, CNRS, LIG, 38000 Grenoble, France
Akram.Idani@univ-grenoble-alpes.fr

Abstract. One of the promising techniques to address the dependability of a system is to apply, at early design stages, domain specific languages (DSLs) with execution semantics. Indeed, an executable DSL would not only represent the expected system's structure but it is intended to itself behave as the system should run. However, in order to make executable DSLs a powerful asset in the development of safety-critical systems, not only a rigorous development process is required but the domain expert should also have confidence in the execution semantics provided by the DSL developer. The challenge addressed in this paper is then to verify whether execution semantics provided by Model-Driven Engineering (MDE) tools comply with the expected behaviour of a given DSL. We experimented existing MDE approaches with associated implementations (QVT, Kermeta, fUML), in order to debug a safety-critical system. This paper presents the lessons learned from this study and provides formal alternatives, based on the B method and CSP process algebra, which are well-established techniques allowing interactive animation on the one hand and reasoning on the behaviour correctness, on the other hand.

Keywords: B Method · Domain specific languages · MDE

1 Introduction

The Model Driven Engineering (MDE) paradigm suggests solutions to the two major problems of software development: (1) the software complexity, and (2) the gap between conceptual models and coding activities. Indeed, on the one hand, MDE advocates for the use of models throughout the engineering life-cycle in order to reduce complexity, and on the other hand, it is assisted by numerous tools (*e.g.* EMF[1], Xtext[2], ATL[3]) dedicated to a clear separation of concerns ranging from requirements to target platforms, and going through several design stages. Interoperability between these tools is favored by the use of standardized meta-modeling formalisms which increases automation especially for developing

---

[1] https://www.eclipse.org/modeling/emf/.
[2] https://www.eclipse.org/Xtext/.
[3] http://www.eclipse.org/atl/.

© Springer Nature Switzerland AG 2020
H. Muccini et al. (Eds.): ECSA 2020, CCIS 1269, pp. 358–373, 2020.
https://doi.org/10.1007/978-3-030-59155-7_27

domain specific languages (called DSLs). In the last decade, several research works have been devoted in order to enhance DSLs by underlying operational semantics which makes them executable. One of the major advantages of executing a DSL is to provide abstractions of the system's behavior and hence allow the domain expert to perform early analysis of the expected system. Indeed, an executable DSL can be simulated and debugged by existing MDE-based tools (*e.g.* the Gemoc Studio[4]) leading to a better quality than a static DSL. Unfortunately, although these advantages show that executable DSLs are a promising paradigm, several issues related to correctness and the level of trust that one can have in execution engines are still challenges for a rigorous development process.

In this paper, we lead an experimental study built on the Petri-net DSL as it is developed by existing works [1,8,10,11] that applied MDE frameworks such as xMOF-fUML, QVT and Gemoc-Kermeta in order to address operational semantics and corresponding simulation/debugging activities. We tried their Petri-net DSLs to debug a safety-critical system and check their ability to address properties such as: correctness, deadlock-freedom, mutual exclusion and fairness. This paper presents a critical review and lessons learned from this study and provides formal alternatives, based on the B method and CSP[5] process algebra, which are well-established techniques allowing interactive animation on the one hand and reasoning on the behaviour correctness, on the other hand.

Section 2 describes the DSL on which we have built our experimental study and gives an overview about tools of our benchmark. Section 3 applies and compares algorithms as they are encoded in existing works for debugging a safety-critical model from the domain expert point of view. In Sect. 4 we provide a formal solution for the definition of execution semantics. Finally, Sect. 5 draws the conclusions and the perspectives of this work.

2   The Petri-Net DSL

In this paper, our case study is that of running Petri-nets. Petri-net is a visual language used for modeling concurrent systems. Its mathematical foundations inspired by the graph theory allow formal calculus about safety properties. The choice of this DSL is motivated by the fact that it was widely addressed by the research works interested in modeling and debugging techniques. This section presents structural and contextual constraints of this DSL as well as its execution semantics and defines a simple safety-critical Petri-net example.

2.1   Structural and Contextual Semantics

Figure 1 shows the Petri-net meta-model as considered by [1][6]. It is composed of three meta-classes: Net (the root class), Place and Transition. These classes are linked by four relationships: places, transitions, input and output.

---

[4] http://gemoc.org/.

[5] CSP: Communicating Sequential Processes.

[6] The ecore file can be found at: https://github.com/gemoc/petrinet/blob/master/
petrinetv1/fr.inria.diverse.sample.petrinetv1.model/model/petrinetv1.ecore.

360   A. Idani

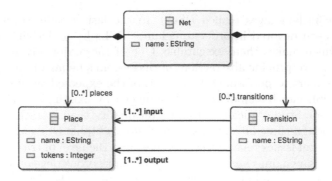

Fig. 1. Petri-nets meta-model

This meta-model defines structural properties of a given Petri-net. For instance, a Transition must be linked to at least one input place and one output place. Attribute tokens represents the number of tokens in a place: it is mono-valuated, optional and without a default initial value. The various references of this meta-model do not admit repetitions. Note that the meta-model is taken from [1] and it is presented without any modification. Furthermore, the DSL must comply with the following contextual invariant written in OCL:

```
context Place inv Token_Is_Natural: self.tokens ≥ 0
```

For illustration we use the simple Petri-net of Fig. 2 which is dedicated to control traffic lights in a crossroads. This model deals with a safety-critical system since failures may lead to loss of life due to accidents that it may cause.

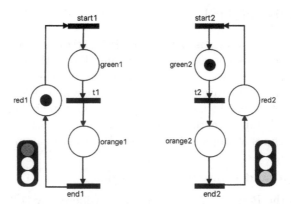

Fig. 2. Traffic light controller in Petri-nets (V1)

The domain expert needs then to have confidence in the provided operational semantics of the Petri-net DSL in order to prove that his model guarantees safety properties such as:

- correctness: asserts that the system does not exhibit bad behaviors, where invariants (structural or contextual) are violated.
- deadlock-freedom: states that the traffic lights can't be blocked in a state in which no progress is possible
- mutual exclusion: states that lights in a road intersection cannot enter simultaneously their critical sections (critical sections are states green and orange in our example).
- fairness: requires that the system gives fair turns to its components (in our example both lights must be able to function).

Model of Fig. 2 deals with two traffic lights (Light A and Light B) which are to be placed in two roads that intersect. Light A and Light B are respectively controlled by the left hand-side and the right hand-side of this figure. Every traffic light sequentially switches from Green to Orange and then to Red, in an infinite loop. This Petri-net model shows concurrent evolutions of traffic lights without any synchronisation between them. Finally, the current state of this model assigns red to Light A and green to Light B.

In this paper we apply existing MDE approaches [1,8,10,11], with associated implementations, in order to debug the traffic light controller especially from the domain expert point of view. The intention is to check the ability of these MDE tools to address safety properties as those mentioned above.

2.2 Execution Semantics

Basic Petri-nets execution semantics are defined by transition firing that holds when a transition satisfies an enabledness property. To check this property, existing MDE techniques call a query defined as:

```
query isEnabled(t : Transition) : Boolean =
    t.input->forAll(p : Place | p.tokens > 0)
```

This query returns true if attribute tokens is greater than 0 for each input place of transition t, false otherwise. Algorithm of Fig. 3, taken from [1], describes how a Petri-net runs. This algorithm chooses non-deterministically a transition t (called $t_{enabled}$) from the set of transitions that satisfy the above property and then calls operation fire(t). As a result, the number of tokens in the input places of t is decreased (operation removeToken) and the number of tokens in the output places is increased (operation addToken). Modifications of tokens, done at every call to operation fire, evolve the set of enabled transitions and then the algorithm may loop or stop when this set becomes empty.

2.3 Benchmark Overview

In order to address safety properties using existing MDE-based Petri-net DSLs, our study applies various approaches which are based on different languages (QVT, Kermeta and fUML). In the remainder, we call these approaches respectively PNet$_{QVT}$, PNet$_{Kermeta}$ and PNet$_{fUML}$.

Algorithm 1: run

Input:

n : the Net object to run

[1] **begin**

[2] $t_{enabled} :\in \{t \in n.\texttt{transitions} \mid isEnabled(t)\}$

[3]   **while** $t_{enabled} \neq null$ **do**

[4] $fire(t_{enabled})$

[5] $t_{enabled} :\in \{t \in n.\texttt{transitions} \mid isEnabled(t)\}$

Algorithm 2: fire

Input:

t : the Transition object to fire

[1] **begin**

[2]   **foreach** $p \in t.\texttt{input}$ **do**

[3] $removeToken(p)$

[4]   **foreach** $p \in t.\texttt{output}$ **do**

[5] $addToken(p)$

Fig. 3. Running a Petri-net [1]

1. PNet$_{QVT}$ [11]: QVT (Query/View/Transformation) is an OMG[7] standard for model transformations. QVT defines: QVT-Relations and QVT-Core which are declarative languages but at two different levels of abstraction, and QVT-Operational which is an imperative language. In [11], the authors used QVT-Relations which is the high-level language of QVT extending OCL and its semantics with imperative features. Unfortunately, there is a lack of tools supporting QVT-Relations. Indeed, the tools that we found are either out of date (Medini QVT) or proprietary (ModelMorf). Then, for our benchmark needs, we encoded a variant of rules proposed by [11] in QVT-Operational using the Eclipse EMF framework.

2. PNet$_{Kermeta}$ [1]: Kermeta [7] is a language workbench that involves different meta-languages for abstract syntax (aligned with EMOF [4]), static semantics (aligned with OCL) and behavioural semantics (via an action language also called Kermeta). In [1], the Gemoc studio was applied together with the Kermeta language to define the Petri-net DSL and debug its execution using an animation technique. In our benchmark we used source-code issued from the Gemoc website: https://github.com/gemoc/petrinet/blob/master/petrinetv1/.

3. PNet$_{fUML}$ [8,10]: fUML is an OMG standard that defines the execution semantics of a subset of UML 2.3. The standard applies, in the form of pseudo Java-code, a basic virtual machine enabling UML models using elements comprised in the fUML subset to be executed. [10] proposes the xMOF tool which integrates fUML with MOF to enable the specification of the behavioural

---

[7] OMG: Object Management Group (https://www.omg.org).

semantics of DSMLs in terms of fUML activities. For our experiments we used the open-source DSL, provided at: https://modelexecution.org/moliz/xmof/.

The above tools use the Eclipse Modeling Framework (EMF), which makes easy their integration and the analysis of the Petri-net DSLs that they provide within a unified framework. Note that their underlying approaches agree on operations fire, addToken and removeToken. However, they differ from each other by: (1) the level of abstraction depending on (meta-)programming languages, (2) the semantics associated to the non-deterministic choice of enabled transitions, and (3) the execution engine.

3   Debugging the Traffic-Light Model

In this section we apply and compare the works of our benchmark for debugging the traffic-light model from the domain expert point of view.

3.1   Results

Starting from the initial state of Fig. 2, PNet$_{QVT}$, PNet$_{fUML}$ and PNet$_{Kermeta}$ produced the same execution trace (Fig. 4) showing that only Light A is functioning. Curiously the transition firing sequence was: $(start1; \quad t1; \quad end1)^+$.

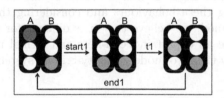

Fig. 4. First execution of the traffic light Petri-net

Often the end user or the domain expert does not have any knowledge about how the Petri-net semantics are encoded, that is why we tried again these tools starting from a more intuitive initial state where lights are set to red. In this second execution, PNet$_{Kermeta}$ and PNet$_{fUML}$ have had the same behaviour than that they exhibited in the previous case but with Light B left in state Red. PNet$_{QVT}$ produced a different trace, presented in Fig. 5:

$$(start1; \quad t1; \quad start2; \quad end1); \quad (start1; \quad t1; \quad end1)^+$$

In this behaviour light B is switched to green after Light A passed to orange and then after firing transition $end1$ the system is engaged in a loop similar to that of Fig. 4. Based on these behaviours it is difficult to conclude about safety properties: dead-lock freedom, mutual exclusion and fairness. In the first

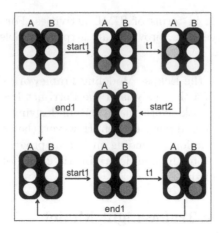

Fig. 5. Second execution of the traffic light Petrinet

execution of PNet$_{Kermeta}$ and PNet$_{fUML}$ both lights reached their critical sections together (middle state of Fig. 4), which violates the mutual exclusion property. Nonetheless, from the second execution one can conclude that this property is satisfied, which is obviously contradictory with the first execution. In the same sense, these two executions show a dead-lock freedom since the corresponding traces did not reach a blocking state, but they show too that the fairness property is not guaranteed since Light B didn't evolve at all, which is also somehow contradictory. Having these behaviours and considering that the semantics of Petri-nets is well-defined, we believe that it is difficult for the end-user − who should be in our case an expert in Petri-nets and formal methods − to adopt these tools and apply them to model a safety-critical system.

3.2   Analysis

In order to explain these behaviours we analysed the source code of our benchmark tools and we found that they do not choose in the same way the enabled transition. Indeed, in our reference algorithm the choice of the transition to fire is non-deterministic, which is not the case for these tools.

Indeterminism in PNet$_{fUML}$ and PNet$_{Kermeta}$: PNet$_{fUML}$ and PNet$_{Kermeta}$ applied a deterministic principle in which the first transition satisfying query isEnabled is fired. In PNet$_{fUML}$ [10] it is stated that: *"The run() operation repeatedly determines a list of enabled Transitions, ..., and calls fire() for the **first** Transition in this list.".* PNet$_{Kermeta}$ source code uses the following instruction in the context of class Net:

```
transitions.findFirst[t|t.isEnabled]
```

The limitation is that collection **transitions** issued from class Net is filled sequentially depending on the order on which the modeling elements are created by the designer. In fact, in EMF references are typed by the EList data structure whose semantics are different from the Set data-structure. Actually for Fig. 2 we created the left hand side (that of Light A) before the right hand side (that of Light B) and hence we get a malfunction of Light B. Based on this observation we changed the order of transitions in the XMI file of the model, and then we get a different behaviour. We think that it is not a judicious choice to condition the DSL behaviour by the order on which modeling elements are created because it may be confusing for the domain expert. Moreover, DSL behaviour variations depending on the XMI file content would not reflect at all the behaviour of the target system, which weakens the debugging functions dedicated to a Petri-net based safety-critical controller.

Indeterminism in PNet$_{QVT}$: In PNet$_{QVT}$, the enabled transition is provided by the following OCL-based query:

```
query getActivated(net: Net): Transition {
        net.transitions -> any(trans | isActivated(trans))
}
```

Semantics of the "any" construct in OCL [3] (section 11.9, page 177) are defined as: "*Returns any element in the source collection for which body evaluates to true... If there are one or more elements for which body is true, an indeterminate choice of one of them is returned*". In the OCL reference manual the operator "any" is rewritten as follows:

```
Set->any(iterator | body) =
   Set->select(iterator | body)->asSequence()->first()
```

Conversion from Set to Sequence is non-deterministic because type set does not cover ordering. However, the EMF/OCL package uses the java structure HashSet[8] for the OCL type Set. Unfortunately, elements of a HashSet are dispersed by means of a hashing function which is called every time a modification operation (*e.g.* add, remove) is applied to the HashSet. Since in our example, the set of transitions is never modified, then this dispersion is not recomputed and the asSequence() operation always produced the same result. The HashSet dispersion produced from our initial Petri-net (Fig. 2) is:

$$[start1, t1, start2, end2, end1, t2]$$

This dispersion allows to understand the weird behaviours of the traffic light. Indeed, in the initial state, the set of enabled transitions gathers $start1$ and $t2$ and hence asSequence()->first() gets $start1$. Then, the same algorithm is applied producing a call to $t1$ followed by $end1$. Transition $t2$ would never be fired because in this dispersion it appears after transition $end1$ which brings back the model to the initial state. The similarity between the output of PNet$_{QVT}$ and that of both PNet$_{fUML}$ and PNet$_{Kermeta}$ when Light A is red and Light B is green is hence a pure luck. This behaviour is not only unsuitable towards a

---

[8] HashSet is an implementation of interface Set in Java.

non-deterministic executable DSL but also dangerous because the failure comes from the execution engine not from the semantics. This failure may reduce the confidence that a domain expert may have in the DSL execution engine. Indeed, besides human errors, it is known that execution engines are the most critical parts in safety-critical systems; that is why several standards exist in order to reduce their capabilities to controllable structures and functions.

4   Formal DSL Semantics: The Meeduse Technique

The disparity between execution tools leads to behaviours that are conformant to the semantics specified by their execution models but may be far from the expected behaviour in accordance with the domain expertise. This is an important problem since the same model may not be executed in the same way on different tools even for deterministic structures. In fact, when designing a model via a given DSL tool, the domain expert focuses on debugging his model rather than debugging the DSL semantics provided by the MDE expert.

We propose an alternative definition of the Petri-net semantics using Meeduse [6], a tool that we developed in order to mix the formal B method and EMF-based DSLs. The use of a well-established formal approach assisted by provers and model-checkers, guarantees the consistency of the Petri-net DSL and its conformance to the expected behaviour. This formal reference model allows then to establish what goes well and wrong in the considered benchmark and can be useful for further improvements of existing DSL definition tools.

4.1   Functional Model

In order to get a functional B specification conformant to the Petri-net meta-model, Meeduse[9] [6] translates the meta-model into a correct by design B specification. Figure 6 gives the heading part of the generated B machine.

```
1. MACHINE
2.     nets
3. SETS
4.     NET; PLACE; TRANSITION
5. ABSTRACT_VARIABLES
6.     Net, Place, Transition,
7.     places, input,
8.     output, transitions, Place_tokens
```

Fig. 6. Heading part of the Petri-nets machine

Every meta-class leads to an abstract set (*e.g.* TRANSITION) and an abstract variable (*e.g.* Transition) which respectively represent the possible

---

[9] Meeduse: http://vasco.imag.fr/tools/meeduse/.

instances and the existing instances of the meta-class. Associations and class attributes lead to variables (*e.g.* places, transitions, etc.). The invariant properties generated by Meeduse are provided in Fig. 7.

9. **INVARIANT**
10. $Net \in \mathcal{F}\ (NET)$
11. $\wedge\ Place \in \mathcal{F}\ (PLACE)$
12. $\wedge\ Transition \in \mathcal{F}\ (TRANSITION)$
13. $\wedge\ places \in Place \twoheadrightarrow Net$
14. $\wedge\ input \in Place \leftrightarrow Transition$
15. $\wedge\ output \in Place \leftrightarrow Transition$
16. $\wedge\ transitions \in Transition \twoheadrightarrow Net$
17. $\wedge\ Place\_tokens \in Place \twoheadrightarrow \mathbf{NAT}$
18. $\wedge\ \mathbf{ran}(input) = Transition$
19. $\wedge\ \mathbf{ran}(output) = Transition$
20. $\wedge\ \forall\ transition \cdot (transition \in \mathbf{ran}(input)$
21. $\Rightarrow input^{-1}\ [\{transition\}] \neq \emptyset\ )$
22. $\wedge\ \forall\ transition \cdot (transition \in \mathbf{ran}(output)$
23. $\Rightarrow output^{-1}\ [\{transition\}] \neq \emptyset\ )$

Fig. 7. Invariant of the Petri-nets machine

This invariant covers structural properties defined by multiplicities and the optional/mandatory character of attributes, as well as contextual constraints like the `Token_Is_Natural` invariant. For example, predicates from line (18.) to line (23.) of Fig. 7 translate multiplicities 1..* associated to references input and output. Attribute tokens, which is single-valued, optional and defined over the set of natural numbers, is translated into a partial function from set Place to the B type NAT (line (17.)).

Tools such as those of our benchmark produce an implementation from a meta-model gathering all basic operations (setters, getters, etc.) and Meeduse generates a B machine gathering similar basic operations but which are written in a theory (set theory, first order predicate logic and generalized substitutions) allowing to carry out proof of correctness. Figure 8 shows the basic setter of attribute `tokens`.

For this specification, Meeduse produced 24 operations and the AtelierB (http://www.atelierb.eu/en/) prover generated 74 proof obligations (POs) for which it was able to automatically prove 62. The 12 other POs were proved manually without improvements of the B specifications.

4.2   Execution Operations

Execution semantics often introduces complex modifications of the domain model. They may create or destroy objects, modify relationships between these objects and also update several class attributes. We are then afraid that the

$$
\begin{array}{|l|}
\hline
\textbf{Place\_SetTokens}(aPlace,\ val) = \\
\textbf{PRE} \\
\quad aPlace \in Place \land val \in \textbf{NAT} \\
\textbf{THEN} \\
\quad Place\_tokens := \\
\qquad (\{aPlace\} \lhd Place\_tokens) \cup \{(aPlace \mapsto val)\} \\
\textbf{END} \\
\hline
\end{array}
$$

Fig. 8. Basic setter of attribute tokens

difficulty in applying executable DSLs in safety-critical systems goes beyond the problem of indeterminism exhibited from our benchmark. We need a clear separation of concerns regarding properties to verify: (1) that of the meta-model with associated modeling operations, (2) that of the execution utility operations (*e.g.* addToken and removeToken), and (3) that of the coordination mechanism (*e.g.* operations fire and run of Fig. 3).

We introduce the execution semantics of the Petri-net DSL by a set of B operations shared in a machine that includes the functional machine. As the Petri-net running algorithm iterates over input and output places of a transition, we add operation getPlaces (Fig. 9) in order to return these sets given a transition tt. Operation getEnabled is a formalisation of query isEnabled presented in Sect. 2.2. The enabledness property of a transition tt should not only be based on the positive value of tokens (relation Place_tokens) for all input places ($input^{-1}[\{tt\}]$) but must also take into account the upper limit of this attribute for all output places ($output^{-1}[\{tt\}]$):

(P1) $Place\_Tokens[input^{-1}[\{tt\}]] \cap \{0\} = \emptyset$
(P2) $Place\_Tokens[output^{-1}[\{t\}]] \cap \{MAXINT\} = \emptyset$

Precondition (P1) is not sufficient because we would like to safely increase the number of tokens in output places. Without precondition (P2), the Petri-net controller may then reach a state in which a transition is enabled, and the tokens in its input places are consumed without producing tokens in the output

$$
\begin{array}{|l|l|}
\hline
tEnabled \leftarrow \textbf{getEnabled} = & src,\ trg \leftarrow getPlaces(tt) = \\
\textbf{ANY}\ tt\ \textbf{WHERE} & \textbf{PRE} \\
\quad tt \in Transition \land & \quad tt \in Transition \\
\quad \{0\} \cap Place\_tokens[input^{-1}[\{tt\}]] = \emptyset \land & \textbf{THEN} \\
\quad \{\textbf{MAXINT}\} \cap Place\_tokens[output^{-1}[\{tt\}]] = \emptyset & \quad src := input^{-1}[\{tt\}] \\
\textbf{THEN} & \quad \|\ trg := output^{-1}[\{tt\}] \\
\quad tEnabled := tt & \textbf{END}; \\
\textbf{END}; & \\
\hline
\end{array}
$$

Fig. 9. Operations getEnabled and getPlaces

places. This would lead to an inconsistent Petri-net because consumption and production of tokens should not be dissociated. Both preconditions are then required in order to be able to call both addToken and removeToken when a transition is enabled.

Figure 10 gives the B specification of operation addToken (operation remove-Token is somehow similar). Note that AtelierB discharged four proof obligations from this machine (two POs for the setter call, and two additional POs for the well-definedness of *Place_Tokens(pp)*) and it was able to prove them automatically.

---

addToken(*pp*) =
PRE
    pp ∈ *Place* ∧ *pp* ∈ **dom**(*Place_tokens*) ∧
    Place_tokens(*pp*) < **MAXINT**
THEN
    Place_SetTokens(*pp*, *Place_tokens*(*pp*) + 1)
END ;

Fig. 10. Operation addToken

4.3 Semantics Coordination

In order to keep reasoning at a high abstraction level, operations run and fire presented as algorithms in Fig. 3, are defined as CSP[10] processes that coordinate the operations of the execution semantics. The process algebra CSP is an event-based formalism that enables description of patterns of system behaviour. In [2] combination of CSP and the B method is defined and integrated within the model-checker ProB [9]. This formalism is then useful for executable DSLs due to its abstraction capabilities and also thanks to the tool availability.

Figure 11 shows the CSP specification of the Petri-net running algorithm. This algorithm is composed of four processes: RUN, FIRE, CONSUME and PRODUCE. Process RUN (line 1.) is a recursion defined by a sequential composition with the prefixed process FIRE. In this sequence channel getEnabled?*trans* is a call to the B operation getEnabled whose output value is registered in variable *trans*. The variable is then transmitted to process FIRE. Concretely, variable *trans* represents an enabled transition provided non-deterministically by operation getEnabled. The simulation of process RUN continues indefinitely or stops when the system reaches a deadlock.

Process FIRE applied to a transition *trans* is a sequencing of processes CONSUME and PRODUCE preceded by the simple action prefix:

    getPlaces!*trans*?*input*?*output*

---

[10] CSP: Communicating Sequential Processes [5].

```
1.  MAIN = RUN
2.  RUN = getEnabled?trans → FIRE(trans) ; RUN
3.  FIRE(trans) =
4.        getPlaces!trans?input?output → (
5.              CONSUME(input) ; PRODUCE(output)
6.        )
7.  CONSUME(input) = |||[x∈input]removeToken!x → SKIP
8.  PRODUCE(output) = |||[x∈output]addToken!x → SKIP
```

Fig. 11. CSP formalisation of run and fire

This action is a call to the B operation **getPlaces** on transition *trans* in order to get its *input* and *output* places, which are further transmitted to processes CONSUME and PRODUCE. The objective is to apply operations **removeToken** and **addToken** to all elements of sets *input* and *output*. Notation $|||_{[x∈S]}$Op!x represents a replicated interleaving which applies all possible combinations of Op having the various valuations of parameter x taken from set S.

4.4   Debugging the Traffic Light

In order to debug the traffic light via our formal semantics we have two possibilities using Meeduse: (1) interactive animation, and/or (2) model-checking. Meeduse integrates ProB and EMF together in order to take benefit of the visualisation capabilities of MDE tools such as Sirius and GMF for DSLs, and the animation and model-checking functions of ProB. In Meeduse, EMF and ProB are continuously synchronised during the animation process.

The right hand side of Fig. 12 provides the ProB view and the left hand side our EMF/Sirius modeler. The ProB view shows CSP guided animation. In the current state of the model two operations are enabled: start1 and t2. In interactive animation, depending on the choice done by the user, the tool fires the selected transition and then changes the model according to the formal B specification. For every animation step, Meeduse gets the B machine state from ProB and translates it back to the EMF model in order to update the graphical view. As presented in Fig. 12, ProB offers model-checking functions allowing to find deadlocks, invariant violations and reachability of CSP goals.

Mutual Exclusion: A traffic light enters its critical section after enabling transition **start** and it leaves it by transition **end** meaning that the critical section includes states Green and Orange. In order to check this property for our petrinet model, we add the following invariant to our B specification and we ask ProB to find invariant violations and produce the corresponding transition sequences. Contrary to the observation issued from our benchmark, ProB quickly found the invariant violation showing that this property is not respected.

$$1 \in Place\_tokens[\{green1, orange1\}]$$
$$\Rightarrow Place\_tokens[\{green2, orange2\}] = \{0\}$$
$$\wedge\ 1 \in Place\_tokens[\{green2, orange2\}]$$
$$\Rightarrow Place\_tokens[\{green1, orange1\}] = \{0\}$$

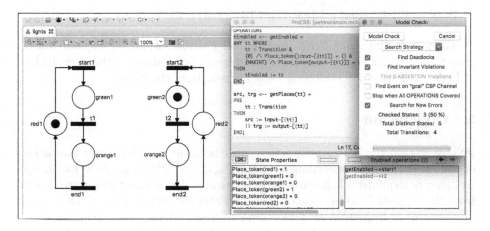

Fig. 12. Integration of ProB within EMF

Fairness: To check this property we apply a parallel composition of process RUN with the process FAIRNESS defined in Fig. 13, line (12.). This process leads to two possible traces: ($step1$; $step2$; $goal$) and ($step2$; $step1$; $goal$). Channel $step1$ (respectively $step2$) is produced from process FIRE when guard $trans = end1$ (respectively $trans = end2$) holds. The objective of this specification is to reach goal STOP when the system produces a trace where both transitions $end1$ and $end2$ are fired by the RUN process.

```
1.  MAIN = RUN |[{step1, step2}]| FAIRNESS
2.  RUN = getEnabled?trans → FIRE(trans) ; RUN
3.  FIRE(trans) =
4.      getPlaces!trans?input?output → (
5.          CONSUME(input) ; PRODUCE(output)
6.      ) ;
7.      ( (trans = end1) : step1 → SKIP
8.      [] (trans = end2) : step2 → SKIP
9.      [] (trans ∉ {end1, end2}) : SKIP )
10. CONSUME(input) = |||[x∈input]removeToken!x → SKIP
11. PRODUCE(output) = |||[x∈output]addToken!x → SKIP
12. FAIRNESS = (step1 → SKIP ||| step2 →SKIP) ;goal → STOP
```

Fig. 13. Fairness checking with CSP

ProB successfully found the expected sequences leading to the goal and showing that the system gives fair turns to lights A and B. However, given that the running algorithm is non-deterministic, it would be interesting to seek for the existence of loops where only one light runs. For this purpose, we can override the getEnabled operation in process RUN as follows:

RUN = FIRE($start1$); FIRE($t1$); FIRE($end1$); RUN

Given this CSP rule, ProB explored all possible situations without finding goal STOP, which shows that the system may stay running without evolutions of Light B. This proof exhibits a weak fairness from the model.

5   Conclusion

PNet$_{QVT}$ gave the better abstraction level however it suffers from limitations of the misuse of non-determinism. PNet$_{Kermeta}$ and PNet$_{fUML}$ have had a controllable deterministic behaviour however this choice makes them quite distant from the original Petri-net semantics. The Petri-net DSL is a "tiny" DSL and it does not allow to present all possibilities of a proof-based approach, but it was sufficient to exhibit several failures from our benchmark. Indeed, in addition to the problem of indeterminism, these tools include other unsafe behaviours due to: the implicit initialisation of the optional attribute tokens, and also the uncontrolled incrementation of this attribute that may produce an integer overflow. Similar simple failures in real-life critical systems have had disastrous consequences. To cope with these limitations, our solution applies a formal model in order to debug the DSL using the ProB animator and model-checker.

Often, in classical development processes, the use of a formal method with proofs is not widespread because it seems to create an overhead for the developer. The Meeduse approach described in this paper targets safety-critical systems where formal reasoning is widely applied even if it requires good skills in mathematics. Integration of a DSL-based solution to this field is interesting since it provides a way for rapid-prototyping of a system's behaviour without a loss of formal proofs. The alliance, favored by Meeduse, between executable DSLs and a formal method such as B, allows to reach a high level of abstraction with a good mix between expressiveness and precision. We believe that this is a promising technique to deal with the dependability of safety-critical systems.

References

1. Bousse, E., Leroy, D., Combemale, B., Wimmer, M., Baudry, B.: Omniscient debugging for executable DSLs. J. Syst. Softw. **137**, 261–288 (2018)
2. Butler, M., Leuschel, M.: Combining CSP and B for specification and property verification. In: Fitzgerald, J., Hayes, I.J., Tarlecki, A. (eds.) FM 2005. LNCS, vol. 3582, pp. 221–236. Springer, Heidelberg (2005). https://doi.org/10.1007/11526841_16

3. Object Management Group: Object Constraint Language (OCL) 2.4 Core Specification (2014). https://www.omg.org/spec/OCL/
4. Object Management Group: Meta Object Facility (MOF) 2.5.1 Core Specification (2015). https://www.omg.org/spec/MOF/2.5.1/
5. Hoare, C.A.R.: Communicating Sequential Processes. Prentice-Hall Inc., Upper Saddle River (1985)
6. Idani, A., Ledru, Y., Vega, G.: Alliance of model-driven engineering with a proof-based formal approach. Innov. Syst. Softw. Eng. 1–19 (2020). https://doi.org/10.1007/s11334-020-00366-3
7. Jézéquel, J.M., Combemale, B., Barais, O., Monperrus, M., Fouquet, F.: Mashup of meta-languages and its implementation in the Kermeta language workbench. Softw. Syst. Model. **14**, 905–920 (2015)
8. Langer, P., Mayerhofer, T., Kappel, G.: Semantic model differencing utilizing behavioral semantics specifications. In: Dingel, J., Schulte, W., Ramos, I., Abrahão, S., Insfran, E. (eds.) MODELS 2014. LNCS, vol. 8767, pp. 116–132. Springer, Cham (2014). https://doi.org/10.1007/978-3-319-11653-2_8
9. Leuschel, M., Butler, M.: ProB: a model checker for B. In: Araki, K., Gnesi, S., Mandrioli, D. (eds.) FME 2003. LNCS, vol. 2805, pp. 855–874. Springer, Heidelberg (2003). https://doi.org/10.1007/978-3-540-45236-2_46
10. Mayerhofer, T., Langer, P., Wimmer, M., Kappel, G.: xMOF: executable DSMLs based on fUML. In: Erwig, M., Paige, R.F., Van Wyk, E. (eds.) SLE 2013. LNCS, vol. 8225, pp. 56–75. Springer, Cham (2013). https://doi.org/10.1007/978-3-319-02654-1_4
11. Wachsmuth, G.: Modelling the operational semantics of domain-specific modelling languages. In: Lämmel, R., Visser, J., Saraiva, J. (eds.) GTTSE 2007. LNCS, vol. 5235, pp. 506–520. Springer, Heidelberg (2008). https://doi.org/10.1007/978-3-540-88643-3_16

FAACS-MDE4SA - Joint Workshop on Formal Approaches for Advanced Computing Systems and Model-Driven Engineering for Software Architecture

Joint Workshop on Formal Approaches for Advanced Computing Systems and Model-Driven Engineering for Software Architecture (FAACS-MDE4SA)

FAACS

The main mission of the workshop is to foster the integration between formal methods and software architecture communities with the purpose of improving their connection in the field of advanced computing systems. This is an emerging class of software systems that expose complex computational models, e.g., mobile, cloud, autonomic, adaptive computing and artificial intelligence based, while exploiting new technologies and infrastructures, e.g., internet-of-things connectivity and smart devices, to deliver services and information to a multitude of end-users. The development of these systems often requires advanced architectural design exploiting the integration of heterogeneous architecture description languages and patterns, qualitative and quantitative assessment of architectures, and solutions already tested in specific contexts. Although significant advancements have been achieved during the last decades, formal methods are still not widely adopted in industry. Ensuring, e.g., reliability, safety, and availability of such systems is a very challenging problem, requiring advanced software architecture design that can be devised by the software architecture community, and rigorous modeling and analysis techniques that can be devised by the formal methods community.

The 4th International Workshop on Formal Approaches for Advanced Computing Systems (FAACS 2020) was held in virtual mode on September 14, 2020. For the third year, the workshop was collocated with the European Conference on Software Architecture (ECSA). The first edition of FAACS was collocated with the 15th International Conference on Software Engineering and Formal Methods (SEFM 2017). This year FAACS received five submissions from authors belonging to six different countries. After an accurate peer-review process involving three members from the Program Committee per submission, three submissions were accepted for publication (an acceptance rate of 60%). The accepted contributions represent a mix of modeling and (design-time and run-time) verification techniques in different application domains such as railway, distributed, and self-adaptive systems. The workshop program included the invited talk entitled "Performance Learning for Uncertainty of Software Systems" given by Catia Trubiani from Gran Sasso Science Institute, Italy.

We would like to thank the Program Committee members that have made the workshop possible with valuable comments received during the review process. We would also like to thank the Steering Committee members and the ECSA workshop chairs for the valuable help and support.

FAACS Organization

FAACS Chairs

Matteo Camilli   Free University of Bozen-Bolzano, Italy
Stéphanie Challita   Inria, France

FAACS Steering Committee

Paolo Arcaini   National Institute of Informatics, Japan
Marina Mongiello   Politecnico di Bari, Italy
Elvinia Riccobene   University of Milan, Italy
Patrizia Scandurra   University of Bergamo, Italy

FAACS Program Committee

Yamine Ait Ameur   IRIT, INPT-ENSEEIHT, France
Paolo Arcaini   National Institute of Informatics, Japan
Simon Bliudze   Inria, France
Georg Buchgeher   Software Competence Center Hagenberg, Austria
Javier Cámara   University of York, UK
Lorenzo Capra   University of Milan, Italy
Julien Deantoni   Inria, France
Stefan Hallerstede   Aarhus University, Denmark
Sungwon Kang   Advanced Institute of Science and Technology, South Korea
Jan Kofron   Charles University, Czech Republic
Elizabeth Leonard   Naval Research Laboratory, USA
Claudio Menghi   University of Luxembourg, Luxembourg
Philippe Merle   Inria, France
Dominique Mery   Université de Lorraine, LORIA, France
Gianfranco Modoni   STIIMA-CNR, Italy
Henry Muccini   University of L'Aquila, Italy
Elvinia Riccobene   University of Milan, Italy
Patrizia Scandurra   University of Bergamo, Italy
Lionel Seinturier   University of Lille, France
Paola Spoletini   Kennesaw State University, USA
Catia Trubiani   Gran Sasso Science Institute, Italy

MDE4SA

Responsiveness to ever-evolving requirements, market needs, customer feedback, and technology are only a few of the challenges posed by modern software systems and impacting software architecture (SA) and its evolution. Such challenges require ad-hoc methodologies, technologies, and tools to mitigate complexity, deal with architectural erosion, and survive the technological evolution. Model-driven engineering (MDE) is a methodology for developing complex software systems, which uses the principle of abstraction and separation of concerns for tackling the complexity of modern software systems. Models are not considered as mere documentation, but as well-defined artefacts (specified through modeling languages) that can be understood, automatically manipulated by automated processes, and transformed into other artefacts. In this context, the interplay between MDE and SA seems natural and of great benefit. Modeling languages, e.g., AADL and ArchiMate, can be used for representing SAs, while model transformations can be used for several different tasks including, e.g., traceability, consistency checking, code generation, and simulation. MDE4SA aims at promoting and fostering discussion on novel ideas and techniques, possibly controversial approaches on the interplay of MDE and SA. The workshop aims at providing a forum for researchers and practitioners from academia and industry in which novel and innovative solutions to current and future challenges of the interplay of MDE and SA can be presented and discussed.

The first edition of MDE4SA was held in virtual mode on September 14, 2020, and was collocated with the European Conference on Software Architecture (ECSA). MDE4SA received three submissions. After a thorough peer-review process involving three members from the Program Committee per submission, only one submission was accepted for publication (an acceptance rate of 33%). The workshop program included the invited talk entitled "(Ab)using MDE for SA" given by Assoc. Prof. Patrizio Pelliccione from University of L'Aquila, Italy, and Chalmers University of Technology, Sweden.

We would like to thank the MDE4SA Steering and Program Committees for making the workshop possible. Additionally, we would like to thank the ECSA workshop chairs, Anne Koziolek and Mauro Caporuscio, for their help and support, ECSA for hosting the workshop, and the CCIS Springer editors for publishing the contributions.

MDE4SA Organization

MDE4SA Chairs

Alessio Bucaioni	Mälardalen University, Sweden
Amleto Di Salle	University of L'Aquila, Italy
Ludovico Iovino	Gran Sasso Science Institute, Italy
Peng Liang	Wuhan University, China

MDE4SA Steering Committee

Alessio Bucaioni	Mälardalen University, Sweden
Amleto Di Salle	University of L'Aquila, Italy
Ludovico Iovino	Gran Sasso Science Institute, Italy

MDE4SA Program Committee

Marco Autili	University of L'Aquila, Italy
Jan Carlson	Mälardalen University, Sweden
Martina De Sanctis	Gran Sasso Science Institute, Italy
Antinisca Di Marco	University of L'Aquila, Italy
Darko Durisic	Volvo Cars, Sweden
Patricia Lago	Vrije Universiteit Amsterdam, The Netherlands
Ivano Malavolta	Vrije Universiteit Amsterdam, The Netherlands
Patrizio Pelliccione	University of L'Aquila, Italy, and Chalmers University of Technology, Sweden
Dalila Tamzalit	LS2N, Université de Nantes, France
Emilio Tuosto	Gran Sasso Science Institute, Italy
Karthik Vaidhyanathan	Gran Sasso Science Institute, Italy
Manuel Wimmer	JKU Linz, Austria
He Xiao	University of Science and Technology Beijing, China
Pengcheng Zhang	Hohai University, China

Defining a Formal Semantic for Parallel Patterns in the Palladio Component Model Using Hierarchical Queuing Petri Nets

Markus Frank[✉], Alireza Hakamian, and Stefen Becker

Univeristy of Stuttgart, 70569 Stuttgart, Germany
{markus.frank,alireza.hakamian,steffen.becker}@iste.uni-stuttgart.de

Abstract. *Context:* With the introduction of multicore processors more than a decade ago, parallel software behavior became also relevant for BIS and end-user applications. This evolution raises several new challenges for **S**oftware **P**erformance **E**ngineering (SPE). One challenge for model-based SPE is to come up with new language concepts to include parallel behavior in the software behavior models (i.e., UML activity diagrams).

Objectives: In this paper we are going to formally describe the semantics of parallel behavior concepts in order to compare existing language extension to that and make an evaluation.

Methods: We use **H**ierarchical **Q**ueuing **P**etri **N**ets to formally describe the general parallel behavior concepts based on the example of the **P**alladio **C**omponent **M**odel.

Results: We give a formal semantic of the parallel behavior elements (like loops, sections, or blocks) for model-based SPE. Further, we evaluate the semantic of introduced parallel language concepts into the PCM.

Conclusion: We show that even if there are syntactic differences between the concepts in PCM and the behavior of the parallel loops, they behave semantically alike.

Keywords: PCM2QPN · Palladio · Parallel langauge concepts · Hierarchical Queuing Petri Nets · Formal semantics

1 Introduction

Around 2003 the first end-user multicore processors were released [9]. Today multicore processors are state of the art—common smartphones have eight cores, and for desktop PCs, up to 32 cores are available. This evolution has a significant impact on the way we develop software. To efficiently use the hardware, the software developers write concurrent code. Thus, current approaches for **S**oftware **P**erformance **E**ngineering have to be reviewed. One well know approach is the **P**alladio **C**omponent **M**odel [3] and the Palladio Bench[1], which are

---

[1] https://www.palladio-simulator.com/home/.

© Springer Nature Switzerland AG 2020
H. Muccini et al. (Eds.): ECSA 2020, CCIS 1269, pp. 381–394, 2020.
https://doi.org/10.1007/978-3-030-59155-7_28

a model-driven performance engineering languages. The PCM has been recently extended with concepts for massive parallel behaviour [5]. These concepts contain language extensions for the PCM to include OpenMP-like parallel loops, sections, and blocks. To the best of our knowledge, such concepts have not been used in SPE before [7] and no formal semantic exist.

In this paper, we use **H**ierarchical **Q**ueueing **P**etri **N**ets [2] to formally describe the semantic of parallel loops, sections, and blocks. Further, we evaluate if the introduced language extensions in [5], follow the same formal semantic.

To achieve this, we comply to and extend the work done by [12] who started to describe the semantics of the PCM elements with HQPNs formally.

As a result, we formally describe parallel loops, sections, and blocks by HQPNs. Further, we show that the previously introduced language extensions [5] do not follow these semantics.

In the following, we start with the foundations in Sect. 2. Here we describe the PCM and the language extension in detail. Further, we give a brief insight into HQPNs. In Sect. 3, we open with a description of the mapping process (PCM to HQPNs). It follows by a summary of the relevant PCM elements for our mapping and a detailed description of the actual mapping (parallel loops, section, and blocks) to HQPNs. Afterwards, we compare the formal semantic with the existing language extension [5] for the PCM and conclude our findings.

2   Foundations

2.1   Software Performance Engineering (SPE)

SPE aims to predict software quality attributes like performance (e.g., response time), cost of operations (costs) and range of capable performance (scalability) [1]. Therefore, SPE uses performance models to estimate quality attributes. In general we distinguish between analytical and simulative approaches. While analytical approaches are usually faster in solving the models, simulative approaches give software performance engineers (SPEs) more freedom in modelling details of the system under study. In analytical approaches the SPEs have to omit many details of the system and make simplistic assumptions. In order, to derive performance metrics, it is necessary to combine the models of the hardware, software (in terms of structure and behaviour) and the usage profile.

The main advantage of SPE is to enable software developers to evaluate performance requirements in the early stage (i.e., during design time). In this phase, decisions and design can easily be changed because no realization has to be made. So, different design alternatives can be evaluated, be compared, and trade-off decisions can be made in an informed and engineering-like manner [20].

2.2   The PCM and the Palladio Bench

The purpose of the PCM and its related tooling, the Palladio Bench [3,17,18], is mainly to analyze quality attributes of a software architecture like performance-related properties, which includes response times of service requests, scalability by changing the demand of a workload to the system, and elasticity (how fast, e.g., a cloud infrastructure scale up to react to an increasing workload) [14]. Within Palladio, the following main aspects have to be modelled. Each representing one of the five viewpoints:

Usage Diagram. The usage environment describes how often and with which kind of data, services are requested. Thus, it describes the user interaction with the system.

Repository Diagram. The available software components are described in a Repository Diagram. The components in this diagram have provided and required interfaces and the logical connections between these interfaces. All in all, the diagram is similar to the UML2 [19] Component Diagram.

Service Effect Specification Diagram. He internal behavior of each component needs to be modeled. The corresponding diagram is called Service **Eff**ect Specification Diagram (SEFF). Thus, for each provided interface, a SEFF has to be modelled. The SEFF is similar to a UML2 Activity Diagram; it can use, e.g., loops, branches, internal actions (to demand hardware resources like CPU cycles) and external actions (usage of other components via required interfaces of the component).

Resource Diagram. Resources are the computing nodes, network connections, etc., which are used to process the requests and provide resources like CPU cycles.

Allocation Diagram. In the Allocation Diagram, the components are deployed or allocated to specific machines and hardware instances. This diagram is similar to the UML2 deployment diagram.

The usage (usage diagram) models the calls to provided interfaces of components (repository diagram). This requires to evaluate the related SEFFs that can call additional interfaces or demand for hardware resources. To evaluate how long, e.g., an internal action takes, the used hardware needs to be considered. Based on the deployment diagram, the actual hardware is identified and utilized. How long it takes to provide the demanded resources depends on the capability of the used hardware, which is described by the resource diagram.

The final model is a Palladio instance model composed out of all the above mentioned sub-models. To analyze such a model, analytic or simulative solvers can be used (see. Sect. 2.1). The result is a (performance) behaviour analysis of the complete system. This behaviour can be further analyzed to identify limitations of the system like bottlenecks or the violation of service level objectives (SLOs). Afterwards, the model can be altered, and the consequences of the changes can be analyzed. This allows to evaluate different versions of a system before the first line of code is written.

Architectural Templates (AT). Next, we describe the Architectural Template (AT) approach in more detail. This is necessary to understand how the

PCM language can be extended and to understand the parallel language extension we evaluate later.

The AT method was introduced by Lehrig [13]. It is a software engineering method that allows software architect to reuse architectural knowledge from pre-specified templates for architectural modelling and analyses. In theory, the AT approach is similar to the UML2 profiling strategy. UML Profile, as well as the AT approach, are using stereotypes and package specialization to extend the meta-model without changing the profiled meta-model. With AT, the software architect can annotate model elements with stereotypes. Next, the engineering method behind AT, transforms the annotated architecture model to a PCM instance, based on pre-defined rules for each AT. The benefit of this approach is that the software architect saves much time, needs less expert knowledge, and errors are reduced [13].

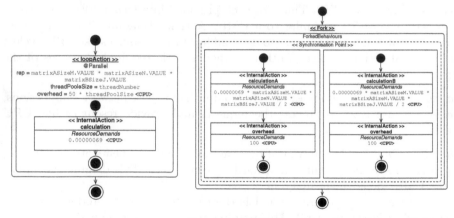

| | Resolved SEFF for a two threaded parallel loop with additional synchronization overhead as extra |
| Parallel Loop AT | internal action |

Fig. 1. Unwrapping of a parallel loop AT (left) to PCM (right)

Parallel ATs. We introduced in previous work [5], an architectural template for parallel loops and sections. The full details can be found in [5]. Here we briefly mention the most relevant concepts to follow the rest of the paper.

Parallel Loop. The basic idea of the parallel AT is to provide an AT to the software architect, which allows him to annotate the parallel behaviour in the model quickly. As an example, in Fig. 1(a) we want to model a matrix multiplication in parallel. Since the matrix multiplication is executed using a loop, we also use the `LoopAction` here. Besides the number of loop iterations, which is in our case specified by the matrix sizes, we also need to use the `@Parallel` stereotype. Further, we need to specify two additional parameters for parallel behaviour. These are the number of threads (i.e., how many software threads should be forked) and the overhead. We introduced the overhead to show that for forking and joining the threads, additional computing resources are required.

Figure 1b shows how the AT approach maps the parallel loop. It performs an in-place model-to-model transformation based on predefined QVTo[2] transformation rules. Due to performance in the Palladio Bench, the mapping resolves the loop action to a fork. This is only possible because the resource demands for the internal action are known at this point. Instead of simulating the loop, we can transform the loop to fork action, by multiplying the resource demands with the number of loop iterations for each thread. Depending on the number of threads, the mapping creates independent forks. Each thread contains the original internal action (with adopted resource demand) and an additional action with the overhead.

Parallel Sections and Blocks: Parallel sections and parallel blocks are conceptually very similar to the parallel loops. Therefore, they are handled in the same conceptual way as we described above.

2.3   Hierarchical Queueing Petri Nets

In this paper, we are using HQPN to formally describe the dynamic behaviour of the parallel language elements in the PCM. HQPNs includes several extensions to the conventional Petri nets (PNs). These extensions include Colored PN, Generalised Stochastic PN, Colored GSPN, and Queueing PN. In the following, we assume the reader is familiar with PNs. Therefore we only give a brief introduction to PNs and HQPNs. Thereby, we follow the definitions given by [2] for PNs and the various extensions [11]. A more detailed overview is provided in [12].

Petri Nets. An ordinary Petri Net (PN) is a 5-tuple $PN = (P, T, I^-, I^+, M_0)$, where:

1. $P = p1, p2, ..., p_n$ a finite and nonempty set of places,
2. $T = t1, t2, ..., t_m$ a finite and nonempty set of transitions $P \cap T = \emptyset$
3. I^- and $I^+ : P \times T \to \mathbb{N}_0$ are called backward and forward incidence functions respectively
4. $M_0 : P \to \mathbb{N}_0$ is called initial marking.

PNs cannot differ between the token type. Coloured PN (CPN) allows binding a type (colour) to each token. Each place is restricted to a set of colours. Furthermore, the transitions of CPNs can fire in different modes based on the colour of the token.

Furthermore, using Stochastic PN (SPN), we can include temporal aspects. SPN assign an exponentially distributed firing delay to each transition. This delay defines the time a transition waits after being enabled until it fires [12].

---

[2] MOF Query/View/Transformation—https://www.omg.org/spec/QVT/.

Queuing Petri Nets. Bause et al. [2] introduced Queueing PN (QPN). Queueing PN is based on CGSPNs and integrates queue concept into places. Therefore QPN is used to express queuing behaviour, which is in the forms of SPE, in PNs. In QPN there is a queueing place, where tokens are queued and a depository for tokens, which have completed their service.

Models in QPN can become quite large. To tolerate the largeness problem of monolithic QPN, it is convenient to divide them into smaller inter-active subnets. For this purpose, HQPN are used. They consist of several QPN subnets and additionally contain subnet places. Each subnet has a dedicated input and output place and another place counting the active population of the subnet, which is the number of tokens fired into the subnet that has not yet left the subnet again.

A Hierarchical Queueing PN is a 4-tuple $HQPN = (N, SP, SA, FS)$, where:

1. N is a finite set, where:
   (a) $n \in N$ is a non-hierarchical QPN $(P_n, T_n, C_n, I_n^-, I_n^+, M_{n_0}, Q_n, W_n)$,
   (b) the sets of net elements are pairwise disjoint:
      $$\forall n_1, n_2 \in N : [n_1 \neq n_2 \Rightarrow (P_{n_1} \cup T_{n_1}) \cap (P_{n_2} \cup T_{n_2}) = \varnothing]$$
2. $SP \subset P_N$ is the set of the subnet places,
3. $SA : SP \to N$ is the subnet assignment function,
4. $FS \subseteq \mathcal{P}(P_N)$ is the set of fusion sets, such that members of a fusion set have identical color sets and equivalent initialization expressions: $\forall fs \in FS :$ $\forall p_1, p_2 \in fs : [C(p_1) = C(p_2) \wedge M_0(p_1) = M_0(p_2)]$

3 Mapping of PCM Instances to HQPN

In this section, we will describe the mapping of PCM Components to HQPNs. The model transformation uses HQPNs as a target model. Thereby, we will start to explain the mapping for essential components of the PCM, which was developed by Koziolek in [12]. Koziolek defined semantic behaviour for most of the PCM elements. However, due to space limitations, we will discuss only the loop and asynchronous fork, which we later reuse. For a full definition of all essential elements of the PCM, we refer to the dissertation of Koziolek [12]. Further, we introduce a mapping for asynchronous for-loop, which was not done by Koziolek. As soon as we know the basic concepts, we discuss mapping of the parallel behaviour to HQPNs in general. Based on that, we will evaluate and compare the semantic behaviour of the parallel AT (from [5]) to the expected parallel behaviour.

3.1 Mapping of General PCM Components

All elements used in the following are part of the Palladio Service Effect Specification, which describes the behaviour of the software model. For the sake of simplicity, we only look at the subnets (QPN) of the HQPN.

Within our HQPN each token represents a single user or request within our system. The token's color is a complex data type named `TokenData` (see Listing 1.1). It contains:

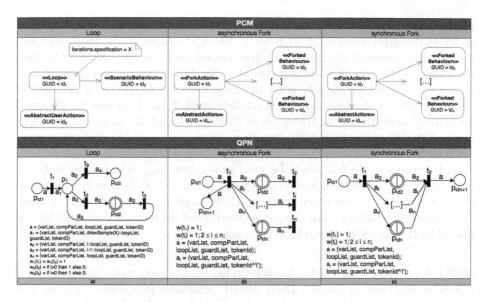

Fig. 2. Mapping of PCM2QPN: (a) LoopAction, (b) asynchronous Fork, (c) synchronous Fork (for a, b cf. [12])

- **VarList**: A list of currently valid parameter characterizations.
- **CompParList**: A list of currently valid parameter characterization specified as component parameter.
- **LoopList**: List of loop iterations. When a token enters a loop, the number is set in the list to show the number of iterations that is left.
- **GuardList**: A List of branching guards. The PN uses them to calculate probability distributions with stochastic dependencies.
- **TokenID**: A unique ID for each token. This can be used to merge tokens after they have been split and firing them into subnets.

In the following we will refer to a `TokenList` as `a`. For more details on mapping the processing resources, stochastic expressions, and distributions see [12].

```
color VarSpec = product string * string;
color VarList = list VarSpec;
color CompParList = list VarSpec;
color LoopList = list int;
color GuardList = list string; color TokenId = int;

color TokenData = product VarList * CompParList *
    LoopList * GuardList * TokenId;
```

Listing 1.1. Color of a token, called TokenData (cmp. [12])

PCM Loop. Figure 2(a) shows the mapping of a PCM Loop Component (above as PCM description) to a QPN (below). The QPN contains the loop head and body. After entering the loop, the first transition t_1 is to evaluate the loop iteration (in this case it is not a constant value, but a distribution or stochastic expression). The transition t_1 adds the loop iteration integer as a list instead of an integer to the LoopList. The reason is that the loop can be executed recursively nested, and the token needs to memorise all the loop counters. The head of the list gives the current iteration count.

Based on that value either transition t_3 (counter $= 0$) or t_2 (counter > 0) fires. In case of t_2 the token will be fired in a subnet p_{id2}, which represents the loop body. As soon as the token returns from the subnet, t_4 fires and a_3 decreases the loop counter and the token enters the loop head. Finally, when t_3 is reached, a_4 removes the counter from the list of loop iteration integers and the token is placed in the successor of the loop (i.e., p_{id3}).

PCM Asynchronous Fork. Asynchronous Forks spawn new threads without synchronising them in the end. Each thread terminates independently from each other. Figure 2(b) illustrates the behavior for the given PCM specification.

First, the transition t_1 fires a copy of the current token into multiple places in QPN p_{idi}, each representing a forked behaviour. During t_1, the values of the current token are modified in a way, that the ID h stays unique. For that, a number i is added for each forked behaviour. The rest of the values stay the same. At the end of each forked behaviour, the transition t_2 - t_n flushes the copied token. To continue, the transition t_1 fires an additional token to the successor represented here by p_{idn+1}.

PCM Synchronous Fork. In contrast to asynchronous, in synchronous forks, the control flow spawn threads and waits for them to finish before continuing with the next steps. Figure 2(c) illustrates the behavior and give the PCM description.

In general, the QPN (Fig. 2(c)) looks very similar to the asynchronous forks. So in the following, we only go into the two main differences:

First, instead of the transitions t_2 to t_n (in asynchronous forks), which flushes the token after the forked behaviour has finished, we now have a transition t_2, which only fires if there is a token available in each place p_{id2} to p_{idn}. Is that condition is fulfilled, t_2 fires and places a token in the successor of the synchronous fork—in our case p_{idn+1}. The token that is placed in the successor place is a merged copy of a_2 to a_n. Further, the ID h is modified in the way that i is removed. Thus, the ID is reset to the original value before entering the fork and stays unique.

The second difference to the asynchronous forks is when and how to pass the token to the successor. While for the asynchronous forks, the transition t_1 immediately passes a token to the successor, the transition in the synchronous forks does not and only passes the tokes into the forked behaviours. The successor is added in the end, and the transition t_2 triggers the successor. In that way, it is ensured that all forked behaviours have finished before continuing.

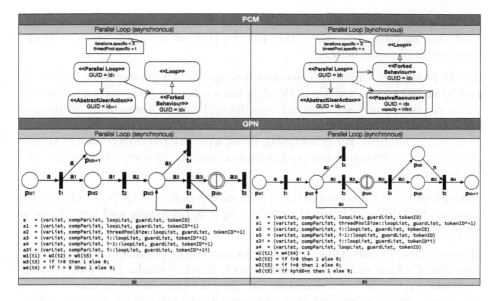

Fig. 3. Mapping PCM2QPN: (a) asynchronous parallel loop, (b) synchronous parallel loop

3.2 Mapping of Parallel Behavior to QPN

In this section, we discuss the behaviour of parallel loops, sections and blocks. Since no native PCM elements are representing these concepts, we give the PCM descriptions based on the parallel AT extensions introduced in our previous work [8]. The description should reflect the way common frameworks like openMP[3] have implemented these concepts. In the next section, we will then demonstrate how parallel ATs have been realised.

Parallel Loops

Behavior: Parallel loops are a parallelisation concept known from different parallel programming paradigms like OpenMP. Simply, a parallel loop executes each loop iterations in a separate thread. Using a thread pool with a fixed or dynamic size, the threads are then scheduled to the physical cores and executed in parallel. For the most scenarios, it is assumed that the threads are data independent. This means that read and write operation of each thread does not influence others. A typical example to illustrate the behaviour of parallel loops is a matrix multiplication [6]. Assuming you have two matrices (10×10) you want to multiply. This would result in a total number of 1000 multiplications to perform. Using, for example, OpenMP parallel loops with a thread pool size of 8, this would split the workload for each thread equally, resulting in 125 calculations per thread.

---

[3] openMP – https://www.openmp.org/.

A parallel loop can either be synchronous (often used when distributing work-loads and realising a master-worker pattern [15]) or asynchronous (i.e., implementing an observer pattern).

PCM Instance: Given the behaviour description of a parallel loop, it is represented similar to a fork action in PCM. It has a successor and a forked behaviour. Since the behaviours are all equal, specifying it once is enough. In addition to the fork action, the information about the thread pool size and the number of iterations is required. For synchronous forks, a passive resource is needed as well. A passive resource can be used to implement require and release behaviours, i.e., for mutexes [12].

Mapping: For the mapping of the behaviour description to QPN, we distinguish between two different kinds of parallel loops: Synchronous and asynchronous loops, which are shown in Fig. 3.

Asynchronous Parallel Loop: The QPN for asynchronous parallel loops is a combination of a loop and an asynchronous fork. It starts similar to a fork with the transition t_1, which fires two tokens: One into the place of the successor p_{idn+1}, which can then continue, and another token into the place of the loop behaviour. Thereby, the id of the token is altered and increased (a_1). Following the description of a loop (see the Fig. 2(a)), the next step, evaluates the loop iteration. In this case, two evaluations are done. One for the outer loop, which forks the new threads. Here the value equals to the value of the given thread pool size. The evaluation of the iteration literal specifies the second loop iteration value and then divided by the thread pool size, to equally share the workload. It is added to the LoopList. Based on that former value, the loop either continues or finally goes to t_4. In case the loop continues t_3 fires a two tokens. One into the subnet p_{idn}, with an adjusted id (cf. Sect. 3.1) and one to p_{id3} with an adjusted loop counter. After that the loop condition is evaluated again. Further, the subnet p_{idn} represents a normal loop as characterized in Sect. 3.1. Finally, when a subnet has finished, t_5 destroys the token.

Synchronous Parallel Loop: In contrast to the asynchronous parallel loop, the synchronous one does not continue until all tokens returned from all subnets. For that reason, there is no fork action in the beginning, and the QPN starts with the evaluation of the loop iteration, which again equals the value for the thread pool size. The loop execution behaves the same way as the asynchronous loop does. In contrast to asynchronous loops, where tokens are flushed after returning from the subnet, in synchronous loops, the tokens are passed on. The transition t_4 fires a token into two places: p_{id5} and p_{id6}. p_{id5} shows a passive resource and X indicates the number of created tokens. So, whenever a subnet is finishes and the token returns, t_4 fires and increases the number of tokes in the places. Thereby, the original token with the corresponding colour is placed in the p_{id5}, and the loop iteration counter is removed from the token's colour. In the very end, transition t_5 fires if there are the number of n tokens in the place p_{id6}. The value of n is equal to the value of the thread pool size. Thus, the transition t_5 fires if all subnets have been returned. Further, the transition

t_5 adjusts the value of the id field, removes the added identifier for the subnet i, and restores the value to its original value.

Please note that we modelled the passive resource (p_{id6}) along with the require (x) and release (n) actions explicit, for reasons of exemplification. It is also possible to combine it with p_{id5}.

Parallel Sections and Blocks

Behavior: Parallel sections or blocks refer to a specific area in the source code that is either explicitly marked for parallel execution (i.e., parallel sections in openMP) or implicitly allow multiple executions of the same block. The former behaves similar to a loop. Most of the time, a parallel section is used to split the workload based on a task set or data structure. The section is specified by the same behaviour but can have different input parameter. The later can be a method that is called by multiple threads.

PCM Instance: In the SEFF, a block, which can be called multiple times form different threads, is modelled with a simple fork action and therefore can be either synchronous or asynchronous. Due to the similarities of a parallel section to a parallel loop, there is no additional concept in PCM and on an abstract level, it can be handled in the same way as a parallel loop.

Mapping: The mapping of PCM Instances for parallel sections to QPN is performed in a very similar way as the mapping of parallel loops. The only difference is that the subnet will not be of type loop but of arbitrary types. This means that not the loop characterisation is passed to the subnet but an adjusted version of the `VarList`, describing the workload for the specific subnet. For blocks, the mapping is the same as for forks. Due to these highly similar concepts, we will skip a full description at this point.

3.3   Evaluation of the Mapping of Parallel ATs to QPN

In the following, we will evaluate the behaviour of the parallel loop ATs. As described in Sect. 2.2, the parallel ATs need to map all elements to the given PCM instances. Thus, the parallel AT method maps all kinds of parallel behaviour (loops, sections, or blocks) to a fork-join scenario (see. Fig. 1). Therefore, we can use the existing mapping of forks to QPNs to express the formal semantic. To show that this is a valid approach, we elaborate on a thought experiment. For that, we assume to have a synchronous parallel loop, which should calculate a matrix multiplication with the matrices of size 10×10. So, in total, 1000 multiplications have to be performed. Further, we assume each multiplication takes 1 ms on a two-core system. In theory, executing the multiplication in a sequential way takes 1 s. Using synchronous parallel loop (as described in Sect. 3.2) needs additional information about the number of worker threads. Assume we use two worker threads for the two core system. The behaviour of the synchronous loop, splits to two separate threads, and share the workload equally. That means each worker threads needs to perform 500 multiplications and needs 500 ms. Since we assume two cores, the overall execution time is 500 ms, due to the fact that both threads can run in parallel. Now let us consider the parallel AT: Here we use the parallel loop action (see Fig. 1a) and specify the number of replications to be 1000, the thread pool size is two, and the resource demand for one calculation is 1 ms on the CPU. The parallel AT approach maps this to a fork behaviour with two parallel threads, which needs to be synchronised in the end. The resource demand for each internal action is still the same 1 ms on the CPU. But this time, it is multiplied by the number of repetitions divided by the number of worker threads (i.e., it shares the workload equally). So, each internal action takes 500 ms, and the total run-time is 500 ms.

This exemplifies that when it comes to the response time, the behaviour is the same. For this, in future work, we plan to provide a mathematical proof based on QPNs.

4   Future Work

In this paper, we formally describe different parallel patterns. This is only one single piece of puzzle fitting in a bigger picture. The overall goal of our research project is to enable software architects to make reliable performance predictions for concurrent software on multicore systems[4]. Including common parallel patterns such as loops, blocks, and sections into the performance prediction languages and thereby giving the formal semantics is only one step. However, there are more parallel paradigms, such as ACTORS, streams, or message passing approaches.

Currently, we are working on identification, categorisation and classification of parallel behaviour patterns in the literature and practice. In future work, we will include further parallelisation patterns in PCM and give a formal definition of the behaviour. It remains an open question if HQPN is suitable to describe other types of parallelisation paradigms.

5   Related Work

When it comes to related work, there are several works, which try to bring a formal semantic to modelling languages by making the models executable. In the following, we name the relevant work for us:

One of the more general approaches is the foundational UML Subset[5] by OMG. The fUML Subset is an executable subset of UML. It can be used to describe the structural and behavioural semantics of the system. It also can be used to define MOF-based modelling languages such as standard UML or its subsets and extensions. For example, the semantics of UML state machines can be specified as a program written in fUML. In addition to that, there are several

---

[4] https://www.researchgate.net/project/Multi-Many-Core-Software-Performance-Engineering.

[5] https://www.omg.org/spec/FUML.

more specific approaches like [16] using fUML to specify the abstract syntax and behavioural semantics of domain-specific modelling languages.

Closer to our topic there is the work from Distefano et al. [4]. In that work, the authors provided and evaluated an approach to map standard UML annotated with OMG Profiles for Schedulability, Performance, and Time Specification to Petri Nets. For this, they use an intermediate representation called a performance context model. They use Petri Nets to evaluate the performance of the software architecture represented by UML models.

Finally, there is also the work from Koziolek [12] and Happe [10], which we have introduced in Sect. 2 and our work relied upon.

In none of the approaches, there is a discussion about the mapping of parallel behaviour concepts.

6   Conclusion

Parallel programming is an essential part of efficiently using state of the art processors. To ensure performance prediction accuracy in parallel execution, current engineering tools need to support the formal definition of elements in parallel behaviour.

In this paper, we first gave a formally defined semantics for parallel loops, blocks, and sections. Second, we evaluated the Parallel Architectural Template method, which is an extension of the Palladio Component Model. Besides, we can list the following contributions:

- Summarize contributions from J. Happe and H. Koziolek.
- Providing a formal specification for synchronous forks using QPN.
- Describing the behaviour for a synchronous and asynchronous parallel loop.
- Describing the behaviour for parallel sections and blocks.
- Provide a formal specification for parallel loops using QPN.
- Provide a formal specification for sections and blocks.
- Evaluate the behaviour of parallel ATs.

As a result, we showed that the parallel Loops provided by the parallel AT method does not follow the same or expected syntax that parallel loops in general have. However, we showed that regarding the aim of the software performance predictions, both concepts deliver the same results and therefore have the same semantics. Thus, the parallel AT method is a valid approach to express parallel behaviour in the PCM.

References

1. Balsamo, S., Di Marco, A., Inverardi, P., Simeoni, M.: Model-based performance prediction in software development: a survey. IEEE Trans. Softw. Eng. 30(5), 295–310 (2004)
2. Bause, F., et al.: Stochastic Petri Nets: An Introduction to the Theory (2002)

3. Becker, S., Koziolek, H., Reussner, R.: The palladio component model for model-driven performance prediction. J. Syst. Softw. **82**(1), 3–22 (2009)
4. Distefano, S., Scarpa, M., Puliafito, A.: From UML to petri nets: the PCM-based methodology. IEEE Trans. Softw. Eng. **37**(1), 65–79 (2010)
5. Frank, M., Hakamian, A.: An architectural template for parallel loops and sections. In: Proceedings of the 9th Symposium on Software Performance 2018, Hildesheim, Germany, 7–9 November 2018, Hildesheim, November 2018
6. Frank, M., Hilbrich, M.: Performance prediction for multicore environments–an experiment report. In: Proceedings of the Symposium on Software Performance 2016, Kiel, Germany, 7–9 November 2016 (2016)
7. Frank, M., Hilbrich, M., Lehrig, S., Becker, S.: Parallelization, modeling, and performance prediction in the multi-/many core area: a systematic literature review. In: Proceedings of the 7th IEEE International Symposium on Cloud and Service Computing (2017)
8. Frank, M., Staude, S., Hilbrich, M.: Is the PCM ready for ACTORs and multicore CPUs? – a use case-based evaluation. In: Proceedings of the Symposium on Software Performance 2017, Karlsruhe, Germany, 9–10 November 2017 (2017)
9. Geer, D.: Chip makers turn to multicore processors. Computer **38**(5), 11–13 (2005)
10. Happe, J.: Predicting software performance in symmetric multi-core and multiprocessor environments. Dissertation, University of Oldenburg, Germany, August 2008
11. Jensen, K.: Coloured Petri Nets: Basic Concepts, Analysis Methods and Practical Use, vol. 1. Springer, Heidelberg (2013). https://doi.org/10.1007/978-3-662-03241-1
12. Koziolek, H.: Parameter dependencies for reusable performance specifications of software components. Ph.D. thesis, Universität Oldenburg (2008)
13. Lehrig, S.: Efficiently conducting quality-of-service analyses by templating architectural knowledge. Ph.D. thesis, University of Stuttgart, Germany (2017, accepted for publication)
14. Lehrig, S., Eikerling, H., Becker, S.: Scalability, elasticity, and efficiency in cloud computing: a systematic literature review of definitions and metrics. In: Proceedings of the 11th International ACM SIGSOFT Conference on Quality of Software Architectures, pp. 83–92. ACM (2015)
15. Mattson, T.G., Sanders, B., Massingill, B.: Patterns for Parallel Programming. Pearson Education, London (2004)
16. Mayerhofer, T., Langer, P., Wimmer, M., Kappel, G.: xMOF: executable DSMLs based on fUML. In: Erwig, M., Paige, R.F., Van Wyk, E. (eds.) SLE 2013. LNCS, vol. 8225, pp. 56–75. Springer, Cham (2013). https://doi.org/10.1007/978-3-319-02654-1_4
17. Reussner, R., et al.: The Palladio Component Model. Technical report, KIT, Fakultät für Informatik, Karlsruhe (2011)
18. Reussner, R., et al.: Modeling and Simulating Software Architectures: The Palladio Approach. MIT Press, Cambridge (2016)
19. Rupp, C., Queins, S., Zengler, B.: UML 2 glasklar: Praxiswissen für die UML-Modellierung. Hanser (2007)
20. Williams, L.G., Smith, C.U.: Making the business case for software performance engineering. In: International CMG Conference, pp. 349–358 (2003)

Model-Based Simulation at Runtime with Abstract State Machines

Elvinia Riccobene[1] and Patrizia Scandurra[2(✉)]

[1] Dipartimento di Informatica, Università degli Studi di Milano, Milan, Italy
`elvinia.riccobene@unimi.it`
[2] Department of Economics and Technology Management, Information Technology and Production, Università degli Studi di Bergamo, Bergamo, Italy
`patrizia.scandurra@unibg.it`

Abstract. Software systems are rapidly growing in complexity and scale, and are subject to different kinds of uncertainties related to the dynamics of resource availability or changes in system objectives. So, many real usage scenarios might be impossible to reproduce and validate at design-time. As envisioned by the Models@run.time research community, the use of models at runtime is fundamental to address this challenge. Our focus is on providing guarantees for changing safety goals at runtime (a form of uncertainty) with the employment of mathematically-based runtime analysis techniques from the area of formal methods (FM@run.time).

In this paper, we propose a novel framework for the runtime simulation of Abstract State Machine models and the on-the-fly changes of safety assertions at the model level to provide software assurance guarantees at runtime. The framework is called AsmetaS@run.time and is being developed as part of the ASM specification and analysis toolset ASMETA.

Keywords: Runtime simulation · Models@run.time · Abstract State Machines · ASMETA

1 Introduction

Modern software systems are rapidly growing in complexity and scale, and many real usage scenarios might be impossible to reproduce and validate at design-time, as they depend on third party off-the-shelf systems and platforms. These systems make the problem of verifying software in-house extremely hard.

To address this challenge, the Models@run.time research community has identified a reference architecture [6,8] to equip a software system with a model running in a "causally connected way" with the system and to allow reasoning about it not only at design time, but also at runtime.

Classically, formal models are built at design time to support system validation and verification. In the new vision, formal models are developed at design

© Springer Nature Switzerland AG 2020
H. Muccini et al. (Eds.): ECSA 2020, CCIS 1269, pp. 395–410, 2020.
https://doi.org/10.1007/978-3-030-59155-7_29

time for an initial assessment that the software system satisfies the initial requirements, but these models are then kept alive at runtime to run in tandem with the real system, and are continuously analyzed to address software runtime assurance [7,13]. Similar ideas have been proliferating in other contexts, such as *Digital twins* in the manufacturing domain [30], and *Living models* [26] in the field of Computer Automated Multi-Paradigm Modelling.

This usage of formal methods requires novel mechanisms for leveraging the efficient applicability of conventional formal analysis techniques at runtime. We share this viewpoint of *continuous assurance* throughout the software lifecycle and in order to support this line of research, we have been investigating the use of *Abstract State Machines* as runtime system models, exploiting their feature of being executable besides being verifiable. Our focus is on providing guarantees for changing safety goals at runtime (a form of uncertainty).

In this paper, we present some preliminary results by introducing the architecture of a runtime simulation platform we have been developing within the ASMETA (ASM mETAmodeling) analysis toolset[1] – a set of tools for the ASM formal method – to check safety assertions of software systems at runtime and support also the on the fly changes of safety assertions. This mechanism exploits the concept of executable ASM models and it is based on a new component, the `AsmetaS@run.time`, that has been designed to manage the ASM model simulation in tandem with the real software system. We also envision a real scenario in the context of safety-critical systems, the so-called *runtime enforcement* [14] of safety assertions, where we are applying the ASM@run.time approach.

This paper is organized as follows. An overview of formal analysis techniques @run.time is given in Sect. 2. In Sect. 3 we provide some preliminary background concepts on the ASM formal method and the ASMETA analysis framework. Section 4 outlines our approach to runtime simulation of ASMs with the new added ASMETA component `AsmetaS@run.time`. In Sect. 4 we provide a model example to illustrate the main features of such a tool, and we conclude this paper in Sect. 5.

2   Related Work on the Use of FMs@run.time

The use of formal and unambigous models at runtime is crucial; the results of model analyses are likely to be more trustworthy than with other types of semi-formal engineering models. However, extending the use of formal analysis techniques at runtime is not trivial. The major challenges are reducing the overheads associated with the execution of formal analysis techniques at runtime and scaling the approach beyond small to medium system sizes. Another challenge is related to the expert knowledge that is required to build the models used in the runtime analysis. In this respect, the adoption of lightweight formal methods (such as state-based formalisms based on set theory and first-order logic) could be helpful, since they may capture or express the required domain concepts more naturally and efficiently for analysis purposes than other heavier formalisms.

---

[1] https://asmeta.github.io/.

We here briefly report the main validation and verification (V&V) approaches relevant to the runtime use of formal methods:

- *Runtime simulation.* Model-based simulation at runtime has been successfully adopted to enable efficient decision making in self-adaptive systems [28,29]. Distinct models for each relevant quality are combined with runtime simulation of the models to select an adaptation option that satisfies the system goals. These last usually refer to extra-functional quality properties (like reliability, availability, expected response time, etc.) and may also change during execution. Simulation, in general, is less time and resource consuming compared with exhaustive verification techniques, and it is, therefore, particularly advantageous at run-time, when time and resources are often constrained.
- *Runtime model checking.* Runtime automated verification checks whether certain properties of interest hold for the system model during system operation. In particular, there is interest in using stochastic models that encode system behaviour and knowledge of relevant qualities [13]. However, this technique puts constraints on the size of the models and on the time and resources required to perform model checking, since exhaustive verification (that exhaustively explores the state-space of a model) suffers from the well-known state-space explosion problem.

Recently, *statistical model checking* has been proposed as an alternative to traditional model checking techniques. It solves the model checking problem differently: it simulates the system for finitely many executions, and uses *hypothesis testing* to infer whether the samples provide *statistical evidence* for the satisfaction or violation of the specification with some degree of confidence [20]. This approach has main advantages in terms of efficiency and simplicity to be used at runtime. It is a compromise between testing and classical model checking techniques. In fact, simulation-based methods are known to be far less memory and time intensive than exhaustive ones, and therefore more appealing to use at runtime. The work in [29], for example, uses statistical model checking at runtime to drive the adaptation of the system by selecting adaptation options that realize the adaptation goals efficiently.

Other runtime verification techniques have been used to ensure the dependability of software systems. They are described in the two following paragraphs since we consider them to be different classes of techniques.

- *Runtime monitoring* is concerned with checking whether a run of a system under scrutiny satisfies or violates given formally-specified properties. Monitors are typically generated automatically from some high-level specification. Examples of such approaches employing state-based formalisms are ASMETA CoMA [3,21] for ASMs and AMOebA-RT [17] for adaptive software, to name a few. These approaches detect violations of correctness properties after they happen and their associated runs are recorded. As they analyse a single run at a time, these techniques scale well. However, unlike the runtime model checking approach, runtime verification cannot guarantee the lack of constraint violations.

- *Runtime quantitative verification* is a mathematically-based technique mostly used to analyse models (such as Markov chains and Markov Decision Processes) of systems that exhibit stochastic behaviour, and to check (through, for example, a probabilistic model checker like PRISM) that they comply with non-functional requirements (such as performance, reliability, and cost/reward system characteristics). These are expressed as combinations of formal quantitative properties (such as in Probabilistic Computational Tree Logic). A runtime use of probabilistic model checking for the dynamic QoS management has been adopted in self-adaptive computer systems with a computation overhead acceptable for realistic system sizes [13,22].
- *Model finding* [19] (as supported by formal specification languages like Alloy, Maude, and FORMULA) is a technique to synthesize a model of the system (or of the relevant parts of the system) that satisfies formally and declaratively specified system constraints and objectives. Model finding over open-world programs uses SAT solvers at the core of the model synthesis process. The synthesised model corresponds to a system configuration that fullfils the system goals given its current state, and is used to drive the system to reach this target configuration. The main challenge of this technique is the limited scalability for systems with a large number of components [13].
- *Runtime certification* (see, for example, the approaches ConSerts [27] and ENTRUST [12] in the context of self-adaptive systems, to name a few) is a technique for the dynamic provision of *assurance cases* [1] arguing the suitability of the software for its intended application at runtime.

3   Abstract State Machines and the ASMETA Toolset

ASMs [10,11] is a state-based formal method, extension of Finite State Machines (FSMs). ASM *states* are algebraic structures, i.e., domains of objects with functions and predicates defined on them. An ASM *location*, defined as the pair (*function-name, list-of-parameter-values*), represents the abstract ASM concept of basic object containers. The couple (*location, value*) represents a machine memory unit. Therefore, ASM states can be viewed as abstract memories.

Location values are changed by firing *transition rules*. They express the modification of functions interpretation from one state to the next one. Note that the algebra signature is fixed and that functions are total (by interpreting undefined locations $f(x)$ with value *undef*). Location *updates* are given as assignments of the form $loc := v$, where loc is a location and v its new value. They are the basic units of rules construction. There is a limited but powerful set of *rule constructors* to express: guarded actions (`if-then`), simultaneous parallel actions (`par`), sequential actions (`seq`), nondeterminism (existential quantification `choose`), and unrestricted synchronous parallelism (universal quantification `forall`).

An ASM *computation* is, therefore, defined as a finite or infinite sequence $S_0, S_1, \ldots, S_n, \ldots$ of states of the machine, where S_0 is an initial state and each S_{n+1} is obtained from S_n by firing the unique *main rule* that represents the starting point of the machine execution and in turn fires other transitions rules. An ASM can have more than one *initial state*.

In a machine computation step, some locations can be updated. Functions are classified as *static* (never change during any run of the machine) or *dynamic* (may change as a consequence of agent actions or *updates*). Dynamic functions are distinguished between *monitored* (only read by the machine and modified by the environment) and *controlled* (read and written by the machine). A further classification is between *basic* and *derived* functions, i.e., those coming with a specification or computation mechanism given in terms of other functions. It is possible to specify state *invariants*.

Running Model Example. Code 1 reports the ASM model of a gate controller for the *Railroad Crossing Problem* [18]. When a train is approaching a railroad crossing, the light, which is off when the gate is open, starts flashing and the gate receives command to close, moving from state open to state closed throughout state closing. When the train has passed, the gate receives command to open, moving from state closed to state open throughout state opening, and the light stop flashing.

This ASM model of the controller mediates between continuous processes (closing and opening of the gate) and discrete computations controlling them.

At any time, an event LIGHT or GATE occurs to provide commands controlling the light status (FLASHING or OFF) and the gate status (CLOSED, OPENED, CLOSING or OPENING). The set of specified invariants guarantee that *The light is off only when the gate is open* and vice versa *the light is flashing if the gate is not open*, and that the only valid traces of the gate behaviour are the sequences *closed, opening, open*, and *open, closing, closed*. Otherwise the gate is not controlled in a safe and correct way (variable *gateStatusUpdateOk* indicated whether the gate has been properly controlled).

ASMETA Modelling Process and Tools. ASMs allow an iterative design process, shown in Fig. 1, based on model refinement. Tools supporting the process are part of the ASMETA framework [4]. Requirements modelling starts by developing a high-level model called *ground model* (ASM 0 in Fig. 1). It is specified by reasoning on the informal requirements (generally given as a text in natural language) and using terms of the application domain, possibly with the involvement of all stakeholders. The ground model should *correctly* reflect the intended requirements and should be *consistent*, i.e., without possible ambiguities of initial requirements. It does not need to be *complete*, i.e., it may not specify some given requirements. The ground model and the other ASM models can be edited in AsmEE by using the concrete syntax AsmetaL [16]. Starting from the ground model, through a sequence of *refined* models, further functional requirements can be specified until a complete model of the system is obtained. The refinement process allows to tackle the system complexity, and to bridge, in a seamless manner, specification to code. At each refinement level, already at the level of the ground model, different V&V activities can be applied, such

```
asm railroadGate
import ../../STDL/StandardLibrary
signature:
   enum domain LightState = {FLASHING | OFF}
   enum domain GateState = {CLOSED | OPENED | CLOSING | OPENING}
   enum domain EventDomain = {LIGHT | GATE}
   dynamic controlled light: LightState
   dynamic controlled gate: GateState
   dynamic controlled gateStatusUpdateOk: Boolean
   dynamic monitored lightMon: LightState
   dynamic monitored gateMon: GateState
   dynamic monitored event: EventDomain

definitions:

   //When the gate is closing, is closed or is opening, the light flashes.
   invariant over gate: (gate=CLOSING or gate =CLOSED or gate =OPENING) implies light = FLASHING

      //invariant over gate: gate != OPENED iff light = FLASHING

   //The light is off only when the gate is open.
   invariant over gate: light = OFF implies gate = OPENED

   //The gate cannot be "closed" after "opening"
   invariant over gate: gateStatusUpdateOk

   main rule r_Main =
      if(event = LIGHT) then
         light := lightMon
      else
         par
            gate := gateMon //lazy evaluation di gateMon
            if( (gate=OPENED and (gateMon=CLOSED or gateMon=OPENING)) or
               (gate=OPENING and (gateMon=CLOSED or gateMon=CLOSING)) or
               (gate=CLOSED and (gateMon=OPENED or gateMon=CLOSING)) or
               (gate=CLOSING and (gateMon=OPENED or gateMon=OPENING)))
            then gateStatusUpdateOk := false
            else gateStatusUpdateOk := true
            endif
         endpar
      endif

default init s0:
   function light = OFF
   function gate = OPENED
   function gateStatusUpdateOk = true
```

Code 1. ASM model of the Gate Controller

as model simulation, scenario-based simulation, property verification by model checking, runtime verification, to name a few. Tools supporting such activities are integrated into ASMETA (see Fig. 1).

Model to code transformation are supported for C++ code [9], and *conformance checking* is possible to check if the implementation, if externally provided, conforms to its specification. The tool ATGT [15] can be used to automatically generate tests from ASM models and, therefore, to check the conformance offline; CoMA [3], instead, can be used to perform runtime verification, i.e., to check the conformance online. The runtime verification approach is supported only for Java code; it consists in observing the behaviour of a Java object and checking

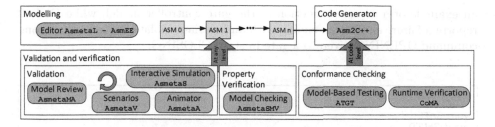

Fig. 1. ASM-based development process

Type	Functions		State 0	State 1	State 2	State 3	State 4	State 5	State 6
M	event		LIGHT	GATE	GATE	GATE	GATE	LIGHT	
M	lightMon		FLASHING	FLASHING	FLASHING	FLASHING	FLASHING	OFF	
C	gateStatusUpdateOk		true	true	true	true	true	true	true
C	gate		OPENED	OPENED	CLOSING	CLOSED	OPENING	OPENED	OPENED
C	light		OFF	FLASHING	FLASHING	FLASHING	FLASHING	FLASHING	OFF
M	gateMon			CLOSING	CLOSED	OPENING	OPENED	OPENED	

Fig. 2. Simulation of the ASM model for the Gate Controller

that it conforms to the expected behaviour captured by an ASM specification. The approach relies on the model checker AsmetaSMV (which, in turn, is based on the NuSMV model checker) and therefore if suffers of all the limitation of a model checker. Our AsmetaS@run.time approach tries to overcome limitations due to system code language and to the size of models.

Model Simulation. Among the others, we here focus on the simulation tool, AsmetaS [16], since its features are exploited by our ASM@run.time approach. Essentially, AsmetaS is an interpreter which makes ASM models (as instances of the Ecore[2] metamodel *AsmM* [16]) executable by navigating the Ecore java object graph (the in-memory representation of AsmM instances) and making computations of the ASM update sets. AsmetaS simulator is used to observe system executions by means of *interactive simulation*. This way of model validation consists in providing inputs (i.e., values of monitored functions) to the machine and observing the computed state. We have different options for model execution: the default one is the *step-by-step* simulation, when a next state is computed from the previous one by applying simultaneously all the possible location updates; a further option (interesting for our future purposes) is the *run Until Empty* to stop the simulation when the update set is empty, i.e., the machine has reached a final state or a fix-point state. The simulator, at each step, performs *consistent updates checking* to check that all the updates are consistent (two updates are inconsistent if they update the same location to two different values at the same time [11]), and *invariant checking*. Figure 2 shows

---

[2] https://wiki.eclipse.org/Ecore.

an example of a correct execution of the gate controller model, while Code 2 reports a failure simulation ending with an invariant violation due to the wrong command OPENING given to a gate in state CLOSING.

```
** Simulation **
<State 1>
event=GATE
gate=OPENED
gateMon=CLOSING
gateStatusUpdateOk=true
light=FLASHING
</State 1>
<State 2>
event=GATE
gate=CLOSING
gateMon=OPENING
gateStatusUpdateOk=true
light=FLASHING
</State 2>
<State 3 (controlled)>
event=GATE
gate=OPENING
gateMon=OPENING
gateStatusUpdateOk=false
light=FLASHING
</State 3>
<Invariant violation>
gateStatusUpdateOk
</Invariant violation>
```

Code 2. Invariant violation of the ASM model of the Gate Controller

4   Runtime Simulation with ASMs

4.1   Overall Approach and Outlook

A system model is an abstract model (or also a multitude of models) describing certain aspects or viewpoints of the system or subsystems of it at different levels of abstraction or detail. The simulation of a system model at runtime with the running software system is crucial in computing the dynamic input/output behaviour in a real setting. It also makes sense that a property of interest concerning some observations of behavior (e.g., about state reachability, order of actions, information exposed, etc.) may be checked more efficiently on the runtime model than on the real system. Correctness policies about resource usage or application interactions could be, for example, formalized and encoded as *enforcement models* to proactively correct misuses and misbehaviours [25].

Regardless of whether the system has been developed incrementally or not from the model, we assume there is a *homomorphic relation* [26] between the model and the system: simulating a model of a real system should yield the same results as performing a real experiment followed by observation and collection of the experimental results. Figure 3 visually illustrates how runtime simulation works, distinguishing the design and the runtime phases. Essentially, a runtime simulation and control tool operates between the system model and the real running system; it traces the state of the model and of the system realizing a conceivable causal relation depending on low level implementation details.

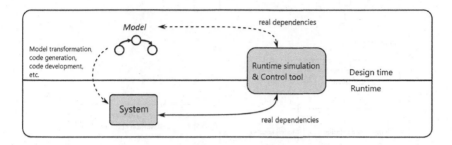

Fig. 3. Runtime simulation

This runtime simulation and control tool could be used in conjunction with an *enforcer* component tool to concretely prevent the execution of unsafe commands in the running system. In this case, the intended use of the runtime simulator is for *input sanitisation* [14], namely to evaluate safety assertions when there is an input event that may change the state of the running system, and prevent the change if it violates an assertion on the runtime model of the system. This safety assertion enforcement mechanism is useful, for example, for cyber physical systems where the environment is only partially observable [23], and, in general, for any safety-critical system, where in certain (possibly transient circumstances/contexts) the effects of not enforcing certain safety assertions would lead to human hazards, as it happens for medical software [2].

We do not here target real-time systems since these systems require dedicated solutions (e.g., real-time operating systems) and pose specific challenges.

4.2   AsmetaS@run.time Simulation Environment

An overview of the overall AsmetaS@run.time simulation framework using ASMs as runtime models is shown in Fig. 4. This framework was recently developed as part of the ASMETA toolset.

The core of the framework is the subsystem `Simulator@runtime`. Its component `Container` supports simulation *as-a-service* features (the interface `IModel-Execution`) of the conventional ASMETA simulator `AsmetaS`, including model roll-back to the previous safe state after a failure of the model execution (e.g., invariant violations, inconsistent updates, ill-formed inputs, etc.) while processing an input event. The container allows also the dynamic adaptation of a running ASM model (the interface `IModelAdaptation`) to add/change/delete safety assertions at runtime and, therefore, guarantee a safer (though possibly temporary) execution of the system.

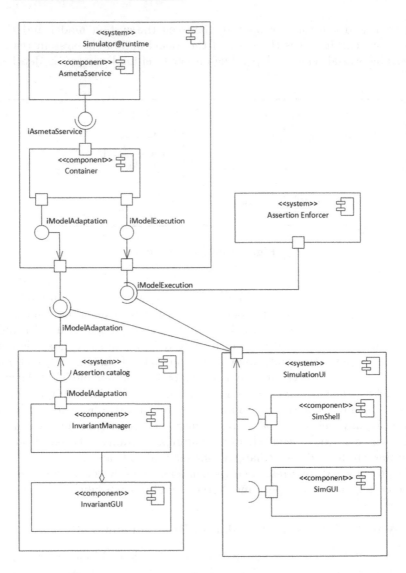

Fig. 4. Runtime simulation with `AsmetaS@run.time`

The subsystems `SimulationUI` and `Assertion Catalog` are based on the interfaces provided by the `Simulator@runtime` subsystem and supports the dynamic *Human-Model-Interaction* (both in a graphical and in a command-line way) to realize a sort of dashboard to visualize the current status of the executing model and to enact commands for changing safety properties respectively.

In the following subsections, more details on the two main functionalities of this platform are described.

Runtime Simulation. An *active simulation* is an entity (an instance of the simulator `AsmetaS`) characterized by an identifier, an associated ASM model and its current execution state, a simulation state (see below), and a set of actions. These last are methods (the operations of the `IModelExecution` interface) labelling the transitions of a protocol state machine that specifies the behaviour of the *simulation life-cycle*: the corresponding UML protocol state machine diagram is shown in Fig. 5. When an action on a simulation entity is executed, the transition labeled by the corresponding method is taken in a synchronized way.

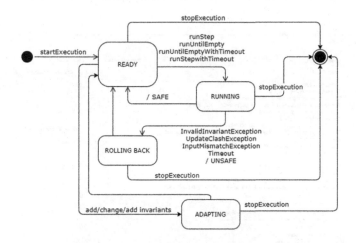

Fig. 5. Runtime simulation lifecycle

A simulation entity could be in only one of the following states: `READY`, `RUNNING`, `ROLLING BACK`, and `ADAPTING`. Once started, the simulation entity is in state `READY`. The simulation entity moves to state `RUNNING` when one of the following operations of the `IModelExecution` interface is called: i) `runStep`, to run the ASM model *step by step* interactively; ii) `runUntilEmpty`, to stop the simulation when the *update set is empty*; iii) `runStepWithTimeout` and `runUntilEmptyWithTimeout`, as i) and ii) respectively, but with a timeout, so the ASM execution is suspended if the timeout period elapses prior to completion of the ASM run. The simulation entity is in state `ROLLING BACK` when the execution timeout or an exception arises. This last could be an `InvalidInvariantException` (when an ASM invariant is violated), or an `UpdateClashException` (when an inconsistent update occurs, i.c. when two updates refer to the same location but are distinct) or an `InputMismatchException` (when the input value the user enters for a monitored function is of a different type than that required by the model). When the ASM model roll-back to the previous (safe) state completes, the simulation entity comes back to the `READY` state. From the `READY` state, the simulation entity can move to state `ADAPTING` for the run-time adaptation (concerning the safety invariants to be verified) of the system model (more details are provided in the next paragraph). From any state, upon the event `stopExecution` the simulation entity is terminated.

Figure 6 shows the ASM model of the gate controller through the UI `SimGUI`. In particular, the central panel shows the ASM runs and the simulation results. The last one produced the verdict `UNSAFE` upon the invariant violation achieved with the same input values reported in Code 2. Then, the model is rolled back to the previous safe state (when the gate is CLOSING); then, a further run step is performed with a right input value for the monitored function `gateMon` (`CLOSED`) and a new safe state is produced as new current state.

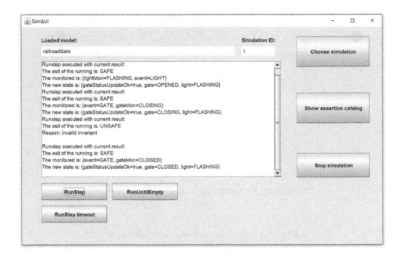

Fig. 6. Runtime simulation UI

Safety Assertion Adaptation. A catalog of safety assertions describing possible situations that may produce a violation of safety are expressed in the ASM runtime model in terms of ASM invariants. The catalog may be dynamically updated at runtime in case dangerous situations have not been foreseen at design time or because of unanticipated changes in the requirements for safety after the system release. So the running ASM model can be adapted dynamically by the simulation container to incorporate the new invariant definitions or simply modify or cancel existing ones. This can be done by an external client program or manually by the user (see the screenshot of the UI `Assertion Catalog` in Fig. 7) through the UI connected to the container.

To the purpose of supporting on-the-fly changes of the underlying ASM model consistently, a separate thread (different from the simulation thread) of the container manages the model adaptation; it observes the status of the simulation to determine when it reaches a *quiescent state* (i.e., it is in the `READY` state), so it is

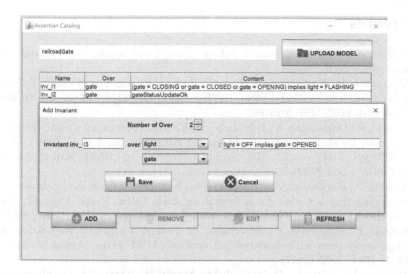

Fig. 7. Assertion catalog UI

not currently in execution and no adaptation activity of it is going on. Once the quiescent state is reached, the adaptation manager thread updates the model to add/change/delete a safety invariant (the state `ADAPTING` in Fig. 5). Then, the ASM model execution continues from its current state. The adding of a safety property that would be immediately violated in the current state of the ASM model would be forbidden at the level of the user interface.

5   Conclusion

In this paper, we have presented our long-term vision of using the ASM executable models as formal support at runtime to assure safe execution of a software system. To evaluate the proposed approach we are conducting a first series of experiments in which we consider as runtime ASM models some case studies available in the ASMETA example repository. Then, as a second series of experiments we are going to execute runtime ASM models in tandem with prototype realizations of systems that these models specify. Our short-term plan is to complete the implementation of a runtime enforcement for *input sanitisation* [14] to protect the system from its (untrusted) environment. A preliminary conceptual view of such a mechanism was presented in [24].

In the future, we plan to apply the ASM@run.time framework in the context of self-adaptive systems [5,29]. Our long term goal is to develop a complete framework able to deal with requirements changes also affecting the model behavior, and therefore providing model adaptation features at runtime. We also want to test its effective operation in the area of safety-critical systems, as for example those in the medical software domain and in the cyber-physical domain, by considering running systems independently developed from the models.

References

1. Defence standard 00–56, issue 4: Safety management requirements for defence systems, June 2007
2. Alemzadeh, H., Kalbarczyk, Z., Iyer, R., Raman, J.: Analysis of safety-critical computer failures in medical devices. IEEE Secur. Priv. **11**(4), 14–26 (2013). https://doi.org/10.1109/MSP.2013.49
3. Arcaini, P., Gargantini, A., Riccobene, E.: CoMA: conformance monitoring of Java programs by abstract state machines. In: Khurshid, S., Sen, K. (eds.) RV 2011. LNCS, vol. 7186, pp. 223–238. Springer, Heidelberg (2012). https://doi.org/10.1007/978-3-642-29860-8_17
4. Arcaini, P., Gargantini, A., Riccobene, E., Scandurra, P.: A model-driven process for engineering a toolset for a formal method. Softw. Pract. Exp. **41**, 155–166 (2011). https://doi.org/10.1002/spe.1019. http://dx.doi.org/10.1002/spe.1019
5. Arcaini, P., Riccobene, E., Scandurra, P.: Formal design and verification of self-adaptive systems with decentralized control. ACM Trans. Auton. Adapt. Syst. **11**(4), 25:1–25:35 (2017)
6. Aßmann, U., Götz, S., Jézéquel, J.-M., Morin, B., Trapp, M.: A reference architecture and roadmap for models@run.time systems. In: Bencomo, N., France, R., Cheng, B.H.C., Aßmann, U. (eds.) Models@run.time. LNCS, vol. 8378, pp. 1–18. Springer, Cham (2014). https://doi.org/10.1007/978-3-319-08915-7_1
7. Baresi, L., Ghezzi, C.: The disappearing boundary between development-time and run-time. In: Roman, G., Sullivan, K.J. (eds.) Proceedings of the Workshop on Future of Software Engineering Research, FoSER 2010, at the 18th ACM SIGSOFT International Symposium on Foundations of Software Engineering, 2010, Santa Fe, NM, USA, 7–11 November 2010, pp. 17–22. ACM (2010)
8. Bencomo, N., Götz, S., Song, H.: Models@run.time: a guided tour of the state of the art and research challenges. Softw. Syst. Model. **18**(5), 3049–3082 (2019). https://doi.org/10.1007/s10270-018-00712-x
9. Bonfanti, S., Gargantini, A., Mashkoor, A.: Design and validation of a C++ code generator from Abstract State Machines specifications. J. Softw. Evol. Process **32**(2), e2205 (2020). https://doi.org/10.1002/smr.2205. https://onlinelibrary.wiley.com/doi/abs/10.1002/smr.2205
10. Börger, E., Raschke, A.: Modeling Companion for Software Practitioners. Springer, Heidelberg (2018). https://doi.org/10.1007/978-3-662-56641-1
11. Börger, E., Stärk, R.: Abstract State Machines: A Method for High-Level System Design and Analysis. Springer, Heidelberg (2003). https://doi.org/10.1007/978-3-642-18216-7
12. Calinescu, R., Weyns, D., Gerasimou, S., Iftikhar, M.U., Habli, I., Kelly, T.: Engineering trustworthy self-adaptive software with dynamic assurance cases. IEEE Trans. Software Eng. **44**(11), 1039–1069 (2018)
13. Calinescu, R., Kikuchi, S.: Formal methods @ runtime. In: Calinescu, R., Jackson, E. (eds.) Monterey Workshop 2010. LNCS, vol. 6662, pp. 122–135. Springer, Heidelberg (2011). https://doi.org/10.1007/978-3-642-21292-5_7
14. Falcone, Y., Mariani, L., Rollet, A., Saha, S.: Runtime failure prevention and reaction. In: Bartocci, E., Falcone, Y. (eds.) Lectures on Runtime Verification. LNCS, vol. 10457, pp. 103–134. Springer, Cham (2018). https://doi.org/10.1007/978-3-319-75632-5_4

15. Gargantini, A., Riccobene, E., Rinzivillo, S.: Using spin to generate tests from ASM specifications. In: Börger, E., Gargantini, A., Riccobene, E. (eds.) ASM 2003. LNCS, vol. 2589, pp. 263–277. Springer, Heidelberg (2003). https://doi.org/10.1007/3-540-36498-6_15

16. Gargantini, A., Riccobene, E., Scandurra, P.: A metamodel-based language and a simulation engine for abstract state machines. J. UCS **14**(12), 1949–1983 (2008). https://doi.org/10.3217/jucs-014-12-1949

17. Goldsby, H.J., Cheng, B.H.C., Zhang, J.: AMOEBA-RT: run-time verification of adaptive software. In: Giese, H. (ed.) MODELS 2007. LNCS, vol. 5002, pp. 212–224. Springer, Heidelberg (2008). https://doi.org/10.1007/978-3-540-69073-3_23

18. Gurevich, Y., Huggins, J.K.: The railroad crossing problem: an experiment with instantaneous actions and immediate reactions. In: Kleine Büning, H. (ed.) CSL 1995. LNCS, vol. 1092, pp. 266–290. Springer, Heidelberg (1996). https://doi.org/10.1007/3-540-61377-3_43

19. Jackson, E.K., Schulte, W.: Understanding specification languages through their model theory. In: Calinescu, R., Garlan, D. (eds.) Monterey Workshop 2012. LNCS, vol. 7539, pp. 396–415. Springer, Heidelberg (2012). https://doi.org/10.1007/978-3-642-34059-8_21

20. Legay, A., Delahaye, B., Bensalem, S.: Statistical model checking: an overview. In: Barringer, H., et al. (eds.) RV 2010. LNCS, vol. 6418, pp. 122–135. Springer, Heidelberg (2010). https://doi.org/10.1007/978-3-642-16612-9_11

21. Liang, H., Dong, J.S., Sun, J., Wong, W.E.: Software monitoring through formal specification animation. ISSE **5**(4), 231–241 (2009). https://doi.org/10.1007/s11334-009-0096-1

22. Moreno, G.A., Cámara, J., Garlan, D., Schmerl, B.R.: Proactive self-adaptation under uncertainty: a probabilistic model checking approach. In: Nitto, E.D., Harman, M., Heymans, P. (eds.) Proceedings of the 2015 10th Joint Meeting on Foundations of Software Engineering, ESEC/FSE 2015, Bergamo, Italy, 30 August–4 September 2015, pp. 1–12. ACM (2015). https://doi.org/10.1145/2786805.2786853

23. Pinisetty, S., Roop, P.S., Smyth, S., Allen, N., Tripakis, S., von Hanxleden, R.: Runtime enforcement of cyber-physical systems. ACM Trans. Embed. Comput. Syst. **16**(5s), 178:1–178:25 (2017). https://doi.org/10.1145/3126500

24. Riccobene, E., Scandurra, P.: Exploring the concept of abstract state machines for system runtime enforcement. In: Raschke, A., Méry, D., Houdek, F. (eds.) ABZ 2020. LNCS, vol. 12071, pp. 244–247. Springer, Cham (2020). https://doi.org/10.1007/978-3-030-48077-6_18

25. Riganelli, O., Micucci, D., Mariani, L.: Controlling interactions with libraries in android apps through runtime enforcement. ACM Trans. Auton. Adapt. Syst. **14**(2), 8:1–8:29 (2019). https://doi.org/10.1145/3368087

26. Tendeloo, Y.V., Mierlo, S.V., Vangheluwe, H.: A multi-paradigm modelling approach to live modelling. Softw. Syst. Model. **18**(5), 2821–2842 (2019). https://doi.org/10.1007/s10270-018-0700-7

27. Trapp, M., Schneider, D.: Safety assurance of open adaptive systems – a survey. In: Bencomo, N., France, R., Cheng, B.H.C., Aßmann, U. (eds.) Models@run.time. LNCS, vol. 8378, pp. 279–318. Springer, Cham (2014). https://doi.org/10.1007/978-3-319-08915-7_11

28. Weyns, D., Iftikhar, M.U.: Model-based simulation at runtime for self-adaptive systems. In: Kounev, S., Giese, H., Liu, J. (eds.) 2016 IEEE International Conference on Autonomic Computing, ICAC 2016, Wuerzburg, Germany, 17–22 July 2016, pp. 364–373. IEEE Computer Society (2016). https://doi.org/10.1109/ICAC.2016.67
29. Weyns, D., Iftikhar, M.U.: ActivFORMS: a model-based approach to engineer self-adaptive systems. CoRR abs/1908.11179 (2019). http://arxiv.org/abs/1908.11179
30. Zhuang, C., Liu, J., Xiong, H.: Digital twin-based smart production management and control framework for the complex product assembly shop-floor. Int. J. Adv. Manuf. Technol. **96**(1), 1149–1163 (2018)

Merging Railway Standard Notations in a Formal DSL-Based Framework

Asfand Yar[1], Akram Idani[1(✉)], and Simon Collart-Dutilleul[2,3]

[1] Univ. Grenoble Alpes, CNRS, Grenoble INP, LIG, 38000 Grenoble, France
asfand.yar@grenoble-inp.org, akram.idani@univ-grenoble-alpes.fr
[2] Institut de Recherche Technologique Railenium, 59300 Famars, France
[3] Univ. Lille Nord de France, IFSTTAR, 59666 Villeneuve d'Ascq Cedex, France
simon.collart-dutilleul@ifsttar.fr

Abstract. The design of a railway signalling system may be validated
using three basic concepts: (1) functional standards, (2) domain specific notations, and (3) safety requirements checking. However, there
is a lack of tools that merge these notions in a unified framework to
be used by standardisation authorities, as well as domain experts and
safety engineers. In this ongoing work we make the bridge between the
three notions using Meeduse, a tool in which the B method is applied
in order to formally reason on the correctness of domain specific languages (DSLs) and simulate their dynamic semantics using the ProB
animator. The application context of this work is that of two well known
standards in the railway field: RailTopoModel and ERTMS/ETCS. We
propose a railway DSL framework whose static semantics are built on
top of RailTopoModel and the underlying dynamic semantics conform
to ERTMS/ETCS. The overall approach is assisted by the B method,
which allows us to define, prove and animate safety-critical behaviors
given domain-centric models.

Keywords: ERTMS/ETCS · RailTopoModel · B method · DSL

1 Introduction

In the railway field, there are several tools that propose Domain Specific Languages (DSLs) to model railroad networks such as RaIL-AiD[1] and SafeCap [7].
They allow the design of readable models thanks to domain specific notations.
However, most of their DSLs are not formally defined and hence they do not
apply formal verification techniques such as theorem proving or model-checking
to guarantee the correctness of the underlying semantics. Furthermore, often
the DSLs they provide are not directly derived from existing standards, such as
RailTopoModel [8] and ERTMS/ETCS [3]. In order to circumvent these shortcomings, we are developing a formally proved railway DSL framework whose

---

[1] Railway Infrastructure and Layout Aided Designer (https://www.rail-aid.com).

© Springer Nature Switzerland AG 2020
H. Muccini et al. (Eds.): ECSA 2020, CCIS 1269, pp. 411–419, 2020.
https://doi.org/10.1007/978-3-030-59155-7_30

static semantics implement RailTopoModel and dynamic semantics comply with ERTMS/ETCS operating rules.

RailTopoModel is the International Railway Standard (IRS 30100[2]) developed by the UIC (International Union of Railways), with the contribution of several railway infrastructure managers and industrial companies, for the sake of optimizing communication between the various actors of the railway sector. It defines and describes the structure of a railway network together with the physical installations that it manages. These structural business assets are intended to be as complete as possible, however the model does not provide operating rules such as route computations and train movements. Our work addresses these behaviours by focusing on the European signalling and train control system ERTMS/ETCS in order to introduce standardized management rules and their underlying safety properties within RailTopoModel. Our approach is assisted by the B method which allows to define, prove and animate safety-critical behaviours given domain specific models designed in our DSL framework.

Section 2 outlines the main principles of this ongoing work. In Sect. 3 discusses how the formal B method will be integrated within our DSL-based framework. Finally, Sect. 4 draws the conclusions and the perspectives of this work.

2   Proposed Approach

2.1   Overall Architecture

Figure 1 gives an overall view about our approach for merging RailTopoModel and ERTMS/ETCS in a formal DSL-based framework. Our framework is composed of the two layers presented at the top and at the bottom of Fig. 1.

The semantics layer covers both static and dynamic semantics of our DSLs: the static semantics are built on meta-models that we derive from RailTopo-Model, and the dynamic semantics are built on ERTMS/ETCS specifications. Regarding the execution layer, it is managed by tool Meeduse[3] that animates behaviours of domain specific models conforming to the semantics layer. Formal B specifications are used in both layers in order to apply formal reasoning techniques to our DSLs: proofs for the semantics definition, and animation/model-checking for models execution. The choice of the B method is motivated by several aspects. First, the B method is widely used in the railway field and there are several success stories that support this fact [9], such as for example Meteor, the automated Paris subway. Recently, a comparative study of several formal methods regarding their industrial suitability [10] has been done and rated B high when it comes to formal constructs like those applied in our work.

---

[2] The IRS 30100 is the foundation for quick, unambiguous and error-free data storage and data exchange inside and between business processes [8].

[3] http://vasco.imag.fr/tools/meeduse.

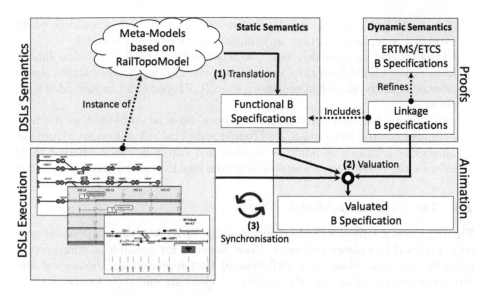

Fig. 1. Architecture of the proposed framework

2.2 Methodology

RailTopoModel is presented in [8] based on a UML class diagram divided into four packages. The Base package of RailTopoModel defines a railway network by an abstraction level (meso, micro, macro) and a composition of railway resources. For example, a network resource can be a NetElement such as line sections, or an InterlockingNetEntity such as signals. Having this reference UML model of RailTopoModel, we introduce two additional meta-models with specific concepts, each of them led to a particular DSL: (1) the Topology DSL allows the domain expert to represent lines, tracks and their connections; and (2) the Infrastructure DSL allows to add objects over a given topology such as physical objects (*e.g.* stations), immaterial objects (*e.g.* speed limits) and logical objects (*e.g.* signals). In order to ensure the conformance of our DSLs with RailTopoModel, our methodology follows the following established rules:

- The Core package contains the exact RailTopoModel: as the semantics of RailTopoModel are defined using a UML class diagram, this step simply introduces the underlying UML concepts within the Eclipse Modeling Framework (EMF), as an EMF meta-model.
- Define the additional meta-models (Topology and Infrastructure) outside the core package and use references. Our aim is to guarantee that the initial RailTopoModel semantics are kept unchanged during the DSL development. The core meta-model remains then low-coupled with the additional meta-models. This rule provides two main advantages: (1) there is no need to modify or extend the core meta-model and therefore it can be considered as

an independent artifact, and (2) the additional meta-models could be easily extended or replaced without any impact on the core meta-model.

– Classes of our meta-models (such as those of ERTMS/ETCS) must inherit from classes issued from the Core meta-model. This inheritance allows one to associate clearly identified semantics from RailTopoModel to any additional class.

– Associations between the additional classes must be computed as much as possible from the elements of RailTopoModel. This rule allows to reduce the number of relations as much as possible and carefully check whether there exists a way to compute these relations from relations of the core meta-model.

2.3 The Core Meta-Model

Figure 2 shows a subset of the Core meta-model. This meta-model applies generic concepts used in railway networks. Class Network for example is composed of network resources (class NetworkResource) that represent its topological and structural properties such as the various net elements and their locations.

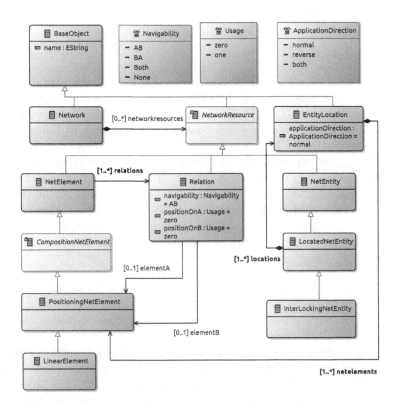

Fig. 2. Subset of the core Meta-model

2.4   Defining the Additional Meta-Models

Figure 3 illustrates the Topology meta-model where the upper part contains the
root class of this meta-model called Topology. It consists of LinearElements and
InterlockingNetEntities. The bottom part of meta-model shows the class Track
(inherited from LinearElement) and the classes Switch and BufferStop (inherited
from InterLockingNetEntity). BufferStop can be used as a start or end of any
network track while Switch is the intermediate junction among three tracks. Each
switch has an attribute called continueCourse which sets the track to be used
(right track or left track). Note that classes LinearElement and InterlockingNetEntity are defined in the core package. On the one hand they are referenced
by the root class and on the other hand they are specialized by the additional
classes Track, Switch and BufferStop. Indeed, these three classes are not initially
defined by RailTopoModel but they are required by a railway DSL especially to
define the dynamic semantics.

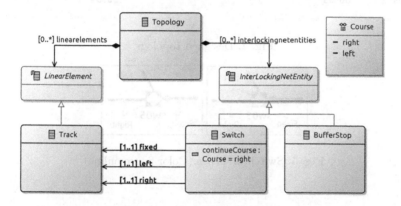

Fig. 3. Topology Meta-Model

Regarding the Infrastructure meta-model, we apply the same principles. This
meta-model contains infrastructure elements to make railway network operational. For this purpose, we introduce concepts from ERTMS/ETCS such as:
movement authority, train, virtual block and track-side.

2.5   Modeling

Our DSL tool allows to instantiate the aforementioned meta-models using
domain specific notations. Figure 4 is an example of a topology designed based
on the Topology meta-model. It represents buffer stops (bus01, bus02, bus03),
switches (sw01, sw02, sw03 etc) and tracks (trc01, trc02, trc03 etc).

As presented by the topology meta-model, each switch has three branches:
the fixed branch, the left branch and the right branch. The fixed branch is a
fixed course for the switch which is not change-able while the continue course is

change-able and can be set to left or right which directs the train either to the left branch or the right branch. In the left hand-side of Fig. 5, the green arrow shows the course assigned to the branches. The arrow to right branch is green as continue course of switch is set to right. The continue course of the same switch shown in the right side of Fig. 5 is set to left which turns the color of arrow to left branch into green and arrow to right branch into red.

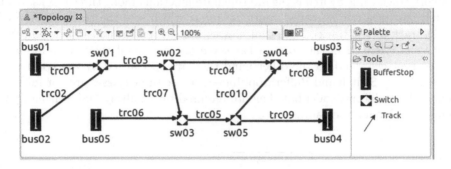

Fig. 4. Designed topology

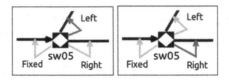

Fig. 5. Switch branches (Color figure online)

3 Formal Semantics

The advantage of a MDE architecture is that it allows to easily develop DSL tools with graphical or textual concrete syntax. This approach puts into practice a clear separation of concerns ranging from requirements to target platforms, and going through several design stages. This is useful especially for railway model editors, because the interoperability between these tools is favored by the use of standardized meta-modeling formalisms. A DSL allows to reduce the risk that human errors such as misinterpretation of the requirements and specification documents lead to erroneously validate the specifications, and produce a wrong real system. Still, while MDE provides solutions to the validation problem, the verification problem remains a major challenge. In this ongoing work we formally define the semantics of our DSL tool using the B method and apply the underlying reasoning tools such as the AtlierB prover and the ProB model-checker. Note that most of the static semantics of our railway DSL tool and the associated graphical concrete syntax are available, and currently we are actively working on the definition of the formal semantics.

3.1   Static Semantics

The formal definition of static semantics is ensured by our tool Meeduse [6]. It applies a classical UML-to-B translation [5] (step (Translation) in Fig. 1) to meta-models and produces a functional B specification covering data structures as well as basic operations (getters, setters, etc). The structure of the resulting B specifications is presented in Fig. 6 where the B machine of the Infrastructure DSL requires data (*sees* dependency) defined in the Topology DSL. The Infrastructure machine is further refined in order to redefine abstract infrastructure objects by means of ERTMS data objects (such as eurobalises, virtual blocks) that are not initially provided by RailTopoModel but which are part of the static semantics. The refinement is then dedicated to guarantee by proofs that this redefinition preserves the infrastructure DSL invariants.

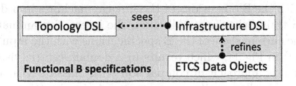

Fig. 6. Formal static semantics

3.2   Dynamic Semantics

The dynamic semantics of a DSL deal with behavioural descriptions that make the DSL executable. In our work, we apply ERTMS/ETCS as a way to introduce execution within RailTopoModel. Indeed, ERTMS/ETCS defines safe train behaviours thanks to the mechanism of movement authority. It describes how and when permissions to enter block sections are assigned to trains. Note that in the last decade, several works have been devoted in order to provide formal models of ERTMS/ETCS. Recently the ABZ'2018 conference [4] has published several B models, which provides us a rich catalog of proved B operations and invariants.

Our objective is to reuse these existing B specifications for the dynamic semantics definition. For this purpose, we create linkage B specifications (Fig. 1) in which we apply two mechanisms from the B method: refinement and inclusion. In the B method, refinements have two main principles: add requirements by going from abstract models to more concrete ones and prove the preservation of the abstract model invariants. The composition, such as inclusion, allows to beak down the system by applying the separation of concerns principle.

In our approach, refinements would guarantee the preservation of the safety invariants of ERTMS/ETCS defined in the re-used B specifications and inclusion provides an access to the B variables that represent the static semantics and use them in place of those of the refined machines. Proved B operations are then refined by DSL-centric operations and hence behaviours that comply with ERTMS/ETCS are applied to our DSLs.

3.3 Execution

DSL execution is intended to perform early validation since the DSL is expected to behave as the target system should run. In our framework, this execution is done by Meeduse given domain-specific models that represent railway topologies and infrastructures conforming to RailTopoModel. First, Meeduse injects these models into the functional B specifications issued from our meta-models. This step, called (Valuation) in Fig. 1, creates enumerations and generates substitutions that assign concrete initial values to the B variables. Then, the tool asks ProB to compute the initial state of the B specifications and the list of operations that can be animated from this state. At this stage, railway experts can start playing with the B operations of the linkage machines in order to simulate ERTMS/ETCS train behaviours. All along the interactive animation, Meeduse synchronises the current state of the B specifications with the input models (step (Synchronisation) in Fig. 1), which results in a domain-centric visual animation. The interest of this approach in comparison with classical visual animation is that our framework allows railway experts to design by themselves the input models and validate their behaviours without being trained in formal methods.

4 Conclusion

The use of Domain-specific modelling languages becomes important in the railway domain as they provide support for railway mechanisms from their semantics definition to their concrete syntax. In the last decade, several tools and platforms [1,2,7,11,12] were proposed in order to allow railway experts to design railway infrastructures and associated signalling systems. However, the limitation with these tools is that either the semantics of their DSLs don't fully comply with international railway standards.

In the railway domain, several specifications are defined by European and national authorities like the ISO[4] specifications from AFNOR[5] or TSIs[6] from EUAR (European Union Agency for Railway). These specifications provide standardised engineering rules and infrastructure guidelines and allow the establishment of common interfaces for railway systems in order to maintain the compatibility among cross-border infrastructure objects. They also provide cost-effectiveness processes to ensure safety by using the best practices.

This paper presents the main principles of our ongoing work for the development and the execution of railway DSLs that comply with current standards: RailTopoModel and ERTMS/ETCS. We apply the B method to formally define the static and dynamic semantics and prove that functional specifications can be

---

[4] https://www.iso.org/.
[5] Association Française de Normalisation.
[6] Technical Specifications for Interoperability.

executed on a given ETCS-based infrastructure, without braking global safety invariants. Our approach is domain-centric, which allows domain experts to design topological views of a railway system and then play with scenarios that comply with ERTMS/ETCS. This work provides two main contributions in comparison with existing railway editors: our DSL is derived from approved railway standard documents (RailTopoModel and ERTMS/ETCS) and the underlying semantics follow a formal method with available reasoning tools.

References

1. Industrial Railway CAD software. https://hwww.railcomplete.com/
2. Railway Infrastructure and Layout Aided Designer. https://www.rail-aid.com/
3. The ERTMS/ETCS signalling system. http://www.railwaysignalling.eu/wp-content/uploads/2016/09/ERTMS_ETCS_signalling_system_revF.pdf
4. Butler, M., Raschke, A., Hoang, T.S., Reichl, K. (eds.): ABZ 2018. LNCS, vol. 10817. Springer, Cham (2018). https://doi.org/10.1007/978-3-319-91271-4
5. Idani, A., Ledru, Y.: B for modeling secure information systems. In: Butler, M., Conchon, S., Zaïdi, F. (eds.) ICFEM 2015. LNCS, vol. 9407, pp. 312–318. Springer, Cham (2015). https://doi.org/10.1007/978-3-319-25423-4_20
6. Idani, A., Ledru, Y., Vega, G.: Alliance of model-driven engineering with a proof-based formal approach. Innovations Syst. Softw. Eng. 1–19 (2020). https://doi.org/10.1007/s11334-020-00366-3
7. Iliasov, A., Lopatkin, I., Romanovsky, A.: The SafeCap platform for modelling railway safety and capacity. In: Bitsch, F., Guiochet, J., Kaâniche, M. (eds.) SAFECOMP 2013. LNCS, vol. 8153, pp. 130–137. Springer, Heidelberg (2013). https://doi.org/10.1007/978-3-642-40793-2_12
8. International Union of Railways (UIC): RailTopoModel - Railway infrastructure topological model (2016). ISBN 978-2-7461-2513-1
9. Lecomte, T.: Applying a formal method in industry: a 15-year trajectory. In: Alpuente, M., Cook, B., Joubert, C. (eds.) FMICS 2009. LNCS, vol. 5825, pp. 26–34. Springer, Heidelberg (2009). https://doi.org/10.1007/978-3-642-04570-7_3
10. Mashkoor, A., Kossak, F., Egyed, A.: Evaluating the suitability of state-based formal methods for industrial deployment. Softw. Pract. Experience 48(12), 2350–2379 (2018)
11. Vu, L., Haxthausen, A., Peleska, J.: A domain-specific language for railway interlocking systems. In: Proceedings of the 10th Symposium on Formal Methods for Automation and Safety in Railway and Automotive Systems, pp. 200–209. Technische Universität Braunschweig (2014)
12. Vu, L.H., Haxthausen, A.E., Peleska, J.: A domain-specific language for generic interlocking models and their properties. In: Fantechi, A., Lecomte, T., Romanovsky, A. (eds.) RSSRail 2017. LNCS, vol. 10598. Springer, Cham (2017). https://doi.org/10.1007/978-3-319-68499-4_7

Continuous Formal Verification of Microservice-Based Process Flows

Matteo Camilli$^{(\boxtimes)}$ (iD)

Faculty of Computer Science, Free University of Bozen-Bolzano, Bolzano, Italy
matteo.camilli@unibz.it

Abstract. The microservice architectural style is often used to implement modern cloud, IoT, and large-scale distributed applications. Here software development processes are characterized by short incremental iterations, where several updates and new functionalities are continuously integrated many times a day in a agile fashion. Such a paradigm shift calls for new formal approaches to systematic (design-time and runtime) verification. This paper introduces a formal framework to apply continuous verification of microservice based applications built on top of CONDUCTOR, i.e., an open source orchestration engine of microservices workflows in use at Netflix, Inc. for their production environment. Our proposal adopts a model-driven paradigm and it leverages solid foundation from Petri nets to specify and verify the behavior of time-dependent workflows. This paper describes our approach, the current implementation, and evaluation activity conducted on a taxi-hailing application example.

Keywords: Microservices · Petri nets · Formal verification · DevOps

1 Introduction

Microservices [11] represents an upward trending architectural style of modern cloud, IoT, or more in general advanced large-scale distributed applications. Even though fundamental principles of microservices are not novel or innovative[1], the migration towards microservices is still a sensitive matter nowadays. In fact, several leading companies applied huge reengeneering activities to adopt this paradigm. As a notable example, Netflix, Inc. [26] moved successfully from a monolithic architectural style to a microservices-based architecture in order to stream multimedia contents to an unprecedented amount of users every day. The adopted architecture builds upon the Netflix CONDUCTOR engine [10], an open source framework designed by Netflix Inc. and used daily in their production environment. CONDUCTOR allows the creation of arbitrary complex workflows in which individual tasks are implemented by microservices. The workflow *blueprint* (i.e., a high level description of the control and data flow) is defined

---

[1] They are comparable to those of service-oriented computing [13] and we can find their roots in the design principles of Unix [15].

© Springer Nature Switzerland AG 2020
H. Muccini et al. (Eds.): ECSA 2020, CCIS 1269, pp. 420–435, 2020.
https://doi.org/10.1007/978-3-030-59155-7_31

using a JSON based DSL and includes a set of *worker* tasks (i.e., pieces of functionality) running on compute nodes and *system* tasks (i.e., the glue composing the workflow) executed by CONDUCTOR. Here, verification activities or even testing can be challenging. In fact, continuous changes in rapidly evolving settings potentially require continuous verification methods where artifacts must be constantly recreated or modified. Moreover, the polyglot nature associated with microservices potentially requires multiple verification/testing tools because of different programming languages and runtime environments. To deal with these issues, we introduce a formal framework to support continuous verification of microservice workflows built on top of CONDUCTOR. Our approach extends our previus work introduced in [6] and it adopts a model-driven [21] paradigm that pushes the usage of formal models through the development as well as operation phases. We foster the integration of the approach in modern software development practices, such as DEVOPS [12], in order to adopt formal methods in agile, continuous delivery, and automation setting. To achieve this goal, we decrease the cost of producing a formal specification by means of an automated model to model transformation technique. Namely, we mechanically obtain a Time Basic Petri Net [16] (or simply TB net) formal model from the CONDUCTOR blueprint. TB nets represents a time-extension of Petri nets (PNs) provided with a clear formal semantics, traditionally considered as effective formal specification of distributed systems with time constraints. The TB nets formalism is supported by powerful off-the-shelf software tools covering both modeling and verification phases [4]. Generated models can be used to perform computer aided verification activities such as model checking by means of well-known techniques. Once the model has been verified, it can be used at runtime, after the deployment of a release build, to monitor and verify the behavior of the target application with respect to its formal specification. Both the model transformation process and the runtime verification technique are currently implemented as part of a open source software toolchain. We used our continuous verification framework to verify both behavioral and temporal properties of a microservice-based taxi-hailing application built upon the CONDUCTOR engine. Results obtained from this preliminary validation activity are presented and discussed.

The paper is organized as follows. In Sect. 2 we give a preliminary high-level overview of our continuous verification approach. In Sect. 3, we introduce background notions to make this paper self-contained and our taxi-hailing microservices-based application running example. In Sect. 4 we provide a detailed description of our framework. In Sect. 5 we discuss the evaluation activity conducted on the taxi-hailing example. In Sect. 6 we present related work. Finally, we draw our conclusions in Sect. 7.

2   Overview of the Approach

Figure 1 shows an high-level overview on the main phases and how they can be integrated into modern software development practices, such as a DEVOPS setting [12]. The guidelines of DEVOPS define a handshake between development

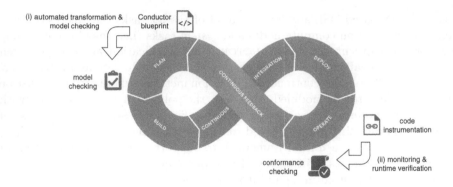

Fig. 1. Overview of our approach integrated into a DEVOPS setting.

and operations that forces a shift in mindset, better collaboration, and tighter integration. Following this trend that emphasizes fading boundaries between design-time and runtime phases, we introduce a continuous formal verification approach based on the iteration of the two phases: (*i*) Model Transformation & Model checking; and (*ii*) Monitoring & Runtime Verification. Although the approach is general, here we focus on microservices and the CONDUCTOR engine. Some of the peculiar characteristics of CONDUCTOR will be leveraged to introduce the rationale and put into place in a natural way some major technical details of our approach.

(i) Model Transformation & Model checking. In this phase we automatically generate the formal specification of the target application by transforming the CONDUCTOR blueprint into a TB nets model which describes both the system under development. The goal of this automatic transformation process is to aid the creation of formal models in rapidly evolving conditions. In fact, every change made to the workflow blueprint during development can be automatically reflected to the formal TB net specification, lowering the cost of keeping it consistent along the software lifecycle. We leverage TB net places to represent the *status* of a service (i.e., scheduled, in progress, timed out, or failed) and transitions to represent both service primitives and events coming from the surrounding environment. We leverage time modeling capability of TB nets to specify temporal constraints on scheduling/execution of tasks composing the overall applications. We defined a complete formal semantics of CONDUCTOR-based workflows, meaning that we cover all the available language constructs to define a CONDUCTOR blueprint. The final model is given by the composition of TB net transformation patterns derived from microservice and execution flow constructs. Such a model can be used to perform formal verification activities, such as interactive simulation (e.g., using token game) and model checking, with the aid of existing off-the-shelf software tools. Our current implementation focuses on the verification of Time Computation Tree Logic (TCTL) formulas [1] to verify *deadlock/livelock* freedom, *invariant*, *safety*, *liveness* and *bounded response-time* properties.

(ii) Monitoring & Runtime Verification. A model (re)generated in the previous step can be used to perform runtime verification upon the production infrastructure (i.e., the CONDUCTOR engine usually running on a cloud platform). The objective here is to run and monitor the execution of the target application in order to check conformance with respect to its own formal specification, thus enabling faster feedback which lays the foundation of every high performing DEVOPS team. The adopted runtime verification technique supplies the ability to map methods of interests (called *action methods*) to specific components of the specification (i.e., TB net transitions). During operations, we perform a monitoring activity through the co-execution of the target application and its formal specification (triggered by observable events). The monitor continuously evaluates the conformance of the execution (timed) trace with respect to the TB net model and it produces a (on-the-fly) report about both functional and temporal conformance failures. The report can be used in turn by developers to extract insights on the failing components. Our current implementation makes use of an JAVA monitoring engine which leverages the ASPECTJ framework to instrument the execution of the CONDUCTOR orchestrator.

It is worth noting that in a continuous integration and delivery pipeline, teams usually have different deployment environments including testing and production. Our RV approach is intended to be integrated in each one of these environments. In fact, common practices in such as load/stress testing can be used to assess to what extent synthetically generated workload intensities affect the ability to verify formal requirements. Furthermore, RV in production can constantly monitor the target system and provide insights on occurring conformance failures.

3 Preliminaries

3.1 Time Basic Petri Nets

TB nets represent an effective formal specification of concurrent (distributed) time-dependent systems. Time constraints are introduced as linear functions associated with each transition representing possible firing instants computed since transition's enabling. Tokens are atomically produced by firing transitions and they are timestamped along with time values ranging over $\mathbb{R}_{\geq 0}$. TB nets support a mixed time semantics, i.e., both *urgent* and *non-urgent* transitions can be used to define mandatory and optional events, respectively.

The structure of a TB net extends the P/T net one (P, T, F), where P is a finite set of places, T is a finite set of transitions such that $P \cap T = \emptyset$, and $F \subseteq (P \times T) \cup (T \times P)$ is a set of arcs (or flows) connecting places to transitions and transitions to places. Let $v \in P \cup T$: ${}^\bullet v$, $v^\bullet$ denote the backward and forward adjacent sets of v according to F, respectively, also called pre/post-sets of v. A timestamp *binding* of $t \in T$ is a map $b_t : {}^\bullet t \to Bag(\mathbb{R}_{\geq 0})$. Moreover, each transition t is associated with a *time function* f_t which maps a binding b_t to a (possibly empty) set of $\mathbb{R}_{\geq 0}$ values, denoted by $f_t(b_t)$. f_t is formally defined as a pair of linear functions $[l_t, u_t]$, denoting parametric interval bounds.

```
{ "name": "access-control",
  "timeoutSeconds": 1200,
  "inputKeys": [ ... ],
  "outputKeys": [ ... ],
  "timeoutPolicy": "ALERT_ONLY",
  "scheduleSeconds": 200
}
```

(a) JSON worker task

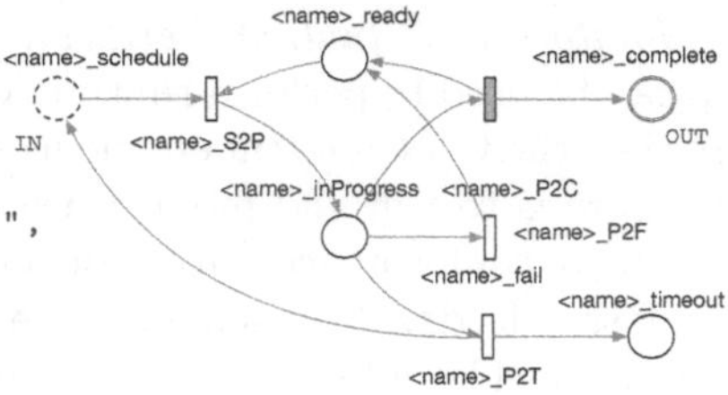

(b) TB net transformation pattern

Initial marking: $\langle name \rangle$_ready$\{T_A\}$

Transition	Time function
$\langle name \rangle$_S2P	$[\tau_e, \tau_e + \langle scheduleSeconds \rangle]$
$\langle name \rangle$_P2C	$[\tau_e, \tau_e + \infty]$
$\langle name \rangle$_fail	$[\tau_e, \tau_e + \infty]$
$\langle name \rangle$_P2T	$[\tau_e + \langle timeoutSeconds \rangle, \tau_e + \langle timeoutSeconds \rangle]$

Fig. 2. Transformation pattern of a ALERT_ONLY timeout-policy worker. Non-urgent transitions are depicted in gray.

A *marking* (or state) is a mapping $m : P \rightarrow Bag(\mathbb{R}_{\geq 0})$, where $Bag(X)$ represents all possible multisets over X. According to the *non-urgent* (or *weak*) semantics, t can fire at any instant $\tau \in f_t(b_t)$. The *urgent* (or *strong*) interpretation states that t must fire at any $\tau \in f_t(b_t)$, unless disabled by the firing of any conflicting transitions before the latest firing time of t. Given a binding b_t, a pair (b_t, τ), with $\tau \in f_t(b_t)$, represents a firing instance of t. The firing instance produces a new reachable marking by applying the traditional PN *firing rules*, but producing tokens timestamped with τ.

Figure 2b shows a TB net example that models the lifecycle of a single microservice. A single token with timestamp $T_0 = 0$ in place $\langle name \rangle$_schedule represents the microservice $\langle name \rangle$ in scheduled state (at time 0). In this marking, the transition $\langle name \rangle$_S2P is the only one enabled to fire by the binding: $\{\langle name \rangle$_schedule $\rightarrow \{1 \cdot T_0\}, \langle name \rangle$_ready $\rightarrow \{1 \cdot T_A\}\}$. The variable T_A represents a special timestamp (i.e., anonymous timestamp) whose time value does not influence the evolution of the system. Possible firing time instants are obtained by evaluating the bounds of $f_{\langle name \rangle\text{_S2P}}$: $[\tau_e, \tau_e + 200]$, where τ_e is the transition's enabling time (the value 0 in this case). Given a valid timestamp value $\tau \in [0, 200]$ (e.g., the value 150), according to the firing rules, we get a new marking with a new token $T_0 = 150$ in place $\langle name \rangle$_inProgress (i.e., the execution of the microservice starts from time 150). In this new marking, three transitions are concurrently enabled to fire: the *non-urgent* $\langle name \rangle$_P2C in the time interval $[0, \infty]$; and the two *urgent* transitions $\langle name \rangle$_fail and $\langle name \rangle$_P2T in the time interval $[1200, 1200]$. This configuration shows that the service can either complete the execution, fail or enter a timeout state. In the latter case, the system increments a counter (by producing a token into place $\langle name \rangle$_timeout) and then schedules again the service. Whenever a final state is entered (i.e., either the place ⟨name⟩_complete or the place ⟨name⟩_fail is marked), the microservice returns in ready state to serve new requests.

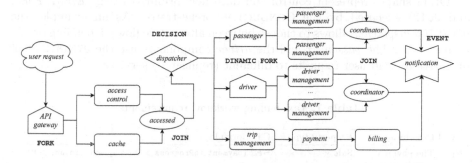

Fig. 3. High-level schema of the taxi-hailing blueprint.

Formally, a marking m_n is *reachable* from m_0 iff. there exists a *path* σ (sequence of firing instances and markings) such that:

$$\sigma = m_0 \xrightarrow{(b_{t_0},\tau_0)} m_1 \xrightarrow{(b_{t_1},\tau_1)} m_2, \ldots, m_{n-1} \xrightarrow{(b_{t_{n-1}},\tau_{n-1})} m_n$$

The transitions associated with the enabled bindings in m are called *enabled transitions* and they are denoted by $enab(m)$.

By using consolidated analysis techniques it is possible to construct a finite symbolic state space of a TB net model, called its *Time Reachability Graph* (*TRG*) [5,7]. The *TRG* construction is fully automated and it relies on a *symbolic state* notion: each reachable state is a pair: $S = (M, C)$, where M (symbolic marking) maps places into multisets of timestamps and C (constraint) is a logical predicate formed by linear inequalities defining time relations between timestamps. Given the *TRG* structure, model checking algorithms can be applied to verify the correctness of the system against requirements expressed as Time Computation Tree Logic (TCTL) properties [1,3]. The model checking technique is fully automated by the GRAPHGEN software tool.

3.2 A Running Example

We introduce here a small taxi-hailing workflow example used to put into place major concepts. Figure 3 shows an high level view of the provided pieces of functionality. This schema follows the notation introduced in [10] and shows both services and their relations in a CONDUCTOR workflow. Each microservice (rectangle) implements an isolated function (e.g., access control, trip management, payment, etc.) and is deployed independently, usually into cloud virtual machines or Docker containers [24]. Microservices expose REST APIs consumed by other services. For instance, *passenger management* uses the *notification* service to notify a passenger about an available driver. The *API gateway* exposes a public API used by mobile clients or web UIs.

Other shapes represent control and data flow primitives (e.g., EVENT, FORK, and JOIN) executed by the CONDUCTOR orchestrator. As an example, the DECISION *dispatcher* allows to choose between alternative flows depending on the request type. The *passenger* and the *driver* components use the DYNAMIC FORK primitive to send user requests to different (replicated) services.

Table 1. Taxi-hailing workflow requirements

Label	Description	Property-type	CTL formula
R_1	The payment service cannot reach an inconsistent state where both in progress and timeout status coexist	Safety	$\neg EF(\texttt{payment\_inProgress} > 0 \land \texttt{payment\_timeout} > 0)$
R_2	Whenever a a user request has been handled correctly, then a task among Driver, Passenger and Trip management is executed	Liveness	$AG(\texttt{accessControl\_complete} > 0 \land \texttt{cache\_complete} > 0$ $\rightarrow AF(\texttt{Passenger\_schedule} > 0 \lor$ $\texttt{Driver\_schedule} > 0 \lor \texttt{TripManagement\_schedule} > 0))$
R_3	Whenever a payment task is scheduled for execution, it is possible to complete the billing process in 2.4 s	Bounded response-time	$AG(\texttt{payment\_schedule} > 0 \rightarrow$ $EF_{\leq 2400}(\texttt{billing\_complete} > 0))$

Finally, let us assume that the taxi-hailing workflow must satisfy the requirements reported in Table 1. Requirements are formally expressed as TCTL properties to verify them upon the TB net specification.

4 Continuous Formal Verification

Figure 4 shows the major components of the toolchain and their existing relations. As anticipated in Sect. 2, the approach builds upon a model-driven iterative paradigm aiming at providing support to both development and operation phases in a formal fashion.

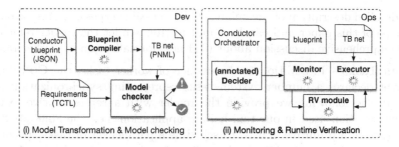

Fig. 4. Toolchain supporting our approach.

4.1 Model Transformation and Model Checking

The first step is a fully automated model-to-model transformation carried out by the *Blueprint Compiler* module as shown in Fig. 4. Our technique follows the approach introduced in [6] and it provides transformation capability for each construct of the CONDUCTOR (JSON-based) specification language. The overall process is guided by the identification of transformation patterns of each individual microservice (worker task) and each workflow primitive (system task). Patterns have input/output elements to compose them each other. The final TB net model is the result of the composition (i.e., the union by connecting input/output elements) of different transformation patterns of the corresponding microservices and primitives.

Worker Tasks – We use TB net places to represent the state of a task, while TB net transitions represent task primitives. Temporal functions associated with transitions are used to specify time concerns of scheduling and execution. Figure 2a shows the definition of a worker task using the CONDUCTOR language. The listing contains a JSON object with a number of control parameters used to tell the orchestrator how to manage the microservice lifecycle. The `scheduleSeconds` parameter sets an upper bound to the scheduling time of each instance of the worker task. The `timeoutSeconds` sets instead an upper bound to the execution time. Thus, if the `access-control` does not complete in 1200 ms, the CONDUCTOR orchestrator must kill the execution and alert the system (by incrementing a timeout counter) because of the `ALERT_ONLY` timeout-policy. Figure 2b shows the corresponding TB net transformation pattern. This pattern must be instantiated by replacing each ⟨`parameter`⟩ with the corresponding value in the JSON object. Dashed line shapes represent the input elements (e.g., `access-control_schedule`). Double line shapes represent output elements (e.g., `access-control_complete`). Three different types of timeout-policy exist: `ALERT_ONLY`, `TIMEOUT_WF` (i.e., put the entire workflow in timeout state), `RETRY` (i.e., reschedule the worker task a fixed number of times). The CONDUCTOR engine handles the execution of worker tasks depending on values assigned to timeout-policy and retry-logic. As a consequence, these control parameters are used to identify the right transformation pattern.

A detailed description of the behavior of all possible types of worker is outside the scope of this paper and can be found in [10]. We let the reader refer to [6] for a comprehensive discussion about (TB net) formalization of worker tasks.

System Tasks – In addition to a sequence of worker tasks, the CONDUCTOR blueprint declares a number system tasks representing synchronization primitives. In the following we provide the reader with a representative example of transformation used in our taxi-hailing application, i.e., the FORK_JOIN *API gateway*. Such a primitive is used to schedule a parallel set of tasks specified in the control parameter `forkTasks` by a list of task sequences. Figure 5a shows the listing used to define this task in our running example. Here the two parallel sequences contain a single worker task: the `access-control` and the `cache`, respectively. This means that upon a user request, performed though the API, the orchestrator triggers a parallel scheduling/execution of both microservices. The control parameter `joinTasks` contains the lists of tasks whose completions determines the end of the fork execution. If both access control and the cache services succeed, the system replies back to the client through a notification event.

```
{ "name": "api-gateway",
  "type": "FORK_JOIN",
  "forkTasks": [[{"taskReferenceName": "access-control", "type": "SIMPLE"}],
               [{"taskReferenceName": "cache", "type": "SIMPLE" }] ],
  "joinOn": ["access-control", "cache" ],
  "forkSeconds": 250,
  "joinSeconds": 250
}
```

(a) JSON FORK_JOIN task

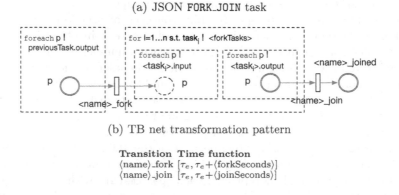

(b) TB net transformation pattern

Transition Time function
$\langle name\rangle\_fork \ [\tau_e, \tau_e + \langle forkSeconds\rangle]$
$\langle name\rangle\_join \ [\tau_e, \tau_e + \langle joinSeconds\rangle]$

Fig. 5. Transformation pattern of a FORK_JOIN system task.

Otherwise, if the required information is not cached, the process continues the execution with the DECISION (req. type decision) system task. Figure 5b show the associated transformation pattern composed of elementary TB net structural elements and *macro substitutions*, delimited by dashed boxes. A `for` macro substitution is a construct used to repeat the inner elements depending on the attached annotation. As an example, the $\langle$name$\rangle$_fork transition represents the starting point of the fork tasks and must be connected to all the input elements ($p \in$ task$_i$input) of all the tasks declared in the listing (task$_i \in$ forkTasks). The parameters forkSeconds and joinSeconds define the maximum time (milliseconds) required by the fork and the join operations, respectively. These values are used to instantiate the time functions of the pattern as shown in Fig. 5b.

Composition and Model Checking – The overall transformation process, executed by the blueprint compiler, reduces to the application of two steps in sequence: transformation of each worker task; and then worker composition, following the definition of transformation patterns associated with the declared system tasks. The result of this process is a TB net model formally specifying the behavior of the overall workflow. The formalization enables the usage of verification techniques to assess design-time requirements satisfaction. In our current approach we use interactive simulation (token game) to support validation, and TCTL model checking to support formal verification. Important properties that can be checked include deadlock/livelock freedom of the workflow, invariant, safety, liveness and bounded response-time properties. For instance, the TCTL properties R_1, R_2 and R_3 reported in Table 1 have been verified on the taxi-hailing workflow specification.

4.2 Monitoring and Runtime Verification

The generated TB net model is kept alive during operations in order to monitor the target workflow. We use the RV technique to verify conformance of behavioral and temporal aspects by first extracting a *timed-trace* of occurring events, from the running workflow, and then verifying whether it corresponds to a feasible *execution path* in the TB net model. A description of the RV approach follows.

Given a workflow ω, we denote a timed-trace π_i as a sequence of *observable events* $\pi_i = \{e_1, ..., e_n\}$, where each event e_k represents the execution of a task (either worker or system) that causes ω to change its global state. An observable event e_k is formally identified by the pair $\langle id(e_k), time(e_k) \rangle$, where id and $time$ map e_k to a identifier (sequence of characters) and a timestamp (in $\mathbb{R}_{\geq 0}$), respectively. An example of timed-trace, extracted from the taxi-hailing workflow, follows.

$$\pi_i = e_0 : \langle \text{api-gateway\_fork}, 450 \rangle, e_1 : \langle \text{access-control\_S2P}, 622 \rangle, \atop e_2 : \langle \text{cache\_S2P}, 630 \rangle, e_3 : \langle \text{access-control\_P2C}, 1550 \rangle, ... \tag{1}$$

Intuitively, the *Monitor* component is in charge of extracting the timed trace π_i from the execution of ω. The *Executor* component incrementally builds the execution path σ_i from the TB net model depending on the occurring observable events. The *conformance relation* is checked by the *RV* module on-the-fly during the co-execution of the workflow and the model by performing a pairwise comparison of occurring events in ω and firing transitions in the mdoel.

Table 2. Taxi-hailing structure.

Conductor blueprint		TB net transformation		
#worker tasks	#system tasks	$|P|$	$|T|$	TRG #states
9	6	57	61	8854

Table 3. Design-time verification.

Transformation		TRG building		Model checking	
Time (s)	Space (KB)	Time (s)	Space (KB)	Time (s)	Space (KB)
2.13	80,304	210.12	273,166	(1) 0.19 (2) 0.38 (3) 0.22	(1) 7,741 (2) 9,522 (3) 7,011

Formally, there exists a *conformance relation* between π_i and σ_i, iff. for each $e_k \in \pi_i$, there exists $m_k \in \sigma_i$ such that:

$$t_k \equiv id(e_k) \wedge time(e_k) \in [l_t(b_{t_k}), u_t(b_{t_k})] \tag{2}$$

To verify such a relation, for each occurring event $e_k \in \pi_i$, the *RV* module verifies that the model transition t named $id(e_k)$ is enabled to fire from the current marking $m \in \sigma_i$. The observed timestamp must conform to possible firing times of t. If this condition holds, the *Executor* component updates σ_i creating a new reachable marking with the proper timestamp.

The workflow execution is made observable by using ASPECTJ instrumentation of the CONDUCTOR DECIDER source code. In fact, the DECIDER contains a number of callback used to handle workflow events, like task scheduling, completion, and failure. The annotation allows the execution of the callback methods to be intercepted by ASPECTJ. Thus, callbacks generate observable events for the *Monitor*. The *Monitor* enqueues the event e_k into the trace π_i, depending on the workflow id. The *RV* module computes $id(e_k)$ by concatenating the task reference name and status. Then, it retrieves $time(e_k)$ by sampling the time from the Java virtual machine. If the conformance relation does not hold, a conformance failure exception is thrown. The exception shows information about the (timestamped) event that generated the exception, along with the set of enabled bindings that represent in this context the expected events predicted by the model.

5   Experimental Validation

We validated the overall continuous verification approach by conducting a number of experiments using our taxi-hailing example both during development and operation phases. Experiments have been conducted on a machine equipped with a Intel Xeon E5-2630 at 2.30 GHz CPU, 64 GB of RAM, the Ubuntu 14.04.3 LTS (GNU/Linux 3.13.0-39-generic x86_64) operating system with a completely fair scheduler, and the Java HotSpot 1.8 64-Bit Server Virtual Machine using the Garbage-First (G1) collector. Here we briefly discuss some significant results and we refer the reader to our implementation[2] for the replicability of the experiments.

---

[2] The main components of the toolchain are available as open source software at https://github.com/SELab-unimi/conductor2pn and https://maharajaframework. bitbucket.io/.

Design-Time Verification – Data describing structural properties of the taxi-hailing blueprint and corresponding TB net transformation are reported in Table 2. This table reports the TB net model size in terms of number of places $|P|$ and number of transitions $|T|$ and the TRG size in terms of number of reachable states. Table 3 reports the execution time (in seconds) and the average memory consumption (in KBytes) of a number of operations required by verification at design-time. Data shows the most expensive operation is the TRG building, while both transformation and verification are orders of magnitude cheaper both in terms of execution time and memory consumption. The transformation process, in particular, is very efficient because its complexity strictly depends on the model size (i.e., the structural complexity of the blueprint and the TB net) which is a small structure with respect to the TRG size ($\sim 10^1$ vs $\sim 10^3$ in our taxi-hailing example).

Table 4. Runtime verification performance.

Frequency (#invocations × s.)	AJO (μs)	AJO jitter (μs)	MIO (μs)	MIO jitter (μs)	DL (μs)	Memory (KB)
1	55.0	23.2	24.0	43.5	1488.6	2,113
2	52.5	20.6	23.6	46.4	1205.9	3,488
4	49.4	24.8	25.0	45.3	1022.7	5,055
8	52.8	27.6	28.1	47.4	755.8	10,066

Runtime Verification – Here we discuss experimental results to evaluate the overhead of the runtime verification module running along with the taxi-hailing CONDUCTOR workflow. Table 4 shows data extracted during runtime verification activities by varying the frequency, i.e., average number of *Monitor* invocations per second. The metrics used during the evaluation include the amount of monitoring overhead added by the instrumentation, the overhead jitter, and the auxiliary memory usage.

The *monitoring overhead* is caused by two main factors: the ASPECTJ instrumentation (AJO) and the monitor invocation overhead (MIO). Table 4 reports the average value of this two variables (in μs) we observed during the execution of the instrumented CONDUCTOR orchestrator by varying the frequency value. The average AJO (i.e., due to the invocation of ASPECTJ advices) strictly depends on the byte code generated from the annotated DECIDER by using the ASPECTJ compiler. The order of magnitude of measured AJO values is approximately 10 μs. The MIO is caused by the amount of time required to enqueue an occurring event into the synchronized event buffer structure. We observed that both the MIO and the AJO have the same order of magnitude, however the average MIO is generally lower ($\sim 50\%$ lower). Namely, the overhead introduced by ASPECTJ dominates the overall monitoring overhead. The monitor invocation frequency impacts on the average MIO. We observed a linear correlation between MIO and frequency values. The *overhead jitter* represents the deviance between the monitoring overhead values. Results show that AJO and the MIO jitter values have the same order of magnitude (i.e., $\sim$10 μs). While the AJO jitter strictly depends on the mechanics of ASPECTJ, the MIO jitter is governed by the *Monitor* status during the observation of events. We observed MIO bursts whenever observable events occur while the *Monitor* is suspended. In fact, in such a case, the MIO includes the time required by resuming the suspended monitoring thread before enqueuing a new event into the empty event buffer synchronized structure. The *detection Latency* value represents the time between an occurring event and the verdict (i.e., either conformance checked or conformance failure) computed by the *RV* module. A bounded detection latency (DL) allows for fast identification of conformance failures, thus making the operations team able to promptly react to degraded situations. During our experimentation we observed the following trend: the higher the frequency, the lower the DL. In fact, a low frequency implies very often an empty event buffer structure, thus increasing the overhead required by resuming a suspended thread. Overall we observed that the *RV* module is able to identify a conformance failure with a very small DL ($\sim$1 ms). The *memory overhead* is the additional space used by the Java virtual machine to run and runtime verification components. Table 4 shows negligible auxiliary memory values (few KBytes on average). We observed a linear correlation between memory overhead and monitor invocation frequency.

6   Related Work

The approach presented in this paper has been mainly influenced by different related works on formal specification and verification techniques of (micro)service-based systems. In particular, we leverage formal methods and integrate them into modern agile practices by following the approach envisioned in [17].

Although modeling formalisms such as timed-automata [2] or finite-state-machines [18] support the modeling of temporal or behavioral aspects, PNs-based approaches are generally more concise and scalable in the specification of concurrency and distribution [23]. Furthermore, aspects such as messaging, communication protocols, which are commonly used in distributed architectures, such as service oriented architectures and microservices, can be difficult to model with the language primitives of automata-based formalisms [20,23]. PNs represent common formal models of service-oriented architecture specified by means of the Business Process Execution Language for Web Services (BPEL) as described in [19]. However, BPEL transformation approaches cannot be directly applied in the context of microservices, where new emerging languages and frameworks, such as CONDUCTOR and JOLIE [25], represent upward trending choices. JOLIE is a microservices workflow interpreter engine equipped with a formal semantics in terms of process algebra [14] that can be used for computer-aided verification at design-time. Another recent line of research aims at leveraging the Event-B modeling language to define microservices architectural patterns [27]. The approach provides formal models of these patterns with the final goal of improving comprehension and enabling correct-by-construction mechanisms. Our runtime verification technique has been built upon the approach presented in [8], i.e., an event-based Runtime Verification (RV) technique for temporal properties of distributed systems leveraging TB nets as modeling formalism. As described in [8] the technique is supported by off-the-shelf tools that outperform comparative other representative state-of-the-art runtime verification Java software tools such as Java MaC [22], and Larva [9].

7 Conclusion

This paper describes an ongoing research activity on the application of formal methods to continuously support the development and operation phases of microservices-based workflows. The approach uses a model-driven paradigm and exploits solid foundation from well-established formal methods. Namely, we use the expressiveness of TB nets to support continuous verification of CONDUCTOR workflows. Model transformation and design-time verification performed during development aims at coping with continuously evolving specifications by keeping (verified) artifacts automatically updated. Runtime verification provides a way to support operation phases by monitoring and checking conformance of the target application with respect to its own formal specification in order to enable fast feedback and support high performing DevOps teams. The major components of our current toolchain have been released as open source software to encourage replication of experiments.

We are currently in the process of extending the RV technique to support (on-the-fly) model-based testing along with different scenario control techniques. We also want to expand the transformation capability by adding stochastic modeling of the intrinsic uncertain aspects of the surrounding environment.

References

1. Alur, R., Courcoubetis, C., Dill, D.: Model-checking for real-time systems. In: [1990] Proceedings. Fifth Annual IEEE Symposium on Logic in Computer Science, pp. 414–425, June 1990. https://doi.org/10.1109/LICS.1990.113766
2. Bengtsson, J., Yi, W.: Timed Automata: Semantics, Algorithms and Tools, pp. 87–124. Springer, Heidelberg (2004). https://doi.org/10.1007/978-3-540-27755-2_3
3. Camilli, M., Bellettini, C., Capra, L., Monga, M.: CTL model checking in the cloud using MapReduce. In: 2014 16th International Symposium on Symbolic and Numeric Algorithms for Scientific Computing, pp. 333–340, September 2014. https://doi.org/10.1109/SYNASC.2014.52
4. Camilli, M., Gargantini, A., Scandurra, P.: Specifying and verifying real-time self-adaptive systems. In: 2015 IEEE 26th International Symposium on Software Reliability Engineering (ISSRE), pp. 303–313, November 2015. https://doi.org/10.1109/ISSRE.2015.7381823
5. Camilli, M.: Petri nets state space analysis in the cloud. In: Proceedings of the 34th International Conference on Software Engineering, ICSE 2012, pp. 1638–1640. IEEE Press, Piscataway (2012)

6. Camilli, M., Bellettini, C., Capra, L., Monga, M.: A formal framework for specifying and verifying microservices based process flows. In: Cerone, A., Roveri, M. (eds.) SEFM 2017. LNCS, vol. 10729, pp. 187–202. Springer, Cham (2018). https://doi.org/10.1007/978-3-319-74781-1_14

7. Camilli, M., Gargantini, A., Scandurra, P.: Zone-based formal specification and timing analysis of real-time self-adaptive systems. Sci. Comput. Program. **159**, 28–57 (2018). https://doi.org/10.1016/j.scico.2018.03.002

8. Camilli, M., Gargantini, A., Scandurra, P., Bellettini, C.: Event-based runtime verification of temporal properties using time basic Petri nets. In: Barrett, C., Davies, M., Kahsai, T. (eds.) NFM 2017. LNCS, vol. 10227, pp. 115–130. Springer, Cham (2017). https://doi.org/10.1007/978-3-319-57288-8_8

9. Colombo, Christian., Pace, Gordon J., Schneider, Gerardo: Dynamic event-based runtime monitoring of real-time and contextual properties. In: Cofer, Darren, Fantechi, Alessandro (eds.) FMICS 2008. LNCS, vol. 5596, pp. 135–149. Springer, Heidelberg (2009). https://doi.org/10.1007/978-3-642-03240-0_13

10. Conductor, N.: Conductor documentation (2019). https://netflix.github.io/conductor/. Accessed Sept 2019

11. Dragoni, N., et al.: Microservices: Yesterday, Today, and Tomorrow, pp. 195–216. Springer, Cham (2017). https://doi.org/10.1007/978-3-319-67425-4_1210.1007/978-3-319-67425-4_12

12. Ebert, C., Gallardo, G., Hernantes, J., Serrano, N.: Devops. IEEE Softw. **33**(3), 94–100 (2016). https://doi.org/10.1109/MS.2016.68

13. Erl, T.: Service-Oriented Architecture: Concepts, Technology, and Design. Prentice Hall PTR, Upper Saddle River (2005)

14. Fokkink, W.: Introduction to Process Algebra, 1st edn. Springer, Heidelberg (2000). https://doi.org/10.1007/978-3-662-04293-9

15. Fowler, M.: Microservices: a definition of this new architectural term (2019). https://martinfowler.com/articles/microservices.html. Accessed Sept 2019

16. Ghezzi, C., Mandrioli, D., Morasca, S., Pezzè, M.: A unified high-level Petri net formalism for time-critical systems. IEEE Trans. Softw. Eng. **17**, 160–172 (1991). https://doi.org/10.1109/32.67597

17. Ghezzi, C.: Formal Methods and Agile Development: Towards a Happy Marriage, pp. 25–36. Springer, Cham (2018). https://doi.org/10.1007/978-3-319-73897-0_2

18. Gurevich, Y.: Sequential abstract-state machines capture sequential algorithms. ACM Trans. Comput. Logic **1**(1), 77–111 (2000). https://doi.org/10.1145/343369.343384

19. Hinz, S., Schmidt, K., Stahl, C.: Transforming BPEL to Petri Nets, pp. 220–235. Springer, Heidelberg (2005). https://doi.org/10.1007/11538394_15

20. Iglesia, D.G.D.L., Weyns, D.: Mape-k formal templates to rigorously design behaviors for self-adaptive systems. ACM Trans. Auton. Adapt. Syst. **10**(3), 151–1531 (2015). https://doi.org/10.1145/2724719

21. Kent, S.: Model driven engineering. In: Butler, M., Petre, L., Sere, K. (eds.) IFM 2002. LNCS, vol. 2335, pp. 286–298. Springer, Heidelberg (2002). https://doi.org/10.1007/3-540-47884-1_16

22. Kim, M., Viswanathan, M., Kannan, S., Lee, I., Sokolsky, O.: Java-MaC: a run-time assurance approach for Java programs. Form. Methods Syst. Des. **24**(2), 129–155 (2004). https://doi.org/10.1023/B:FORM.0000017719.43755.7c

23. Lee, W.J., Cha, S.D., Kwon, Y.R.: Integration and analysis of use cases using modular Petri nets in requirements engineering. IEEE Trans. Softw. Eng. **24**(12), 1115–1130 (1998)

24. Merkel, D.: Docker: lightweight Linux containers for consistent development and deployment. Linux J. **2014**(239) (2014). http://dl.acm.org/citation.cfm?id=2600239.2600241
25. Montesi, F., Guidi, C., Lucchi, R., Zavattaro, G.: JOLIE: a Java orchestration language interpreter engine. Electr. Notes Theor. Comput. Sci. **181**, 19–33 (2007). https://doi.org/10.1016/j.entcs.2007.01.051
26. Netflix, I.: The Netflix Service (2019). https://www.netflix.com/. Accessed Sept 2019
27. Vergara, S., González, L., Ruggia, R.: Towards formalizing microservices architectural patterns with Event-B. In: 2020 IEEE International Conference on Software Architecture Companion (ICSA-C), pp. 71–74 (2020)

IoT-ASAP - 4th International Workshop on Engineering IoT Systems: Architectures, Services, Applications, and Platforms

International Workshop on Engineering IoT Systems: Architectures, Services, Applications, and Platforms (IoT-ASAP)

In 2017, we organized the First International Workshop on Engineering IoT Systems: Architectures, Services, Applications, and Platform (IoT-ASAP 2017). Given its success, we organized the second, third, and fourth editions – this year under the special conditions of the COVID-19 pandemic that affected the entire world.

The Internet of Things (IoT) is characterized by billions of heterogeneous, distributed, and (intelligent) things – both from the digital and the physical worlds – running applications and services from the Internet of Services (IoS). Things span, for instance, simple RFID tags, sensors, actuators, as well as computers, autonomous robots, and self-driving vehicles. Often, things are connected through heterogeneous platforms also providing support for, e.g., data collection and management and applications deployment. Additionally, things can offer their functionalities as (web) services, facilitating them to interact with each other dynamically.

Since IoT systems are composed of a variety of things and services, the architecture is a key aspect of their engineering. While designing and managing IoT systems, services, and platforms has some challenges when it comes to tacking heterogeneity, adaptability, reusability, interoperability, uncertainty, security, and privacy, it also takes into account the human in the loop, bringing needs of the systems' functionalities and qualities. Additionally, challenges lie in the artificial intelligence area and include, e.g., data analytics and machine learning. Novel software architecture principles are needed to overcome all these challenges for IoT systems.

The objective of IoT-ASAP 2020 was, once again, to bring together researchers and practitioners from several areas (e.g., architecture, IoT, service-oriented computing, self-adaptive systems, multi-agent systems, data analytics, user interaction, and experience) to deepen and consolidate the latest R&D trends, principles, challenges, and (interdisciplinary) approaches for engineering IoT systems. This year, the workshop received two submissions of which one was accepted. Both papers were reviewed and discussed by three reviewers from our Program Committee, following a single-blind process. Furthermore, we invited the authors of the other paper to present and discuss their ongoing work. Both works were in the area of architecture composition: one about patterns for IoT APIs and the other about composition in dynamic industrial IoT systems.

The program included a mixture of presentations as well as extensive interactive parts with interesting discussions. The attendees of IoT-ASAP 2020 represented an international mixture of people and the discussions contributed to gain an increased, shared understanding of the IoT research field, with a focus on software architecture (e.g., what is (not) part of IoT systems), suitable models for IoT systems considering all challenges, and properties analysis and enforcement in IoT. We consider this a very good continuation of this workshop series.

We would like to thank all the people who contributed to make this workshop a success, including the Program Committee, the ECSA 2020 workshop chairs, Anne Koziolek and Mauro Caporuscio, all the presenters, authors, and participants. Thank you!

Organization

Workshop Chairs

Romina Spalazzese   Malmö University, Sweden
Marie Platenius-Mohr   ABB Corporate Research, Germany
Ilias Gerostathopoulos   Vrije Universiteit Amsterdam, Netherlands
Steffen Becker   University of Stuttgart, Germany

Workshop Steering Committee

Romina Spalazzese   Malmö University, Sweden
Marie Platenius-Mohr   ABB Corporate Research, Germany
Gregor Engels   University of Paderborn, Germany
Steffen Becker   University of Stuttgart, Germany

Workshop Program Committee

Marco Autili   University of L'Aquila, Italy
Antonio Bucchiarone   Fondazione Bruno Kessler, Italy
Tomáš Bureš   Charles University, Czech Republic
Federico Ciccozzi   Mälardalen University, Sweden
Ivica Crnkovic   Chalmers University of Technology, Sweden
Paul Davidsson   Malmö University, Sweden
David Garlan   Carnegie Mellon University, USA
Nikolaos Georgantas   Inria, France
Sebastian Götz   University of Technology Dresden, Germany
Panagiotis Katsaros   Aristotle University of Thessaloniki, Greece
Jan Kofron   Charles University, Czech Republic
Heiko Koziolek   ABB Corporate Research, Germany
Pankesh Patel   National University of Ireland, Ireland
Per Persso   Ericsson, Sweden
Christian Prehofer   Technical University of Munich, Germany
Alessandro Ricci   Universitá di Bologna, Italy
Magnus Standar   Ericsson, Sweden
Kenji Tei   NII University, Japan

Danny Weyns   KU Leuven, Belgium
Uwe Zdun   University of Vienna, Austria

Sponsor

Knowledge Foundation (KKS) through the Internet of Things and People research profile, Malmö University, Sweden.

Defining Design Patterns for IoT APIs

Rasmus Svensson, Adell Tatrous, and Francis Palma[⊠]

Department of Computer Science and Media Technology,
Linnaeus University, Kalmar, Sweden
{rs222tg,at222ux}@student.lnu.se, francis.palma@lnu.se

Abstract. Smart devices (or *things*) in the realm of IoT (Internet of Things) talk to each other and transfer data over the Internet. IoT vendors provide APIs for their clients to send data to the gateways and application servers. However, there is a lack of guidelines on how a vendor would design its API and resource URIs (Uniform Resource Identifiers). A generic design solution – *design patterns* – would make the API design and development easier for the vendors. Design patterns are reusable solutions to recurring problems and provide improved reusability and understandability. Currently, there are no design patterns for IoT APIs that IoT vendors can use. In this paper, we analyzed more than 1,300 URIs from 13 IoT APIs including IBM Watson and Microsoft Azure, and proposed eight novel design patterns for IoT APIs. We analyzed two datasets: (1) analysis set with 70% of all our URIs to define design patterns for IoT APIs and (2) validation set with the remaining 30% of the URIs to verify the prevalence of defined design patterns. We found that design patterns are prevalent in the IoT domain.

Keywords: IoT · APIs · Design patterns · Reusability · Maintainability

1 Introduction

Design patterns are reusable solutions to recurring design problems in software engineering [3]. Among numerous benefits, design patterns make the systems easier to understand and maintain. Design patterns work as a common language for designers and developers, which is essential to build a system efficiently. Design patterns are also useful in designing and developing Web services, *e.g.*, RESTful APIs. RESTful Web services are designed and developed based on the resources, where resources are identified using URIs (Uniform Resource Identifiers) [9]. The success of a RESTful Web service depends on the ease with which its clients can adopt the provided API, which includes understandability. Essentially, this would benefit the reusability of the API, which is why design patterns were proposed originally.

Researchers proposed design patterns for RESTful Web services [10]. However, those design patterns focus more on ensuring the RESTful-ness of the

© Springer Nature Switzerland AG 2020
H. Muccini et al. (Eds.): ECSA 2020, CCIS 1269, pp. 443–458, 2020.
https://doi.org/10.1007/978-3-030-59155-7_32

APIs, *i.e.*, suggest guidelines to design APIs that make the APIs truly REST-ful. Moreover, the design patterns for REST APIs proposed in the literature are micro-level patterns, *e.g.*, how the versioning should be done, the endpoint should be designed, a service contract can be made uniform, and so on. Thus, design patterns at the URI-level are still missing. However, there are some contributions to defining design patterns for REST APIs [1].

In the era of the Web, an emerging domain called IoT (Internet of Things) relies on smart devices or *things* that communicate over the Internet and talk to each other using an application layer protocol like HTTP or MQTT. The IoT paradigm is heavily things-oriented and the design guidelines for APIs should focus more on IoT-centric architecture [4]. Yet, there are no defined design patterns for IoT APIs. This is the first study that thoroughly analyzes IoT APIs and proposes relevant design patterns based on a subset of existing IoT APIs. The prospective IoT vendors can benefit from this by designing and developing their APIs based on our suggested design patterns, which would increase the reusability and understandability of their IoT APIs.

Our key contributions include: (1) a thorough manual analysis of more than 1,300 URIs from 13 IoT APIs including IBM Watson IoT and Microsoft Azure; (2) the definition of eight novel design patterns for IoT APIs that IoT vendors can use, and that would work as a common language for IoT APIs designers; and (3) a case study that shows the defined design patterns indeed are prevalent among the IoT APIs with 84% of URIs mapped to at least one design pattern.

The remainder of the paper is organized as follows: Sect. 2 presents a brief discussion on relevant studies in the literature. Section 3 details our methodology and discusses each step in detail. Section 4 presents eight novel design patterns for IoT APIs, while Sect. 5 shows the results of our case study. Finally, Sect. 6 concludes the paper and highlights our plans.

2   Related Work

Researchers proposed design patterns for REST APIs (Application Programming Interfaces) [1,13]. For example, Abbas and Ojo [1] proposed a set of eight design patterns by consolidating existing URI design rules and then abstracting the rules into a set of URI design patterns specifications. However, the proposed design patterns are domain-specific, *i.e.*, geospatial data that describe information related to locations on Earth. For this, the authors used the vocabulary of inter-linked datasets and best practices for URI construction. Li *et al.* [6,13] proposed some design patterns for northbound APIs in the software-defined networking, *i.e.*, the APIs between the network applications and the controller in software-defined networking. However, the goal of this was to ensure that APIs conform to REST constraints [2]. Besides, the proposed design patterns are not applicable in other domains, *i.e.*, only for the network applications. Other studies to improve the URI design include Wilkinson *et al.* [12], where the authors proposed the SADI approach (Semantic Automated Discovery and Integration) that consists of a set of recommendations on how the services should be implemented and described in order to achieve high interoperability. More specifically,

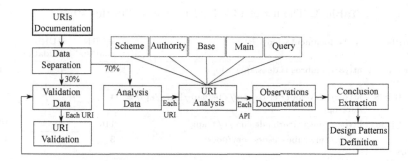

Fig. 1. Our methodology of defining design patterns.

SADI proposed a set of conventions and best-practices for developing APIs in the bioinformatics domain. Some books discussed the best practices for URI design [7,10]. However, they defined best practices in the forms of design rules to help designers in designing readable and understandable URIs at the micro-level, *i.e.*, how the version number should be provided, the pagination should be used, name the resources to avoid confusions. Yet, design patterns at the URI-level are still missing, which would work as a common language for the designers. McEwen and Cassimally [8] described the design of the Internet of Things (IoT) at the application level that combines hardware and software.

Our study is the first to provide a set of usable design patterns for the IoT APIs regardless of the domain. Moreover, our design patterns can work as a common language among the API designers. The following section details our methodology of defining design patterns for IoT APIs.

3 Methodology

As depicted in Fig. 1, our methodology includes the collection of APIs documentation (*e.g.*, URIs), analysis of URIs, definition of design patterns, and finally, manual validation of the newly defined design patterns with a set of unseen URIs. The subsequent sections present our patterns defining strategy, our observations, and the template that we used to present the design patterns.

3.1 Strategy for Design Pattern Definition

The steps undertaken include the following:

- We manually gather more than 1,300 URIs (regardless of the HTTP methods) from 13 IoT REST APIs, as listed in Table 1. In this first step, we also randomly split all the collected URIs into two sets: (1) the analysis set with 70% of all URIs to be used for defining design patterns and (2) the validation set with the remaining 30% of the URIs to be used for validating the defined design patterns. We perform this split for each IoT API. Table 1 shows the number of URIs in the analysis and validation set.

Table 1. The list of 13 IoT APIs analyzed in this study.

IoT APIs	APIs documentation URLs	#URIs analysis	#URIs validation	Total
Ambrosus Gateway	https://ambrosus.docs.apiary.io/#	10	4	14
Cisco IPICS	https://developer.cisco.com/site/flare/learn/api/#flare-api	4	1	5
Clear Blade	https://docs.clearblade.com/v/4/api/	116	50	166
Cube Sensors	https://my.cubesensors.com/docs	3	1	4
Droplit.io	https://docs.droplit.io	142	61	203
IBM Watson	https://docs.internetofthings.ibmcloud.com/apis/swagger/index.html	189	80	269
Losant	https://docs.losant.com/rest-api/overview/	152	65	217
Microsoft Azure	https://docs.microsoft.com/en-us/rest/api/iothub/	124	52	176
Particle	https://docs.particle.io/reference/device-cloud/api/	77	33	110
Sonos	https://developer.sonos.com/reference/	46	20	66
thethings.iO	https://developers.thethings.io/reference	23	10	33
The Things Network	https://www.thethingsnetwork.org/docs/applications/manager/api.html	8	4	12
Toon	https://developer.toon.eu/toonapi/apis	18	8	26
Total		**912**	**389**	**1,301**

- We proceed with the analysis set for the definition of the design patterns. At this point, we analyze and document more detailed information about each URI in the analysis set. This information includes, for example, the HTTP request method used for the resource URI, query and path parameters used, a full description of the nodes involved in the URI, and the position of these nodes in the URI. A node represents the smallest unit in a URI separated by a forward slash (/). According to IETF RFC 3986 [5], a URI can be divided into five sections: `Scheme://Authority/Path?Query#Fragment`. To be able to analyze further, we extended this structure by dividing the `Path` section into `Base` and `Main` sections, and disregard the `Fragment` section since it is not found in any URIs. Thus, the resulting URI sections will instead be `Scheme://Authority/Base/Main?Query`.
- Based on the newly defined URI structure, we analyze the analysis set for each API by documenting observations in each section.
- Observations gathered for all the analysis set are grouped, and then, we determine obvious, common, and repeated patterns among all APIs. Design patterns are concretely defined based on the findings in this step.
- Finally, we use the validation set to validate the patterns, *i.e.*, to find the prevalence of newly defined design patterns among the unseen validation set. For this, we manually map each URI in the validation set to see if they fit any newly defined patterns, and if yes, to which pattern(s). We found that

Table 2. The definitions of node types.

Name	Description
Access Node	A node that is used only to direct the following parts of the URI to a certain section of the API, *i.e.*, it is not a resource or data that could be fetched
Parent Node	A node that usually represents a category, a resource that includes resources or an object. In the API and the URI, this node exists in a hierarchy. Here, we tend to mention only the end of the hierarchy. For instance, when a resource is accessed by these ways `/parentnode1/{var1}.../parentnodeN/{varN}` or `/parentnode1/{var1}.../parentnodeN` we only mention `/parentnodeN/{varN}` or `/parentnodeN`
Indicative Node	A node that represents an order, query or action to be taken on a certain resource to apply this action or know a specific information about this resource, *e.g.*, filtering the results of a request made on a certain resource. We can think of it as an endpoint that triggers a function. It is usually a conventional word such as 'info', 'create', 'last', 'status', etc. *Indicative Nodes* can be divided into three categories: *Action Nodes*, *Filtering Nodes*, and *Informational Nodes*
Action Node	A node used to trigger a specific function or apply classic CRUD functionalities on a resource, using any HTTP request method. In most cases, these nodes take a form of an order to perform an action, *e.g.*, 'create', 'clone', 'upload', or 'consume'
Filtering Node	A node used to target a specific group or state of the requested resources
Informational Node	A node used to get information about metadata for a single or multiple resources. These metadata cannot be directly modified nor accessible through the resource

most URIs from the validation set fit at least one class of design patterns. Thus, we show that the design patterns are prevalent in the IoT domain.

3.2 Our Observations on URI Sections

For the `Scheme` section that incorporates the protocol used in the URI, all analyzed APIs have one of two following variants:

- `HTTP` in CubeSensors and The Things Network;
- `HTTPS` in Ambrosus Gateway, Cisco IPICS, ClearBlade, Droplit.io, IBM Watson, Losant, Microsoft Azure, Particle, Sonos, thethings.iO, and Toon;

The `Authority` section incorporates the host and, rarely, the port, *i.e.*, `host:port` used in the URI. The `Authority` section also includes all the possible variables required to redirect the URIs at specific services, areas, organizations, and so on. Two variants are found among all the analyzed APIs:

- **Static:** the `Authority` section has the same string for all users of the API.
- **Dynamic:** the `Authority` section consists of a variable constructed for each user, *e.g.*, 'servername' in Cisco IPICS represents a qualified host name provided by the user. Alternatively, the `Authority` section includes a variable in

it that is placed at the beginning of the section, *e.g.*, 'orgId' in IBM Watson that represents a 6-character string ID to identify the organization within this API. Also, 'fully-qualified-iothubname' in Microsoft Azure represents a unique name string that is provided by the user and follows the API standards. The 'region' in The Things Network represents the area code string that users provide depending on the geographical area of their application.

The `Base` section usually incorporates the version of the API, among other *Access Node(s)* (as defined in Table 2), that are used in the majority of the URIs provided by an API. The `Base` section, in contrast to the previous sections, does not have to be included in the URI, *e.g.*, as in Ambrosus Gateway, Microsoft Azure, The Things Network, and Losant. But if it does, it can take the whole section as *Access Node(s)* only. For example, the `/ipics_server/handsetservice` in all URIs provided by Cisco IPICS, and `/admin` or `/codeadmin` in some of the URIs provided by Clear Blade.

Another form the `Base` section might take when providing the version of the API. This could be done by providing the version as a single node, and this node represents the whole `Base` section, *e.g.*, `/v1` in all URIs of Cube Sensors, `/v1` in most URIs of Particle, and `/v2` in all URIs of thethings.iO. The *Access Node(s)* and the version of the API could be mentioned together to represent this section. The version could be:

- A single node after the Access Node(s), *e.g.*, `/api/v0002` in all URIs of IBM Watson, `/control/api/v1` in most URIs of Sonos and `/toon/v3` in all URIs of Toon;
- A single node before the Access Node(s), *e.g.*, `/v0/api` in most URIs of Droplit.io;
- Multiple nodes after the Access Node(s), *e.g.*, `/admin/v/4`, `/codeadmin/v/2`, `/api/v/1`, `/api/v/2`, `/api/v/3` or `/api/v/4` in some URIs of ClearBlade;

The `Query` section incorporates all the required and optional query parameters that an API needs or provides in its URIs to make it possible to send, filter, and sort data and information. The version of the API might be provided in this section, instead of the conventional way within the `Base` section. The version is provided as a required query parameter, *e.g.*, `api-version=2018-01-22` in all URIs of Microsoft Azure. Another behavior found in this `Query` section is when the authentication string is added as a required query parameter. For example, the `access_token=`, in most URIs of Particle. One observation worth mentioning for this section is that all query parameters in all the URIs from all APIs follow the same structure `?key1=value1&key2=value2&...` rather than other forms like `?value1&value2&...` or `?value1,value2,...`, etc.

The `Main` is the most crucial section to define the purpose of the URI. Besides the HTTP request method used in the URI, this section makes the URI unique for serving its purpose. The *Indicative Nodes* presented in Table 3 are found in URIs to apply the CRUD functionalities or other processes on resources and their metadata. These nodes could be placed inside this section in various ways.

Table 3. The list of all found *Indicative Nodes* in analysis set URIs for all APIs.

Indicative nodes	Action node	Filtering node	Informational node
Ambrosus Gateway	/info, /create, /list, /modify	–	/nodeinfo
Cisco IPICS	/join, /uploaddata, /leave	–	/userdirectory
ClearBlade	/putpass, /regensystemsecret, /publish, /reg, /auth, /anon, /checkauth, /execute, /logout	/history, /failed	/count, /connectioncount, /logs, /userinfo, /definitions
CubeSensors	–	–	/current
Droplit.io	/create, /consume, /undelete, /reactivate, /activate, /start, /export, /disable	–	/state
IBM Watson	/add, /remove, /cancel, /download, /multiple, /request, /restore	/draft	/edgestatus, /connection, /data-traffic, /service-status
Losant	/clone, /export, /search, /import, /delete, /query, /truncate, /setConnectionState, /mqttPublishMessage, /release, /bootstrap, /upload, /changePassword, /disableTwoFactorAuth, /disconnectGithub, /disconnectTwitter, /refreshToken, /transferResources, /verify-email, /execute	–	/archiveData, /fullDataTablesArchive, /payloadCounts, /state, /fullEventsArchive, /mqttSubscriptionStream, /linkedResources, /stats, /logs
Microsoft Azure	/applyConfigurationContent, /testQueries, /abandon, /cancel, /create, /query, /checkNameAvailability, /exportDevices, /importDevices, /verify, /search	–	/statistics
Particle	/ping, /device_claims, /password-reset, /test, /release	–	/current, /last, /metadata, /status, /data_usage, /impact
Sonos	/access, /subscription, /relative, /mute, /match, /lineIn, /play, /pause, /seek, /skipToNextTrack, /skipToPreviousTrack, /togglePlayPause, /join, /joinOrCreate, /loadCloudQueue, /skipToItem, /loadStreamUrl, /refreshCloudQueue, /suspend, /getPlaylist	–	/playbackMetadata
thethings.iO	–	–	/latest
Toon	/states	–	/flows, /data

For example, an *Indicative Node* can be placed either before, after, or in the middle of a chain of *Parent Node(s)*, which are described in Table 2, depending on the purpose of this node. It is worth mentioning that most of the URIs studied have a conventional structure that does not have any extra nodes apart from the *Parent Node(s)*.

3.3 Template for Design Patterns Definition

Based on the observations found in each section (*i.e.*, Scheme, Authority, Base, Query, and Main) in analysis set URIs, we present the obtained design patterns in Sect. 4. The template of our design pattern is inspired by the widely known

GoF design pattern template by Gamma et al. [3]. The template includes the following sections:

- **Name:** States the chosen name of the design pattern.
- **Description:** Provides some background about when, why, and how this pattern could be useful.
- **Affected Sections:** Mentions the sections that this pattern applies to.
- **Forms:** Enumerates the variants that this pattern might take in a URI, *i.e.*, the different positions that nodes and variables might take in the URI.
- **Sources:** Mentions the APIs that this pattern was found in.
- **Examples:** Enumerates some realistic examples from the studied APIs.

In the following section, we present each of the design patterns for IoT APIs.

4   Design Patterns

This section presents eight design patterns that are abstracted from the URIs from our analysis set. For each design pattern, we also represent them graphically to show the relationships among the various constituents in the pattern, *i.e.*, how they are associated to form a design pattern. Tables 4, 5, 6, 7, 8, 9, 10 and 11 describe our eight design patterns using the template presented in

Table 4. *Early Directed URI* pattern.

Name	Early Directed URI (ED_URI)
Description	To direct the requested URI at a specific or unique subsection of the API, such as an organization ID, an area code or a custom server name, use a variable at the beginning of the *Authority* section followed by a period
Affected sections	*Authority* section
Forms	`Scheme://{variable}.../Base/Main?Query`
Sources	IBM Watson IoT, The Things Network, and Microsoft Azure
Examples	https://myiothub.azure-devices.net/jobs or http://eu.thethings.network: 8084/applications

Sect. 3.3. The tables also include the graphical representation of each design pattern. In summary, among our eight defined design patterns: one is related to the `Authority` section, one is related to both `Base` and `Query` sections, five are related to the `Main` section, and one to the `Query` section.

5   Case Study

We performed this case study with our validation set, which is 30% of our initially gathered data. To avoid the bias, the validation set was not exposed until all the URIs in the analysis set are analyzed, and the definition of design patterns is done. This case study aims to see whether our newly defined design patterns are meaningful, *i.e.*, whether we can map each URI from the unseen validation set to the certain design pattern(s) that are defined based on the known analysis set. We are able to map 84% of the URIs (325 out of 389 URIs) to at least one defined design pattern, *i.e.*, the IoT design patterns are indeed prevalent.

We follow an iterative and manual validation using the first-past-the-post[1] technique by the maximum voting system. For a URI in the validation set, if the first two authors (who are involved in defining design patterns) agree on a design pattern, the URI is assigned to that design pattern class. In the case of a tie, the third author of this paper (not involved in defining patterns) gets involved.

Table 5. *Expressive Request* pattern.

Name	Expressive Request (ER)
Description	To perform the classic CRUD functionalities or trigger a specific function on a resource while clearly stating the purpose of the URI and not just relying on the method used, add an *Action Node* in the *Main* section.
Affected sections	*Main* section.
Forms	1. `Scheme://Authority/Base/../ActionNode?Query` or 2. `Scheme://Authority/Base/../ParentNode/ActionNode/{variable}?Query`
Sources	Ambrosus Gateway, Cisco IPICS, thethings.iO, Particle, ClearBlade, Losant, Droplit.io, IBM Watson IoT, Microsoft Azure, Sonos, and Toon
Examples	https://platform.clearblade.com/admin/checkauth or https://ioe.droplit.io/v0/api/zones/123/behaviors/456/start or https://hermes.ambrosus-test.com/account2/modify/123

---

[1] http://aceproject.org/main/english/es/esd01.htm.

Table 6. *'me' Accessible Resources* pattern.

Name	'me' Accessible Resources (MAR)
Description	To point at the currently authenticated user when requesting resources or performing actions that this user has access to, use a "me" node at the beginning of the *Main* section
Affected sections	*Main* section
Forms	`Scheme://Authority/Base/me/..?Query`
Sources	thethings.iO and Losant
Examples	https://api.losant.com/me/refreshToken or https://api.thethings.io/v2/me/resources/123

We performed the case study on the validation set with 389 URIs, *i.e.*, 30% of all collected URIs from 13 IoT APIs. Table 12 shows the distribution of URI counts over the design patterns for each API from the validation set. The results show that the majority of the URIs follow the *Versionized API* and *Early Directed URI* patterns regardless of the APIs, which is 75% and 31%, respectively. The *Expressive Request* pattern is also moderately common among the APIs. Although *'me' Accessible Resources*, *Metadata Retrievability*, and *Versionized Resources* are less frequent among the APIs, this might be subject to the gathered URIs, and thus, the validation set. However, at the beginning of the pattern defining process, we split the dataset randomly to avoid biasing the pattern frequency both in validation and analysis set. The quantitative observation in Table 12 suggests that the thresholds for detecting a pattern are rather low, *i.e.*, QA is only found in one API (with 2% of URIs), but MAR/PF/VR in only two APIs, and ED_URI in three APIs. Thus, only half of the patterns included in the paper comply with Will Tracz's *'rule of three'* [11].

Table 7. *Metadata Retrievability* pattern.

Name	Metadata Retrievability (MR)
Description	To read information, mostly using the GET method, about metadata for a single or multiple resources such as: count, state, status or other data that cannot be directly modified nor accessible through a resource, the URI can have a meaningful *Informational Node* at the end of the *Main* section as an indication for the requested information
Affected sections	*Main* section
Forms	`Scheme://Authority/Base/../InformationalNode?Query`
Sources	Ambrosus Gateway, Cisco IPICS, CubeSensors, thethings.iO, Particle, ClearBlade, Losant, Droplit.io, IBM Watson IoT, Microsoft Azure, Sonos and Toon
Examples	https://platform.clearblade.com/admin/user/123/roles/count or https://api.particle.io/v1/sims/123/status

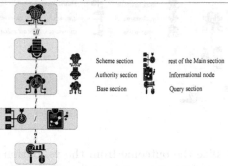

Table 8. *Proactive Filtering* pattern.

Name	Proactive Filtering (PF)
Description	To target a specific group or state of the requested resource without relying on a dedicated query parameter, use a *Filtering Node* in the *Main* section
Affected sections	*Main* section
Forms	1. `Scheme://Authority/Base/../FilteringNode/ParentNode/..?Query` or 2. `Scheme://Authority/Base/../ParentNode/FilteringNode/..?Query`
Sources	ClearBlade and IBM Watson IoT
Examples	https://123456.internetofthings.ibmcloud.com/api/v0002/draft/schemas or https://platform.clearblade.com/codeadmin/failed

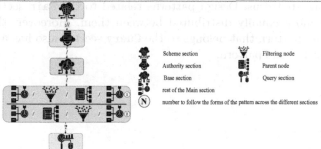

Table 9. *Querified Authentication* pattern.

Name	Querified Authentication (QA)
Description	To provide the authentication string of the user in the URI when using the GET method, instead of providing it in the header or the body when using other methods, use a dedicated query parameter
Affected sections	*Query* section
Forms	`Scheme://Authority/Base/Main/?{authentication-key}={authentication-string-value}`
Sources	Particle
Examples	https://api.particle.io/v1/events/123?access_token=456789

To further generalize the outcome from the validation set, we also tag each URI from the analysis dataset to at least one design pattern. Table 13 shows the distribution of URI counts over the design patterns for each API from the analysis set. We found similar pattern usage frequency regardless of the API, *i.e.*, we still have the *Early Directed URI* and *Versionized API* as the most common pattern, and *Expressive Request* pattern as the third most frequent design pattern applied in the design of IoT APIs.

Figure 2 shows the relative frequency of design patterns for the analysis and validation set. Compared to each other, analysis and validation set seem to follow the same trend when it comes to the number of URIs using each of the patterns. The *Versionized API* pattern that belongs to the `Base` section and *Early Directed URI* pattern that belongs to the `Authority` section is the most common design patterns. Design patterns related to the `Main` section are used less and are more equally distributed between them. Moreover, the *Querified Authentication* pattern that belongs to the `Query` section also has a low number of URIs following the pattern.

Table 10. *Versionized API* pattern.

Name	Versionized API (V_API)
Description	To add the version of the API in a selected single section to differentiate between the updated types of the API, use either a dedicated version number in the *Base* section, that could be put in different places, or a date-string as a query parameter
Affected sections	*Base* and *Query* sections
Forms	1. Scheme://Authority/v{number}/Main?Query or 2. Scheme://Authority/AccessNode(s)/v{number}/Main?Query or 3. Scheme://Authority//AccessNode(s)/v/{number}/Main?Query or 4. Scheme://Authority/v{number}/AccessNode(s)/Main?Query or 5. Scheme://Authority/Base/Main?{version-key}={version-data-value}
Sources	CubeSensors, thethings.iO, Particle, ClearBlade, Droplit.io, IBM Watson IoT, Microsoft Azure, Sonos, and Toon
Examples	http://api.cubesensors.com/v1/devices or https://123456.internetofthings.ibmcloud.com/api/v0002/device or https://api.ws.sonos.com/control/api/v1/groups/123 or https://platform.clearblade.com/api/v/3/code or https://ioe.droplit.io/v0/api/clients or https://myiothub.azure-devices.net/configurations/123?api-version=2020-03-13

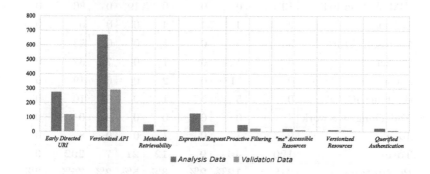

Fig. 2. Pattern frequency in validation and analysis data.

Table 11. *Versionized Resources* pattern.

Name	Versionized Resources (VR)
Description	To add the version of a resource in the URI to differentiate between the various types of updated functionalities that the API provides on the requested resource, use a dedicated number in the same resource node or as a separate node
Affected sections	*Main* section
Forms	1. `Scheme://Authority/Base/../ParentNode{number}/..?Query` or 2. `Scheme://Authority/Base/../ParentNode/v{number}/..?Query`
Sources	Ambrosus Gateway and Microsoft Azure
Examples	https://hermes.ambrosus-test.com/account2/info/accountAddress or https://myiothub.azure-devices.net/jobs/v2/123

Table 12. Patterns frequency in **Validation Set** for all studied URIs.

IoT APIs/Patterns	ED_URI	ER	MAR	MR	PF	QA	V_API	VR
Ambrosus Gateway	0	4	0	0	0	0	0	4
Cisco IPICS	0	0	0	0	0	0	0	0
ClearBlade	0	5	0	1	2	0	29	0
CubeSensors	0	0	0	1	0	0	1	0
Droplit.io	0	10	0	0	0	0	61	0
IBM Watson IoT	80	0	0	0	19	0	80	0
Losant	0	4	4	4	0	0	0	0
Microsoft Azure	36	5	0	1	0	0	52	4
Particle	0	1	0	1	0	7	32	0
Sonos	0	11	0	2	0	0	19	0
thethings.iO	0	5	5	1	0	0	10	0
The Things Network	4	0	0	0	0	0	0	0
Toon	0	1	0	1	0	0	8	0
Total	**120**	**46**	**9**	**12**	**21**	**7**	**292**	**9**
Percentage	**31%**	**12%**	**2%**	**3%**	**5%**	**2%**	**75%**	**2%**

Table 13. Patterns frequency in **Analysis Set** for all Studied URIs.

IoT APIs/Patterns	ED_URI	ER	MAR	MR	PF	QA	V_API	VR
Ambrosus Gateway	0	6	0	1	0	0	0	6
Cisco IPICS	0	3	0	1	0	0	0	0
ClearBlade	0	12	0	9	5	0	55	0
CubeSensors	0	0	0	1	0	0	3	0
Droplit.io	0	11	0	1	0	0	142	0
IBM Watson IoT	189	10	0	5	41	0	189	0
Losant	0	25	10	12	0	0	0	0
Microsoft Azure	78	22	0	2	0	0	124	5
Particle	0	5	0	7	0	23	72	0
Sonos	0	30	0	1	0	0	45	0
thethings.iO	0	1	9	1	0	0	23	0
The Things Network	8	0	0	0	0	0	0	0
Toon	0	1	0	8	0	0	18	0
Total	**275**	**126**	**19**	**49**	**46**	**23**	**671**	**11**
Percentage	**30%**	**14%**	**2%**	**5%**	**5%**	**3%**	**74%**	**1%**

6   Conclusion and Future Work

Design patterns are widely accepted as reusable solutions to recurring design problems with benefits of reusability and easy to understand and maintain [3]. Design patterns can be useful in RESTful Web services and, in particular, for IoT APIs. The prospective IoT vendors can benefit from IoT APIs design patterns by designing and developing their APIs based on our suggested design patterns, which would increase the reusability and understandability of their APIs. In this paper, we analyzed a set of 13 IoT APIs and proposed eight relevant design patterns based on the existing IoT APIs. Our key contributions are: (1) a thorough manual analysis of more than 1,300 URIs from 13 IoT APIs including IBM Watson and Microsoft Azure; (2) the definition of eight novel design patterns for IoT APIs that IoT vendors can use, and that would work as a common language for IoT APIs designers; and (3) a case study that shows the defined design patterns are prevalent among the IoT APIs with 84% of URIs in our validation set being mapped to at least one design pattern.

Our plans include analyzing more APIs and extending our list of design patterns. Our case study needs to be extended with more URIs from the selected APIs. We also plan to develop a tool that can automatically detect design patterns in the URIs and recommend design patterns for API designers.

Acknowledgment. We would like to thank The Knowledge Foundation that partially supported this research through two projects with ref no. 20150088 and 20170176, respectively. This study is conducted with support from Linnaeus University Centre for Data Intensive Sciences and Applications (DISA).

References

1. Abbas, S., Ojo, A.: Applying design patterns in URI strategies-naming in linked geospatial data infrastructure. In: 2014 47th Hawaii International Conference on System Sciences, pp. 2094–2103. IEEE (2014)
2. Fielding, R.T., Taylor, R.N.: Architectural Styles and the Design of Network-based Software Architectures, vol. 7. University of California, Irvine (2000)
3. Gamma, E.: Design Patterns: Elements of Reusable Object-Oriented Software. Pearson Education India (1995)
4. Grønbæk, I.: Architecture for the Internet of Things (IoT): API and interconnect. In: 2008 Second International Conference on Sensor Technologies and Applications (Sensorcomm 2008), pp. 802–807. IEEE (2008)
5. Network Working Group: Uniform Resource Identifier (URI): Generic Syntax (2005). https://tools.ietf.org/html/rfc3986
6. Li, L., Chou, W., Zhou, W., Luo, M.: Design patterns and extensibility of rest API for networking applications. IEEE Trans. Netw. Serv. Manag. **13**(1), 154–167 (2016)
7. Masse, M.: REST API Design Rulebook: Designing Consistent RESTful Web Service Interfaces. O'Reilly Media Inc., Newton (2011)
8. McEwen, A., Cassimally, H.: Designing the Internet of Things. Wiley, Hoboken (2013)
9. Richardson, L., Amundsen, M.: RESTful Web APIs. O'Reilly (2013). https://books.google.se/books?id=ppEVtAEACAAJ
10. Subramanian, H., Raj, P.: Hands-on RESTful Web API Design Patterns and Best Practices: Design, Develop, and Deploy Highly Adaptable, Scalable, and Secure RESTful Web APIs. Packt Publishing (2019)
11. Tracz, W.: Where does reuse start? ACM SIGSOFT Softw. Eng. Notes **15**(2), 42–46 (1990)
12. Wilkinson, M.D., Vandervalk, B., McCarthy, L.: The semantic automated discovery and integration (SADI) web service design-pattern, API and reference implementation. J. Biomed. Semant. **2**(1), 8 (2011)
13. Zhou, W., Li, L., Luo, M., Chou, W.: REST API design patterns for SDN northbound API. In: 2014 28th International Conference on Advanced Information Networking and Applications Workshops, pp. 358–365. IEEE (2014)

SASI4 - 2nd Workshop on Systems, Architectures, and Solutions for Industry 4.0

Workshop on Systems, Architectures, and Solutions for Industry 4.0 (SASI4)

Industry 4.0 (I4) is the next software revolution from computerized systems to digitalization of industry solutions, which aims at efficient manufacturing of small lot sizes, even lot size one, by transforming the traditional PLCs (programmable logic controllers) based interleaved structures into logical artifacts that are easy to change, maintain, and adapt. To enable this, the fourth generation of the industrial revolution attempts to automate as much as possible all industry processes and manage an unprecedented amount of data where cyber-physical systems (CPSs) interact with humans to produce software-intensive systems more efficiently. From a software engineering perspective, such complex systems must be produced in many cases using continuous software engineering approaches and multiple releases demanding continuous integration and delivery. From the software architecture point of view, flexible and open architectures are required to integrate the diversity of platforms and technology in support of I4 processes and manage the vast amount of data required by complex engineering processes.

Also, the realization of smart factories demands high digitalization and integration of each phase of the production process, the de-hierarchization of the traditional automation pyramid, and the reconsideration of the different entities from the production process, e.g., shop flop operators, factory management, providers of raw materials, and electromechanical and computational equipment like robots, logistics companies, and end users. Nowadays, many companies are replacing or upgrading old rigid architecture approaches in favor of the greater flexibility supported by platforms (e.g., microservice architectures) to provide higher scalability, but also domain-specific architectures (e.g., robotics and automotive domains) demand new technologies and software solutions to produce more efficient and versatile systems.

This workshop is relevant to the software architecture field to understand how to design and maintain complex software architectures in different application domains where multiple stakeholder's concerns and multiple quality attributes must coexist to produce complex systems. Along with the need to create more open systems, the requirements will evolve often during the lifetime of the systems, either because new functionality is required that was not anticipated during creation of the systems or because new needs are identified based on requirements monitoring. This workshop aims to increase the awareness combining software architecture and complex systems engineering processes to understand how modern systems under the I4 umbrella must be designed and efficiently built at lower costs.

In this edition we received four full submissions (a lower number than usual perhaps caused by the COVID-19 pandemic) and we accepted three out of them. The papers where each reviewed by three Program Committee members and selected based on their novelty and on their relevance to the scope of the workshop.

Organization

Workshop Chairs

Rafael Capilla   Rey Juan Carlos University, Spain
Klaus Schmid   University of Hildesheim, Germany
Patrizio Pelliccione   University of L'Aquila, Italy
Andreas Burger   ABB Corporate Research, Germany
Pablo Oliveira Antonino   Fraunhofer IESE, Germany

Workshop Program Committee

Christian Berger   University of Gothenburg, Sweden
Hongyu Pei Breivold   ABB Corporate Research, Sweden
Juan Luis Carús   TSK, Spain
Jan Bosch   Chalmers University of Technology, Sweden
Christoph Elsner   Siemens AG, Germany
Thomas Fogdal   Danfoss, Denmark
Sten Grüner   ABB Corporate Research Germany, Germany
Mike Hinchey   Lero, Ireland
Frank Van Der Linden   Philips, The Netherlands
Thomas Kuhn   Fraunhofer IESE, Germany
Jabier Martinez   Tecnalia, Spain
Frank Schnicke   Fraunhofer IESE, Germany
Dimitrios Serpanos   University of Patras, Greece
Elisa Yumi Nakagawa   University of São Paulo, Brazil
Rick Rabiser   Christian Doppler Lab. MEVSS, JKU Linz, Austria

Additional Reviewer

Virendra Ashiwal

Access Control for Smart Manufacturing Systems

Björn Leander[1,2](✉) ®, Aida Čaušević[1] ®, Hans Hansson[1] ®,
and Tomas Lindström[2]

[1] Mälardalen University, Västerås, Sweden
{bjorn.leander,aida.causevic,hans.hansson}@mdh.se
[2] ABB Industrial Automation, Process Control Platform, Västerås, Sweden
tomas.lindstrom@se.abb.com

Abstract. In the ongoing 4th industrial revolution, a new paradigm of modular and flexible manufacturing factories powered by IoT devices, cloud computing, big data analytics and artificial intelligence is emerging. It promises increased cost efficiency, reduced time-to-market and extreme customization. However, there is a risk that technical assets within such systems will be targeted by cybersecurity attacks. A compromised device in a smart manufacturing system could cause a significant damage, not only economically for the factory owner, but also physically on humans, machinery and the environment.

Strict and granular Access Control is one of the main protective mechanisms against compromised devices in any system. In this paper we discuss the requirements and implications of Access Control within the context of Smart Manufacturing. The contributions of this paper are twofold: first we derive requirements on an Access Control Model in the context of smart manufacturing, and then asses the Attribute Based Access Control model against these requirements in the context of a use case scenario.

Keywords: Access control · Industrial automation and control systems · Smart manufacturing · Industry 4.0 · Cybersecurity

1 Introduction

Smart manufacturing [1,2] is a development of traditional manufacturing implying a shift from production of big series of identical units towards a highly dynamic manufacturing environment that is tuned to extreme customization, fluctuating markets, and specific customer needs. The technology to enable this

This work is supported by the industrial postgraduate school Automation Region Research Academy (ARRAY), funded by The Knowledge Foundation. The authors would like to acknowledge Andrea Macauda and Axel Haller for valuable discussions and feedback.

H. Muccini et al. (Eds.): ECSA 2020, CCIS 1269, pp. 463–476, 2020.
https://doi.org/10.1007/978-3-030-59155-7_33

dynamic behavior includes an increasing amount of interconnected sensors, actuators and related services in the manufacturing environment, in combination with e.g., cloud technologies, data lakes, artificial intelligence, etc., for inference and aid to decision-makers [3].

In the dynamic smart manufacturing environments of today and tomorrow, the traditional view of the manufacturing networks being air-gapped and protected by proprietary technologies no longer holds [4]. Considering that a great number of these devices introduced in a smart manufacturing system have wireless connectivity, are living on the edge of the network, possibly with direct connections to unprotected networks, there is an increasing risk that any of these devices become compromised. This has been illustrated in a number of attacks targeting industrial systems over the last ten years [5]. To protect the manufacturing environment from compromised devices, there is a need to introduce a number of security measures in the form of e.g., Intrusion Detection Systems (IDSs), end-to-end security for sensitive data, malware detection and fine-grained access control.

In this article we focus on *access control*, as one of the basic security functions in any system, enabling access restriction to operations on resources only to legitimate authorized subjects. The models for access control that are currently in use are tailored to authorize human subjects performing operations on digital assets, mainly supporting use-cases for rather static sets of resources and subjects or roles. These traditional models do not provide a high level of flexibility for expressing fine-grained policies [6], as frequently needed in smart manufacturing. Attribute Based Access Control (ABAC) is a relatively new model for policy formulation, potentially useful for machine-to-machine authorization [7,8]. Our aim in this paper is to derive requirements on access control in smart manufacturing systems, and evaluate ABAC against those requirements.

The remainder of this paper is structured as follows: Background is presented in Sect. 2. In Sect. 3 we identify a compilation of requirements on access control. In Sect. 4 a use cases scenario for smart manufacturing is presented, including suggestions on policy formulations for ABAC in this context. A discussion on how ABAC relates to the requirements are provided in Sect. 5. Scientific work related to our findings is presented in Sect. 6. Finally the work is summarized and some remaining challenges and future areas of research are described in Sect. 7.

2   Background

2.1   Smart Manufacturing Concepts

The term *smart manufacturing* is used for describing the 4th industrial revolution from a manufacturing perspective, with origin in a joint work by several agencies in the US [3]. Smart manufacturing is sometimes also referred to as Cyber Physical Production Systems (CPPS) [9] and Intelligent Manufacturing Systems (IMS)[1].

---

[1] More information available at http://ims.org.

In general, smart manufacturing encompasses the whole manufacturing chain, from supply to production and logistics. Data collected from sensors within the process are used for advanced data analytic in order to improve the overall operations. A key aspect of smart manufacturing is to provide flexibility and dynamicity in the manufacturing environment by modularization of process steps, so that process steps can be combined and re-combined based on current production requirements [10]. Integrating modular process steps in the manufacturing system enables Workflow as a Service (WfaaS), where vendors of production equipment could sell pre-fabricated process-steps as a service, allowing the factory owners to easily adapt to fluctuating market demands.

2.2 Cybersecurity Threats to Smart Manufacturing Systems

The increasing amount of connected and interconnected devices required for the data acquisition together with external stakeholders in need to access the data, considerably increases the attack surfaces of a smart manufacturing system. Furthermore, as different modules within the system are dynamically connected to each other, the authorization of privileges between devices and services must be equally dynamic to allow continuous secure operation. According to Tuptuk et al. [4], cybersecurity is rather seen as a characteristic than as a design principle within the development of smart manufacturing systems, a misconception that may lead towards many systems being insufficiently protected.

The CIA-model is often used to describe desired security characteristics of a system (**C**onfidentiality, **I**ntegrity and **A**vailability [11]). In the context of smart manufacturing, a cybersecurity attack may breach any of these characteristics, e.g., leading to possible loss of Intellectual Property (IP), costly errors in production due to unreliable or faulty data, and down-time or potentially safety-related threats to production machinery, workers and the environment.

2.3 Access Control Definitions

There are a number of guiding principles for access control, the most notable ones being [12]:

1. **Least privilege**, requires that a subject should only have the minimum possible privileges needed to perform its tasks.
2. **Complete mediation** requires that any access to a resource must be monitored and verified.

Following these principles in a smart manufacturing system will help minimize the harm an adversary can do after gaining an initial foothold within the system, and even shorten the detection time, since failed access attempts typically are logged and monitored.

Sandhu et al. [13] describe access control as being comprised of models at three different layers, **P**olicy, **E**nforcement and **I**mplementation (PEI). Policy models are used to formalize high level access control requirements, enforcement level models describe how to enforce these policies from a systems perspective, and the implementation level models show how to implement the components and protocols described by the enforcement model. Following the PEI-model, this work is focusing on the policy-layer models, meaning that we will discuss how rules can be expressed, rather than mechanisms to enforce the rules.

A prerequisite for robust access control is reliable authentication of entities. In this work we assume that a trustworthy solution for authentication is used.

Historically, Mandatory Access Control (MAC) and Discretionary Access Control (DAC) have been the two main paradigms within access control [14]. MAC is based on security classifications of resources, combined with security clearances for subjects, e.g., top-secret content only readable for subjects with the highest security clearance. In DAC on the other hand, the privileges are defined as a relation between the resource and subject, often with the subject allowed to transfer its privileges.

Role-Based Access Control (RBAC) is a model building on principles from both DAC and MAC, where subjects are assigned to one or several roles that may be hierarchically ordered. Privileges are derived from the roles rather than from the subject. In a number of studies it has been shown that the traditional access control schemes are not sufficient for, e.g., cloud-connected cyber physical systems [15] and IIoT [16].

2.4   Attribute Based Access Control (ABAC)

A relatively novel scheme in access control is ABAC. In the work of Yuan and Tong [17], the application is aimed at providing access control in web services. They show that the granularity of the traditional RBAC scheme is not fine enough, in order to formulate certain policies easily expressed in natural language. The following example is extracted from [17], and provided here to introduce ABAC and illustrate that such natural language rules are difficult to express using the traditional Access Control models:

Let us assume we need to grant a user access to movies in an online streaming service. In this example we consider a movie *rating* (R, R-13, G) and *freshness* (New release, Normal), mapped to the user *age* and subscription *category* (Budget, Premium). The following to rules apply for a user to be allowed to watch a movie:

1. To watch movies with rating R, user must be over 17 years old, and for movies with rating R-13, over 12 years.
2. To watch a New release, the user subscription category must be Premium.

In ABAC, the subject s's right to perform operation o on a resource r in environment e is calculated based on attributes of the subject, resource and environment, A_s, A_r, A_e respectively:

$$allow_o(s, r, e) \leftarrow f(A_s, A_r, A_e)$$

For the movie streaming service, the following policy rules can be expressed, based on the viewer and movie attributes:

$$f_1(s,r,e) = (rating(r) = \text{G}) \vee (age(s) > 12 \wedge rating(r) = \text{R-13}) \vee (age(s) > 17)$$

$$f_2(s,r,e) = (freshness(r) = \text{normal}) \vee (category(s) = \text{premium})$$

allowing for rules to be further combined:

$$allow_{view}(s,r,e) = f_1(s,r,e) \wedge f_2(s,r,e).$$

Several works on ABAC have been conducted, including two major standardization efforts in the area: eXtensible Access Control Markup Language (XACML) by OASIS [18], and Next Generation Access Control (NGAC) by NIST [19]. A comparison between NGAC and XACML is provided by Ferraiollo et al. [20].

Authorization architectures for ABAC typically contain a number of standard components [8,18,20]: A subject can only access a resource through the the the Policy Enforcement Point (PEP), which acts as a mediator for any privilege request. The PEP queries an authorization decision from the Policy Decision Point (PDP) that reads policy information from the Policy Information Point (PIP), which has access to Policy Data. An administrator maintains Policy Data through a Policy Administration Point (PAP).

3   Access Control Requirements on Smart Manufacturing

In this section we formulate a list of requirements on access control for a smart manufacturing system. To provide such a list we have studied the literature, using an adapted version of the method presented by Kitchenham [21]. We have selected relevant requirements guided by the basic principles for access control. For details regarding the literature review and used protocol we refer the reader to [22].

3.1   Requirements Related to a Traditional Manufacturing System

A traditional manufacturing system can be described as an Industrial Automation and Control System (IACS) which typically supports safety- and security critical processes [23]. IACS are used to control and monitor a wide range of different types of physical processes, e.g., in chemical industries, power plants, and discrete manufacturing.

An illustration of a generic traditional manufacturing system architecture can be seen in Fig. 1a, inspired by the Purdue Enterprise Reference Architecture (PERA) [24]. These systems contain a number of essential functions that cannot be disrupted, and that are required to maintain health, safety and availability of the equipment under control. In principle, a security measure must not result in a state of the system that could lead to Health, Safety or Environmental (HSE) consequences. A number of requirements on the access control arise from the need to support essential functions [23]:

R1 Availability: The manufacturing system should be operable even if some components fail, e.g., a failed server or a disruption in network connectivity between shop floor and cooperate network should not interfere with production.

R2 Security measures must not have a negative impact on essential functions. Specifically, HSE-related incidents shall not happen as a result of loss of control due to lack of privileges.

Non-Repudiation is also an important characteristic of access control that is required by e.g., IEC 62443[2]. We choose not to list it as a requirement in this context, as the focus of this work is on mechanisms for access control at a policy level and non-repudiation refers to logging and auditing of execution of granted privileges.

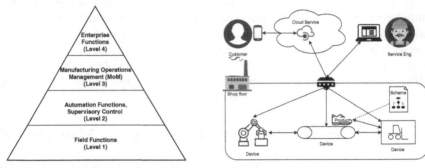

(a) A traditional manufacturing system architecture based on PERA

(b) A simplistic smart manufacturing scenario

Fig. 1. An overview of a traditional and a smart manufacturing architecture. (a) PERA illustration and (b) SM scenario

3.2 Requirements Related to Smart Manufacturing Systems

A number of requirements on access control are shared between the smart manufacturing domain and other dynamic systems of interconnected cyber-physical systems. These requirements arise through the evolution of the traditional automation pyramid towards a service oriented and decentralized system [10,15]:

R3 Diversity: A system should provide support for several different kinds of applications to be integrated throughout the whole life-cycle. This implies that multiple categories of users, usages of services and production related data shall be supported by the system.

---

[2] Part 3-3: System security requirements and security levels, Ed 1.0, 2013.

R4 Scalability: A system should be scalable with regards to users and policies. Management of a huge amount of devices, services and users must be simple and cost efficient, still providing necessary transparency.

R5 Flexibility: The access control mechanism shall provide an easy way of defining new policies.

R6 Efficiency: The computational cost of inferring privileges should not negatively impact the performance of the system as a whole.

From [16,25–27] we have derived the following requirements specific to the smart manufacturing domain:

R7 Temporal policies: The required privileges to perform a task may shift between each batch, or even between each produced unit. The access control model shall be equally flexible, following the principle of least privilege.

R8 Logical ordering: Production in a manufacturing environment is usually described as a workflow, meaning that the order of the actions, and the number of times an action can be executed could be limited. The access control model shall be able to express such logical ordering at a policy level.

3.3   Generic Access Control Requirements

In the following we describe generic access control requirements not covered in earlier sections. These requirements are the result of discussions with industrial experts:

R9 Transparency: From the perspective of an administrator, it must be easy to deduce current state of granted privileges, and historical changes to privileges. This transparency requirement could also extend to other privileged users.

R10 Delegation: For certain scenarios, it should be possible to transfer privileges from one subject to another through delegation.

4   A Smart Manufacturing Scenario

In this section we describe a generic smart manufacturing scenario to be analyzed from an access control perspective. We provide a discussion on how ABAC can be applied to the scenario in Fig. 1b. The scenario essentially follows the set-up of a service-driven architecture for manufacturing, described in [10,26], connected to the IEC 61499 [28].

Let us assume that a product p is to be manufactured. p is associated to a set of devices $\mathbf{D}$ that must perform tasks on p for it to be finalized. In order to perform the actions there is a need for a device $d \in \mathbf{D}$ to share information, and execute operations on one or more other devices in $\mathbf{D}$, according to the manufacturing scheme defined specifically for p.

The customer c wants to read information from the system for data related to product p via a cloud service, e.g., production status and expected delivery time. A 3rd party service organization o is responsible for maintaining some of the devices in $\mathbf{D}$, and must therefore be able to read status and perform service-related actions on the devices, e.g., reading health records and performing firmware upgrades.

In practice, the rules we describe in the following would be implemented using e.g., XACML [18]. For brevity, we choose to describe only the logical expressions of the policies, following the formalism introduced in [17]. The following attributes will be used in the ABAC policy formulations below:

- $batch_{id}(x)^3$ is the value of the batch attribute, related to a produced entity p or related to the current context of execution for a device d.
- $batches(e)$ is the set of all active batches in the manufacturing environment e.
- $purchases(c)$ is the set of batches that customer c has purchased. In this example we assume a one-to-one connection between customer and batch.
- $contract_{id}(d)$ is the value of the service-contract attribute related to a device d.
- $contracts(o)$ is a set of contracts under which the service organization o is working.
- $idle(d)$ is a Boolean attribute indicating that device d is currently idle if TRUE or busy if FALSE.
- $*$ is used to indicate an unassigned attribute value.

Given the example, we are able to show some interesting characteristics regarding access control in smart manufacturing systems.

C1 Machine to Machine (m2m) cooperation is limited by the current entity/batch attribute.
C2 Customer outside organization read rights are limited by a purchase.
C3 Service organization personnel (possibly 3rd party) having read and e.g., firmware-update rights limited by a contract.

Using ABAC, a policy to satisfy characteristic C1 could be expressed as:

$$allow_{op}(d_1, d_2, e) = (batch_{id}(d_1) = batch_{id}(d_2)) \wedge batch_{id}(d_1) \in batches(e) \quad (1)$$

Stating that the privilege to perform the operation will be granted only if the devices d_1 and d_2 have the attribute $batch_{id}$ assigned with the same id, and that id is among the active batches in the environment. Similarly, the customer could be granted privileges based on a combination of attributes of the data and attributes of the customer, which would allow a very fine-grained model for authorization (i.e., related to characteristic C2). One simple example of an authorization rule could be:

$$allow_{read}(c, p, e) = batch_{id}(p) \in purchases(c) \quad (2)$$

Note that in this specific rule, as well as the following, no environment attributes are used. Entity e will still be used in the declaration of the formula for consistency reasons. The above equation is stating that reading information about

---

^{3} Here x is used as variable representing either an entity p or a device d.

product p is allowed if the $batch_{id}$ for p is present in the set of *purchases* that the customer c has done. Typically such information is retrieved through filtering, i.e., the privilege is enforced by the application or API implementation, which is a much weaker condition than granting privileges through the access control mechanism. In fact, following the traditional practice, the access control mechanism will grant read-access to any valid customer and rely on the application to perform the correct filtering.

The privileges of personnel from the service organization (i.e., related to characteristics C3) is an interesting issue, since there may be many factors within the manufacturing environment that should prevent interruption or additional load on devices or services related to direct operation. In a classical service operation scheme, privileges to perform maintenance related operations may not be allowed except when the production unit is halted for planned maintenance or similar. However, in a smart manufacturing environment, this may be a common case, especially for WfaaS scenarios, i.e., it is up to the service organization to make sure that the workflows are running as needed. In these cases, an ABAC policy could be used to minimize the risk of disturbing ongoing operations. For example, an attribute indicating that the device is currently in use could inhibit the right to perform disruptive actions, and attributes indicating a need to perform an update or a similar disruptive maintenance action could inhibit the device from being assigned to a batch. The following rule could be set up for intrusive service operations:

$$allow_{op}(o, d, e) = (contract_{id}(d) \in contracts(o)) \land idle(d) \qquad (3)$$

Stating that the operation is allowed if the service contract for the device d is in the set of contracts the service organization o is working under, and d is currently idle.

5 Fulfillment of Requirements

A summary of the requirements and the fulfillment levels with regards to ABAC is provided in Table 1. The fulfillment level *Fulfilled* denotes that ABAC is well suited to fulfill the requirement; *Possible* denotes that fulfillment is possible, but depends on the implementation; and *Unclear* denotes a requirement where the fulfillment level is difficult to assess from available documentation. In the following we discuss the reasoning behind the fulfillment assessment.

ABAC is able to express fine-grained rules due to the use of attributes on subjects, objects and the environment, as well as the possibility to set up policy-rules as functions of these attributes. This granularity and expressiveness will allow a very high level of flexibility, leading to fulfilling **requirement R5**. As illustrated in the Sect. 4, it seems possible to express rules in ABAC so that the principle of *least privilege* is satisfied, something that would be more challenging using e.g., RBAC. The **requirement R3** on diversity is also fulfilled, provided that policies can be easily added and adapted for different applications and user

Table 1. Requirements fulfillment for ABAC

ID	Requirement	Description	Fulfillment
R1	Availability	Work in spite of degraded functionality	Possible
R2	Critical events	No HSE impact	Possible
R3	Diverse	Many user categories and usages of services and data	Fulfilled
R4	Scalable	Management of huge amount of devices, services, users	Unclear
R5	Flexible	AC must allow easy policy creation for new scenarios	Fulfilled
R6	Efficient	Cost of AC cannot impact system performance	Unclear
R7	Temporal policies	Quick shift in policies, due to customization	Fulfilled
R8	Logical ordering	Workflow based access control	Unclear
R9	Transparency	Administrator to see what privileges are granted and why	Possible
R10	Delegation	Privileges transferable through delegation	Possible

categories. Here the enforcement and implementation considerations are of great importance.

The reasoning used for **R5** is also valid for **requirement R7**, as it arises as a result of quick shifts in policies, due to e.g. customization. Hence, it can be fulfilled since it is possible to express very fine-grained rules based on attributes. As demonstrated in the scenario description, it is possible to express policies so that they are meaningful in the context of shifting production schemes.

The management effort of an ABAC-model may not scale well with increasing size and complexity of the system (**requirement R4**). It may be the case that policy rules can be expressed in such a general way, as suggested in Sect. 4, but there are certainly more complex scenarios including a potentially larger set of rules. Any privilege request needs to evaluate all rules applicable for that specific request, demanding logic for handling combinations of rules. In a system with a complex set of policies, the implications of adding or altering a policy can be difficult to foresee. Attribute provisioning is also a management issue in a dynamic system. There is a need for trusted Attribute Authorities to provide the integrity of claimed attributes.

A low computational cost (**requirement R6**) is not a general property of ABAC. Depending on the implementation and how the policy base is formulated, the operation of granting or denying a privilege request may be computationally expensive. In case of using e.g., XCAML [18] for policy expression, there does not seem to be a bounded cost for inference [20, 29]. The total cost of inference must also include the time for attribute enumeration, which may need additional communication rounds with Attribute Authorities.

Requirement R1 implies that there should be a distributed architecture for access control in smart manufacturing applications, possibly including redundancy for key entities. This characteristic is uncommon in most available access control enforcement models. An ABAC architecture consist of several authorities, which all must be available to provide continuous privilege enforcement. However, it is possible to fulfill the requirement of a functioning access control mechanism during degraded mode using an enforcement architecture with local caches for attributes and policies that can be used in isolation. Another possibility is using a distributed architecture of policy- and attribute-authorities.

Requirement R2 concerns the possibility for a system to stop (e.g., operator lock-out during a critical scenario), and could possibly be met by ABAC using an environment attribute indicating a *system state* within the plant. This would however not be the first option for designing the system to protect it from HSE-related incidents. Instead, secondary control-units are typically used for essential functions, e.g., an emergency stop. Those controls are not dependent on standard user authentication and authorization, and will have a very limited functionality. Therefore, the fulfillment of this requirement can be seen as *possible*, even though it is not directly dependent on the access control model.

Requirement R8 is stating that the access policies should follow the workflow in the process. This is currently not supported by ABAC. There are mechanisms in e.g., NGAC and UCON [7] called obligations, which may alter privileges based on previous policy decisions. However, it is not clear if obligations can be used to describe a state-machine altering attribute assignments to mimic a process workflow.

A generic requirement on an access control model is to provide transparency (**requirement R9**). For ABAC it is unclear if such functionality is available neither with regards to an administrator, nor to a user. A solution on the implementation-model level could possibly be able to answer to the transparency needs of an administrator, but it is not intrinsic to the access control scheme, as in the case with e.g., the access control list (ACL) ability to perform per-resource review, or the RBAC ability to perform a per-subject review.

To be able to transfer privileges between subjects, as stipulated by **requirement R10**, is common during delegation in industrial systems. In the case of ABAC, this would require a subject to be able to transfer a set of attributes to another entity, as the privilege inference is based on attribute values. In principle there is nothing in ABAC that specifically prohibits this. However, it may prove a challenge in practice, as the subject needs to know precisely which attributes to transfer in order to achieve the intended privilege delegation. Detailed knowledge on how the policy-rules are expressed is needed to perform privilege delegation in ABAC. Looking at the examples from our use case scenario in Sect. 4, it would be quite easy to allow delegation by e.g., transfer the $contract_{id}$ attribute to a service engineer temporarily working with maintenance under a specific contract, but there are more complex scenarios in which several rules concurrently may influence a privilege decision. Furthermore, when transferring attributes there is a need to limit the usage of the attributes to the actual scope of the delegation, otherwise there is an apparent risk that the attribute transfer will grant other privileges than was intended. Our conclusion is that additional mechanisms in the enforcement and implementation layers are needed to make this requirement practically achievable.

6   Related Work

Salonikas et al. discuss the concept of access control requirements in a dynamic industrial system with focus on the wider concept of IIoT [16], while Lopez et al. target cloud connected cyber physical systems [15]. Both articles discuss different access control models at the policy level, very similar to our work. However, these articles do not consider modular system characteristics specific for a smart manufacturing, as we do.

Watson et al. [6], discuss the use of different access control models in conjunction with OPC UA. They advocate the use of ABAC or a combination of ABAC and RBAC as a good match for protection against privilege escalation for both inside and outside attackers within IACS. Their work can be seen as a suggestion for the enforcement layer, whereas our work provides guidance applicable to the policy layer.

Some of the existing work present variations of ABAC suitable in different domains. Lang et al. [8] suggest a proximity based access control (PBAC), well suited for intelligent transportation systems. It originates from the ABAC model, but uses the mathematical proximity between subject and resource as one of the deciding factors for granting privileges. To derive policy rules, Model Driven Security (MDS) is used. MDS usually relies on a modeling tool in which the policy can be described at a high level of abstraction and the actual enforcement rules are then generated based on that model. Park and Sandhu [7] present the Usage CONtrol (UCON$_{ABC}$)-model, which can also be seen as an extension of the ABAC model with obligations. In this approach, an access-control event could alter attributes or conditions for future access controls. This mutability of attributes, or a variation thereof, could possibly be used to model the behavior of temporal workflows required by smart manufacturing. Next Generation Access Control (NGAC) [20] is the NIST proposal on how ABAC should be described. Compared to the traditional ABAC, in this variant attributes are provided as hierarchical labels (i.e., similar to RBAC group hierarchies), rather than properties with values as described in the initial ABAC-models. All of these approaches have interesting features useful in a smart manufacturing system, e.g., the model driven approach from PBAC and the obligations from UCON$_{ABC}$. As a future work, we aim to investigate the possibility to combine the beneficial concepts from these approaches in a practical smart manufacturing scenario.

7   Conclusions

Smart manufacturing is a technology that has a huge economical potential, transforming manufacturing towards servitization and extreme customization. However, the technologies that such systems are built upon bring new challenges, especially as the increasing attack surface expose the system to additional cybersecurity threats. As we have argued in this paper, one of the largely neglected mechanisms for security within manufacturing systems is access control between devices and services. Since the dynamic properties of smart manufacturing require a similarly dynamic model for access control, additional attention must be directed to this issue.

In this article we have derived a number of requirements on access control within smart manufacturing systems, based on knowledge related to traditional manufacturing systems, interconnected cyber-physical systems, and industrial expertise. These requirements are considering both the guiding principles for access control and the basic safety principles of an industrial control system.

Illustrated by a use-case scenario we have mapped the requirements to the ABAC model, and shown that the model aligns well with the requirements. However, there are still several open questions to be answered. How to handle scalability with regards to management of policies and attributes in large systems seems to be the most difficult issue to deal with, especially for complex sets of access control policies. The management process must be sufficiently light-weight in order for the model to be adopted in real applications. Transparency and efficiency are other areas where additional efforts are needed to make the ABAC model a feasible alternative for modern industrial manufacturing systems.

As future research we envision conducting a simulation study with use-cases from the smart manufacturing domain, together with e.g., the Policy Machine, which is the reference implementation of NGAC from NIST[4]. The management issue of security policy generation could possibly be handled using model driven security, as discussed by Lang et al. [8].

References

1. Mittal, S., Khan, M.A., Wuest, T.: Smart manufacturing: characteristics and technologies. In: Harik, R., Rivest, L., Bernard, A., Eynard, B., Bouras, A. (eds.) PLM 2016. IAICT, vol. 492, pp. 539–548. Springer, Cham (2016). https://doi.org/10.1007/978-3-319-54660-5_48
2. Davis, J., Edgar, T., Porter, J., Bernaden, J., Sarli, M.: Smart manufacturing, manufacturing intelligence and demand-dynamic performance. Comput. Chem. Eng. **47**, 145–156 (2012)
3. Thoben, K.-D., Wiesner, S., Wuest, T.: "Industrie 4.0" and smart manufacturing - a review of research issues and application examples. Int. J. Autom. Technol. **1**, 4–16 (2017)
4. Tuptuk, N., Hailes, S.: Security of smart manufacturing systems. J. Manuf. Syst. **47**(April), 93–106 (2018)
5. Slowik, J.: Evolution of ICS attacks and the prospects for future disruptive events. Technical report (2017)
6. Watson, V., Sassmannshausen, J., Waedt, K.: Secure granular interoperability with OPC UA In: INFORMATIK 2019: 50 Jahre Gesellschaft für Informatik - Informatik fr Gesellschaft (2019)
7. Park, J., Sandhu, R.: The UCON$_{ABC}$ usage control model. ACM Trans. Inf. Syst. Secur. **7**(1), 128–174 (2004)

---

[4] https://csrc.nist.gov/Projects/Policy-Machine.

8. Lang, U., Schreiner, R.: Proximity-based access control (PBAC) using model-driven security. ISSE 2015, pp. 157–170. Springer, Wiesbaden (2015). https://doi.org/10.1007/978-3-658-10934-9_14
9. Sadeghi, A.-R., Wachsmann, C., Waidner, M.: Security and privacy challenges in industrial internet of things. In: The 52nd IEEE Annual Design Automation Conference (2015)
10. Lu, Y., Ju, F.: Smart manufacturing systems based on cyber-physical manufacturing services (CPMS). IFAC-PapersOnLine 50, 15883–15889 (2017)
11. Whitman, M., Mattord, H.: Principles of information security. In: Cengage Learning, 4th edn. (2012)
12. Saltzer, J., Schroeder, M.: The protection of information in computer systems. IEEE 63(9), 1278–1308 (1975)
13. Sandhu, R., Ranganathan, K., Zhang, X.: Secure information sharing enabled by trusted computing and PEI models. In: Proceedings of ACM Symposium on Information, Computer and Communications Security (2006)
14. Sandhu, R.S., Samarati, P.: Access control: principles and practice. IEEE Commun. Mag. 32, 40–48 (1994)
15. Lopez, J., Rubio, J.E.: Access control for cyber-physical systems interconnected to the cloud. Comput. Netw. 134, 46–54 (2018)
16. Salonikias, S., Gouglidis, A., Mavridis, I., Gritzalis, D.: Access control in the industrial internet of things. In: Alcaraz, C. (ed.) Security and Privacy Trends in the Industrial Internet of Things. ASTSA, pp. 95–114. Springer, Cham (2019). https://doi.org/10.1007/978-3-030-12330-7_5
17. Yuan, E., Tong, J.: Attributed based access control for web services. In: Proceedings of IEEE International Conference on Web Services (2005)
18. eXtensible Access Control Markup Language (XACML) version 3.0 plus errata 01, standard, OASIS (2017)
19. Hu, V.C., et al.: Guide to attribute based access control (ABAC) definition and considerations. Technical report, NIST (2014)
20. Ferraiolo, D., Chandramouli, R., Kuhn, R., Hu, V.: Extensible access control markup language and next generation access control (2016)
21. Kitchenham, B.A.: Procedures for undertaking systematic reviews. Technical report, Keele University (2004)
22. B. Leander, "Towards an access control in a smart manufacturing context," tech. rep., Mälardalen Real-Time Research Centre, Mälardalen University (2020)
23. IEC 62443 security for industrial automation and control systems, standard, Internation Electrotechnical Commission, Geneva, CH, 2009–2018
24. Williams, T.J.: The purdue enterprise reference architecture. Comput Ind. 24(2), 141–158 (1994)
25. Ladiges, J.: Integration of modular process units into process control systems. IEEE Transactions on Industry Applications 54, 1870–1880 (2018)
26. Faller, C., Höftmann, M.: Service-oriented communication model for cyber-physical-production-systems. Procedia CIRP 67, 156–161 (2018)
27. Ayatollahi, I., Brier, J., Mörzinger, B., Heger, M., Bleicher, F.: SOA on smart manufacturing utilities for identification, data access and control. Procedia CIRP 67, 162–166 (2018)
28. IEC 61449 function blocks, standard, Internation Electrotechnical Commission, Geneva, CH (2012)
29. Turkmen, F., Crispo, B.: Performance evaluation of XACML PDP implementations. In: ACM Conference on Computer and Communications Security (2008)

Industrie 4.0 Virtual Automation Bus Architecture

Thomas Kuhn[⊠], Pablo Oliveira Antonino, and Frank Schnicke

Fraunhofer Institute IESE, Fraunhofer-Platz 1, 67663 Kaiserslautern, Germany
{thomas.kuhn,pablo.antonino,frank.schnicke}@iese.fraunhofer.de

Abstract. Many Industrie 4.0 use-cases require end-to-end communication between layers of the automation pyramid. Converting the existing layered communication into a peer-to-peer architecture does however require the functional bridging between protocols. In this article, we discuss Industrie 4.0 communication scenarios, constraints of the automation domain, as well as device communication requirements, and present our end-to-end communication approach based on our information bus concept, the virtual automation bus (VAB).

Keywords: Industrie 4.0 · Industrial IoT · Security · End-to-end communciation · Software platform · Production · Changeability

1 Introduction

The fourth industrial revolution is driven by digitalization and networking of production processes. This is a challenge for system architects, as they have to consider platform and communication aspects in addition to traditional system requirements [9]. One central scenario of Industrie 4.0 is improvement of the changeability of production processes. Changeable production is considerably different from existing flexible production lines, which enable the manufacturing of products with a preprogrammed range of changes. Flexible car manufacturing lines produce cars with normal or adaptive cruise control. Switching a production within this range of planned flexibility requires only minor efforts. Changeability in production addresses unplanned changes, e.g. the manufacturing of chassis elements with changed set of drilling holes. Changeable production lines reduce downtimes due to production changes to a minimum value.

Changeability today is limited by the basic principles or operation in factory automation. In most cases, PLC controllers realize the factory automation. They execute cyclic programs that read sensor values and control actuators to automate manufacturing steps. Program execution is affected e.g. by sensors or Manufacturing Execution Systems (MES systems) [8] that select variants from the preprogrammed flexibility range. A changeable production requires the MES system to change the programming of a PLC controller in a much more flexible manner, e.g. by orchestrating production steps. In context of the BaSys 4.0 project[1], we did develop a service-based production that enables this kind

---

[1] www.basys40.de.

© Springer Nature Switzerland AG 2020
H. Muccini et al. (Eds.): ECSA 2020, CCIS 1269, pp. 477–489, 2020.
https://doi.org/10.1007/978-3-030-59155-7_34

of changeable production. Our service-based production deploys atomic, configurable production steps on PLC controllers that implement services; service orchestration is performed by higher-level components.

Realization of this concept requires an operational end-to-end communication between all production assets. Ideally, a peer-to-peer communication between all devices that are relevant for the production should be possible. This includes devices located in the shopfloor, but also servers in the IT, or (mobile) interfaces to human operators. Today, the automation pyramid prevents this. Field devices, e.g. sensors and actuators often use proprietary busses to communicate. Data is encapsulated in proprietary formats. PLC controllers communicate via Modbus or OPC-UA, which are standardized technologies, but target shopfloor applications. The IT communicates using http/REST services. In many installations, additional proprietary busses are used in addition for specific purposes. Moreover, different data types and data encodings further limit interoperability.

We did therefore develop the virtual automation bus (VAB) concept [10] as end-to-end communication solution in production environments. It defines communication primitives, and enables inter-network communication with existing infrastructures. The VAB is therefore not another protocol, but a common language to bridge existing protocols and (heterogeneous) network topologies into one virtual network.

In this paper, we describe an Industrie 4.0 use-case with respect to communication needs. We devise our VAB concept and describe the VAB architecture, as well as its operation in Industrie 4.0 settings with heterogeneous networks and with inter-company communication. We furthermore analyze the VAB in context of common communication scenarios.

2   Industrie 4.0 Virtual Automation Bus

Asset administration shells (AAS) [6] are one main concept of Industrie 4.0 for providing information hiding and higher levels of abstraction for assets. An AAS has a unique identifier and contains sub-models. Sub-models define properties and services, and implement a reflexive interface. They provide high-level information, e.g. regarding offered services of assets, asset status models, or plant topology models. Low-level PLC controllers implement the implement service-oriented interfaces of an AAS. High-level controllers invoke services, but do not need to know about service implementation. To enable re-use, orchestration functions should be able to set-up real-time connections between controllers, e.g. by assigning PROFINET IO application relationships (AR).

2.1   Virtual Automation Bus Concept

Our virtual automation bus (VAB) should support the communication with and between asset administration shells across network borders. It should also support service-based and functional abstraction of production systems to support service-based production systems for changeable production. To this end, we follow the proposals made in the Industrie 4.0 community [5] to separate the different concerns for accessing data models, managing asset functions, and for transporting data. The VAB hides the distributed deployment of information, one of the main features of an asset administration shell.

Figure 2 illustrates this functional abstraction in context of an aluminum cold rolling mill as example. It consists of Light Barriers (LBxx), Engines that move conveyor belts (Ex), and PLC Controllers (Pxxx).

Aluminum cold rolling mills move aluminum coils through a system of conveyor belts and other transport mechanisms between storage and the milling process, and perform the milling with given quality and thickness values. Our example highlights the proposed I4.0 interconnection between devices of the cold-rolling mill.

Controller runtime environments (Controller RTE) execute control algorithms that control e.g. the milling process with real-time capabilities. Controller runtime environments offer services and invoke services of other controller RTEs. They also communicate e.g. sensor values to other entities and receive setpoint values. Application runtime environments (Application RTE) execute high-level applications that interact with the office-floor, or that implement e.g. transport strategies. Application RTEs host applications that offer service calls and use service calls to interact with other functions.

Asset administration shells (AAS) provide a unified interface for assets. They consist of sub models that logically structure information and services. Each sub model therefore covers a specific aspect of an asset (Fig. 1).

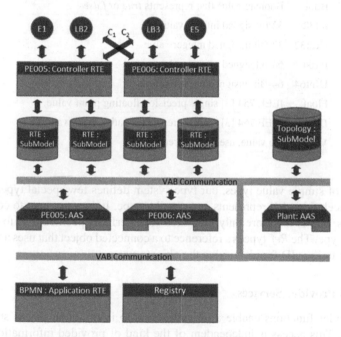

Fig. 1. Functional components of plant (cold rolling mill) automation

The VAB therefore provides the communication backend for controller RTEs and for AAS. It therefore needs to implement data and message transport services and connect automation components. It also needs to map the VAB communication primitives to concrete communication technologies. This also require the mapping of network specific addresses. The illustrated *Registry* therefore defines a unified way to map technology independent identifiers to concrete technology specific communication endpoints.

The VAB hides nature and deployment location of sub models behind administration shell interfaces. To ensure end-to-end connectivity between different device types, the VAB sub models are based on a common, technology independent type system. Technology mappings realize the mappings to platform types, e.g. OPC-UA data types. Platform types must at least support the value ranges and accuracy of the defined technology independent types. Table 1 defines our technology independent types, combining elementary types for strings, integers, and real values with specific value ranges.

Table 1. Technology-independent data types

Any	Represents any type
Ref	Unambiguous reference to an element
Str	String (sequence of characters) of unconstrained length
Str(x)	String (sequence of characters) of maximum length x
Bool	Boolean value that represents *true* or *false*
Int32	32-bit signed integer value
UInt32	32-Bit unsigned integer value
Int64	64-bit signed integer value
UInt64	64-Bit unsigned integer value
Float	IEEE 754 [3] single precision floating point value
Double	IEEE 754 [3] double precision floating point value
Void	No value, used e.g. as return type

Besides of simple value types, our type system defines few special types: The *Any* type is a placeholder that represents any possible type. It does not map to communication systems, and is therefore only permitted for interface specifications to express an unspecified type. The *Ref* type is a reference to a connected object that uses a technology independent unique ID for identifying the object.

2.2 Model Provider Services

Model provider functions enable a unified access to information that is structures in sub models. This access is independent of the kind of provided information and it is independent of how an information item is stored. Model providers map native data formats into a specialization of the common structure that is shown in Fig. 2. This common model representation is accessible through a service API, which enables its exploration without knowledge of the underlying data format.

Model providers manage a set of elements and values of element properties. They organize elements hierarchically, yielding a tree of elements. Elements therefore have one parent and any number of contained elements. Properties describe element details,

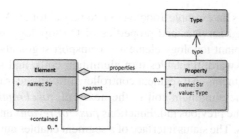

Fig. 2. Reflexive presentation of data as hierarchical model

e.g. its value. The predefined *type* property supports reflexive access to type information via a reflexive type description. The reflexive type description conforms to the meta-model in Fig. 3. Every model provider defines five primitives that enable interaction with sub models.

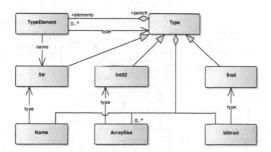

Fig. 3. Reflexive type description

- Ref create(Ref parent, Str name, Any value)
  Create a new model element with parent element *parent*, name *name*, and value defined by *value*.
- Ref delete(Ref parent, Str name)
  Delete model element with name *name* from element *parent*.
- Any read(Ref el, Str prop)
  Return value of property *prop* from element *el*.
- void update(Ref el, Str prop, Any value)
  Change value from property *prop* of element *el* to new value *value*.
- Any invoke(Ref prov, Str id, Any[] par)
  Invokes service with ID *id* on service provider *prov* with parameter array *par*. The result will be returned when service execution is completed.

A type is described at runtime by the information model shown in Fig. 3. Every type is described by a model element that defines the technology independent type name, an optional array of array sizes, and a flag that indicates whether the type is a structure or not.

Figure 4 illustrates an example Topology meta model for an Aluminum cold rolling mill. It defines offered services and properties of the topology sub model. The meta model defines three plant topology elements: Transport segments transport aluminum coils forward or backward, turntables turn aluminum coils, and shift tables vertically connect transport segments. All segment controllers offer basic transportation services: *passToNext* passes the aluminum coil to the next rail, *takeFromPrevious* receives an aluminum coil from the previous rail. Functions *passToPrevious* and *takeFromNext* provide likewise services. The status interface of a segment enables automation engineers to query whether the segment is free, i.e. no transport pallet is on the segment, or occupied. Turntables additionally turn to angular positions between 0° and 180°. Shift tables drive to specified positions.

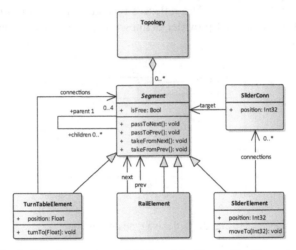

Fig. 4. Topology meta-model of a cold rolling mill with services

3   Evaluating Deployments and Technologies

We did evaluate the Virtual Automation bus in several deployment scenarios. In this section, we present two of them: the first scenario connects Industrie 4.0 devices with an Ethernet network and uses HTTP/REST web services for communication. The second scenario consists of two Ethernet networks that use HTTP/REST and OPC-UA for communication. Both networks are connected via a BaSys gateway that couples networks. The third Scenario consists of a deployment with an Ethernet network that realizes BaSys VAB communication and a CAN bus network that implements a proprietary communication. The shown implementation were created with the Open-Source implementation of the VAB that is available for download from [7].

3.1   Simple HTTP/REST Deployment

Figure 5 illustrates the first deployment scenario that we evaluate. Field devices connect via Profibus to controllers; all other devices connect to one Ethernet network. Asset

Administration Shells of controllers and the plant reside on an AAS server, servers and PLC controllers provide AAS sub models. The VAB therefore forms a virtual bus that connects all AAS and sub models on the network.

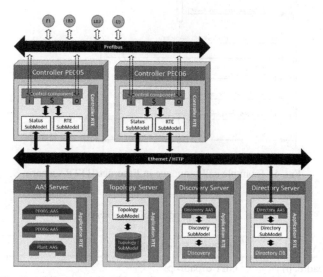

Fig. 5. Ethernet technology mapping example for Cold-Rolling Mill

The sequence diagram in Fig. 6 illustrates an example interaction between the topology server and controller *PE005*. The topology server exports the topology sub model that contains the *isFree* property for each segment of the plant. The value of *isFree* depends on the status of four light barriers that every controller exports in its status model. The Topology server queries the status sub model of controller *PE005* to check the status of the light barriers. The example sequence illustrates the message sequence via the VAB that queries the first light barrier *LB2*.

In the first step, the topology server queries a reference to the AAS with id *PE005* using the VAB *invoke* primitive. The query is sent to a known directory instance that tracks the addresses of all connected components. The directory returns a URL with the local top-level domain *.loc* that points to the AAS provider. The topology server then reads the available sub models of the AAS of controller *PE005* using a HTTP GET request. Then it invokes the directory server again to query the address of the sub model provider. The topology server then uses the defined model provider API to read the reference to the *Status SubModel* and subsequently the status of the light barrier. The VAB hides the communication details of the AAS and sub models, it abstracts concrete network locations through URLs.

Asset Administration Shells and Controllers implement a defined mapping from logic meta models (cf. Fig. 4) to HTTP REST. An URL identifies every AAS and sub model provider that realizes an HTTP REST service. Model provider services map to HTTP requests as illustrated in Table 2.

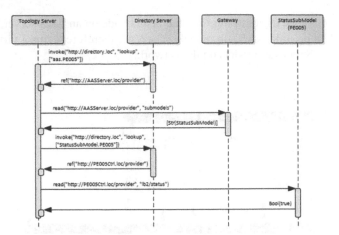

Fig. 6. Example call sequence in Ethernet/HTTP scenario

Table 2. HTTP mapping of VAB service calls

VAB call	HTTP/REST mapping
read(e, p)	GET e?path=p
update(e, p, v)	PUT e?path=p [body: v as JSON]
create(e, p, v)	POST e?path=p&op=create [body: v as JSON]
delete(e, p)	DELETE e?path=p
invoke(p, id, par)	POST p?path=id&op=invoke [body: par as JSON]

The defined mapping maps VAB calls to HTTP service primitives. Small values, e.g. the path to the element and an operation ID are transmitted in the header, while complex objects, e.g. parameters are transmitted in the HTTP body, which has no size limitation.

3.2 Multi Network Scenario

The second deployment in Fig. 7 illustrates a situation with two different Ethernet networks. Shop floor devices communicate via OPC-UA, which is an automation protocol to connect shop floor devices. Enterprise components in the office floor communicate via HTTP/REST web services. Similar to the first deployment, Asset Administration Shells and sub models represent all components and their information and services through a common interface. In contrast to the first deployment, the virtual automation bus needs to bridge different networks. In the illustrated deployment, a gateway is instantiated between both networks. The gateway implements technology mappings from both connected networks. The used gateway realizes http/REST mappings, as illustrated in Table 2 for HTTP. For OPC-UA, a similar mapping was defined in context of the evaluation.

The sequence diagram in Fig. 8 illustrates the call sequence with a gateway. The Topology server asks for the *Status SubModel*, and receives a reference as response that

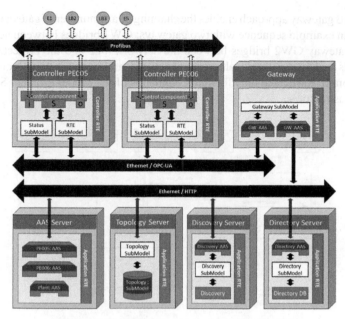

Fig. 7. Complex deployment with two networks

points to the gateway and encodes the OPC-UA address of the controller in the different network. The topology server invokes the HTTP GET command via the received URL in the same way as in the first scenario, the presence of the gateway is transparent. The Gateway processes the GET command, transforms the requested property address in the *dest* field to the appropriate OPC-UA call, and invokes the OPC-UA *ReadValue* operation that reads the status of light barrier *LB2*. When invoking *ReadValue*, the Gateway has to add the namespace ID (3 in the example), which therefore needs to be known to the Gateway.

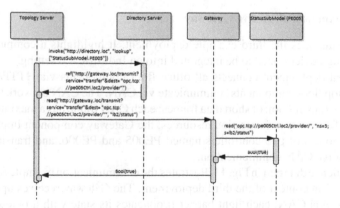

Fig. 8. Example call sequence in two networks scenario

Our VAB gateway approach enables the chaining of any number of gateways. Figure 9 illustrates an example sequence with two gateways: GW1 bridges between networks *loc* and *loc2*, gateway GW2 bridges between the network *loc2* and the protected network *hidden*. This enables e.g. the development of network architectures that decouple critical sections from IP traffic and only forward commands of the Model Provider Services for critical infrastructures.

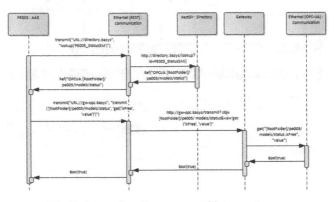

Fig. 9. Example call sequence with two gateways

The directory server returns the path with all necessary gateways as response to the lookup request. This path is either pre-configured or is dynamically looked up by the directory server. Gateways do not need to perform any activity besides forwarding the call, and possibly translating the request, a read request in the illustrated example, into the language of the target protocol. Every gateway forwards the request to the address in field *dest*, which marks the destination. HTTP REST protocols encode the requested operation in the request type. The illustrated HTTP/REST gateways therefore need to support HTTP GET, POST, DELETE, and PUT requests.

3.3 Deployment with Active Gateway

Figure 10 illustrates the third example deployment. It highlights a common situation when existing devices need to be integrated into an Industrie 4.0 setting.

Our third deployment connects all office floor components via HTTP/REST web services. Shop floor components communicate via CAN. The CAN network is optimized for real-time transmission of short data frames; each CAN frame has a maximum payload of 8 bytes. To save communication resources, the Gateway component implements the status sub models of two controllers named PE005 and PE006, and translates service calls into native CAN communication.

The sequence diagram in Fig. 11 illustrates the communication example from deployments 1 and 2 in context of the third deployment. The Gateway receives updates of the light barriers via CAN; each light barrier propagates its state with a unique CAN ID. Light barrier LB2 propagates its status in this example with CAN ID 16. The gateway manages the controller sub model and stores the light barrier status. The gateway

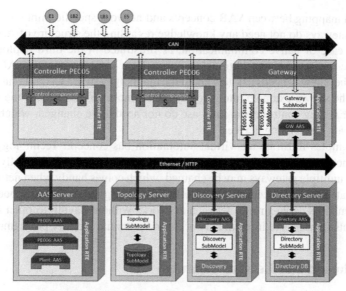

Fig. 10. Complex deployment with CAN bus

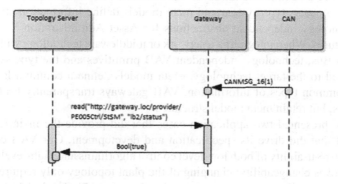

Fig. 11. Example call sequence in CAN bus deployment scenario

did register this sub model with the directory server. The *StatusSubModel* of controller *PE005Ctrl* is available at:

http://gateway.loc/provider/PE005Ctrl/StSM

The stored status is returned when the respective property is queried via the HTTP query illustrated in Fig. 11. The gateway in this case performs an active translation between native CAN bus traffic and the defined VAB communication semantics.

3.4 Discussion

Our deployment examples show how the VAB concept is realized in context of concrete technologies, and that is proves useful in different deployment scenarios. The VAB is able to transparently bridge between networks as long as every network implements one defined mapping between VAB concepts and network specific implementations. In this case, gateways do not need any knowledge regarding the structure of AAS and sub models. In case of native communication, as illustrated in the third deployment, the gateway needs to provide an additional mapping. Data is propagated via CAN bus using CAN IDs, the gateway needs to know about the mapping between CAN IDs and property names. In the shown example, the gateway furthermore did implement the sub model structures. Existing controllers in this case do not need to be changed, which realizes a migration path for existing devices.

Our examples illustrate the virtual automation bus concept. Technology independent reference types encode network specific paths, addresses, and optionally gateways. Optionally, multiple gateways may be chained, which comes handy when networks need to be separated, e.g. for security reasons. In this case, gateways copy model provider calls as human readable strings between networks without having to open an IP port. This prevents IP access to internal networks, and potential security problems.

4   Conclusion and Lessons Learned

During the development of our Virtual Automation Bus architecture, we put emphasis into creation of a communication layer that connects Asset Administration Shells and sub models. A basic type system and meta models define information structures and enable technology independent abstractions for Asset Administration Shells and sub model structures. When integrating a network or middleware technology with the Virtual Automation Bus, technology independent VAB primitives and the type system needs to be mapped to the target technology. Meta models define a common language that structure common types of information. VAB gateways transparently bridge network technologies, but retain meta model structures.

We have presented two application cases that did provide the main requirements to our VAB that did drive its specification and development. Our VAB considerably improves the re-usability of both low-level control algorithms and high-level controllers. It also improves changeability: changing of the plant topology only requires an update of topology models. It is not necessary to update Low-level PLC code. This significantly lowers the time that is necessary for adapting code to new plant installations. Furthermore, the VAB enables the integration of legacy devices. For existing devices that do not support Asset Administration Shells, the AAS and sub models are provided by gateways that translate between the VAB and the (proprietary) protocol of the native device.

Future work includes the evaluation of our Virtual Automation Bus in context of other application cases, as well as the implementation of more complex Asset Administration Shell use-cases that cover for example handing over of Asset Administration Shells and the serialization of complex sub models.

References

1. Scheid, O.: AUTOSAR Compendium - Part 1: Application & RTE (2015). ISBN 978-1-5027-5152-2

2. Alves, T.R., Buratto, M., de Souza, F.M., Rodrigues, T.V.: OpenPLC: an open source alternative to automation. In: IEEE Global Humanitarian Technology Conference (GHTC 2014), San Jose, CA, pp. 585–589 (2014)
3. IEEE 754-2008: Standard for Floating-Point Arithmetic, IEEE Standards Association (2008). https://doi.org/10.1109/ieeestd.2008.4610935
4. Lehnhoff, S., Rohjans, S., Uslar, M., Mahnke, W.: OPC unified architecture: a service-oriented architecture for smart grids. In: First International Workshop on Software Engineering Challenges for the Smart Grid (SE-SmartGrids), Zurich, pp. 1–7 (2012)
5. Epple, U., Schulz, D., et al.: Industrie 4.0 service architecture: basic concepts for interoperability. VDI/VDE, November 2016
6. Adolphs, P., et al.: Structure of the administration shell – continuation of the reference model for the industrie 4.0 component. VDI/VDE, April 2016
7. The Eclipse BaSyx Project. https://projects.eclipse.org/projects/technology.basyx
8. McClellan, M.: Applying Manufacturing Execution Systems. CRC Press, Boca Raton (1997). ISBN 9781574441352
9. Antonino, P.O., Morgenstern, A., Kuhn, T.: Embedded-software architects: it's not only about the software. IEEE Softw. 33(6), 56–62 (2016)
10. Kuhn, T., et al.: Industrie 4.0 virtual automation bus. In: Proceedings of the 40th International Conference on Software Engineering: Companion Proceedings (2018)

Enabling Industry 4.0 Service-Oriented Architecture Through Digital Twins

Frank Schnicke$^{(\boxtimes)}$, Thomas Kuhn, and Pablo Oliveira Antonino

Fraunhofer IESE, Fraunhofer-Platz 1, 67633 Kaiserslautern, Germany
{frank.schnicke,thomas.kuhn,pablo.antonino}@iese.fraunhofer.de

Abstract. A major goal of Industry 4.0 is to increase changeability of production processes, and to reduce the additional cost for individualized products. A service oriented production architecture can enable this goal. However, it demands changes in the software-based systems that compose the different levels of automation in a factory. Additionally, it requires a multitude of data to reflect the demands of service-oriented manufacturing processes. In this paper, we detail the minimal data to be contained in digital twins to enable an Industry 4.0 service-oriented architecture. We use two central Industry 4.0 use cases as drivers for deriving this data. We describe services by detailing their capabilities and their quality of service in terms of time, money and resulting product quality. Using these descriptions, we detail customer's order and the included product to be manufactured. Additionally, we describe challenges of the orchestration process like incompleteness of business processes and detail, how they can be solved using digital twins of the product, the service providers and the plant. Finally, we validate the proposed models by implementing the use cases on two model plants and give an experience report.

Keywords: Service-oriented architecture · Industry 4.0 · Digital twin · Service-based production · Asset Administration Shell

1 Introduction

Industry 4.0 (I4.0) is the fourth industrial revolution [1]. Unlike previous revolutions, it does not introduce a singular new technology, but covers a more groundbreaking change, which is the end-to-end digitalization of manufacturing processes. A major benefit of I4.0 are changeable processes. Today, changing of a manufacturing process yields high cost [2], which is distributed over the lot size of a production. Consequently, the cost for the production of small lot sizes is much higher than that of mass-produced assets. If the cost for changing a manufacturing process decreases significantly, the production of small lot sizes will become economically feasible.

The high cost for changing production processes originates in their federated architectures. Today, programmable logical controllers (PLCs) control production processes steps. The used IEC 61131 [3] languages however were developed to automate simple processes. Due to the grown complexity of manufacturing processes and inter-PLC

© Springer Nature Switzerland AG 2020
H. Muccini et al. (Eds.): ECSA 2020, CCIS 1269, pp. 490–503, 2020.
https://doi.org/10.1007/978-3-030-59155-7_35

communication, automation engineers that change production processes face similar issues as software engineers that maintain large software systems: changes yield unpredictable side effects, that are difficult to locate, and that require time and effort to resolve (cf. Sect. 2.3). The efforts for reprogramming PLCs are therefore a big part of process changing costs.

We apply a Service-oriented Architecture (SOA) to automation to remove side-effects when changing manufacturing processes. SOA provides a clear separation between service providers and consumers. PLCs implement stateless, callable services that must only depend on the explicit service parameters that are passed during invocation. Orchestration of services into process steps is no longer performed by the PLCs, but by designated orchestrators. Only the service orchestrator has knowledge about the final sequence of services that are required for the manufacturing of a specific product. Information about products and PLC services are provided in Asset Administration Shells (AAS) [23] that provide information about assets with a unified interface.

In this paper, we analyze I4.0 use cases as drivers to devise the minimum required information for integrating SOA into production processes. We define AAS base models with the amount of information that is at least required for supporting I4.0 use cases, and that may be extended to tailor them to other manufacturing processes. We describe the integration of agreed I4.0 technologies to enable a unified inter-device communication, and describe the application of our framework in context of example implementations.

This paper is structured as follows: Sect. 2 introduces the state of the art and the state of the practice of I4.0 and SOA. Section 3 describes use cases of I4.0 that drive the development of our architecture framework. Section 4 describes the minimum information. The proposed digital twins and orchestration is assessed in Sect. 5. Section 6 presents an overview of related work. Finally, Sect. 7 draws conclusions and provides an outlook on future work.

2   State of the Art and State of Practice

I4.0 is about the end-to-end digitalization of the manufacturing industry. Today, manufacturing devices already collect large amounts of sensor data. They are however only locally available. Data processing is only possible along the layers of the "automation pyramid", which refers to the strictly separated layers and protocols in automation systems and the difficulties for implementing cross-layer interaction. I4.0 instead advocates a peer-to-peer architecture that enables cross-layer interaction that, for example, enables enterprise resource planning (ERP) systems to directly interact with sensors, e.g. for tracking the quality of manufacturing processes.

2.1   Industry 4.0 and Digital Twins

Cross-layer interaction requires a structured approach for representing and exchanging data. The concept of digital twins, whose origin is in the testing of avionics systems [4] is a key concept for a cross-layer communication in Industry 4.0 [5]. A digital twin is a representation of the state of an asset, i.e. a physical entity. It enables unified access to asset data and services. As defined by the IIC [6], *"a digital twin is a formal digital representation of some asset, process or system that captures attributes and behaviors of that entity suitable for communication, storage, interpretation or processing within a certain context.".*

Digital twins will describe all relevant assets in an I4.0 production. Assets are for example products-to-be-produced, work pieces and devices. DTs aggregate data generated in the physical world, enable experimenting with this data in digital representations of I4.0 assets (physical or non-physical entities), and provide insights that may be deployed back to the physical world as updated configurations. Thus, the data provided by the digital twins can be used to orchestrate and optimize the plant.

2.2 Service-Oriented Architecture

A Service-Oriented Architecture (SOA) is defined as *"a set of architectural tenets for building autonomous yet interoperable systems"* [2]. An autonomous system is defined as one that [2]: Is created independent of other systems, operates independent of their environment, and provides self-contained functionality. Interoperability is defined as *"a characteristic of a product or system, whose interfaces are completely understood, to work with other products or systems, present or future, in either implementation or access, without any restrictions"* [7]. SOA builds upon services, realizing this autonomy and interoperability. Services are defined as *"an act or performance offered by one party to another. Although the process may be tied to a physical product, the performance is essentially intangible and does normally result in ownership of any of the factors of production"* [8]. These services are understood to have several properties, such as having a transaction concept [9] and being stateless [2, 10], which need to be transferred to process automation. Even when using SOA, architects need to keep communication times, platform resources, and scalability in mind [34].

2.3 Architecture of Plant Automation

Currently, automation is implemented using the "automation pyramid" reference architecture as defined by IEC 62264 [11]. This architecture consists of separate layers with defined interaction points. PLCs perform the specific steps in predetermined cyclic programs. Supervisory control and data acquisition (SCADA) realize the distributed control of several PLCs. Manufacturing Execution Systems (MES) manage the overall production by controlling high-level manufacturing steps. Enterprise Resource Planning (ERP) systems manage resources, for example the number of items in stock. Cross layer interaction in the automation pyramid is difficult, as every layer can only access information that is provided by lower layers. Changes therefore require modifications in all layers. Industry 4.0 propagates instead a peer-to-peer communication to enable device-to-device communication. However, this change in architecture only addresses the data acquisition part and does not introduce changeability on its own.

PLCs are programmed using languages defined by IEC 61131 [3]. These languages impose several challenges, e.g. unclear semantics [12]. If process parameter needs to be changed and the needed variant is not already implemented, the code on the PLC needs to change, which may affect PLC cycle times and therefore real-time constraints of the program. Predecessor and successor devices of the changed device depend on this cycle time, and inter-PLC communication through networks also must be considered during reprogramming. In consequence, a change of a single PLC may produce side effects in other PLCs [13], which lead to downtimes, and therefore to a loss in time and money.

Thus, a change in architecture is necessary. Currently, there are several reference architectures for Industry 4.0. IIRA [14] is not only a reference architecture for Industry 4.0, but also addresses other domains like energy, smart cities and health care. It presents the architectural viewpoints of business, usage, functionality and implementation. RAMI 4.0 [15] defines a three dimensional model decomposed into hierarchy levels, lifecycle and value stream, and layers. It is a framework for a common understanding between stakeholders. SITAM [16] decomposes its architecture into three middlewares: integration, mobile and analytics with a focus on SOA.

3 Industry 4.0 Use Cases

Industry 4.0 is driven by major use cases that exemplify potentials and challenges. These use cases are the architecture drivers that steer our design decisions regarding our I4.0 SOA information model. For the overall goal of process changeability, we emphasis on use cases that focus on *flexibility* and *productivity* [17]. Flexibility is the automatic reconfiguration concerning products and used devices. Productivity is about optimizing the production process with respect to business goals, e.g. equally distributed degree of capacity utilization.

3.1 Use-Case 1: Integration of New Devices

When a manufacturing process changes, the integration of new devices into the plant quickly becomes necessary. As described in Sect. 2.3, this requires considerable efforts for updating PLC and for testing. Industry 4.0 aims to drastically reduce this integration time [18]. When applying the service-oriented principle, a device will register itself with the manufacturing system and exposing provided services. Orchestrators will integrate the new device dynamically into the process. The AAS describes additional information regarding e.g. the required time and cost of process steps.

3.2 Use-Case 2: On-The-Fly Product Change

An efficient support of small lot sizes requires more efficient approaches for the changing of manufactured products [17]. Process changes should be possible with low, and predictable effort and down times. Ideally, PLCs only need re-programming when new base-services and tools are integrated. SOA enables this by separating service providers, and orchestrators as service users. Furthermore, the SOA principle must be realized to ensure stateless services and the transaction principle. It must support the controlling of individual production lines, as well as complete factories.

4 Enabling Industry 4.0 Service-Oriented Architecture

Major I4.0 applications therefore depend on information exchange between heterogeneous devices. Harmonizing data structures used for this information exchange enables the definition of an overall Industry 4.0 architecture. Our architecture supports this heterogeneous exchange by using digital twins. Digital Twins (DT) are digital entities that store data in well-defined information models, called sub-models. Using the use cases described in the Sect. 3 we identify the following required sub-models: Service, Order, Product and Plant model to create an executable production plan.

4.1 Service Model

Our service-based production approach decouples the implementation of services that is provided by PLCs from the service orchestration. Orchestration of PLCs requires a defined interface that enables the activation and monitoring of services. As PLC services may be concurrent and long-running, we decided to use asynchronous call semantics. The DT of a service provider therefore needs to provide a sub-model that provides an interface I_{serv} for all provided services, which enables their controlling. Interface I_{serv} is defined as following: $I_{serv} = (u_{Occ}, c_{Exec}, i_{Exec}, c_{OpMode}, i_{Work})$.

This interface definition resembles the interface of a control component. The *Control component* concept was first introduced by Pohl, Krumm, Holland, Stewing and Lueck [19] to provide generic access and control of service providers. The control component defines several status variables of the service provider. These are:

- Occupation u_{Occ} – The occupation state of the service provider indicates the current occupier of a control component. Only one user may occupy a service provider at a time. Sensitive operation modes may only be selected by the occupier of a component to prevent interfering users. Property write access attempts to set an occupier, reading back the property value indicates whether component occupation was successful.
- Execution Mode c_{Exec} – Defines the execution mode according to *ISA-88.00.01-2010* [20], e.g. installation, automatic, or manual mode.
- Execution State i_{Exec} – Describes the current state of the service execution, e.g. idle, execute or aborted. The corresponding state machine is defined by *ISA-88.00.02* [21] and originates from the Batch Control Industry. State transition commands may be written to this property, read access returns the current state.
- Operation Mode c_{OpMode} – Enables selection of the service to be executed. Services are identified by a control-component specific name. Writing the property attempts to select an operation mode, reading returns the selected operation mode.
- Work State i_{Work} – Describes the current step of the service provider. In case of a service of higher order, this can be for example the name of the current sub-step.

The service interface therefore defines five properties that support controlling and monitoring of the Control component. A Control component may expose all services through a single interface, or it may define multiple interfaces for independent services. The use of a generic state machine for execution state i_{Exec} enables orchestrators to monitor any control component for ready, running, completed services, as well as for error indications. The control component concept is arbitrarily nestable to create services of higher order while still exposing the same interface. A control component interfacing other control components is called a group control component. In extreme, the whole plant can be thought about as a service provider offering a "manufacture product" service.

In addition to an interface for invoking a service, service orchestrators need to know about the capabilities of a service. We define a service by the service capabilities D_{cap}, associated cost C_{serv}, achievable quality Q_{Serv}, the control component interface for invoking the service I_{serv}, and the service name *name* that must be given as operation mode: $serv = (D_{cap}, C_{serv}, Q_{Serv}, I_{serv}, name)$.

Because the definition of a generic semantic capability model that covers all possible services is difficult, we therefore use a straightforward approach for the implementation of a semantic description of offered services: Tags (e.g. Strings) describe the services and identify them by names. In addition to this information, it is also important to describe the quality that a service provider guarantees, e.g. in the sense of quality and cost in form of money or time consumption. This may vary over time: For example, when considering a milling machine, the service duration and tool wear will depend on work piece material, tool material, and previous milling times. In some combinations, e.g. metal tool and metal work piece, it may not even be possible to provide a successful service at all. Service descriptions therefore need to be able to refer to machine and product properties.

We therefore add (non)functional requirements to service descriptions to address additional service constraints. Boolean logic enables creation of semantic relations between tags and requirements. Requirements describe constraints imposed by the service provider. Such constraints can be for example the maximum dimension of a work piece a milling machine can process or the minimum temperature a hot rolling mill needs for sufficient service execution. The following example d_{drill} illustrates a service description with tags: $d_{drill} = \{((dev.heat < 80\ °C)\ \&\ (drill.diameter < 5\ mm))\}$

Service "drill" is available if property *heat* of asset *dev* is less than 80 °C, and requested product property *drill diameter* does not exceed 5 mm. Control component service definitions may contain several definitions of this kind for provided services. The overall capability definition D_{cap} is therefore a set of multiple definitions d_n. The service quality set Q_{Serv} is a dynamic provided information that describes the currently provided service quality. It consists of service-tag specific properties $q_{prop.n}$ that describe the possible service quality, e.g. depending on measured tool quality.

The cost model C_{serv} describes cost associated with using the service. We define two initial cost properties c_{time} and c_{money} that refer to the required time and associated monetary cost for executing a production service. With this model, we assume that the cost for invoking a service are the same, regardless of the processed product. If this is not the case, e.g. because different materials are processed, explicit services need to be defined that represent different use cases.

4.2 Order and Product Model

An order consists of a set of products to be manufactured in combination with bounded cost, a deadline expectation, and quality requirements. Products are characterized by a sequence of manufacturing steps, rec_{prod}, and associated cost C_{prod} that definine deadlines c_{dl} and monetary cost c_{money}.

$$order = (\{product_1, \ldots, product_n\}, C_{prod}), product = (rec_{prod}, P_{Group}), C_{prod} = \{c_{dl}, c_{money}\}$$

The product group P_{Group} defines a set of tags that identify similar products, e.g. products of similar dimensions and weight, with similar recipes that may for example be transported together. A recipe describes a product in a device independent way. As stated in Sect. 4.1, we describe services with tags and constraints. Consequently, the recipe should also identify requested services by tags, and define required product properties, and quality requirements. Product properties and quality requirements are specific to the service, and define for example the required diameter and accuracy when drilling a hole. We apply the Business Process Model and Notation (BPMN) to define recipes, which has been proven feasible for describing the interdependence of manufacturing steps. Each BPMN node details one needed skill in combination with product and quality parameters.

In order to keep the product recipe independent of the plant topology, the recipe must only include transforming services, and no supporting services. A transforming service is a service that changes the work piece itself, e.g. drilling a hole. In contrast, a supporting service does not change the work piece but instead performs an action that is necessary to enable transforming services in their execution. The most prominent example of a supportive service is a transport service. Another example is a change of temperature in the work piece. These supportive services should not be included in the BPMN since the need for them depends on the plant setup on which the BPMN will be instantiated. Thus, the orchestration step described in Sect. 4.4 will insert them where necessary.

4.3 Plant Model

Orchestration of a production process based on a recipe needs knowledge regarding plant topology to plan e.g. work piece transportation. A plant model details the plant by providing a logical topology model that specify possible connections between production resources. A cold-rolling mill for example transports an aluminum coil while milling, and changes the position of that work piece. We therefore represent plant topologies with directed graphs that describe transport mechanisms.

An incoming edge from a transport mechanism indicates that this mechanism is able to serve the input of a production resource. Similarly, an outgoing edge indicates that the transport service provider can retrieve a work piece from a production resource. For an example of this directed graph, see Sect. 5.2. A major challenge for creating a cost model for transportation is the large amount of transportation systems with their characteristics: conveyor belts transport a steady stream of work pieces between fixed end points. They transport several work pieces at a time with constant delays. Autonomous transport vehicles (ATVs) are able to transport several work pieces at a time as well, but will wait until e.g. a palette is filled. Work pieces in this case suffer a significant delay in transportation. Cranes are very flexible and can transport between numerous end-points. They however may yield long delays, depending on their load. All transportation might require buffer zones to store work pieces that are awaiting transportation. Additionally, transport mechanisms may influence each other, e.g. by obstructing a path.

A unified model for a DT needs to abstract from the specifics of individual transport systems. We therefore approximate the cost and delays associated with the transportation of a work piece, and define whether a transportation device is exclusively (ATV, crane) or not exclusively useable (e.g. conveyor belt). A plant topology model T_{Plant} consists of a set of tuples that describe devices and outgoing connections with transportation services:

$$T_{Plant} = \{dev_1, \ldots, dev_n\}, t_{dev} = (\{serv_1, \ldots, serv_n\}, \{trans_1, \ldots, trans_n\})$$

$$trans_{Ex} = (t_{typeEx}, n_{cap}, t_{del}, P_{Group}), trans_{Nex} = (t_{typeNex}, f_{prod}, P_{Group})$$

Plant topology T_{Plant} describes all devices dev_n. Each device dev describes its services $serv$, and available transportation for products. Transportation may either be exclusive $(trans_{Ex})$ or non-exclusive $(trans_{Nex})$. Exclusive transportation is characterized by work piece capacity n_{cap} and transportation delays t_{del} for product groups P_{Group}. Non-exclusive transportation is characterized by supported product frequency f_{prod}. For any transportation, we identify permitted product group tags P_{Group}.

4.4 Industry 4.0 Orchestration

The Industry 4.0 orchestration uses the previously described Digital Twins during the orchestration process to identify a set of feasible service providers out of all service providers. It assesses the following properties when creating the set: Functional matching (i.e. is the provided service the needed service), matching of constraints, quality, and cost requirement.

Functional service matching is performed by finding appropriate services through matching of tags. Afterwards, supporting service providers are scheduled based on constraints and on the plant topology sub-model to create a set of execution plans. Each of these plans is a possible alternative product manufacturing. After a sufficient set of plans are created, they need to be validated and judged. Thus, identification of likely candidate plans based on property values from digital twins is crucial.

The minimum cost C (independent of cost in time or cost in money) is derived by adding the cost of each service call. Additionally, product quality requirements have to be considered. Similar to cost calculation, the maximum product quality is derived based on the maximum quality estimate given by each provider. The maximum achievable quality Q is calculated by multiplying the estimated maximum quality of each involved service provider.

Finally, each execution plan will have minimum cost and a maximum quality estimate assigned. By removing plans which do not meet cost or quality requirements, the orchestrator creates a set of plans that meet the requirements. Figure 1 provides a high-level overview on the orchestration and DT models.

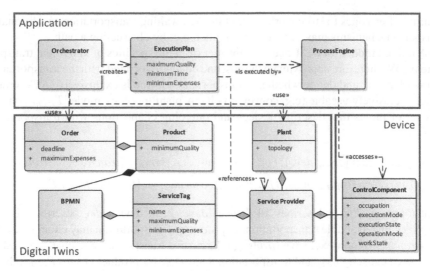

Fig. 1. The Digital Twins and their contained data needed to enable Industry 4.0 SOA.

5   Approach Implementation and Experience Report

We did implement our approach with the BaSys 4[1] middleware [22]. It provides concepts needed to implement Industry 4.0 in production systems. A major artifact of BaSys is the Digital Twin that is realized with the Asset Administration Shell (AAS) [23]. Ongoing standardization activities aim at creating a common meta-model, and runtime interface for the AAS. BaSys 4.0 supports the open-source reference implementation Eclipse BaSyx[2] that implements AAS and Digital Twins. In particular, the Eclipse BaSyx framework was used to describe the digital twins through the concept of the AAS and to communicate with the used devices through control components.

5.1   Demonstrator Description

We did evaluate our approach in context of a demonstrator setup that was shown at Hannover Messe (HMI) 2018. It did consist of devices representing different function-alities of a milling line for the production of screws: two feeders acting as work piece sources, two mills processing the work pieces by providing several services, and one packager acting as a work piece sink. A human worker was integrated into the workflow to provide a transport service. The demonstrator did evaluate our architecture in context of the use cases from Sect. 3: Failure of devices was simulated by disabling the devices. Repairing of devices was simulated by enabling the devices again. Through a GUI, it was possible to define and order new products on-the-fly using the available services. Additionally, the orchestration was configured to support the business goal of having a maximum throughput.

---

[1] The German joint research project BaSys 4.0 tackles the lack of maintainability and portability of current manufacturing applications by implementing a middleware as compatibility layer.

[2] https://eclipse.org/basyx.

For HMI 2019, we did created a second demonstrator using a plant model provided by Fischertechnik[3] that did implement a changeable production of brake disks. This demonstrator evaluated our architecture in a second setting consisting of a high-rack storage, a transport robot, an oven, and an ERP system. Through an order dialog, a customer could order a brake disk that then would be produced on the plant model.

5.2 Example Implementation of Digital Twins and Orchestration

Our demonstrators did create Digital Twins with the BaSys 4 middleware. We did create a Digital Twin using an AAS for each device and product, and did structure relevant information into sub-models. The plant AAS did define the plant topology as a sub-model. Each AAS registers itself with the AAS Registry, thus making its data and services available to other applications. AAS reference control components to provide a unified interface for controlling production processes[4].

Figure 2(a) illustrates the HMI 2018 demonstrator topology graph. The central transport service connects all devices (service provider). Figure 2(b) illustrates the recipe for a screw. First, a metal cube is milled into a cylindrical shape. Next, the screw head is created by creating a cavity on the top of the cylinder. Finally, the screw thread is created and the screw is packaged. Additionally, in the figure the orchestration of the abstract recipe to an executable plan is shown by incorporating the plant topology to derive supporting transport services. In the demonstrator context, Mill 2 did provide both profile milling and spiral milling services, while Mill 1 was able to provide round milling. The necessary data for service orchestration were retrieved from the product AAS. Device services were implemented by control components as described in Sect. 4.1. The orchestration provides an execution plan in form of a BPMN model. We did use the Activi[5] engine to execute the BPMN model.

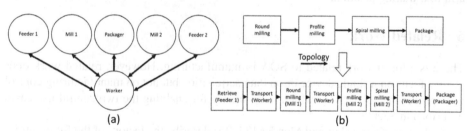

(a)   (b)

Fig. 2. (a) The HMI 2018 demonstrator topology as a directed graph. (b) The execution plan is derived from the recipe by mapping it to service providers while incorporating the demonstrator topology.

The HMI 2019 demonstrator implements similar AAS and sub-models. When ordering a new product, the ERP system creates a new AAS detailing the order as described in Sect. 4.2.

---

[3] https://www.fischertechnik.de/en/service/elearning/simulating/fabrik-simulation-9v.

[4] For an illustration of the architecture, see https://wiki.eclipse.org/File:BaSyx.BaSyx10Mins_8.png.

[5] https://www.activiti.org/.

5.3 Experience Report

We did implement our architecture successfully in both demonstrators. Modeling production recipes with a BPMN has proven its worth. Instead of changing PLC behavior, only a BPMN describing a new product needs to be introduced to the system to implement a process change. Thus, a low-level code change is replaced by a much more simplistic high-level change. By adding and removing device AAS from the registry, devices can quickly be integrated or removed, and are immediately usable by the orchestrator. This was also proven while designing the demonstrators: Initially, the HMI 2018 demonstrator should use a robot for transportation. Due to organization constraints, this was not realizable. Instead, the visitor was integrated into the demonstrator to transport a workpiece. However, this fact emerged at a late point of development when most of the system was already integrated. As result of the changeability introduced by the I4.0 SOA architecture, it was possible to quickly exchange the initially planned *transport* service provider (i.e. the robot) with a worker guidance system that did communicate with the user. The overall plant planning and description did remain the same. Thus, the scope of a complete device exchange was only limited to the device integration into the existing AAS infrastructure. No side effects did emerge. This underlines that even in demonstrator development the proposed architecture provides a huge benefit.

Additionally, several challenges needed to be addressed during the implementation. In the HMI 2019 demonstrator, service definition was not straightforward. An exposed service should be as complete and simple to use as possible. However, in the interest of process optimization, exposition of service details was necessary. Specifically, separating the transport service in $transport_{prepare}$, $transport_{perform}$ and $transport_{reset}$ steps allowed to greatly decrease time needed for a manufacturing execution. *Prepare* moves the robot arm to the source location, *perform* performs the transport step and *reset* moves the robot arm to a waiting position.

6 Related Work

There is a lot of work related to SOA in manufacturing. However, related work does mostly focus on a single device or on data acquisition but not on manufacturing control through the means of SOA, which is necessary for enabling the two central use cases described in Sect. 3.

Colombo, Karnouskos and Mendes [24, 25] describe the factory of the future utilizing SOA. The authors propose viewing the factory of the future as a system of systems organized by means of SOA. Additionally, they describe a methodology for dynamic reconfiguration of a SOA-based shop floor using high-level petri nets to describe the control of devices. Additionally, the authors illustrate the composition of services as a vectorial composition. Karnouskos et al. [26] propose an SOA-based architecture for collaborative cloud-based industrial automation. The authors describe design considerations such as backward/forward compatibility and system simulations. Based on these considerations, they propose a service-based architecture built upon different user roles and service groups. Using this architecture, they present the next generation of the concepts of Supervisory Control and Data Acquisition (SCADA) and Distributed Control System (DCS).

Jammes and Smit [2] describe a SOA approach using web services. They evaluated their approach using a dose-maker device, focusing on an SOA approach in the device itself. The topic of orchestration is described by Jammes, Smit, Lastra and Delamer [27] and addressed through the use of OWL ontologies. Additionally, SOA is described in the context of agent-based, self-orchestrating manufacturing systems. Both works evaluated their proposal in the context of the SIRENA project. Jammes, Mensch and Smit [28] describe an approach for service-oriented device communication using Devices Profile for Web Services (DPWS). Additionally, they describe how to integrate legacy devices into SOA. Pohl, Krumm, Holland, Stewing and Lueck [29] describe SOA in distributed automation and control systems with a focus on service-oriented control architectures. They describe a lease mechanism used for flexible service binding.

Thramboulidis, Vachtsevanou and Solanos [30] propose a microservice-based IoT-based framework for manufacturing systems. The authors introduce the idea of a plant-independent model (PIM) and a plant-specific model (PSM). Additionally, they describe how to transform a PIM into a PSM. The paper details the description and discovery of microservices. Ciavotta, Alge, Menato, Rovere and Pedrazzoli [31] propose a microservice-based middleware for data acquisition using the MAYA platform. They focus on the aspect of plant simulation in their proposed architecture.

Delamer and Lastra [32] describe device-level SOA with the focus on engineering knowledge descriptions based on ontologies. They propose four interrelated ontologies: process taxonomy, product ontology, equipment ontology, and service ontology. Varga et al. [33] propose the Arrowhead framework, which builds upon the concept of local clouds. Each local cloud is a system providing and consuming services.

7 Conclusion and Future Work

SOA is a viable approach for solving the requirements of Industry 4.0. However, to enable I4.0 SOA, a multitude of data is needed, and data structures must be agreed upon. In this paper, we have described a core of digital twins that enable changeable production and organize data and interfaces of service providers, services, products, plant topologies, and transportation. We have illustrated the applicability of our approach to changeable production. We purposely perceive our approach as technical core rather than a fully defined set of models: due to the large amount of different processes, it is likely that real-world deployments will have to add additional properties, constraints, and digital twins to achieve their I4.0 scenarios. We however believe that our core will provide a valuable structuring and initial framework as foundation for these activities. We did implement and validate our approach in context of the BaSys 4.0 project by implementing it to two demonstrators, both shown at the Hannover Messe (HMI). The implementation shows the potential of adopting the proposed digital twins and I4.0 orchestration.

A topic of future interest is the transformation of the plant-independent model into a plant-specific model similarly to the addition of transport steps. It is possible, that a single step in the product recipe is mapped onto a multitude of steps within the factory. We assume that future research will focus on how to enable this mapping when different levels of service granularity are described by recipe and service provider.

References

1. Lasi, H., Fettke, P., Kemper, H.-G., Feld, T., Hoffmann, M.: Industry 4.0. Bus. Inf. Syst. Eng. **6**(4), 239–242 (2014). https://doi.org/10.1007/s12599-014-0334-4
2. Jammes, F., Smit, H.: Service-oriented paradigms in industrial automation. IEEE Trans. Ind. Inform. **1**, 62–70 (2005)
3. Programmable Controllers—Part 3: Programming Languages, International Electrotechnical Commission, IEC, International Standard IEC61131-3 (2003)
4. Glaessgen, E., Stargel, D.: The digital twin paradigm for future NASA and US air force vehicles. In: 53rd AIAA/ASME/ASCE/AHS/ASC Structures, Structural Dynamics and Materials Conference 20th AIAA/ASME/AHS Adaptive Structures Conference 14th AIAA (2012)
5. Rosen, R., Von Wichert, G., Lo, G., Bettenhausen, K.D.: About the importance of autonomy and digital twins for the future of manufacturing. IFAC-PapersOnLine **48**(3), 567–572 (2015)
6. Definition of Digital Twin. https://www.iiconsortium.org/pdf/IIC_Digital_Twins_Industrial_Apps_White_Paper_2020-02-18.pdf. Accessed 20 July 2020
7. Definition of Interoperability. http://interoperability-definition.info/en/. Accessed 05 Dec 2019
8. Lovelock, C., Vandermerwe, S., Lewis, B.: Services Marketing. Prentice Hall Europe, London (1996)
9. Turner, M., Budgen, D., Brereton, P.: Turning software into a service. Computer **36**, 38–44 (2003)
10. Perrey, R., Lycett, M.: Service-oriented architecture. In: Proceedings of the 2003 Symposium on Applications and the Internet Workshops, 2003, pp. 116–119. IEEE January 2003
11. International Electrotechnical Commission: IEC 62264-1 Enterprise-control system integration–Part 1: Models and terminology. IEC, Genf (2003)
12. Bauer, N., Huuck, R., Lukoschus, B., Engell, S.: A unifying semantics for sequential function charts. In: Ehrig, H., et al. (eds.) Integration of Software Specification Techniques for Applications in Engineering. LNCS, vol. 3147, pp. 400–418. Springer, Heidelberg (2004). https://doi.org/10.1007/978-3-540-27863-4_22
13. Vyatkin, V.: Software engineering in industrial automation: state-of-the-art review. IEEE Trans. Ind. Inform. **9**(3), 1234–1249 (2013)
14. Industrial Internet Consortium: Industrial internet reference architecture. Technical Article (2015). http://www.iiconsortium.org/IIRA.htm. Accessed 05 Mar 2020
15. DIN specification 91345: 2016-04 (2016). Reference Architecture Model Industrie 4.0 (RAMI4. 0)
16. Kassner, L., et al.: The Stuttgart IT architecture for manufacturing. In: Hammoudi, S., Maciaszek, L.A., Missikoff, M.M., Camp, O., Cordeiro, J. (eds.) ICEIS 2016. LNBIP, vol. 291, pp. 53–80. Springer, Cham (2017). https://doi.org/10.1007/978-3-319-62386-3_3
17. Wang, S., Wan, J., Li, D., Zhang, C.: Implementing smart factory of Industrie 4.0: an outlook. Int. J. Distrib. Sens. Netw. **12**(1), 3159805 (2016)
18. Böhm, B., et al.: Challenges in the engineering of adaptable and flexible industrial factories. In: Modellierung (Workshops), pp. 101–110 (2018)
19. Polke, M., Epple, U., Heim, M.: Process Control Engineering, VCH Verlagsgesellschaft mbH, D-69451 Weinheim (1994). ISBN 3-527-28689-6
20. American National Standards Institute. ANSI/ISA-88.00.02 (2001). Batch Control Part 2: Data Structures and Guidelines for Languages
21. American National Standards Institute: ANSI/ISA-88.00.02 (2001). Batch Control Part 2: Data Structures and Guidelines for Languages
22. Kuhn, T., et al.: Industrie 4.0 virtual automation bus. In: ACM ICSE 2018, Göteborg, Schweden (2018)

23. Grangel-González, I., Halilaj, L., Coskun, G., Auer, S., Collarana, D., Hoffmeister, M.: Towards a semantic administrative shell for industry 4.0 components. In: 2016 IEEE Tenth International Conference on Semantic Computing (ICSC), pp. 230–237. IEEE, February 2016

24. Colombo, A.W., Karnouskos, S., Mendes, J.M.: Factory of the future: a service-oriented system of modular, dynamic reconfigurable and collaborative systems. In: Benyoucef, L., Grabot, B. (eds.) Artificial Intelligence Techniques for Networked Manufacturing Enterprises Management. SSAM, pp. 459–481. Springer, London (2010). https://doi.org/10.1007/978-1-84996-119-6_15

25. Karnouskos, S., et al.: A SOA-based architecture for empowering future collaborative cloud-based industrial automation. In: IECON 2012-38th Annual Conference on IEEE Industrial Electronics Society. IEEE (2012)

26. Bedenbender, H., et al.: Examples of the Asset Administration Shell for Industrie 4.0 Components–Basic Part. ZVEI White Paper (2017)

27. Jammes, F., Smit, H., Lastra, J.L.M., Delamer, I.M.: Orchestration of service-oriented manufacturing processes. ETFA (2005)

28. Jammes, F., Mensch, A., Smit, H.: Service-oriented device communications using the devices profile for web services. In: Proceedings of the 3rd International Workshop on Middleware for Pervasive and Ad-Hoc Computing, pp. 1–8 (2005)

29. Pohl, A., Krumm, H., Holland, F., Stewing, F.J., Lueck, I.: Service-orientation and flexible service binding in distributed automation and control systems. In: 22nd International Conference on Advanced Information Networking and Applications-Workshops (AINA workshops 2008), pp. 1393–1398. IEEE, March 2008

30. Thramboulidis, K., Vachtsevanou, D.C., Solanos, A.: Cyber-physical microservices: an IoT-based framework for manufacturing systems. In: 2018 IEEE Industrial Cyber-Physical Systems (ICPS), pp. 232–239. IEEE, May 2018

31. Ciavotta, M., Alge, M., Menato, S., Rovere, D., Pedrazzoli, P.: A microservice-based middleware for the digital factory. Procedia Manuf. 11, 931–938 (2017)

32. Delamer, I.M., Lastra, J.L.M.: Loosely-coupled automation systems using device-level SOA. In: 2007 5th IEEE International Conference on Industrial Informatics, vol. 2, pp. 743–748. IEEE, June 2007

33. Varga, P., et al.: Making system of systems interoperable–the core components of the arrowhead framework. J. Netw. Comput. Appl. 81, 85–95 (2017)

34. Oliveira Antonino, P., Morgenstern, A., Kuhn, T.: Embedded-software architects: it's not only about the software. IEEE Softw. 33(6), 56–62 (2016)

WASA - 6th International Workshop on Automotive System/Software Architecture

International Workshop on Automotive System/Software Architecture (WASA)

This volume contains the papers presented at the 6th International Workshop on Automotive System/Software Architecture (WASA 2020) held on September 14, 2020, in L'Aquila, Italy. WASA was organized as part of the 14th European Conference on Software Architecture (ECSA 2020). Due to the worldwide COVID-19 pandemic, the main conference and the workshop were hosted virtually.

WASA is concerned with topics related to the appropriate automotive system/software architecture and engineering techniques, which can be accepted by the automotive industry. Therefore, to bring together researchers and practitioners in the automotive system/software architecture and engineering area, WASA was organized with ECSA, the premier European software architecture conference.

The papers submitted covered topics such as a verified systems engineering process, system health indicators in the automated driving context, a simulation platform for an autonomous driving truck, an emotional model of a car, and experiences and practical guidelines to conduct experiments with real cars. In particular, the 2020 edition of WASA saw an increase of papers focusing on automated driving in the broadest sense. WASA 2020 had no separate abstract submission deadline, and we received six submissions on the paper deadline with four full and two short papers. The submissions came from The Netherlands and Germany. We conducted a single-blind review process with three to four reviews per paper. Out of these submissions, we accepted four papers (two full and two short papers, 67% acceptance rate). Besides these paper presentations, we were happy to start the workshop day with a keynote given by Erik Coelingh. He is a Technology Advisor and Vice President at Zenuity and an Adjunct Professor Mechatronics at Chalmers University, Sweden. Erik gave an inspiring talk on the future of intelligent vehicles.

We thank the ECSA 2020 organizers, in particular, Henry Muccini, the general chair. We also thank Anne Koziolek and Mauro Caporuscio, the ECSA workshop chairs, for managing the whole process and for swift feedback on several questions. Moreover, we want to thank our Program Committee for doing an excellent job. The workshop would not have been possible without these volunteer experts, who provided reviews of such high quality. We appreciate this work very much!

We hope that you will enjoy reading this volume.

Organization

Workshop Chairs

Darko Durisic   Volvo Car Corporation, Sweden
Stefan Kugele   Technische Hochschule Ingolstadt, Germany
Yanja Dajsuren   Eindhoven University of Technology,
     The Netherlands
Miroslaw Staron   Chalmers – University of Gothenburg, Sweden

Workshop Program Committee

Harald Altinger   Audi, Germany
Klaus Becker   BMW Group, Germany
Christian Berger   University of Gothenburg, Sweden
Reinder Bril   Eindhoven University of Technology,
     The Netherlands
Alessio Bucaioni   Mälardalen University, Sweden
Thomas Galla   Elektrobit, Germany
Uwe Honekamp   Vector, Germany
Yaping Luo   Eindhoven University of Technology,
     The Netherlands
Corrado Motta   Volvo Car Corporation, Sweden
Marta Olszewska   Abo Akademi University, Finland
S. Ramesh   General Motors, USA
Karsten Schmidt   Audi, Germany
Tetsuya Tohdo   Denso, Japan
Mark Van Den Brand   Eindhoven University of Technology,
     The Netherlands
Andreas Vogelsang   Technische Universität Berlin, Germany
Ji Wu   Beihang University, China

System Health Indicators in Mixed Criticality E/E Systems in Automated Driving Context

Friederike Dollinger[1]([✉])[iD], Rinat Asmus[3][iD], and Marc Dreiser[2][iD]

[1] Technical University Munich, Boltzmannstrasse 3, 85748 Garching, Germany
friederike.dollinger@tum.de
[2] Fraunhofer Institute for Cognitive Systems IKS, Hansastraße 32, 80686 Munich, Germany
marc.dreiser@iks.fraunhofer.de
[3] BMW Group, 80788 Munich, Germany
rinat.asmus@bmw.de

Abstract. One problem standing in the way of fully automated vehicles is the question of how to ensure vehicle safety and the safety of all traffic participants. Standards like ISO 26262 and ISO/PAS 21448 tackle those issues from different viewpoints by defining safety measures and mechanisms. While ISO 26262 focuses on safety hazards arising from malfunctioning of E/E systems, ISO/PAS 21448 stresses hazards due to technological limitations. However, it is an open challenge how system-wide safety can be monitored and validated at run-time. To complement those safety specifications we propose a system-wide run-time safety analysis. Our System Health Management concept is based on so-called Health Indicators (HIs) to propagate knowledge about detected errors and trigger appropriate error reactions. We analyze probable information sources to define meaningful HIs in automated driving context and investigate influence factors, of both ISO 26262 and ISO/PAS 21448. We apply our approach to a case study demonstrating its applicability in an automated driving scenario.

Keywords: Safety · Automated driving system · Health indicator

1 Introduction

To classify different levels of automation, SAE International released the standard J3016 defining "Levels of Driving Automation" [4]. Current cars realize levels 0 up to level 2, which offer driver support features. For instance, level 2 features can automatically accelerate and decelerate the vehicle. However, the driver must always supervise and take over in case of critical situations, ergo he serves as a safe fallback state. Transitioning from level 2 to level 3 increases system complexity as the vehicle operates autonomously in dedicated Operational

© Springer Nature Switzerland AG 2020
H. Muccini et al. (Eds.): ECSA 2020, CCIS 1269, pp. 509–517, 2020.
https://doi.org/10.1007/978-3-030-59155-7_36

Design Domains (ODDs) without requiring driver supervision. Only after notification, the driver must take over within a specified time span. Level 4 can master all driving tasks within the ODD; the automated driving system of level 5 vehicles is capable to handle all environmental conditions. ISO 26262 [2] provides necessary processes and mechanisms for realizing functional safety by avoiding design faults and offering error detection and handling mechanisms, among other things. Nonetheless, these mechanisms do not automatically account for the absence of functional insufficiencies. To close this gap, ISO/PAS 21448 [3] defines the term 'Safety of the Intended Functionality (SOTIF)' as absence of unreasonable risk due to hazards caused by performance limitations of the intended behavior or by reasonably misuse by the user. And yet, the safety standards only support vehicle development up to automation level 2 as many open issues, such as how to validate and verify functional safety, remain [11]. The diversity of error sources like random hardware faults or software design faults gives an indication of why designing level 3 systems is so challenging. Furthermore, the causal safety chain becomes a system-wide property as the failure of one element impacts the rest of the system. For instance, sensor limitations could lead to erroneous environment perception and dangerous driving maneuvers. These safety violations must be identified at run-time in order to trigger respective mitigation actions. To tackle this problem, we present an approach for system-wide safety monitoring at run-time.

This paper is structured as follows. In Sect. 2 we present a detailed description of the proposed concept. Section 3 provides an example of how this concept can be applied in an automated driving context. In Sect. 4 we compare our concept to related work. At the end we give a conclusion and outlook.

2 Proposed Approach

Introducing the notion of Health Indicators shall increase system safety by enabling system degradation and Quality of Service (QoS) mechanisms. HIs on system-level enable system-wide recovery and degradation. Especially automated driving systems rely on mechanisms of redundancy and diversity to improve system safety. Thus, a standardized approach for degradation, not locally but on system level, has to be defined. In case of failure, this allows switching to hot-standby instances. Moreover, the principal idea of QoS is adopted to a safety perspective. Attaching QoS values containing HIs permits service receivers to instantly decide how far they trust the received service and how to process this data. Current vehicle architectures integrate diverse platforms like AUTOSAR or Genivi confirming to different safety and criticality levels. The QoS approach facilitates coordinating safety mechanisms beyond the borders of single platforms and standards.

2.1 Meta-Model

We introduce a System Health Management concept to target system-wide run-time safety analysis. Figure 1 depicts a meta-model of the considered system.

Its goal is to formally express vehicle abstraction levels and system properties used for run-time health analysis. This model enables partitioning the vehicle into different domains that group dependent features. According to safety analysis conducted for ISO 26262 and ISO/PAS 21448 all functional features and domains must have well-defined safety properties. These properties can include redundancy and configuration information for the purpose of analyzing valid configurations and possible degradation strategies. At domain level, those requirements result in a rule set for functional degradation rules. Depending on available features, this rule set allows continued system operation despite failures by reducing the set of active functional features (graceful degradation). For deciding which features to terminate, functional features have an assigned priority. In case of failure, features can implement adaptation strategies to save resources by performance degradation. Functional features are composed of different subsystems, defined by hardware, software, redundancy, and capability properties. The performance degradation rules are based on the subsystem's availability and performance. Our concept considers the described properties of the meta-model as basis to define constraints and models for run-time Health Indicators. Thus, run-time monitors check those properties at subsystem, functional feature, and domain level. Those monitors are tailored to their underlying systems. Subsystems for example have monitors that supervise critical hardware and software resources. Domains or functional feature monitors may check degradation and availability properties of platforms. Run-time Health Indicators shall enable run-time system degradation strategies. Possible structures of health models are defined in Sect. 3.

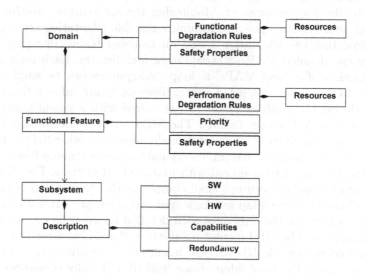

Fig. 1. Meta-model for considered vehicle

2.2   Health Indicator

Within our concept we define Health Indicators as a triple of Performance, Reliability and Degradation: HI = (Per, Rel, Deg). The three parameters capture different aspects required by different safety standards. The Degradation parameter is a system specific set of degradation levels, which are based on availability requirements. ISO 26262 demands supervision and monitoring functionalities to assess the health state of E/E systems with respect to random or system errors. The health state of ISO 26262 related safety considerations is captured in the Performance parameter. The Reliability parameter evaluates how much to trust the system due to uncertainties. Therefore, it encompasses SOTIF related safety considerations by including the vehicle's interaction with its environment, users, and other cars to capture uncertainties introduced by them.

The main purpose of Health Indicators is to monitor system-wide safety properties at run-time in order to trigger appropriate mitigation actions. Safety violations can be mitigated by reducing the system's functionality or performance. Our Health Indicator triple supports both degradation strategies. The Degradation parameter gives an overview on available system resources for functional degradation. The Performance and Reliability parameters of features or domains are a valuable information source to trigger performance degradation strategies.

2.3   Run-Time System Health Management

The self-adaptation strategy of the SHM is implemented as MAPE-K loop. It refers to the five activities of Monitoring the environment and/or system, Analyzing data for discrepancies, Planning possible adaptation strategies, and finally Executing the adaptation based on modeled Knowledge [10]. Figure 2 illustrates the planned MAPE-K adaptation architecture. Each managed subsystem consists of a local MAPE-K loop. Subsystems can be single software platforms, ECUs, or sensors, for instance. Relevant health information is locally collected during the analysis phase and is shared with a global analysis unit, the System Health Manager (SHM). The SHM receives information from one or multiple local analysis units and optionally also from other SHMs. Based on this information, HIs on subsystem, functional feature or domain level are determined. The HIs are in turn shared with managed subsystems. For clean architectural structuring, the concept shall comply to the "separation of concerns" principle. Therefore, the adaption logic and execution are left with local state managers, as they are the only ones with detailed information on, for instance, running processes. The SHM focuses on abstract global health analysis and provides this information via HIs to local managers. Extensive system analysis is required to ensure the local adaptations lead to a globally consistent state as for instance presented in [5]. For safe global recovery, it may be necessary for dependent subsystems to exchange current states.

As a standalone solution, our concept cannot guarantee safe system behavior but rather acts as one measure to enable system degradation strategies by

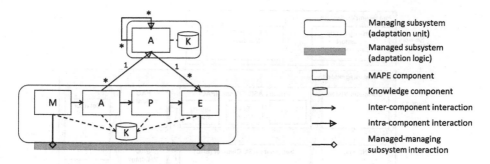

Fig. 2. Adaptation mechanism structure

providing self-awareness on the system's health status. For example, one SHM is a single point of failure and might violate safety requirements. To circumvent this problem, two redundant global SHMs can be implemented. The second SHM serves as hot-standby instance and can take over in case of failure of the first instance. Therefore, compliance with safety requirements is dependent on combining safety mechanisms tailored to the underlying problem statement.

3 Health Indicators in Automated Driving Context

3.1 Use Case

This section presents an example for determining HIs on subsystem level. The paper is taken from the thesis [6], refer to it for more refined Health Indicator examples. Figure 3 shows a simplified logical architecture of the Automated Driving domain adapted from [1]. The system enables level 3 features like a "highway pilot", to autonomously navigate vehicles on highways with structurally separated roads with a maximum velocity of 130 km/h. In case of severe system failures, the vehicle can either continue its operation with a reduced velocity of 60 km/h, request the driver to take over after a specified time, or stop the vehicle at the emergency lane. To define HIs the presented E/E system architecture is analyzed and divided into subsystems. In the following, the nominal integration platform is taken as an exemplary subsystem for calculating HIs. The nominal integration system is responsible for trajectory calculation. The computer vision platform provides information to the PAC and the SAC ECUs. Both channels generate independent environment models. Based on this environment model, the PAC application computes a collision-free vehicle trajectory. In parallel, SAC also uses computer vision information to determine a minimal risk trajectory. Afterwards, the PAC Validator and the SAC Validator each check both trajectories for collisions. According to several performance and safety requirements, the trajectories are associated with a score. The Selector uses those scores to choose the best trajectory.

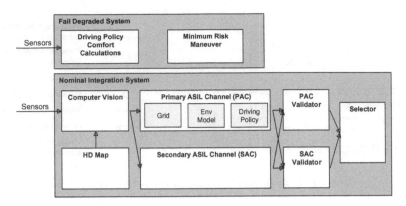

Fig. 3. Example logical architecture for Automated Driving domain

3.2 Health Indicators of Automated Driving System

The Degradation represents different levels based on the availability and causal dependencies of hardware and software resources. PAC and SAC have different purposes; PAC shall continuously operate and compute trajectories while SAC is supposed to take over in case of PAC failure. SAC is not intended for continuous operation. As soon as SAC is activated a handover to the driver is initiated. Those differences shall be visible in different degradation states:

$$Deg_{Nom} = \begin{cases} 0 & \text{Ok} \\ 1 & \text{Minimal Risk} \\ 2 & \text{Failed} \end{cases} \tag{1}$$

For determining the Performance parameter, we propose a rule-based approach based on software monitor results. The nominal integration system is considered safety-critical and different software monitors supervise the timely arrival of sensor information and whether logical and deadline constraints are satisfied. An error tolerance for failed reference cycles can be configured for Alive Supervisions. For instance, all supervision results are summed up in a supervision status, which can have one of four states:

- OK: No supervision failed.
- FAILED: An Alive Supervision failed and the error counter is below the configured error tolerance.
- EXPIRED: A Deadline or Logical Supervision failed or the error counter is equal or above the configured error tolerance.
- DEACTIVATED: A mode switch deactivated the Supervised Entity.

Those supervision states can be mapped to performance levels as shown in Eq. 2. OK and DEACTIVATED suggest application performance is good (0). A delayed sensor input might decrease overall performance of the highway pilot regarding its driving smoothness but is not considered a safety risk. Thus, FAILED is in this case mapped to medium performance (1). EXPIRED indicates a severe error or even functionality loss and is mapped to poor performance (2).

$$Per_{Sen} = \begin{cases} 0 & \text{if } LSS = OK \vee LSS = DEACTIVATED \\ 1 & \text{if } LSS = FAILED \\ 2 & \text{if } LSS = EXPIRED \end{cases} \tag{2}$$

The nominal integration system is a poster example of uncertainty introduced by SOTIF for the Reliability parameter. Using machine learning algorithms in computer vision and grid fusion yields high uncertainties as unfamiliar environments might be interpreted the wrong way. The probability values of both machine learning algorithms are indicators of how good the reliability of the environment model is. In addition, the cross-validation of both trajectories evaluates how much the computed trajectories can be trusted. The reliability is influenced by whether the validators agree on the trajectory score and by the number of the score itself. Disagreeing should decrease reliability, agreeing should increase its values. Equation 1 considers the elaborated influence aspects.

$$Rel_{Nom} = (\alpha * Prob + \beta * \frac{\#agree}{\#disagree}) * \frac{score}{score_{max}} \tag{3}$$

3.3   Health Indicator Models

In the following, we outline general aspects for determining Health Indicators on subsystem, feature and domain level. For Degradation and Performance rule-based health models prove valuable. They can encompass supervision results of already installed monitoring mechanisms of safety-relevant software and hardware components like software supervision results or sensor measurements. Possible subsystem failure dependencies are included by inspecting fault trees. The uncertainty mirrored by the Reliability cannot be categorized in concrete states. Instead we propose numerical evaluation with values ranging from 0 to 100. This way, different influence factors can be weighted and put into relation with each other. In general exist two main uncertainty causes: aleatoric and epistemic uncertainty [9]. Epistemic uncertainty covers the uncertainty of unknown situations as there is no guarantee the artificial intelligence system will react safely. Aleatoric uncertainty is caused by inaccurate sensor measurements and results in a misrepresentation of the actual environment. To grasp aleatoric uncertainty, it is important to capture the current environment state as well as the capabilities and availability of different sensors. For measuring epistemic uncertainty diverse and redundant information is used and compared as presented in the example with PAC and SAC. Therefore, results of different validator and plausibility checkers can be weighted to measure Reliability. Another uncertainty factor are human operators. Consequentially, results of driver monitoring systems are a good information source on the current driver state and could be included in the Reliability analysis.

4   Related Work

Most self-adaptive strategies in the industry and the scientific community focus on application- or component-level analysis. In the following we compare our concept with three system-level solutions. In the avionics domain, [7] presents a two-level approach for software health management. The authors suggest combining Component-level Health Managers with a high-level System Health Manager. Similar to our approach, the Component-Level Health Manager is responsible for monitoring subsystems and reporting the anomalies to the System-Level Health Manager. The System-Level Health Manager conducts a system-level analysis on anomalies and executed mitigation actions. In contrast to our runtime mitigation strategies based on HIs, the overall system diagnosis identifies the root cause and an appropriate coping strategy is selected. Afterwards, the Component-Level Health Manager is informed about the strategy and executes the mitigation actions [7]. This work does not define any abstraction levels for system health as we do with subsystem, features and domains.

In the automotive domain, the "SafeAdapt - Safe Adaptive Software for Fully Electric Vehicles" project presents a decentralized concept for safe runtime reconfiguration. All core nodes cyclically exchange health states of running applications. The knowledge of application health states is used for coordinated global adaptions [12]. We propose collecting health information to determine HIs on feature and domain level in a centralized instance. Our SHM only provides relevant HIs to local instances, which execute the adaptations.

Frtunikj proposes in [8] a decentralized fault management layer to handle system failures. Each local node collects health information to determine a health state of multiple system functions. Those health states are cyclically exchanged. Taking the health state and additional information like redundancy types of a subsystem, its degradation level as well as the system function degradation level is calculated. On this basis the system reconfiguration manager chooses an appropriate adaption option [8]. The proposed system functions are similar to the features of this concept. We further consider the domain level for HIs. Additionally, the HIs do not only give an indication on the current degradation state but include knowledge on Performance and Reliability states.

5   Conclusion and Outlook

To complement existing standards, we set up a generic System Health Management concept for run-time safety analysis based on Health Indicators. Moreover, HIs can help tackling other open challenges for automated vehicles. To bring automated driving into practice without compromising safety requirements, sophisticated verification and validation methods are required. It is yet an unsolved problem how to generate test scenarios and test data that capture all relevant hazards. Virtual simulation environments are a promising strategy and could further be used for validating our concept in a risk-free environment.

But this is only part of the solution. Bringing verification and testing to run-time appears a valid approach to complement the vehicle's safety argumentation. HIs can be seen as a first step in the direction of run-time verification. Our concept currently does not consider security issues. Information corruption of sources like backend servers, other vehicles, infrastructure, or apps would result in severe hazards. Including a run-time security evaluation is as important as the run-time safety assessment. Future work could extend the existing HI with security parameters that indicate external intrusions.

References

1. BMW Group Safety Assessment Report - SAE Level 3 Automated Driving System. https://www.bmwusa.com/content/dam/bmwusa/innovation-campaign/autonomous/BMW-Safety-Assessment-Report.pdf. Accessed 05 11 2020
2. ISO 26262 - Road Vehicles - Functional Safety, December 2018
3. ISO/PAS 21448 - Road vehicles – Safety of the intended functionality, January 2019
4. SAE Standard J3016 - Taxonomy and Definitions for Terms Related to Driving Automation Systems for on-Road Motor Vehicles, June 2018
5. Becker, K.: Software Deployment Analysis for Mixed Reliability Automotive Systems. Dissertation, Technical University Munich, Munich (2017)
6. Dollinger, F.: Definition of System Health Indicators in Mixed Criticality E/E Systems in Automated Driving Context. Master's thesis, Technical University Munich, Munich (2020)
7. Dubey, A., Karsai, G., Mahadevan, N.: Model-based software health management for real-time systems. In: 2011 Aerospace Conference, pp. 1–18, March 2011. https://doi.org/10.1109/AERO.2011.5747559
8. Frtunikj, J.: Safety Framework and Platform for Functions of Future Automotive E/E Systems. Dissertation, Technical University Munich (2016)
9. Hüllermeier, E., Waegeman, W.: Aleatoric and epistemic uncertainty in machine learning: a tutorial introduction. ArXiv abs/1910.09457 (2019)
10. Kephart, J.O., Chess, D.M.: The vision of autonomic computing. Computer **36**(1), 41–50 (2003). https://doi.org/10.1109/MC.2003.1160055
11. Kirovskii, O.M., Gorelov, V.A.: Driver assistance systems: analysis, tests and the safety case. ISO 26262 and ISO/PAS 21448. In: IOP Conference Series: Materials Science and Engineering 534, June 2019. https://doi.org/10.1088/1757-899x/534/1/012019
12. Weiss, G., Schleiss, P., Drabek, C.: Towards flexible and dependable E/E-architectures for future vehicles, September 2016

How to Conduct Experiments with a Real Car? Experiences and Practical Guidelines

Thomas Hutzelmann$^{(\boxtimes)}$, Dominik Mauksch, and Alexander Pretschner

Department of Informatics, Technical University of Munich,
85748 Garching b. München, Germany
{t.hutzelmann,d.mauksch,alexander.pretschner}@tum.de

Abstract. Higher computational power, new dimensions of interconnectivity and modern machine learning techniques are necessary for building a fully autonomous car, but exhibit an enormous technical complexity. Research about new approaches and technology for handling this complexity raises a problem: On the one side, researchers advocate transitions and replacements for the current systems mainly without deploying them in real cars on the streets. On the other side applying theoretical approaches without clear evidence of their practical benefits is risky for the practitioners. As a solution to close this gap, researchers should bring their ideas more often into physical cars and support their proposals with measurements from realistic experiments.

With this paper, we share our insights from an academic perspective about connecting scientific prototypes with a real car. (1) We discuss three interface designs for setups with differing connectivity to a running car; (2) We provide a checklist for planning and organizing real car experiments including a discussion of involved trade-offs; (3) We give practical advice and identify best practices learned from our own experiments inside a car. In sum, we demonstrate that even with a short budget and a small team size it still is possible to bring prototypes into real cars.

Keywords: Automotive · Car interface · Experimental evaluation

1 Introduction

The automotive domain is in the process of a huge technological change for turning a vehicle from a basic machine into a fully autonomous transport mean with included infotainment systems [3]. Although academic research and industry both work towards the same goal, there is a gap between academia focusing on new ideas and approaches, whereas industry must naturally focus on the most promising and applicable ideas [11].

As an academic research team in the area of Software and Systems Engineering, we have developed various new algorithms and approaches for modern cars in the last years. These software prototypes span from profiling of driving scenarios to different approaches for intrusion detection. However, we have ended

© Springer Nature Switzerland AG 2020
H. Muccini et al. (Eds.): ECSA 2020, CCIS 1269, pp. 518–526, 2020.
https://doi.org/10.1007/978-3-030-59155-7_37

up with the same problem in all these prototypes: They cannot be evaluated realistically without being used inside a real car. Nevertheless, putting research prototypes into a car has seemed risky, expensive and a plenty of work.

We are aware of various work from bigger research teams, ranging from building their own car [8] to collaborations between multiple universities [7]. Such projects, budgets and team sizes were not available for us, but still we aimed for a realistic evaluation. Through various iterations we experimented with different approaches and realized several experimental setups: Starting with small dongles for passive data-recording, over Raspberry Pis with acoustic feedback to the driver, to partially controlling the car's driving behavior through attacks with a connected laptop. In retrospective all these experiments are based on the same decision process and follow the same schema in approaching a car.

In this work, we summarize our experiences from experiments with real cars under tight budget and human resource constraints. Based on practical advice, guided by checklists and best practices, we advocate experiments with cars while keeping the risk controllable and the budget and workload low. Thus, our paper dedicated to small research groups complements the already documented effort of bigger research teams and projects. Thereby, we want to demonstrate that our initial concerns as a small team were not justified, and we hope to encourage academic researchers to put their experimental prototypes earlier and more often into real cars. Thus, we make an important step away from pure paperwork and artificial toy setups, towards real systems. Consequently, all research findings have higher significance and provide meaningful validation of the new approaches.

During this paper we use several terms that we define as follows: The implemented research prototype that is designed for operating with a car is labeled as an *experimental setup*. An *experiment* is the process to collect empirical data with the experimental setup. *Research team* refers to all people taking part in the planning and conduction of the experiment. The *track* is the physical location where the car is driven during an experiment. Finally, *conducting an experiment* denotes all the required steps for getting results from the experiments—from planning and organizing, to driving the car to elicit data.

2   Constraints and Requirements

Due to their dependency on expensive and potentially dangerous equipment, experiments with real cars are strictly limited by external factors. In the following discussions about decisions made before and during experiments, we distinguish between constraints and requirements: *Constraints* identify the general limitations that are invariant for all experiments. These constraints are imposed by rationality and by good scientific practice. *Requirements* on the experiment are based on specific trade-offs and vary in different usages. All requirements reflect the affected constraints, but are influenced by decisions of the research team.

2.1   Constraints

Assured Safety: During the experiments, no human must be harmed. Damage to the car or used setups might be acceptable but should be avoided if possible. Therefore, it must be assured that the used setup is controllable at all times and in all circumstances.

Minimal Budget: The cheaper the conduction of an experiment is, the better. It is impossible to avoid some minimal costs, but if there are two approaches with comparable outcome, the cheaper approach is preferable.

Sound Documentation: After the experiment, the documentation of the used setup, and all collected data need to be as comprehensive and complete as necessary for supporting or rejecting the hypothesis. The experiment needs to be reproducible in the future, and the data is required as proof for the results and support for the conclusions.

2.2   Requirements

Acceptable Risks: While working with physical hardware, it is impossible to avoid all possible risks and dangers. However, it is important to consider which scenarios are acceptable and which are not. There is no guarantee or full insurance. Therefore, all parties involved during the conduction need to agree on the maximum acceptable risk during the experiments. This especially applies if regular traffic participants are involved, as no additional risk can be put on them.

Available Budget: The physical car, the experimental setup as well as the track and the used equipment cost money. With smart ideas, there are often strategies that reduce costs and enable low budget setups. Some of these tips will be highlighted during this paper.

Usage of the Car: At the beginning of the experiment planning, it is important to consider what to actually do with the car. This includes the driving scenarios as well as how the experimental setup interacts with the car. Since the researchers can focus only on relevant aspects, this offers big space for decisions.

3   Candidate Interfaces Between Setup and Car

For putting an experimental setup into the car, the first decision is about the interaction with the car. The information exchange is highly dependent on the experiment, but for the interfaces, in general, there exist three different choices depicted in Fig. 1 and discussed in this section. Hybrids and combinations of these interfaces for different parts of the setup are also possible.

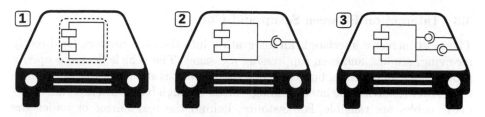

Fig. 1. Three interfaces for experiments: (1) Isolation, (2) Receiving, (3) Interaction

3.1   Isolation of Setup and Car

A simple approach is not to connect the experimental setup with the car at all. Just through operating inside the car and driving around with the setup already enables several experiments. Various sensors like cameras, gyroscopes, or GPS dongles enable a realistic data collection without direct connection to the car.

When the experimental setup is completely isolated from the car, the only risk results from a potential interaction with the driver. The setup will behave inside the car exactly as it does during the preparation, and the operation of the car is not influenced at all. However, the isolation might require using redundant sensors, which is more expensive than reusing the sensors inside the car. Furthermore, the usage of the car is limited as the setup is never connected with any network or realistic data from the car. For example, this type of interface has been used to collect GPS traces around a city area to improve privacy issues [4] and several variants to detect driver fatigue [10].

3.2   Receiving Data from the Car

Another approach for an interface is to connect the experimental setup with the car, but only to receive information out of the network through the On-Board Diagnostic (OBD) [9]. This standardized interface provides access to various information from the vehicle, especially the engine, for example, the current speed, the driven distance or the engine's intake and exhaust.

As the OBD-port is designed for receiving information during the operation of the car, the risk of this approach is rather minimal, when the experimental setup is robust against delays or gaps in the received information. There exist diverse OBD-adapters and—due to the standardization—they are rather cheap. For example, this type of interface has been used to determine the fuel consumption in osculating traffic [12] and to analyze the driving behavior to spot unsafe driving [1]. Unfortunately, OBD does not offer access to advanced sensors as video streams, lidar or radar. For receiving such data, the approach described for interaction between setup and car is also applicable for just listening to the network. However, it remains more intrusive so the provided assessment of this other approach still applies.

3.3   Interaction Between Setup and Car

The most intrusive interface is an integration into the car's network for directly receiving, sending and even suppressing messages. The vehicle does not openly provide such an interface, but from our experience, it is still accessible reasonably easy. After removing the interior lining—often through basic click mechanisms—many cables are tangible. For instance, behind the rear mirror or under the central console are convenient choices that expose various networks and do not impede the driving. The concrete layout differs between manufacturers and car models, but in our case, the information was always easily accessible online.

Such an interconnection with the experimental setup is very dangerous, if the setup is not tested thoroughly and carefully. Wrong network interactions can potentially disable or permanently destroy the car's electronic components. Therefore, this approach has two major prerequisites: First, the setup needs a physical connection to the relevant network in the car. Most cables inside the car have standardized plugs that are cheaply available, but the concrete connector might still need to be handmade or at least customized. Second, the setup needs to understand the network protocol and the relevant payload in order to communicate with syntactically valid and semantically meaningful messages. Although the full message matrices are kept confidential by the manufacturers, there exist open communities trying to reverse engineer the networks, for example, the opendbc project [2] for CAN. Overall, the available information from the network as well as the potential to integrate the experimental setup directly into the car enables a huge potential for use cases, that might be worth the implied risk and effort to establish this interface. For example, this type of interface has been used for excessive security penetration testing [6] and to develop extensible prototypes for autonomous driving [5].

4   Checklist of Organizing Experiments

After the experimental setup is prepared and provides a suitable interface to the car, the concrete experiments need to be organized. This section discusses the most important questions for devising the experiments. Each question refers to requirements introduced in Sect. 2 and provides multiple alternatives with different degrees of risk, budget, or usage of the car.

4.1   How to Compose the Research Team? (Risk, Budget, Usage)

Some experimental setups can be operated by a single person—the driver of the car. For keeping the risk defensible with this, the experimental setup needs to be very automatic and should only require close to no interaction by the driver. So, this is only an option if the experimental setup mostly collects data while not interfering with the drive. With experiments that require at least some interaction or control during the drive, having two researchers in the car is reasonable to keep the risk manageable without full automation: one for focusing on driving the car and the other for controlling the experimental setup.

If the experiment requires equipment or observations from outside the car, adding a third person to the team might be reasonable to assist with the setup or to focus on documentation. Such assistance is comfortable, but from our experience, stationary cameras permanently recording are also a suitable alternative. Additional people watching the experiment could be distractive and disturb the focus. Therefore, too many people should be avoided as they also imply a safety risk during the experiment.

4.2 Where to Get a Suitable Car? (Budget, Usage)

Only if the usage requires a permanent modification to the car that cannot be undone without damage, then buying a car is the only option. Without these, there also exist cheaper alternatives. If the usage scenario is not limited to specific cars or car models, mainly when the setup is in isolation from the car, big rental services are the best option as they offer cars for short periods and very small budget. If the experiment requires a specific car model, for example, because of some sensors incorporated in an interactive interface, big rental services to our experience do not provide a broad choice between distinctive car models.

However, there also exist various smaller car and repair shops that have a fleet of cars for rental. Most of the time, they focus on a specific brand and offer all the recent models to similar conditions as the big rental services. After contacting a few shops in our surrounding, we were always able to find the model that we needed. No matter how the car is rented, it is crucial to check that the planned usage is legally permitted.

4.3 Where to Do Experimental Rides? (Risk, Budget, Usage)

Non-interaction setups with no major risk may just be driven on regular streets as the car still has a permission to operate there. Modified cars do lose their permission to operate on regular streets and need an isolated, private place to not endanger regular traffic. Furthermore, the specific driving scenario—the speed, traffic, maneuver—is limiting the useful types of location. Industry corporations, bigger research institutes or driving schools have specially designed tracks for test drives. If the research team has a more flexible time schedule, there are also options to build their own track on a private parking place. For example, the parking side of a university is crowded during the week, but on the weekend it is mostly empty. So with some barrier tape, parts of the parking places can be separated and used for the experiments. These separated tracks lack street signs or road markings, but the research team can build them. For the road marking, washable color or barrier tape fixed straight on the ground has worked the best for us. Street signs can be emulated with paperboard stabilized by water-filled plastic bottles. If the car detects obstacles through radar, in our experience wrapping the paperboard in aluminum is a simple solution. Nevertheless, separated tracks limit the usages as their length is limited, and the driving scenarios are monotonic.

5   Best Practices and General Advice

This final section provides general considerations for experiments with cars. Depending on the concrete experiment, this list is not complete, but it provides a baseline to prevent basic mistakes.

5.1   Structure the Available Time in Advance

A clear structure of what to do is essential for assuring that the spent time leads to results. Therefore, the minimum is at least a temporal order of the concrete experiments. The most important part of the schedule is to agree on limits: This phase will end at this time, or during the experiments the car will not drive above this speed and not outside this area. Additionally, the schedule should consider breaks with snacks and food explicitly. It is important to get out of the car regularly as it is not comfortable to work with the laptop on the knees for longer hours. When the experiments—success or failures—bring strong emotions, these breaks are valuable to calm down again.

5.2   What If the Setup Does Not Work?

None of our experiments has worked on our first attempt. Often there were only small errors, but identifying them can be very time-consuming. Hence, it is important to include self-checks into the experimental setup, for example, if all the cables are connected properly. Also, a simple interface eases the experiments as for example fast and precise typing is problematic during drives with higher speed. Ideally, these interfaces also offer debugging options and provide meaningful error messages if something goes wrong. Last but not least, never try to hack something quick and dirty during the conduction. These hacks can influence the whole experimental setup, ruin all measurements and have severe safety impacts.

5.3   Enduring Power Supply

Especially conducting or preparing experiments in an idle car exhausts the batteries of the equipment as well as of the car. While there are external chargers for the car battery, these are expensive and there exist cheaper alternatives. In our cases, it was the easiest to find one member of our team that drove the car to his home and back to work in the morning. This procedure refilled the batteries and was sufficient for day long experiments.

The other equipment inside the car can use two different forms of power supply: When the component is running on batteries, bringing replacement batteries or a power bank is sufficient to operate during the day and to recharge during the night. Alternatively, the battery of the car can also be used to power the experimental setup. There exist various adapters for USB or laptops to the vehicle input and also the OBD-Port provides a small source of power.

6   Conclusion and Outlook

With this paper, we documented our experiences with connecting experimental setups with running cars. Starting with a refinement from general constraints to competing requirements, the report elicited three different interface designs to connect the experimental setup with the car. These requirements and interfaces are used as a foundation for a checklist of the organization and best practices for conducting the experiments. The car usage can vary from driving around with a small single-board computer to partially disassembling the car to connect new components. Although the implied risk cannot be avoided completely, the discussions provide guidance for keeping it controllable. A bigger budget is helpful, but with focus on the minimal realizations the overall budget can be cut down.

To balance conflicting requirements is difficult as long as the constraints and their implications remain abstract. Hence, this paper provides a foundation for discussions in the researcher team in order to decide about each aspect individually and eases the agreement about the shape of the experiment. Thereby, our checklists and best practices are a foundation for conducting academic experiments in various research domains.

We would like to end this experience paper with a personal comment: Before we touched a physical car, we expected it to be a big challenge to connect our experiments with a driving car. However, after we gave it a try it always turned out to be relatively easy. The insights that we gained from a few drives with our experimental setups changed our understanding completely. Sensor data and measurements of the real physical behavior and real inaccuracy; a real time operation and realistic information flow workload; and most importantly authentic interactions with the driver and the driving behavior, in combination spotted several misconceptions in our research prototypes and provided valuable validation. Therefore, we highly recommend that academic researchers more often aim for putting their research into a real car. With these guidelines we hope to provide enough support to encourage more researches to follow our direction and gain—as we did—richer and more applicable insights through their projects.

A   Key-Questions from the Paper in Condensed Form

A.1   Candidate Interfaces between Setup and Car

1. What kind of interaction from the setup with the car is required?
2. What sensor data does the setup require?
3. What makes the deployment inside a car different from without a car?
4. How does the driver interact with the setup?

A.2   Checklist of Organizing Experiments

1. Is there need for a co-driver to assist with the experiments?
2. Does the experiment require additional documentation, e.g. by an additional video from outside the car?

3. Is some special car model, e.g. with a specific sensor, required?
4. Does the car need to be permanently modified?
5. What characteristics need to be present on the street?
6. What interaction with other traffic participants is needed?

A.3   Best Practices and General Advice

1. Has the setup been tested extensively before the experiment?
2. Does the schedule contain regular breaks?
3. Does every experiment have limits (time, speed, location, etc.)?
4. Does the setup provide a debug interface?
5. Are there replacement batteries for the setup?
6. How is the battery of the car regularly recharged?

References

1. Chen, S.H., Pan, J.S., Lu, K.: Driving behavior analysis based on vehicle OBD information and adaboost algorithms. In: Proceedings of the International Multi-Conference of Engineers and Computer Scientists (2015)
2. Comma.ai: opendbc. https://github.com/commaai/opendbc
3. Coppola, R., Morisio, M.: Connected car: technologies, issues, future trends. ACM Comput. Surv. (2016). https://doi.org/10.1145/2971482
4. Hoh, B., Gruteser, M., Xiong, H., Alrabady, A.: Preserving privacy in GPS traces via uncertainty-aware path cloaking. In: Computer and Communications Security (2007). https://doi.org/10.1145/1315245.1315266
5. Kato, S., Takeuchi, E., Ishiguro, Y., Ninomiya, Y., Takeda, K., Hamada, T.: An open approach to autonomous vehicles. IEEE Micro (2015). https://doi.org/10.1109/MM.2015.133
6. Miller, C., Valasek, C.: Adventures in automotive networks and control units. Def. Con. (2013). http://www.illmatics.com/car_hacking.pdf
7. Van Oorschot, P.F., Besselink, I.J.M., Meinders, E., Nijmeijer, H.: Realization and control of the Lupo EL electric vehicle. World Electr. Veh. J. 5(1), 14–23 (2012)
8. Ploeg, J., et al.: Cooperative automated maneuvering at the 2016 grand cooperative driving challenge. IEEE Trans. Intell. Transp. Syst. (2018). https://doi.org/10.1109/TITS.2017.2765669
9. SAE International: E/E Diagnostic Test Modes (2017). https://doi.org/10.4271/J1979_201702
10. Sikander, G., Anwar, S.: Driver fatigue detection systems: a review. IEEE Trans. Intell. Transp. Syst. (2019). https://doi.org/10.1109/TITS.2018.2868499
11. Vuori, T., Piik, J.: The co-evolution of academic research and industry practice: evidence from the US car industry. Int. J. Soc. Syst. Sci. (2010). https://doi.org/10.1504/IJSSS.2010.035567
12. Wu, F., et al.: Measuring trajectories and fuel consumption in oscillatory traffic: experimental results. In: Transportation Research Board 96th Annual Meeting (2017). https://hal.archives-ouvertes.fr/hal-01516133

Towards a Systems Engineering Based Automotive Product Engineering Process

Hassan Hage[1,2]([envelope]), Vahid Hashemi[2], and Frank Mantwill[1]

[1] Helmut-Schmidt-University, Holstenhofweg 85, 22043 Hamburg, Germany
hassan.hage@hsu-hh.de
[2] AUDI AG, Auto-Union-Straße 1, 85057 Ingolstadt, Germany

Abstract. Deficit and redundancies in existing automotive product development hinder a systems engineering based development. In this paper we discuss a methodical procedure to eliminate deficits in the current product development and in turn to enable the introduction of a new systems engineering based development methodology. As the core part of our approach, we discuss how to transform an opaque heterogeneous product development to a homogenous consistent product development taking into account existing disciplines. Our approach paves the way to achieve a process structure that is more amenable to verification and validation. We show the effectiveness of our proposed solution approach on an automotive use case.

Keywords: Business process · Systems engineering · Verification & Validation

1 Introduction

The ever-increasing demand for technology and connectivity in automotive industries has led automakers to invest heavily in the electronics and software development. The interaction of the three components hardware, electronics and software is becoming increasingly important, which in turn increases the complexity of a vehicle development [3, 20]. The complexity arises due to the fact that safe, environmental friendly, economical and easy accessible vehicle is demanded in the market [8]. At the same time, the legal requirements, which are required for an initial vehicle registration, are tightened [16]. Despite increasing complexity in a vehicle, a reduction in development times due to competition is necessary [1, 20]. Hence, automotive manufacturers are facing an exponentially growing challenge for which a reformation of their development strategy is required [20, 25]. To account for the latter, manufacturers orient themselves according to the standard of the "Automotive Software Process Improvement and Capability Determination" (A-SPICE), which should enable a mastery of the development complexity [8]. Hence, the development methodology of Systems Engineering (SE) plays an important role, since this methodology will help to master the complexity. Systems engineering approach has been exploited for many years in avionics industries for product development. The increasing product complexity in automotive industries solicits application of this method [4] which in turn is associated with complications.

© Springer Nature Switzerland AG 2020
H. Muccini et al. (Eds.): ECSA 2020, CCIS 1269, pp. 527–541, 2020.
https://doi.org/10.1007/978-3-030-59155-7_38

Firstly, vehicle manufacturers have grown dramatically since they were founded in the past few decades. Due to the drastic and rapid expansion of the company, a partly heterogeneous company structure was formed. Domain-specific departments independently developed their own processes, methods and tools [14]. As a result, it was no longer possible to ensure a homogeneous, consistent and transparent product development. Therefore, the traceability in the product development is sometimes challenging and hence, the high product quality can be only ensured with difficulty. The recent vehicle software manipulation for incorrect exhaust values is an example of a product development in which such manipulations were difficult and time consuming to be traced [7, 11]. The reason for such a difficultly is the heterogeneous processes of the product development.

Moreover, in the automotive industry, the Product Engineering Process (PEP) traditionally consists mainly of individual phases and control points/milestones. Behind the phases are processes that have to be reached at certain milestones [12, 24]. Generally a PEP is saved in a company as a specific document format, which is available for retrieval. However, the processes presented in the PEP do not provide the domain-specific departments with process-related, sufficiently detailed information. In particular, the necessary detailed process steps to reach the milestones are not apparent. Consequently, there exists no product development process overview which could deliver sufficient information and the interdependency of all relevant groups of a product development. In addition, the scheduling for domain-specific departments is very rough and dependencies between these departments and intermediate milestones are not clear. Finally, the use of the SE method requires a radical change in the corporate culture as well as parts of the corporate roles, processes, methods and tools as the current product engineering process is not designed based on the SE.

The present paper presents a methodological approach that arose out of necessity during the attempt to introduce SE at an automotive manufacture and resolves current deficits in existing automotive developments that make it difficult to introduce new development methods such as the SE.

Summarizing, the main contributions of this paper are as follows.

- We introduce and integrate milestones in process models to capture temporal aspects of the product development.
- We show that by means of a unified modelling language in a heterogeneous product development, the connectivity from the highest level of abstraction down to the lowest level of abstraction can be ensured. This way we provide consistency and traceability in the entire product development.
- We provide an approach which enables SE in the automotive product development. We show promising results on the feasibility of our solution approach, obtained by its implementation on an automotive use case.

Structure of the Paper. Section 2 provides a brief overview of the related works and highlights the research gap. In Sect. 3, a solution approach is described. This approach promises the elimination of deficits of an automotive product development and presents a method to enable the introduction of SE in an existing product development. We then validate the feasibility of our proposed approach on a use case. Finally, Sect. 5 discusses the solution approach and concludes the paper.

2 Related Work

This section provides an overview of related works. Existing methodologies, which should provide transparency and consistency in the product development, are briefly examined for advantages and disadvantages. This leads us to identify the current gap and therefore, to propose a solution approach.

2.1 Methodology for Product Planning

The organization of German engineers a.k.a. *"Verein der Deutschen Ingenieure (VDI)"* proposes a methodical procedure according to VDI 2220 guideline to plan the life cycle of a product [22, 23]. This life cycle is referred to as a product planning or in a corporate level as a product process (PP) [12]. It starts with a market research through the PEP and finally, up to the product disposal [9, 22]. The actual product development takes place in the PEP and includes the planning, drafting, designing and realization of a new product. To account for the latter, the VDI guideline presents a methodical approach on a detailed level. Finally, following the guideline leads to a consistent and traceable product process. Product developments of automotive manufactures are roughly similar (see Fig. 1).

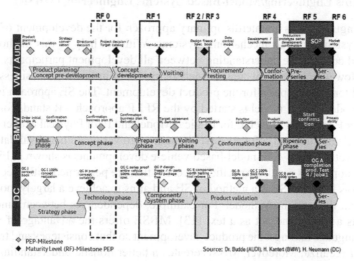

Fig. 1. Product engineering process of various automotive manufactures [19].

As mentioned in Sect. 1, a product process as well as a PEP consists of phases and milestones. This is a crucial bottleneck as product development according to VDI 2220 does not consider the temporal aspect of a development. Moreover, the guideline VDI

2220 specifies a strict method; however, in practice a development consists of huge amount of methods. Therefore, following such a strict method is hardly realizable. After all, the VDI 2220 guideline is not designed for complex mechatronic products [22, 23].

2.2 Design Methodology for Mechatronic Systems

The organization of German engineers introduced the guideline VDI 2206 for designing of mechatronic systems [23]. This guideline consists of elements problem-solving cycle as a micro-cycle, the V model as a macro-cycle as well as process modules for recurrent working steps. The first problem-solving element is based on the method of SE but further considers disciplines such as business administration which are necessary for a product development. Target of this element is to analyze the initial problem as well as to determine the actual and desired state. The second element consists a problem solution and plans the further procedure based on the V model of SE for developing mechatronic systems [23]. Finally, the third element defines and deepens a part of the V model with the use of process modules. This approach enables a consistent and traceable development of complex mechatronic products by strictly following the guideline. Nevertheless, this approach similarly to the VDI 2220 guideline enables a theoretical approach based on a completely new product development. Therefore, already established processes, methods and tools could not further be used and an existing development has completely to be changed. The latter is unrealizable due mainly to the high product complexity as well as the lack of consideration of temporal aspects.

2.3 Systems Engineering/Model-Based Systems Engineering (MBSE)

Systems Engineering is an interdisciplinary approach for the development of multidisciplinary systems such as mechatronic systems. With the help of this methodology, a holistic and cooperative understanding between all development participants is created [15, 21]. However, it does not consider necessary disciplines such as business administration and temporal aspects for the product development. The SE approach is oriented on the V model. The V model is started by the RFLP approach – R stands for Requirements, F for Functional Model, L for Logical Model and P for Physical Model – through hardware, electronics and software development up to verification and validation of the entire product [17, 18]. A V model-based vehicle developments is shown in Fig. 2. This development process requires specific processes that are performed with specific methods and tools [18]. MBSE is a method of SE and aims to achieve a largely model-based development through the V model. For example, dependencies between functions are recorded as a model and not as a text [13]. MBSE offers the advantage of a uniform standard language amongst the product development so that consistency and traceability are easier to realize. Moreover, MBSE creates a better holistic understanding between developers [13]. Nevertheless, using MBSE over the entire existing product development needs a radical change of processes, methods and tools. In particular, use of this approach is not realizable when the existing development is not transparent as detailed in Sect. 1.

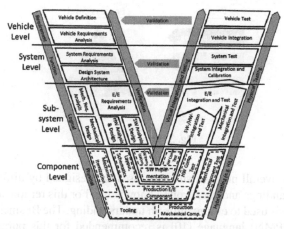

Fig. 2. V-model of SE for developing a vehicle [17].

2.4 Research Gap

Following strictly the aforementioned approaches enables a consistent and traceable product development. The main issue is that all approaches are based on a new product development including specific processes, method and tools. However, a method for reaching consistency and traceability in an existing development is required. Additionally, necessary disciplines such as production, marketing, finance, temporal aspects etc. shall be considered in a product development. To account for the latter, a method shall be developed to enable transformation of an opaque heterogonous product development to a homogenous consistent product development taking into account existing disciplines as well as processes, methods and tools. The latter is clearly identified as a research gap which is the core focus in this paper. It is worthwhile to note that the required method has to inevitably consider a development based on SE as automotive manufactures orient themselves according to A-SPICE guidelines and the approach of SE. However the integration of the SE approach shall be incremental as already developed processes, methods and tools are not possible to change abruptly.

3 Solution Approach

In order to record the actual state of the product development in terms of processes, the top-down approach "from rough to detail" is used. This approach recommends breaking down an overall problem to be solved into logical and interrelated sub-problems. The sub-problems are further broken down until small manageable problems are obtained which can then be solved [2]. The bottom-up approach could also used but for the target of this paper the bottom-up approach is more time intensive. The recording of the actual state is done in a similar way as the top-down approach. At the beginning the business process is defined. Subsequently, the specification of the main process takes place. After that associated sub-processes are specified until the last process workflow level is finally recorded. Figure 3 reflects the process hierarchy where X means the last specified sub-process and Y the last specified process workflow.

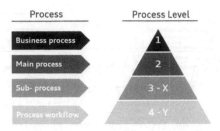

Fig. 3. Process levels.

In a complex overall process, sub-processes are designed by different people with different understandings and background knowledge. For this reason, an existing specification language is used to ensure uniform understanding. The Business Process Model and Notation (BPMN) language [10] is recommended for this purpose because this language enables a sufficiently described process through its notations. All recorded processes are represented using the BPMN specification language. It is also possible to create logical dependencies between the main- and sub-processes. In practice, the success of a development does not only depend on the process flow but also on the adherence to the time component and milestones. For this reason, it is necessary to take the time component into account at the process specification and modeling phase. Specification languages like BPMN do not offer suitable symbols to capture milestones in the process model. Therefore, we provide symbols from the BPMN language with a different context in this approach.

The top-down process modeling and specification are prerequisite for enabling the inevitable usage of SE. However, as already discussed in Sect. 2, the application is not straightforward for an existing automotive development. To this end, and with the aim of enabling the SE approach, we discuss a methodical approach to transform an existing product development to achieve consistency and, in the case of e.g. changes, the possibility of traceability. The high level idea of our approach takes the prepared process modeling and specification and compares that with the prescribed processes of the SE to observe similarities and deviations. The procedural changes cannot be avoided during the implementation of the SE as the nature of SE is up to a certain extent, theory-based. Therefore, it is necessary to obtain a constant overview of the quality of the changed processes in order to remain within the scope of the prescribed SE process standard. Our approach includes implementation of five phases detailed as follows.

3.1 Phase 1: *SP – Setting a Pyramid*

A product is described as an entire system which in turn consists of several subsystems, each of which are composed in components. The development of such systems or components requires a large number of specialist, who are simply responsible for the system or component. In order to achieve a consistent product development, it is necessary to make the existing structure transparent, such that transparency is realized through the cycle shown in Fig. 4.

The starting step *Determine Level* identifies a sub-process of the product process and determines its hierarchical assignment (see Fig. 3) to the entire process. Then, the

Fig. 4. Cycle of process transparency.

next step *Determine Docs* captures all required documents that are needed to perform the associated process. The focus here is especially on process flow overview including timing dependencies. Finally, the last step *Adding to Pyramid* takes all processes including documents to the associated level in a notional pyramid down.

3.2 Phase 2: *NL – Neutralizing the Language*

Complex product developments usually involves a large number of different, independent processes, methods and tools. For example, Microsoft Excel (ME) is used in a certain sub-process. Therefore, results are generated and forwarded in an ME format. On the other side, an in-house developed tool is used to generate results in another sub-process. The large number of sub-processes and their complexities result in a difficult communication between different processes. Therefore, a lot of time is invested in translating technical terms from other domain-specific departments [5]. Besides, it is not possible to assign a domain-specific process to the entire process chain or product development. As an immediate consequence, there are often unwanted, redundant sub-processes. To avoid these problems, a common holistic modeling language is required, which is performed in this phase. All processes recorded in the first phase has to be translated in a holistic language. This requires a graphical specification language as process design is done by various people with different understandings and background knowledge. Therefore, a specification language accessible to all process-involved persons is necessary. As mentioned earlier, the solution approach of this paper recommends the BPMN language for process modeling.

In order to obtain an expressive enough process model, some qualitative requirements has to be taken into account to ensure that all for a consistent product engineering process required information are for the further procedure guaranteed:

1. Only necessary process steps are recorded.
2. Each process step has a defined *input* and *output*, and a specified *execution time*.
3. All *actors* within a process are assigned to a specific *role* description.
4. Milestones are in the process model equal to *events* [10]. A start milestone is equal to a *start event*, an intermediate milestone (see Fig. 5b) is equal to an *intermediate event* and an end milestone is equal to an *end event*. For covering the temporal aspect, the event symbol is always followed by a time symbol, depicted in Fig. 5a. This symbol describes the time that is needed to reach an event. In total, the time and event symbol cover a milestone.

(a) time symbol   (b) intermediate event

Fig. 5. The symbols depicted here are captured by the software *Enterprise Architect*.

These qualitative requirements must be observed when creating process models. All of the processes captured in phase 1 are continuously modeled according to these requirements.

3.3 Phase 3: *LD – Logical Dependency*

This phase deals with the development of a logical process structure to achieve the entire consistent process. For this purpose, all relations between processes with each other are encoded by means of the specification language. Figure 6 shows a quantitative representation of logical dependencies.

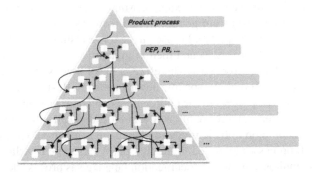

Fig. 6. An entire logical and coherent process.

In general, the lowest level of the pyramid has the highest level of detail, since this is the place of the domain-specific development. In contrast, the top pyramid level has the highest level of abstraction. Following the top-down approach, the highest level of abstraction is used to create the logical process structure. Starting from the uppermost process of the pyramid level, this process has to be connected to the process of the subsequent pyramid level. Due to a uniform specification language, a connection between the processes is possible without any complications. Afterwards, the second pyramid level is connected to the third level. This process is carried out from level to level until the last pyramid level is reached. An entire continuous process is achieved when the dependency of a process on all other processes at all levels can be shown. Dependencies among processes at the same pyramid level are given at the next higher level and denoted as implicit dependencies. Section 3.4 deepened the way to reach these dependencies.

3.4   Phase 4: *CBM – Controlled by Milestones*

The phase *Controlled by Milestones* aims to detect implicit dependencies of processes and provides all target groups of the pyramid with all common process relevant information. This is realized by symbols of a graphical specification language. The time symbol shown in Fig. 5a describes a specific time or date that supports an intermediate process to trigger or completes a process. Each event that occurs between the beginning and the end of an event is called an intermediate event as depicted in Fig. 5b.

An event is equated with a milestone in the present context. In other words, a milestone in a process model is reached when an event is reached after the process steps have been successfully completed. Since a milestone always has a temporal dependency, a time symbol is added to the intermediate event symbol in order to transfer the meaningfulness of a milestone completely in a process model.

As mentioned before, milestones are represented in the process model with the help of the time and event symbols. The milestone *Project Start (PS)* is equal to an intermediate event and the time specification fictionally indicates that the milestone PS occurs at the specified time before *Start Of Production (SOP)*. It is worthwhile to mention that the idea of covering temporal aspects is partly considered in the work of [6]. This work describes the usage of time symbols for every process step in a BPMN model. Each process step/task obtains a time symbol that describes the time needed for performing the step/task. Nevertheless, this approach does not take into account the idea of milestones into a process model such as the BPMN model. The latter has been addressed in our approach through simultaneous use of time and event symbols.

An example for introducing a milestone into a process model is depicted in Fig. 7. It is quite often that milestones are represented in the shape of inverted triangles with a given name and time.

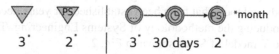

Fig. 7. Capturing milestones in BPMN. In this example, a previous time event occurs for three months before SOP and one month passes until the intermediate event PS is reached. The intermediate event PS thus occurs two months before SOP.

Every process model has a process flow which is performed by defined roles with the help of one or more tools at a given time.

In order to start a process, at least one input variable is required. The process in turn provides at least one output variable. A milestone life cycle is depicted in Fig. 8. It describes all necessary information which a milestone should have in order to detect implicit dependencies and to realize a consistency. A milestone requires answering of the eight *Golden Questions (GQ)* for obtaining all relevant information to build up a consistent and traceable BPMN model:

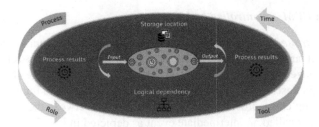

Fig. 8. Milestone life cycle.

- GQ1 - Which process has to be performed?
- GQ2 - Which role is responsible for the process?
- GQ3 - Which tools are required?
- GQ4 - How much time is necessary for performing the process?
- GQ5 - Which input is required?
- GQ6 - Which output is generated?
- GQ7 - For which milestone is the generated output of GQ6 required as an input?
- GQ8 - On which file are the inputs/outputs saved?

If the eight GQs are answered for each milestone of the process, the processes at various levels are able to know interdependencies through the milestones. The answers of the eight GQs have to be linked to each milestone. According to the BPMN standard, inputs and outputs could be described in a process model with the symbol Data Object.

3.5 Phase 5: *CSEA – Compliance with Systems Engineering Approach*

This phase deals with the qualitative changes of processes, methods and tools. The processes, methods and tools that have been established for years need to be revised or reformed for introducing the methodology of Systems Engineering. This is done based on the automotive V model of SE as shown in Fig. 2.

The linked processes from the pyramid of phase 4 are compared with the processes of the V model for similarities and deviations. Four aspects are considered in this comparison; namely, *Process steps/tasks, Roles, Methods and Tools*.

The processes at the lowest level of the pyramid need to be compared with similar processes of the V model. For example, in an automotive development components of a vehicle are tested before approval. The V model also provides a component test. All necessary process steps in the existing process for testing a component has to be compared with the process steps for component test according to SE. If process steps differ, a revision of the old process according to the V model process is required. It should be revised for the entire process otherwise a consistent product engineering process according to SE is not ensured. This applies also to the roles, methods and tools. This comparison including changes is elaborated for each individual process. It is possible that old processes deviate strongly from processes of SE but then new process has to be added and old one removed.

The V model of SE is characterized by verification and validation of developed systems and functions. For ensuring that characteristic, processes at the right side of the V model has to be linked to the processes of the left side of the model. Consequently, roles that are responsible for testing obtain the possibility of verification and validation by calling up e.g. the target requirements. Moreover, during revising the product engineering process sufficient iterations for verification and validation of different degrees of maturity have to be considered. In addition, in further procedure methods and tools of the corresponding processes could be used to stabilize verification and validation. This requires a comprehensive networking in the entire product engineering process of all tools which is out of the focus of this paper. It is worthwhile to note that in order to ensure the possibility for verification and validation during the implementation of the SE processes the retaining of the entire milestones in the model shall be considered. The latter is due to the fact that exchange of the performance and content of the processes are triggered by means of milestones. This guarantees verification and validation of the process at a proper time with the corresponding process content. Iterations of verification and validation can be increased arbitrarily by adding intermediate milestones in the process model. Through a successful implementation of SE processes a traceability on each process level of abstraction can be ensured through the entire process. This in turn enables recognizing process changes and obstacles in time.

4   An Automotive Use Case

The feasibility of the proposed approach in Sect. 3 has been tested to a certain extent on an automotive use case. Since such a check is not feasible for the entire vehicle development within the framework of a research project, we chose *testing process of a park pilot* as a use case. The aim is to integrate and demonstrate this use case in the context of the entire product development and to design its SE compatible process. Initially, phases 1 and 2 of the solution approach are applied. Thereby all levels of product development, which are relevant for the use case could be determined. Following the top-down approach, the Product Process is linked through the product engineering process to the Function Chart which in turn is linked through a Test Plan down to the lowest level where the required department was located as depicted in Fig. 9.

In parallel, all interdependent processes, methods and tools are recorded. Information about the processes at different levels are obtained from various stakeholder with different data formats. After determining all necessary processes and their contents, phase 3 to 5 are applied, so that finally a uniform overall BPMN model is created that starts from the Product Process. From the Product Process all levels can be broken down and navigated until finally the process of the use case testing of a park pilot is reached on the lowest level.

The corresponding BPMN model in a coordinate system is described in Fig. 10. The overall process of vehicle development, the Product Process, begins at the origin. To reach the process of the testing of a park pilot, a constant deepening of the processes

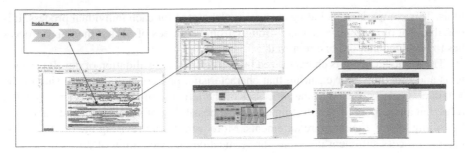

Fig. 9. Current product process.

is necessary. At the same time the complexity of the processes increases due to the technical details. Finally, the importance and dependence of the testing of a park pilot use case in the overall context could be determined. More precisely, if this process is changed the effect of this change on the overall process can be tracked.

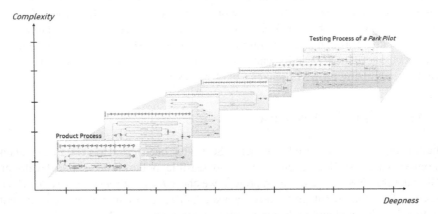

Fig. 10. BPMN model of the entire process in a coordinate system.

Each BPMN diagram in the model is given a timeline which can be seen as milestones, as depicted in Fig. 11. This figure describes the timeline of the entire product process at a high level with its associated milestones. Hence the time aspect in the process could be taken into account. Furthermore, the timeline helps to enable dependencies between the processes by means of input and output variables. The differences between the existing process of the testing of a park pilot use case and the processes to be achieved according to SE are determined in the last phase. For this use case we analyzed the testing process of a park pilot and could notice only small deviations between the existing process and the process according to SE. According to the deviations the old process has been revised to be SE compatible.

In this use case only small process modifications were required. However, this is not always the case. Integration of different SE processes may require massive modifications which in turn are time consuming. A further investigation may be needed to automate

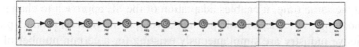

Fig. 11. Timeline of the product process.

adaptation of the old processes to the SE ones. However, such an automation is not in the focus of the present paper. It is very important to follow the structure of revising processes step by step. Otherwise, the idea of verification and validation by means of milestones is hindered. Therefore, during the implementation of SE milestones correct interdependencies are needed as depicted in Fig. 12. In this figure, a cutout of the interdependencies of the milestones at several levels of abstraction of the entire product is presented. The third rectangle in Fig. 12 depicts a reference timeline of milestones in one month step for the entire product process. This reference timeline ensures the correct link between milestones of higher and lower levels of abstractions. Moreover the link between different levels of timelines supports the transparency about inputs/outputs between various processes.

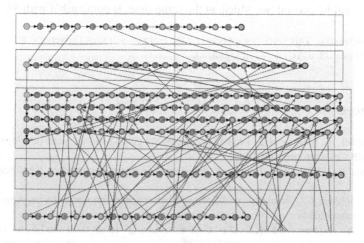

Fig. 12. Excerpt from the networked milestones at different process level.

5 Conclusion and Future Work

Due to the increase in product complexity, the introduction of the SE methodology for vehicle manufacturers is inevitable as this methodology is necessary for achieving a high A-SPICE standard where the strong focus is on process qualities. In this paper, we identify deficits in the development process at vehicle manufacturers that impair process quality and develop a methodical approach to address this issue. Our proposed solution turns existing processes into a consistent structure and thus increases the existing process quality. At the same time, it enables adaptation of the SE approach to change development methodologies of a decade-old product development. Several product processes in the automotive industry are simultaneously existing for a certain number of products. In this regard, our solution approach enables exchange between different product processes through the phases discussed in Sect. 3, especially the use of a uniform modelling language. Our proposed, unlike conventional methodologies, offers direct practical relevance. The effectiveness of the solution approach has successfully been tested on an automotive use case.

The SE is characterized by iterative verifications and validations on different development levels (e.g. components or subsystems). In order to make this possible, an extension of phase 5 is needed to be provided as the industrial PEP does not further consider the verification and validation methodology of the SE. Moreover, the identified processes shall be checked for their process-related and temporal implementation in practice. For this purpose, a logic is required that can record individual process steps, including the executed time of a developer and assign them in the entire process. This way deviations between the prescribed process and the executed processes in terms of content and time are to be detected and eliminated at an early stage. Furthermore, this logic should contribute to the optimization of the processes. Finally, an automated verification and validation shall be carried out which, at the same time, is compatible with SE.

Acknowledgments. This work is supported by the Helmut-Schmidt-University in Hamburg and by the AVAI project at AUDI AG in Ingolstadt.

References

1. Bögemann, B., Siegmund, I.: Product life cycles are getting shorter, your development times too? MB Collaborations (2018)
2. Brugger, R.: IT-Projekte strukturiert realisieren. Springer Fachmedien Wiesbaden GmbH (2003)
3. Brünglinghaus, C.: Elektronik und Software beherrschen Innovationen im Auto. Springer Professional (2014)
4. Busch, A.: Automotive SPICE: Die "Gewürzmischung" für System- und Softwareentwicklung. Continental Automotive GmbH (2020)
5. Düchting, C.: Aufbau eines freigabe- und kommunikationsbasierten Assistenzsystems im Produktentstehungsprozess. University of Dortmund (2005)
6. Duran, F., Camilo, R., Gwen, S.: Stochastic Analysis of BPMN with Time in Rewriting Logic (2018)
7. DW Made for minds. www.dw.com, https://www.dw.com/en/bmw-searched-over-suspicious-emissions-software/a-43055629. Accessed 20 Mar 2018
8. e.V., Verband der Automobilindustrie (2020). www.vda-qmc.de
9. Eßmann, V.: Planung potentialgerechter Produkte. Springer Fachmedien Wiesbaden GmbH (2013)
10. Group, Object Management (2020). www.omg.org, https://www.omg.org/spec/BPMN
11. Hans-Dieter, Z., Michael, K., Raimund, P.: Lexikon Qualitätsmanagement: Handbuch des Modernen Managements auf der Basis des Qualitätsmanagements. De Gruyter Oldenbourg (2016)

12. Hans-Hermann, B., et al.: Produktentstehungsprozess. Springer Fachmedien (2013)
13. Hart, L.E.: Introduction to Model-Based System Engineering (MBSE) and SysML (2015)
14. Hutterer, P.: Reflexive Dialoge und Denkbausteine für die methodische Produktentwicklung. Technical University Munich (2005)
15. Gausemeier, Jürgen, et al.: Studie: Systems Engineering in der industriellen Praxis. Carl Hanser Verlag GmbH & Co, Munich (2013)
16. Klöckner, J.: Autohersteller kämpfen gegen EU. WirtschaftsWoche (2013)
17. Groll, M.W., Heber, D.: E/E-Product Data Managment in Consideration of Model-Based Systems Engineering. IOS Press (2016)
18. Stelzer, R. et al.: EEE Methoden und Werkzeuge in der Produktentwicklung. TUDpress Verlag der Wissenschaft GmbH, n.d
19. Reuter, M.: Technischer und wirtschaftlicher Vergleich von Herstellungsverfahren bei der Entwicklung von Kunststoffhohlkörpern in Automobilanwendungen (2013)
20. Schömann, S.O.: Produktentwicklung in der Automobilindustrie. Springer Gabler (2012)
21. Shortell, T.M.: INCOSE Systems Engineering: A Guide for System Life Cycle Processes and Activities. John Wiley, Hoboken (2015)
22. VDI Fachbereich Produktentwicklung und Mechatronik: Systematic approach to the development and design of technical systems and products. Beuth Verlag GmbH (1993)
23. Verein Deutscher Ingenieure: Design methodology for mechatronic systems. Beuth Verlag GmbH (2004)
24. Walla, W.: Standard- und Modulbasierte digitale Rohbauprozesskette. KIT Scientific Publishing (2017)
25. Watanabe, K.: Toyota Motor Corporation (2007)

Development of a Virtual Simulation Environment and a Digital Twin of an Autonomous Driving Truck for a Distribution Center

Ion Barosan$^{(\boxtimes)}$, Arash Arjmandi Basmenj, Sudhanshu G. R. Chouhan, and David Manrique

Eindhoven University of Technology, Eindhoven, The Netherlands
{i.barosan,a.arjmandi.basmenj,s.g.r.chouhan}@tue.nl,
d.a.manrique.negrin@student.tue.nl

Abstract. This paper presents the development of a Virtual Simulation Environment (VSE) and a Digital Twin (DT) of an autonomously driving truck for a distribution center. While autonomous driving on public roads still faces various technical and legal challenges, within a distribution center, which is a confined area, some of these restrictions do not apply. Therefore, distribution centers can be the first environment where the autonomous driving of trucks is possible. A distribution center is a closed environment with no, or minimal generic traffic, where the trucks have relatively low speeds, short stopping distance and layout precisely known. Dedicated sensors locate the trucks. This paper addresses the mentioned aspects of driving in the distribution centers describing the necessary steps taken for the design, implementation, and testing of a VSE for a distribution center, and a DT of an autonomously driving truck. The development of the VSE is based on the integration of a SysML modeling tool – IBM Rhapsody, MATLAB Simulink, and Unity Game Engine using a Model-Based System Engineering approach. The paper also presents the test and the validation of a driving scenario used in a distribution center, using the TruckLab setup of the Eindhoven University of Technology, The Netherlands. The VSE and the DT showed considerable potential as testing and validation tools for automotive engineers, making it possible to define driving test scenarios for different types of tractor and trailer combinations.

Keywords: Digital Twin · Autonomous driving truck · Model-Based System Engineering · Virtual Simulation Environment · Distribution center · SysML · MIL (Model-In-Loop) · DTIL (Digital-Twin-In-Loop)

1 Introduction

The automotive industry is facing a fundamental change by moving its focus from a mechanical to a software-intensive approach [1]. This fundamental change

© Springer Nature Switzerland AG 2020
H. Muccini et al. (Eds.): ECSA 2020, CCIS 1269, pp. 542–557, 2020.
https://doi.org/10.1007/978-3-030-59155-7_39

affects many aspects related to the way customers envisage vehicles and mobility. The constant introduction of innovations and functionality in modern automobile rely mostly on software engineering model-based competence [2]. As part of the automotive industry's innovation, autonomous driving trucks offers a significant area of technological advancement. Companies like Amazon, Daimler and many others [3–5] have started testing their autonomous truck technologies. However, the mentioned companies are majorly focused on driving on a highway, and not in the areas of the warehouses or the distribution centers.

Distribution centers are the basis of a supply network, and often one of the essential parts of a production or manufacturing operation. In distribution centers goods arrive in bulk, are stored until needed, retrieved, and then assembled into shipments [5]. Moreover, the distribution centers are equipped with the latest technology for order processing, warehouse management, transportation management.

The efficient processing of a distribution center greatly impacts the final price of the product delivered to the end-user. In general, a distribution center has three main areas: the receiving, the storage, and the shipping area. It may also have additional specialized areas. In the shipping area, each store can have dedicated dock doors. The receiving area can also be specialized based on the handling characteristics of freight being received, on whether the product is going into storage or directly to a store, or by the type of vehicle delivering the product [6].

While autonomous driving on public roads still faces various technical and legal challenges, within a distribution center, which is a confined area, some of these restrictions do not apply. It may very well be the first environment where autonomous driving trucks can be possible. In container terminals Automated Guided Vehicles are already driving for many years. As future trucks can be controlled by wire, they will be well equipped for autonomous driving.

A distribution center is a closed environment with no/minimal generic traffic, such as pedestrians or cyclists. In the distribution center, the trucks have relatively low speeds, short stopping distance and layout precisely known. To manage all these aspects dedicated sensors may be used to locate the vehicles within the distribution center, for example cameras and LIDAR. However, ensuring safety in the distribution centers is a critical aspect of both software and hardware deployed in the vehicle.

This paper presents the development of a Virtual Simulation Environment, and a Digital Twin of an autonomously driving truck used to simulate different use-case driving test scenarios in distribution centers. Moreover, the VSE and the DT can be used to simulate many types of tractor and trailer combinations, making the VSE a very flexible environment for testing their maneuverability at low speeds in small areas.

This paper is organized as follows: Section 2 gives more background and motives this work further. Section 3 reviews the related work. Section 4 covers the design of the TruckLab's virtual environment and the Digital Twin of the autonomous driving truck. Section 4.3 presents the development of the VSE. Also, this section presents the integration of different tools necessary for Model-In-Loop and Digital Twin-In-Loop. Section 4.4 covers the results of a driving test scenario in the distribution center. Finally, Sect. 5 presents the conclusions, discussions and future work.

2   Context and Motivation

The significance of Logistics to the Economy of The Netherlands is around 10% of its GDP (Gross Domestic Product per capita), making Logistics a key sector of the Netherlands economy [7]. The Autonomous Vehicles Readiness index of 2019 ranks the Netherlands as the global leader in terms of preparedness to deploy autonomous vehicles [8]. This circumstance suggests that the scope for autonomous vehicles to be deployed practically is ample.

Fig. 1. Left, The TruckLab at Eindhoven University of Technology. Right, the Jumbo distribution center in Veghel, The Netherlands.

The Netherlands has the highest number of distribution centers in Europe [7]. INTRALOG project - Intelligent Truck Application in Logistics has been started for identifying the potential of automated driving within the Logistics domain [9]. INTRALOG is a consortium of companies and universities, with a focus on docking semitrailers in distribution centers.

There is a shortage of truck drivers in the Netherlands and other parts of Europe [10], which stimulates the opportunity for deploying autonomous trucks in the Logistics sector, without the concern of displacing human jobs.

In the distribution centers, the movement of trucks is done by human drivers, who could be time-dependent due to their non-availability past work hours. Thus, autonomous trucks can improve the efficiency of a distribution center and make their operation less dependent on human drivers. The most challenging driver's professional skill is the docking of a truck. An automated docking could be a significant step towards easing the manual effort required to perform the docking. With the advancement in modern sensor technology, autonomous trucks are becoming more viable for operation within short distances as that of a distribution center [11].

There have been a few attempts to develop systems that assist the driver to maneuver inside a distribution center. Eaton has developed a dock assist system as presented in [13]. With the supervision of a human driver, assistance is provided only for the case of docking. It is reported that the dock assist system made far more corrections and was slower compared to a human driver. Also, the most important limitation is that the driver needs to park the semitrailer parallel to the docking station initially.

Another major aspect of the distribution centers is safety. Besides collision between vehicles, collision avoidance is needed with objects located in the distribution centers area. With increasing attention to cooperative driving, scenarios like vehicles working together at a crossing become important. To guaranty the safety inside the distribution center, it is necessary to create the optimum path planning for the vehicles. This challenge increases the complexity of the automation in the distribution center and of the truck. When the path is predefined, it is known what kind of maneuvers the truck will execute in a specific situation. Being able to control the truck's maneuvers, we can avoid unsafe situation. We can plan the driving of the truck to the dock stations, based on the optimum path, the dock stations positions and the initial truck's parking position. In this way the safety in the distribution centers will increase.

The trucks driving between distribution centers have an increased overall length, 25 m or more, and multiple articulations. These so-called, high-capacity vehicles lead to an increase in transport efficiency both regarding costs and reduction of CO_2 emissions. The truck can be actuated fully electrically, 100% by wire, which will facilitate autonomous driving. The throttle, brake, clutch, and gearshift are already operated electrically, and the first trucks that have electric steering actuation are appearing on the market.

As a consequence, future scenarios for distribution centers can be defined, taking into account that in a distribution center:

- Safety is a crucial component for every employee.
- Articulated vehicles load and unload at a fast rate, making the distribution center a high-risk area.
- Multiple vehicles driving around each with a destination rely on the truck drives smooth maneuvers ability in a small area.
- More commonly used to increase the loads on trucks, larger vehicle combinations, which leads to an increase in complexity around distribution centers. For example, a double or triple tractor-trailer can quickly get stuck when making wrong maneuvers.
- Localization systems are needed to determine the position of the trucks and of the objects.
- Using the localization system, articulated vehicles can be monitored and position data could be made available.
- Using the vehicle's dynamics a control system for a truck can be created; a path-following controller can use the sensor information to maneuver the vehicle.

To test all the aforementioned aspects of autonomously driving trucks in a distribution center, a lot of financial and human resources are needed. It is rather difficult to build a real setup for testing and taking into account all the specified aspects. However, building a virtual testing and simulation environment for a distribution center is an affordable solution.

To design control systems that can support articulated vehicles in distribution centers, a virtual testing environment is needed. Currently, at Eindhoven University of Technology (TU/e) scaled models of articulated vehicles were developed. This is a necessary foundation for creating truck controllers before using them on large scale vehicles. These scale models are integrated into a setup called TruckLab, shown in Fig. 1 (left). The TruckLab represents a scaled model with scale 1:13.3 of the Jumbo distribution center in Veghel, The Netherlands, Fig. 1 (right).

To efficiently use the testing facilities of the TruckLab, an entire Virtual Simulation Environment was developed, which implements the supervisory control of the distribution center, the controllers of the autonomous driving trucks and the communication between the trucks and the distribution center.

To simulate the functionality of the distribution center, a Digital Twin (DT) of an autonomous driving truck was developed. Our DT is based on a five-dimensional framework approach [12], which consist of:

- *Physical Entity* (**PE**) - the mock-up truck, which contains various subsystems, sensory devices, and actuators. The sensors collect real-time states of the mock-up truck.
- *Virtual Entity* (**VE**) - the digital truck, a faithful mirror image of the physical entity containing the geometric parameters of the physical entity, such as shapes, sizes, and assembly relations. Also, the physical properties (e.g., speed, wear, and force) reflecting the physical phenomena of the entity, are part of the virtual entity. Moreover, we implemented in the VE the truck's dynamics, the numerical multi-body capabilities, and collision detection mechanism. The VE was integrated into the Unity Game Engine.
- *The Connection* (**CN**) - connects the PE and the VE. Also, the CN connects both entities to the provided services. All the connection are bidirectional.
- *The Digital Twin Data* (**DD**) - is denoted as the data from the PE, mainly including the operation states and working conditions. Also, the DD refers to the data from the VE and consists of model parameters and model operation data.
- *The Services* (**SRs**) - the services for both the PE and the VE. The SRs make the PE work as expected through real-time regulation, and sustains high fidelity of the VE with the PE through model parameters calibration. In our paper we consider only the monitoring service for the PE. For the VE, the SRs consist of construction service, calibration service, and test service for the SysML and Simulink models.

The development of the Digital Twin implied the integration of four major automotive domains: vehicle dynamics, real-time software engineering, power trains and human machine interface. To tackle the complexity of the Digital Twin, we used a Model-Based Systems Engineering (MBSE) approach based on SysML. As a MBSE methodology the SYSMOD [14] was applied. For the elicitation and understanding of the requirements, the Thinking in Time TRIZ tool [15] was used. For the analysis of the Digital Twin solutions space we used the TRIZ Contradiction Toolkit. We model the requirements, the use cases, and the architecture and the behaviour of the Digital Twin in a SysML modeling environment using the IBM Rhapsody and MATLAB Simulink. Also, base on the Unity Game Engine, a Virtual Environment of the TruckLab was created - The Virtual Truck Lab, which represents the scaled Jumbo distribution center. In addition, the Digital Twin and the Virtual Truck Lab were integrated into VSE.

3   Related Work

Several projects have been implemented in the TruckLab related to cooperative driving, collision avoidance, autonomous controlling, and localization of the trucks [17,18]. The main objective of the projects was to autonomously control the vehicle using a prerecorded input of a joystick controller [20]. The results of the tests were not optimal. The vehicle was not able to follow the course while driving backward [19]. This was because of poor road surface conditions and the limited accuracy of the localization system used. However, the path-following controllers implemented were capable of controlling an articulated vehicle both forward and backward. These path-following controllers were integrated into our VSE for testing purposes.

Hertogh had created a virtual environment and supervisory control for the TruckLab [20]. He integrated the following components in his virtual environment: a path-following controller, a VRML 3D representation of the TruckLab, and the scaled mock-up of a tractor semi-trailer combination. Hertogh made the first attempt to create a Digital Twin for a truck semi-trailer combination. However, the virtual environment and supervisory control were not flexible enough to facilitate the configuration of vehicle physics: a rigid body, collision detection, the wheels controllers, the vehicle's suspension and the axles. Moreover, the 3D virtual environment is not easily adjustable. In VRML every object needs to be defined with an orientation, position and visual components, making the creation of a large 3D scene difficult and time-consuming.

In our implementation, we use the Unity Game Engine, which is flexible and optimized for large and complex 3D scenes. Moreover, a SysML modeler is integrated into the VSE, which makes possible the development of any test driving scenario in the TruckLab or the virtual TruckLab using the Digital Twin.

The idea of creating a virtual environment for testing is not new. Coupling a 3D virtual environment with simulation tools have been used in different domains [21,22]. There is a large variety of vehicle driving simulators using virtual environments. These vehicle driving simulators are built and used to obtain insights that will be relevant to future real-world applications [23–25]. However, they are custom made and do not provide a comprehensive development platform for modeling and simulating new applications.

In recent years, autonomous driving has become an important research area. Many new tools have been developed to support autonomous driving research. The predominantly used open-source simulation engines to simulate training data in autonomous driving research are CARLA [26], TORCS [27] and AirSim [28]. CARLA is an open-source simulator developed from the ground up to support the development, training, and validation of autonomous driving systems. CARLA provides open digital assets for urban layouts, buildings, vehicles. AirSim, is released by Microsoft to support the development of autonomous vehicles like drones, cars and more. AirSim main goal is to narrow the gap between simulation and reality. TORCS, The Open Racing Car Simulator is a highly portable multi-platform car racing simulation. TORCS can be used as an ordinary car racing game, as an AI racing game, and as a research platform.

From the three mentioned simulation engines, CARLA was a good candidate for our virtual simulation environment. However, the already available integration between the Unity Game Engine and MATLAB Simulink was decisive for our design decision to use Unity Game Engine instead of CARLA.

To conclude, we created a general flexible and robust VSE for comprehensive testing of driving scenarios, by integration of three primary environments:

- IBM Rhapsody - a SysML modeling tool.
- MATLAB Simulink - a graphical programming environment for modeling, simulating and analyzing multi-domain dynamical systems.
- Unity Game Engine - a virtual reality and games development platform.

4   System Design

4.1   The Virtual Truck Lab and the Digital Twin

The TruckLab setup at the Eindhoven University of Technology is a demonstrative setup that allows testing of autonomous articulated vehicles. The TruckLab consists of two tractor-semitrailers combinations, a distribution center with a docking station, a video camera-based localization system, a computational unit and a communication system.

To address the design and test complexity of the Virtual Truck Lab, we used a SysML based Model Driven System Engineering approach. All the aspects related to requirements, structure and behavior of the Virtual Truck Lab had been modeled using the SysML diagrams. Figure 2 (right), present the overall architecture of the Virtual Truck Lab, where the *DigitalTwinTruck* component implements the Digital Twin of the truck, *EnvironmentDC* implements the 3D environment of the distribution center, *Obstacles* implements the collision detection management for the truck, and the *LocalizationSystem* component implements the localization system of the TruckLab.

To create a 3D virtual environment for the TruckLab set up a suitable 3D virtual framework development was need. The framework must support and bring

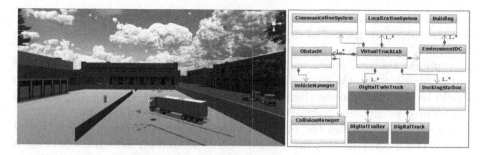

Fig. 2. Left, the 3D representation of the Truck Lab, including all the 3D assets: the buildings, the docking stations, the parking area, the obstacles inside the distribution center and the digital twin truck. Right, the high level components of the Virtual Truck Lab's architecture containing: the virtual Truck lab, the digital twin truck with its truck trailer combination, the truck manager, the collision manager.

together several core areas. We needed to add 2D and 3D graphical objects and assets in our 3D environment; assembled those assets into scenes and environments; adding lighting, audio, special effects, physics and animation, interactivity. The framework should be flexible enough to allow the development of plug-ins for MATLAB/Simulink and SysML modelers, by example IBM Rhapsody or Enterprise Architect. Also, because it was nearly impossible to simulate the truck's dynamics and collision detection of the truck with objects of any shapes in the Simulink, it was required to use a more general simulation environment. Taking these aspects into consideration, Unity Game Engine was selected for this purpose. Also, Unity Game Engine is using NVIDIA PhysX engine to simulate the multi-body problem in real-time, in the presence of collision, friction and joint constraints. Besides its efficient numerical multi-body simulation capabilities, Unity Game Engine can render the scene with state-of-art technologies and provide a realistic graphical output of the scene that can be used for demonstration purposes. This graphical output can also be used to feed autonomous driving algorithms in the possible future use-cases.

Using the Unity Game Engine framework a 3D replica of the TruckLab was built, as presented in Fig. 2 (left). In the 3D scene the docking station, a dummy pedestrian and the 3D representation of the Digital Twin of the truck are rendered.

The vehicles used in the TruckLab setup are tractor-semitrailers. The autonomous movement of the tractor-semitrailer in a distribution center requires making an autonomous movement from the parking station to one of the docking stations and back. The initial movement requires forward mode driving, whereas docking requires reverse mode driving as the semi-trailer must be presented to the docking station to unload the goods into the distribution center.

The Digital Twin must behave in the same way as its real counterpart vehicle, the mock-up truck. The Digital Twin must allow inputs and outputs for different parameters, which are needed to control the vehicle autonomously in the distribution center. For example, two critical parameters, the steering angle and the speed are generated by a path-following controller which uses a reference path, so that the vehicle maneuvers to the reference path and follows it. To replicate the real truck, we needed to design the Digital Twin's structure and integrate it into the Unity Game Engine. Every aspect of the actual vehicle should be modeled into the Digital Twin counterpart such that the Digital Twin can be used in different testing scenarios in the distribution centers.

Figure 3 (left), shows the top level view of the architecture of the Digital Twin's Truck component using a SysML Block Definition diagram. There are a few Truck's components which are worthwhile to mention. The *VehiclePhysicsTruck* contains the key aspects necessary for the numerical multi-body simulation capabilities of the truck. The *VehiclePhysicsTruck* is based on NWH's Physics Package [16], suitable for a wide range of vehicles including a wheel controller 3D for wheel physics used by the *WheelController* component.

The *TrailerAttachementPoint* controls the attachment of the semi-trailer to the tractor, which allows the coupling and decoupling of the semi-trailer from the tractor. The *Camera* component presents different views from the 3D scenes to the user: one from the cabin, one from the front of the truck. The *Body* component describes the main components of the truck's body. Every component of the Digital Twin has its data attributes and behavior, which are implemented in Unity Game Engine using C# scripts. Also, every component has a GUI which facilitates the interaction between the user and the component. Similar to the *DigitalTruck* component, the *DigitalTrailer* architecture is shown in Fig. 3 (right). The Digital Trailer has a body, wheels, wheels controllers, lights, an attachment point, and physics properties. The body has a suspension, doors, and a trailer interior and exterior components. Also, the *VehiclePhysicsTrailer* is implemented based on NWH's Physics Package [16].

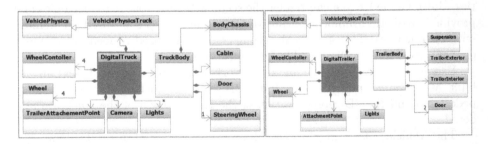

Fig. 3. Left, the high level Digital Truck's Architecture containing the wheels controllers, the trailer attachment point, the vehicle physics, the cameras, the lights and the truck body. Right, the abstract architecture of the Digital Trailer's Architecture, modeling the same abstract components as for the Digital Truck's Architecture.

4.2   Setting Up a Vehicle

After the Truck and the Trailer component have been defined, we need to set up a vehicle. In our case, the following components have to be set up for the *VehiclePhysicsTruck* and the *VehiclePhysicsTrailer*: a rigid body, collision detection, wheels controllers, vehicle's suspension and the axles. For example, the axle's functionality is implemented in a C# script that contains variables defining how much torque the axle will receive, and all the geometry related data for each of the axle and its wheels, like the steer coefficient, Ackermann percent, toe angle, caster angle, camber at top and the Anti Roll Bar Force. The amount of power an axle will receive is stored in a variable as a ratio for both the front and the rear axles. Similarly, we have variables storing the braking coefficient along with the hand brake coefficient that defines what fraction of the total brake and hand brake torque the axle will receive.

For setting up a truck, the Vehicle Physics provides the following parameters: **Sound, Steering, Effects, Engine, Transmission, Axles, Brakes, Tracks, Driving Assists, Traction control system, Damage, Trailer Handler, Ground Detection.** NWH's Physics Package [16] presents a complete description of these parameters and theirs scripts.

4.3   The Virtual Simulation Environment - VSE

After the Virtual Truck Lab and the Digital Twin of the autonomous truck were developed, a Virtual Simulation Environment was built, as presented in Fig. 4 (left). VSE integrates these two components for testing different driving use-cases in the distribution center. The intended simulations shall be able to simulate truck dynamics and collision detection of the truck with its environment, which in this case is the docking station and the distribution center area.

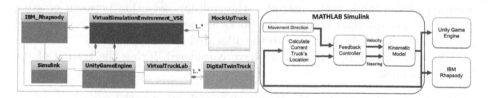

Fig. 4. Left, the architecture of the Virtual Simulation Environment. Right, the Simulink implementation of collision detection. The colors indicate: the truck's digital components (yellow), the tools we integrate (blue) and the Visual Simulation Environments (green). (Color figure online)

The VSE is made up of a SysML modeling tool - IBM Rhapsody, a simulation tool - Simulink, the Virtual Truck Lab, and the actual mock-up truck. Using the Simulation Environment different scenario-based can be implemented for Digital-Twin-in-Loop testing. The structure and behavior of the VSE is modeled in IBM

Rhapsody, including the structure and behavior of the distribution center, and the structure and behavior of the Digital Twin of the autonomously driving truck.

The path planning and path-following, the kinematic model of the tractor-semitrailer combination, and the collision detection mechanism are implemented in Simulink, as presented in Fig. 4 (right).

The communication between IBM Rhapsody and Simulink is implemented by a Functional Mock-up Interface (FMI). Rhapsody-Simulink integration does not provide interaction with Unity. Therefore, TCP/IP is used to establish a reliable connection between Rhapsody-Simulink and Unity, which is necessary for the DTIL testing.

A TCP/IP interface is provided to control the Digital Twin and the mock-up trucks. The steering and acceleration control signals are sent through this interface. The mock-up trucks use Raspberry Pi hardware controllers and different sensors and actuators. The truck's linear velocity and position of three ArUco markers, placed on top of the trucks, are sent back as feedback. It is possible to use any external tools to communicate and control the muck-up trucks in the simulated docking station. Collision information of the truck with objects in the scene are also available through a similar interface. As mentioned in Sect. 4, using the Virtual Truck Lab environment, it is possible to customize vehicle dynamics parameters such as engine characteristics, suspension system, steering, transmission. For the customization of the parameters the Vehicle Physics by NWH is used.

4.4   Testing of VSE

To test and validate the VSE, including the Virtual Truck Lab and the Digital Twin, a few use-cases scenarios were implemented. We have implemented different scenarios in which some boundary conditions were tested, including the accuracy of the truck path controller, the collision detection between crossing trucks, etc. For example, when all the docks are occupied, based on a predefined priority list, the trucks can leave to the allocated parking places.

There are many aspects that we have considered during the testing of the DT, for example:

- What is happening when the trucks cross each other path?
- Should the truck's path be computed dynamically of predefined?
- What is happening when the communication between the DC and the trucks, or V2V failed?

In all mentioned situations the DT behaved accordingly. However, during the tests, we encountered some challenges related to the path-controller. Once a path is generated using the specific algorithm, it is essential to ensure that the truck follows that designed path. To facilitate the tracking of the truck and reduce any deviations from the path, specific control strategies need to be defined. Specific control strategies need to be defined to facilitate the tracking of the truck and reduce any deviations from the path. Before the controller design, it is essential to understand the truck model. During the forward motion of the truck, its position is monitored by monitoring the location of the front axle of the tractor. In case, it is required, a correction input, a steering angle, and velocity should be given to reduce deviation from the path. This correction input leads to a stable system as the point of measurement and the point of control coincide and so the trailer perfectly follows the tractor. However, during reverse driving, since the truck's position is monitored by monitoring the rear axle of the trailer, the required correction input should be given as a steering angle, otherwise, the system is unstable. Therefore, for designing control strategies, the two motions that are forward and reverse, are treated separately. This is enabled by defining the direction of motion at each instant of time, which is done in the path panning phase.

In this paper, we presented the following use cases scenario, as example:

- After arrival at the distribution center, the driver parks the truck in a designated location.
- The controller of the distribution center calls the truck to the dock at a specific location.
- A route is determined, the truck drives to the correct dock and communicates with other trucks for optimization and collision prevention, and reverses to allow access to the rear doors.
- The cargo is unloaded from the truck.
- After unloading, the truck is directed to another dock to load goods.
- The truck drives autonomously to the parking spot again.The driver pick up the truck and drives towards the supermarket.

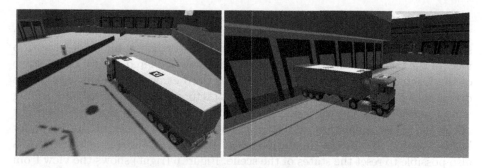

Fig. 5. Left, the initial parking position of the Truck inside the distribution center. Right, the truck parked at the designated docking station.

To test the mentioned scenario an actual simulation of tractor semi-trailer system was done. The simulation controlled the tractors velocity using a path-following controller. The throttle signal was going to be the control signal produced by the speed controller. During the simulation, the tractor semi-trailer combination started to move from its initial position until it arrived at the designated docking station.

Figure 5 (left), shows a screen-shot of the truck parked at the designated location inside the distribution center. After parking, the driver was able to monitor and to interact with the truck using a GUI. Figure 6 (left), presents an example of a GUI implemented in IBM Rhapsody, which displays information about the state of the truck. Also, using the GUI the DC operator can: allocate a docking station or a parking location for a specific track, monitor the state of the docking station, assign a parking place for the truck, halt the entire system in case of a emergency, monitor the truck driving autonomously, change the camera view of a truck and monitor the environment. Moreover, the driver can switch on/off the autonomous mode of the truck.

Fig. 6. Left, a GUI used: to monitor the truck's state, to select a docking station and monitor its state, to select a parking destination for the truck. Right, cabin camera view showing the environment from the driver's perspective.

While running, it was possible the choose between 3 cameras available in the scene. The first and default camera provided a 2D (orthographic projection) top view of the truck parking station. The second camera offered a third perspective of the tractor semi-trailer combination. The third camera provided view of the driver, which included a cockpit view of the tractor with a dashboard and driving wheel, and also the tractor's side mirror. Switching between camera's does not affect the scene simulation and only provides different views of the truck for better viewing the current simulation state. While the scene was running, it was also possible to reset the states of the scene. Figure 6 (right) shows the view from the cabin using the second camera.

The user could select between manual control of the tractor semi-trailer combination or using a network interface to control it by an external program, by example, Simulink or IBM Rhapsody. Figure 7 shows a collision test of the truck with an external object, in this case, a pedestrian. When the truck touched the bounding box of an object, it stopped. Also, the color of the cylinder around the pedestrian changes from green to red in case of a collision, as seen in the Fig. 7 (right).

Fig. 7. The collision detection mechanism in action: left, the green cylinder indicates no collision; right, the red cylinder indicates an eminent collision with a pedestrian. (Color figure online)

After a route is determined, the truck drove to the correct dock and communicated with other trucks for optimization and collision prevention, and reversed to allow access to the rear doors. Figure 5 (right), shows the truck parked at the designated docking station. During docking time the truck was unloaded or loaded with specific goods and then drove to the designated parking location.

5   Conclusions and Future Work

Research in autonomous driving in distribution centers is hindered by infrastructure costs and logical difficulties of training and testing of the system in the physical world. This paper presented an overview of the development of a VSE for an autonomously driving truck in a distribution center. Also, the paper described the steps taken for the development of a DT for an autonomous driving truck.

The DT was designed using a Model-Based System Engineering approach based on SysML. The VSE, based on the Unity Game Engine, Simulink, and IBM Rhapsody offers considerable possibilities for testing. The pairing of the Digital Twin model with the physical world was realized at the TruckLab of the Eindhoven University of Technology. Different kinematics models for the truck and trailers were used. Also, different path-controllers were implemented and tested. The tests showed good accuracy of the truck's localization, dynamics and collision detection with objects located in the distribution center. Using the DT, many scenarios related to docking, driving, and parking in the Distributed Center's areas were tested and simulated, making the VSE a vital testing tool for engineers.

The Virtual Simulation Environment allows the integration of many trucks making possible the development and testing of applications using platooning and multi-trucks driving scenarios. Also, it is possible to define different truck and trailer combinations using the setup mechanism for vehicles, making the Virtual Simulation Environment very flexible for testing different use-case scenarios. However, a future improvement of the VSE will be to create a live-link between the SysML modeling tool and the Unity Game Engine. The live-link will allow a direct conversion of the SysML architecture and behavior of trucks and the distribution center as a 3D object into Unity Game Engine. In this way, the entire structure and the behavior of the truck will be visualized together with its 3D representation; in the same environment, in this case, the Unity Game Engine. Also, the path-controller, which ensures that the trucks follows the designed path during the reverse driving, need to be improved. Therefore, the forward and reverse motions have to be treated separately for designing control strategies. This is enabled by defining the direction of motion at each instant of time, which is done in the path panning phase. Also, the integration of CARLA simulation tool in our VSE is another area of future research.

References

1. Dajsuren, Y., van den Brand, M.G.J.: Automotive Systems and Software Engineering State of the Art and Future Trends. Springer, Heidelberg (2019). https://doi.org/10.1007/978-3-030-12157-0
2. Ebert, C., Favaro, J.: Automotive Software **34**, 33–39 (2017)
3. Frangoule, A.: Self-driving trucks are being tested on public roads in Virginia, September 2019. https://www.cnbc.com/2019/09/10/self-driving-trucks-are-being-tested-on-public-roads-in-virginia.html
4. Baum Hedlund Law, SAmazon Tests Self-Driving Trucks, Invests in Tech Startup, August 2019. https://medium.com/@baumhedlund/amazon-tests-self-driving-trucks-invests-in-tech-startup-a39ba986162b
5. O'Dell, J.: Daimler starts highway test of autonomous freightliner truck, September 2019. https://www.trucks.com/2019/09/09/daimler-starts-highway-test-autonomous-freightliner-truck
6. van Duin, J.R., van Kolck, A., Anand, N., Taniguchi, E., et al.: Towards an agent-based modelling approach for the evaluation of dynamic usage of urban distribution centres. Procedia-Soc. Behav. Sci. **39**, 333–348 (2012)
7. Netherlands office for Science and Special Report Technology, Smart logistics in the Netherlands, Association for Computing Machinery, pp. 5–6 (2018)
8. KPMG: Autonomous Vehicles Readiness Index 2019, pp. 5–6 (2019)
9. Gerrits, B.: Multi-agent system design for automated docking of semi-trailers by means of autonomous vehicles, University of Twente, pp. 5–6 (2016)
10. Trans. Info, November 2019. https://trans.info/en/lack-of-drivers-in-the-netherlands-every-second-company-has-trouble-finding-workers-79697
11. Rosen, R., Von Wichert, G., Lo, G., Bettenhausen, K.D.: About the importance of autonomy and digital twins for the future of manufacturing. IFAC-PapersOnLine **48**(3), 567–572 (2015)
12. Tao, F., Zhang, M., Liu, Y., Nee, A.Y.C.: Digital twin driven prognostics and health management for complex equipment. CIRP Ann. Manuf. Technol. **67**(1), 169–172 (2018)
13. Berg, T.: Driver keeps hands off as eaton system docks a trailer, May 2017. https://www.truckinginfo.com/159971/driver-keeps-hands-off-as-eaton-system-docks-a-trailer
14. Weilkiens, T.: SYSMOD - The Systems Modeling Toolbox, 2nd edn. MBSE4U (2016)
15. Gadd, K., Goddard, C.: TRIZ for Engineers: Enabling Inventive Problem Solving. Wiley, Hoboken (2011)

16. NWH Vehicle Physics Manual. http://nwhcoding.com
17. Rajagopalan, S.: MATLAB based Control of a Scaled Tractor Semi-trailer, D&C 2017031, Eindhoven University of Technology (2017)
18. Hertogh, M.A.M.: Automatic docking of articulated vehicles, D&C 201703, Eindhoven University of Technology (2017)
19. Lousberg, T.A.H.: Building a MATLAB/Simulink-based truck simulator, D&C 2016012, Eindhoven University of Technology (2016)
20. Hertogh, M.A.M.: Development of a virtual environment and supervisory control for TruckLab, D&C 2018.031, Eindhoven University of Technology (2018)
21. Waas, T., Kucera, M., Földi, A.: Simulation environment for real-time applications 3D visualisation/simulation environment for testing real-time electronic control units. In: 2013 Proceedings of the 11th Workshop on Intelligent Solutions in Embedded Systems (WISES) (2013)
22. Tsai, P.-S., Wu, T.-F., Hu, N.-T., Tang, J.-H., Chen, J.-Y.: Virtual reality to implement driving simulation for combining CAN BUS and automotive sensors. In: IEEE International Conference on Information, Communication and Engineering IEEE-ICICE (2017)
23. Lindemann, P., Rigoll, G.: A diminished reality simulation for driver-car interaction with transparent cockpits. In: IEEE Virtual Reality (VR) (2017)
24. Kucera, E., Haffner, O., Leskovský, R.: Interactive and virtual/mixed reality applications for mechatronics education developed in unity engine. In: Proceedings of the 29th International Conference Cybernetics & Informatics (K&I) (2018)
25. Yang, C.-W., Lee, T.-H., Huang, C.-L., Hsu, K.-S.: Unity 3D production and environmental perception vehicle simulation platform. In: Proceedings of the IEEE International Conference on Advanced Materials for Science and Engineering IEEE-ICAMSE (2016)
26. Dosovitskiy, A., Ros, G., Codevilla, F., Lopez, A., Koltun, V.: CARLA: an open urban driving simulator. In: Proceedings of the 1st Annual Conference on Robot Learning, pp. 1–16 (2017)
27. Shah, S., Dey, D., Lovett, C., Kapoor, A.: AirSim: High-Fidelity Visual and Physical Simulation for Autonomous Vehicles. In: Hutter, M., Siegwart, R. (eds.) Field and Service Robotics. SPAR, vol. 5, pp. 621–635. Springer, Cham (2018). https://doi.org/10.1007/978-3-319-67361-5_40
28. Wymann, B., Dimitrakakisy, C., Sumnery, A., Guionneauz, C.: Torcs: the open racing car simulator (2015)

Author Index

Printed in the United States
By Bookmasters